The Good Skiing Guide 1992

THE GOOD SKIING GUIDE

The 300 best
winter sports resorts
in Europe and America

Edited by **Chris Gill**

Published by Consumers' Association
and Hodder & Stoughton

Which? books are commissioned and researched by
The Association for Consumer Research
and published by Consumers' Association
2 Marylebone Road, London NW1 4DX and
Hodder & Stoughton
47 Bedford Square, London WC1B 3DP

First edition 1985
New edition 1991

The *Guide* has been prepared with the help of the Ski Club of Great
Britain, which is gratefully acknowledged. But the views expressed herein
are those of the Editor, and not necessarily those of the Club.

Assistant editor Julia Letts
Research assistants Amanda Crook, Jane Austin
Contributing editor Adam Ruck
Specialist contributors Konrad Bartelski, Martin Bell, David Goldsmith,
Elisabeth Hussey, David Smallwood

Design Patrick Nugent and Val Fox
Cover design Tim Higgins
Maps David Perrott and Bristol Illustrators

Acknowledgements to The Image Bank for the cover photograph

British Library Cataloguing-in-Publication Data:
A catalogue record for this book is available
from the British Library

ISBN 0 340 55001 5

Typeset by Fox + Partners, Bath,
and PCS Typesetting, Frome

Printed and bound in Great Britain by
Pindar Print Ltd, Scarborough

Contents

About this guide

This is the seventh edition of *The Good Skiing Guide*. It resembles earlier editions in concentrating above all on one question: where to go skiing. It differs from earlier ones not only in being up-to-date for 1992, but also in covering more resorts than ever – we have added new chapters on several minor European resorts, and have continued the gradual process of covering major American ones. At the front of the book, there are some new feature chapters; at the back, an expanded reference section. To make room for these improvements, we have dropped several 'background' chapters which have been in the *Guide*, more or less unchanged, since the first edition.

The pace of change in ski resorts shows little sign of slackening, despite economic and ecological constraints, and the *Guide* has been thoroughly updated to reflect the developments of the past year. Practically all the piste maps have been amended to show new lifts and runs, and of course all the resort descriptions, factual details and verdicts have been revised.

For the new reader, what matters is not how much this edition differs from earlier ones but how it differs from other sources of information about ski resorts. First, it is independent and thus impartial: we have a modest research budget which allows us to travel under our own steam, and we prefer to ask holiday-makers rather than tourist offices or tour operators for their opinions of resorts. Secondly, it is consistent: we are a very small team, and we have a very broad recent experience of European resorts to draw on for comparative purposes. Thirdly, it is discriminating: by spelling out the drawbacks of each resort as well as its attractions, our descriptions highlight the differences between resorts instead of blurring them.

The *Guide* was born of a conviction that skiers planning a holiday lacked impartial, clear and relevant information, particularly about resorts. Its success confirms that belief, and gives us some confidence that we have gone the right way about filling the gap: since its first publication in 1985, reviewers have received the *Guide* warmly, and holiday skiers have bought the book in sufficient numbers to support annual publication. We have our critics, of course; some tourist offices have been distressed to find that their resorts' write-ups are not good advertisements – which only goes to show how rarely they encounter any published reference to the drawbacks of resorts. We hope they will accept that our intention is to review critically, not simply to criticise, and forgive us for not deleting all references to lift queues and over-size ski school classes.

Not everyone finds our maps as immediately comprehensible as the more widespread style of piste map – that is, an artist's impression of a mountain landscape – but they are a unique aid in the difficult process of comparing ski resorts. Like any conventional map, they take a vertically downward view of the ground, showing its ups and downs by means of contour lines and shading. These maps do not distort many-faceted mountains to make them fit the picture, but show clearly whether runs face north, south, east or west. All but a couple of special maps are drawn to a single scale – so you can easily compare one ski area with another, for size at least. When comparing ski areas for difficulty, bear in mind that resorts differ in their understanding of 'easy' and 'difficult', and that the piste grades on our maps are those used by the resorts. Comparisons between European and American resorts (mapped for the first time in this edition) are particularly tricky because of the different grading systems used. We make it clear in the description of the ski area when we feel runs are incorrectly graded.

The information and judgements the *Guide* contains are largely the result of our own inspection trips. But we are well aware that some aspects of a resort are not easy to judge on brief working visits, and the *Guide* has been greatly strengthened by the observations of the many correspondents who have sent in reports on their own holiday experiences. The more of these reports we receive, the more useful the *Guide* will be. Towards the back of the book is a check-list that shows how your resort reports can be most helpfully organised. This year we have again enjoyed the collaboration of the Ski Club of Great Britain in bringing the book up to date.

A book calling itself *The Good Skiing Guide* might be expected to include 'good' resorts and to exclude 'bad' ones, but it doesn't. There is no such thing as a 'bad' resort; every ski resort can properly claim to be good for someone. But we have started leaving out resorts – including some quite major ones – in which (to judge by the reports we receive) readers appear to have little interest. From this edition we have dropped the following: Bardonecchia, Engelberg, Le Grand-Bornand, Gstaad and neighbours, Leysin, Madonna di Campiglio, Madesimo, Les Orres, Serfaus, Val Cenis and Zell am Ziller. By cutting them out, we have been able to give more space to many other resorts.

If you think there is a resort we should be restoring or adding to the book, write and tell us about it. On the other hand, do pause and reflect before you write to ask why we seem so unenthusiastic about the slopes where you had that wonderful afternoon's skiing in March. We try to produce a balanced view of each resort, but we do aim to find faults where they exist, and to spell them out. So it is inevitable that our reports will seem negative compared with what you might read elsewhere – or compared with what you might write about your own favourite places. We know that skiing is tremendous fun, that high mountains in winter are entrancing, and that any ski resort is a fabulous place on the right day. We could have prefaced each resort entry with a statement to that effect; but we hope that saying it once is enough.

Introduction

The season past, the season ahead

After three very disappointing seasons, last winter did a lot to restore the confidence of Europe's skiers and ski industry in the weather. It was not a perfect winter; it was not even the good winter that it was made out to be by some commentators. There is no denying that there was a lot of good skiing to be had at most stages of the season, but spring came much too early for comfort, particularly in low resorts. High resorts got the benefit of the late burst of cold snowy weather in April which seems to have become an established feature of the Alpine scene.

For UK tour operators, the season was overshadowed by the Gulf War and the recession. It was clear during the season that some companies were having trouble selling their holidays – we encountered high-season chalets entirely filled by people travelling on half-price deals. And with the season over it is clear that business was appreciably down on the previous season. This has left some companies financially weak (and owing money to resort staff, for example).

As we prepare this edition in May, it is difficult to be confident that next season will be entirely free of the effects of the recession. Even if one wintery winter is enough to give skiers a renewed appetite for skiing holidays, there may be a shortage of skiers with the spare cash to buy those holidays.

The significance of this is that many tour operators need that cash, and if they don't get it companies that have held on to life through the summer may give up the ghost during the autumn. No one should book a holiday for next winter that is not bonded or bought via a credit card, so that your prepayments will not be lost if the company fails. (Bonding is explained in the 'Package holidays' chapter, towards the back of the book.)

Zermatt update

Regular readers may recall that for several years now we have been protesting in these pages about the indifferent standards of the Zermatt ski school. This year's verdict? Steady progress, but plenty of room for further improvement. Readers who have experience of the school are about equally divided into those in favour and those against – a marked improvement on earlier years, when reports have been almost universally damning. There are still complaints of poor organisation and irresponsible or incompetent individual instructors. But it is a rare school indeed that generates no complaints at all, and we are encouraged to think that perhaps the recent changes to the management of the school are paying off.

It would, however, be hasty to conclude from this that Zermatt's managers are entirely reformed characters. Last season, they took the bizarre step of removing an appreciable number of runs from the piste network. The runs still exist, and are still shown on the piste map, but are shown in yellow instead of their original black or red. Last season's piste map identified the yellow runs as ski routes or itineraries, but failed to explain properly what this meant. It turns out to mean that the runs are marked and subject to avalanche checks, but not patrolled.

This development seems to us undesirable in itself; it does not make the runs any more challenging, nor does it serve the alternative purpose of distinguishing the resort's most difficult runs. From the skier's point of view, it simply makes the affected runs less safe than proper pistes, and in particular much less safe for lone skiers. It will save the resort the trouble and expense of patrolling the runs concerned, but what probably motivates the change is a desire to cultivate the right sort of image abroad, and specifically in the USA, where many resorts have a grade of run beyond black – either double-diamond black or yellow.

Of greater concern is the fact that the change adds to the confusion about the status of non-piste runs, and who can safely ski them. Perhaps the new Zermatt piste map will offer clear guidance; but even if it does, the resort's yellow-run convention is yet another addition to the already abundant catalogue of non-piste run definitions employed in Europe. It is time that the resorts which provide such runs got together to agree on standard terms, standard meanings and standard marking conventions.

Off-piste, off-course

These are not simply academic concerns. Obviously, if you are on a run that is not patrolled (eg a ski route in Zermatt) you are less likely to be rescued quickly after an accident. If you are on a run that is not safe from avalanches (eg a high-alpine ski touring route in St Anton) you could be exposing yourself to great dangers. If you are on either, you may not be covered by your insurance. Believe it or not, at precisely the time when more skiers are being tempted to go off-piste and more resorts like Zermatt are encouraging them to do so, some vendors of winter sports insurance are categorising off-piste skiing as an unacceptably dangerous activity, like mountaineering and hang-gliding.

You may be shaking your head in disbelief at this, confident that your own cover had no such exclusion. If you still have the paperwork, dig it out and have a look: you may be in for an unpleasant surprise. More than one skier we lectured on this subject last winter found that they had a duff policy, and had to make hurried arrangements to buy another.

Sowzy fights back

Last year, we took the unprecedented step of demoting a resort from 'major' to 'minor' status; this year, Sauze d'Oulx is back. The readers' reports we appealed for have come in, in modest numbers; the lift system has been taken over by neighbouring Sestriere, and the tourist office has provided the information we need to bring our piste map up to date; and an editorial visit confirmed our long-standing affection for the extensive intermediate skiing that the resort has to offer. The village is no prettier than it was, although it did strike us as being much less rowdy than of yore. But much remains unchanged: the lifts are still slow, old and creaky; the organisation of the resort is still infuriating. We arrive at midday, and buy an afternoon pass; we ask for a piste map; sorry, signor, we don't have piste maps – you have to get them from the tourist office; we enjoy a five-minute walk to the tourist office; it is closed until 4pm.

Lager shouts
There may be some doubt about where lively young Brits are doing their après-skiing, but there cannot be much doubt about the form that their après-skiing takes. In the last edition, it didn't rate a mention; in this one, it crops up in resort after resort. What is it? Karaoke. We have to confess that our knowledge of the matter is still theoretical, our winter bases having been too quiet, too sophisticated or too conservative to provide this latest craze. It consists of punters taking turns to sing popular songs to the accompaniment of pre-recorded backing tracks; it is, apparently, very amusing.

Delays: who pays?
If bad weather or some other uncontrollable factor prevents your tour operator getting you out of your resort and on to the right plane, who is responsible for any costs arising? The question arose in conversation with a tour operator, who instinctively took the view that it would be your misfortune, and your loss, and that it was therefore important to have insurance against that risk. We instinctively took the view that the tour operator had a contractual obligation to get her holiday-makers home, and that bad weather would be her misfortune. Has anyone put this to the test?

Pack 'em in
We have never been fans of 'ski packs' – the deals offered by tour operators whereby you book your ski hire, lift pass and ski school (or some of those components) through the operator, and pay for them in advance, in sterling. By committing yourself in advance, you limit your ability to make choices on the spot. But we had always innocently assumed that ski packs were at least cheap. Not so, readers have pointed out. Some operators do not adhere to the resorts' definition of low and high season, with the result that you may be charged for a high-season lift pass when it is actually still low season. More seriously, some operators simply charge more than the local price for lift passes and school lessons; if you're not careful, you can pay £30 a head more than you need to by buying a pack.

If you are tempted to buy a ski-pack, ask the operator whether his prices represent a discount on the local prices; if not, steer clear.

Skiing costs
Skiing is an expensive way to spend your time. Some skiers are reconciled to that, while some have no need to give it a second thought. For most of us, though, the high cost of most things associated with skiing is at least an irritant and for some it is a problem. The reports we

200 winners wanted

We don't doubt that most reporters to the *Guide* give us the benefit of their wisdom for entirely altruistic reasons. But to encourage the others, two years ago we started giving free copies of the *Guide* to reporters. The incentive seems to help, and for the moment it continues.

You are not guaranteed a copy of the next edition if you send in any old resort report; but you stand a good chance of winning one if you make a thorough job of it. As we go through your reports in the process of revising the *Guide*, we rate each one for its usefulness, and at the end of the process sift out the 200 most useful reports. Quantity can in some circumstances make up for quality: we are quite likely to reward the author of three moderately useful reports as well as the author of one outstandingly useful one. But sending in half a dozen reports devoid of information does you no good.

There is a check-list, to help you structure your reports, towards the back of the *Guide*.

have had from readers this year suggest some ways of making economies.

In eastern Europe, and particularly Bulgaria and Romania, prices are so low as to seem ridiculous by comparison with the Alps or Pyrenees. If the budget is really tight, putting up with the privations that go with the low prices may be worthwhile.

Within the mainstream of European skiing, your choice of resort is more important than your choice of country: in Austria, France, Italy and Switzerland you can pay widely varying amounts for everything from lift passes to beer. To pay more, follow the international spotlight; to pay less, go where the locals go, or where only downmarket or small-time international operators go.

Car hire rip-offs

We have long emphasised the attractions of having a car to get around or between ski resorts. For trips of two weeks or more, driving out to the Alps is the way to do it – throw the kit in the back of the car, and you're on your way. But for the week-long trips that most people take, the 15 hours travelling out and back are more than many people are likely to want to face. Solution: car hire at the arrival airport. It is not difficult to arrange (phone any of the international companies) but there are pitfalls for the unwary.

You need snow-chains or special tyres, and perhaps a ski rack. The car hire companies are quite used to providing these items, but they are also quite used to charging outrageous amounts for them. Before you book, ring all the companies you can track down; you will find pronounced differences in price, and the differences will vary according to the country you're heading for. Bear in mind that it might be worth tailoring your arrival point to get cheaper hire.

The ideal would be to hire a four-wheel-drive car. Such cars are now reasonably cheap to buy; sadly, for reasons we cannot fathom, they cost a great deal to hire – more than most people can justify for business purposes, never mind holiday purposes.

Top of the pops

Bestseller lists make compulsive reading, whatever the part of the market they relate to. They don't tell you much about the quality of the books (or whatever) being bought, but something about the people doing the buying. Here, for what it's worth, is a list of *Good Skiing Guide* readers' top 30 resorts, as indicated by the numbers of resort reports we received last spring (given after the resort name):

1	Obergurgl 22
	Val d'Isère 22
3	Méribel 21
4	Valmorel 16
	Verbier 16
6	La Plagne 15
	Val Thorens 15
	Zermatt 15
9	Courchevel 14
	St Anton 14
11	Les Arcs 13
	Flaine 13
13	Courmayeur 12
	Les Deux Alpes 12
15	Breckenridge 11
	Borovets 11
	Ischgl 11
18	Livigno 10
	Tignes 10
	Vail 10
	Wengen 10
22	Chamonix 9
	Saalbach Hinterglemm 9
	Whistler 9
25	Aonach Mor 8
	Alpe d'Huez 8
	Châtel 8
	Serre-Chevalier 8
29	Avoriaz 7
	Galtur 7

We hesitate to draw any conclusions from this list. Many of the resorts are ones you would expect: the big names of the ski world that are on any keen skier's agenda. We are at a loss to explain the prominence of Valmorel; and intrigued by the relatively poor showing of Alpe d'Huez, which in recent years has been much more popular. Whistler – covered in the *Guide* this year for the first time – has enjoyed a meteoric rise.

French queues

The French have poured a lot of money into preparations for the coming Winter Games, not least to provide serious road access to the Tarentaise region. The new roads were not complete for this winter, but large parts of them were, and the jams were worse than ever. Perhaps that is what the computer model predicted for this season; and perhaps the same computer model has accurately predicted that when the roads and junctions are complete they will be able to cope with the unprecedented volume of traffic that the Olympics will surely generate next season. But we wonder. There are something like 250,000 visitor beds in the region; when the occupants are on the move, they have to be funnelled through the crucial junctions at Albertville and Moûtiers. They will have to be very cleverly designed junctions indeed to handle volumes of that kind without serious queues.

Next winter, we shall know just how effective the junctions are. Until then, there is still a lot to be said for travelling to and from these resorts on Sundays.

Hire shop hassles

We and our companions have hired skis in several resorts over the last two seasons, and generally have not enjoyed the experience. We have had timid intermediate skiers equipped with smart, high-performance (and high-price) skis. We have been offered a choice between badly-maintained skis at the regular price or brand-new ones at three times that rate. We have been 'accidentally' charged for five days' hire instead of four. We have been 'accidentally' charged for the hire of our own boots. It has been an interesting experiment, but we've had enough – next season, it's back to lugging our own skis to and from airports.

1992 Olympics

Between the 8th and 23rd of February 1992, the XVI Winter Olympic Games are being held in the French Savoie. For European holiday skiers – especially the British, who flock to the region every winter – these Games represent a clear departure from the recent norm. They are being held in a range of resorts, practically all of which are major holiday destinations – so many skiers watching on TV will be able to recognise the slopes on which the racers perform; some may even be tempted to combine a skiing holiday with a bit of live spectating.

Getting there
For the first time in many years, holiday skiers from Britain are likely to be thinking of going to watch some of the Olympic events in the flesh. Not only are the Olympic resorts of major interest to holiday-makers, but they will also be within easy reach of our shores – provided that the improvements in access to the Tarentaise region turn out to be effective.

Three road improvement schemes (the new free *autoroute* from Chambéry to Albertville, the up-grading of the RN90 from Albertville to Moûtiers, and the improvements to the section between Moûtiers and Bourg-St-Maurice) should improve the notorious weekend congestion in this area. Apparently private cars will not be allowed beyond Bourg-St-Maurice during the games and holiday-makers staying in either Val d'Isère or Tignes will have to proceed from there by bus. Free buses will shuttle between the resorts 24 hours a day, but priority will be given to competitors, officials and press, and holiday-makers could face delays of up to four hours – not a very good start to the holiday.

Direct flights to Lyon should be more readily available after the opening of the new terminal, at Lyon Satolas airport. The comparatively short transfer time to the Tarentaise resorts is a big incentive to fly here rather than Geneva. The really lazy can now fly directly to Courchevel altiport, on scheduled flights from various European cities. A slight (but multi-million franc) shift in the axis of the runway has made it possible to extend and widen it so that it can accommodate larger aircraft.

Train enthusiasts from the UK can reach the region by catching the overnight service from Calais to Moûtiers (or Bourg-St-Maurice).

Staying there
The Olympic Committee (COJA) has commandeered all normally privately let accommodation for the period of the games, making it illegal for property owners in the area to rent out accommodation unless they do so through the Committee. This means that although prices may be high, they will at least be controlled. 'Official' hotels, we are told, will cost something in the region of £90 per night. The Olympic village is at Brides-les-Bains, in the valley below Courchevel and Méribel.

Olympic timetable

Event	Resort	Dates
Men's Downhill	Val d'Isère	9 Feb
Giant Slalom		18 Feb
Super Giant Slalom		16 Feb
Combined Slalom		10-11 Feb
Men's Slalom	Les Menuires	22 Feb
Women's Downhill	Méribel	15 Feb
Giant Slalom		19 Feb
Combined Slalom		12-13 Feb
Slalom		20 Feb
Super Giant Slalom		17 Feb
Freestyle Moguls	Tignes	12-13 Feb
Freestyle Ballet		9-10 Feb
Freestyle Aerials		15-16 Feb
Speed-skiing	Les Arcs	18-19,21-22 Feb
Ski Jumping	Courchevel	9, 14 & 16 Feb
Combined Nordic		11-12,17-18 Feb
Cross-country	Les Saisies	9-22 Feb
Biathlon		11-20 Feb
Bobsleigh	La Plagne	15-16,21-22 Feb
Luge		9-14 Feb
Freestyle skating	Albertville	9-22 Feb
Speed-skating		9-20 Feb
Short-track speed-skating		18-22 Feb
Ice hockey	Méribel	8-23 Feb
Curling	Pralognan	17-22 Feb

The opening and closing ceremonies are taking place on the 8th and 23rd of February in Albertville

Val d'Isère

A new Olympic course down the face of Bellevarde has replaced the old Downhill run from the top of Bellevarde to La Daille. Its steepness has caused a certain amount of controversy; in order to keep down speeds, there are number of turns in the course which have prompted critics to compare it to a Giant Slalom. It is 3km long and descends over 1000 metres, with maximum pitches of 63°. On sections of the course, the racers will be going at speeds of over 60 mph.

The GS course starts just to the right of the Downhill and descends sharply (around 50°), almost parallel to the Santel Express chair-lift, before joining the downhill course lower down. The event is likely to cause a lot of local attention as Franck Piccard, born in Les Saisies, will be defending his Olympic title from Calgary.

The courses have apparently been designed with the public in mind; it is possible to see 80% of the Downhill from the finish line.

Les Menuires

Les Menuires' new slalom stadium, to be used for the men's event, has been in operation since 1988. It is on the west-facing slopes directly above the village and can be reached from nearly all the lower lifts.

Méribel

Not to be out-done by Val d'Isère, Méribel has constructed a new Downhill course for the women's events, on the east-facing slopes below Roc de Fer. The descent is 2.7km long and drops 800 metres, with some pitches of 45°. It is a highly technical course and promises to be exciting to watch – if the World Cup events last year are anything to go by. The other women's events (Giant Slalom, slalom, Combined Slalom) will be held on the same slope, all finishing at Chaudanne.

Beside the finish-line at Chaudanne is Méribel's new ice-rink complex, built for the ice-hockey competition, which, for the first time, will be a knock-out tournament. There will be three games a day, each lasting 60 minutes. A new gondola will connect the 6,000-seat stadium with the Olympic village, Brides-les-Bains, with mid-stations at Les Allues and Raffort. When the competition is over, the complex will be modified to include a nursery, a squash court, a swimming pool, a restaurant, a climbing wall, a golf practice hall and a gym.

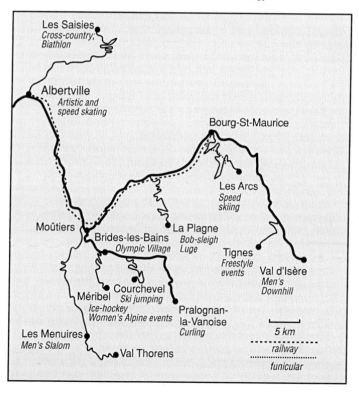

Tignes

Tignes is the venue for the *Ski Artistique* or freestyle events. These include the Olympic 'moguls' discipline (*Les Bosses*), a testing race down a bumps run on the lower slopes of the Col du Palet. The aim of the game is to cover the course as quickly – and therefore as directly – as possible, which involves leaping from bump to bump. It is an excellent spectator sport, as are the two demonstration events, ballet (the skiing equivalent of ice-dancing) and aerials (air-borne acrobatics, using a snowy ramp in place of a trampoline). There are several British hopefuls in all the freestyle disciplines.

Les Saisies: a star is born?

All of the Olympic resorts are banking on a higher profile in the skiing world as a result of the Games; but none stands to gain as much as little old Les Saisies. You may have heard of it in 1988, when local hero Franck Piccard won a super-G gold and a downhill bronze at Calgary. You may have heard of it in 1990, when British instructors based in other resorts but here in search of decent snow were charged with teaching illegally. But in 1992 it will hold centre-stage as the venue of the Olympic cross-country skiing and biathlon events.

The organisers have grasped this opportunity with both hands and intend to revolutionise the previously dull spectacle of cross-country skiing. The model for the innovation was the biathlon, where the athletes return to the stadium after each lap to fire five shots at a target, and have to complete a short penalty lap if they miss. With this in mind, Hervé Nicot, a local man who is the 'chargé de mission' for the Games, has devised a cross-country course of revolutionary design. Instead of leaving the stadium and battling for places out on the course, where the public sees nothing until the final sprint, the competitors will finish each of four laps in front of the 15,000 spectators. Within the stadium there are five rings, representing the Olympic emblem, where the public will have ample opportunity to witness the changes of position as they occur.

This is by far the most impressive of the many changes which this alpine pass has seen in its history. In 1936, an Austrian refugee from Hitler's regime saw the potential of the vast snow fields at the meeting of the Arly and Beaufortain valleys, converted one of the few alpine chalets into a rudimentary hotel, constructed a makeshift ski lift, and the rest, as they say, is history. Erwin Eckl still lives here, ageless, holding court in his son's bar, telling stories of his resistance days in Les Saisies and the famous parachute drop of arms for the 'maquisards'. In 1963, the four communities of the region pooled their resources, and the resort was really on its way.

In the 1970s, Les Saisies grew quickly. The accommodation capacity reached 1,200 in 1977, and 5,800 in 1983. The Alpine ski area was then enlarged by linking it up with Crest Voland and Cohennoz, thereby creating the 'Espace Cristal'. There are now 110 kilometres of downhill pistes. It was at this time, too, that the fateful

Les Arcs

In 1988 Michaël Prüfer entered the record books as '*l'homme le plus rapide du monde*'. Without any mechanical help, he reached a speed of 140mph on Les Arcs' speed-skiing course. Even greater speeds have been predicted for the Olympic demonstration, on a new, longer course, close to the old one on the slopes of the Aiguille Rouge above Arc 2000.

Courchevel

Courchevel is hosting the ski jumping events, for which a new stadium has been built at Le Praz (1300m). The stadium seats 23,000 and has

---

decision was taken to add a Nordic ski area of international stature.

The announcement in 1986 that Les Saisies was to be the Olympic venue provided the impetus – and the money – to construct at a breathtaking pace to prepare for the 1992 Games. Some say that the resort has become too big for its ski area; it now has 8,800 beds, with a projected limit of 10,000. One aspect of this rapid growth is that large developers have moved into what was a locally owned resort. As a reward for virtually giving their land away to create the initial ski area, the local farmers were allowed to construct, and open shops and restaurants. 70% of the commercial outlets in Les Saisies are owned by locals from the villages of Hauteluce and Villard. Franck Piccard has been rewarded, too, for his efforts; the three-star hotel which he was given was built by local craftsmen, mostly friends of the family, and it shows. It's a pity that the same cannot be said of the rather brutal four-star hotel in the prime site overlooking both valleys.

There are only three hotels in Les Saisies. Most of the accommodation is in apartments, about half of which are in converted chalets. The Alpine ski area is very suitable for beginners, especially children, and for those skiers who prefer gentle slopes without having to go too far, but who like the occasional more challenging run. The 'Espace Cristal' boasts four such black runs, with a couple of pretty demanding reds thrown in. The cross-country section is beautiful, with trails meandering gently through the forest, and it caters for all levels of nordic skier. Standing as it does in the impressive shadow of Mont Blanc, Les Saisies enjoys a micro-climate ideal for a ski resort; loads of snow – even in these years of relative dearth – but also of sun. The restaurants provide simple fare at the usual inflated resort prices. There are a couple of late-night bars, and the inevitable disco, but these hardly represent the feel of the place. It is primarily a family resort.

It must be said that the advent of the 'Coca Cola Games' has hardly enhanced the appeal of Les Saisies, but it does still have a certain rustic charm. Although no British tour companies operate here, it is perhaps a sign of the times that many of the villagers are participating in an extensive English teaching programme; so, if you should decide to venture up the Beaufortain valley and try Les Saisies, the locals are ready and waiting!

two jumps (90m and 120m). As well as the individual and team jumping events (judged on length and style), there are combined Nordic events, which involve 10-15km of cross-country skiing as well as a 90m jump.

Just along from the stadium on the road to Méribel is the new mini-resort of La Tania, at the foot of the lifts up to Col de la Loze. La Tania will be used by the Press during the Games.

Courchevel has also invested in a big new sports centre, the Forum (1850m). This contains an array of sports and leisure facilities, including an Olympic-sized ice-rink (where the ice-hockey teams will practise).

Les Saisies

If you haven't heard much about Les Saisies before, you soon will. It is a small resort right on the edge of the Olympic arena, in fact rather closer to Megève than to the Tarentaise resorts. It is the site of all the Olympic cross-country and biathlon events (the latter will be open to women for the first time ever). See the feature box in this chapter.

La Plagne

The new bobsled and luge track in La Roche, La Plagne, caused a few problems during its test runs at the World Cup last year. In their efforts to be environmentally friendly, the French used ammonia instead of CFCs in the track's refrigeration plant – and then had to ban spectators from the track area because of the risk of fumes. No doubt the problem will have been solved in time for the Olympics. The track is 1500m long and has 19 corners. Bobsleighs descend it in about 60 seconds, travelling at speeds of over 80mph. Not surprisingly, it takes them a further 200m to stop. Luge competitors reach similar speeds.

Albertville

A massive new ice-hall and Olympic oval have been built in Albertville to hold the skating events. 9,000 spectators will be able to watch the figure skating, while a further 10,000 can see the speed-skaters flash past at over 30mph. New to the Olympics this year is sprint skating on a specially designed short track. The opening and closing ceremonies will also take place in the massive new 'ceremonies' stadium in Albertville.

Pralognan-la-Vanoise

Pralognan, a delightful village between Les Arcs and La Plagne, is hosting the demonstration curling event at its new 2,000-seat sports complex. This extremely skilful game, played between teams of four, involves sliding stones across an ice-rink to a target, 38 metres away.

Equipment news

David Goldsmith brings us up to date on what's new in the shops, and on the pitfalls awaiting the unwary buyer of ski equipment.

Caveat emptor

In late February and early March each year, the ski equipment trade lays out its wares at large international trade shows in the cities of Munich and Grenoble; a British show also takes place in Manchester. Just as one ski season is at its height, retailers are feverishly buying goods which will be delivered to the shops six to nine months later, in time for the next. Hardly has one winter's sales pattern developed before the next one has to be predicted.

Equipment retailing is thus a tricky business for all involved, including the consumer. Relatively few products are tried by those who end up selling them to the public. Boots are a particular problem: usually, boot manufacturers do not make a range of sizes until their sales book has filled (an individual mould for a single size of boot costs thousands of pounds). Although the more professional equipment distributors in Britain organise 'dealer trips' in January, with testing of next year's gear, relatively few retailers take advantage of them. And there is little opportunity for comparative testing between brands.

The result is that many mediocre and some downright unskiable products are sold to the public. The marketing bandwagon goes into action, the trade buyers are carried along on the wave of hype, and the design deficiencies of the product don't become apparent to thousands of consumers until they are on a cold mountainside many months later.

Of course, the more responsible companies (the ones that tend to survive in the longer term) take years to develop and test their equipment, in all conditions, and do not launch a new model until they are convinced that it works. But this general lack of adequate testing is certainly an argument for taking a cautious attitude to radical new products.

One recent example of a product that showed initial promise but subsequently produced universal disappointment was the Lange Mid, a boot with a novel system of enveloping the overlapping shell with a cable system that could be tightened at the rear. The Lange Mid has since been re-designed twice, the cable system has been scrapped, and hopefully the latest version works. It now features a fairly conventional row of clips but retains its unusual method of entry and 'locking up' the forward lean into position for skiing.

Perhaps the boot was ahead of its time, because two larger boot manufacturers are now making boots which could be described as 'hybrid rear-entries'. Read on....

The new trend in boots

The argument between those who believe feet should enter ski boots from the rear and those who believe they should enter from the front has raged for years, and has now become more involved with the appearance of the 'mid' and the 'overlap rear-entry' boot.

Rear-entry boots first appeared in the mid-1970s but were initially (and justifiably) dismissed as gimmicks because they did not provide any effective hold over the instep. In the early 1980s, however, they grew in popularity when Salomon entered the boot market with their SX90, followed by the classic SX91. Other brands – notably Nordica and Raichle – also improved the design qualities of rear-entry boots by fitting internal cable loops, 'pressure distribution plates' and other features that held the foot firmly.

Two or three years ago it seemed that rear-entries (which at that time accounted for 80 per cent of sales) would clinch the argument and win over the remaining professional skiers and racers who stuck out for conventional front-entry boots. But a surprising reverse trend has occurred. A strong revival in front-entry boot sales has prompted manufacturers to make new designs and moulds.

Our experience of testing and using rear-entry boots has been largely positive. Provided the design works – and many rear-entry boots, sadly, have been poorly designed – the result can be an extremely comfortable well-fitting product. The convenience of slipping the foot in from the back without fiddling with a tongue and stiff overlapping flaps, and the ease of walking with the back of the boot open, cannot be equalled by a conventional front-entry clipped boot. In our experience Salomon's specialisation in this type of boot – they have never made a front-entry model – has produced the best designs, though the original two-clip closure is to be preferred to the single downward-closing lever, used on some current models, which is over-elaborate.

But there is a valid argument for front entry; a shell that overlaps along its front section can close around the foot better than a rear-entry shell, where the volume of the shell is normally fixed. Hence the new Nordica and Raichle designs, which are attempts to combine the virtues of front- and rear-entry. The back of the new (and, on first examination, well designed) Nordica Syntech works like a normal rear-entry boot, by opening to let the foot inside. But the front section of the boot has a row of clips like a traditional front-entry boot. It has a good quality inner boot and an attractive matt finish. Raichle have a different solution, with a new series called FX. They have a 'variable volume shellfit', produced by a cable connected to both sides of a split shell at the front of the boot. Turning a dial at the back of the boot pulls both sides of the boot together for a tighter fit.

Only skiers' experience this winter will tell whether these latest attempts to resolve the debate have been successful.

New ski construction: better performance?

It will not have escaped the notice of keen window shoppers that skis with unusual shapes and designs have started to appear on the racks recently. Plastic tips, rounded top surfaces, 'monocoque' construction techniques, dazzling graphics and multi-coloured base materials are all part of a new chapter in ski manufacture. These new ski models, from makers such as Fischer (with the CAD), Kastle (X1), Rossignol (DVE) and Salomon (9000 series) and others, are the result of competition to simplify construction and reduce the cost of materials, finishing and labour. Because the skis are moulded in a different way, there are new opportunities for creating such features as inset sections for mounting the bindings.

Since the prices being demanded for these new skis are often well above average, an obvious question arises: Do these simplified processes have any associated benefit in terms of performance, or is there, on the contrary, a loss in performance which makes the new models clearly worse value than traditional ones?

Since World War II, when the demands of the aircraft industry revolutionised the use of metals and other materials, skis have enjoyed the spin-off: wood (although not displaced altogether) has been largely replaced by metal laminates, lightweight glassfibre and (in the past fifteen years) high-strength 'composite' materials – carbon fibre and so on. These materials have reduced the weight of skis and increased the ability of designers to vary flex patterns, twist and vibration characteristics, and so tune the performance of skis.

The new wave of ski models can certainly turn heads. Our verdict on their performance, however, gleaned from some comparative testing in past seasons, is that there is no appreciable difference in performance. Good skis of conventional laminated or 'torsion box' manufacture have reached such impressive levels of performance that one is left grasping at subtle niceties when making comparisons. The new Salomon skis, for instance, of which so much has been written, are certainly very fine in terms of their carving qualities and responsiveness (the 2S model is probably best for all-round conditions) but for £50 or so less a racing ski of comparable quality can be obtained from other makers. We also hear some reports of breakage or bending of Salomon skis in the tip/shovel area.

The crucial factor, whatever you buy, is to keep the edges and soles away from rocks, and have them serviced every few days. Even a £350 pair of skis can be wrecked in a matter of minutes on a worn piste.

Floating in powder

One of the disadvantages of modern skis – particularly racing skis – is that they perform poorly in powder snow. As skis have become narrower to achieve superior 'edge to edge' speed and quickness of response, so their surface area has declined. There has been a general reduction of around 5 to 10 per cent in the width – and hence surface area – of skis over the past decade. And for powder skiing this is clearly bad news: narrow skis sink.

At the same time, ski makers (in comparison with golf club makers, for example) seem strangely reluctant to promote the idea of specialised skis for specialised conditions, in spite of the profusion of double ski bags. The myth of the 'all-round' ski, so heavily marketed and yet essentially a hopelessly ambitious idea, continues.

But there are exceptions, and a radical one is launched this winter by Atomic: the Magic Powder. This model, which has a waist of 100mm (most skis are around 65mm wide), should provide dramatic improvements in buoyancy in powder, similar to those experienced by monoskiers. The length of the skis is a standard 180cm, which is probably quite sensible because most skiers reached the heights of confidence in powder snow when 'compact' skis were around in the mid-1970s. The only immediate problem with the Magic Powder (apart from its rather alien breadth for skiing the piste) is the necessity to saw off one arm of each pair of ski brakes, since the two of them cannot overhang the ski's edges.

Fun on piste

In complete contrast to super-wide skis are two other equipment developments of possible interest to those who like to skid around on super-short skis. The elitists of the ski business (of which there is no shortage) will undoubtedly turn up their noses at the Dalbello Snowrunner and Kneissl Big Foot, but they warrant comment.

The Dalbello Snowrunner has a smooth sole capable of sliding downhill with no other attachment. The sole has a slightly turned-up and extended 'toe' so that it does not snag as it slides, but it has no steel edges. The Kneissl Big Foot, which enjoyed large sales in its native Austria last winter, is a 60cm ski in the shape of a slim foot (strongly waisted) complete with stubby toes on its tip. This is, in essence, a modification of the 'figl' ski, which several Austrian makers have traditionally turned out for ski patrollers and mechanics who require an extremely manoeuvrable and light ski.

Neither of these short sliding objects can be recommended for deep or soft snow because they get bogged down, but on a well-packed piste they can be great fun, presenting their own challenges and requiring their own techniques. Whether you're likely to find them worth the cost of purchase (around £100) is of course another matter.

Attached to your snowboard?

Snowboard bindings are screwed solidly to the deck, like ski bindings, but there the similarity ends. The boots clip on, without the conventional automatic step-in or release components, and there they stay however serious the fall. Designing an effective mechanism has preoccupied inventors for years. Unlike a ski binding, a snowboard binding has to allow for considerable sideways stress and leverage during normal use. And when a fall takes place it is pretty essential that both boots release simultaneously to avoid the hazards of 'one foot in, one foot out'.

Two bindings from new sources have now appeared which offer solid construction and what appear to be sensibly designed release mechanisms. They are made by Meyer and Galde, and availability in Britain may be limited.

Readers report

The foundation of the *Guide* is the consistency of its appraisals of resorts, and in the past we have in the main resisted the temptation to report on resorts that have not been visited by one of the editorial team. But two years ago we introduced a short chapter summarising several resorts largely on the basis of reports sent in by readers. By doing so we hoped to encourage more readers to report on those resorts, and on other resorts not previously covered by the *Guide*.

We judged the experiment a success; we now know enough about some of the resorts covered in this way to promote them to short chapters of their own in the main body of the book. And we have had reports on another set of 'new' resorts, described here.

If you ski in any other resort that is not covered by the *Guide* but deserves to be brought to the attention of British skiers, please do send us a report. It helps if you describe the village and the skiing in more detail than we normally expect (if we have visited a resort, we prefer to stick to our own view of these aspects) and if you send in whatever resort literature you have retained – particularly the piste map. These reports, like all other resort reports we receive, stand a fair chance of winning you a free copy of the resultant edition.

Note that readers' reports on American resorts not covered 'properly' in the *Guide* have been fed into our American round-up chapter.

Ovronnaz, Switzerland

Ovronnaz (1350m) is a traditional-looking village spread across a sunny, sparsely wooded plateau, on the opposite side of the Rhône valley to Verbier. Situation is about the only thing the two resorts have in common. Ovronnaz is small, undeveloped and cheap – 'don't tell too many people about it' says our enthusiastic reporter, who loved the peaceful, uncommercial atmosphere and the lack of Verbier-type tourists. There are a couple of hotels in the village, and it is possible to rent apartments – at uninflated prices. The local supermarket is reasonably stocked and there are a handful of bars and restaurants. There is also a new thermal swimming pool complex, with its own shop and restaurant – 'well worth a visit'.

The lift system ('delightfully antiquated – a step back in time from Verbier') serves a small but interesting ski area on the west-facing slopes of the Six Armaille (2430m). An ancient chair-lift takes you up to Ovronnaz's only mountain restaurant, and from here a series of drags serve a variety of pistes, including one long descent around the back of the mountain to Petit-Pré. Several proposed lifts will open up the mountains beyond Six Armaille, at present a popular touring area. On the other side of the village is a single red run, served by a long drag-lift. There is a scenic cross-country circuit just above the village and plenty

of 'very pleasant' walking paths. The resort is probably best suited to unambitious intermediates, elderly skiers or ski-mountaineers (there are several guides available). It also makes a welcome day-trip from Verbier and its satellite resorts if you have a car.
Tourist office ✆ (027) 864293.

Meiringen, Switzerland

Meiringen is an unremarkable valley town, situated at the end of the Brienzer See in the Bernese Oberland and easily accessible by car or train. It operates as a resort in summer and winter, and has an abundance of small hotels and apartments, catering for mainly Swiss and German families. English is not widely spoken (except in the large finishing school nearby).

The skiing is in two well connected areas – Meiringen and Hasliberg, for which there are separate or joint lift passes. Most of the skiing is in the shade in the morning, and our reporter found the exposed top chair-lifts an interminably long and bitterly cold experience. There are, however, plenty of enclosed lifts: a cable-car and two consecutive gondolas from the valley to Magisalp (1710m) and a gondola on the Hasliberg side to Kaserstatt.

The skiing above Magisalp consists of a variety of blue, red and blacks runs plus ample off-piste opportunities down the sides of a large bowl. The bottom section is steep and black, 'a fine run to Magisalp', which you can avoid by using the drag-lift from just above it. The high-point of this area, Planplatten (2245m), is the starting point of a long, scenic red to the Bidmi gondola station, some 280m below Magisalp. A women's downhill is held on part of this run, which has some steep and awkward sections. There are easy runs down to Reuti, from where you catch the cable-car to the valley. Access to the Hasliberg area is either by chair-lift through the trees or via a run to the bottom of the Hasliberg gondola. The most interesting skiing here is served by the long, cold Kaserstatt chair, which goes through a wide valley and then up a ridge to the top of the Hochstrass (2120m). There is a choice of routes down; a 'good run down the valley' or an off-piste route to Magisalp.

Our reporter came across very few queues and found the lift system well laid out and efficiently run by pleasant lift attendants. There are plenty of adequate mountain restaurants; prices are considerably lower than in the better-known resorts nearby. For those who want plenty of worthwhile skiing, but prefer a non-resort atmosphere and non-resort prices, Meiringen seems an excellent choice of destination.
Tourist office ✆ (036) 713622.
Package holidays Made to Measure (h) Ski Sutherland (h) SnowRanger (h).

St Wolfgang, Austria

Three reports on this picturesque village on the northern shores of Lake Wolfgang have prompted us to include it in this chapter, despite the fact that its ski area is a forty-minute drive away at Postalm. All three reporters were pleased with their choice of resort and hope to return to it – as good a recommendation as any. But then, they were all looking for a quiet, family resort which didn't focus only on skiing – which St Wolfgang doesn't.

The village is just over an hour's drive east of Salzburg and would definitely come into our category of 'good for short airport transfers'. Excursions to Salzburg and Vienna are readily available. Our reporters enjoyed walking along the beautiful lake shore and wandering through the village, although they complain that many of the shops were closed by the time they got back from the ski slopes. There is a fair choice of hotel accommodation, of which the Wolfgangerhof ('good food and facilities, friendly but slightly chaotic service') and the Seehotel Cortisen ('quiet, family-run, very relaxing') are recommended. Après-ski seems to centre around the Wolfgangerhof, where there are different tour-operator activities organised every night. The 'Pub' apparently closes when the last person leaves. There is an expensive nightclub and a bowling alley.

The drive to the ski area 'is a joy in itself', according to our reporters. Buses leave promptly at 9am every morning and wind through beautiful Alpine scenery to Postalm (1290m). They return equally promptly at 4pm. Postalm's skiing is on easy undulating slopes, served by short drag-lifts for which there are seldom queues. It suits beginners well, and has two nursery areas, a special beginners' lift pass and, by all accounts, an excellent ski school (run by Walter and Marianne Pistorius) with patient, flexible, English-speaking instructors. All but one of the runs are graded blue.

Tourist office ✆ (6138) 2239.
Package holidays Austrian Holidays (h) Crystal (h) Inghams (h) Thomson (h).

Altenmarkt, Austria

Altenmarkt is a pleasant old market town, on the edge of the Grossarltal in the eastern corner of Austria. It has a small skiing area of its own (a couple of lifts on one side of the Kemathöhe (1680m), linking with lifts from Radstadt on the other side) but of greater appeal to reporters are the ski areas of other nearby villages, all covered by the same lift pass.

Just round the corner to the south-west of Altenmarkt is Flachau, a village in the most easterly of three linked valleys, with Wagrain in the middle and Alpendorf (a satellite of St Johann in Pongau) on the western edge. These resorts are all described in greater detail in the Wagrain resort chapter. Of equal interest to skiers based in Altenmarkt is the small village of Zauchensee (due south of Altenmarkt), which has a variety of pistes on either side of the valley and is linked westwards to another two valleys, Flachauwinkl and Kleinarl. All this adds up to an extensive but fragmented ski area of mainly short, intermediate runs, all of which need to be reached by bus. This has not deterred our reporters, who generally liked the scope and nature of the skiing and were reasonably satisfied with the bus network, despite the peak-hour sardine-like conditions and some frustrating delays.

All three of our reporters went on the five-day instruction course run by New Zealanders Jo and Kevin Dent, which they unanimously recommend – 'small groups, clear explanations and demonstrations, enlightening video sessions, tremendous fun'; 'I seem to have made five years' progress in one year'. There are at least two other locally-run ski schools.

One reporter was pleasantly surprised to find that Altenmarkt is 'a town which happens to accommodate skiers', rather than a resort. It is a friendly place, with a modest range of restaurants and tea shops, one disco, a swimming pool and a tennis hall. Recommended hotels are the Lebzelter ('central and modern but not without character, friendly staff, good varied food') and the Lugin's Land, an ancient building set in lovely countryside about ten minutes' uphill walk from the town centre. The walk is apparently worth it for 'the views, the exceptional friendliness of the proprietor and his Welsh wife, and the superb four-course meals'.

Tourist office ✆ (6138) 2239.
Package holidays Austro Tours (h) Made to Measure (hs) Mogul Ski Holidays (hr) Ski Europe (h) Waymark (h).

Arêches, France

Not far from the Olympic cross-country venue of Les Saisies (described in another of the *Guide's* introductory chapters), Arêches is an unspoilt village in a beautiful agricultural area south of Beaufort. It shares a ski area with the neighbouring village of Le Planay, on two adjacent mountains, inconveniently separated by a valley. The mountain directly accessible from Arêches, Grand Mont (2690m), has the smaller share of the skiing – predominantly blue runs and paths, both above and below the tree-line. A fast new chair from the edge of the village climbs over wooded slopes to Le Cuvy (1710m), a small flatish clearing in the woods which has nursery slopes, a short cross-country circuit and a restaurant. It is also the starting point of the Bonnets Rouges chair-lift which serves open north-facing runs back to Le Cuvy. From here, there is a choice of routes down: blue 2 is a windy path which opens out towards the bottom; the more direct red is reportedly 'steep and challenging' and has an alternative black section; and blue 7 descends down the Combe de Perches to Le Planay, a long, attractive run with some awkward sections and a narrow gully.

Le Planay has altogether more scope and challenge than Grand Mont. There is no easy way down the mountain, which is why the 'easy motorway pistes' at the top are marked red – to discourage beginners from attempting them before they are ready to tackle the challenging intermediate lower runs (steep reds and two wooded blacks). From the high-point of the system, Grande Combe (2080m), there are several off-piste opportunities, one of which joins the Combe de Perches run half-way down. There are nursery slopes in Le Planay and a cross-country trail. A pleasant green path follows the road back to Arêches beside a mountain stream. There is also a regular navette between the two resorts.

Arêches is a sleepy village, apparently 'dead' at night, with few tourist facilities (the nearest foreign exchange is in Beaufort). It is reportedly dominated by a huge lodge accommodating employees of the French telecoms system. (Employees of British Telecom and related services can also stay there at very favourable rates.) The chalet-style lodge has all its own facilities (a shop, bar, games room, disco etc) and organises après-ski and excursions. For other visitors, there are several agencies with rooms and apartments to let in the village and a couple of small hotels and B&Bs. Beaufort offers more choice of accommodation – the Grand Mont hotel is recommended. Arêches has a well-regarded ski school, though English is not widely spoken, and kindergarten facilities. **Tourist office** © 79381533.

Sainte-Foy, France

You may be surprised to learn that the latest addition to the Tarentaise region is neither purpose-built nor attached to a vast ski area. It consists of a handful of old stone farm houses clustered around the base of the first of three consecutive chair-lifts above the village of Sainte-Foy, on the east side of the Isère valley. 'Le dernier grand domaine inexploité de Tarentaise' has finally been christened, 40 years after the first plans were drawn up to develop it. We must hope that the intervening years will have taught the developers a thing or two about resort expansion, and that Sainte-Foy will be built in a controlled, sympathetic and environmentally friendly way. It has certainly started along the right lines.

A newly surfaced road leads up from the village of Sainte-Foy to a car-park at the base of the ski area (1550m). A nursery drag, not in operation when our reporters visited, takes you to the main chair-lift. Just above it is a small ticket office next to a delightful restaurant, La Becqua, which has a sunny terrace and panoramic views of Mt Pourri on the other side of the valley. The main chair, a fast four-seater, rises over wooded slopes, dotted with old stone chalets, to a gentle plateau and another small restaurant. Runs back to the car-park consist of straightforward reds on the left-hand side of the lift and a long green track on the right (a road in summer). Two further chairs take you up to the Col de l'Aiguille (2620m), a sharp ridge between the peaks of Fogliettaz and Pierre d'Arbine. According to the piste map, there are black runs down either side of the top chair-lift, but in reality you can ski virtually anywhere on this wide, consistently steep and extremely beautiful mountainside before plunging into the woods lower down. It is wild, daunting, empty and 'a totally unique experience'.

From the ridge, there is a magnificent off-piste run down the south-facing side of the Col de l'Aiguille into a vast white wilderness. The route then follows the Clou river, past a deserted hamlet of the same name, to the beautiful and ancient village of Le Monal, deserted in winter. From here an easy and extremely scenic path, in and out of the woods, brings you back to Sainte-Foy. The Col de l'Aiguille is also the starting point for several ski touring routes.

Despite attempts to publicise itself (anyone driving up the Isère valley will have noticed the huge bill-boards), Sainte-Foy has had a very quiet first season. Both our reporters found that there were more lift-attendants than lift-users. The pisteurs are 'delightfully friendly', as are the staff of the La Becqua restaurant, who will put on a superb evening meal for you if you book in advance. The village of Sainte-Foy has a couple of simple hotels and rooms for rent, and there are several

other restaurants nearby. The smart Le Miroir restaurant in Miroir is particularly recommended.
Tourist office ✆ 79069170.

Lake Louise, Canada

Impressive numbers of reports on Canadian resorts this year have prompted us to create a new chapter on Whistler, British Columbia and to include Lake Louise, one of several small resorts around Banff in Alberta, in this chapter. Readers who think that a skiing holiday across the Atlantic is way out of their budget will be surprised to learn from one reporter that 'a two-week trip to Lake Louise, staying in a very upmarket hotel, actually cost less than it would have done to take the family to a typical hotel in Mottaret over Easter'. If this inspires you, read on.

Lake Louise (1650m) may not be in the same league as the well-known American resorts, but it has suited most of its visitors down to the ground. One reporter has made a list of its advantages: a good choice of runs of different grades from most lifts, so that almost everybody can ski from virtually any of the eleven lifts; a superb ski school and no language barriers; negligible lift queues (if you have to queue for more than ten minutes, the cost of your lift pass will be refunded); excellent cross-country trails through impressive Rockies scenery; high standards of accommodation in a superb setting; relatively low cost of living. The main disadvantage, mentioned by all our reporters, is that of extreme cold. In January last year the resort had to close for a few days when the effective temperature (with wind chill) dropped below -40°. This is unusually low, but it would pay to take many layers of clothing and to time your trip later, rather than earlier, in the season.

The lift system comprises three virtually parallel chair-lifts from the Base Area to various points on a wooded slope half-way up Mount Whitehorn (2660m) – the parallel gondola operates only in the summer. Three further chairs take skiers above the tree-line; to the summit of Mount Whitehorn on the left and to the ridge below it which divides the South Face skiing from the Back Bowls. A couple of further chairs extend the skiing into a third sector, the Larch area. There are extensive snow-making facilities. Those who want to get to know the resort can join a group led by one of the 'Friends of Louise', volunteers who give free guided tours of the area. Ski buses connect Lake Louise with the other resorts around Banff, principally Mount Norquay and Sunshine Village. A reporter who tried out Sunshine found the views better, the runs shorter and queues longer than at Lake Louise.

Lake Louise village is hardly more than a collection of hotels (Chateau Lake Louise, one of the famous Canadian Pacific hotels, is highly recommended by several reporters). Skating and ice-hockey take place on the lake and there are a few cleared paths, but après-ski and non-skiing facilities are limited. There is far more on offer in Banff (45 minutes away).
Package holidays Canada Air Holidays (hs) Hickie Borman (h) Neilson (h) SnowRanger (h) Sportsworld Travel (h).

WHICH SKI RESORT?

The heart of the *Guide* starts here. In this 500-page section, we describe and assess the 300 or so ski resorts in Europe and North America which, one way or another, have the biggest claims on your attention.

We have arranged the resorts not in national or alphabetical order, but geographically – so that resorts which are close together on the ground are close together in the book. We are aware that some people like to decide first which country to go to, and then to choose within it – and our geographical order *will* be a bit painful if pasta and Chianti are your main priorities. But countries other than Italy form almost solid blocks of the book, and the geographical order has the great advantage that it allows you to consider sensibly the several shared ski areas which cross boundaries both alphabetical and national – chief among them the Portes du Soleil (France and Switzerland), the Milky Way (France and Italy), the Matterhorn area, between Zermatt (Switzerland) and Cervinia (Italy), and the area shared by La Thuile (Italy) and La Rosière (France). Even where there is not shared skiing, there is sense in choosing your resort in the knowledge of what other resorts nearby have to offer. The skier who likes to explore can easily run up against borders – from the Chamonix valley in France, for example, the sunny slopes of Courmayeur in Italy lie only half an hour away, through the Mont Blanc Tunnel. If you want to know what lies over the hill, you need only look over the page.

To find a resort by name, turn to the **resort index**, almost at the back of the book.

To find the resorts of a particular region, turn over the page to the **list of chapters**, which is in page (and therefore geographical) order, or look at the **location maps** starting on page 54.

To find a resort to suit your needs, turn first to the **verdicts chart** starting on page 47, which summarises the pros and cons of the major resorts covered by the *Guide*.

Resorts chapter by chapter

The resorts are grouped into short chapters which are ordered geographically. First, north-east Italy is dealt with from east to west; then the sequence goes through the Alps in an anti-clockwise sweep via Austria and Switzerland to France – taking in further parts of Italy on the way. After the most southerly resort in the French Alps come chapters on the Pyrenees; then Spain; then Scotland; then Norway; then Eastern Europe; then the USA; then finally Canada.

Major resorts – those which attract a lot of British visitors or which have undeniably major ski areas – are covered in detail, with information on lift passes, ski school and so on, as well as a full description of (and judgements on) the resort; the names of these resorts are printed in **bold type** below and on our maps of the Alpine countries. Minor resorts, which are summarised in a few lines (or even a few words) in the *Guide*, appear in ordinary type below – very minor ones are not listed here at all. The skiing of each major resort (and of most minor resorts linked in to a major area) is described in detail, and shown on a map; the key to these maps is on page 61.

The chapters on Alpine resorts follow a standard pattern. Those on resorts elsewhere are less consistent: as well as fully detailed resort reports on the Alpine pattern, you will find general reports (or at least general sections) on what it is like to go skiing in the Pyrenees, Scotland, Eastern Europe, Norway and America.

Some resorts new to the *Guide* are described (on the basis of readers' reports) in a chapter starting on page 25.

In the list below, recognised names of ski areas are given in *italic type* after the resort names. Where an area bridges two chapters, we have applied the label to both with the addition of a suffix 1 or 2.

Choosing your resort

Choice of resort may not be the most important reason for the success or failure of a holiday – luck with the weather and snow, and perhaps with companions, is probably more decisive – but it is one aspect of the holiday over which you have some control. Every ski resort is somebody's ideal resort; on the other hand, none suits everyone. In this chapter our aim is mainly to provoke thought about what constitutes your own ideal – so that with the help of the main resorts section of the *Guide* (and the comparative chart following this chapter) you can arrive at your own short-list.

The time-of-year factor
The shifting patterns of weather and crowds affect resorts in different ways: timing of a holiday should weigh heavily in the balance when choosing your resort.

Going skiing **before Christmas** means going before the skiing season is properly under way. Choose a large, well-known resort popular with good skiers. Val d'Isère has a famous pre-Christmas downhill race, is lively and as reliable for snow as anywhere. A few resorts (Verbier and St Anton are the best-known examples) are popular places for pre-season ski courses known as *Wedelkurse* or *Cours de Godille*. The resorts offer all-in packages of accommodation, lift pass and ski school just as they do at other low-season periods. There is an undeserved mystique about these courses, which are in fact no more than an intensive course of ski school tuition which can be undertaken by fit skiers of all standards.

If you are going skiing over **Christmas/New Year** mainly in order to be away from home for the festivities, then resort charm and specific choice of hotel count for a lot. Little Austrian resorts such as Alpbach and Serfaus (not covered in this edition) have a delightfully festive atmosphere at this time of year and are justifiably popular, despite their limited skiing. In general, lower resorts which have a permanent as well as a casual population are attractively Christmassy. Skiers who have had snowless skiing over the holiday in the few past years may be tempted to aim high – though lack of precipitation has often been the problem. Those who do so shouldn't be surprised to find bleak, low-visibility conditions if the weather is more traditional. They must also be prepared to find not much of a Yuletide atmosphere – though a jovial chalet party can make up for that. One clear advantage of a high, purpose-built resort is shorter queues, because of better-organised lifts.

Some long-established Swiss resorts have a special appeal; the British have been spending Christmas in resorts such as Wengen and Mürren for over half a century, and there's still nowhere more suitable for living out your own Christmas-card idyll – beautiful old log-cabin chalets, no cars, and magnificent scenery.

Continental skiers stay at home in **January**, unless tempted on to the slopes by good weather at the weekend. Keen British skiers, lured to the Alps by keen British package prices, should go to places with a big British trade – such as Val d'Isère, Courmayeur, Verbier and Söll – if they want to be sure of finding much life in the resort.

Although recent winters have not conformed to the pattern, January has traditionally been expected to bring more than a fair share of blizzards. In these conditions, medium-altitude resorts with plenty of skiing below the tree-line come into their own, because visibility is better among trees and the slopes are sheltered from wind – so lifts are less likely to be closed. In general the Alpine tree-line is at about 1800 to 2000m; resorts such as Kitzbühel and Söll in the Austrian Tirol offer a full 1000 metres of skiing (measured vertically) in more-or-less friendly woodland surroundings. Chair-lifts and drag-lifts are less prone to closure than cable-cars, but riding them can be bitterly cold. The ideal is to have a choice of kinds of lift.

January is a tempting time to visit big-name resorts notorious for their lift queues. If you have a week of good weather, you'll get very fit and be an immediate convert to January holidays. With a car, you could even sample several such resorts in one trip, fixing up accommodation as you go – you'll have no trouble finding a bed.

The disappointing skiing conditions of recent years (and particularly of 1988, 1989 and 1990) have been far from uniform; but one clear characteristic they have had in common is a pronounced lack of January snow. 1991 did not follow this 'new' pattern. Heaven knows what we should expect in 1992.

You can hope to find decent skiing wherever you go in **February**; but you must expect crowds. The French, Swiss and Germans have holidays during the month. The concentration of French holidays is particularly heavy, and although the French resorts are better able to cope with peak loads than most, the roads leading to them are not. In 1992 there is the further complication of the Winter Olympics in the Tarentaise resorts from 8th to 23rd February. Most people will want to avoid the region during that period. The national tourist office can tell you which particular school-holiday weeks to avoid.

For a holiday in **early March**, it is advisable to choose a resort with plenty of skiing above 2000m on slopes facing north and east. In high resorts you can be pretty sure of snow and reasonably hopeful of good snow; conditions are often excellent for exploring off-piste. (Many of the lower Austrian resorts, on the other hand, offer low-season prices for March, because they are regarded as increasingly risky for snow as the month progresses.)

To be confident of finding decent skiing in **late March** or **April** you have to go high – as a rule of thumb, you need slopes in the range 2500m to 3500m, and preferably north-facing. The resorts which can provide such slopes are few, with the result that skiers are concentrated in those resorts and the crowds at Easter are the worst of the season – particularly in France, where many of the reliable late-season resorts are to be found.

The tail end of the season in the Alps is often the time when conditions are at their best in Scotland; in the depth of winter the weather is often discouragingly bad, while in spring the sun is not so strong as to ruin the snow.

The ability factor

It's important that your choice of resort takes account of the kind of skier you are. We've called this the ability factor, but it's actually rather broader, embracing your skiing appetite as well as aptitude.

The first requirement of a resort for **beginners** is that it should have a gentle nursery slope on which to take those first faltering steps on skis. It should ideally not be much of a slope at all (part of it should be completely flat); it should be big enough to cope with however many beginners there are, and it should not be part of a piste used by other skiers on their way down the mountain. It should have a gentle, slow lift, not one which non-nursery skiers are tempted to use. It should get some sunshine, and there should be a bar close by.

Most resorts have such slopes beside the village, at the foot of the main ski slopes. If the nursery slopes are high up, beginners face the cost of getting to and from them each day. On the other hand, high-level nursery slopes are usually sunnier than village ones; they are usually more convenient for mid-day meetings with other skiers; and they are extremely valuable if snow is in short supply in the village – the lower the resort is, the more likely this is, especially late in the season. Many purpose-built resorts have achieved the best of both worlds by siting themselves high up, with excellent wide-open nursery areas immediately at hand. Alpe d'Huez, Sestriere and Isola 2000 are spectacularly good in this respect.

Nursery slopes are for the first few days only – perhaps even the first few hours if you make good progress with an adventurous instructor. For a painless graduation to real skiing, you need easy, unthreatening pistes – graded green in those resorts which sensibly adopt four categories of run – on which to build up confidence. Many resorts which have perfectly good nursery areas – Selva, for example – are very uncomfortable places for a near-beginner because they lack such runs.

It is equally important to bear in mind that not all beginners are dedicated piste-bashers by the end of their first week. Some don't take to skiing at all, and throw in the towel (and their crippling hired boots); others find skiing all day a bit exhausting, and like to mix skiing with other things. So it's important to consider the charm factor, and the non-skiing factor – dealt with later in the chapter.

Fashionable resorts with enormous ski areas, where lift passes and ski hire are expensive, are wasted on most beginners. Affluent beginners – or beginners joining parties of more experienced skiers – need not avoid them altogether. But some big-name resorts which appeal strongly to good skiers *are* best avoided for your first trip – see our comparative chart.

In practically any resort **intermediate** skiers will find skiing suitable for their ability. Even in resorts that appeal mainly to good skiers, most of the pistes will be negotiable under good snow conditions by plucky (and that does not mean fearless or reckless) intermediates. Plenty of them ski around the toughest skiing resorts in the Alps without a qualm. These resorts do not provide very much scope for relaxing, flattering skiing – you have to enjoy a challenge, and be prepared to take a lift down if you're not up to it.

Many intermediate skiers are keen and adventurous without relishing the challenge of difficult skiing, and the modern resorts with big ski areas have bred a species of skier for whom variety in skiing is very much the spice of life. These piste-freaks look for resorts where 'you can ski for a week without doing the same piste twice'; and provided you're not too literal about it there is now quite a range of resorts which conform to the specification. Many are modern French resorts in the Tarentaise or the northern Alps. Piste tourism at its most beautiful is to be found in the majestic scenery around the Sella Group in the Dolomites. In all these areas, no very difficult runs have to be skied in the course of skiing from resort to resort. Our comparative chart identifies several other traditional resorts with extensive skiing areas where intermediates can cover lots of ground without terrifying themselves. And the *Guide*'s piste maps are in a way tailor-made for the intermediate piste-basher, who can now see at a glance what a resort means when it claims to possess 'le plus grand domaine skiable du monde'.

We hesitate to prescribe what the **expert** skier should look for in a resort – we imagine that anyone who has become expert at negotiating steep slopes will also have become expert at identifying them, and at figuring out what other resort characteristics are desirable. But our comparative chart shows which resorts we would turn to first for tough skiing and for off-piste skiing.

Any grade of skier may have an interest in the quality of the **ski-school**. In the *Guide*'s resort assessments, we have drawn what conclusions we can about individual ski schools from our readers' experiences, but it is impossible to generalise except in a few respects. First, standards within any one school are likely to vary widely, and schools with long-standing reputations are no exception to this. Secondly, it's important for most British skiers that they are taught in English; this means not only that the instructor must speak English well, but also that there must be enough English-speaking clients to justify an English-speaking class – and that means going to a resort with a big UK trade (or to America). Thirdly, it doesn't matter how skilled the instructor is if there are 20 people in the class – your progress will be slow, or nil. We've paid particular attention to class size in our resort reports but there are precious few resorts which do not at some time or another permit classes of ludicrous sizes.

The access factor

Holiday-makers who are used to a 30-minute ride from package airport to package hotel in their summer resorts get a bit of a shock when they first go skiing. Coach transfers of less than two hours are exceptional. Most of the very easily accessible resorts are in two areas – close to Geneva, where France, Switzerland and Italy meet, or in the eastern part of the Austrian Tirol, within easy motorway reach of Munich and Salzburg airports. Resorts in Western Austria and Eastern Switzerland are all much further away from airports. Most Italian resorts involve very long airport transfers – some as long as eight hours, even without delays; the exceptions are the resorts in the extreme west of the country, which are about two hours from Turin. Enthusiastic supporters of resorts in the Tarentaise region of the French Alps – Méribel, Val d'Isère and so on – admit that the transfers are a drawback. In theory the journey from Geneva takes three or four hours, culminating in tortuous climbs from the valley to the high resorts – but weekend traffic jams can double the theoretical journey times. New road-building for the 1992 Olympics may or may not solve the problem.

If you're going by car, don't pay too much attention to slight differences in distance to resorts; winter weather (in the Channel as well as the Alps) and holiday traffic are more likely to determine how long the journey takes. But some of the differences are not slight: it's an appreciably longer-than-average journey to Italian resorts east of Milan, to St Moritz, and to southern French resorts – especially Isola 2000 and its neighbours, which are best reached via Nice.

In the Reference section chapter we list the major resorts which have railway stations. Many can be reached with only one or two changes of train, and some can be reached with no changes at all. The Austrian resort of St Anton is outstanding in this respect: you can board a train at Victoria after lunch, and disembark next morning about 100 yards from the cable-car station which gives direct access to some of the best skiing in the world.

The convenience factor

Most skiers would like to have ski-lifts going up from their front door and pistes coming back down to it. Most would also like to spend their holiday in a community rather than a holiday camp. But it is very rare to find a village or town which is ideally placed as a skiing base *and* has grown up naturally for some other reason. St Anton is one example – a travellers' rest at the foot of the Arlberg Pass, and coincidentally at the foot of excellent ski slopes. Its village centre is a very convenient base for skiers. Obergurgl is another – a high village which might have been purpose-built, but didn't need to be. In most other traditional resorts, you need to choose your location with care, and with one eye firmly on the public transport system.

If the convenience factor really matters, though, you will almost certainly be better off choosing a modern resort which has been designed solely for skiers. Convenience is not just a question of getting around; planned resorts, provided they are sufficiently remote, can in theory achieve an approximate balance between the supply of uphill transport and the demand for it. Although resort developers make no money out of blissfully uncongested lifts, many purpose-built resorts have managed to put this theory into reasonably effective practice; what's more, many have also managed to plan lift and piste networks so as to avoid bottle-necks.

Skiing convenience dictates a style of building and a resort layout which have little in common with real communities. In most ski areas there is one situation which makes a more convenient base than any other, and the logical plan is one which concentrates skiers there. The landmarks of the first purpose-built resort, Sestriere, show the logic in action: tall, round towers full of very cramped accommodation.

Some small resorts – Puy-St-Vincent, Isola 2000 – consist of little more than one single-building complex, with flats, shops, bars, restaurants and resort offices under one roof. The walking you have to do is along carpeted corridors, the lift queues are to get to and from the 32nd floor. They're a bit like ocean liners – except that low standards of design, finish and maintenance have made them more like troop ships than the QE2. But a single such unit cannot simply be expanded to accommodate any number of skiers, or to service any size of ski-area. Thus, in the much larger resort of La Plagne (which claims to sell more lift passes than any other resort), half a dozen clusters of buildings are scattered far and wide, high and low, around an enormous skiing area – including several old hamlets far below the main purpose-built resort centres.

There is no shortage of skiers who welcome the effortlessness of holidays in these new resorts. There are keen skiers who are obliged to take their holidays in high season, when many resorts cannot handle the crowds; they ski hard, value the lift system which enables them to do so, and are not too bothered about après-ski or sleigh rides. Then there are skiing families, who find that the freedom and economy of the apartment formula suits them and their pockets well, and that many of the new resorts (especially in France) are the most relaxing places to take children.

Needless to say, resorts such as these do not suit everyone; one man's convenience food is another man's junk. Non-skiing activities (day-time and night-time) are rarely as fully developed as in traditional resorts. What they lack more than anything else is life, the feeling of being a community, which by definition they are not. Hoteliers, shop-keepers and ski instructors are foreigners hired for the season or commuters from the valley, who leave the place deserted in the evening except for holiday-makers at a loose end, who may search in vain for a café with some local atmosphere.

Other big resorts have been developed differently, to have some resemblance to a real village – in overall structure even if not in style. It is no coincidence that these resorts – of which Méribel is the clearest example – are ones where you need to take care about where in the village you stay, just as you do in traditional resorts.

It may not be possible to give a new resort the vitality of an established community, but it is possible to build one which is both convenient and appealing – provided it is not also required to be large. That, at least, is the conclusion we draw from the example of Valmorel, recently developed not far from the Three Valleys. Its designers have obviously set out to synthesize an Alpine village atmosphere, and if the buildings mature rather than decay as they age, that objective seems likely to be achieved.

In many ways the most successful of the big purpose-built resorts is one of the first – Courchevel. It is no beauty, but under snow its ugliness is not obtrusive and it is much less shoddy than many younger resorts. It has a lively centre, with comfortable hotels (it pre-dates the great self-catering boom), restaurants and varied nightlife. Chalets and more hotels are spread around the mountainside in a broad horseshoe so that nearly everyone can get to and from home on skis. The terrain is such that the skiing around the resort itself is spacious and very easy, and snow is usually reliable at resort level. For bad weather there is good skiing below the resort among the woods. Queues build up at the main lift departure point, but there are alternative ways into the system. The only thing it isn't easy to do in Courchevel is economise.

The crowds factor

You don't have to be a super-keen skier to prefer skiing in a resort which is relatively free of lift queues; they are boring, tiring, often stressful, and disruptive of the best-laid plans. Tourist offices like to produce statistics giving the ratio of resort beds to lift capacity in persons per hour, but these figures rarely tell you what you need to know about queues – and can be highly misleading. The *Guide's* resort reports contain what concrete information we have about queues in recent seasons, but it is also helpful to have an appreciation of what makes a resort more likely or less likely to suffer from bad queues in high season.

A resort will be relatively queue-free if it is small (relative to its skiing area) and remote from centres of population; or if it has a lift system without bottle-necks (a shortage of lifts leaving the resort is the usual problem – and most of the resorts which don't suffer from bottle-necks are purpose-built ones); or if it attracts a high proportion of non-skiers and cross-country skiers; or if it doesn't attract many people at all. A few examples will serve to show how these factors operate in practice.

Obergurgl is very popular and its lift system is mainly old and slow; it often has good snow when other places are short; but it very rarely has lift queues, because it is a very small place and, equally important, it is remote. Valmorel is small and rarely gets crowded; other resorts in its neighbourhood are much more powerful magnets. Val d'Isère is large and very popular, but remote and very well served by lifts from the valley floor; queues are rarely serious, except in bad weather when higher lifts are closed by wind.

Famous, large resorts which provide inefficient access to excellent skiing areas normally have substantial queues. Kitzbühel is a prominent example: a fashionable, international resort with a lot of visitor beds, easy access from Munich in southern Germany and a quite inadequate access lift from the town to the main ski area. In Cortina d'Ampezzo the ratio of beds to lift capacity (especially capacity from the resort) is also discouraging; but queues are usually not serious, because so many people do things other than skiing, and because many skiers are late starters in the morning.

The queueing for lifts in most of the long-established resorts is in fact not the problem it used to be, now that new lifts have relieved their notorious bottle-necks. But the result of all this efficiency is that the pistes in many resorts are becoming crowded, instead of the lifts; this is just as unpleasant and much more dangerous. At least in the Chamonix valley (where the hostility of terrain and ecologists have for years combined to frustrate initiatives to alleviate the queueing problem), when you do get to the top of the mountain you don't have to ski all the way down in a crowd.

The accommodation factor

Most skiers choose the style of their holiday accommodation before considering where to look for it – indeed many skiers go to the same sort of accommodation year after year. Such single-mindedness predetermines to some extent your choice of resort.

Nearly all package holidays in Italy and Austria employ **hotel** accommodation. In most Italian resorts there are plenty of cheap, mostly very simple hotels and guest-houses, which make other forms of accommodation look expensive. Cheap as they are, not all these places represent good value, unless your requirements are minimal. Most of our reporters' disappointment with hotels has come from Italian holidays. Most Italian resorts have one or two large, comfortable hotels; few of these are stylish or cheaper than comfortable hotels in other countries.

In Austria (and in most of the Dolomite resorts – which are in many ways more Austrian in character than Italian) the standard of hotel accommodation is high and uniform. Not only are most hotels well kept, clean and comfortable, but also they tend to be attractive (outside and in) and welcoming. For many of our reporters, the attraction of a particular hotel is a powerful reason to return to an Austrian resort which they might otherwise desert. Lots of not-very-luxurious Austrian hotels have saunas and pools. In (and near) the largest and most famous resorts, such as Kitzbühel and St Anton, many package operators offer cheap holidays in simple bed-and-breakfast accommodation (the prefix 'Haus' often indicates this); even the simplest are usually attractive and adequately comfortable. In most skiing regions of Austria there are lots of small villages within easy driving distance of skiing, where almost every family takes in bed-and-breakfast guests.

In traditional Swiss and French resorts there is a much greater variety of style, standard and price of hotel accommodation, ranging from very simple boarding houses, where ski-bums cram several to a room and live very cheaply, to simple family hotels and (mostly in Switzerland) large, expensive palaces which are almost self-sufficient resorts in themselves. In the new purpose-built resorts there are usually few hotels, and not much of a range of comfort and cost. Courchevel is one of the few purpose-built French resorts with a lot of hotels, some of them very comfortable and expensive.

There are **self-catering** chalets and apartments for rent in most resorts, but the majority of self-catering package holidays are in French resorts, mostly purpose-built. Shopping facilities, more important for self-caterers than other skiers, are usually good and convenient, but demand for them in the early evening is heavy, and prices are of course higher than in valley-bottom *hypermarchés*. It is quite possible to arrange self-catering holidays in other resorts – write to the local tourist offices for information, and get hold of the Interhome brochure for the country you're looking at; if nothing else, it will give you a clear idea of the possibilities.

Verbier and the French Tarentaise resorts are the great homes of the **chalet** holiday, and now of the 'club' or 'jumbo' chalet which has sprung off from the original animal; all are very fashionable among gregarious young and not-so-young keen skiers who like the staffed chalet formula. Chalets are also to be found (usually in smaller numbers) in a few other Swiss and Italian (mainly Dolomite) resorts, and in a very few Austrian ones. The cost of chalet holidays doesn't vary much from country to country, which makes them a particularly attractive way to holiday in Switzerland and France, and not very attractive in Italy and Austria. Our resort verdicts pick out the small number of resorts with a wide range of chalet holidays on offer.

The charm factor

Keen skiers who piste-bash themselves to exhaustion every day may well scorn the idea that the style, looks and diversions of a ski resort could make any difference to them. But for most people the very word 'Alpine' has connotations of Christmas-card charm, and an Alpine holiday with no trees, no log cabins, no jingle bells, and no skaters – only bare rock and snow and concrete – adds up to a sadly incomplete holiday. Resort charm has seven major ingredients.

A year-round community – probably a village, but sometimes a town, with a life independent of skiing; preferably farming buildings and hamlets dotted around the valley and hillsides. This is most easily found in Austria, where many ski resorts have grown out of farming communities, at relatively low altitude. It is not a matter of prettiness, more a matter of people – a sense of place, of character.

A picturesque setting – not too enclosed, with some woodland. The beauty of the mountain scenery is a major contribution, for example, to the appeal of Zermatt and St Moritz. It is an even greater element of the appeal of the Dolomites. Not all high mountain scenery is particularly beautiful – on the contrary, it is often merely bleak, hostile and monotonous. Resorts in balcony settings half-way up the flanks of wide, deep valleys benefit from broader, longer views and usually more sunshine than resorts at the bottom of valleys, which may be better placed for multidirectional skiing; examples are Crans-Montana, Sauze d'Oulx, Wengen and Mürren – surely the most beautifully set ski resort of all.

Absence of cars – or at least an absence of busy through-routes; preferably snowy streets. Here most high, remote resorts naturally have the advantage. Most purpose-built resorts restrict or banish cars; and most car-free resorts are purpose-built – the main exceptions are Zermatt, Saas Fee, Mürren, Wengen (all in Switzerland) and Serfaus (not covered in this edition).

Traditional winter sports activities – horses and sleighs, walkers, outdoor skating and curling, tobogganers, cross-country skiers to give the place something other than the brutal downhill atmosphere. Most often found in long-established winter sports resorts, mainly in

Switzerland (St Moritz and Arosa among others). Seefeld is a departure from the pattern – in Austria, and mainly of recent development.

Decent mountain restaurants – plentiful in number, with outside terraces for good weather and mountain-refuge-style (rather than cafeteria-style) interiors for bad weather. Long-established resorts, and especially ones popular for summer walking, tend to be well and attractively catered for – Klosters, Zermatt, Courmayeur, the Dolomites, even Sauze d'Oulx.

Dignified clientele – as opposed to a clientele consisting of rowdy international youth. Undoubtedly the popularity of resorts such as Sauze d'Oulx, Mayrhofen, Söll, Val d'Isère and St Anton with rowdy young people, not necessarily British, spoils the atmosphere for others.

Chalet-style buildings – with balconies and pitched roofs. In Austria, not only are many resorts attractive old villages, they have also been developed in a carefully pseudo-traditional style; very few – not even resorts which grew from almost nothing, such as Obergurgl and Zürs – are eyesores. Not all 'traditional' resorts can claim this, especially in Switzerland: Davos, Arosa, Crans-Montana, even St Moritz, can rival any purpose-built resort for architectural bleakness.

The non-skiing factor

The needs of non-skiers are largely covered under the charm factor. For variety of spectacle as well as variety of activity, there is no beating the Engadine (St Moritz and its surroundings); part of its great appeal is the scope it offers for escaping the paraphernalia and mechanics of a modern ski resort to explore beautiful wooded valleys where no skiers (or at least no Alpine piste skiers) venture.

Many people like to get out of the resort for a day to go shopping or sightseeing, or simply for a change. Resorts near Innsbruck are the very good for this, with plentiful day-trips to Innsbruck and to the various places of interest, cultural and material, over the Brenner Pass in Italy. Non-skiers in the Dolomites not only have these interesting excursions within reach, they can also do their own Sella Ronda spectacular by public bus and can just about fit in visits to Venice or Verona. By contrast, a non-skier in one of the resorts of the French Tarentaise region – Val d'Isère or Méribel, say – is practically confined there for the duration of the holiday.

The family factor

Properly speaking, there is not a separate family factor. If you are taking children skiing, you will want to take account of the matters we have considered under charm, convenience, ability, access (long coach transfers can be a nightmare with children), non-skiing and accommodation. But there remains the distinct question of how resorts actually look after children. In general, purpose-built resorts aim for family business, and the skiing requirements of beginners, and especially junior beginners, are very well looked after. Parents can dump their offspring for the day or half-day in trained hands and enjoy their own skiing. Consider also where you will want to spend your skiing day, and how far away it is from the nursery areas.

The après-ski factor

The skiing day is rarely longer than eight or nine hours, and often appreciably shorter. This leaves plenty of time for activities other than skiing, and some skiers find it leaves plenty of energy as well – though our attempts to glean information on nightlife from your resort reports leave no doubt that few *Guide* readers fall into this category. For those who care about it, après-ski is a crucial consideration: ski resorts vary more in the range, quantity, style and expense of their evening social activities than in practically any other respect. The key factor for most skiers, probably, is the presence in the resort of plenty of like-minded, socially well matched compatriots. Go to well known resorts which are widely advertised by tour operators as offering the sort of nightlife you like, and with luck you will find it in full swing.

The snow factor

Good snow is an important element in a satisfactory skiing holiday; in general, where you should go to find it varies with the time of year, and that factor is dealt with at the beginning of the chapter. But with most resorts there is always a risk that the snow at a normally dependable time of year will turn out to be disappointing, and if you're prepared to travel out of high season it's tempting to think that you can avoid this risk by fixing your holiday at the last moment and going to a resort which is doing well in the newspaper snow reports.

Newspapers carry two main kinds of snow report. Resort tourist offices issue figures for the depth of snow on the upper and lower slopes, which are distributed to the press by national tourist offices; even if these figures were reliable (which they are not) they would give only a crude idea of the snow cover. Much more valuable are the reports sent home by the Ski Club of Great Britain's representatives (based in about 30 Alpine resorts). These incorporate the figures, but add brief comments which are very illuminating once you learn to read between the words. The Club has to tread carefully in order to provide helpful information while meeting its obligation to the resorts, which sponsor the reps in the expectation that having a rep in town will attract British skiers. So the comments (which are often sent via the tourist office telex machine) have to be delicately written: 'Good skiing above 2,500 metres' and 'Good skiing on upper slopes' are favourite ways of describing wash-out conditions on the lower slopes.

Naturally, reps vary in how they handle these difficulties, and in how they perceive snow conditions. Some resort officials take a much closer interest in the reports than others, too. So resort-to-resort comparisons are unlikely to tell you much. But you can certainly use the reports to build up a general picture of broad areas of the Alps.

Ski Club reports are also among those 'published' via telephone services promoted by newspapers. These services are expensive (especially if you are interested in a particular resort which comes toward the end of the recorded message), but the best of them carry a lot of illuminating detail, usually provided by tour operators' reps.

Since the 1986–87 season, *The Independent* has carried (on Saturday mornings) a general review of snow conditions, drawing on all the available sources including telephone reports from readers on holiday. This innovation has been widely imitated by other newspapers.

The cost factor

For most people, the cost of a skiing holiday can be broken down into three parts – your package of transport, accommodation and perhaps meals; your skiing 'overheads' (equipment, lift pass, tuition); and incidentals (drinks, meals other than those included in the package).

Our studies of package holiday prices lead us to the not very helpful conclusion that it is difficult to generalise about which resorts or which countries are cheap and which expensive, and still more difficult to generalise about which places offer good and bad value for what you pay. So much depends on the particular deal assembled by the tour operator that even such plausible assertions as 'Italy is less expensive than Switzerland' should not be accepted without question.

Overhead costs vary very widely between resorts; they are not so much the result of fundamental economic characteristics of different countries as of the place in the market that different resorts occupy – though of course exchange rates (and rapid changes in those rates) can have a marked effect on comparisons. Nevertheless, it is broadly true that most skiers going to Switzerland or France should expect to spend more than those going to Austria or Italy – and much more than those going to Spain, Andorra and eastern Europe. There are places in Switzerland and France where a modest budget can be made to suffice, but they are in the main not internationally known.

The most expensive Swiss resorts (Verbier or Zermatt) may charge three or four times as much as the cheapest down-market resorts for lift passes, ski school tuition and equipment hire, making a difference of perhaps £150 to the total cost of a week's holiday.

Incidental costs also vary widely. The differences are surprisingly difficult to pin down, but again you will find France and Switzerland more expensive than Austria and Italy; and again you will find smart international resorts much more expensive than less well-known neighbours.

Major resort verdicts

The chart spread over the next six pages shows our verdicts on the attractions and drawbacks of the major resorts of Europe, and the few American resorts we have so far covered in detail. It is intended as an aid to making your own shortlist. Do not rely exclusively on the chart for resort selection. Use it as a short-cut to the resort chapters, which explain and sometimes qualify the verdicts. Also remember that there are plenty of good smaller resorts in the *Guide* but not in this chart.

The chapter on 'Choosing your resort', starting on page 35, explains what we mean by some of the less obvious concepts used here, such as *Alpine charm* (a concept which we extend outside the Alps), *chalet holidays*, *family holidays* and *skiing convenience*. The chapter also explains some of the seasonal variations, which the chart cannot convey. These are especially important when considering such matters as *lift queues* (where 'good for queues' means queues are rare), *après-ski* and *resort-level snow* (which refers to the likelihood of snow in the village streets, as well as on the runs down to village level). Some resorts are low and unreliable for snow in and around the resort, but have high, absolutely reliable glacier runs; this is why we have a separate *late holidays* category. It is when snow is falling in abundance that the shelter of *woodland runs* is particularly welcome.

For most aspects of a resort we employ a simple scale of three unashamedly subjective judgements – good, bad and average. But for some aspects, where the distinction between average and poor has little meaning, we use only the good rating. These include *ski touring* (which means climbing on skis, not travelling around various resorts by car), *off-piste skiing, artificial snow* or direct *rail access* (in which we include resorts such as Verbier, where the station and the village are linked by cable-car).

By a *big ski area*, we mean a large, linked lift network making it possible to cover lots of ground without removing your skis, as exemplified by the Trois Vallées resorts. By *easy runs* we mean not nursery slopes but long easy runs which can give near-beginners and timid skiers some variety, satisfaction and confidence. In assessing how good or bad a resort is for *tough runs*, we have concentrated on whether a resort as a whole is likely to appeal to skiers who relish a challenge. By good for *not skiing*, we do not mean useless for skiing, but good for a non-skiing holiday. The *sunny slopes* category refers to ski areas well endowed either with south-facing slopes or with both east-and west-facing ones.

Resorts rated good for *easy road access* are ones which are not too far from the Channel *and* which present no local difficulties for drivers. To be judged good for *freedom from cars*, a resort must also not be over-run by other vehicles – such as Zermatt's electric taxis.

Major Resorts
our verdicts summarised

✔ good
○ average
✗ bad

	Big ski area	Tough runs	Off-piste skiing	Ski touring	Lift queues	Skiing convenience	Woodland runs	Late holidays	Artificial snow	Summer skiing
Adelboden		✗			○	○	✔	✗		
Alpbach		✗			○	✗	○	✗		
Alpe d'Huez	✔	✔	✔		○	○	✗	○	✔	
Andermatt		✔	✔	✔	✗	✗	✗	○		
Les Arcs	✔	✔	✔		○	✔	○	✔		
Arosa		✗		✔	○	○	✗	○		
Avoriaz	✔	○			✗	✔	○	✗		
Badgastein	✔	✔			✗	✗	✔	○	✔	
Barèges	✔	✗			○	○	○	✗		
Bormio		✗			○	○	✔	✗	✔	✔
Breckenridge		✔			✔	○	✔	○	✔	
Cervinia	✔	✗			✗	○	✗	✔		✔
Chamonix		✔	✔	✔	✗	✗	✗	✔		
La Clusaz		○			○	✗	✔	✗		
Cortina d'Ampezzo		○			○	✗	✔	✗	✔	
Courchevel	✔	✔			✔	✔	✔	○	✔	
Courmayeur		✗	✔	✔	○	✗	✔	○	✔	
Crans-Montana	✔	✗			○	✗	✔	✗		
Davos	✔	○	✔	✔	○	✗	○	○		
Les Deux Alpes		○	✔		○	○	✗	✔		✔
Flaine	✔	○			✔	✔	✗	✔		
Flims	✔	✗			○	✗	✔	✗		
Hintertux		✗			○	✗	✗	✔		✔

Easy runs	Nursery slopes	Family holidays	Mountain restaurants	Sunny slopes	Freedom from cars	Alpine charm	Resort-level snow	Beautiful scenery	Apres-ski	Not skiing	Cross-country	Chalet holidays	Short transfers	Easy road access	Rail access
○	○	✔	○	✔	○	✔	○		○	○	✔		○	○	
○	○	✔	○		○	✔	○		○	○			✔	✔	
○	✔	✔	○	✔	✗	✗	✔	✔	○	○			○	○	
✗	✗		✗		○	✔	✔		✗	✗			○	○	✔
○	○	✔	✗	✔	✔	✗	✔		✗	✗			✗	✗	✔
✔	✔		○	✔	○	○	✔		○	✔	✔		○	✗	✔
○	✔	✔	○		✔	✗	✔		○	✗			✔	○	
✗	✗		○		✗	✗	✗		✔	✔			○	○	✔
○	✔		✗	✔	○	✔	✗		○	✗			✔	○	
✗	○		✔		✗	○	✗		○	✔			✗	✗	
✔	○	✔	✗		○	○	✔		○	○			○		
✔	✔		✗	✔	✗	✗	✔		○	✗			○	○	
✗	✗		✗		✗	○	✗	✔	✔	○	✔		✔	✔	✔
○	○		✔		✗	○	✗	✔	○	○	✔		✔	✔	
○	✔		✔	✔	✗	○	○	✔	○	✔	✔		✗	✗	
✔	✔	✔	○		○	✗	✔		✔	✗		✔	✗	✗	
✗	✗		✔		○	✔	○	✔	✔	○	✔		✔	✔	
✔	○		○	✔	✗	✗	○		○	✔	✔		○	✔	✔
✔	○		○	✔	✗	✗	○		○	✔	✔		○	○	✔
✔	○		✗	✔	✗	✗	○	✔	✔	✗			○	○	
✔	✔	✔	✗		✔	✗	✔		✗	✗			✔	○	
○	○		○	✔	○	○	✗		✗	○	✔		○	○	
○	✗		○		○	○	✔	✔	✗	✗			○	○	

Major resorts
our verdicts summarised

- ✔ good
- ○ average
- ✘ bad

	Big ski area	Tough runs	Off-piste skiing	Ski touring	Lift queues	Skiing convenience	Woodland runs	Late holidays	Artificial snow	Summer skiing
Ischgl	✔	○		✔	✘	○	✘	○		
Isola 2000		✘			○	✔	○	○		
Kitzbühel	✔	✘			✘	✘	○	✘		
Klosters	✔	○		✔	○	✘	○	○		
Lech		✘	✔		✘	○	✔	○	✔	
Lenzerheide	✔	✘			○	✘	✔	○		
Livigno		✘			○	✘	○	✔	✔	
Mayrhofen		✘			✘	✘	✘	○		
Megève	✔	✘			○	✘	✔	✘		
Les Menuires	✔	✔	✔		○	✔	✘	○	✔	
Méribel	✔	○			✔	○	○	○	✔	
Montgenèvre	✔	✘			○	✔	✔	✘		
Morzine	✔	✘			○	✘	✔	✘		
Murren		○			○	○	○	○		
Niederau		✘			○	○	✔	✘		
Obergurgl		✘		✔	✔	○	✘	✔		
Obertauern		○	✔		○	✔	✘	○		
Park City		✔	✔		○	✘	✔	○	✔	
La Plagne	•✔	○	✔		○	✔	○	✔		
La Rosière		✘			✔	○	✘	○		
Saalbach	✔	✘			○	○	✔	✘	✔	
Saas Fee		○		✔	✘	✘	✘	✔		✔
Sauze d'Oulx	✔	✘			○	✘	✔	✘		

Easy runs	Nursery slopes	Family holidays	Mountain restaurants	Sunny slopes	Freedom from cars	Alpine charm	Resort-level snow	Beautiful scenery	Apres-ski	Not skiing	Cross-country	Chalet holidays	Short transfers	Easy road access	Rail access
✓	○		○	✓	○	✓	○	✓	✓	○			✗	○	
○	✓	✓	○	✓	✓	✗	✓		✗	✗			○	✗	
✓	○		✓		✗	✓	✗		✓	✓			✓	✓	✓
○	○		✓	✓	○	○	○		✗	○	✓		○	✓	✓
✓	○		✗	✓	○	✓	✓		○	○			✗	✗	
✓	○		○	✓	○	○	○		✗	✓	✓		○	○	
✓	✓		✗	✓	✗	○	✓		○	✗			✗	✗	
○	○		○		○	○	✗		✓	✓			✓	✓	✓
✓	○		✓	✓	✗	○	✗	✓	✓	✓	✓		✓	✓	
○	○		○		○	✗	✓		✗	✗			✗	✗	
○	✗		✓	✓	○	○	✓		○	✗		✓	✗	✗	
✓	○		✗		✗		✓		✗	✗			○	○	
✓	○		✓		✗	○	✗	✓	○	✓	✓		✓	✓	
✗	○	✓	○		✓	✓	✓	✓	✗	○			○	○	✓
✓	✓	✓	○		○	○	✗		○	○	✓		✓	✓	
✓	○	✓	○		○	✓	✓		✓	✗			○	✗	
✓	✓		○	✓	○	✗	✓		✗	✗			○	○	
✓	✓	✓	✗		✗	○	✓		○	○			✓		
✓	✓	✓	✗	✓	✓	✗	✓	✓	✗	✗			✗	✗	
✓	✓	✓	○	✓	○	○	○	✓	✗	✗			○	○	
✓	○		✓	✓	○	○	○		✓	○			✓	✓	
○	✓	✓	○		✓	✓	✓	✓	○	○			✗	✗	
○	○		✓	✓	✗	○	✗		○	✗			✓	○	

Major resorts
our verdicts summarised

✔ good
○ average
✖ bad

	Big ski area	Tough runs	Off-piste skiing	Ski touring	Lift queues	Skiing convenience	Woodland runs	Late holidays	Artificial snow	Summer skiing
St Anton	✔	✔	✔		✖	✖	✖	○	✔	
St Johann in Tirol		✖			○	✖	✔	✖	✔	
St Moritz	✔	○			✖	✖	✖	✔	✔	
Schladming	✔	✖			○	✖	✔	✖	✔	
Seefeld		✖			✔	✖	✔	○	✔	
Selva	✔	○			○	✖	✔	✖	✔	
Serre-Chevalier	✔	○	✔		✔	✖	✔	○		
Sölden		✖			✖	○	○	✔		✔
Söll	✔	✖			○	✖	✔	✖		
La Thuile		✖			✔	✔	✔	○		
Tignes	✔	✔	✔		✔	✔	✖	✔		✔
Vail	✔	✖	✔		○	○	✔	○		
Val d'Isère	✔	✔	✔		✔	✖	✖	✔	✔	✔
Valmorel		○			✔	✔	○	○		
Val Thorens	✔	✔	✔		✔	✔	✖	✔		✔
Verbier	✔	✔	✔	✔	✖	✖	○	○		
Villars		✖			○	○	○	○		
Wagrain	✔	✖			✔	○	✔	✖		
Wengen	✔	✖		✔	○	✖	✔	✖		
Zell am See		○			✖	✖	○	✖	✔	
Zermatt	✔	✔	✔	✔	○	✖	✔	✔	✔	✔

Easy runs	Nursery slopes	Family holidays	Mountain restaurants	Sunny slopes	Freedom from cars	Alpine charm	Resort-level snow	Beautiful scenery	Apres-ski	Not skiing	Cross-country	Chalet holidays	Short transfers	Easy road access	Rail access
✗	✗		○	✓	○	○	○		✓	✗		✓	○	✓	✓
✓	○	✓	✓		✗	○	✗		✓	○	✓		✓	✓	✓
○	✗		✓	✓	○	○	✓	✓	✓	✓	✓		✗	✗	✓
✓	✓		✓		○	✓	✗		○	○	✓		✓	✓	✓
○	○	✓	○		○	○	○		○	✓	✓		✓	✓	✓
○	✓		✓		✗	○	○	✓	✓	✓	✓	✓	✗	✗	
○	✓		○		✗	✗	✗		○	○	✓		○	○	
○	✗		○		○	○	○		✓	✗			✗	○	
○	○		○		○	○	✗		✓	○			✓	✓	
✓	○		○		○	✗	○	✓	✗	✗			✓	○	
○	○		✗		○	✗	✓		✗	✗			✗	✗	
✓	○		✗		○	✓	✓		○	○			○		
✓	○		✗	✓	○	✗	✓		✓	✗		✓	✗	✗	
○	✓	✓	✗	✓	✓	✓	✓		✗	✗			○	○	
○	✓		○		○	✗	✓		✗	✗			✗	✗	
✗	○		○	✓	○	○	○	✓	✓	○		✓	○	✓	✓
✓	○	✓	○	✓	✗	○	○	✓	○	✓	✓		✓	✓	✓
✓	○		✓	✓	✗	○	✗		○	✗	✓		✓	✓	
✓	✓	✓	○		✓	✓	○	✓	○	✓		✓	○	○	✓
✓	○		○		✗	○	✗		✓	✓	✓		✓	✓	✓
○	✗		✓		○	✓	✓	✓	✓	✓		✓	✗	✗	✓

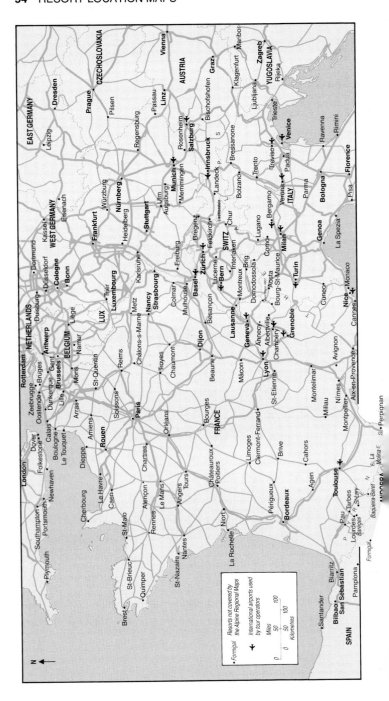

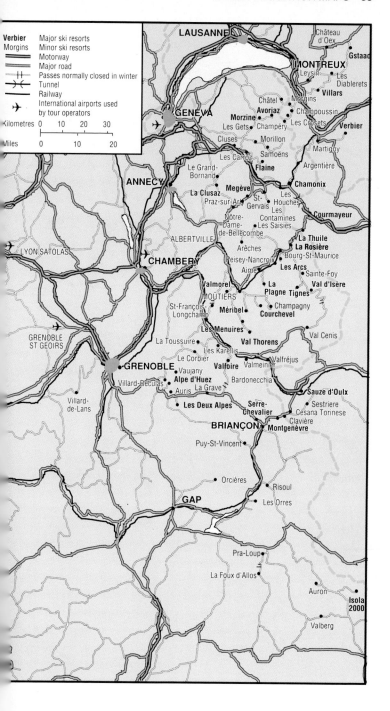

Verbier Major ski resorts
Morgins Minor ski resorts
　　　　 Motorway
　　　　 Major road
　　 ++　 Passes normally closed in winter
　 ✕ ✕　 Tunnel
　　　　 Railway
　 ✈　 International airports used
　　　　 by tour operators
Kilometres 0 10 20 30
Miles 0 10 20

LAUSANNE

Château
d'Oex

MONTREUX

Gstaad

Leysin

Les
Diablerets

Villars

Châtel

Morgins

GENEVA

Morzine

Avoriaz

Champoussin

Les Gets

Champéry

Les Crosets

Verbier

Cluses

Morillon

Martigny

Les Carroz

Samoëns

ANNECY

Le Grand-
Bornand

Flaine

Argentière

La Clusaz

Megève

Chamonix

Praz-sur-Arly

St-
Gervais

Les
Houches

Courmayeur

Nôtre-
Dame-
de-Bellecombe

Les
Contamines

Les Saisies

La Thuile

ALBERTVILLE

Arêches

La Rosière

Bourg-St-Maurice

CHAMBERY

Peisey-Nancroix

Les Arcs

Aime

Sainte-Foy

Valmorel

La
Plagne

Tignes

Val d'Isère

MOÛTIERS

St-François-
Longchamp

Méribel

Champagny

Courchevel

Les Menuires

Val Cenis

La Toussuire

Val Thorens

GRENOBLE
ST GEOIRS

Les Karellis

Le Corbier

Valfréjus

LYON SATOLAS

Valloire

Valmeinier

GRENOBLE

Vaujany

Alpe d'Huez

Bardonecchia

Villard-Reculas

Bardonecchia

Sauze d'Oulx

Auris

La Grave

Sestriere

Villard-
de-Lans

Les Deux Alpes

Serre-
Chevalier

Cesana Torinese

BRIANÇON

Clavière

Montgenèvre

Puy-St-Vincent

Orcières

Risoul

GAP

Les Orres

Pra-Loup

La Foux d'Allos

Auron

Isola
2000

Valberg

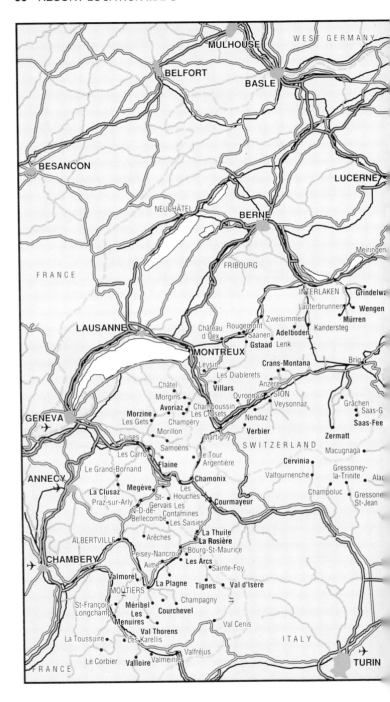

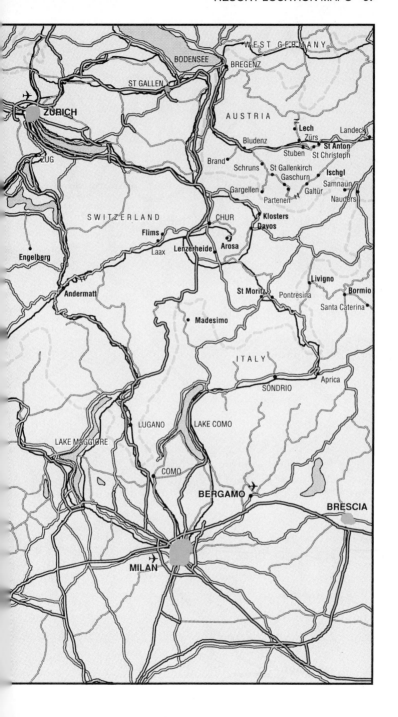

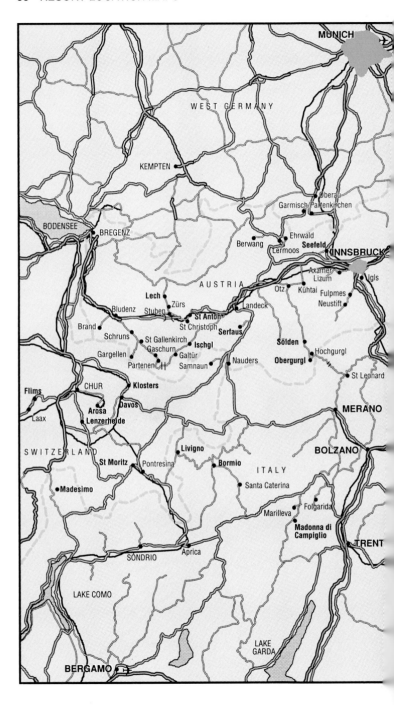

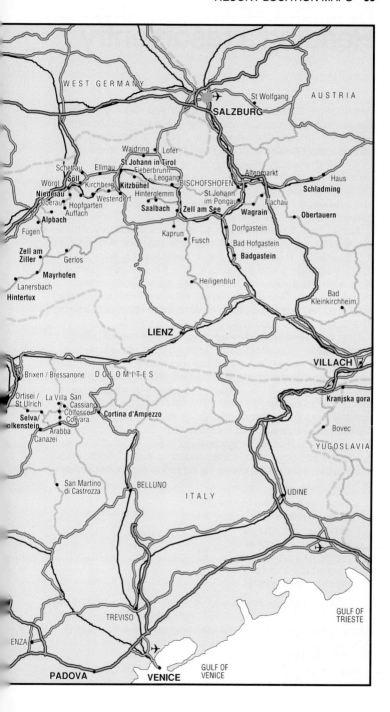

Reading a resort entry

Resorts in the *Guide* are divided into 'major' and 'minor' ones. These categories are not meant to indicate the size or the absolute worth of any resort. Alpbach, although small, is a 'major' resort because it attracts a great number of British skiers for very good reasons.

In the first resorts chapter, for example, Cortina is the major resort. Its name is picked out in large type, and is followed by a list of verdicts – the things it is 'good for' and 'bad for'. If the Cortina chapter covered any minor resorts, these would be listed under the verdicts – as in the Selva chapter that follows, for example.

The first part of the chapter text gives a general summary of the area, aiming to convey something of its character and more of its attractions and drawbacks. Then follows a detailed description of the major ski area – including the skiing of minor resorts, if it is linked to the major area. After that comes a description of the major resort village or villages. As part of this description you will find a 'factbox', occupying most of a page and giving details of ski school, lift passes and so on. This factbox needs explanation in a couple of respects.

Near the start of the factbox we say if the resort has a Ski Club representative – a volunteer skier stationed in the resort to help members get the most out of their stay. Each week the rep advertises a varied skiing programme of group skiing, so that you can join a group of similar ability, skiing in the company of the rep, who will have been trained to lead such groups safely. The service is free, and non-members may try it for a day. The programme might include 'Gentle tour of the resort', 'Mogul mania day', 'Easy piste cruising' and 'Introduction to off-piste', for example.

Under 'Package holidays' we list the tour operators offering holidays in the resort, with codes showing the kinds of accommodation they provide:

h: hotels and hotel-like guest-houses
c: catered chalets
j: 'jumbo' or 'club' chalets
s: self-catering apartments
r: rooms in private homes
a: catered apartments
y: youth accommodation.

Our lists of tour operators are as up to date as we can make them, but in most cases are based on 1991 rather than 1992 programmes. There is more information about each operator in the 'Package holidays' section towards the back of the book – including addresses and numbers for further information.

All the prices we give are for 1991-92, and are in the local currency (named at the top of the factbox). The price of the main lift pass is converted into pounds at a rate of exchange current in late winter 1991. Among recent improvements and additions to our factboxes are these points: we now say whether the lift company accepts payment by credit card; we say whether ski school classes have priority over other skiers in lifts queues; and at the end of the factbox we summarise major changes in the resort last season or this.

After the description of the major resort or resorts covered by the chapter, there are brief descriptions of the most significant minor resort villages in the area, and of their skiing if it is separate from that of the major resort.

The ski area of each major resort (and linked minor resorts) is shown on a map. All but a couple of these maps are drawn to a consistent scale, and use colour tints to show height above sea level – see the scale and key below. The arrows on the runs indicate the resorts' own gradings, not our assessment of difficulty. The maps are meant to help you compare resorts, not to find your way around the mountains.

In a few resorts with very well known downhill race courses, we include an assessment of the course by the British racer Martin Bell ('Bell's View'), based on the chapter on ski racing which appeared in earlier editions of the *Guide*.

Both the text and the maps are based mainly on the 1990-91 ski season; but where a new lift is virtually certain to be in place for the 1991-92 season we have included it.

Two final points of clarification. When we say a resort is good for lift queues, we don't mean that it's a resort where queues are easy to find; we mean that from the queuing point of view it's a good resort. And when we talk about a run of 1600m vertical, we don't mean a mile-high precipice; we mean that the bottom is 1600m lower than the top.

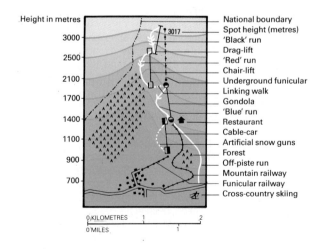

Ageing beauty

Cortina d'Ampezzo Italy 1220m

Good for *Nursery slopes, mountain restaurants, beautiful scenery, sunny slopes, cross-country skiing, not skiing, artificial snow, woodland runs*
Bad for *Skiing convenience, late holidays, short airport transfers, easy road access, freedom from cars*

Cortina is Italy's most fashionable ski resort and, unlike many Dolomite resorts, thoroughly Italian in atmosphere and style. It is one of the most remote resorts for visitors from north and west, and although it is very cosmopolitan the bulk of its clientele is cosmopolitan Italians. It hosted the 1956 winter Olympics and ranks with St Moritz and Chamonix as one of the most complete winter sports resorts in the world.

Its downhill skiing includes some of the best nursery slopes anywhere and a few long, challenging runs for good skiers, all in dramatically beautiful scenery. Much of the most recent development of the resort was generated by the Olympics, and it is showing its age – though lifts are gradually being upgraded now. It is a large sunny town in a wide valley; the skiing areas are widely separated on the surrounding mountains, and travelling between them is tiresome – our reporters' major grumble.

Cortina has a very glamorous reputation which may deter skiers who look to Italy for informal, cheap holidays. One recent reporter described it as 'far more a general purpose winter watering-hole for northern Italy's *haute bourgeoisie* than merely a ski resort'. In high season there are plenty of beautiful people to match the shop windows ('the incredible number of fur coats was rather a shock'), but it is not an exclusive or uniformly expensive resort: there are plenty of small, attractive, not outrageously expensive hotels, and simple, friendly bars full of character. Most reporters stress the friendly atmosphere.

The resorts ringing the Sella massif are within reach by car, and the Dolomiti Superski lift pass covers all of them (and many other resorts). A car is useful around the resort, too, but parking is 'a nightmare'.

The skiing top 2930m bottom 1220m

The skiing is typical of the Dolomites in being broken up by cliff faces. There are excellent open fields of very easy runs and a few steep and narrow gullies which verge on the extreme. Between the two there is a variety of intermediate skiing. The main Tofana-Socrepes skiing area is west of the town. On the other side of the large resort, the Staunies and Faloria areas are just about linked, despite the road between them, and provide a few interesting runs. A long way out of town, by the Passo Falzarego road, are several unconnected little ski areas, well worth visiting for a change of spectacular scenery.

The bottom station of the **Tofana** cable-car is a long walk from the centre of the resort. Between the resort and Col Druscié (1774m) the cable-car goes over gentle woodlands and open fields with wide, easy trails complicated only by several danger points where piste crosses rough roads with unobtrusive warnings for skiers and drivers which are easily missed. Snow conditions often make these home runs fairly tricky and account for their red and black gradings. The second stage of the cable-car climbs an impressively steep and rocky mountain side to Ra Valles, in the middle of an excellent sheltered bowl of intermediate runs between 2828m (the top of the skiing on this side of the valley) and 2216m; this area is reportedly often closed in poor weather. The top section of the cable-car is for sun-bathing and sightseeing only. Near the bottom of the bowl there is a breach in the rock which allows skiers a narrow path down – graded black because there is a fairly steep south-facing stretch in the middle. The run ends up at the bottom of the Pomedes chair-lifts, about 100m lower than Col Druscié, which is set on a little peak. You get up to it by skiing on down to Colfiere and taking the Col Druscié chair-lift which itself has an interesting short black run underneath it. The Pomedes chair-lifts, which can usually be reached by car, add an excellent series of more-or-less direct runs, including a couple of genuine blacks and the spectacular downhill race-course which starts down a narrow *canalone* between massive pillars of rock. There is also a very long circuitous blue trail from the middle station. The Pomedes runs and lifts link up via long, panoramic woodland paths with the splendid open skiing above Pocol and Lacedel – a vast area of very easy and nursery slopes, usually referred to by the general name of **Socrepes**.

A cable-car goes up to **Faloria** from the ring road, the first stage over flat ground, the second over a cliff to 2120m. There are no runs under the cable-car, but an area of short intermediate runs beyond it, including several challenging pitches. These runs are served by a series of chair-lifts, the most westerly of which recently replaced an old drag-lift. You can ski through attractive woods to the Tre Croci road at Rio Gere, either directly from Faloria, or with less effort by means of a little-used red run from Tondi, served by a quad chair.

On the other side of the Tre Croci road are south-facing slopes which are served by a slow and long chair-lift going up to the foot of the cliffs of the Cristallo massif. The run back down is wide and easy. A two-stage chair-lift climbs to **Staunies**, one of the steep and narrow chutes so characteristic of the Dolomites. The run under the top section starts narrowly and steeply, faces south and is often unskiable. Its beauty is rather spoilt by lift pylons. The bottom section, accessible from the chair-lift mid-station, is less complicated and continues down to Rio Gere and then runs beside the Tre Croci road back to Cortina. There is no link with the extensive area of easy runs served by a number of lifts beneath **Mietres**.

An isolated two-stage chair-lift (1900–2400m) beside the road up to Passo Falzarego serves the little-used north-facing intermediate runs of **Cinque Torri**, surrounded by beautiful scenery.

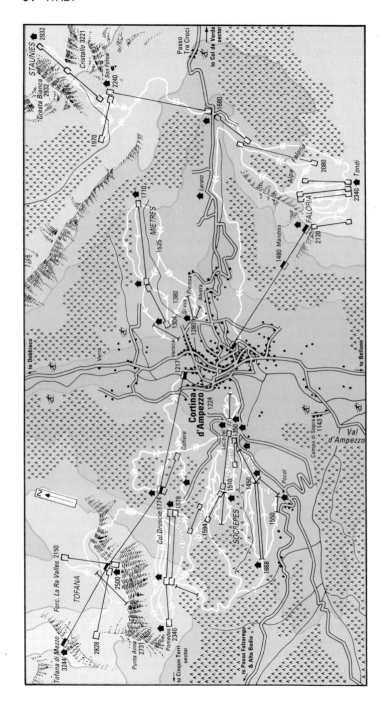

One of the Dolomites' extremely dramatic cable-cars soars up a cliff face from Passo Falzarego (2105m) to **Lagazuoi** (2746m). The run back down is mostly bluish in difficulty with a short red section in the middle. Much more worthwhile is the run down the back to Armentarola, near San Cassiano in the Alta Badia (see the Selva chapter). This is an 11km run of no great technical difficulty, but wild and exceedingly beautiful, and punctuated by restaurants. There are buses from Cortina and Armentarola to Falzarego.

Mountain restaurants are plentiful in all the skiing areas, mostly excellent and not particularly expensive. There are particularly delightful restaurants at Pomedes, Col Druscié and Tondi. There are several expensive places for serious gastronomic lunches near the Socrepes lifts, notably El Camineto. Reservations needed at weekends.

Getting around Cortina's ski areas can be extremely time-consuming. Morning **queues** for the Tofana cable-car are not as serious as you might expect (Cortina skiers are notoriously late risers); but cable-cars reportedly run to timetables, regardless of demand. Reporters complain that some runs are graded too leniently, particularly the narrow, twisty forest trails, marked blue, but of considerable difficulty to inexperienced skiers.

There is a fair amount of **artificial snow** equipment in all the ski areas except Faloria – including Cinque Torri, not within the area of our map.

The resort

Cortina is a handsome small town of 8,000 inhabitants set in a beautiful broad bowl, a busy crossroads with plenty of through, as well as local, traffic. The attractive main street, Corso Italia, is sheltered from this as a pedestrian precinct, and traffic streams around a central one-way circuit. There are lots of very stylish shop windows and lots of elegant fur-clad people strolling up and down in the early evening. Outside the centre the resort spreads widely up and down the valley, with comfortable chalets beside the main road out towards Dobbiaco, and some development across the river on the hill which climbs more steeply up towards Falzarego.

The ski-bus service is said to be unreliable, circling anti-clockwise between the two cable-car stations and leaving many parts of the resort unserved. There are other, less frequent buses from the centre to outlying ski-lifts; there are only three buses a day to and from Cinque Torri. Taxis are 'very reliable and not expensive'.

Accommodation consists of a great variety of hotels from international conference comfort to very simple, and large numbers of private apartments and chalets, usually empty. The most attractive hotel is the absolutely central, comfortable Poste, right at the heart of fashionable Cortina life – 'excellent service, large rooms, consistently good food'. Also comfortable, central and stylish, but cheaper, is the Ancora. Two small, attractive chalet hotels within walking distance of the main cable-car are the Capannina, with a well-reputed restaurant, and the inexpensive Barisetti. Although its position is not convenient, the Menardi has been repeatedly recommended – attractive, friendly, good food, medium price. The Montana and the 'simple and friendly' Olimpia are among the cheapest and most central B&B hotels. The Fiames is a one-star hotel, placed conveniently for the cross-country trails.

Après-ski is very varied, but evenings are generally quiet outside high season – 'we found it difficult to find anywhere open after 10.30pm'. There are a dozen discos, and numerous bars with a lot of character – the Poste hotel bar being the smartest rendezvous in the early evening. There are also several excellent restaurants, notably the Meloncino al Lago at Laghi Ghedina, north-west of the town, and the very expensive Toula, beside the road up towards Falzarego, and those in the Capannina and Da Beppe Sello hotels. A reporter recommends the Buca dell Inferno pizzeria – 'central and full of character'. There is an ice disco on the Olympic rink, and bobsleigh practice and horse jumping to watch. The Mietres chair-lift serves a toboggan run.

Facts on Cortina d'Ampezzo   Belluno **Italy**

Prices in lire

Tourist office
Piazzetta S. Francesco, 8
Postcode 32043
Tel (436) 3231
Fax (436) 3235
Tlx 440004

Getting there
By road 1,335km from Calais. Via Munich, Brenner, Dobbiaco; chains occasionally needed.
By rail Calalzo (30km) or Dobbiaco (32km); frequent buses from station.
By air Treviso; transfer 2½hr. (Or Venice.)

Staying there
Visitor beds 22,500; breakdown: 4,500 in hotels; 18,000 in apartments.
Package holidays Citalia (h) SnowRanger (h) Supertravel (h) .
Medical facilities In resort: Fracture clinic, doctors, chemists, dentists. Hospital: Pieve di Cadore (30km).

Non-skiing activities
Indoor Olympic ice-stadium (2 rinks), swimming pool, saunas, museum, art gallery, cinema, indoor tennis court.
Outdoor Sleigh rides, horse-riding school, ski-bob run, 6 km walking paths, toboggan run, heli-skiing.

Special skiing facilities
Summer skiing At Marmolada's glacier: 40km from Cortina.
Cross-country Extensive trails, total length 74km, of varying difficulty (graded green, red and black) in the valley north of Cortina, with a base and ski school and equipment rental facilities at Fiames (5km from Cortina). Small circuit at Campo (S of Cortina) plus 200km cross country trail from Cortina to Villach (Austria). Instruction available.

Lift passes
Cortina Skipass
Covers all the Cortina lifts and the ski bus. (52 lifts in total.)
Cost 6 days 186,700.00 (£87.24). Low season: 158,900.00 saving 15%.
Credit cards accepted Yes.
Senior citizens 149,360.00 (over 60) saving 20%.
Children 130,690.00 (under 14) saving 30%.
Beginners Coupons.
Short-term passes Day passes available.
Other passes Superski Dolomiti Skipass, which covers 464 lifts in the Dolomites (194,300.00 for adults, 165,300.00 for children).

Ski school
Scuola Sci Cortina
Classes 9.30-4.30. Cost: 400,000.00 (6 days). Alternatively, 2½hr am costs 170,000.00 per week; 2hr pm costs 140,000.00 per week; 4hr pm costs 200,000.00 per week.
Lift priority No.
Children's classes Ages: any. Cost: 400,000.00 (6 days).
Private lessons available Hourly. Cost: 42,000.00 per hour. 7,000.00 per each additional person.
Special courses Ski-mountaineering weeks.
Scuola Sci Azzurra Cortina
Classes 9.30-12.30. Cost: 200,000.00 (6 half-days).
Lift priority No.
Children's classes Ages: up to 15. Cost: 420,000.00 (6 full days, 9.30-4.30).
Private lessons available Hourly, 1-2 people. Cost: 47,000.00 per hour. 9,000.00 per each additional person.

The **cross-country** trails are long and beautiful and varied, although the Fiames base is a long way from central Cortina and the trails do not link with any of the Alpine skiing areas. One very long trail follows the old railway track to Dobbiaco, another all the way to Villach, in Austria. There is a marathon in early February, ending in the Corso Italia. For **non-skiers** there are good walks along the valley and to restaurants in and around the skiing area. Excursions are easily arranged around the Dolomites and to Venice. The resort is varied, interesting and colourful, with an excellent skating rink.

Nursery slopes (and long green runs for early post-nursery stages) are excellent. Most beginners use the very extensive area above the Falzarego road at Pocol. The Pierosa and Mietres area is equally broad and gentle and even more secluded – but it is also isolated.

The main **ski school** has an office in the centre of the resort, and a meeting place for adult beginners at the Socrepes lift. Reports speak well of the school. There is a smaller ski school (the Azzurra Cortina) with an office at the foot of the Faloria cable-car.

Selva Italy 1550m

Good for *Big ski area, beautiful scenery, artificial snow, nursery slopes, cross-country skiing, mountain restaurants, après-ski, chalet holidays, not skiing, woodland runs*
Bad for *Skiing convenience, late holidays, short airport transfers, easy road access, freedom from cars*

Linked resorts: Ortisei, Corvara, Canazei, San Cassiano, Arabba, Colfosco, Campitello, Santa Cristina, La Villa

For the few British skiers who do it, skiing in the Dolomites generally means skiing in the area around the massive Gruppo Sella, Europe's Table Mountain. The Sella Ronda is the name of the trip around the mountain. It is piste tourism at its most spectacular, with as much of the enjoyment coming from the dramatic spectacle of the landscape as from the skiing itself.

The Dolomites typically have gentle lower slopes surmounted by vertical cliffs, which means a large proportion of easy runs and a few extremely steep, narrow chutes between towers of rock, with few runs between the two extremes. Although the peaks are high, not much skiing takes place near the tops, and the range of altitude is not great. A more important reservation is that the Dolomites have a very erratic snow record; snowfalls can be heavy, but they are not reliable. 1989 was an extreme example: two virtually snowless months were followed by a massive dump at the beginning of March. Until that point, the resorts were reliant entirely on their artificial snow, which is now very extensive (particularly around Selva) and provided good pistes when there would otherwise have been no skiing.

Although the Sella region is entirely in Italy, holidays there have very little Italian about them. Much of the area was Austrian until 1918 (many villages have dual names as a result) and the area as a whole is dominated by car-borne visitors from Germany. Nightlife consists of beer-swilling and tea-dances to the sound of zither and squeeze-box. Standing slightly apart from most of the German-speaking Dolomites is the Val Gardena (Gröden), and particularly its main town of Ortisei (St Ulrich), where the Ladin dialect and crafts are proudly perpetuated.

It is not an area of big resorts. Accommodation is spread widely around the valleys in hamlets at the foot of the slopes or in complete isolation – clean, simple B&B houses and new chalet-style hotels. The Val Gardena does have two large resorts. Ortisei is a long-established town of considerable charm, detached from the main Sella Ronda circuit. The major resort is Selva (Wolkenstein), a good base for exploring the region, but a disappointingly characterless and inconvenient roadside resort. Its local runs include long and challenging ones, and both après-ski and accommodation are plentiful and varied.

Perhaps the most convenient base for moderate skiers is Corvara, the most major of the minor resorts in the Alta Badia region, with its infinity of blue and red runs. For good skiers the choice destination is Arabba, with its big, steep, north-facing non-Dolomitic mountain (and an impressive new access lift due to open this season).

The Sella Ronda can be skied in either direction. Either way, it consists predominantly of easy blue runs; the red sections are not very severe, but poor snow conditions may make them difficult – there is no escaping south-facing slopes at some stage. The tour involves about 20km of uphill transport, and 26km and 4000m vertical of skiing. It takes about five hours, not allowing for queues or rests. Getting between resorts by car is not much quicker than by lift and piste, but recent reporters are agreed that a car is nevertheless an asset in the area.

The skiing top 2950m bottom 1225m

Ortisei: Alpe di Siusi A cable-car from the southern edge of Ortisei scales a very steep wooded mountainside. The only piste down is a red-graded track engineered into the face, with netting to protect skiers from long drops. The cable-car delivers you to Punta Mesdi (2006m), on the rim of the remarkable Alpe di Siusi (Seiseralm) – a broad, high, gently sloping basin which claims to be the biggest alp (in its sense of high pasture) in the Alps. It is an idyllic area for the under-confident and for those who enjoy pottering around in beautiful mountain surroundings, with sleigh rides, extensive cross-country trails, walking paths and dozens of hotels and restaurants dotted around the spacious sunny slopes. Behind Punta Mesdi there is an extensive and confusing arrangement of short drags and chair-lifts which make it just about possible to ski down to a collection of hotels at 1850m (Kompatsch). To the north of here is a lift-served hill which is moderately steep but less than 300m vertical; to the south, very gentle terrain served by some longer lifts with a top station of 2238m. Getting from lift to lift here involves walking. Further round the basin still, the Florian lift serves longer intermediate pistes through woods; from the top, it is possible to ski (and walk) across to Monte Pana above S Cristina.

Ortisei/Santa Cristina: Seceda Two lifts from the edge of Ortisei give access to sunny slopes with long runs which often lack snow and are little skied. The two-stage cable-car to Seceda may involve long waits for a quorum to assemble, even in high season. The top section scales an impressive cliff to the main skiing area – south-facing slopes above the Col Raiser and S Cristina offering open intermediate skiing and advanced sunbathing, with several very welcoming restaurant chalets. Below Col Raiser there is a single easy run down to the edge of S Cristina, served by a gondola; it is also possible to ski (off-piste) to the edge of Selva. The long run back to Ortisei skirts the rock face with a narrow path and runs on through woods easily and prettily.

Santa Cristina: Monte Pana This small community of hotels and restaurants is reached by road or chair-lift from S Cristina, with a fan of nursery lifts and a chair-lift which serves two short woodland runs (black and red) which in themselves hardly merit a detour. There is no marked run down to S Cristina.

Santa Cristina/Selva: Ciampinoi Efficient stand-up gondolas have recently replaced the cable-cars from the edge of S Cristina and the centre of Selva giving access to this splendid skiing mountain, with a spray of broad, long, challenging north-facing runs cut through the woods below its bald, rounded peak – windswept and often treacherously icy. There is no easy way down to the valley. From Ciampinoi and from Piz Sella at the top of the Plan de Gralba skiing it is possible to ski round to Monte Pana – though this pleasant ski-ramble is not easy to follow.

Selva: Plan de Gralba Plan de Gralba is a roadside skiing service area with a network of short, easy intermediate runs. It can be reached either by bus in a few minutes from Selva, or via Ciampinoi. The skiing route gets a lot of sun, is rarely in good condition, and is usually crowded, which adds to the difficulty of negotiating the ice and stones and roots. It is quite steep enough for long falls. The Ciampinoi chair-lift very usefully cuts out queuing and the most awkward slope. The landscape above Plan de Gralba is pleasantly wooded, with restaurants and an outdoor ice bar. Unfortunately the peaks of the Sasso Lungo block out the sun early in the afternoon. There is a very easy run beside the road to Selva, skirting the Ciampinoi mountain.

The Selva Downhill: Bell's view

The Val Gardena race almost always comes after Val d'Isère. It's a really tough course, a real test of physical fitness. Lots of racers end up with sore backs from all the jumps and bumps. The most famous section consists of three jumps in a row – peculiarly called the Camel Humps. The first jump is a little way away from the second and third, which are the tricky ones because they're so close together – though you've got to take the first jump just right to stand a chance with the others. What you can do is suck up the first bump to fly as short a distance as possible, then spring off the second like a ski jumper and land just on the far side of the third bump. The classic thing is that someone who jumps over the camels gains maybe half a second; then he's so relieved that he managed to clear the third jump that he totally loses concentration for the turns that follow and loses two seconds on those!

The turns on the course after the Camels, called the Meadows, are incredibly bumpy. I think they must be bumps in the ground, but it might have something to do with the way the man-made snow piles up overnight – every year the bumps seem to be in different places. One day I'll go there in summer and check! I already mentioned that the man-made snow holds up well and gives late starters a good chance. Another factor in their favour is a huge Dolomite peak which shades the course until about start number 20. After that the sun moves round and hits the course just on these bumpy turns after the Camels, and the good visibility makes this section quite a bit easier.

Passo Sella The link from Plan de Gralba to Passo Sella is called Rock City or the Moon Walk – a track through a chaos of enormous boulders which does indeed involve some walking. It finishes at the foot of the Sasso Lungo bucket lift, which climbs to a refuge in a narrow breach between two pinnacles and serves only off-piste runs. The notorious run under the lift is steep, rocky and narrow – not exceedingly difficult in good snow, but a dangerous slope on which to fall. Much less often skied, less steep (after the start) but prone to avalanche danger is the beautiful run down behind the mountain to Monte Pana and S Cristina. To the south of the Sasso Lungo lift is a modest area of bleak, easy intermediate runs, north and east-facing. This area is most easily reached by cable-car from Campitello. Chair-lifts complete the link in both directions between Passo Sella and the Canazei skiing via Lupo Bianco (1721m), a roadside restaurant.

Selva: Passo Gardena The Dantercepies gondola goes from the top end of Selva to 2298m above Passo Gardena, serving a couple of long and satisfying red runs back to Selva and a more challenging narrow unofficial run between the pylons – splendid skiing in good snow.

Colfosco From Passo Sella a very gentle run drops down to the lifts and pistes of Colfosco, much of it a straight schuss. The last kilometre to Corvara is almost flat; many skiers take the chair-lift in both directions. Set apart from this main skiing thoroughfare, the little village of Colfosco has its own nursery area and a few attractive runs above it between 2125m and 1650m, served by a series of drag-lifts. This is a secluded ski area with enjoyable intermediate runs and a particularly delightful sun-soaked bar among the trees at the top.

Corvara: Boè On the western side of the road over Passo di Campolongo, a chain of lifts provides connections to and from Arabba. The runs to Arabba face south and tend to be icy in the mornings; apart from this there is no great difficulty about the skiing, although most of it is graded red. The long run down to Corvara beneath the Boè cable-car is wide and fast. The blackness of the run down from the top chair is mainly to do with its being unprepared.

Corvara/San Cassiano/La Villa: Alta Badia The bulk of Corvara's skiing is in the wide area, east of the Campolongo road, which it shares with the smaller villages of La Villa and San Cassiano. The not very high, round-topped, wooded mountain is covered with little drags and chair-lifts and an endless number of very gentle runs, individually short but adding up to a great deal of skiing. The great exception is the excellent north-facing black run above La Villa of nearly 700m vertical – there is also a challenging red variant. At the other end of the web of lifts and runs, the area around Pralongia and Cherz is always uncrowded. This provides an alternative, slower way to and from Arabba.

Arabba The attraction of this small area is a series of long, steep, north-facing runs on a wide, fragmented mountainside served by a cable-car which climbs nearly 900m from the village to the Porta Vescovo (2478m). A two-stage chair-lift has been installed to relieve the cable-car (and to enable moderate skiers to proceed towards Pordoi without tackling the slightly daunting slope, often icy and stony, at the top of the cable-car), and the long-awaited new gondola is now

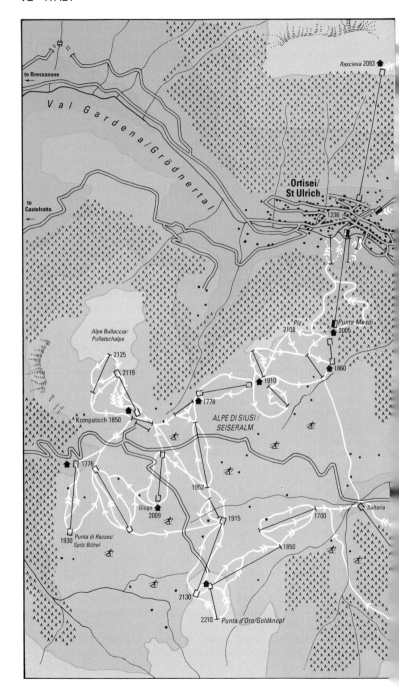

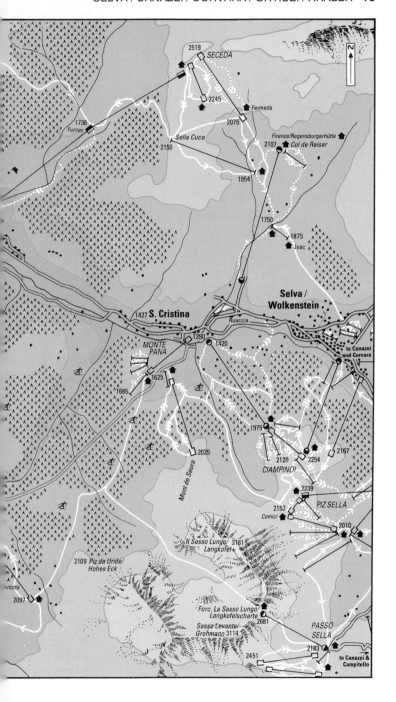

2519

SECEDA

2245

Fermeda

2075

Sella Cuca

2150

1736
Furnes

Firenze/Regensburgerhütte

2107 Col de Raiser

1954

1750

1875
Juac

**Selva /
Wolkenstein**

1427 **S. Cristina**

Ruaccia

to Canazei
and Corvara

1390 1420

**MONTE
PANA**

1625

1685

1975

2120 2254 2167

2025

CIAMPINOI

Mont de Seura

2239

2153 *PIZ SELLA*

Comici

2010

*Il Sasso Lungo/ 3181
Langkofel*

2109 Piz de Uride/
Hohes Eck

rlotta

2097

*Forc. La Sasso Lungo/
Langkofelscharte*

2681

*Sasso Levante/
Grohmann 3114*

*PASSO
SELLA*

2451

2183

to Canazei &
Campitello

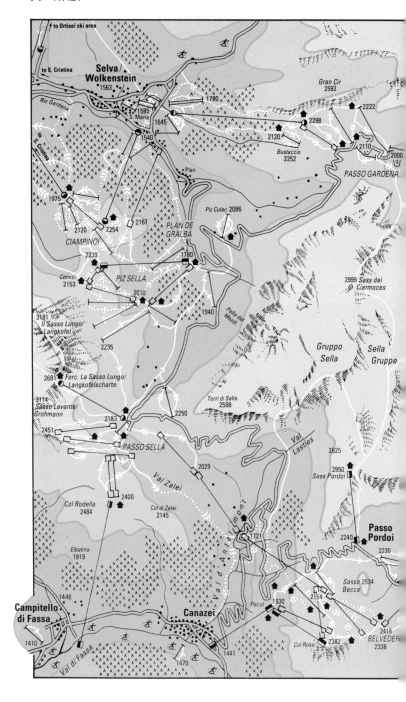

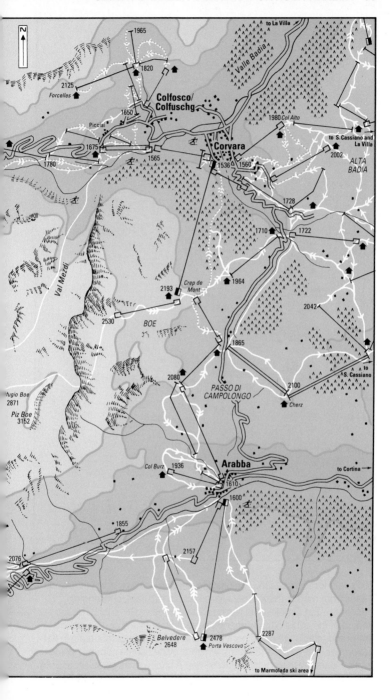

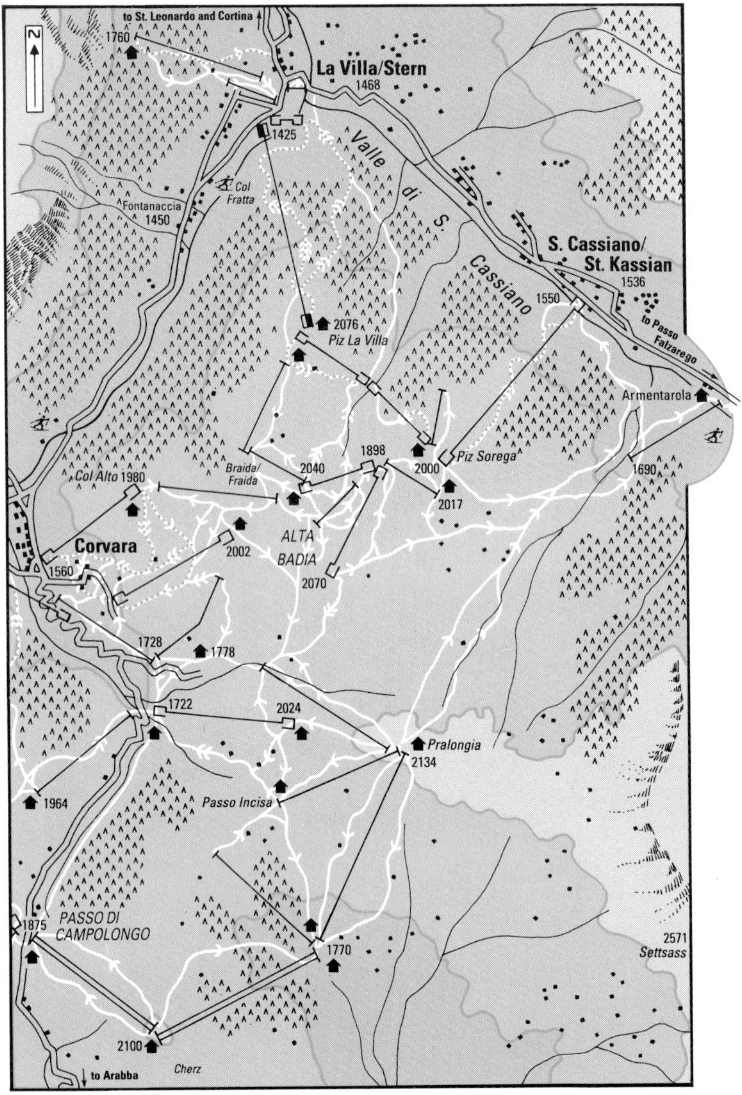

N

to St. Leonardo and Cortina
1760

La Villa/Stern
1468

1425

Valle di S

Col Fratta

Fontanaccia 1450

S. Cassiano/ St. Kassian
1536

Cassiano

1550

to Passo Falzarego

2076
Piz La Villa

Armentarola

Braida/ Fraida
2040
1898
Piz Sorega
2000

Col Alto 1980
2017

Corvara
2002
ALTA BADIA
2070

1560

1728
1778

1722
2024

Pralongia
2134

1964
Passo Incisa

PASSO DI CAMPOLONGO
1875

2571
Settsass

1770

2100
Cherz
to Arabba

promised for this season. The grading of the runs back down to Arabba varies from map to map. They are in fact all excellent, challenging descents – the Ornella blue run has an impressive 25° pitch. The top station of the cable-car commands a magnificent view southwards to the grand, glacier-covered northern flank of the highest mountain in the Dolomites, Marmolada (3342m), which provides some summer skiing and exhilarating long runs in late winter. A chain of lifts gives access via Passo Padon to the sunny slopes above Marmolada's resort, Malga

Ciapela. They are covered by the lift pass, but Marmolada itself is not.

Passo Pordoi As well as being the link between Arabba and Canazei, Pordoi has a cable-car which climbs very steeply up to 2950m. This is the only lift which penetrates the fortifications of the mighty Gruppo Sella. It serves no pistes, but several notorious runs. The obvious one is the Forcella, under the cable-car. This faces due south and includes a narrow, steep top section which must very often be dangerously icy or bare, as we found it. Longer off-piste routes which mix easier stretches with steep, narrow and rocky pitches include the Val Lasties down to near the Lupo Bianco restaurant and lifts above Canazei; and the Val de Mesdi, the great adventure which involves a 45-minute walk across the massif, before entering a very long, enclosed north-facing valley which drops, steeply in parts, down towards Colfosco.

Canazei: Belvedere The local skiing is confined to the open, not very large, north-west-facing bowl above Pecol (1933m), reached either by road or by cable-car. The top of the skiing is 2426m, so runs served by the fan of lifts up to the rim of the bowl are not long. They are mostly of intermediate difficulty, with a couple of short nursery lifts. There is a long, gentle descent (graded red) to Canazei via Lupo Bianco.

   Mountain restaurants are one of the great joys of skiing in the Dolomites. There are plenty of them (except at Arabba), the views are beautiful and most are welcoming, with generally reasonable prices. A recent visitor based in Arabba particularly recommends Saas Becce, Belvedere, Dantercepies and Capanna Bill (Marmolada).

   In the past there have been serious lift **queues** at various points on the Sella Ronda circuit; latest reports suggest that the problem is now more-or-less confined to the Boè cable-car at Corvara. The Selva blackspot has reportedly been removed by the gondola to Ciampinoi. The Porta Vescovo cable-car at Arabba has in the past been crowded in the morning and early afternoon, especially when snow elsewhere is poor, but the new 25-person gondola expected to come into service this winter should put paid to that problem. An excellent, highly detailed topographical piste map is sold locally.

   The **artificial snow** installations of Selva and neighbouring resorts is about the most comprehensive in Europe, covering practically all the main runs from top to bottom.

The resort

Selva is a long, shapeless village which suffers from having grown along the road. From the centre it extends far down towards S Cristina with an uninterrupted succession of shops and hotels, and chalets spreading back from the road. It is mostly modern and has no very obvious village character, but the style of building is generally attractive, and when full in winter it is a lively place, with the western wall of the Sella group providing a magnificent fiery sunset backdrop.

   There is now a free ski-bus service between Ortisei and Selva, and ordinary valley bus services elsewhere. There are no evening buses.

   Selva lacks the charm factor, but in most respects the Val Gardena as

Facts on Selva Bolzano **Italy**

Prices in lire

Tourist office
Postcode 39048
Tel (471) 795122
Fax (471) 794245
Tlx 400359

Getting there
By road 1,226km from Calais. Via Munich, Brenner, Bressanone; chains occasionally needed.
By rail Chiusa (27km); frequent buses from station.
By air Verona; transfer 4hr. (Or Munich, Treviso or Milan; transfers about 5hr.)

Staying there
Visitor beds 8,000; breakdown: 4,500 in hotels, 3,500 in apartments.
Package holidays Inghams (h) Ski Whizz Small World (c) SnowRanger (h) .
Medical facilities In resort: Fracture clinic, doctors, chemists. Hospital: Bolzano (42km). Dentist: Ortisei (7km).

Non-skiing activities
Indoor Swimming, sauna, solaria (in hotels), bowling alley, squash, artificial skating-rink, ice-hockey, curling, museum, indoor golf, skittles, concerts, cinema, billiards, tennis, curling.
Outdoor Sleigh rides, torch-light descents, horse-riding, extensive cleared paths around Selva and above S Cristina and Ortisei, ski-bob.

Kindergartens
Ski kindergarten
Tuition: Possible. Hours: 8.30-4.00. Ages: 2½-6. Cost: 228,000.00 per week (with meals).

Special skiing facilities
Summer skiing On the Marmolada (3342m), a cable-car and several lifts. Access via Malga Ciapela, south of Arabba.

Cross-country 12km trail in Vallunga with abbreviations to create shorter trails. Also trails in Val Gardena between S Cristina and Ortisei. Over 40km trails at Alpe di Siusi. Two trails, 5km and 8km on Monte Pana.

Lift passes
Superski Dolomiti
Covers all lifts in the Dolomites. (464 lifts in total.)
Cost 6 days 194,300.00 (£90.79). Low season: 165,300.00 saving 15%.
Credit cards accepted Yes.
Senior citizens 155,600.00 (over 60) saving 20%.
Children 136,300.00 (under 14) saving 30%. Free pass up to age 6.
Notes Free ski bus between Selva and Ortisei.
Beginners Points tickets.
Short-term passes Half-day (from 1.00pm) and day pass for individual areas; single tickets for some lifts.
Other passes Skipass Val Gardena, covers Gardena lifts only, (178,300.00 for adults, 125,000.00 for children).

Ski school
Ski-School Selva
Special family ski-school available.
Classes 9.30-4.00. Cost: 160,000.00 (6 days, Sun-Fri). Full-day excursions twice a week. 5-day courses also available.
Lift priority No.
Children's classes Ages: 4-12. Cost: 280,000.00 (6 days, Sun-Fri). including ski-pass, 240,000.00 excluding ski-pass.
Private lessons available Hourly. Cost: 35,000.00 per hour. For one person. For 2 people 42,000.00.
Special courses Mono, snowboard and telemark.

What was new in 91
Saslonch cable-car (from S Cristina to Ciampinoi) changed to a 12-seater gondola.

---

a whole is excellent for **cross-country** and **non-skiers**.

Accommodation is mainly in modern comfortable hotels, none of them very stylish, and simple B&B houses; staffed chalet accommodation is offered by a few companies. The Aaritz and Antares are comfortable, expensive hotels near the Ciampinoi gondola. Even better placed for access to both Ciampinoi and the Costabella chair-lift are the comfortable, functional Laurin, the Genziana and the large and fairly simple Stella. But about the best location of all is across the river, near the very useful Ciampinoi chair-lift, where several inexpensive B&B hotels include the Somont and the Eden; the more comfortable Savoy is just by the lift and has a restaurant.

Après-ski is one of Selva's main advantages over the other mostly small and peaceful resorts in the Sella area. There are several discothèques (reporters have in the past recommended the Club Stella), one or two places with live music, and plenty of bars and inexpensive restaurants.

Selva's nursery slopes are excellent – a wide open area with snow-making machines near the resort centre and beneath the Dantercepies lifts. Unfortunately the slopes and lifts are often busy with skiers in transit. We have no recent reports on the quality of Selva's **ski school**.

Minor resorts

Ortisei   1240m
The main town in the Val Gardena is not convenient as a base for keen Alpine skiers, but it is charming and well placed for access to the Alpe di Siusi (for walks and cross country skiing) and for excursions to the Adige valley reaching as far as Verona. There is a local museum as well as a display of religious wood-carving for which the valley is famous. Another tradition which adds to the charm of the village streets is ice sculpture.

The town centre is by-passed by the main valley road, but this busy highway still has to be crossed on foot to get to and from the ice rink and Alpe di Siusi cable-car. The main street is a long one and includes a short, fairly steep hill between the church and main square and bus terminal. As in Selva, staying in Ortisei usually involves quite a lot of tiresome walking. Ortisei nightlife is less lively than Selva's, but there are some good bars and restaurants, especially the delightful Zur Traube/all'Uva, and a disco. A local passion is ice hockey; there are often evening league matches. Most of the many hotels in the centre of the resort are simple, except for the smart and expensive Adler. Opposite it is the Posta, a large, solid, central old village hotel. The Snaltnerhof is simple, inexpensive and welcoming, and very well placed beside the main bus stop. The Alpe di Siusi offers varying degrees of retreat. The main community is Kompatsch, at the top of the road up from Castelrotto, where there are several hotels, a ski school with kindergarten and a skating rink. Two large, comfortable and secluded hotels are the Floralpina at the S Cristina end and the Sonne near the top of the cable-car from Ortisei.
Tourist office ✆ (471) 796328. Fax ✆ (471) 796749. Tx 400305.
Package holidays SnowRanger (s).

Arabba   1600m
A small, quiet and attractively unspoilt village in the Italian-speaking sector of the Sella region (and therefore relatively German-free), Arabba is the best resort in the area for good and adventurous skiers, thanks to its excellent home slopes and to the ease of access Cortina (by road) and to Marmolada (by piste) – though it's important to remember that the Superski pass does not at present include Marmolada.

Although the main operator from Britain, Beach Villas, offers chalets (Casanova is 'spacious and comfortable'), most of the accommodation is in apartments, pensiones and hotels; the Sport is about the most comfortable but slightly out of the way; the Porta Vescovo is central, modern and smart, with the resort's one disco. This apart, there is nothing much to do except ski, skate (on a modest natural rink), eat (there is a good choice of restaurants), drink (Bar Peter, Pensione Erica and Albergo Pordoi are recommended) and sleep – though the brighter lights of Corvara are not far away. Shopping is very limited – one small supermarket, but also a bank, pharmacy and three ski shops. The ski school has only three English-speaking instructors, and arranging a class in English can therefore be tricky, but they are apparently highly competent and committed.

Tourist office ✆ (436) 79130. Fax ✆ (436) 79300. Tx 440823.
Package holidays Beach Villas (cs) SnowRanger (h).

Corvara 1550m

From the skiing point of view, Corvara has great attractions – direct access to the Alta Badia area, coupled with probably the best location on the Sella Ronda. Selva and Arabba are easily reached, and the most remote segment of the available skiing (Canazei) is the least interesting for intermediate skiers. The village is a characterless sprawl of modern chalets and chalet-style hotels, large and small, spread across a large area beside the roads down from the Gardena and Campolongo passes. The centre and most convenient place to stay is near the Col Alto chair-lift (for access to the Alta Badia) which is a manageable walk from the Boè cable-car (for Arabba) and the scene of most of Corvara's limited après-ski. This usually includes dancing (at tea-time and in the evening) at the Posta, the biggest, smartest and most central of the hotels (pool and sauna). The Veneranda is much smaller and less expensive and also conveniently placed. The Eden is 'comfortable, with good food'. There is a short cross-country track between the Boè cable-car and Colfosco and an ice rink with facilities for curling.

Tourist office ✆ (471) 836176. Tx 401555.

Colfosco 1650m

A small holiday village which has grown up beside the road between Corvara and the Gardena pass, with easy access to Selva and Corvara and a small skiing area of its own (including a good nursery area) beside the village. There are a couple of plush, modern, expensive hotels at the top of the village, of which one, the Kolfuschgerhof, boasts a swimming pool and squash court. Most hotels are more modest; the Centrale is large and comfortable and, as it sounds, well placed for skiing and also for après-ski.

Tourist office ✆ (471) 836145.

San Cassiano 1537m

A small roadside village in typical Dolomite style with a lot of mostly new chalet buildings, largely consisting of hotels and B&B houses. San Cassiano has some of the best of the local skiing for beginners and timid skiers, who can enjoy the very long, easy runs down to the village itself from Pralongia and from Piz Sorega before venturing further afield. The Rosa Alpina is a large, comfortable, modern hotel (with pool) at the centre of the village and the focus of après-ski (live bands afternoon and evening). There is not much else going on. There are cross-country possibilities at Armentarola, a cluster of quiet hotels and restaurants about 1km east. Cortina is less than an hour away via Valparola and

Falzarego passes – a spectacular drive through a rocky wilderness.
Tourist office ✆ (471) 849422. **Package holidays** Ski Whizz Small World (c).

Canazei 1440m

Canazei is a large, noisy village in the Italian-speaking Val di Fassa, cut
through by the busy main road. It is the only real alternative to the Val
Gardena resorts for skiers wanting varied off-slope activities and a
range of nightlife. Its local skiing is inconvenient – even the nursery
slopes involve taking the cable-car, which starts a long walk from the
resort centre, and is often crowded. But once up the mountain you can
soon be in Arabba.

The village centre is an attractive jumble of busy narrow streets with
some rustic old buildings as well as new hotels and shopping precincts
which have sprung up with the Dolomites' tourist boom. There are
plenty of bars, restaurants and evening entertainment (mostly hotel-
oriented), with discos and jokey contests. There is a large public pool
and sauna, a natural ice rink beside an attractive wooded playground in
the centre, and a long chain of cross-country trails (mostly easy) along
the shady side of the river. The Val di Fassa hosts a 70km X-C
marathon (the Marcialonga) between Canazei and Cavalese; some
stretches of the course are open only at the time of the race.

In the centre, the Croce Bianca is a long-established hotel,
substantial and comfortably refurbished. The Bellevue is better placed
for the cable-car. The Laurin is on the wrong side of town for skiing
purposes, but is otherwise attractive. Two hotels offer greater skiing
convenience. The comfortable and friendly Bellavista is at Pecol, near
the top of the Canazei cable-car. Higher up (2100m), the inexpensive
80-year-old Pordoi is somewhat Spartan. It has a modern self-catering
annexe with pool and sauna. The Tyrol is 'comfortable, with good food'.

Buses in the Val di Fassa are reportedly regular and frequent, but
overcrowded in the mornings. Taxis are affordable for outings (eg to
Cortina).
Tourist office ✆ (462) 61113. Tx 400012. **Package holidays** Citalia (h) Enterprise
(h) SnowRanger (hs).

Campitello 1440m

Canazei's close neighbour is a quieter and much smaller village, its
centre set back from the main road, an attractive collection of old
buildings beside a stream running down into the main river. A cable-car
goes up to the Passo Sella skiing, but there is no piste back down. The
Fedora is a comfortable hotel beside the cable-car station – others may
be quite a walk away. There are limited shopping facilities in the village,
and we are informed that there is nightlife, too. There are secluded
nursery slopes in the valley, conditions permitting, and an ice rink.
Tourist office ✆ (462) 61137.
Package holidays Enterprise (h).

Bormio Italy 1225m

Good for *Summer skiing, mountain restaurants, not skiing, artificial snow, woodland runs*
Bad for *Easy runs, tough runs, resort-level snow, late holidays, easy road access, short airport transfers, freedom from cars*

Separate resort: Santa Caterina

Bormio, host of the 1985 skiing World Championships, is a small town in a remote corner of Lombardy at the foot of the Stelvio pass which separates Italian Italy from Germanic Dolomite Italy and serves some of the best summer skiing in the Alps. Bormio's history as a spa goes back to Roman times, and the centre is old, unaffected and very Italian, with a greater variety of everyday shops, cafés and restaurants tucked away in the back-streets than in most ski resorts, and good open-air markets. The skiing that matters is on one tall mountainside whose slopes provide long runs, mostly intermediate. New lifts and a battery of snow-guns have helped to relieve the associated problems of queues and not being able to ski down to the valley, but have not opened up any new skiing on what is, by today's standards, a narrow skiing area. We get few reports on Bormio, but it seems to inspire great affection in the reporters it suits.

The Superpool lift pass covers Santa Caterina, a pretty nearby village with more reliable snow, less queuing and intermediate skiing which is a match for Bormio's when snow low down is poor. A car is mainly of use for exploring the other skiing areas; parking in Bormio is not problematic. The road to Livigno (also covered by the pass) has been improved, but is still long and often requires chains. Reaching Bormio by road via Milan is very time-consuming.

The skiing top 3012m bottom 1225m

The north-west-facing slopes of the tall Monte Vallecetta rise evenly from the riverside near Bormio to its 3148m summit just above the top of a two-stage cable-car from the edge of town. The middle station is Bormio 2000, an upper mini-resort, usually accessible by car (a car park separates the two stages of cable-car). An alternative access route is by gondola to Ciuk (1620m), followed by chair-lifts or the long Graziella drag to the top. When conditions permit there are very long runs from top to bottom, up to 14km and nearly 1800m vertical. On the open top half alone the runs are long and satisfying, but the range of difficulty is limited; the easy runs are a bit tough for skiers just off the nursery slopes, and only when they are icy do the more difficult ones (two short blacks) excite skiers hungry for a challenge. Immediately below the top cable-car station and to the west of the pistes, a fairly steep, wide and

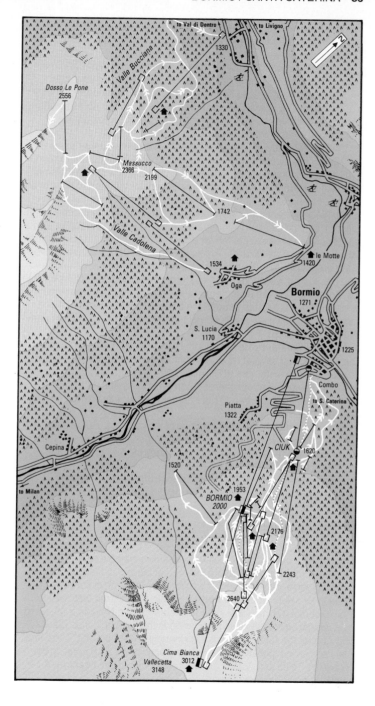

sunless bowl provides excellent off-piste skiing when conditions are safe, which is not often. Take a guide and check that the Ornella drag-lift is working before embarking on the lower section.

Most skiers spend the day on the top half of the mountain, and the wide, undulating trails through the woods below Ciuk are little used except in bad weather and for skiing home in the afternoon, when they are crowded. The Stelvio World Championship downhill course starts steeply just above La Rocca and runs down past Ciuk to near the bottom of the gondola 1000m below.

On the other side of the valley a worthwhile new ski area has been created by the recent building of lifts on the west-facing slopes above the villages of Oga and Le Motte, linking up with those above the small resort of Valdidentro. A chair-lift from the edge of Valdidentro rises over the wooded north-facing slopes of Masucco (2366m) to a restaurant and a small nursery area. From here two consecutive lifts ascend to the summit, serving pleasant intermediate runs back down the valley, with a couple of blue variants. On the other side of the valley from Masucco is the high point of the ski area, Posse le Pone (2550m), reached by two short drag-lifts. From the top there are a number of off-piste routes and one marked run descending the east side of the mountain. Runs back to Le Motte and Oga are disrupted by a number of lifts up; they are mainly short intermediate pistes through the trees, with the exception of one long blue run down the south side of the Val Cadolena to Oga (of nearly 800m vertical drop).

Mountain restaurants are plentiful, considering the limited size of the ski area, and several reporters commented on good food, even in the self-service restaurant at Bormio 2000. La Rocca is recommended for 'food, value and atmosphere'. Cedrone is apparently 'ideal for families with small children'. There are two restaurants in the Valdidentro area.

Peak-time **queues** for both sections of the cable-car can usually be avoided, except when the bottom runs are unskiable. Several of the drag-lifts are steep and very long, particularly the Nevada and the important linking lift, the Graziella.

Bormio was one of the first to invest in **artificial snow**, and its installation is still quite impressive, extending from 2600m to the town.

The resort

The outskirts of the town, much less attractive than the centre, include numerous modern hotels along the road at the foot of the slopes between cable-car and gondola station. This is the most convenient location for skiers' **accommodation**, within 10 or 15 minutes' walk of the old centre. Of the hotels near the cable-car, the Nevada is favoured by a regular visitor who also recommends the Funivia, Larice Bianca and Aurora; the Ambassador is also friendly and welcoming. The Cima Bianca is an inexpensive, attractive and convenient B&B hotel. In the centre the Posta and Astoria are both comfortable and attractive. A couple of reporters recommend the Girasole, despite its isolated

Facts on Bormio   Sondrio **Italy**

Prices in lire

Tourist office
Via allo Stelvio, 10
Postcode 23032
Tel (342) 903300
Fax (342) 904696

Getting there
By road 1,146km from Calais. Via Mont Blanc Tunnel, Milan, Sondrio; chains rarely needed. Via Livigno; chains often needed.
By rail Tirano (40km); 15 daily buses from station.
By air Milan; transfer 4½hr. (Or Verona, Bergamo.)

Staying there
Visitor beds 6,100; breakdown: 3,165 in hotels; 2,935 in apartments.
Package holidays Enterprise (hs) Inghams (h) Neilson (h) Quality Ski Tours (h) Ski Global (hs) .
Medical facilities In resort: Hospital, doctors, chemists, dentists.

Non-skiing activities
Indoor 2 museums, library, thermal baths, squash, swimming pool, sauna, massage, sports hall, tennis, artificial skating rink.
Outdoor Ski-bob, toboggan run, horse-riding, walks in the Stelvio National Park.

Special skiing facilities
Summer skiing Extensive area at Stelvio Pass (20km), 2760m to 3420m.
Cross-country 10km trails near resort (easy).

More difficult trails (up to 25km) in Valdidentro, Insolaccia and S. Caterina Valfurva (25km).

Lift passes
Alta Valtellina (Superpool)
Covers Bormio, Santa Caterina, Livigno, Valdisotto, Valdidentro. (24 lifts in total.)
Cost 6 days 160,000.00 (£74.77). Low season: 140,000.00 saving 13%.
Credit cards accepted Yes.
Senior citizens 115,000.00 (over 65) saving 28%.
Children 115,000.00 (under 12) saving 28%.
Beginners Points tickets.
Short-term passes Day pass (half-day available for Bormio only); tickets for single rides on a few lifts.
Other passes Bormio only (day pass 33,000.00 for adults, 25,000.00 for children).

Ski school
Various
5 ski schools all with similar times and prices: Anzi, Bormio 2000, Capitani, Nozionale, Sertorelli. (Sertorelli specialises in children's classes).
Classes 2hr. Cost: 100,000.00 (6 days).
Lift priority No.
Children's classes Ages: From 5. Cost: 80,000.00 (6 days).
Private lessons available Hourly. Cost: 30,000.00 per hour.

What was new in 91
2-seater chair-lift at Ciuk-La-Rocca and a new baby-lift at Bormio 2000.

---

position at Bormio 2000 (very convenient for the slopes) – 'basic but excellent value for money', 'the owners were superb hosts and couldn't have done more to make our stay comfortable'. A half-hourly bus does a circuit of the town.

Après-ski is generally quiet, but there are a few discos and a wide range of bars and restaurants outside hotels. The Aurora has a 'very popular' piano bar. The Cristall Bar, near the gondola station, does 'wonderful' pizza. Organised outings may include the excellent Baiona restaurant, beside the road up to Bormio 2000. Many skiers enjoy easing their joints in the thermal baths.

Bormio offers a lot to the **non-skier**, with new spa and sports facilities generated by the World Championships (a bus ride from the centre), and is itself an interesting town. Reporters recommend the excursions to Livigno and St Moritz. The **cross-country** trails at Valdidentro are more reliable for snow than those around Bormio itself.

There are no village **nursery slopes** but good areas up the mountain at Ciuk and Bormio 2000, the first being larger and more tranquil, but sometimes short of snow, the latter marred by a 'dreadful' rope-tow lift. There is not very much easy skiing for the post-nursery stages.

There are several **ski schools**, with numerous English-speaking instructors. Our few reports are generally favourable. Several reporters commented on the off-piste run to Santa Caterina – long but not difficult.

Santa Caterina   1750m

Santa Caterina is a quiet little resort in the pretty, wooded Valfurva, a dead-end in winter when the exciting Gavia pass is closed. When snow conditions are good, adventurous skiers based here are tempted to bus down to Bormio, but when snow is in short supply the traffic flows the other way; weekend queues can occur. The local skiing is on the north-east-facing slopes of the Sobretta between the village and a top station of 2725m. The higher slopes are fairly steep and graded black, but most are intermediate, with a beautiful long run behind Cresta Sobretta, and good wide woodland trails. There is a good but often overcrowded nursery area above the woods and an easy way home via the Gavia road. A recent reporter commends all the mountain restaurants, but especially the Paradiso and the Bella Vista. There is some attractive cross-country skiing (up to 10km) in quiet surroundings beyond the resort, and skating on the natural rink. The resort itself is picturesque and its inhabitants are 'very welcoming'. A reporter recommends the Parc hotel. The Sport is clean but fairly basic and serves 'good and plentiful' food. None of the hotels is far from the slopes. Night-life revolves around several 'comfortable' bars (particularly recommended is the central Camino) and two discos (Queen's is apparently the better of the two).

Tourist office ✆ (0342) 935598.

Package holidays Enterprise (hs) Neilson (h) Quality Ski Tours (h) SkiTonic (h)

High skiing, low spirits

Livigno Italy 1820m

Good for *Nursery slopes, easy runs, resort-level snow, late holidays, sunny slopes, duty-free, artificial snow*
Bad for *Skiing convenience, tough runs, short airport transfers, easy road access, mountain restaurants, not skiing, freedom from cars*

Livigno is a very strung-out series of villages in a long, wide, high and exceedingly remote valley – a lost world to which the easiest access from mother Italy is the 2290m pass from Bormio, over an hour's drive away. British skiers sent by their tour operators via Milan airport can face coach transfers of over six hours in which to build up a thirst for Livigno's much-vaunted duty-free drink.

The high and wide slopes along both sides of the valley above the resort provide a lot of uncomplicated intermediate skiing for a long winter season. In good weather and good snow it is splendid; in bad weather 'Piccolo Tibet', as Livigno is known locally, is extremely bleak. Whatever the weather, the lift system is poorly conceived and the ski areas are largely unconnected. Moving from one area to another usually involves a fair amount of walking or waiting. The village is old and interesting, but modern building has spoilt some of its charm – happily, more thought and planning now seems to be going into its development. A large number of reports this year indicate that the resort is becoming very popular with younger British skiers, who seem consistently impressed by the resort's good value for money.

Thanks to a road tunnel from Switzerland, Livigno is no longer seriously inaccessible to motorists. Tour operators are also taking advantage of this and transferring clients from Zurich rather than Milan, a marginally shorter and more scenic route. Having a car is handy in the resort and for excursions, though parking may be a bit of a headache. The lift pass covers Bormio and Santa Caterina, and includes a free half-day in St Moritz; all are within easy reach by road.

The skiing top 2800m bottom 1816m

Skiing takes place on both flanks of the valley. Although there are many more lifts on the south-east-facing side of the valley, most of them are short nursery drags, and the north-and west-facing Mottolino slopes above the winding road to Bormio offer a similar amount of skiing. Most of the skiing is above the tree-line, and only a couple of the lifts offers protection against the elements.

The two-stage **Lago Salin** gondola from the southern end of town spans the longest slopes in the ski area, a wide open, south-east-facing mountainside with several possible variations of the run back down; none is severe, but snow is often difficult on the lower slopes, which are fairly steep and poorly marked. Behind the top station is a quiet area of short runs beside the Federia drag-lifts, with reliably good snow. A very long and gentle blue run northwards along the mountain ridge links up with the **Costaccia** chair-lifts above the northern end of the resort (S Maria), which serve a small area of shorter wooded runs, often worn (but now benefiting from snow-guns).

The drag-lift up to the **Mottolino** skiing has recently been replaced by a twelve-man gondola, which has greatly eased congestion at this regular bottle-neck. There are various other access points along the Bormio road, serving a spectrum of intermediate runs complicated only by poor signposting and by the road itself which cuts awkwardly through the skiing area. The wide slope above Trepalle (little more than a few houses, including a bar, beside the road to Bormio) faces east, and the red run beneath the chair-lift can be quite a challenge as it freezes at the end of a sunny day. There is tempting off-piste skiing below the Monte della Neve, but it is difficult to stay within reach of lifts. From the top of Monte della Neve, there is reportedly a 'particularly satisfying blue' via Monte Sponda right down to the bottom of the new gondola (one section of it is marked red on the piste map).

For an Italian resort, Livigno is not well equipped with **mountain restaurants**. Reporters agree that they are no more than adequate in number, and unremarkable in style. Two exceptions are the Carosello 3000 and the Mottolino, both recently refurbished and very popular. Other recommendations include Tea Bock in the Carosello area, the Tea del Vidal at Mottolino, and the charming unmarked place about half-way down the tricky run from Lago Salin to the village. The rustic cow shed at Tea del Plan (Costaccia) is as popular as ever.

The main problem with lifts is the difficulty of getting to them. We have no reports of serious **queues**, except for the buses at peak times. The new Mottolino gondola, replacing the cold fifteen-minute drag-lift, has relieved peak-time congestion, though the slopes above it can be very crowded at weekends. Despite tourist office claims that the piste map is 'very easy to follow', virtually all our reporters found it confusing, unreliable and out of date. It unhelpfully does not give the run numbers.

Artificial snow now extends to all three sectors of the ski area. There are snow guns on virtually all the Costaccia slopes, on the run to Trepalle and the red down the Mottolino gondola, and on a short piste in the Lago Salin area.

The resort

Originally three separate communities (Santa Maria, San Antonio and San Rocco) spread out along the western side of the long flat valley, Livigno is now an unbroken three-mile straggle of hotels, bars, garages and duty-free supermarkets. They are interspersed by many beautiful old buildings and barns full of animals, but there is no real old village centre. Spirits cost from £3 a litre, petrol is about half the normal Italian price and there are small savings to be made on cosmetics, electrical goods and ski equipment (though to be sure of a saving you need to be very well informed about prices at home before you depart). One reporter found that prices in the supermarkets were somewhat lower than in the so-called special duty-free shops.

The main road (a surprisingly busy thoroughfare between Italy and Austria) by-passes the southern end of the village (San Rocco) but central San Antonio is a very busy road junction. Because of the road tunnel and the duty-free goods, Livigno is one of the few Italian resorts outside the Dolomites to attract many German skiers (for holidays and shopping day-trips). They all come by car, and day-time traffic nuisance is considerable. The free ski-bus is an essential link between the two main skiing areas; it runs frequently, but reporters complain of sardine-like conditions at peak times. There are also regular buses to Bormio and St Moritz, which may be cheaper than taking an organised excursion.

Accommodation is mostly in hotels and apartments along the resort's single axis from Santa Maria (within reach of the Costaccia and Mottolino lifts) to San Rocco (near the Lago Salin lifts). Most of our reporters recommend staying somewhere between these extremes, and suggest the Camana Veglia ('small, family-run, bags of character, convenient'), the Steinbock ('excellent restaurant') and the Piccolo Tibet. A regular visitor continues to praise the family-run Silvestri

Facts on Livigno   Sondrio **Italy**

Prices in lire

Tourist office

Plaza Dal Comun
Postcode 23030
Tel (342) 996379
Fax (342) 996881
Tlx 350400

Getting there

By road 1,107km from Calais. Via Munich, Innsbruck, Landeck, Zernez; chains may be needed; toll tunnel open 8am to 8pm. Alternative route via Bormio; chains often needed.
By rail Tirano; 4 daily buses to resort (3hr).
By air Zurich; transfer 6hr. (Or Milan; transfer 6hr plus.)

Staying there

Visitor beds 7,770; breakdown: 4,155 in hotels, 3,615 in apartments.
Package holidays Citalia (hs) Crystal (hrs) Enterprise (hs) Falcon (hs) Inghams (hs) Neilson (hs) Panorama's Ski Experience (hs) Ski Global (hs) SkiTonic (h) Thomson (hs) .
Medical facilities In resort: Doctor, dentist, chemist. Hospital: Sondalo (60km).

Non-skiing activities

Indoor Sauna, gym, body-building, games room.
Outdoor Cleared paths, skating rink, snow buggies, snowmobiles, sleigh rides.

Special skiing facilities

Summer skiing No.
Cross-country 30km green and 10km red trails along valley floor. Instruction available.

Lift passes

Superpool pass
Covers all lifts at Livigno, Bormio, S Caterina, Val di Dentro and Val di Sotto, and local ski bus. (28 lifts in total.)
Cost 6 days 160,000.00 (£74.77). Low season: 140,000.00 saving 13%.
Credit cards accepted No.

Senior citizens 125,000.00 (over 65) saving 22%.
Children 125,000.00 (under 12) saving 22%.
Notes 7-day or longer passes give one free day in St Moritz.
Beginners Coupons.
Short-term passes Afternoon pass for Livigno only.
Other passes Livigno only pass (per day 32,000.00 for adults, 26,000.00 for children).

Ski school

Interalpen
Classes 2hr: 9.00-11.00 or 11.00-1.00. Cost: 73,000.00 (6 days).
Lift priority Yes.
Children's classes Ages: From 9. Cost: 65,000.00 (6 days).
Private lessons available Per hour. Cost: 32,000.00 per hour. Each additional person 5,000.00.
Inverno/Estate
Classes 2hr am or pm. Cost: 73,000.00 (6 days (from Sun or Mon)).
Lift priority Yes.
Children's classes Ages: 6. Cost: 65,000.00 (6 days (from Sun or Mon)).
Private lessons available Per hour. Cost: 32,000.00 per hour. Each additional adult 5,000.00.
Livigno
Classes 2hr daily. Cost: 73,000.00 (6 days, Mon to Sat).
Lift priority Yes.
Children's classes Ages: 8. Cost: 65,000.00 (6 days, Mon to Sat).
Private lessons available Per hour. Cost: 29,000.00 per hour. Each additional adult 5,000.00.

What was new in 91

1. New Mottolino gondola (opened 28/12/90) cutting out 15 minute drag-lift to Mottolino.
2. New short drag-lift parallel to top section of gondola.

('comfortable, friendly, good food'). The very central St Anton and Galli's are not recommended. We've had one glowing report of the Tananai Beii apartments – 'would be surprised to find anywhere as nice, let alone better'.

Après-ski is mainly bar-oriented and lively, but far from riotous. There are half a dozen discos but most of these are inconveniently situated on the outskirts of town. The British tend to congregate at Galli's bar in San Rocco, where the ski school give out their awards. Other popular night spots include Foxi's in San Antonio ('vaulted ceiling and a slide at the entrance'), Il Ceilo ('expensive, up-market, Italian clientele'), the Underground Bar ('not all it's cracked up to be'), Marco's Video Bar ('raves on into the small hours') and the popular Black Out disco. Our reporters, conscious of the resort's duty-free status, have been surprised by the range of prices – from the very reasonable to the rather expensive. Most restaurants are in hotels, though there are several cheap and cheerful places to eat for the budget conscious (Foxi's, Galli's and Mario's all serve pizzas and burgers). The Tea del Plan organizes evening parties twice a week; you take the last chair-lift up and ski down afterwards by torchlight.

For **non-skiers** there are few diversions except drinking and regular excursions to St Moritz and Bormio. In January and February, international dog-sled races are staged. Several reporters warmly recommend the skidoo rides through the valley. There is an indoor golf and tennis club. The **cross-country** trails are convenient, running along the valley, and reliable for snow.

Nursery slopes and lifts cover a large expanse of the lower slopes on the western side of the resort. They are open and gentle, and easily accessible from accommodation in the main strip of village, with bars close at hand, including the Bar Scuola, the lively headquarters of the main ski school.

There are at least five **ski schools**, all officially recognised, and according to recent reports, all of a high standard. The only general complaint is that the classes are too short (just two hours a day). The Livigno Inferno school is particularly recommended for children's classes. Private lessons are said to be 'excellent value for money', and video sessions are available. There is no **kindergarten**.

Paradise reinvented

Schladming Austria 750m

Good for *Nursery slopes, Alpine charm, easy runs, big ski area, woodland runs, artificial snow, cross-country skiing, short airport transfers, easy road access, rail access, mountain restaurants*
Bad for *Skiing convenience, late holidays, resort-level snow, tough runs*

Linked resorts: Rohrmoos, Haus in Ennstal

This world-famous ski racing town became familiar to Sunday afternoon television viewers before it started attracting British holiday skiers – a process which justly continues to gather momentum. Schladming is the furthest east of Austria's major skiing centres and the only one in Styria, and differs from the Tyrolean norm in giving the attractive impression of being an ordinary old town with a life of its own, independent of tourism; as well as wooden chalets with painted shutters there are sober old stone buildings, including a splendid medieval town gate.

The town lies in the middle of a broad valley on a main east-west road and rail route. To the north are the spectacular rocky peaks of the Dachstein, with summer skiing (Alpine and cross-country) on its very gentle expanse of glacier. But Schladming's skiing, forming the heart of the 'Skiparadies', is on the gentler wooded foothills of the Tauern mountains to the south of the Ennstal – long, broad runs through woods from around 2000m to the valley floor at 750m. It offers a great deal of intermediate skiing, but there is a pronounced lack of variety in the many blue and red runs, and they are spread over four mountains which for all practical purposes are separate. The first of these flaws is probably not remediable; the second is, to some degree, and the first steps towards building linking lifts have apparently been taken.

There are further substantial areas of skiing within easy reach by car at high, purpose-built Obertauern and the resorts in the valleys around Wagrain, all covered by the Top Tauern Schischeck lift pass. A car helps to make the most of the local skiing, too.

Rohrmoos is a straggling satellite community with no village focus, on an extensive, gentle shelf, slightly above Schladming, at the foot of one of the main skiing areas – near-ideal for beginners. Haus is a quiet village offering direct access to the most easterly major ski area.

The skiing top 2015m bottom 750m

The four mountains lined up on the south side of the valley are for practical skiing purposes quite separate – the two mountains in the centre of the range and closest to Schladming (Planai and Hochwurzen) are linked awkwardly by chair-lift and not at all by piste. The lie of the land is such that improvements in this link will be difficult to achieve. In contrast, there is obvious scope for linking Planai to Hauser Kaibling and Hochwurzen to Reiteralm, and the necessary lifts may be in place by 1992. The Tourist Office will not confirm this and we remain sceptical. Most of the slopes face north and provide good, long red runs which are difficult to distinguish from one another; there is also some added skiing on the east-and west-facing flanks, at higher altitudes. The ski-bus service (including routes going up into the skiing) is essential for adventurous skiers without cars; it is covered by the lift pass, but most reporters have wished for a more frequent service.

For skiers based in Schladming, the closest skiing is on the **Planai**, served by a two-stage gondola to 1894m from the edge of town, a manageable walk from the centre. The middle station (Kessleralm) of the gondola can be reached by car; a chair-lift runs in parallel with the top half of the gondola. Beyond the top station of the gondola are open east-facing slopes served by drag-lifts – good, sustained runs, with moguls in places, but not particularly steep.

The **Hauser Kaibling** (2115m) lies above the delightful village of Haus in Ennstal. The main means of access is a gondola from a huge car-park beside the main road (a long walk east of the village) to a big congregation area half-way up the mountain, also reachable by bus. Motorists can drive up to the eastern edge of the system (Knappl, 1100m) to avoid queues. Beyond the gondola, a series of three drags is necessary to reach the minor peak of Krummholzhütte, also reachable directly by a small and inefficient cable-car from the top of Haus. A gentle path leads from here along the side of the mountain to the Gipfellift, serving an easy black slope, and on to a remote area of gentle skiing at Kaiblingalm, with two short drags, no crowds, excellent snow and a friendly restaurant. The snag is the very long walk back. It is in this area that the new lift from Planai will arrive. The Gipfellift also gives access to a short, well marked and very popular off-piste route down to the lifts at the eastern extremity of the system – slightly awkward at the top and quite steep, but not terrifying. Hauser Kaibling has been slow to modernise its lifts and restaurants, but our reporters find this 'a refreshing change after the glitzy installations on Planai'.

Hochwurzen offers several long red runs (and a toboggan run) between 1100m and 1850m, served by two steep drags and a new hybrid gondola/cable-car (marked on our map as a cable-car, at the Tourist Office's insistence). Below the cable-car station, a selection of chairs and drags serve an extensive network of easy and beginners' slopes around the village of Rohrmoos – and below it down to the western edge of Schladming.

The westernmost of the four local ski areas is the **Reiteralm**, with skiing from 1860m to the banks of the Enns over 1000m below. Access is either by gondola from the edge of Gleiming village or by chair-lift from an isolated riverside lift station across the valley from the hamlet of Pichl – more convenient for motorists. The skiing is spread over a wide area, with yet more long woodland trails, as on the other mountains, and more red than of blue difficulty. There are plans to extend the area upwards, above the tree-line.

Mountain restaurants are more than adequate in number (several of

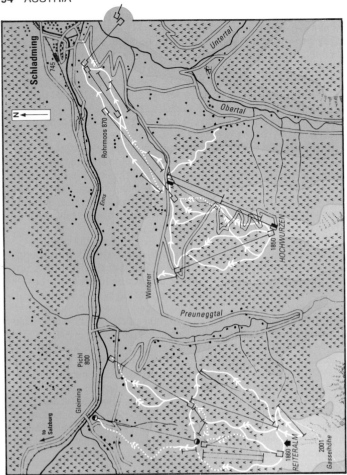

them are not marked on the resort piste map) and generally attractive. Recommendations on Planai include Mitterhausalm, Schladmingerhütte ('for access, original menu and, in spring, the snow-bar') and the ever-popular Onkel Willi's Hütte ('for live music and large sun terraces'); on Hauser Kaibling, Krummholzhütte; on Reiteralm, Eiskarhütte. On Hochwurzen, one reporter recommends the Seiterhütte – 'an efficiently-run, large pine restaurant with excellent food' – and another recommends the Hochwurzenhütte. The ski school area is particularly congested at lunch-time despite the addition of a large new restaurant.

The lift system is not prone to **queues**, and the resort organisation as a whole has impressed recent reporters – though the crowded piste map has been found unclear and confusing.

There is now an extensive network of **artificial snow** on several long runs on all four of the mountains.

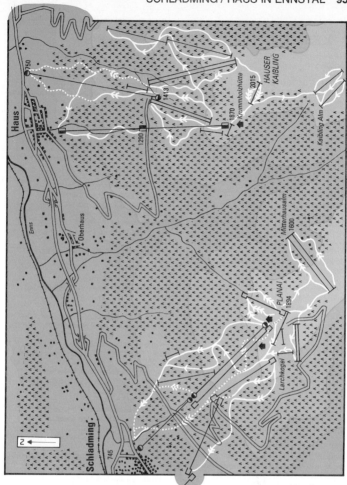

The resort

Schladming is a fairly compact town, with most of its shops and a good many of its hotels, restaurants and bars concentrated around the attractive, broad main street, the Hauptplatz. There are two supermarkets on the outskirts, and a good market on Mondays.

Most of the **accommodation** is in private rooms, guest-houses and hotels. Location is important and many of our reporters found themselves quite a long way from the town centre and the lifts. Apparently the most desirable place to stay, also about the most convenient and among the most expensive, is the Alte Post in the Hauptplatz. But a reporter much impressed by the food describes the rooms as basic, and another judges the hotel over-rated, and prefers the Zum Stadttor – 'lovely rooms, excellent food'. The Sporthotel

Facts on Schladming Steiermark **Austria**

Prices in schillings
Ski Club represented

Tourist office
Postcode A-8970
Tel (3687) 22268
Fax (3687) 2226821
Tlx 38276

Getting there
By road 1,235km from Calais. Via Munich and Salzburg; chains normally unnecessary.
By rail Main-line station in resort.
By air Salzburg; transfer 1½hr. (Or Munich.)

Staying there
Visitor beds 3,300; breakdown: mainly in hotels and pensions.
Package holidays Crystal (hrs) Kings Ski Club (cj) Neilson (hr) Quality Ski Tours (h) Quest Total Ski (h) Quest Travel (schools) (h) Ski Party Snow World (h) SkiBound (h) Thomson (hr) .
Medical facilities In resort: Hospital, doctors, chemists, dentists.

Non-skiing activities
Indoor Swimming, sauna, bowling, tennis court.
Outdoor Ice-rinks in all villages, skating, curling, 13km toboggan runs, sleigh rides, 50km of cleared paths in the surrounding area of Untertal, Rohrmoos and Schladming.

Kindergartens
Miniclub Rohrmoos
Tuition: Yes, for over 4yr. Hours: 9.00-5.00, 5 days. Ages: 18 mth-12yr. Cost: 1,500.00 per week (meals and lunchtime supervision possible).
Hubertas Spieleck
Tuition: No. Hours: 9.15-12.15, 1.15-4.15, 5 days. Ages: 1-10. Cost: 850.00 per week (meals and lunchtime supervision possible).

Special skiing facilities
Summer skiing Several lifts on the Dachstein glacier at 2700m. Access via cable-car above Ramsau. Glacial cross-country trail.
Cross-country Long trails down the valley to Pruggern and beyond. Higher, more interesting trails from Rohrmoos: 4km easy, 6km medium, 17km medium up Obertal, 32km medium up Untertal. Ramsau: 24km easy, 44km medium, 55km difficult.

Lift passes
Skiparadies
Covers all lifts in the Dachstein/Tauern region and ski bus. (75 lifts in total.)
Cost 6 days 1,435.00 (£71.93). Low season: 1,310.00 saving 9%.
Credit cards accepted Yes.
Children 915.00 (under 15) saving 36%. Free pass up to age 5.
Notes Discounts for families, invalids and senior citizens available.
Short-term passes Half-day from 11.00am; 'Try-out' ticket valid for 2½hr costs 290.00 (100.00 refunded if returned within 2½hr).
Other passes Day passes for Ramsau, Reiteralm or Hauser Kaibling areas only; Top-Tauern Skischeck covers Obertauern, Schladming, Wagrain, Pongau, Dachstein etc. (6 days 1490.00 for adults, 860.00 for children).
Other periods 21/2-day passes available.

Ski school
WM (Keinprecht Kahr)
Classes 4hr: 2hr am and pm. Cost: 1,000.00 (5 days).
Lift priority No.
Children's classes Ages: Over 4. Cost: 1,000.00 (5 days). One day 'trying' ticket 400.00; lunchtime supervision and meals available for 450.00.
Private lessons available 2hr or 4hr per day. Cost: 800.00 per hour. Each additional person 250.00.
Schladming-Rohrmoos/Tritscher
Classes 10.00-12.00 and 1.30-4.00. Cost: 1,000.00 (5 days).
Lift priority No.
Children's classes Ages: 4-14. Cost: 1,000.00 (5 days). One day 'experiment' tickets (400.00).
Private lessons available 2½hr or 5hr per day. Cost: 900.00 per hour. Each additional adult 150.00.
Special courses Snowboard school, 1hr to 4-day lessons.

What was new in 91
1. New gondola/cable from Rohrmoos to Hochwurzen, GUB.
2. New 4-seater chair-lift at Planai, Burgstallalmlift.

Royer's location is not convenient, but it is recommended as 'everything one could ask for on an activity holiday': as well as comprehensive sports facilities of its own, it is next to the swimming pool and ice-rink. At the cheaper end of the market is the family-run Starchlhof – 'excellent but a fair hike from the centre of town'. Reports on the Plattner apartments are generally favourable; 'comfortable and spacious but with limited cooking facilities'.

Reports suggest that **après-ski** is better in the early evening than in the small hours – though there are a couple of discos ('the one under the Rossl hotel is good, the other looks seedy'). Charly's Treff (at the bottom of the Planai) is the most popular tea-time bar, but there are also many cafés doing a roaring trade in hot chocolate and cakes; later on, the Hanglbar and the Siglu (on the main square) come into their own. Recent reporters have commented on a good evening's entertainment at the bowling alley (behind the Hanglbar). The charming Zum Kirkenwirt gasthof serves excellent food in a traditional setting.

The good sports facilities, easy access to mountain restaurants, amiable town and good excursion possibilities (eg by train to Salzburg) make Schladming a sound bet for **non-skiers**. There is a very popular toboggan run from top to bottom of the Hochwurzen, down the hairpin road. It is open only at night (when the road is closed). Reporters recommend the café half-way down for hot drinks – 'or something stronger'. And for **cross-country** skiers there is enormous scope.

Rohrmoos consists almost entirely of **nursery slopes**, and beginners should not consider starting elsewhere. There are two main **ski schools** – the Keinprecht-Kahr (more commonly known as Charly Kahr) school at Planai and the Tritscher at Rohrmoos. We have had favourable reports on both. The former has several English-speaking instructors and tuition is apparently good, though somewhat disorganised. The Tritscher school has some native English-speakers but large classes. There is also a snowboard school, Dachstein-Tauern, apparently the largest in Austria.

Rohrmoos   870m

This diffuse satellite suburb has easy skiing to and from many hotel doorsteps. Among its many good-value hotels and guest-houses is the Austria, well placed at the point where the lower gentle slopes of Rohrmoos meet the steeper slopes of Hochwurzen proper. The smarter Schwaigerhof has a good position on the edge of the pistes, and is one of the few places with a pool. A recent reporter stayed at the Alpenkrone, which is clean and comfortable but an inconveniently long way from the village centre. Après-ski is 'informal and unsophisticated' and centres around hotel bars. The café at the Tannerhof is a tea-time favourite. One of the the most popular nightspots is the atmospheric Barbara's bar; another is the Alm bar, apparently the 'in' place this year. For comments on the ski school, see Schladming.
Tourist office ✆ (3867) 61147.

Haus in Ennstal   750m

Haus is a quiet village with its farming origins still in evidence – though it has quite a lot of holiday accommodation, particularly in guest-houses and chalets. There are a couple of shops and cafés, one of which has jazz nights. The smart Hauser Kaibling ('super food and entertainment') is one of the two or three hotels with a pool. The Gasthof Reiter is a fine old chalet, much cheaper. The Gürtl is 'a lovely family-run hotel', convenient for the cable-car. There is a gentle, open nursery slope between the village and the gondola station. The two ski schools and their respective kindergartens are reportedly satisfactory.
Tourist Office ✆ (3686) 2234. Tx 038254. **Package holidays** Austro Tours (h).

Take the high road

Obertauern Austria 1740m

Good for *Resort-level snow, sunny slopes, skiing convenience, nursery slopes, off-piste skiing, easy runs*
Bad for *Not skiing, Alpine charm, après-ski, woodland runs*

Until quite recently, the Niedere Tauern – the mountains at the eastern extremity of the Austrian Alps that separate Villach and Klagenfurt in southerly Carinthia from northerly Salzburg – were all but impassable in winter. Now, a motorway tunnel goes through the mountains, and the only point in the chain where they drop below 2000m is no longer an important pass. Obertauern, built right on the summit of the pass, is not a mightily important ski resort either. But it is certainly finding its place on the British market and over the last few years we have had a very worthwhile number of readers' reports. This is doubtless due in part to its reputation for good snow (it is higher than most Austrian competitors, which often helps). But we imagine it also reflects the resort's other qualities. Obertauern is a high, modern village which exists almost entirely for skiing, and which has densely mechanised slopes allowing skiers to do complete circuits, in either direction, of the mountain bowl surrounding the village. What's more, most hotels give more-or-less direct access to the snow. Such a thing may be common in France, but not in Austria.

Although the village is high, the skiing does not go much more than 500m higher – so although it is an excellent February resort it may not be a very satisfactory April one. Our map makes it evident that the area is not very extensive, either. But there is more to it than there is to most ski areas of such a size – partly because it is quite steep and heavily mogulled (at least around the rim of the bowl), partly because it crams in a lot of lifts and partly because the terrain is interestingly varied and suits most grades of skier. There are even slopes to test experts, though there are not many of them and they are not always open.

The resort is not as hideous as many French purpose-built resorts, and many reporters have commented on the friendliness of the inhabitants, if not the architecture. But it is no beauty, and the largely treeless setting is bleak – and many lifts close when the weather turns bad. Après-ski, similarly, is more entertaining than the French purpose-built norm, but by Austrian standards is distinctly limited. The range of non-skiing activities is even more so.

A car is not of much use in Obertauern, and although the access road is a good one it often requires chains. But taking a car opens up the possibility of making wide use of the Top Tauern Skischeck lift pass, giving access to Schladming and many other resorts.

Not surprisingly, the combination of relatively reliable snow and easy road access results in a daily invasion of cars and coaches when lower resorts are short of snow.

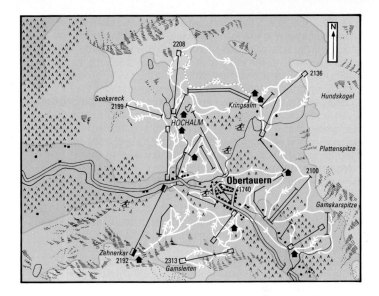

The skiing top 2313m bottom 1640m

The skiing circuit is concentrated on the north side of the resort, spread around a broad, undulating, largely treeless bowl ringed by rocky peaks. Around the bowl there are four main lifts going up to points near the rim. Two of them go up to about 2200m from more-or-less the same point at Hochalm (1940m) – the Seekareck drag-lift over a steep east-facing slope, and the Panorama chair-lift over a more varied south-facing one. As the altitudes suggest, neither run is long, but both are challenging and entertaining, often with moguls. The chair also gives access to a couple of longer, varied runs down to Kringsalm.

The Hundskogel chair-lift serves a slightly longer slope offering a choice of routes down – a moderately steep piste away from the lift on the north side, and off-piste routes more directly down on its south side. The Plattenkar drag-lift goes up from a point just below the village to 2100m, giving a good intermediate run of 400m vertical. Beyond this drag, a little further down the pass, the Schaidberg double chair-lift serves the steepest run on the north side of the resort, but also gives access to a short drag gentle enough to be used as a high-altitude nursery. An easy roundabout way back to the valley from here is apparently available.

Supplementing these lifts going up to the outer edges of the skiing are lifts and pistes linking one with another. These offer less experienced skiers plenty of scope, and a clockwise circuit of this northern part of the area need not involve any of the higher, more difficult runs. But the pistes of most interest to timid skiers are the easy, open runs across the middle of the bowl, served by drag-lifts including the long Zentral lift from just below the village.

On the south side of the resort, the mountains rise more immediately, keeping the village in shade for much of the day in mid-winter. The major lift is the Zehnerkar cable-car, climbing over 500m from the western extremity of the village and giving access to a long, moderately testing run branching to various points along the pass. The lower Gamsleiten chair-lift serves a straightforward piste across the mountainside to the foot of the cable-car, which is part of the clockwise circuit, and more challenging ones back to the base. The upper Gamsleiten chair-lift serves a seriously steep, unprepared run from the high point of the system. When snow is in short supply, this rocky slope may lack adequate cover despite its north-east orientation.

Mountain restaurants are more than adequate for an area where there is such easy access to village restaurants, though more than one reporter has felt prices were high. The Seekarhaus at Kringsalm is particularly cosy, with waitress service, good food and cheap drinks, but it can be crowded. Other recommendations include Schaidberg Hütte ('extensive menu'), Gamsmilch bar at the top of the cable-car and Edelweisshütte at the top of lift 12, reportedly the scene of lively tea-dancing, with only an easy piste to negotiate thereafter.

The incidence of **queues** depends largely on the extent of day-trip invasions. At Fasching time, if lower resorts have poor snow, you can expect trouble; at other times – even in high season – the system works well. The weak points in the chain are the Zehnerkar cable-car, which forms a blockage on the anticlockwise circuit, and the nearby Grünwaldkopf double chair-lift, due to be replaced by a more efficient lift. Even at off-peak times the short Seekar button lift just below Kringsalm restricts the clockwise flow.

The circular piste map (which has received plenty of criticism – 'must have been drawn up by a non-skier') now gives piste gradings, which are reflected in our own map. Reporters are not altogether happy with the gradings – 'some reds were nursery standard, while at least one blue was very steep and challenging, another narrow and mogully'. Other reporters have complained of poor piste marking and too many pistes crossing drag-lift tracks. But reporters have been greatly impressed by the careful piste grooming ('all night, every night'). There is **artificial snow** on one long piste from Seekarspitze down to Kringsalm, and on the short Schaidberg black run at the eastern end of the village.

The resort

The main part of the resort is spread along the road gently dropping down to the east from the summit of the pass, where there is a big open parking area. There are buildings dotted along lanes off the road on the north side, and there is a distinct cluster where these lanes rejoin the road on the west side of the village. There is a much smaller community some way down the road to the west, at the foot of the chair-lift to Hochalm and the cable-car to Zehnerkar. A lot of the buildings are in chalet style, but without the conviction the Austrians normally manage in lower, more comforting settings. The result is a village which is neither offensive nor charming to the eye. Shopping is limited – there are two 'moderately well stocked' supermarkets, but no specialist shops to speak of.

Nearly all the **accommodation** is in hotels and guest-houses, few of them cheap by Austrian standards. Location is not critical unless children are involved, but a good compromise position for skiing both sides of the road, for swimming and tennis and for evening atmosphere

---

Facts on Obertauern Salzburg **Austria**

Prices in schillings

Tourist office

Postcode A-5562
Tel (6456) 252
Fax (6456) 515
Tlx 67560

Getting there

By road 1,222km from Calais. Via Munich and Salzburg; chains often needed.
By rail Radstadt (20km); connecting buses and taxis. Also direct bus service from Salzburg station.
By air Salzburg; transfer 2hr.

Staying there

Visitor beds 5,200; breakdown: mainly in hotels and pensions.
Package holidays Austro Tours (h) Inghams (h) Thomson (h) .
Medical facilities In resort: Fracture clinic, doctor, dentist, chemist.

Non-skiing activities

Indoor Swimming, sauna, massage, golf, tennis hall.
Outdoor Ski-bob, curling, biathlon.

Kindergartens

Sud-Krallinger
Tuition: Yes. Hours: 10.00–3.30. Ages: 4 up. Cost: 1,600.00 per week (with lunch and lunchtime supervision).
Skipi-Club
Tuition: Yes. Hours: 10.00–3.30. Ages: 3 up. Cost: 1,700.00 per week (with lunch and lunchtime supervision).
Nord-Koch
Tuition: Yes. Hours: 10.00-3.30. Ages: 3 up. Cost: 1,600.00 per week (with lunch and lunchtime supervision).

Special skiing facilities

Summer skiing No.
Cross-country 18 km loop from top of village into downhill ski area. Instruction available.

Lift passes

Tauernrunde
Covers all Obertauern's lifts. (25 lifts in total.)
Cost 6 days 1,350.00 (£67.67). Low season: 1,240.00 saving 8%.
Credit cards accepted Yes.

Children 845.00 (under 14) saving 37%.
Notes Discounts for disabled skiers.
Beginners Points cards.
Short-term passes Half-day pass available.
Other passes Top-Tauern Skischeck covers Obertauern, Schladming, Wagrain, Pongau, Dachstein etc. (6 days 1490.00 for adults, 860.00 for children).
Other periods Passes available for 5 out of 7 days, and 10 days.

Ski school

Süd-Krallinger
Classes 4hr: 2hr am and pm. Cost: 1,100.00 (6 days).
Lift priority No.
Children's classes Ages: Any. Cost: 1,100.00 (6 days). Special prices over half-term holidays.
Private lessons available Full-day or hourly. Cost: 400.00 per hour. Private lessons have priority in lift queues.
Nord-Koch
Classes 4hr: 2hr am and pm. Cost: 1,100.00 (6 days).
Lift priority No.
Children's classes Ages: Any. Cost: 1,100.00 (6 days).
Private lessons available Full-day or hourly. Cost: 400.00 per hour. Private lessons have priority in lift queues.
Smily Company
Classes 10.00–3.30. Cost: 1,300.00 (6 days).
Lift priority No.
Children's classes Ages: 4-12. Cost: 1,700.00 (6 days).
Private lessons available Full day or hourly. Cost: 400.00 per hour. Private lessons have priority in lift queues.
Snowwave-surf school
Classes From 10.00am. Cost: 780.00 (3-day course).
Lift priority No.
Children's classes Ages: Any. Cost: 780.00 (3 days).
Private lessons available Hourly. Cost: 400.00 per hour.

What was new in 91

New Schaidberg double chair.

What is new for 92

Plans to replace three drag lifts (Plattenkar, Seekarspitzlifte and Seekarecklift) with 4-seater chairs.

is close to the foot of the Gamsleiten chair-lift, towards the south end of the resort. Closest of all is the Gamsleiten, which has not impressed reporters in the past, but has recently improved – 'comfortable spacious rooms, spotlessly clean, dinner rather hurried'. The Enzian, down the road a little, enjoys repeated recommendations – 'superb food, comfort and position'. Other recommendations include the Marietta ('first-class, well located'), the Wisenegg ('excellent meals and rooms, but a mile out') and the Taurach ('cheap and not fancy but in a superb position on the sunny side of the resort, good for groups and families'). The Kohlmayr is apparently regarded as the best in town.

The resort's limited **après-ski** pivots around hotel bars, of which over 15 claim to offer music and dancing. The Gasthof Taverne reportedly has the most lively disco, as those who have tried to sleep above it can confirm. It operates at tea time (as well as at night), when it faces competition from the LA bar at the foot of lift 22. The Edelweiss has a live band and suits the 'middle-aged crowd' well; the Enzian has a lively bar.

The **non-skiing** sports facilities are good, provided you want to swim or play tennis: more traditional winter sports are not in evidence, and the video golf simulation is reportedly a rip-off. Excursions to Salzburg are possible (starting with a taxi down to Radstadt). The **cross-country** skiing trail in the heart of the sunny bowl covers quite interesting terrain but lacks scenic variety. The very long trails of the Tauernloipe can be reached from Untertauern, 9km down the road.

The **nursery slopes** are excellent. There is a short, gentle drag-lift in the heart of the village, just north of the road, and another rather longer one on the lower slopes at the east end. There is an even longer one parallel to and just south of the road, though it is shaded for much of the day in mid-winter. The high Gamskarlift, at the top of the steep Schaidberg chair-lift, is anything but shaded.

The **ski school** arrangements are as different from the Austrian norm as the resort itself, with several apparently competing schools in different locations. The Krallinger Obertauern Süd school, favoured by most tour operators, receives conflicting reports, from the mightily impressed to the acutely disappointed. We also have varying reports on Obertauern Nord, which seems to be very short of English-speaking instructors. Both schools will allow enormous class sizes when demand exceeds supply.

Wagrain Austria 900m

Good for *Big ski area, easy runs, woodland runs, cross-country skiing, short airport transfers, easy road access, lift queues, mountain restaurants, sunny slopes*
Bad for *Tough runs, late holidays, resort-level snow, not skiing, freedom from cars*

Linked resorts: St Johann im Pongau, Flachau

The success of the French resorts operating under the Trois Vallées banner has not gone unnoticed elsewhere, and any ski area which can claim to offer linked skiing in three or even four adjacent valleys is now likely to want to climb aboard their bandwagon. The skiing of the *3-Täler-Skischaukelland* in the Pongau region, south of Salzburg, is much more modest in scale, and is practically devoid of challenge for the expert (though far from ideal for the nervous intermediate), but by Austrian standards it is a very extensive system. Wagrain is the Méribel of the area, well placed in the central valley for full exploration of the skiing. It is a busy village, not notably charming in Austrian terms, but pleasant and adequately convenient. St Johann is more widely sold by UK tour operators, but is linked in to the skiing only via its satellite of Alpendorf. Flachau, at the eastern end, is scarcely sold at all in Britain, but is in some ways the most attractive base.

These low resorts are easily reached by car, and having one permits exploration of various other resorts nearby, all covered by the affordable Salzburger Sportwelt Amadé pass, as is another three-valley system just to the south – Zauchensee, Flachauwinkl and Kleinarl (easily reached by bus, too).

The skiing top 2015m bottom 800m

Wagrain sits in a valley with ski-lifts rising on either side. Those to the east approach the ridge of Griessenkareck, on the shoulder of the Saukarkopf; on the far side of this is Flachau and its suburbs, with a range of lifts on its flank of the same mountain. To the west of Wagrain is a slightly lower but more complicated mountain, the Sonntagskogl, fragmented at altitude by two mini-valleys. This is reported to be the most reliable area for snow when conditions are poor. There are lifts and pistes on the St Johann side of this mountain, but they stop short of the town at the slightly elevated community of Alpendorf. St Johann has some further, separate skiing of its own on the Hahnbaum, closer to the town.

The lifts for **Griessenkareck** start from a spacious suburb of Wagrain (Kirchboden), a few hundred metres east of the centre. The first stage is a chair-lift; the second is a 12-place gondola which gives access to the skiing over on the Flachau side. From the top you can also ski a little bowl, provided with two drags, beneath the Saukarkopf; the drag towards the Saukarkopf summit serves a short, moderately challenging north-facing slope, graded black.

All the runs from Griessenkareck are broad swathes through the woods, of intermediate difficulty. The reds are not difficult, and the blues are not the simplest of blues, but the gradings do separate the more difficult from the less so. There are no really easy ways down to Flachau or to its outposts of Moadörfl and Reitdorf, but it is possible to ride down by lift. From Flachau there is a free bus service to Flachauwinkl where the Tauern motorway divides the south-easterly 3-valley lift chain into two: Zauchensee to the east, Kleinarl to the west. The two halves are in turn linked by a jolly toy train shuttle via a subway. Zauchensee's slopes provide good open intermediate skiing, with plenty of space for off-piste forays, and reliable snow.

The **Sonntagskogl** side of Wagrain's skiing is reached by an efficient six-seater gondola starting from a roadside station a little way out of the town and going up to Grafenberg. Most of the easy slope underneath it can be skied repeatedly by using chair-and-drag-lifts rather than returning to the village. Stretching westward from Grafenberg is an

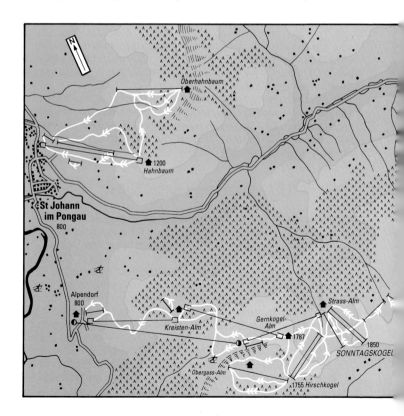

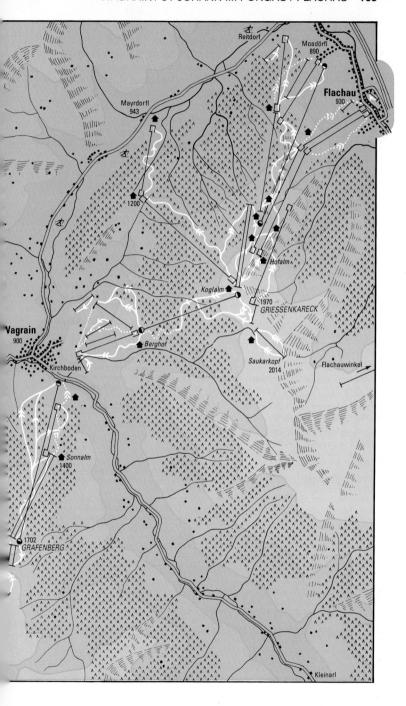

Reitdorf

Moadörfl
890

Flachau
930

Mayrdorfl
943

1200

Hofalm

Koglalm

1970
GRIESSENKARECK

Vagrain
900

Berghof

Kirchboden

Saukarkopf
2014

Flachauwinkel

Sonnalm
1400

1702
GRAFENBERG

Kleinarl

attractive, open landscape of minor ridges and troughs with lifts making the necessary skiing links and serving additional north-facing runs on the Sonntagskogl. There is little here to challenge the good skier, but the skiing is not trivially easy on the runs down to Sonnalm, or on the attractive runs (one red, the other an unjustified black) from Hirschkogel down to the bottom of an isolated drag-lift. The run down to Alpendorf (above St Johann) is graded red, but requires only a moderate amount of confidence. From Alpendorf a new lift system, comprising a six-seater gondola and a four-seater chair-lift, runs up to the Strass Alm below Sonntagskogl, duplicating the old chairs toward Gernkogel-Alm.

There are plenty of **mountain restaurants** all over the ski area except in the middle of the Sonntagskogl; the easy slopes above Flachau are peppered with places. The local speciality of plate-sized

---

Facts on Wagrain Salzburg **Austria**

Prices in schillings

Tourist office
Postcode A-5602
Tel (6413) 8265/8448
Fax (6413) 8449
Tlx 67563

Getting there
By road 1,207km from Calais. Via Munich and Salzburg; chains sometimes needed.
By rail St Johann (8km), 5 daily buses to resort.
By air Salzburg; transfer 1hr.

Staying there
Visitor beds 4,500; breakdown: mainly in hotels, pensions and private rooms.
Package holidays Thomson (h) .
Medical facilities In resort: Doctor, chemist, dentist. Hospital: Schwarzach (15km).

Non-skiing activities
Indoor Hotel swimming pools.
Outdoor Curling, toboggan run, sleigh rides, floodlit ski slope in Flachau.

Kindergartens
Kinderskischule
Tuition: Yes. Hours: 10.00-3.00, 5 days per week. Ages: 4 up. Cost: 1,500.00 per week (with lunchtime supervision).
Gästekindergarten
Tuition: No. Hours: 11.30-4.00, Mon-Fri. Ages: 3 up. Cost: 990.00 per week (with lunch).

Special skiing facilities
Summer skiing No.
Cross-country Tauernloipe 50km. Many other trails varying from easy to medium, ranging from 2km to over 20km. Also, the more difficult Gasthofalmloipe from Flachau (26km). Instruction available.

Lift passes
Salzburger Sportwelt Amadé
Covers all lifts and the ski bus in Wagrain, St Johann and Flachau, and in several other ski areas nearby, and the ski bus. (120 lifts in total.)
Cost 6 days 1,270.00 (£63.66). Low season: 1,145.00 saving 10%.
Credit cards accepted No.
Senior citizens 1,143.00 (over 60/65) saving 10%.
Children 780.00 (under 15) saving 39%. Free pass up to age 6.
Beginners Points cards; try-out tickets.
Short-term passes Half-day passes (morning until 12.00 or 1.00, afternoon from 11.00 or 2.00).
Other passes Top-Tauern Skischeck covers Obertauern, Schladming, Wagrain, Pongau, Dachstein etc. (6 days 1490.00 for adults, 860.00 for children).
Other periods Passes available for 5 out of 6, 6 out of 7 and 12 out of 14 days.

Ski school
Moser
Classes 10.00-12.00 and 1.30-4.00. Cost: 1,050.00 (5 days).
Lift priority No.
Children's classes Ages: 4 up. Cost: 1,050.00 (5 days). 1500.00 with lunchtime supervision.
Private lessons available Per day or hour. Cost: 400.00 per hour. 1650.00 per day, 250.00 for additional person.
Special courses On request.
Huber
Classes Full day. Cost: 1,100.00 (6 days).
Lift priority No.
Children's classes Ages: 3 up. Cost: 1,100.00 (6 days). 110.00 for lunchtime supervision.
Private lessons available Per day or hour. Cost: 400.00 per hour. 1650.00 per day, 250.00 per additional person.

What was new in 91
1. Toboggan run at Schwaighof.
2. Snow guns (now cover 2.6km of piste).

doughnuts (*Krapfen*) is recommended.

High-season lift **queues** have been serious at times in the past but, to judge by recent reports, new lifts have solved the problem. There is **artificial snow** on three lower pistes at Flachau, and two at Wagrain.

The resort

Wagrain is a tight, compact and busy little place with a fair amount of traffic on the minor road from St Johann to Flachau and Radstadt running through on the north side. Fortunately the village has been able to develop away from this road, along the dead-end road up the valley to Kleinarl, and into the fields at the foot of the Griessenkareck lifts and pistes (Kirchboden) – though traffic and parking are still problematic. Location within the resort is not critical; there is a free ski-bus linking the centre and the lift stations frequently.Everyday shopping is adequate.

Most of the **accommodation** is in modern, chalet-style hotels, *pensions* and private houses. In the centre, the Wagrainerhof is smart, and not very expensive. A little way out, the Enzian is recommended by a reporter. Simpler and more atmospheric places include the Gasthof Grafenwirt (recommended) and the modest Gasthof Steinerwirt. The simple Gasthof Kalkofen is well placed for the Griessenkareck lifts, as is the 'very good' Haus Ruperti.

Après-ski is mainly traditional ('several cafés for good hot chocolate and strudel'), with musical events organised by the resort, and tobogganing evenings. Bars range from 'quiet and reasonable' to 'noisy rip-offs'. The Bierstube at the lower end of the village is recommended for dark beer and unlabelled schnapps, the Café Bosek for sticky cakes. Restaurant reservations are advised; recommendations include the Alpina and Tatzelwurm. There is dancing in at least one of the central hotels (the Wagrainerhof), with 'semi-live' music. The World Cup Café at Kleinarl, with Annemarie Moser behind the bar, is one of the great local tourist attractions.

Wagrain is rather too small to be a particularly good place for **non-skiers**, though there are limited sports facilities and other diversions; excursions to Salzburg are easily arranged. It is a much better resort for **cross-country** skiers; a trail starting at Kirchboden links with the very extensive Tauernloipe network.

There are excellent broad **nursery slopes** at Kirchboden, at the foot of the main lift for Griessenkareck. Reports of the **ski school** (based there) are good, 'most instructors speak some English'.

Flachau   930m

Flachau is very much a holiday village – a spacious, relaxed place with chalets and apartment blocks spreading along the valley and up the slopes away from its somewhat nebulous centre. There are countless comfortable, modern and quite big chalet-style hotels and guest-houses. The central Reslwirt is mid-priced, and partly old and traditional in style. Flachau is well placed for the long, widely varying Tauernloipe cross-country trails, and there are walks, toboggan runs

and sleigh rides. Après-ski activity includes traditional musical events and three or four discos in hotels. The nursery slopes are excellent: a very gentle area in the village, separated from the main pistes (its only drawback that it is shaded early in the morning in mid-winter) and more extensive and slightly steeper areas at the foot of the main slopes.
Tourist office © (6457) 214. Tx 67698. **Package holidays** Austro Tours (h).

St Johann im Pongau 800m

St Johann is a town rather than a village, with a thriving existence independent of skiing. The small but not worthless Hahnbaum skiing starts close to the centre: it has a nursery lift at the bottom, but there is a much better nursery area – gentler, more spacious and with better snow – part-way up the mountain (reached by bus). The nursery slope at Alpendorf is uncomfortably steep for beginners. Alpendorf is the way into the main ski area – a hillside collection of chalet-style hotels and guest-houses. There are short cross-country trails near Alpendorf and down in the valley bottom. The resort as a whole offers cleared walks, tennis and squash, skating and curling on natural rinks, toboggan runs and sleigh rides. There are traditional après-ski events (some of them in Alpendorf), and half a dozen discos. Toni's ski school at Alpendorf is highly recommended by a recent group leader, as is its rival the Baumgartner school – 'meticulous in improving our technique, became a friend'.
Tourist office © (6412) 6036. Tx 67502.
Package holidays Austrian Holidays (h) Kings Ski Club (c) Ski Party Snow World (h).

No rest cure

Badgastein Austria 1080m

Good for *Big ski area, tough runs, après-ski, not skiing, rail access , woodland runs, artificial snow*
Bad for *Skiing convenience, easy runs, lift queues, Alpine charm, nursery slopes, resort-level snow, freedom from cars*

Linked resort: Bad Hofgastein
Separate resorts: Dorfgastein, Sportgastein

Badgastein is one of three widely differing resorts in a long and beautiful valley in western Salzburgerland. It is one of the most ponderously grand of spa resorts, but in a remarkable setting – stacked on a steep hillside (a regular source of complaints from exhausted reporters) at the head of the valley. The river cascades down between the hotel blocks at the heart of the resort, which is still rather sedate and formal, though now more dependent on the conference than the *Kur* business. A second Badgastein has grown up for skiers – a sprawl of hotels and apartment buildings beside the railway station and main ski-lift departure, and on up the valley from there. It is not at all beautiful, but practical, and lively in the evenings.

Dorfgastein, just inside the narrow gateway into the valley, is an unspoilt rustic village near a lot of pleasant intermediate skiing. A few miles upstream, Bad Hofgastein is a spacious and comfortable spa, without any grandiose pretensions, which has greatly impressed recent reporters as a quiet, pretty resort, suitable for families.

Lift links between Badgastein and Bad Hofgastein have created one of Austria's major ski areas – big and varied, with very long and mainly challenging runs from top to bottom. Although a few blue trails wind across the slopes, these mountains are in general best suited to experienced skiers. Problems are not confined to the pistes – some of the drag-lifts are intimidating, too.

In Badgastein, parking space is inadequate and driving is hazardous, but having a car is very useful for making the most of the skiing and après-ski. It is quite a long drive to any other major resorts.

The skiing top 2686m bottom 850m

In addition to the main ski area on the west side of the valley between Badgastein and Bad Hofgastein, there are three other separate areas, with differing attractions. The Graukogel runs above Badgastein are few, but long and satisfying for good skiers. Sportgastein has some good runs in a very different style: high altitude, open ground and no development. And the friendly skiing shared by Dorfgastein and Grossarl adds greatly to the area's appeal for leisurely skiers.

From a milling concourse of car park, ski school meeting-place and

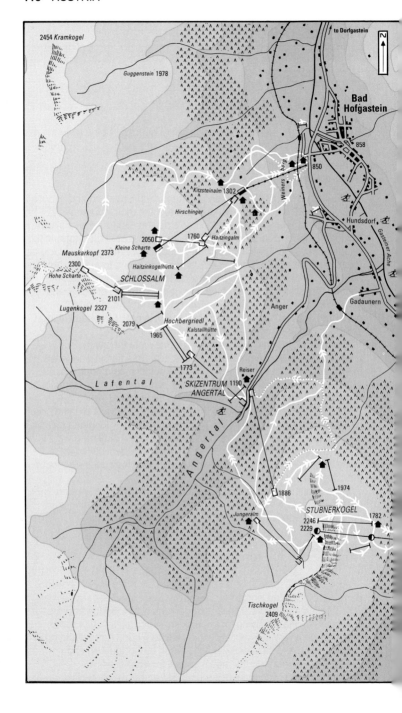

2454 Kramkogel

Guggenstein 1978

Bad Hofgastein

to Dorfgastein

858

850

Weinersberg

Hundsdorf

Gasteiner Ache

Kitzsteinalm 1302

Hirschinger

2050

Kleine Scharte

1760

Haitzingalm

Mauskarkopf 2373

Haitzinkogelhütte

2300

Hohe Scharte

SCHLOSSALM

Anger

Gadaunern

2101

Lugenkogel 2327

2079

Hochbergriedl

Kalstallhütte

1965

L a f e n t a l

1773

Reiser

SKIZENTRUM ANGERTAL 1190

A n g e r t a l

1886

1974

STUBNERKOGEL

Jungeralm

2246

1782

2229

Tischkogel 2409

nursery area, squeezed between the steep mountain and Badgastein station, a two-stage gondola climbs to the **Stubnerkogel** (2246m), a tangled junction of lift arrivals at the top of a long ridge. The east-facing runs to Badgastein provide good, tough skiing with a mixture of open ground above half-way and woods below – mostly graded red, but difficult when conditions are poor. There is a blue run winding down the mountain, but this too is often icy and crowded. The open top half of the slope gives plenty of opportunity for skiing off-piste between the runs. The Ahorn drag-lift back up is particularly steep. The west-facing back side of the ridge is broken ground with some impressive rocky drops and gullies, and skiing options down to Jungeralm are limited; the piste tends to be crowded. The north-facing runs down into the Angertal provide some of the best skiing in the region. From Jungeralm a long, undulating black run drops directly through the woods. The alternatives are to traverse to and fro on the 'Skiweg' from Jungeralm, or take the famous, much more satisfying red run from Stubnerkogel. Both the Angertalbahn and the Jungeralmbahn back up are fast new chairs.

From the Angertal, a chair and drag-lift go up over south-facing slopes to the **Schlossalm** skiing – also accessible by funicular railway starting a long walk from Bad Hofgastein. This is a very spacious basin above the tree-line providing a lot of similar intermediate runs, not very long and mostly easier than on the Stubnerkogel. For good skiers the

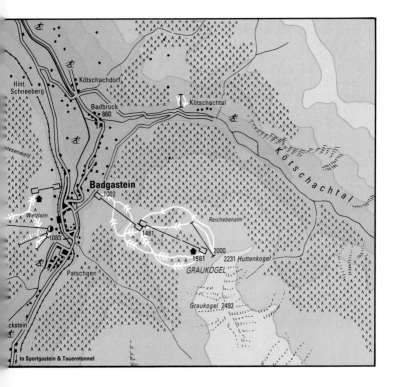

main interest is the beautiful long run round the back of the mountains, reached either from Höhe Scharte (2300m) or from Kleine Scharte (2050m). In good snow the run goes to the bottom of the railway, an 8km descent of 1450m vertical.

The thickly wooded, north-west-facing slopes of **Graukogel** are served by a slow two-stage chair-lift. This is the local racing hill and, apart from one easy run round the top of the mountain, all the trails are challenging variants of the direct descent under the chairs of 900m vertical. Not all of them are prepared. Snow conditions are as good as you'll find locally, and the surroundings and views are delightful.

Sportgastein is a valuable asset if snow elsewhere in the valley is poor – when (unusually) it can become crowded. The high, narrow, dead-end valley is empty and undeveloped save for a couple of restaurants. A chair and then a drag go up from 1600m to Kreuzkogel at 2686m, most of it above the trees and facing west. The top half may be exposed and cold, but usually has good snow on its gentle runs. The great attraction to good skiers is the long north-facing off-piste run over the back down to the toll-gate above Böckstein (where you catch a bus). The slopes beneath the chair-lift are steeper, with some good off-piste skiing among the thinly scattered trees as well as a stiff red run.

Dorfgastein and **Grossarl** share a friendly, wooded ski area, the high-points of which (at about 2030m) are Fulseck and another Kreuzkogel. Although most of the runs are classed red and some are of over 1000m vertical, few of the runs are steep except the black to Dorfgastein. The Grossarl side is mostly gentle, with long, wide runs and some easy off-piste skiing among the trees. After crowded and often icy Stubnerkogel, intermediates may find all this attractive. It is now served by a new two-stage gondola from the village.

Mountain restaurants are plentiful and generally pleasant, with charming alternatives to the big cafeterias at the main lift stations. There are several very attractive huts on the lower slopes of the Stubnerkogel and of the Schlossalm. We have glowing reports of the Hamburger Skiheim above Bad Hofgastein (especially its ice-bar barbecue); other recommendations include the Schlossalmhütte, the Aeroplanstadl and the Kitzsteinalm. But a reporter puts the cosy Wengeralm above Dorfgastein at the top of the list – 'first-rate food, great views and waitress service'; he also rates highly the new Panorama at Kreuzkogel which has a children's slide between its two floors. Toni's Almgasthaus at the top of Graukogel serves garlic soup in bowls hollowed out of bread loaves.

Recent reports do not indicate any serious **queues** at Badgastein. At Bad Hofgastein, the main problem in getting to the top is the cable-car (30min queues in high season). On the way to Badgastein, the Schlosshochalm drag is inadequate.

There are small **artificial snow** installations at the bottom of the Stubnerkogel, at Bad Hofgastein and Dorfgastein. Snow-guns have recently been installed on the 11km Angertal run.

The resort

Badgastein is built in a cramped, claustrophobic position on the steep wooded slopes which abruptly close the southern end of the Gastein valley. The main road and railway by-pass the resort centre, which is more simply negotiated by the steep footpaths and stairways than by car. The focus of the resort is a smart new complex including hotel, shopping precinct, casino and conference hall projecting from the hillside beside the waterfall. In the vicinity there are glossy shop windows, coiffeurs and tea shops for those with expensive tastes. The resort's upper level (a steep but short walk away) is a rather ordinary collection of unfashionable spa hotels, which attract skiers in winter because of their convenient location, and newer accommodation which has grown up there for the same reason. Most of our reporters were not happy with the bus services that link the village centres and lift stations; the two bus companies do not appear to coordinate their arrivals, which can result in long waits before several buses arrive at once.

Accommodation is mostly in hotels, of which there are hundreds in the valley, many of them with hot and cold running radioactive water. Among the hotels at the top of the resort, within easy walking distance of the Stubnerkogel lifts, the new Bärenhof is the most comfortable and expensive. The Krone and the Goethehof are ideally placed but very uninspiring middle-range hotels. Much more charming and in a quieter position is the simple Fischerwirt. In the centre, the Straubinger is not in the grand league but handsomely traditional; the map of Europe was redrawn in room seven, so they say. At the foot of the Graukogel lift is the Schillerhof, recommended for 'splendid views, clean and comfortable rooms'. Of the cheaper places to stay, 'you couldn't do better than the Tirolerhof, a very reasonable B&B'. The Grüner Baum (or Hoteldorf) deserves special mention – an idyllic, self-contained tourist colony in the beautifully secluded setting of the Kötschachtal.

Après-ski is very varied. In the centre there are quiet tea rooms, plush hotel bars with formal dancing, and a casino . The big hotels put on live shows (fashion displays, beauty contests, cabaret, rock bands). There are plenty of discos, pubs, simple bars and restaurants but recent reporters have found the resort to be surprisingly quiet at night. We have enthusiastic reports of tea-dances, and of a lack of the usual Austrian thigh-slapping. The Bahnhof restaurant is particularly recommended.

Although Badgastein itself is not an ideal base, the valley as a whole has an excellent amount and variety of **cross-country** skiing. There are lots of things for **non-skiers** to do apart from inhale radon. A vast range of aquatic activities (from thermal bathing to water gymnastics) are on offer and there are long and beautiful walks in the woods (maps available from the tourist office).

Nursery slopes at the foot of the Stubnerkogel, Angertal and Bad Hofgastein lifts are rather cramped, and there are not many runs suitable for skiers making the transition from nursery slopes to pistes. The area as a whole is not good for beginners.

Recent reporters have been impressed by the **ski school**, and particularly by its native English-speaking instructors and the evident close involvement of its director, Werner Pflaum – 'he did the class selection himself, and popped into our hotel most evenings'. The advanced class did not greatly impress one regular *Guide* reporter. There is an alternative for skiers who want to be led around the slopes but not formally taught – the *Ski-gäste-guides* (apparently they now operate only on Mondays).

Facts on Badgastein Salzburg **Austria**

Prices in schillings

Tourist office

Postcode A-5640
Tel (6434) 25310
Fax (6434) 253137
Tlx 67520

Getting there

By road 1,221km from Calais. Via Munich; chains rarely needed.
By rail Main line station in resort, hourly buses.
By air Salzburg; transfer 1½hr. (Or Linz or Munich; transfer about 2hr.)

Staying there

Visitor beds 7,000; breakdown: 6,000 in hotels, 1,000 in apartments.
Package holidays Inghams (h) Made to Measure (h) Ski Europe (h) Ski Global (h) SkiTonic (h) Thomson (h) .
Medical facilities In resort: Doctors, dentists, chemists. Hospital: Schwarzach (25km).

Non-skiing activities

Indoor Fitness centre (swimming, sauna, gym), thermal baths, squash, bridge, chess, tennis, bowling, golf, darts, casino, museum, theatre, concerts.
Outdoor Natural ice-rinks (skating and curling), sleigh rides, horse-riding, toboggan runs, ski-bob, 35km cleared paths.

Kindergartens

Werner Pflaum
Tuition: yes. Hours: 9.00-4.00. Ages: 3-7. Cost: 1,800.00 per week (with meals).

Special skiing facilities

Summer skiing No.
Cross-country Of varying length and difficulty along the main valley floor between Bad Hofgastein and Badbruck (over 20km), around Dorfgastein (12.5km) and Sportgastein (over 20km); also at Böckstein, Angertal and Kötschachtal.

Lift passes

Gastein-Super-Ski-Pass
Covers all lifts, buses and trains. (51 lifts in total.)
Cost 6 days 1,510.00 (£75.69). Low season: 1,280.00 saving 15%.
Credit cards accepted Yes.
Senior citizens 1,430.00 (over 65/60) saving 5%.

Children 910.00 (under 14) saving 40%. Free pass up to age 6.
Notes Student rates (up to age 26) available; group discounts.
Beginners Day- and points-tickets for baby-lifts.
Short-term passes Half-day, time-tickets (reimbursed when handed in), single ascent tickets on some lifts.
Other passes ½-2½ day passes for Bad Hofgastein and Badgastein only (per day 310.00 for adults, 190.00 for children).
Other periods 5 or 10 days in one season.

Ski school

Werner Pflaum
Classes 5hr: 2hr am, 3hr pm. Cost: 1,380.00 (6 days).
Lift priority No.
Children's classes Ages: up to 14. Cost: 1,380.00 (6 days).
Private lessons available On request, per 55 mins. Cost: 360.00 per hour. Each additional person 120.00.
Special courses 3-day snowboard course (2 hr per day) 600.00.
Hofgastein
In Bad Hofgastein.
Classes 10.00-12.00 and 1.00-3.15. Cost: 1,150.00 (6 days).
Lift priority No.
Children's classes Ages: from 4. Cost: 1,150.00 (6 days).
Private lessons available Hourly. Cost: 420.00 per hour. Up to 2 people.
Luigi
In Sportgastein.
Classes 10.00-3.00. Cost: 1,150.00 (6 days).
Lift priority No.
Children's classes Ages: Any. Cost: 1,150.00 (6 days).
Private lessons available Per day or 55 mins. Cost: 400.00 per hour. Each additional adult 100.00.
Special courses Powderskiing course (2,200.00 per day for 4-7 people).

What was new in 91

1. There are 10 snow-guns in resort which can move position as necessary.
2. New ski school in Sportsgastein – Luigi.

What is new for 92

Plans for a new lift in Sportgastein.

Bad Hofgastein 870m

Bad Hofgastein has neither the inconveniently steep and dark setting nor the stodgy grandeur of Badgastein; it is smaller but still a sizeable resort, spread along the broadest part of the valley. The Kitzstein funicular is inconveniently distant, and the resort is not very ski-oriented: it attracts lots of non-skiing visitors who potter about in the very agreeable, spacious, sunny surroundings. It is a good base for the valley's walks and cross-country trails, and busy skating and curling rinks complete the winter scene. There is an outdoor, naturally-heated swimming pool, and a new sports centre (tennis and squash). Evenings are generally quiet, though an energetic reporter claims that there is action to be found – eg at Georgie's and Sherwood's. Other recommendations include Franky's and Miles pubs, the Kaiser Franz café and the restaurant of the Hotel Austria. The most convenient hotels are the mostly new ones lining the road from the centre to the river; but many more remote hotels have courtesy buses. One recommended B&B is the Haus Monuth – 'clean and simple, lovely young Austrian owners'.

Tourist office ✆ (6432) 6429. Tx 67796.
Package holidays Austrian Holidays (h) Mogul Ski Holidays (h) Thomson (h).

Dorfgastein 835m

Dorfgastein is a charming, villagey resort, untouched by the depressing influence of spa-hood. Horses and carts clatter along the narrow, arcaded main street past the old church, more often taking local folk about their business than taking tourists for jaunts. There are several well-kept, friendly and comfortable medium-priced hotels in the centre; the Steindlwirt and Kirchenwirt are two of the larger hotels, typically comfortable although without much character. The ski-lift departure is at least a 5-minute walk from the village; the Gasthof Schihäusl stands at the foot of the slopes. Dorfgastein does not lack bars, music and animation in the evening.

Tourist office ✆ (6433) 277. Tx 67737.

Beside the seaside

Zell am See Austria 750m

Good for *Easy runs, not skiing, après-ski, easy road access, short airport transfers, cross-country skiing, artificial snow, rail access*
Bad for *Skiing convenience, resort-level snow, late holidays, freedom from cars, lift queues*

Separate resort: Kaprun

Zell am See enjoys a splendid geography-textbook setting on a gentle promontory where a mountain stream flows into a lake. The town predates tourism by many centuries and its car-free old centre has great charm. Many of our reporters were surprised to find such a pretty, compact centre to this large and sprawling town, It has built up around a main road and rail thoroughfare, and is very different from what many British skiers expect of an Austrian ski resort (unless they are used to Kitzbühel).

Zell is busy all the year round and has most of the ingredients of an all-round winter resort: pistes steep and gentle, good nightlife, a vast network of cross-country skiing, lots for non-skiers to do, and even a snow guarantee in the form of glacier skiing half an hour's drive away on the Kitzsteinhorn, above Kaprun. But the ingredients do not blend perfectly. The town is separated from one access lift by the main road and from the main ones by over a mile. Most of the skiing is either very easy or fairly challenging and, being the snow guarantee for many low resorts, the glacier gets extremely crowded when snow is scarce.

Kaprun has a small ski area of its own, but is mainly of interest as the closest resort to the glacier and as a base for cross-country skiers. Saalbach is also nearby. A recent reporter who had a car found it extremely useful, particularly for getting to Kaprun before the queues.

The skiing top 1965m bottom 750m

The two arms of a mountain horseshoe rise gently from the ends of the lake to the rounded peak of **Schmittenhöhe**, giving long easy runs, especially along the southern limb. Steeper wooded slopes facing south, north and east drop down from Schmittenhöhe into the pit of the bowl, providing some challenging skiing. There would be good off-piste skiing, but in the interest of the trees little is allowed.

From close to the resort centre a gondola goes up to the southern limb of the horseshoe, and from the suburb of Schüttdorf a six-seater gondola does likewise. A third lift station is in the pit of the bowl, about 2km from the centre of Zell. One of the two cable-cars from here goes directly to (indeed into) the Schmittenhöhe Berghotel, where an elevator delivers you to the sunny summit plateau.

Behind the summit is a small area of pleasant intermediate runs, of

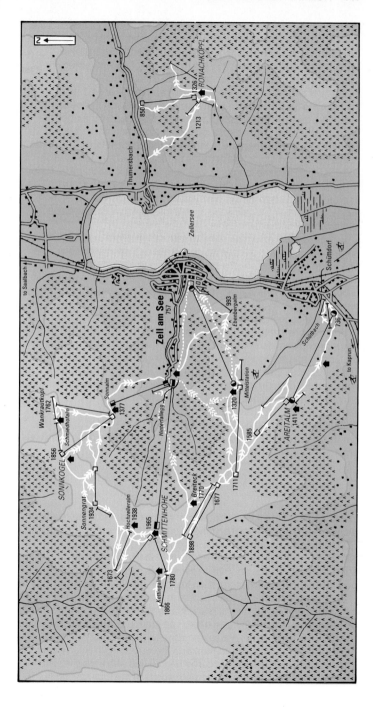

varying difficulty. Turning right at the top takes you along a flattish ridge
to a sunny area, also reachable via the other cable-car from the valley to
Sonnalm. None of the skiing here is difficult; the black run below
Sonnalm is no steeper than 25°, but it does get very worn and icy or
slushy. Lifts and pistes link Sonnalm with Schmittenhöhe.

South of Schmittenhöhe there is a succession of gentle, broad, sunny
pistes along the horseshoe ridge. A right fork takes you to **Areitalm**,
where the gondola from Schüttdorf arrives; the pleasant intermediate
piste to Schüttdorf doesn't keep its snow for long and ends steeply.
Taking the left fork brings you to the top of the gondola from Zell. At two
points on the horseshoe, black pistes branch off into the bowl. These
soon steepen into fine long runs, challenging but not too intimidating for
adventurous intermediates (the steepest is from Breiteck, about 28°).
The other two runs to the bottom stations are less steep, but get more
sun. The Ebenberglift, little used except for slalom practice, gives a
splendid view of the town, and a short, fairly steep run.

There are quite a number of **mountain restaurants** around the ski
area, most of them in pleasant surroundings and sunny positions. The
one at the top Schmittenhöhe cable-station has particularly good views.
Those off the beaten track tend to be less crowded and less expensive.
Glöcknerhaus, on the way down to Schüttdorf, is particularly
recommended.

In high season there can be long **queues** all day for the
Schmittenhöhe cable-car. The efficient gondola access lift from the town
has morning queues and one reporter suggests getting the bus to
Schüttdorf and taking the efficient six-seater gondola from there. When
snow is sparse, there are long delays to get back down to Zell from
Mittelstation. But one regular high-season visitor to Zell has not
encountered any serious queues in the last three years.

There is **artificial snow** on two runs down into the pit of the
Schmittenhöhe horseshoe, on the nursery slope there and the home
run from there, and on the runs down from the Mittelstation to Zell. It has
apparently made 'a huge difference'.

The resort

Zell is a town rather than a village, with shops catering for the needs of
residents and the whims of summer tourists rather than just for skiers.

Post buses run regularly to the lifts and once an hour to the
Kitzsteinhorn glacier. We have reports of 'unbelievable chaos'
surrounding these bus services at peak times, and queues of three
hundred people waiting to get back to Zell in the afternoons.

Accommodation is in hotels, some in the centre, others in the
quieter streets towards the lake and the north end of the town. For
après-ski the centre is the best base. The Traube is a comfortable,
friendly small hotel in the pedestrian zone, with an atmospheric
bar/restaurant. A long way up-market is the very smooth Neue Post.
The Grüner Baum has been recently refurbished with attractive pine
bedrooms. We have received glowing reports of the four-star Tirolerhof,

Facts on Zell am See

Salzburg **Austria**

Prices in schillings

Tourist office

Postcode A-5700
Tel (6542) 2600
Fax (6542) 2032
Tlx 66617

Getting there

By road 1,184km from Calais. Via Munich; chains rarely needed.
By rail Station in resort.
By air Salzburg; transfer 1½hr. (Or Munich; transfer about 2hr.)

Staying there

Visitor beds 9,400; breakdown: 8,900 in hotels, 500 in apartments.
Package holidays Austrian Holidays (h) Austro Tours (h) Crystal (hr) Enterprise (h) Horizon (h) Inghams (h) Neilson (h) Panorama's Ski Experience (hr) Quality Ski Tours (h) Ski Global (h) SkiBound (h) SkiTonic (h) Snobiz (h) Thomson (hr) .
Medical facilities In resort: Doctors, chemists, dentist, fracture clinic. Hospital: Prielau (41 km).

Non-skiing activities

Indoor Swimming, sauna, solarium, fitness centre, tennis, squash, bowling, shooting range, museum.
Outdoor Riding, skating, curling, floodlit toboggan runs, plane flights, sleigh rides.

Kindergartens

Guests Kindergarten
Tuition: No. Hours: 8.00-4.00, Mon-Fri. Ages: 3 up. Cost: 400.00 per week (with lunch).
Snow Kindergarten
Tuition: No. Hours: 9.00-4.30. Ages: 3 up. Cost: 1,000.00 per week (own common room and snow field). On the Areitalm.
Ski-Kindergarten Ursula Zink
Tuition: Yes. Hours: 9.00-4.00. Ages: from one year. Cost: 1,000.00 per week (with lunch).
Other childcare facilities
Part-time baby-sitting service, 8.00-12.00, costs 40.00 per hour.

Special skiing facilities

Summer skiing Extensive area on Kitzsteinhorn, above Kaprun.
Cross-country Easy and medium loops totalling 350km on the valley floor and 2.3km at middle station of Zellerbergbahn. Also very long trails along the Salzach valley east and west of Kaprun. Instruction available.

Lift passes

Europa-Sportregion Kaprun–Zell am See
Covers all lifts in Zell and Kaprun, and buses between them. (55 lifts in total.)

Cost 6 days 1,530.00 (£76.69). Low season: 1,270.00 saving 17%.
Credit cards accepted Yes.
Senior citizens 1,377.00 (over 60/65) saving 10%.
Children 995.00 (under 15) saving 35%. Free pass up to age 6.
Notes 10% discount for disabled skiers.
Beginners Coupons or limited pass.
Short-term passes Half-day passes for Zell only, getting cheaper the later you start in the day.
Other passes Zell am See only; Kaprun glacier; Golden Skicard (which covers several nearby ski regions including the Dolomites).
Other periods Flexibility tickets: 5 in 7 days and 10 in 14 days.

Ski school

Schmittenhöhe
Classes Full day; start 9.30 for beginners, 10.00 for others. Cost: 1,100.00 (6 days).
Lift priority No.
Children's classes Ages: 4 up. Cost: 1,100.00 (6 days). Free lunch-time supervision, lunch costs 60.00-80.00 per day.
Private lessons available Full day or hourly. Cost: 400.00 per hour. 100.00 for each additional person.
Special courses Swing-bo courses by appointment.
Wallner Prenner
Classes Full day; start 9.30. Cost: 1,100.00 (6 days).
Lift priority No.
Children's classes Ages: 4 up. Cost: 1,100.00 (6 days). Free lunch-time supervision.
Private lessons available Full day or hourly. Cost: 400.00 per hour. 100.00 for each additional adult.
Areitbahn
Classes Full day; start 10.00. Cost: 1,100.00 (6 days).
Lift priority No.
Children's classes Ages: 4 up. Cost: 1,100.00 (6 days). Lunch-time supervision if required.
Private lessons available Full day or hourly. Cost: 400.00 per hour. 100.00 for each additional person.
Thumersbach
Classes Half day. Cost: 700.00 (6 half-days).
Lift priority No.
Children's classes Ages: Any. Cost: 700.00 (6 half-days).
Private lessons available Hourly. Cost: 300.00 per hour. 1-3 people.
Special courses Ski safaris.

What was new in 91

1. Two new lifts on the Kitzsteinhorn glacier at Kaprun.
2. New snow-making facilities on the Standard and Trassabfahrt runs.

recently renovated in the same traditional style – 'difficult to fault it, we will certainly return'. The Eichenhof is also recommended, although it is a little way from the centre at the top of a hill. For skiing purposes there is much to be said for staying close to the cable-car station; the Schwebebahn or the Waldhof St George are the obvious choices. Staying in dreary Schüttdorf puts you close to cross-country trails, tennis and riding facilities – and gives easy access to the skiing if you're based close to the gondola.

There is plenty of **après-ski**, at least in season: restaurants at every price level, bars, discos, *Weinstüberl*, tea-dancing, and the standard 'evenings' – Tyrolean, fondue, zither, tobogganing. There is even a Macdonalds in the centre of town. The nearby Café Kofe has a 'lovely old-fashioned atmosphere and serves delicious apfelstrüdel'. Bar 33 has a range of 33 beers to try, but they don't come cheap. One reporter recommends the Feinschmeck for 'splendid cakes and coffee' and judges that it is worth waiting for a table at the very popular Giuseppe's for an excellent Italian meal. The Crazy Daisy pub appears to be popular with the British, as is the Diele bar, which has an extended happy hour. More upmarket nightspots are the Wunderbar (above the Grand Hotel) and the expensive Visage disco. In Prielau (a suburb at the northern end of the lake), the Finka-Wirt is a 'comfortable, reasonably priced restaurant with a relaxed family atmosphere'. In Schüttdorf, the popular Cafe Latini plays live music every night. Tobogganing at Brück (a village to the south of the lake) is reportedly well worth the effort of getting there – 'the run was excellent and the farmhouse bar at the bottom full of Austrian atmosphere'. Several reporters have enjoyed watching big-time ice-hockey matches.

The extent of **cross-country** trails in the valleys around Zell is enormous; Kaprun hosts a famous marathon race. There is lots for **non-skiers** to do, with very good sports facilities, and easy access by train to Salzburg. When the lake is frozen (from mid-January to the end of February in a good year) you can walk across to Thumersbach.

There are **nursery slopes** at the bottom cable-car station and more at Schüttdorf, but the snow is often in poor condition. Beginners then go up by gondola or chair to higher nursery lifts.

The **ski schools** in Zell tend to vary in quality. We have had more good than bad reports – one reporter had the 'best ever' instruction, but a couple of others have complained about the bad attitudes of their instructors.

Kaprun 770m

Kaprun is a spacious, pleasant holiday village with a splendid sports centre (the pool is 'excellent'), a kindergarten and a few shops including a 'well-stocked' supermarket. The Hotel Toni is recommended for its 'exceptionally friendly staff', the Salzburgerhof for its rooms and position. Après-ski is confined to a few discos and bars; the Baum bar just out of Kaprun is about the most lively, the Underground is also popular, Nindls serves beer by the boot (a two-foot glass shaped as a boot) and reserves one night a week for the older generation. The local skiing on the Maiskogel consists of easy-intermediate runs (facing roughly east) served by a chain of drag-lifts starting near the village and a cable-car starting quite a way out. A further couple of drags going up to 1737m serve less straightforward north-facing runs. The Kitzsteinhorn glacier skiing (2450m–3029m) is reached by cable-car or funicular starting several miles up the valley. Not surprisingly, when snow is short and every skier in this part of Austria wants to ski here, these lifts are not up to the job – queues of up to four hours are reported. Another access cable-car is at the planning stage. The glacier is an exposed area of mainly easy-intermediate skiing, without great variety of terrain but with some reddish blue runs. The interesting red to the middle station of the underground funicular ends in a tiring push along the plastic floor of a long tunnel. A new four-seater chair has just been installed on this run. We have conflicting reports on the Kaprun ski school; there is a separate Kitzsteinhorn school, which has met with recent approval.

Tourist office © (6547) 8643. Tx 66763.

Package holidays Austro Tours (h) Crystal (hrcs) Enterprise (h) Made to Measure (h) Ski Global (h) Ski Partners (h).

Circus interruptus

Saalbach Austria 1000m

Good for *Easy runs, big ski area, sunny slopes, mountain restaurants, après ski, easy road access, short airport transfers, artificial snow, woodland runs*
Bad for *Tough runs, late holidays*

Linked resorts: Hinterglemm, Leogang

The essentially friendly mountains of the Kitzbühel Alps are familiar territory to British skiers, who have long formed a large part of the winter clientele of such resorts as Alpbach, Söll and Kitzbühel. Until they fell under the media spotlight for the World Championships last season, the two resorts of the east–west Glemm valley, at the eastern extremity of the range, were less well known in Britain. They are at least as worthy of our attention, combining a fairly convincing replication of Austrian Alpine village charm, an extensive network of easy and intermediate skiing (the 'Skicircus') which links the two resorts and the two sides of the valley with almost French efficiency, and adequately varied non-skiing diversions – and all this amid pleasant though unspectacular scenery. As our cautious choice of words implies, the area is a compromise, unlikely to suit those who seek the ultimate in rustic village atmosphere, reliable snow or challenging skiing. But it is a very smooth confection, with which most recent reporters have been well satisfied. Some have expressed the view that the villagey veneer is rather thin, and have persuaded us that we should no longer rate Saalbach 'good for Alpine charm'.

Saalbach and Hinterglemm are 4km apart but growing towards each other. They now style themselves as a single resort called Saalbach Hinterglemm, but the distinction is one which shouldn't be forgotten when choosing where to stay, so we're persisting with it – and our non-skiing verdicts apply only to Saalbach. It is larger and more expensive than Hinterglemm, but more villagey, prettier and much more fun for keen après-skiers. Leogang is a small, diffuse village in the next valley, which offers a back-door way into the skiing.

Zell am See is close, and worth a visit for a pronounced change of scene. The Kitzsteinhorn glacier (described under Kaprun) is within reach by car or bus. A car is of no great advantage within Saalbach.

The skiing top 2096m bottom 930m

Spread along both sides of the valley, the interlinking lifts enable you to ski comfortably from either village to the other, or to perform a circuit of the valley – hence the area's 'Skicircus' label. Circuits can be performed in either direction, but the clockwise one is shorter, missing out the extreme eastern end of the system. The south-facing slopes are mostly open and undemanding, but can deteriorate rapidly in good weather, especially low down, despite snow-making machinery. This ruins the circuits and adds to congestion on the north-facing slopes, which offer more challenging skiing. Austria's largest cable-car (100 people per car) rises 1000m from the centre of Saalbach to the eastern summit of the **Schattberg**. Behind the peak is some fairly easy skiing on the sunny slopes served by two drag-lifts and a beginners' lift, and below the cable-car is a fine 4km black north-facing run to the village which is nowhere excessively steep (about 29˚ at its steepest), but often icy and/or crowded. Tracks bypass the steeper sections near the bottom and make it possible to ski back either to the base station or to accommodation upstream of Saalbach. The easy alternative is a delightful long round-the-mountain blue run through the woods to Vorderglemm, where a gondola now makes the link with the Wildenkarkogel slopes on the other side of the valley. The easy run back from here to Saalbach completes a splendid long outing for near-beginners. The third option from Schattberg is to turn right towards a connecting lift up to Schattberg West, at 2096m the top of the lift system. The black grading of the runs between the two summits is misleading: this crucial link in the circus holds no terrors. There is then a fine wide 5km red run down to Hinterglemm, partly open and partly wooded, and often busy, passing the rock-blaring Bergstadl restaurant at half-way, below which snow cover is unreliable. The run emerges above the Hinterglemm nursery slopes, next to the village; a two-stage double chair-lift goes back up.

From the nursery slopes it is only a short walk to Hinterglemm's base lift station, with parallel double and single chair-lifts rising over 1000m in two stages to the summit of **Zwölferkogel** at 1984m, the site of the men's downhill championship last winter. There are two-drag lifts and some fairly easy skiing on the open south-east facing slopes near the top. The main run back to Hinterglemm is a broad intermediate piste facing north-east, with steeper and easier variants; the final stretch was the men's slalom course. The alternative is to take a black run directly into the Glemm valley, which presents no serious difficulties until the steep final section where most skiers stick to a narrow zigzag path. A new and uncrowded gondola (also reached by a woodland path signed near the bottom of the main run down to Hinterglemm) returns speedily to Zwölferkogel, and makes a two-way link with the **Hochalm** lifts on the north side of the valley. These serve a range of broad, smooth pistes, all graded red, though only the more direct runs justify the grading. From the top you can traverse across to Hinterglemm, or use the series of drags north of the village on **Reiterkogel** to progress along the valley. You can also traverse in the opposite direction from Hasenauer to Hochalm. This whole area has wide intersecting pistes of varying intermediate steepness, but with little challenge. Eventually, via Bernkogel, you come to a long straightforward blue run down to Saalbach.

There are lifts from Saalbach back up these south-facing slopes on Bernkogel (a useful upland nursery area) and onward to **Kohlmaiskopf** – the latter served by a lift that looks like a gondola but works more like

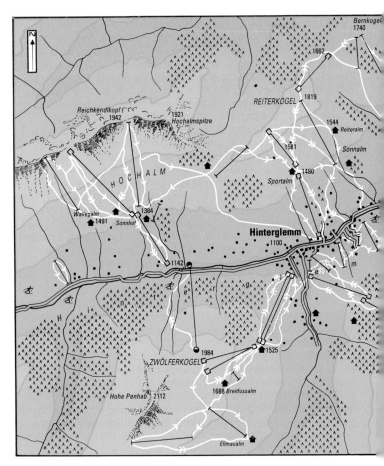

a cable-car. The uncomplicated red run back to Saalbach from here was the site of most of the women's World Championship races in 1991. It is at the centre of another area criss-crossed by intersecting pistes and paths, with some worthwhile intermediate runs, which links on the eastern side with **Wildenkarkogel**, also accessible by the new Schönleiten gondola from Vorderglemm. From the top you can traverse westwards towards Saalbach, or take a connecting lift to the **Leogang** ski area, on the north side of the ridge. The upper Leogang slopes have wide, open pistes ideal for most intermediates, and the runs down to the village are also straightforward. The return ascent requires four lifts. From Schönleiten there is a run down to Saalbach's neighbour Viehhofen but, for the time being, no lift back.

Although nor clearly marked on the otherwise admirable piste map, **mountain restaurants** are profusely distributed around the slopes – though you can eat more cheaply and quite conveniently down in Hinterglemm. They are generally attractive, in traditional style, and we

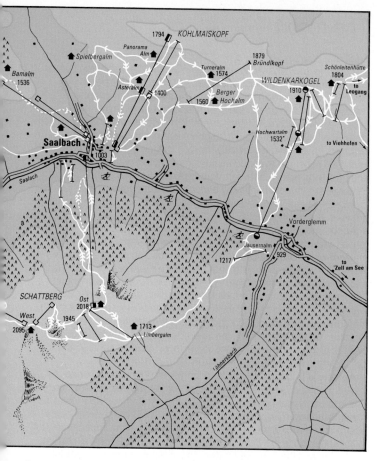

have too many recommendations from readers to include them all. The Wildenkarkogel Hütte has 'exceptionally good' food.

The main blackspot for **queues** is the Schattberg cable-car, despite its capacity. How serious they are depends less on how busy the resort is than on the state of the snow on the opposite (sunny) side of the valley. Queues at Hinterglemm are usually shorter. Minor bottle-necks can occur on the connecting lifts on the south-facing slopes (less at Hochalm than elsewhere). And there can be serious jams on the way back from Leogang.

There is **artificial snow** on three main pistes down to Saalbach, and on Zwölferkogel and the bottom of the Schattberg runs at Hinterglemm. Piste marking and maintenance are generally good, but some reporters have judged some of the lower blue runs to be undergraded.

The resort

Saalbach is almost entirely a post-War development, though built very much in the traditional Austrian village manner. The traffic-free central zone is pleasantly compact, with shops (a lot of glitzy expensive clothes), restaurants and hotels lining the steepish, narrow main street leading past the onion-domed church and square (with the main supermarket, which gets very busy after skiing) towards the Bernkogel lifts and nursery slope. The atmosphere is lively and friendly; some reporters have found it positively rowdy. Daytime buses (now covered by the ski pass) run every 20 minutes (and more frequently at morning and afternoon peaks) between Vorderglemm, Saalbach and Hinterglemm, supplemented by a much less frequent post bus. The buses are severely overcrowded at times and do not run in the evening, but there are plenty of taxis.

Accommodation includes a mixture of stylish, modern hotels (chalet-style rather than concrete blocks) and cheaper guest-houses, many of which straggle out along the main road on either side of the village. It's well worth staying near the centre if you can, close to the lifts and the main life of the village. The most stylish hotel is the Ingonda. Other recommendations include the Alpen (with an 'excellent' nightclub), the Kristall ('old-fashioned, good amenities, excellent food'), the Kohlmais ('excellent food and rooms'), the Haider ('modest rooms, excellent English breakfast'), the Sport Bergerhof ('very good food, lively at night') and the Reiterhof, for its food, location, service, and hot-air jets in the boot room.

Après-ski is loud and lively for a long evening, but not enormously varied: Saalbach's population of flash German yuppies prefers loud rock music to traditional Tyrolean thigh-slapping. At Berger's Sporthotel the dancing gets going at about 6 and continues well into the small hours after a brief lull for dinner. Other favourite locales, often impenetrably full in season, include the Zum Turm, under the church, Bauer's Schi Alm, Heli's Bar, and the Zum Herr'n Karl Bar. A reporter recommends the Old Fashion Bar – 'cheapest in town'. The glass-fronted Cafe Bauer on the main street is a more civilised tea place, with classical music and a good view of the world going by, and also recommended for meals. The Ingonda hotel's restaurant is excellent, at a price, as is the more cosy Peter, famous for its massive Felsensteaks. Book in advance. The Schattbergstube serves food until 4am. The bowling alley is reportedly 'a grotty rip-off'.

Both **cross-country** trails are along the flat floor of the valley and are overshadowed by the Schattberg and Zwölferkogel respectively. Zell am See has more extensive opportunities. Valley walks are also shaded, even in February, and all in all these are not ideal resorts for **non-skiers**. But there are alternatives to skiing – there is a good public pool and sauna, for example.

The **nursery slopes** at Saalbach are central and gentle but south-facing, and deteriorate badly as the season progresses. Beginners must then use the open slopes on Bernkogel or Schattberg.

There are now four **ski schools** in Saalbach, and more in Hinterglemm. Fritzenwallner is the biggest and, with Furstauer, attracts most of the British business – probably the best bet unless you prefer to learn in German.

Hinterglemm   1100m

Although Hinterglemm has also stuck to the proper Alpine style in most of its development, it has achieved a less satisfactory result than

---

Facts on Saalbach   Salzburg **Austria**

Prices in schillings

Tourist office

Postcode A-5753
Tel (6541) 7272
Fax (6541) 7900
Tlx 66507

Getting there

By road 1,193km from Calais. Via Munich; chains rarely needed.
By rail Zell am See; hourly buses from station.
By air Salzburg; transfer 1½hr. (Or Munich; transfer about 2hr.)

Staying there

Visitor beds 17,500; breakdown: 14,500 in hotels, 3,000 in apartments.
Package holidays Crystal (h) Enterprise (h) Horizon (h) Inghams (h) Made to Measure (h) Neilson (h) Quality Ski Tours (h) Sally Holidays (h) Ski Europe (h) Ski Sutherland (h) Ski Unique (h) Ski-Tal (h) SkiBound (h) SkiTonic (h) Snobiz (h) Thomson (h).
Medical facilities In resort: Doctors, dentist, chemists. Hospital: Zell am See (18km).

Non-skiing activities

Indoor Swimming (free for holders of 6-day or longer lift passes), sauna, massage, solarium, bowling, billiards, squash (Hinterglemm), tennis.
Outdoor Floodlit tobogganing, sleigh rides, skating, curling, 35km cleared paths.

Kindergartens

Hotel Theresia
Tuition: with ski school. Hours: 9.45-4.15, Mon-Fri. Ages: 1½-6. Cost: 1,600.00 per week (with meals). Guests only.
Other childcare facilities
Lunch-time care/meal at ski school for ages 4 up, (100.00 per day). Special offers for children at Christmas and Easter.

Special skiing facilities

Summer skiing No.
Cross-country 8km from Saalbach to Vorderglemm, 10km trail from Wiesernfeld (Hinterglemm) to Lengau.

Lift passes

Saalbach Hinterglemm
Covers all the lifts in Saalbach, Hinterglemm and Leogang and the ski bus. (60 lifts in total.)
Cost 6 days 1,555.00 (£77.94). Low season: 1,240.00 saving 20%.
Credit cards accepted No.
Senior citizens 925.00 (over 60/65) saving 41%.
Children 925.00 (under 15) saving 41%. Free pass up to age 4.
Notes 6-day pass for 4-10 yrs 685.00. Special rates over Christmas and Easter (free passes for children under 16 at Easter). 15% reduction for women aged 55-59 and men aged 60-64.
Beginners Books of tickets.
Short-term passes 'Hourly' day pass, refundable when handed in; single and return tickets on main lifts.

Ski school

Hannes Furstauer
Courses start Sun or Mon. 3-day courses available.
Classes 4hr: 2hr am and pm. Cost: 1,200.00 (4-6 days).
Lift priority No.
Children's classes Ages: 5 up. Cost: 1,200.00 (4-6 days).
Private lessons available Per hour. Cost: 450.00 per hour. Each additional person 100.00.
Wolfgang Zink
Courses start Sun or Mon (at 9.30).
Classes 10.00-12.00 and 1.00-3.00. Cost: 1,200.00 (4-6 days).
Lift priority No.
Children's classes Ages: 6 up. Cost: 1,200.00 (4-6 days).
Private lessons available Per hour. Cost: 450.00 per hour. Each additional person 100.00 (up to 5 people).
Willi Fritzenwallner
Classes 4hr per day. Cost: 1,200.00 (4-6 days).
Lift priority No.
Children's classes Ages: Any. Cost: 1,200.00 (4-6 days).
Private lessons available per hour. Cost: 450.00 per hour. Up to 2 people.
Ski and Rennschule
3-day courses 900.00.
Classes 4hr per day. Cost: 1,200.00 (4-6 days).
Lift priority No.
Children's classes Ages: 4 up. Cost: 1,200.00 (4-6 days).
Private lessons available per hour. Cost: 450.00 per hour. Up to 2 people.
Special courses 6-day racing course 1,750.00.

Saalbach. The road along the valley runs through the centre, and even though it goes nowhere it interferes with both safety and atmosphere. There are big apartment blocks at the west end of the village, which are rather out of things but close to the 'excellent' swimming pool and sports centre (tennis, skating). The nursery slopes are extensive, free from passing traffic and much more snow-sure than the Saalbach nursery slope. As well as the main Lechner ski school, the erstwhile 'ski guides' have become the Wolf school, and there is also a special racing school – Gensbichler. The Haus Wolf is recommended by a reporter as a 'good, convenient but expensive' hotel, the Hochleiten as 'friendly, with excellent food'. Other recommendations include the Sonnalp, Sonnblick and Pinzgauerhof. Hinterglemm has its own all-day kindergarten. There are adequate everyday shops, 'definitely cheaper' than in Saalbach. Après-ski is muted.

Tourist office As Saalbach.
Package holidays Crystal (hr) Enterprise (h) Horizon (h) Inghams (hr) Ski Global (h) Snobiz (h) Thomson (h).

Leogang 840m

Leogang is a quiet village which sprawls along the next valley to the north-east of Saalbach, its lifts up towards Schönleiten starting a bus-ride away from the centre. It has little après-ski or shopping, and reporters are agreed that the key thing is to choose a hotel close to the lifts with its own après-ski life and sports facilities if you want them. (Buses are infrequent, some hotels are a long walk from its route, and taxis are expensive.) The Salzburgerhof hotel is recommended, though the Krallerhof (scene of the ski school awards) has better facilities including the main local après-ski focus, the Kralleralm; the St Leonhard is 'extremely comfortable'. There is cross-country skiing in the valley and at altitude, and sleighs and toboggans are advertised. We have an eulogistic report of the Altenberger ski school.

Tourist office ✆ (6583) 234
Package holidays Crystal (hr) Enterprise (hr) Ski-Tal (hrcjas).

Kitzbühel Austria 760m

Good for *Easy runs, big ski area, mountain restaurants, après-ski, Alpine charm, not skiing, easy road access, rail access, short airport transfers*
Bad for *Lift queues, skiing convenience, late holidays, resort-level snow, freedom from cars, tough runs*

Linked resorts: Kirchberg, Jochberg, Pass Thurn

Linking lifts and runs to form a ski 'circus' is no longer the novelty it was when they first created one at Kitzbühel. As modern circuses go this one is imperfectly linked and low, with the result that its lower slopes are often icy, and washed out long before spring; and it suffers from lift bottle-necks – mainly in Kitzbühel itself. But with those provisos it is a very attractive skiing area, possessing a delightful mixture of friendly woodlands (with chalet restaurants playing jolly Tyrolean tunes) and open upper slopes commanding magnificent views – a surprise, considering the altitude. When snow is plentiful, the shared skiing of Kitzbühel and Kirchberg makes an impressive ski region by all but the most testing standards – though the Ski Safari linking with Jochberg and Pass Thurn can hardly be called big game, and little of the skiing is tough.

Kitzbühel is a beautiful old town on a main road and rail thoroughfare. It is one of the oldest and most famous of Austrian ski resorts and, along with Lech and Zürs, one of the most fashionable. Unlike the other two, it is large (much bigger than the Austrian resort norm) and not exclusive, and attracts large numbers of young British skiers who make a lot of noise in the streets after closing time at the Londoner pub (1.45am).

There are several quieter villages which give the chance to enjoy the skiing, without having to submit to the tumult of the town – Kirchberg most important among them. Although rustic by Kitzbühel's standards, it is nevertheless a large, busy resort. If you want a haven of tranquillity, Kirchberg is not it. But it is certainly more attractive as a base than bargain hotels 'near' Kitzbühel, which in terms of skiing and après-skiing convenience are a long way from anywhere.

Taking a car has the undoubted benefit of being independent of the bus system, but this may be outweighed by the difficulty of driving and parking – and other major resorts within reach for day trips are not particularly tempting.

The skiing top 2000m bottom 760m

The skiing is in three main areas. Kitzbühel and a bus ride or a 20-minute walk separate two of them – the Kitzbüheler Horn and the much more extensive Hahnenkamm/Ehrenbachhöhe/Pengelstein area

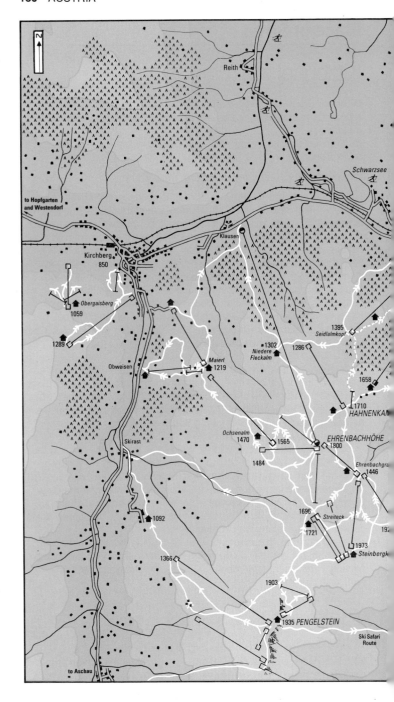

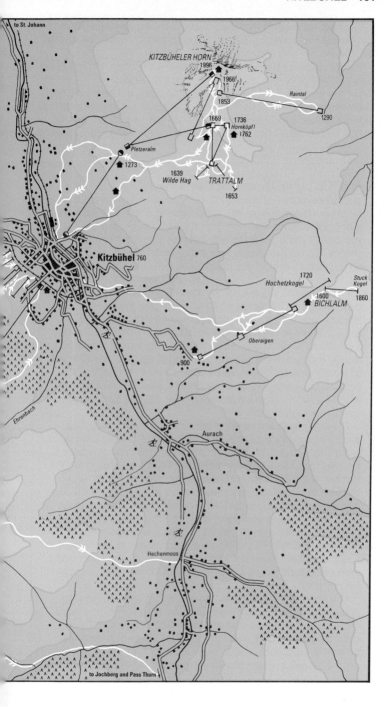

(shared with Kirchberg). The third, above Jochberg and Pass Thurn, can be reached almost entirely on skis from the Hahnenkamm, via the 'Ski Safari'.

The **Kitzbüheler Horn** is a big and beautiful mountain, its peak rising over 1200m from the valley floor and giving tremendous top-of-the-world views. There is good gentle skiing, but for experienced skiers the Horn is less good than it looks; its pistes are much easier than they are graded except when conditions are bad – which towards the bottom means quite often, since they face mostly south-west. The skiing

The Kitzbühel Downhill: Bell's view

The Hahnenkamm is probably the only course that frightens most experienced downhillers, which includes me. Even in a year when a lot of the courses aren't really stimulating enough, at Kitzbühel you know if you make a slight mistake you've got a very good chance of crashing. On the other hand, if you're aggressive and don't let the course get you down, Kitzbühel is the supreme thrill to ski. When I'm getting it right here I have virtually no fear of it.

The start is the steepest of any downhill. You hardly need to push out of the start – it's almost a free fall. Inspecting the course for the first time, you think the first couple of turns are steep, then you come to an edge where it gets even steeper. That's the Mausfalle: a gradient of virtually one in one. It's really frightening, but not that difficult once you know you can do it. You fly about 20m over it, land on it and go straight down. Every year you get the butterflies because you've forgotten that it's actually possible. I never like to watch the racer before me disappear over that cliff; it makes you wonder how anyone can do it.

The really difficult bit is about ten seconds after the Mausfalle – the Steilhang (which just means steep slope). A compression leads into a 180° turn, technical but not that steep, then you dive down to the Steilhang with a left-hand turn down into it. This is definitely the hardest turn in any downhill because it goes on for so long and because the slope runs away from you as you try to turn. I made a mistake here in 1987. In the middle of the turn I was doing really well, carving cleanly and high, then I got too aggressive: I moved my weight back too much, started to sit back and also got twisted – the dreaded rotation. I found myself heading straight for the net and had to do a slalom turn at 60mph, which killed off all my speed and probably lost me a couple of seconds. But at least I stayed out of the net, just!

You never see the long flat road on TV. This is where the skis and gliding ability come into play. If you're not a very experienced racer you just sit on the road and thank God you made it. Once you get more experienced you wish you hadn't messed up the turns before the road, because you seem to be going so slowly at this point. Still travelling very slowly, you come round the mountain, see is reached (after a bus-ride or a walk from the town centre across the main road, river and railway) by a lengthy combination of gondola and cable-cars – one to the Horn itself, the other towards the lower Hornköpfl, nearby.

Most flanks of the Horn are steep and rocky, which explains the lack of a lift link with nearby St Johann. At the top there is no obvious alternative to the single piste (now served by an efficient double chair-lift), which soon branches to give access to the Raintal bowl on the back of the mountain. Although the runs are black and red, there isn't

---

the village a long way below, and realise it's going to take all of 20 seconds to get down to that level – the hill just drops away. You're tired by then and, what's worse, you've had time to think about it, and to wonder how your legs are going to cope with the compression below.

The finish is really steep again, not as technical as the top, but incredibly bumpy: you just hang on. Anyone could catch an edge on those bumps; Todd Brooker's fall here was probably one of the worst I've seen. Sometimes I think they deliberately don't make it as smooth as they could, just to keep their reputation going. But that's how it should be – demanding. Even more than Wengen, Kitzbühel is a course which couldn't be introduced to the circuit today – trainers would throw up their hands in horror and say 'too dangerous'.

At Kitzbühel (as at Wengen) they usually have the downhill on Saturday and the slalom on Sunday. The best place for setting warm-up courses for the slalom is on the downhill course just after the race, so the national slalom trainers have their own race to secure the best piece of piste. Literally as the last racer is going through the finish the trainers dash out on to the course with their drills and poles; it's a free-for-all.

One of the funnier aspects of Kitzbühel is the sight of all the spectators climbing over the fence after the race. The course becomes an absolute madhouse, with hundreds of people sliding on their bums down the steep sections, which are unskiable if you don't have razor-sharp edges. Once, when my ski pre-released at the top after about five seconds (despite special springs and the top release setting of 20 DIN) I had to wait until the race was over before I could ski down the course. It was definitely more dangerous than doing the race itself, trying to avoid people skidding out of control.

One thing you notice here (as in Switzerland) is the huge numbers of supporters: they have to run special trains into places like Kitzbühel, which gets incredibly full for the Hahnenkamm race. Generally the Austrian supporters are very knowledgeable, and generous with their applause.

much to this area (the red is almost a schuss). Beyond a briefly dense network of short lifts and mostly easy runs around the Trattalm (a good post-nursery area), the run back down to Kitzbühel splits into black, red and blue. The black isn't steep, but may present a stern test of skating ability. The red is exhaustingly flat for a long way at the bottom.

Just along the hill, the little-used Bichlalm lifts above the hamlet of Aurach serve limited straight-up-and-down pistes facing south-west, and an off-piste route to Fieberbrunn. In good conditions there is a blue piste back to the edge of the town.

The **Hahnenkamm** is the site of the world's most feared downhill race (see Box), but most of the runs are easily managed by intermediates, as long as the snow is good. It is more easily reached from the centre than the Horn, but still a five-minute walk. Direct access is by cable-car over a steep mountainside to an open ridge about 900m above. The preferable alternative (in all but the worst weather) is to take the two Streifalm chair-lifts, thus avoiding not only the cable-car queue but also some plodding at the top. There are a couple of good, long, northish-facing runs back to the town from the Streifalm, the most direct approximately following the downhill race-course but by-passing the steepest sections. For a brief period after the race the course can easily be identified, and less easily skied.

The Hahnenkamm gives access to the heart of the skiing on and around **Ehrenbachhöhe** (a busy meeting place with several hotels and restaurants around the summit) which Kitzbühel shares with Kirchberg. It offers lots of variety, some good off-piste runs, and some long and beautiful pistes. There is an easy run with mogulled reddish alternatives down into the Ehrenbachgraben dip, where three chair-lifts fan out. The skiing here, beneath Steinbergkogel, is the most challenging in the region – a genuinely black 500m drop, facing north, with a number of variants and often big moguls. From the top of the ridge there are apparently good off-piste runs, a long run down through the woods to Hechenmoos and an easy connection to **Pengelstein**. On the north-western flank of Pengelstein there are now two chair-lifts (one an efficient four-seater) serving open, easy, uncrowded runs which continue down to a bus stop beyond Kirchberg. There is also an unpatrolled route (which involves some initial walking) down to Aschau.

From Ehrenbachhöhe there are easy connections to and from Hahnenkamm skiing, and long runs down north-west-facing slopes to Kirchberg (mostly gentle) and down the north-facing slope to Klausen (with more scope for challenge and off-piste adventure), served by a six-seater gondola.

On the south-east flank of Pengelstein is a recently built four-seat chair-lift which is the first in a chain of lifts designed to link this area fully with the skiing of Jochberg and Pass Thurn. For the moment, the 'Ski Safari' remains a basically one-way affair. A very long, easy run from Pengelstein takes you to the fringes of Jochberg, where (after a fair walk or short taxi ride) you embark on a long series of lifts and pistes to complete your Safari to the slopes above Pass Thurn. Recently added lifts make it possible to retrace your steps as far as Jochberg, but from there you still have to take the bus back to Kitzbühel.

The **Pass Thurn** skiing (1265m to 1999m) is a great asset when conditions are poor lower down. It is a simple network, mostly of drag-lifts but with a couple of double chairs, serving mostly easy, wide open skiing, again with beautiful views from the top lifts towards the distant Kitzbüheler Horn, and with one stiff mogul-field to provide a change from gentle cruising. There is good off-piste skiing on the open slopes of the head of the valley, reached from the Zweitausender chair or the Trattenbach chair on the opposite (Jochberg) slope, sunny and often short of snow.

Mountain restaurants are liberally scattered around the slopes and peaks of the area and greatly approved by recent reporters: 'wonderful selection' ... 'superb loos, good food, splendid views, sunny locations'. Recommendations include the Trattenbergalm (between Jochberg and Pass Thurn), the Ochsalm (waitress service), the Berggasthaus, the Birchalm, the Horngipfelhaus, and the Brandseit (cheap and uncrowded) near the bottom of the Fleckalm gondola.

Kitzbühel is large, easy to get to, and fashionable. The result has traditionally been serious **queues** to get up the mountains. The authorised Tourist Office view is that the gondola from Klausen (half-way to Kirchberg) into the Hahnenkamm skiing, built a few years ago, has solved the problem. Erratic snow conditions in the last couple of seasons have kept German skiers away in droves, with the result that some reporters have met negligible queues. Last season, the Gulf war hit Kitzbühel's American business to similar effect. But not everyone has been so lucky: on occasion, the cable-cars out of the town still attracted monstrous queues. 'Arrive at 9 or take sandwiches', writes one dissatisfied mid-February customer. A new and more efficient gondola should be in place to relieve queues on the way up to the Horn this season. When conditions are generally poor, Pass Thurn gets crowded with skiers from Kitzbühel and resorts on the other side of the pass.

There is supposed to be **artificial snow** on the Streif-Familienabfahrt, from the Hahnenkamm to the town, but reporters have not found any.

The resort

Kitzbühel is set splendidly between its main ski areas, spreading across a wide and busy junction of valleys. It is a large and colourful old town enclosed by walls and, less prettily, by main roads and a loop in the railway. The old town with its twin-towered church, cobbled streets and gaily painted houses is one of the few ski resorts you might choose to visit just for a look. Shopping is sophisticated and international. The centre is, by day at least, traffic-free, but only at the cost of a complicated and often congested one-way ring-road system, which doesn't prevent traffic seriously impairing the quality of Kitzbühel life throughout the season – for drivers and pedestrians alike. Getting from the centre of town to either ski area involves crossing the railway line and a long walk or slow bus ride. The daytime buses around the resort and to other villages in the ski area are efficiently organised, though seriously oversubscribed at peak times. The service (with several

Facts on Kitzbühel Tirol **Austria**

Prices in schillings
Ski Club represented

Tourist office

Postcode A-6370
Tel (5356) 2155
Fax (5356) 2307.
Tlx 5118413

Getting there

By road 1,130km from Calais. Via Munich; chains rarely needed.
By rail Main-line station in resort. Postbus every 15 mins from station.
By air Salzburg; transfer 1½hr. (Or Munich; transfer about 2hr.)

Staying there

Visitor beds 8,500; breakdown: 8,000 in hotels, 500 in apartments.
Package holidays Austrian Holidays (h) Austro Tours (h) Bladon Lines (hrcj) Crystal (hrcs) Enterprise (h) Horizon (h) Inghams (hs) Kings Ski Club (j) Made to Measure (h) Neilson (hr) Quality Ski Tours (h) Quest Travel (schools) (h) Ski Global (h) Ski Unique (h) SkiBound (h) SkiTonic (h) Snobiz (hr) Supertravel (h) Thomson (hr) .
Medical facilities In resort: Hospital, doctors (including specialists), chemists, dentists.

Non-skiing activities

Indoor Aquarena Centre (2 pools, sauna, solarium, mud baths, aerated baths, under-water massage – free entry with lift pass), also tennis hall, 2 squash courts, fitness centre, bridge, bowling, casino, 2 riding schools.
Outdoor Ice-rink (curling and skating), horse-riding, sleigh rides, wildlife park, toboggan run, ski-bobs.

Kindergartens

Red Devils
Tuition: Yes. Hours: same as ski school, but can baby-sit until 5.00pm. Ages: from 3. Cost: 1,050.00 per week (meals 60.00 per day). Enclosed area with children's restaurant.
Snow Adventure (Total ski kindergarten)
Tuition: Yes. Hours: 9.30-11.30 and 1.00-3.00. Ages: 3 up. Cost: 1,050.00 per week (meals 80.00 per day). Facilities in Marco Polo hotel.
Other childcare facilities
Baby-sitting list available from Tourist Office.

Special skiing facilities

Summer skiing No.

Cross-country 14km trail to and from Hechenmoos (medium), 12km of loops around Reith (mixed), 8km at Bichlach (difficult), 3km at Schwarzsee (easy). Instruction and free guided excursions (thrice weekly).

Lift passes

Kitzbühel local pass
Covers all lifts in Kitzbühel, Kirchberg, Jochberg, Pass Thurn, Aschau and Bichlalm and linking buses and swimming pool. (62 lifts in total.)
Cost 6 days 1,500.00 (£75.19). Low season: 1,300.00 saving 13%.
Credit cards accepted No.
Senior citizens 1,350.00 (over 60/65) saving 10%.
Children 750.00 (under 15) saving 50%. Free pass up to 1.10m (3ft 6in) in height on certain T-bars if accompanied by adult.
Notes Children over 1.65m (5ft 4in) must have proof of age. 20% reduction for disabled skiers. Group discounts for 15 or more people.
Beginners Punch cards, valid on 20 lifts; single ascent tickets on some lifts.
Short-term passes Hourly reductions on day passes bought after 11.00am.
Other periods 4 in 6 days and 10 in 14 days.

Ski school

Red Devils
Classes 4hr: 2hr am and pm. Cost: 1,050.00 (6 days).
Lift priority No.
Children's classes Ages: 3 up. Cost: 1,050.00 (6 days).
Private lessons available Full- or half-day. Cost: 1,850.00 per hour.
Special courses 'Golden Ski' touring; race training, 1,800.00 for 6 days.
Ski School Total
Classes 9.30-11.30 and 1.00-3.00. Cost: 1,100.00 (6 days).
Lift priority No.
Children's classes Ages: 4-11. Cost: 1,050.00 (6 days).
Private lessons available Full- or half-day. Cost: 1,850.00 per hour. Half-day 1,300.00.
Special courses Ski trekking, 400.00 per person per day; snowboard courses, 500.00 for 3 days.

What was new in 91

Nothing.

What is new for 92

Vague plans to improve links between Jochberg and Pengelstein.

Key to types of package holiday
h: hotels and guest-houses
c: catered chalets
j: 'jumbo' or 'club' chalets
s: self-catering apartments
r: rooms in private homes
a: catered apartments

different routes) is complicated by the one-way system and hampered by the traffic. For the evening, there are plenty of taxis.

Accommodation consists equally of hotels large, comfortable and expensive, and guest-houses cheap and simple, with little in between. The town has spread far beyond the old core, and because of the far-reaching coverage of the lift pass lots of (mostly cheap) accommodation which is a long way from Kitzbühel itself is sold under its name. Because skiing on the Horn is of secondary interest, the best location is either in the old centre (certainly the most attractive place to stay) or near the Hahnenkamm lifts, most people's starting point for the skiing, and where the nursery slopes are. The Goldener Greif, Tenne and Tiefenbrunner are the most prestigious town centre hotels, the Strasshofer equally well-placed, friendly and good value. The Maria Theresia is recommended for 'first-class cuisine', the Schwarzer Adler as being 'very comfortable' and the Klausner ('distinctively Austrian food'). Hotels near the Hahnenkamm include the Haselsberger, Montana (both good value) and Schweizerhof ('very good food'). Two regular visitors recommend the family-run Mühlbergerhof, a B&B on the edge of town, not far from the Hahnenkamm lifts.

Après-ski is extremely lively and varied, from the horrifically crowded Londoner pub ('by 10pm the place was a bit emptier, and everyone was standing on the chairs dancing to English oldies') to the Casino (jacket, tie and passport). There are plenty of tea-bars (some with outdoor tea-dancing), discos, smoky dives, and more traditional musical venues, and organised outings. Seppi's Pub, once very quiet, is now said to be 'friendly and relaxing'. A reporter has recommended the Mockingstube, near the Hahnenkamm lift, for happy-hour bargains. Other recommended bars include the Big Ben ('cheap and friendly') and the Glockenspiel. Restaurants are numerous and varied, the Tenne (cabaret, band) most fashionable. The Sport Bar is recommended for 'the best Jagertee and steaks'. The Hüberbraustube opposite Praxmair's Cafe is good value, and convincingly local.

Although Kitzbühel is low and its surroundings rather built up, its **cross-country** trails are good and the guided excursions recommended. **Non-skiers** will find a great variety of things to do, including excursions, organised or DIY by train. The museum is recommended. The Aquarena pool is excellent, but free only to those with a lift pass.

The **nursery slopes**, across a broad area at the bottom of the Hahnenkamm and Streifalm lifts, are adequate, but often short of snow, when beginners are taken up the Horn. There are easy runs to move on to. We have had mixed reports, over the years, of the **ski school** and its famous Red Devils. This year is no exception, despite the existence of a competing school, Total. Some pupils have been impressed by good Aussie and American instructors, but others rightly complain that there is no excuse for over-large classes when large numbers of instructors had been laid off because of the poor conditions and attendant down-turn in trade. We lack reports on the new school. Recent reports on the **ski kindergarten**, run by one-time champion and film star Toni Sailer, are inconclusive: 'uninviting, and German spoken', or 'Brilliant!'.

Kirchberg 850m

Kirchberg is a big, busy village 5km from Kitzbühel, centred on a road junction, with river and railway nearby. It shares some of its more interesting neighbour's problems, as well as its skiing – it is full of traffic, and its lifts are a bus-ride away from the centre of the village. The idea that you can do Kitzbühel on the cheap by staying in Kirchberg is misguided, but it is an attractively lively resort in its own right, and has long been popular among British skiers with no taste for the glamour of Kitzbühel. It has plenty of good traditional Tyrolean nightlife and lively bars, good facilities for cross-country skiing (not only along the valley to Westendorf but also a short, difficult loop at higher altitude), long cleared paths, tobogganing, skating and curling (natural rinks), tennis, squash, sleigh rides and swimming, and plenty of organised excursions. If staying on B&B terms, be prepared for queues and early closing in the village restaurants. Most of the hotels and guest-houses are in the centre, though there are a handful by the lift departure for Ehrenbachhöhe. There are nursery slopes at that same place, and both skiing and non-skiing kindergartens. Among the most charming of the town hotels is the mid-priced Gasthof Unterm Rain, on the Kitzbühel road. Kirchberg has its own small ski area on the Gaisberg – a modest slope, now sensibly graded red, notable mainly for a lack of crowds. Reports on the ski school are favourable.

Tourist office ✆ (5357) 2309. Tx 51371.
Package holidays Crystal (h) Enterprise (h) Falcon (hr) Horizon (h) Inghams (h) Neilson (h) Thomson (hr) Top Deck (hjs).

St Johann in Tirol Austria 650m

Good for *Easy runs, mountain restaurants, après-ski, short airport transfers, easy road access, rail access, cross-country, family holidays, artificial snow, woodland runs*
Bad for *Tough runs, late holidays, skiing convenience, resort-level snow, freedom from cars*

Separate resort: Fieberbrunn

St Johann is a substantial, bustling valley town, just over the hill from Kitzbühel. The hill in question is the Kitzbüheler Horn, and the mainly gentle skiing of St Johann covers a north-facing wooded shoulder of it, from the modest height (even by local standards) of 1700m all the way down to various points along the valleys. But proximity to Kitzbühel should not be taken to indicate similarity. St Johann has little of the gloss of its famous neighbour, and none of the fashionable following. Its appeal (like its skiing, which suits beginners and early intermediates well) is much more straightforward – it is a pleasant chalet-style setting for a lively and quite varied winter holiday at reasonable prices.

Only a few miles up the road from St Johann, but seemingly much further from the bustle of the busy junction of main roads and valleys, lies the small village of Fieberbrunn, covered along with St Johann by the area lift pass. When skiers argue about snowfall, it always seems to be the name of lowly little Fieberbrunn that crops up to illustrate the point that higher does not always mean snowier.

Kitzbühel is only a ten-minute train-ride away, and there are few other obvious targets for skiing expeditions – so a car is of no great value, though it can be useful for exploring other valley towns and ski areas further afield. The problems of parking in the town are considerable.

The skiing top 1700m bottom 680m

A two-stage gondola goes up from a point on the fringes of the resort all the way to Harschbichl at 1700m. From this point, runs fan out down three gentle rounded ridges, separated by wooded glades, some of them splitting and linking further down the mountain. Practically all the skiing on the top half of the mountain is graded red, and properly so. These are good intermediate slopes, varied and occasionally challenging. Most runs can be extended to the valley, but there are plentiful drags and chair-lifts to allow red-run skiers to stay high and leave blue-run skiers in peace lower down. The long Penzing chair is a fast four-seater, making its red run particularly attractive.

The bottom sections of the runs are all easier, and constitute excellent terrain for building the confidence of near-beginners. The main run back to the village has the additional attraction for nervous novices of

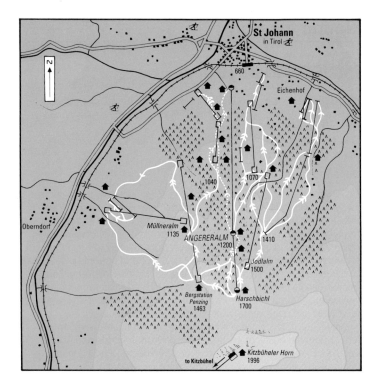

involving no tricky lifts and being littered with restaurants.

Only one black run is marked on the piste map – a pleasant long run almost from top to bottom of the hill on the west side – and its grading is an exaggeration. There is a moderately steep, sunny pitch part-way down, where poor snow can make things tricky for a few yards, but the run is otherwise easy, and manageable by many skiers who normally baulk at reds. It may be closed, even in high season, for racing practice.

The choice of reasonably priced and welcoming **mountain restaurants** is very wide. Practically every piste has a hut at the top or bottom, or part-way down, or all three – in one run down from Harschbichl to the village it is possible to include no less than eight restaurants. Many of them have excellent views over the town. Several of the restaurants are also hotels.

Queues are generally not a problem at village level or up the mountain – the system of lifts and pistes fanning out down a conical mountain is not prone to bottle-necks. But the balance can be upset by visitors from other resorts and (at weekends) from nearby cities when the snow here is better than elsewhere. There is **artificial snow** on the main piste down from above Angereralm to the town, and on the piste of the short Hochfeld chair-lift nearby. This, combined with the northward orientation of the slopes and reportedly 'superb' piste grooming, generally keeps the skiing here in good condition, despite the weather.

The resort

St Johann is at a junction of valleys, rivers and roads, and has a railway line running through; the centre is a triangle neatly defined by this railway on the south side and by the two rivers which meet to the north. The ski slopes are across the railway line, and there are spreading suburbs outside these boundaries on all sides. Eichenhof, an easterly suburb, has some accommodation and is convenient for the ski lifts but is 'an unattractive 15- to 20-minute walk from the town centre along a busy, dusty road'. The main road from Kitzbühel bypasses the centre of St Johann. It is an old town much developed, and a popular summer resort as well as a winter one. It is lively with a bit of character, but not particularly pretty or charming. There are plenty of everyday shops. A free ski-bus serves the main lift station, so location is not critical.

Most of the **accommodation** is in hotels, *pensions* and private rooms. Among the smarter hotels, the Dorfschmiede is attractively rustic, in parts at least, and in a good compromise position just on the

---

Facts on St Johann in Tirol Tirol **Austria**

Prices in schillings

Tourist office

Postcode A-6380
Tel (5352) 2218
Fax (5352) 5200
Tlx 51606

Getting there

By road 1,133km from Calais. Via Munich; chains rarely needed.
By rail Main-line station in resort.
By air Salzburg; transfer 1½hr. (Or Munich; transfer about 2hr.)

Staying there

Visitor beds 6,000; breakdown: mainly in hotels, pensions and private rooms.
Package holidays Austro Tours (h) Crystal (hr) Enterprise (h) Horizon (h) Ski Europe (h) Ski Partners (h) Ski Party Snow World (h) SkiBound (h) Thomson (hr) .
Medical facilities In resort: Hospital, doctors (including specialists), dentists, chemists.

Non-skiing activities

Swimming, sauna, steam baths, solarium, indoor tennis hall, fitness centre, massage, bowling, air-gun range.
Outdoor Natural skating rink, curling, sleigh rides, horse-riding, joy-rides, toboggan run, 40km cleared paths.

Kindergartens

Skikindergarten
Tuition: Yes. Hours: 9.30-4.30. Ages: One yr up. Cost: 3,360.00 per week (with lunch). Lunchtime baby-sitting at the Hotel Park 80.00 per day.

Special skiing facilities

Summer skiing No.
Cross-country 74km total – easy, medium and difficult trails both on east and west sides of the town. Instruction available.

Lift passes

St Johann lift pass
Covers all lifts and ski bus. (18 lifts in total.)
Cost 6 days 1,220.00 (£61.15). Low season: 1,100.00 saving 10%.
Credit cards accepted No.
Children 640.00 (under 15) saving 48%. Free pass up to age 6.
Beginners Points card, and half-day passes for nursery drags.
Short-term passes Half-day pass (morning valid until 12.30, afternoon valid from 12.30); 'late sleeper' pass from 11.00am; 'try out' pass from 2.00pm.
Other passes Schneewinkl 6-day pass also covers Fieberbrunn, Waidring and other small resorts (6 days 1,350.00 for adults, 820.00 for children).
Other periods 5 in 6 days and 11 in 13 days.

Ski school

Schischule Arpe
Classes 4hr: 2hr am and pm. Cost: 1,100.00 (6 days). Special rates for small classes (no more than 7 people).
Lift priority No.
Children's classes Ages: 4 to 15. Cost: 1,100.00 (6 days). Race training for teenagers, 6 days costs 1050.00.
Private lessons available Full day or half-day. Cost: 1,500.00 per day for 1-2 people (1,000.00 per half-day).

town side of the railway. The much cheaper Gasthof Bären is right in the centre on the Hauptplatz; it is a popular après-ski meeting place, and reportedly very comfortable. We have an enthusiastic report of the 'very friendly family atmosphere' at the Pension Noella, right on the piste.

The **après-ski** scene is lively in season, with such dignified proceedings as Mr and Miss St Johann competitions, as well as charming old bars and restaurants (the Speckbackerstub'n is reportedly a good example) and towny tea-rooms. There are youth-oriented discos as well as more traditional musical venues. When the resort is quieter, the Aussie-staffed Bunny's (the 'in' place last season) and Klomp bars are recommended. The Tyroller Keller has traditional Austrian music played on the piano, accordion and zither and is very atmospheric. The local brewery has a top-floor bar, with good views.

For **non-skiers** St Johann has a wide range of sporting activities, including an excellent pool and a tennis hall. It is ideally placed for excursions to Kitzbühel, Innsbruck and Salzburg. The resort is a good base for **cross-country** skiers, who have a choice of long trails of all degrees of difficulty on two sides of the resort. A cross-country centre (the Koasa-stadion) has been built just across the main road.

The gentle pistes coming down to the village and its outposts have excellent **nursery slopes** at the bottom, provided there is snow. Past reports on **ski school** have been generally favourable, with reservations about hasty allocation to classes and large groups. The ski school based in Eichenhof earns high praise – 'imaginative, native English-speaking instructors coped magnificently'.

Fieberbrunn 800m

Fieberbrunn's village centre is set back from the road and has the usual ingredients of Tyrolean charm: clean and cheerful hotels and guest-houses, a pretty church and a very jolly après-ski atmosphere (tea-dancing and beauty contests) in the Alte Post and one or two other bars, with Dutch visitors much in evidence. Recent reports suggest that the noisy Londoner bar has gone downhill, and that the Windmill is now the most popular evening venue. The River House is also recommended. Overall the resort is small, but it is also highly inconvenient – strung out along the road for over a mile but at no point within walking range of the main ski area; much use is made of the efficient free ski-bus service (packed at peak times). A few chair- and drag-lifts cover a small and very attractive, lightly wooded mountainside between the base station near the road at about 800m and the bald Lärchfilzkogel (1655m), with a chair-lift on the slopes beyond this peak reaching 1870m. A new gondola is planned for next season. There are several long, very easy runs, some easy off-piste skiing on the open eastern side of the mountain, and steeper north-facing slopes dropping from the summit down into a wide and empty valley. An unpisted route leads back to the nursery slopes on the edge of the village. Ski tours between Fieberbrunn and the Kitzbühel valley are popular. There is a swimming pool and an indoor ice-rink, and kindergartens.

Tourist office ✆ (5354) 6304. Tx 51560. **Package holidays** Enterprise (h) Hoverspeed Ski-Drive (s) Inghams (h) Ski Global.

Wilder still and Wilder?

Söll Austria 700m

Good for *Short airport transfers, après-ski, easy road access, big ski area, woodland runs*
Bad for *Tough runs, late holidays, skiing convenience, resort-level snow*

Linked resorts: Scheffau, Going, Ellmau, Brixen, Hopfgarten, Itter
Separate resort: Westendorf

Like nearby Kitzbühel, Söll shares with several less well-known neighbours a broad ski area which is spread around a pleasantly wooded, mostly round-topped ridge – more hilly than mountainous in Alpine terms. The area's name of Grossraum is increasingly overshadowed by the suffix Wilder Kaiser Brixental – the Wilder Kaiser being the spectacularly soaring mountain seen to the north of the area, and Brixental being the valley that bounds it to the south.

The skiing is friendly in general, with lots of villages dotted along the broad low valleys below. Söll is still the main centre for British visitors, although Ellmau and Westendorf also attract large numbers of package holiday-makers from the UK. In the past, these have included quite a high proportion of lager louts, but we are persuaded by recent reporters that Söll is not as wild a place as it was, and that these days it can safely be categorised as lively but not rowdy.

The recent introduction of a big gondola access lift seems to have put an end to the queues to get out of the valley which have spoiled Söll for many skiers in the past. Last winter the erratic weather was a more major cause for complaint. Several of our March reporters found no snow at all in Söll and had to be bussed to St Jakob, two hour's drive away, where the ski school had set up base. Set low, and beside a main road very near the motorway system, Söll is admirably accessible both for motorists and for air travellers. Having a car is very valuable for skiing and non-skiing excursions, and for going to glacier areas when local conditions are poor – Hintertux is the nearest, the Kitzsteinhorn a bit further away, the Stubai further still.

Many other holiday villages also give access to the Grossraum skiing. Of those close to major lifts, Scheffau is the most charming, and probably the best base for exploring the whole ski area; Ellmau is closer to lifts but less well placed for the area as a whole; quiet little Itter is also on the same side of the main road as the ski area, and its access lift has recently been upgraded to a gondola; despite improved links, the village of Going is peripheral for skiing, but has charm and regulars who swear by it; Hopfgarten, on the south-west side of the area, is young and lively, with good but south-facing runs; Brixen has excellent access to the Grossraum ski area as a whole, with a powerful lift up into the heart of it, and its home slopes are steep but sunny.

Westendorf is a charming and civilised resort with its own separate

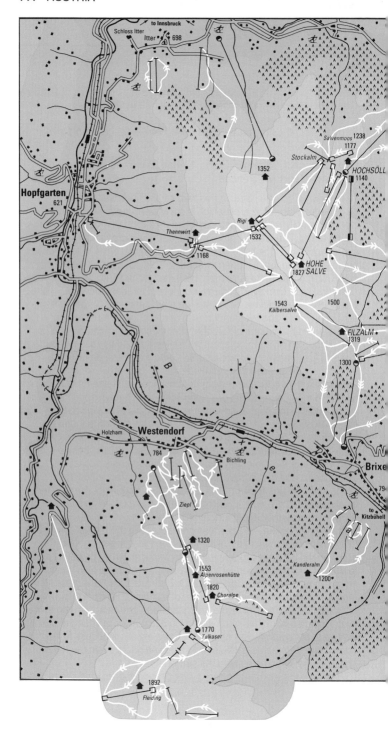

to Innsbruck

Schloss Itter
Itter 698

1352

Salvenmoos 1238
1177
Stockalm
HOCHSÖLL
1140

Hopfgarten
621

Rigi
Thennwirt
1532
1168

HOHE
SALVE
1827

1543
Kälbersalve

1500

FILZALM
1319

1300

Holzham
Westendorf
784
Bichling

Brixe

79

to
Kitzbühell

Ziepl

1320

1553
Alpenrosenhütte
1820
Choralpe

Kandleralm

1200

1770
Talkaser

1892
Fleiding

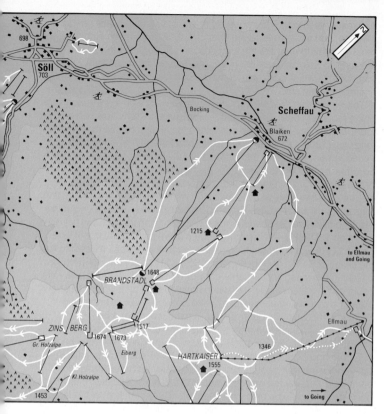

ski area, just along the valley from Brixen but on the opposite (south) side; it is deservedly popular with inexperienced skiers, and now covered by the Grossraum pass, facilitating exploration via Brixen. To judge by the flood of reports we have received over the last couple of years, it is enjoying a revival of British interest.

The skiing top 1827m bottom 621m

The Grossraum ski region is spread around broad, medium-altitude mountains separating two wide valleys. One side consists of north-facing slopes above Söll, Scheffau, Ellmau and Going, the other of south-facing ones accessible from Hopfgarten and Brixen im Thale. The skiing above Itter, between Söll and Hopfgarten, faces west.

For most people, **Söll**'s skiing starts with a long walk from the village centre to the lifts (there are ski-buses, but they can't be relied on). An eight-seater gondola goes up to Hochsöll, an open but not very flat shelf, with a few short drags and chairs on the easier slopes at the foot of the impressively steep Hohe Salve, the top of which is reached by chair-lift. Runs down from this beautiful, panoramic peak (with church and restaurant on top) are not easy; there is a genuine black run down the face, and a tricky red to the right of it. Apart from these high runs, the most interesting runs are the long descents through the trees from Hochsöll to Söll, an excellent red and a more roundabout 'family run' blue, both of which can be treacherous or unskiable when icy – as they not infrequently are.

The easiest ways down from the Hohe Salve are on the western flank of the mountain down to Rigi above **Hopfgarten** – runs now served by a four-person chair-lift. In good conditions these runs can be extended a long way (1200m vertical) down to Hopfgarten itself, over interestingly varied terrain. From Rigi there are easy runs round to Hochsöll and it is possible to ski down to **Itter** under the new gondola. From Thennwirt, below Rigi, a chair-lift makes the connection with the south-facing slopes at Kälbersalve and thus with the wide area of almost flat lifts and runs around Filzalm above Brixen. The runs down to **Brixen** (including blacks beside the big gondola) are excellent, given good snow; but don't count on it. There are more direct routes down to this area from Hohe Salve, but they are either steep or likely to be icy, or both. If heading for the skiing of Brixen or Scheffau from Söll, you can cut out Hohe Salve by taking the recently built cable-car from Hochsöll to the east of it. This cable-car and the chair-lift it leads to have opened up a worthwhile new area of skiing on the east flank of Hohe Salve, as well as improving Söll's connections with other resorts in the Grossraum area.

From Filzalm there are easy although time-consuming connections to the top of Scheffau's skiing at Brandstadl via the gently rounded knolls of Eiberg and Zinsberg – now reached by from Filzalm by an efficient (and enclosed) four-seater chair-lift. Runs down to **Scheffau** are long open trails through the woods, steep and fast enough to be a challenge, but wide enough to be easily manageable. Consistently over the last few years, Scheffau has had the best snow conditions in the Grossraum – indeed for much of last season it had the only snow conditions in the region. The alternative is to ski further along to Hartkaiser, for similar runs down to **Ellmau**, where lower-slope lifts link up with the skiing of **Going**, below Astberg (1267m). Getting back to Söll from these places means retracing your steps. Many skiers prefer to ski these parts of the system by taking the valley bus in the morning or the evening. But plan with care: taxis can be expensive.

Mountain restaurants are generally considered by reporters to be pleasant and adequate in number – though there are often crowds and queues at the busier spots, particularly Hochsöll. Particularly recommended are Gemütlich (below Hartkaiser), the restaurant between the chair-lifts from Scheffau to Brandstadl and the Jochstub'n in Scheffau. The Gipfel restaurant (Söll) has marvellous views of the Brixental and beyond.

A high-season reporter says that the Söll gondola has relieved the serious **queues** to get into the skiing from there. But the system as a whole is not free of queues – particularly when conditions are poor. Reporters complain of regularly waiting 20 to 30 minutes for some key lifts. The main link between Brixen and Söll is reportedly a bottle-neck. Hopfgarten's chair-lifts are rarely over-subscribed, but Scheffau's gondola is very popular when snow low-down is poor.

Navigation around what is an extensive and complicated area is hindered by the 'incomprehensible' piste maps provided locally. The latest version unhelpfully shows only the lifts.

Söll has a couple of movable guns for the application of **artificial snow** where necessary (they must have been kept busy during the past three winters); Brixen has some on the red run to the valley, as does Ellmau, on the run down the Hartkaiser.

The resort

Söll is not a very large village but it has spread considerably across its wide valley. The buildings are attractive, in a neat neo-Tyrolean way, but do not add up convincingly to a village with any real character. A main road by-passes the village, between it and the ski slopes, which are a long walk or a taxi-ride away. There is a bus, free to 'residents', but high-season reporters found it too infrequent and the drivers too unhelpful to be relied on. There are good every day shops close together in the centre – one reporter was disappointed to find that all the shop assistants firmly spoke English.

Accommodation is in hotels, mostly simple but satisfactory. The Postwirt is an attractive old hotel right in the centre (of the nightlife as well as the village). The Eggerwirt ('very pleasant staff, very good food') and Austria are quieter central recommendations; and a regular visitor says the Tenne and Tyrol can also be safely recommended. The Dorfstubn ('drafty and lacks atmosphere') and the Agerhof ('3km from town') can not. We have an enthusiastic report on the Pension Kaiserblick, run by a friendly husband-and-wife team on the edge of the village. There are several hotels lining the nursery slopes (which also makes them handy for the main lift).

As we've said, latest reports encourage us to portray Söll **après-ski** as lively rather than outrageous. The Whisky Mühle remains the popular disco, the boisterous Pub 15 the most popular bar. The Austria has a 'brilliant' upstairs bar with guitarists and the bars of the Poste and Tyrol are recommended. There are all sorts of organised evening amusements, from bowling at the Tenne (recommended) to zither performances. With a large B&B population, queues are common for restaurants as well as for lifts. The Söller Stuben (opposite the Whisky Mühle) has 'very good food and friendly service'.

The **cross-country** trails, on the valley floor, look satisfactory to our untutored eye, but one reporter pronounces them uninteresting. There are organised 'try out' cross-country evenings. The resort is not very exciting for **non-skiers**, but the swimming pool (with a heated outdoor section) is highly recommended – though it gets very busy in the evenings. There are lots of organised excursions.

Söll's **nursery slopes** are beside the chair-lift departure – open fields between the bottom of the wooded mountain and the village. They are splendidly wide and near-horizontal, but often short of snow, when the gentle slopes at Salvenmoos have to be used. There are always lots of people around, and often lift queues. A regular reporter says that two beginners in his party found the transition from the nursery slopes to the Hochsöll area very difficult; they made much better progress on easy runs in the Brandstadl area. There are now two **ski schools**; recent reports are generally favourable – good organisation, good English spoken – but there are exceptions. We have one enthusiastic report on kindergarten care.

Scheffau 750m
Scheffau itself is poorly placed for skiing, a little way up the wrong side of the valley, but there are hotels close to its main lift into the Grossraum skiing at Blaiken. For many visitors the rustic seclusion of the spacious village more than compensates for any inconvenience: hotels and pensions are dotted around in the pastures, and there is also a

Facts on Söll   Tirol **Austria**

Prices in schillings

Tourist office
Postcode A-6306
Tel (5333) 5216
Fax (5333) 6180
Tlx 51449

Getting there
By road 1,114km from Calais. Via Munich; chains rarely needed.
By rail Wörgl (13km) or Kufstein (15km); bus to resort.
By air Salzburg; transfer 1½hr. (Or Munich; transfer about 2hr.)

Staying there
Visitor beds 4,200; breakdown: 1,400 in hotels, 2,800 other.
Package holidays Crystal (hr) Enterprise (h) Falcon (hr) Horizon (h) Inghams (hr) Neilson (hr) Sally Holidays (hr) Ski Global (hr) Thomson (hr) .
Medical facilities In resort: Doctor, dentist, chemist. Hospital: Wörgl (13km) or Kufstein (15km).

Non-skiing activities
Indoor Swimming, sauna, solarium, massage, bowling, rifle range.
Outdoor Swimming, natural skating rink (skating, curling), horse-riding, sleigh rides, 3km floodlit toboggan run.

Kindergartens
Ski School Soll
Tuition: Yes. Hours: 9.30-4.15. Ages: under 5. Cost: 1,410.00 per week (includes ski school and lunch). Learn to ski in 'fairytale ski meadow'.

Special skiing facilities
Summer skiing No.
Cross-country A total of 100km of easy runs between Söll, Scheffau, Going and Ellmau; 35km around Söll alone. Instruction available.

Lift passes
Grossraum pass
Covers all lifts in the Wilder Kaiser Brixental area and the Scheffau/Hopfgarten bus. (85 lifts in total.)
Cost 6 days 1,300.00 (£65.16).
Credit cards accepted Yes.
Children 735.00 (under 15) saving 43%. Free pass up to age 5.
Notes No low-season pass but you can get a voucher worth 120.00 off meals in mountain restaurants with a pass of 6 or more days in low season.
Beginners Points tickets.
Short-term passes Half-day from 11.00 or 12.00; single ascent tickets.
Other passes Local resort passes (eg 6-day Söll only pass 1,145.00 for adults, 640.00 for children).
Other periods 5 in 7 days, 7 in 10 days and 10 in 14 days.

Ski school
Soll Skischool
Ski schools in all the Grossraum villages.
Classes 4 hr; 10.00-12.00 and 2.00-4.00. Cost: 990.00 (6 days).
Lift priority No.
Children's classes Ages: 5-12. Cost: 950.00 (6 days). Lunch available for 80.00 per day.
Private lessons available Full- or half-day, or hourly. Cost: 360.00 per hour. Each additional person 120.00.
Special courses Guided tours around the Grossraum region; racing introduction course, 700.00 per half-day; snowboarding courses; limited groups of 3-7 people, 2,300.00 per day.
Hohe Salve
Classes 2hr am and/or pm. Cost: 990.00 (6 days).
Lift priority No.
Children's classes Ages: 4 up. Cost: 990.00 (6 days).
Private lessons available Full- or half-day, or hourly. Cost: 360.00 per hour.
Special courses Racing practice.

recognisable village centre, where the old Gasthof Maikircher offers good-value accommodation. The Alpin is recommended by one recent reporter, but has been condemned for overbooking by two others. At Blaiken, the Wilder Kaiser and the more modest Pension Aloisia and Gastehaus Waldrand (free sauna) are recommended. The Wilder Kaiser has various entertainments during the week. There is little going on at night, although there are a couple of bars (the Pub Royale is the most lively, the Coco is rather chic) and one 'quiet' nightclub. There are two fairly new bowling alleys. There is an adequate sunny nursery slope close to the village, and ski and non-ski kindergartens which have been recommended. The ski school has received favourable reports. The ski-bus service is described in a report as 'diabolical in the morning, non-existent at the end of the day'; only when snow is good can you ski down to Blaiken.

Tourist office ✆ (5358) 8137.
Package holidays Crystal (hr) Enterprise (h) Falcon (hr) Thomson (hr).

Ellmau 820m

Ellmau is not a big place, but it has grown substantially over the last few years and is the most towny of the Grossraum resorts, with more shops and bars ('friendly, not too trendy') than elsewhere. It attracts more Dutch and German than British skiers, but we have many reporters happy with its low-key friendly family atmosphere. The centre is compact, but the resort sprawls widely up the hillside between the valley station of the main lift on the west – an efficient funicular to Hartkaiser – and an enormous area of nursery slopes spreading across to Going on the east; you need to pick your location. The Pension St Christoph is very convenient for access to the funicular and has suited many visitors, but the recent abysmal treatment of one reporter by the hotel's management has made us wary of recommending it. The Claudia ('quiet and comfortable') is a good alternative. The Sport is recommended for families. There are at least two discos; bowling alleys, curling rinks and a good swimming pool in various hotels; and a 3km toboggan run and ski bob run. The Rendez-vous pub is quite lively, as is the Buchinger Stuberl, which has a real mountain-hut atmosphere. The ski instructors gather in the Memory bar; verdicts on their daytime performance vary. A new ski school opened last season, no doubt introducing a welcome element of competition. Recent reports speak well of the lack of lift queues, but not so well of the 'atrocious' ski-bus service, which many reporters found useless.

Tourist office ✆ (5358) 2307. **Package holidays** Crystal (hr) Enterprise (h) Inghams (h) Kings Ski Club (j) Neilson (hr) Sally Holidays (h) SkiBound (h) Thomson (hr) Waymark (h).

Going 800m

Going is a charming rustic village with the Goinger Bach flowing through between its mellow old chalets. Its mountain, Astberg, is low (1267m) and connected to the rest of the Grossraum skiing only at resort level (Ellmau) – a connection recently much improved by a chair-lift from the Ellmau funicular station across to the flanks of Astberg. One reporter who wishes he had discovered Going (and skiing) 60 years ago warmly recommends the 'cosy and very inexpensive' Retthäusl. The Schablwirt has recently been upgraded. Après-ski is confined to sleigh and toboggan rides.

Tourist office ✆ (5358) 2438. **Package holidays** Enterprise (h).

Westendorf 790m

Westendorf is a small village (though big enough to justify a ski-bus) in the Brixental, within sight of the Grossraum skiing but not linked to it. It attracts numerous British (and Irish) skiers, but also Dutch and German ones. Practically all our reporters agree that it is a very friendly and charming village, though some old hands complain that it is becoming too busy and boisterous. There is certainly plenty of nightlife, both imported (Andy's disco, Andy's piano bar, Gerry's Inn) and traditional. The local skiing is a small area of mostly easy runs, reached by an efficient two-stage gondola going up from the very extensive nursery slopes at the edge of the village (about five minutes' gentle walk from the centre) to about 1800m. It is pretty skiing, on broad, mostly woodland pistes and snow-covered roads, and suits inexperienced or leisurely skiers very well. Two short black runs parallel to the gondola add some challenge for experts. Beyond the top gondola station is a further area of intermediate skiing on Fleiding mountain (1890m) reached by the new Talkaser four-seat chair-lift. Snow-guns are apparently going to be installed on the lower runs for this season. There are several pleasant restaurants on the mountain.

In the daytime there is not much to do other than ski, though there are beautiful walks in the area, open-air skating and plenty of excursion possibilities. The key factor in choice of accommodation is remoteness from the church, whose bells wake the dead at 6.45am. The Haus Wetti ('friendly, good value') meets this criterion. Most people stay in small family-run pensions or B&Bs, which offer simple, clean accommodation at very reasonable prices. Recommendations include the Ingeborg (next to the gondola station), Pension Schneerose (handy for the nursery slopes), Zirmheim (friendly B&B, 10 minutes from village centre) and the Alpenhof. Tables often need to be reserved for evening meals in the village restaurants; reporters recommend the Wastlhof ('quiet, congenial and reasonably priced') and Chez Yves ('best in town, on the square'). The Lendwirt, three miles west of the village in a narrow river valley, serves delicious trout. We have a number of positive reports on the ski school, though classes tend to be on the large side.

Tourist office ✆ (5334) 6230. Tx 51237.

Package holidays Crystal (h) Enterprise (h) Horizon (hs) Inghams (h) Neilson (hr) Ski Global (hrs) Thomson (hr).

For want of a better name

Niederau Austria 830m

Good for *Easy runs, nursery slopes, cross-country skiing, family holidays, short airport transfers, easy road access, woodland runs*
Bad for *Tough runs, late holidays, resort-level snow*

Separate resorts: Oberau, Auffach

Wildschönau is a savage-sounding name, but it is attached to an area of mainly amiable skiing on low, mostly wooded mountains south of the Inn valley, between Alpbach and Söll. The area embraces several resorts, all very small. Niederau is the main one on the UK market – a sprawling village at the foot of one of the two small main ski areas, its modern hotels and guest-houses built in traditional style but with no central focus. As Tyrolean villages go, it is not particularly charming – but it can be convenient, with skiing to some hotel doors. One reporter describes it as 'an unsophisticated family resort, unchanged since we first visited almost 15 years ago'. The skiing is limited in extent and challenge, but offers plenty of scope for beginners and timid intermediates.

The valley road climbs gently beyond Niederau to a low col on which sits Oberau, a more established and attractive village with its own nursery slopes. Beyond it, around a bend in the valley, is Auffach, a tiny but growing village with a gondola up to the Schatzberg (1900m).

The skiing top 1900m bottom 830m

The skiing immediately above **Niederau** is in two small areas, each reached initially by a chair-lift from the valley. You can ski from the higher Lanerköpfl to the lower Markbachjoch.

The chair-lift for Lanerköpfl leaves from the western extremity of Niederau. The two runs from it are graded red, and the more westerly one (which connects with the Lanerköpfl drag) is given the status of skiroute, which we hope is an excuse for not grooming the run rather than not patrolling it. In practice they are both good intermediate trails through the trees. The top drag-lift to Lanerköpfl itself serves a short slope which is not a lot steeper, but is graded black.

From the top an easy-intermediate run, with some leg-work involved, links with Markbachjoch, where, beyond the hotels and restaurants and linking lifts, there are two drag-lifts serving a sunny open slope, correctly graded blue. From the lower of these two easterly lifts, a run goes through the trees down to a drag on the lower slopes above an outpost of the village, or on to the village itself. A central section is sensibly graded red, but the run as a whole is harmless. Steeper runs go down directly from Markbachjoch to the village. There is a black skiroute variant on the attractive main red run, but it is not difficult. Nor, in terms of steepness, is the black route down under the chairs.

The **Auffach** gondola goes up from a busy car park area south of the village. Its top section is duplicated by a very long drag-lift. Parallel drags on the high open flank of the Schatzberg serve easy slopes of around 200m vertical and give access to long off-piste runs to the valley, outside the piste network. The slope under the gondola is properly graded red – much of it is easy, but occasional pitches are moderately steep. At the top and middle stations there are worthwhile drag-lifts on the northern flanks of the mountain which do serve easy runs, but there is no genuinely easy way back to the village.

Many skiers have lunch in the villages; the hotel Alpenland is very popular. There are **mountain restaurants** in both main ski areas, but they tend to be overcrowded. The one at the top of the Markbachjoch chair has stunning views and reasonable food.

There may be **queues** for the village lifts at ski school time. A couple of reporters have been surprised to find 'tricky red sections on many blue runs'. The area has no **artificial snow**.

The resort

Niederau spreads across the gentle north-facing slope at the foot of its skiing, with no very clear distinction between village and not-village. All the buildings have a veneer of chalet style applied, but it is a thin one.

Most of the **accommodation** is in hotels and guest-houses, with which our reporters have no complaint. The smartest in the village (there are also hotels up the mountain) is the big, comfortable, central Austria – 'without doubt the place to stay,' says one reporter. Another very central hotel is the Staffler – 'excellent for children and very reasonably priced'. A little further from the lifts is the Sonnschein – 'food very good, service excellent'. The Gasthof Wastlhof at the western end of the village is 'comfortable and friendly, with excellent traditional food'.

Small though it is, the village does not lack lively **après-ski** in its tea rooms, cafés, bars and discos, largely based in hotels. The Vicky is still one of the pivots of the nightlife and has live music on Tuesdays and Thursdays ('go early if you want a seat'). Also recommended are the Alm pub ('fairly traditional with a good compère') and the popular Cave bar. The Tennladen is a particularly good restaurant.

Non-skiers who are not content to potter along gentle paths between the villages will find the Wildschönau limited. A recent visitor was disappointed in the horse-riding, after booking three days in advance for an expensive hour in a small indoor school. The **cross-country** trails linking the villages are attractive and varied, and those beyond Auffach at Schönanger are peaceful and pretty.

There are **nursery slopes** right next to the village which represent a reasonable compromise between sun and snow. More extensive slopes can be found at Oberau. Views on the **ski school** are generally favourable – 'excellent English- speaking tuition and a good mix of activities' – but the groups tend to be fairly large (10 to 15 people). The **kindergarten** has a flexible arrangement with the ski school for skiing toddlers; a reporting parent was very happy with the arrangements.

Facts on Niederau Tirol **Austria**

Prices in schillings

Tourist office
Postcode A-6311
Tel (5339) 8255
Fax (5339) 2433
Tlx 51139

Getting there
By road 1,114km from Calais. Via Munich; chains rarely needed.
By rail Wörgl (7km), 9 daily buses from station.
By air Salzburg; transfer 2hr. (Or Munich; transfer about 2hr.)

Staying there
Visitor beds 2,900; breakdown: mainly in hotels and pensions.
Package holidays Enterprise (h) Falcon (hr) Horizon (h) Inghams (h) Neilson (h) Ski Europe (h) Ski Global (h) Thomson (h) .
Medical facilities In resort: Doctor, chemist. Hospital: Wörgl (7km). Dentist: Oberau (3km).

Non-skiing activities
Indoor Sauna and solarium (between Oberau and Niederau), bowling (in hotel).
Outdoor Curling, horse sleigh rides, floodlit toboggan runs, horse-riding, cleared paths.

Kindergartens
Gastekindergarten
Tuition: No. Hours: 9.30-4.30. Ages: over 2. Cost: 1,460.00 per week (with lunch).

Special skiing facilities
Summer skiing No.

Cross-country Over 35km in total, linking the villages and beyond Auffach at Schönangeralm. Practice track from Oberau and Niederau. Instruction available.

Lift passes
Wildschönau
Covers all lifts in Niederau, Oberau, Auffach and smaller resorts. (37 lifts in total.)
Cost 6 days 1,135.00 (£56.89).
Credit cards accepted Yes.
Senior citizens 735.00 (over 60) saving 35%.
Children 735.00 (under 15) saving 35%.
Notes Discounts for large groups.
Beginners Coupons.
Short-term passes Half-day.
Other periods Passes for 5 days in 7 or 10 days in 14.

Ski school
Ski School Wildschonau
Classes 4hr: 2hr am and pm. Cost: 990.00 (6 days).
Lift priority Yes.
Children's classes Ages: 4 up. Cost: 950.00 (6 days). 15% reduction if parent also taking lessons; 110.00 for lunch-time supervision.
Private lessons available Hourly. Cost: 340.00 per hour. Each additional person 130.00.

What was new in 91
Nothing.

What is new for 92
1. New beginners lift in Niederau planned.
2. Possible installation of snow guns.

Oberau   935m
Oberau is a friendly little village with no direct access to the main ski areas (which are served by a free ski-bus). It has good broad nursery slopes close to hand and slightly further away, along the hillside towards Auffach, at Roggenboden. And it has one short intermediate piste above the main nursery slopes, served by a drag-lift. The resort attracts elderly walkers and cross-country skiers as well as downhill beginners.
Tourist office ℗ (5339) 8255. Tx 51139. **Package holidays** Enterprise (h) Inghams (h) Quality Ski Tours (h) Ski Europe (h) Ski Sutherland (h).

Auffach   870m
Auffach has developed relatively little as a resort, despite its convenience for the major lift in the area. It consists mainly of a fairly tight gathering of chalets around the church, and a line of hotels and guest-houses along the road beyond the gondola station. There is also an elevated outpost at Bernau, with its own nursery lifts and cross-country loops. The Auffacherhof is a comfortable modern chalet hotel, convenient for the gondola and moderately priced. There is a toboggan run from the middle station of the gondola to Bernau.
Tourist office ℗ (5339) 824420. **Package holidays** Enterprise (h) Ski Europe (h) Ski Sutherland (h).

Is love at first sight blind?

Alpbach Austria 1000m

Good for *Alpine charm, family holidays, easy road access, short airport transfers*
Bad for *Tough runs, late holidays, skiing convenience*

Alpbach is a small village in attractive although unspectacular country between Kitzbühel and Innsbruck. Its skiing area is inconveniently located, and is limited in extent, variety and challenge. Yet Alpbach has a special corner in the affections of many British skiers who return year after year to meet their friends, both locals and regular visitors like themselves. Among so many picturesque little Tyrolean villages, Alpbach stands out as one of the prettiest of them all, and it wins visitors over from the moment they arrive (unless they arrive at the same time as a great many other people, and meet one of the small-scale traffic jams to which the village is prone). It is a particularly good place for a family holiday at Christmas, and for beginners, who stand to benefit more than most skiers from its welcoming, charming atmosphere.

As our map makes clear, the ski area of Alpbach is modest in scale – basically only two main mountain slopes, neither measuring more than 4km from top to bottom as an intermediate skier flies. It will not suit the piste-basher reared on the *domaines skiables* of the northern French Alps. But no one should make the mistake of dismissing it as being suitable only for beginners. Provided skiing the same pistes repeatedly does not worry you, there is plenty of interest to be found in Alpbach's several red runs and couple of short blacks. And the lift system has recently been improved appreciably.

Having a car in Alpbach seems rather anti-social, but many visitors (including not a few British visitors) take one; as a result, parking in the village is not easy. A car does help you get to and from skiing, both locally and further afield – expeditions are possible westward to the Zillertal (Mayrhofen, Hintertux) and eastward to Söll or even beyond to Kitzbühel. In Inneralpbach a car is very useful for après-ski purposes.

The skiing top 2025m bottom 830m

Apart from a small nursery area beside the village, all Alpbach's skiing is on the slopes of the Wiedersbergerhorn, a short bus-ride away. The usual starting point is the Achenwirt lift station, beside the road up from Brixlegg. A six-seater gondola has recently replaced the chair-lifts going up from here across wooded north-facing slopes to Hornboden. There are broad trails down either side to the Kriegalm half-way station, including a race-course marked black. From here a red run continues down to the bottom, giving an excellent long, fast course of over 1000m vertical – used by British racing clubs for annual competitions. Around

Hornboden the views are splendid, the terrain is open and gentle, with several short drag-lifts suitable for near-beginners. But this area does not lack steeper slopes, both down the Brandegg drag-lift (marked black) and down the short but efficient three-seater Gmahbahn. There is an easy blue run (mostly pathway) down as far as Kriegalm.

Lifts from Inneralpbach join up with the skiing above Hornboden and serve a long, not very tough red run back down. Two substantial drags have recently been built on the eastern flank of the mountain below the peak of the Wiedersbergerhorn, taking the skiing up to a new high point of 2000m. The higher of these lifts, Hornlift 2000, provides some challenging sunny skiing for intermediates; access to this, and the return to the valley, depends on the long red ski-route leading down to Inneralpbach. Conditions on this run are not off-piste for long, and neither this nor the added possibility of skiing over the hill to Hygna (buses back) make Alpbach a resort for ski adventurers.

There are several **mountain restaurants**; the self-service one at Hornboden has been recently extended to include 'an excellent new *à la carte* restaurant upstairs, with a sunny balcony'; it can easily be reached by non-skiers. The Gmah restaurant, just down from the top of the mountain, is also popular, as are the restaurants down in the valleys at Achenwirt and Inneralpbach.

Queues are generally not a problem except first thing in the morning and at busy weekends for access to the Wiedersbergerhorn. There is artificial snow on one nursery run and on one run down to Reith.

The resort

Alpbach is a small village in a sunny position set on an elevated and quite steep hillside, but compact enough for that not to matter too much, even in ski boots. At the heart of the village is its spotlessly clean green-and-white church, surrounded by traditional chalet buildings large and small. Tradition is a very evident part of Alpbach life, especially at Christmas and New Year, which is when many of Alpbach's family regulars prefer to visit. A good many such regulars are British; there is even a British ski club, the Alpbach Visitors, based in the resort. Regular

---

Facts on Alpbach Tirol Austria

Prices in schillings

Tourist office
Postcode A-6236
Tel (5336) 5211
Fax (5336) 5012
Tlx 51380

Getting there
By road 1,127km from Calais. Via Munich; chains rarely needed.
By rail Brixlegg (10km) 7 daily Postbuses to Alpbach.
By air Innsbruck; transfer 1hr. (Or Munich; transfer about 2hr.)

Staying there
Visitor beds 2,400; breakdown: 700 in hotels and guest-houses, 1,700 in apartments.
Package holidays Enterprise (h) Horizon (h) Inghams (h) Made to Measure (hs) Ski Europe (h) Ski Global (hs) Ski Sutherland (h) Ski Unique (h) Thomson (h) .
Medical facilities In resort: Doctor, chemist (at doctor's). Dentist: Brixlegg (9 km). Hospital: Wörgl (28km).

Non-skiing activities
Indoor Swimming, sauna, solarium, massage, museum of mountain farming.
Outdoor 20km cleared paths, skating, curling, horse-sleigh rides, toboggan runs.

Kindergartens
Rudi Lederer
Tuition: Yes. Hours: 9.30-4.15. Ages: 4 up. Cost: 1,650.00 per week (with lunch).

Special skiing facilities
Summer skiing No.
Cross-country 17km of trails near Inneralpbach.

Instruction available.

Lift passes
Alpbachtal
Covers all lifts in the Alpbach valley and the ski bus. (21 lifts in total.)
Cost 6 days 1,090.00 (£54.64). Low season: 1,040.00 saving 5%.
Credit cards accepted No.
Senior citizens 750.00 (over 65) saving 31%.
Children 740.00 (under 15) saving 32%. Free pass up to age 6.
Beginners Points tickets.
Short-term passes Half-day passes (am or pm); hourly reductions on passes bought after 11.00am.
Other periods Passes for 5 days out of 7 and 7 days out of 10.

Ski school
Rudi Lederer
Classes 4hr: 2hr am and pm. Cost: 1,050.00 (6 days).
Lift priority No.
Children's classes Ages: up to 14. Cost: 1,050.00 (6 days).
Private lessons available Per hour. Cost: 350.00 per hour. Each additional person 120.00.
Special courses Ski touring on Saturdays.
Tiroler
Classes 2 or 4 hr per day. Cost: 1,020.00 (6 days). 6 half-days 760.00.
Lift priority No.
Children's classes Ages: 5 to 14. Cost: 920.00 (6 days). 1,430.00 with lunch and supervision.
Private lessons available Per hour (and only outside ski school hours). Cost: 340.00 per hour.
Special courses Combined deep snow and ski touring course (5 day course 1,950.00); powder course (100.00 per day).

visitors have noticed a lot of new building recently. Shopping is limited, although the two Spar supermarkets are 'well stocked'. There are a couple of shops in Inneralpbach.

The free ski-bus to Achenwirt runs frequently enough for the needs of the small village, but gets crowded in the mornings; the service to Inneralpbach is frequent until mid-morning.

Accommodation is mostly in hotels, with a wide variety of comfort and cost between simple B&B houses and spacious, very comfortable hotels. The centre of the village is the most convenient for the ski-bus, but location isn't a serious worry. The three most comfortable hotels (all with pools) are the Böglerhof, and the less central Alphof and Alpbacherhof – the last recommended by two reporters ('lovely room, caring staff, especially considerate of my young children'). Among less expensive hotels, reporters recommend the Post, the Haus Elisabeth, the Haus Angelika and the Haus Erna. Keen skiers may prefer to stay in Inneralpbach – 'very quiet, ideal for families' (though there is a disco). One reporter recommends the Galtenberg as being pleasant and ideally situated for the lifts. For direct access to the gondola there is no beating the old Gasthof Achenwirt, with simple rooms above its panelled *stube*.

Après-ski has all the typically Tyrolean ingredients – notably the Tyrolean Evening itself, plus sleigh rides, skating and curling, bowling, very lively tea-time bars in central hotels (notably the Messnerwirt and Jakober) and a disco in the Alphof Hotel, fifteen minutes' walk from the centre. This may sound like a wide choice, but devotees of Mayrhofen or Kitzbühel would find the diet monotonous. Reporters staying on B&B found little variety of restaurants – most are in hotels. Several reports this year have warmly recommended the Reblaus, a cellar restaurant in the Haus Elisabeth. There is a new pub, the Waschstub'n, next to the Jakober, which is apparently open until 3am for late-night revellers. Inneralpbach has a couple of lively bars (particularly the Hornbeisl) and live music at the Galtenberg twice a week.

Cross-country skiers should stay in Inneralpbach. The trails are low and not entirely reliable for snow, but very attractive. **Non-skiers** can enjoy plenty of attractive walks, although not many within rendezvous range of skiers – one reporter suggests trying organized 'Gourmet walks' ('all day wandering around the valley sampling farmers' fare and schnapps'). There is a wide choice of interesting excursions (Salzburg, Kitzbühel, Innsbruck, and over the Brenner Pass to Vipiteno in Italy). The public swimming pool and sauna are good, but a long walk from the centre of the village, as is the ice rink and health centre.

The **nursery slopes** close to the village centre are very good, being sunny and offering a variety of terrain from flat to slightly challenging. When snow is short, as it may be on this south-facing shelf, beginners are taken up to Hornboden.

We have had generally favourable reports on the **ski schools** ('very rewarding, our instructor was a real character') and glowing reports on the children's classes and the kindergarten facilities. Hours coincide with adult classes, which is often not the case elsewhere. Guides are available for day ski tours (with skins).

Still waiting

Mayrhofen Austria 630m

Good for *Not skiing, après-ski, easy road access, rail access, short airport transfers*
Bad for *Tough runs, lift queues, skiing convenience, woodland runs, resort-level snow*

Linked resort: Finkenberg
Separate resort: Lanersbach

Mayrhofen remains one of the great British favourites in Austria although several reporters have found it less Anglo-dominated than we had led them to expect. It enjoys a splendid setting enclosed by the steep wooded walls of the Zillertal (a busy, touristy valley of which Mayrhofen is the main focus), its hotels are clean and comfortable, there is lots to do off the slopes and plenty of evening action in the bars and discos. Its popularity must rest on these things (and on the reputation of the ski school, particularly its caring for young children), because the large, towny resort is only moderately attractive and its skiing is far from ideal – being limited in variety for experienced skiers and yet awkward for the inexperienced, who have to take cable-cars to and from skiing, and notoriously queue-prone. These are important drawbacks in the era of purpose-built resorts, and in the past reporters have been almost unanimous in recommending Mayrhofen only to inexperienced skiers and in remarking on the length of the lift queues. 'Enough to put you off skiing for life – in Mayrhofen anyway' writes a recent reporter.

Improvements have been made. The Zillertaler Superskipass opens up enormous possibilities within day-trip range; school hours are designed to relieve the pressure on the main lifts up to and back from the skiing; and new lifts have been built giving speedier access to the main ski area from other points in the valley.

Mayrhofen does not generally suffer the snow problems common to many other low Tyrolean resorts, because most skiers have to spend most of their time on the sunny slopes at the top of the ski area; so although it is hardly an ideal late-season resort – its skiing does not reach 2300m – it is not merely an early-season resort either.

South of Mayrhofen the Zillertal splits into three small glacier valleys and the Tuxertal – a high, narrow valley, very different from the broad Zillertal. Several small resorts line the road up to and along it. Just above Mayrhofen, Finkenberg is a cramped village sharing Mayrhofen's main ski area, the Penken. Vorderlanersbach and Lanersbach have plans to link up with the same lift system, and already have interesting skiing of their own. For keen skiers happy or even eager to forgo après-ski, these resorts have the advantage over Mayrhofen of easier access to the excellent glacier skiing of Hintertux, described in the next chapter. Mayrhofen also has bus services to Hintertux, but like the lifts

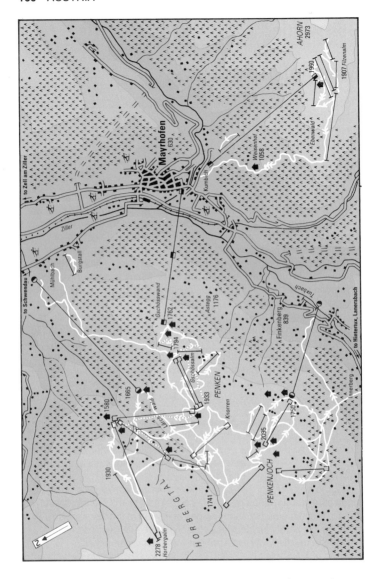

they are oversubscribed: having a car is an enormous advantage for skiers wanting to make the most of the region. Mayrhofen is the terminus of the Zillertal railway, which can be used to get to Zell or down to the Inn valley.

The skiing top 2278m bottom 640m

Mayrhofen skiing is on two separate mountains enclosing the Zillertal with their steep, wooded walls. The main skiing is on the Penken, reached by cable-car from the resort centre or by gondola from Schwendau (a bus-ride away to the north) or from Finkenberg (to the south). The Ahorn, on the other side of Mayrhofen, is accessible only by cable-car from a point which is a long walk from the centre of the village. For all these lifts (except Finkenberg's) there is a regular free ski-bus; but it is often over-subscribed – in particular, it cannot cope with crowds coming down the Horberg gondola in the afternoon.

The **Ahorn** faces mainly west, but so gentle are the slopes around the top of the cable-car that orientation doesn't matter much. This is an excellent open, spacious beginners' area, with a broad and beautiful panorama. There is one run down from the upper slopes to the bottom, the top of it served by drag-lift. This trail through the woods is graded red, but only as far as a restaurant (served by occasional buses). The steeper, but not extreme, bottom stretch is officially off-piste.

For most skiers, Mayrhofen skiing means the **Penken**. The notoriously crowded cable-car climbs over an unskiable wooded mountainside to a shelf at the top of the trees; chair-lifts starting an awkward distance from the top of the cable-car then go up to Penkenjoch. From Penken there is a long ungraded run, some of it difficult, down to the bottom of the Horberg gondola: excellent skiing for good skiers in good snow (which is rare). The main skiing area consists of a relatively narrow band of open and lightly wooded skiing on the north and south sides of the wide ridge that peaks at the rounded Penkenjoch, where there are merry ice bars and restaurants. The runs are short and mostly more red than blue, with easier ones (and some nursery slopes) back along the ridge towards Penken. A easy run links Penken and the top of the Horberg lift, allowing inexperienced skiers to take the gondola down at the end of the day. From just below the gondola, a chair-lift climbs up to 2278m on the sunny Gerent side of the Horbergtal. Apart from the sunshine, the interest of the area is the unpisted run underneath the chairs, relatively long and steep (about 27°), usually mogulled and littered with bodies. It branches right half-way down to the top of the Tappenalmchair, from where it is possible to connect (via two baby drags) to the chair-lifts back to Penkenjoch. There is a red run back down to Finkenberg, mostly path.

The Penken has a liberal scattering of **mountain restaurants**, most of which are sunny and attractive. But they can be crowded and noisy – a reporter recommends making for the extreme ends of the system (Horbergalm and Penkenjoch) for more peace. A couple of people have recommended the Vronis Skialm at the top of the Penkenjoch. There is a popular new restaurant at Gerent though reports suggest that it is expensive. Crowds are even more of a problem on the Ahorn, where there is only one restaurant. Going down to the resort for lunch is not something you want to do if you can avoid it.

The problem of serious **queues** for Mayrhofen's cable-cars has been only partly relieved by the installation of the gondola up to the Penken skiing from Finkenberg and by a ski school scheme which offers a choice of morning, afternoon or all-day lessons – a recent reporter sums up the high season thus: 'start queueing at 8 to be up at Penken by 10; get down at 6 if you ski later than 3.30'. We also hear of two-hour waits for Ahorn (coming down as well as going up) and pretty long queues for the Horberg gondola too. Improving access to Penken can only increase the considerable high-season congestion there (in restaurants and on pistes, as well as on lifts).

There is an increasing amount of **artificial snow** on Penken's nursery slopes and intermediate runs, but not on the run down to the valley.

The resort

Mayrhofen is a large traditional-looking Tyrolean village with many handsome painted and timbered buildings. It is not totally given over to tourism, but the long, wide main street between the market place near the station and the Penken cable-car is busy and touristy. The main valley road by-passes the resort centre and, although there are always plenty of cars around, congestion isn't unpleasant. There is no evening public transport. It is a lively place, full of young people; the 'fun resort' atmosphere is the main reason for Mayrhofen's enduring popularity.

Accommodation is mostly in attractive, traditionally styled hotels (with traditionally clad staff), and most reports we have are favourable, although light sleepers are advised to avoid the Sporthotel and the Brücke, which are well placed for the lifts but also uncomfortably close to the noisiest night spots. One reporter had stayed in four different cheap B&B houses and found them all excellent. Another suggests the Gastehaus Binder as a cheap, pleasant and convenient guest-house, its only drawback being the communal showers. The large Neuhaus is central, calmer and highly rated by reporters although less beautiful inside than out. The Elisabeth, just off the main street, is the most luxurious and expensive hotel in the town, and has had favourable reports, as have the Kramerwirt and the Kristall – 'a small and friendly hotel with balconies overlooking the mountains'. The St George, five minutes' walk from the centre, is also popular and has its own pool and sauna. We have several enthusiastic reports of the Strass, ideally placed for the Penken cable car, but one highly critical – particularly of the food served to package holiday-makers.

Après-ski is very lively either side of an 8-11pm hiatus for dinner. There are venues for traditional live music as well as deafening discos, and tobogganing, sleigh-riding and Tyrolean evenings are regularly organised by operators. Hotel bars see most of the après-skiing custom, though they are not very atmospheric; the great British haunts are the Sporthotel ('as inviting as an airport lounge'), the more pub-like Scotland Yard ('recommended if you fancy imitating a sardine in a tin'), and the Schlüssel, probably the best of the Mayrhofen discos. There is a less British, less noisy and less anonymous style of local nightlife: the

Kramerwirt's Andreas Keller has a live band for cheek-to-cheek dancing, and at the Elisabeth's stylish nightclub seated conversation is possible. Most guests eat in the hotel restaurants, though there are several cheap and cheerful places about town, especially the Grillkuchel which serves 'excellent good-value food, though you may have to wait

---

Facts on Mayrhofen Tirol **Austria**

Prices in schillings
Ski Club represented

Tourist office
Postcode A-6290
Tel (5285) 2305
Fax: (5285) 230533
Tlx 533850

Getting there
By road 1,200km from Calais. Via Munich; chains rarely needed.
By rail Local line through in resort; 25 daily buses from station.
By air Munich; transfer 2hr. (Or Innsbruck; transfer about 1hr.)

Staying there
Visitor beds 8,000; breakdown: mainly in hotels and pensions.
Package holidays Austro Tours (h) Crystal (hr) Enterprise (h) Falcon (hr) Horizon (h) Hoverspeed Ski-Drive (s) Inghams (h) Neilson (hr) Quest Travel (schools) (h) Sally Holidays (hr) Ski Global (h) Ski Party Snow World (h) Snobiz (h) Snowcoach Club Cantabrica (hrc) Thomson (h) .
Medical facilities In resort: Doctors, dentists, chemist. Hospital: Schwaz (40km).

Non-skiing activities
Indoor Bowling, 3 hotel pools open to the public, massage, sauna, jacuzzi, Turkish baths (in hotels, but open to non-residents), squash, 4 fitness centres, chess, tennis centre at Hotel Berghof (3 courts, coaching available), riding-school (150.00 per hour), pool and billiards, stamp- swapping, cinema..
Outdoor Natural skating-rink, curling, horse-riding, horse and dog sleigh rides and racing, 45km cleared paths, hang-gliding, paragliding, tobogganing (2 runs of 2.5km).

Kindergartens
Riki's (Spiess)
Tuition: Yes. Hours: 9.00-4.00. Ages: 4-12. Cost: 1,650.00 per week (with lunch and supervision). At the Ahorn.
Dwarfland (Gager)
Tuition: Yes. Hours: 9.00-4.00. Ages: 4-14. Cost: 1,650.00 per week (with lunch and supervision). At the Penken.
Wuppy's Childrenland
Tuition: Possible. Hours: 8.30-5.00 Sun to Fri. Ages: 3mth-7yr. Cost: 1,300.00 per week (with lunch).
Other childcare facilities
Trial ticket for 4-6 year olds 485.00; baby-sitting

available, contact Tourist Office.

Special skiing facilities
Summer skiing Large and interesting area at Hintertux – see separate chapter.
Cross-country 20km of nine easy trails along valley floor to Zell am Ziller. One trail floodlit. Instruction available.

Lift passes
Zillertal Superskipass
Covers all lifts in Ziller valley, including the Hintertux glacier, ski bus and Ziller Valley railway. (151 lifts in total.)
Cost 6 days 1,500.00 (£75.19).
Credit cards accepted No.
Children 900.00 (under 15) saving 40%. Free pass up to age 6.
Short-term passes Half-day for Mayrhofen only pass.
Other passes Superskipass without Hintertux glacier (6 days 1,280.00 for adults, 770.00 for children); Skipass Mahrhofen, covers all lifts belonging to the Mayrhofen Cableways: the Ahornbahn and Penkenbahn cable-cars and the Horbergbahn gondola, and their respective chair-lifts and drag-lifts (per day 250.00 for adults, 150.00 for children).

Ski school
Spiess
Classes 10.00-12.00 and/or 1.00-3.00. Cost: 1,140.00 (6 days). 6 half-days cost 790.00; special small classes (4-7 people) cost 2,100.00 for 6 full days.
Lift priority No.
Children's classes Ages: 4-14. Cost: 1,140.00 (6 days).
Private lessons available Hourly. Cost: 350.00 per hour. 2 people 500.00, 3 people 750.00.
Special courses Yeti Club and High-Life Programme – huge range of courses available, 6 days 790.00, 2hr per day.
Gager
Classes 10.00-12.00 and/or 1.30-3.30. Cost: 1,140.00 (6 days). 6 half-days cost 790.00; special small classes (4-7 people) cost 2,100.00 for 6 full days.
Lift priority No.
Children's classes Ages: 4-14. Cost: 1,140.00 (6 days).
Private lessons available Hourly. Cost: 350.00 per hour. Each additional person 150.00.
Special courses Yeti Club and High-Life Programme.

What was new in 91
New artificial snow on the Penken.

for a table'. The pizzeria on the main street serves food late and has an enthusiastic live band.

One **cross-country** skiing reporter was well pleased with the long valley floor trails, but they are mostly easy and not reliable for snow cover. Mayrhofen is a good place for **non-skiers**, although the pool is small and the natural ice unreliable. Walks are clearly signed and good maps are readily available, and there are plenty of attractive excursions, within the local area and further afield to Innsbruck and Salzburg. Several people have mentioned the excellent Tourist Office, which is very well   stocked with local information.

Nursery slopes on the Ahorn are excellent – sunny, high, and pleasantly free from bombers on skis. Even so, the slopes, lifts and restaurant are often crowded, as is the cable-car up and down. The small nursery area on the Penken, often used by the adult ski school, is more convenient for meeting up with other skiers.

The Spiess **ski school**, Mayrhofen's pride and joy, now faces competition in the form of the Gager school – similar uniform, similar prices, similar hours. Most operators still use Spiess. Reports vary from 'absolutely superb' to 'Uli Spiess is living on his reputation', but are generally favourable. Many reporters had Australasian instructors, and appreciated them. We still hear of large classes despite tourist office denials. Both schools have all-day **kindergartens**, also highly satisfactory.

Lanersbach   1300m

At the entrance to the Tuxertal, and at about 1300m, Lanersbach and Vorderlanersbach share a wide skiing area in two halves, linked in both directions. A double-chair from Lanersbach takes you up to the skiing on Scheidegg (2030m) which is pleasantly open and uncrowded and includes enjoyable, fast and fairly long runs served by a series of drags. Runs down to the village are easier and more reliable for snow than those to Mayrhofen. A triple chair from Vorderlanersbach, just down the road, gives access to the Lammerbichl skiing, above the tree-line – wide, open and mostly gentle. From here a drag-lift and chair take you up to the Wanglspitz at nearly 2500m. A projected lift will eventually connect this area with the Penkenjoch and Mayrhofen's skiing, which will greatly increase the appeal of Lanersbach (the largest and most attractive of the villages in the Tux valley) as a base for skiers; at present it is possible to get across to the Penken only by skiing off-piste. Accommodation is largely in pretty chalet-style guest-houses, and there are a number of bars and cafés, hotel facilities open to the public and a ski school and kindergarten.

Tourist office ✆ (5287) 606. Fax (5287) 60629 Tx 5239111.
Package holidays Alpine Tours (hr)

Deep-freeze delights

Hintertux Austria 1500m

Good for *Late holidays, summer skiing, beautiful scenery, resort-level snow*
Bad for *Nursery slopes, skiing convenience, après-ski, not skiing, tough runs, woodland runs*

Near the head of the Tuxertal (an offshoot of the Zillertal, of which the major resort is Mayrhofen) lies Hintertux, a quiet and rather sunless spa blessed with one of the best glacier ski areas in the Alps. On several visits we have been impressed by the extent, beauty and variety of the skiing (with much more challenge than is common on glaciers). Normally, it is also relatively free of serious queues. But, despite its remote location 50km from the main east-west Inn valley, Hintertux serves as a safety-net for many resorts, and when Austrian snow is in short supply, it can become crowded at peak times. Many reporters have mentioned long lift queues, crowded restaurants and pistes resembling the M25 on a bank holiday, probably because they have resorted to Hintertux for safety-net purposes. As a place to stay, there is no denying its limitations: there is very little to do other than ski, and in bad weather residents must head down the valley in order to do that. The local waters are said to be 'efficacious in the treatment of general exhaustion'.

The skiing top 3250m bottom 1500m

The foot of the Hintertux ski area is about half a mile from the edge of the village. A slow gondola and chair-lift climb in parallel over woods to Sommerbergalm, a sunny platform with restaurants and a small area of easy east-facing skiing directly above it, beneath the Tuxerjoch. The main glacier area is separated from here by a shallow gorge. Its runs are long and the ride up beside the glacier to Gefrorene Wand ('deep-frozen wall') is slow and cold. A three-seater chair-lift on the back of the mountain has opened up 350m vertical of sunnier skiing. There are easy runs near the top of the glacier and down to Tuxerfernerhaus, but the skiing is less uniformly easy than on many glaciers, with fairly tough runs on the western side and below glacier level – over 30° in places, and deserving of the black grading which is now reportedly in evidence on the spot; the piste maps show only reds. A short T-bar returns to Sommerbergalm, from which point there are two runs down – an ungraded route, easy to follow and not very steep, but narrow in places and often difficult, and a red down the western flank of the mountain through the trees. The much more attractive alternative for experienced skiers is to take the Tuxerjoch chair-lift and then traverse an unnervingly steep slope to get to the beautiful run down the bowl of

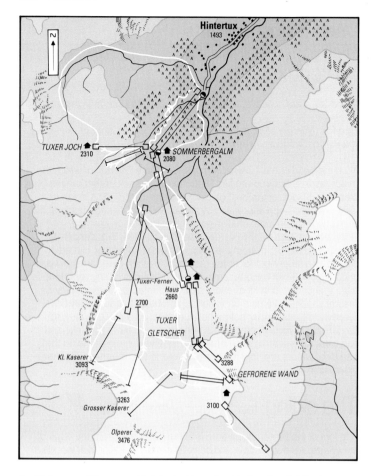

the Schwarze Pfanne – off-piste, but heavily skied and not difficult.

Hintertux **mountain restaurants** are generally uninspiring, and inadequate for the demand in high season. The Spannagelhaus, near the piste below Tuxerfernerhaus, is about the most attractive and least crowded, the Gletscherhütte (just below the top station), recently rebuilt after storm destruction, the most panoramic.

In normal circumstances, the Hintertux glacier is pleasantly free of **queues**. When snow low-down is poor, however, there may be long waits at each stage of the ascent, and for the descent from Sommerbergalm at the end of the day.

Not surprisingly, Hintertux has not installed any **artificial snow.**

The resort

Hintertux is a small spa, without much village atmosphere, at the head of the Tuxertal. Mountains rise steeply to the east, west and south, leaving the village in the shadow for much of the day in mid-winter. Cars and coaches on their way to and from the glacier ski area detract from the charm of the village, as they do all along the Tuxertal. Shopping is limited and there is no bank. Apart from the indoor pool of the Badhotel Kirchler, indoor tennis at the Hintertuxerhof and a good toboggan run down from the Bichlalm restaurant (above the village, out of the ski area), there is little for **non-skiers** to do. Nor is there much **après-ski** once the tea-time open-air disco bar at the foot of the lifts has subsided at about 6pm – just a few cafés, a couple of bars with dancing, and bowling in the Neu Hintertux hotel. The Mühlbach at nearby Juns is

---

Facts on Hintertux   Tirol **Austria**

Prices in schillings

Tourist office
Postcode A-6293
Tel (5287) 6060
Fax (5287) 60629
Tlx 533155

Getting there
By road 1,175km from Calais. Via Munich; chains may be needed.
By rail Station in Mayrhofen (17km), 18 daily buses from station.
By air Munich; transfer 3hr. (Or Innsbruck; transfer about 3hr.)

Staying there
Visitor beds 4,500; breakdown: mainly in hotels and guest houses.
Package holidays Alpine Tours (hr) Austro Tours (h) Snobiz (hr) .
Medical facilities In resort: Doctor and chemist: Lanersbach (5km). Hospital: Schwaz (56km) (5km). Dentist: Mayrhofen (17km).

Non-skiing activities
Indoor Thermal pool, 2 other swimming pools, bowling alleys (in Hintertux and in Lanersbach), fitness centre with hot whirlpools, sauna, solarium, massage, shooting range, tennis hall, squash.
Outdoor 20km walks in Tuxertal, tobogganing (2 tracks, length 3 miles), open-air swimming pool.

Kindergartens
Skikindergarten
Tuition: Yes. Hours: 9.00-4.30. Ages: 4 up. Cost: 1,660.00 per week (without meals).
Gastekindergarten
Tuition: No. Hours: 9.00-4.30. Ages: 2 up. Cost: 1,140.00 per week (with lunch).
Both kindergartens are in Lanersbach.

Special skiing facilities
Summer skiing Extensive area on glacier, embracing much of the winter skiing.
Cross-country 23km trails along valley between Vorderlanersbach and Madseit (about half a mile away). Instruction at Madseit.

Lift passes
Zillertal Superskipass
Covers all lifts in Ziller Valley, including the Hintertux glacier, ski bus and Ziller Valley railway. (151 lifts in total.)
Cost 6 days 1,500.00 (£75.19). Low season: 1,280.00 saving 15%.
Credit cards accepted No.
Children 900.00 (under 15) saving 40%. Free pass up to age 6.
Short-term passes Half-day for Tuxer pass only.
Other passes Tuxer ski pass (Hintertux lifts only) per day 340.00 for adults, 200.00 for children.

Ski school
Hintertux/Madseit
Classes 10.00-12.00 and 1.00-3.00. Cost: 1,090.00 (5 days).
Lift priority No.
Children's classes Ages: 15. Cost: 1,530.00 (5 days). 9.00-3.30.
Private lessons available Hourly. Cost: 360.00 per hour. Each additional person 150.00.
Lanersbach
Classes 10.00-12.00, 1.00-3.00. Cost: 1,180.00 (6 days).
Lift priority No.
Children's classes Ages: 4-12, includes meal. Cost: 1,660.00 (6 days).
Private lessons available Hourly. Cost: 360.00 per hour. Each additional person 150.00.
Special courses 2- and 3-day ski tours around Zillertal.

recommended: 'cheap, with a great atmosphere and dancing into the small hours'. **Cross-country** skiers are better catered for, with a long and reliably snowy trail down the valley.

There is **accommodation** in a few hotels around the village's single square, and at the foot of the lifts about half a mile away, the obvious base for downhillers to choose for convenience. The Rindererhof is comfortable and has a sauna and use of the pool in the Badhotel Kirchler (in the village). Its neighbour, the Neu Hintertux, has bowling and more elaborate facilities (steam bath, sauna, whirlpool and solarium). The Vierjahreszeiten is the least expensive of the ski-convenient hotels, all modern and comfortable. Buses are free for anyone staying locally.

Hintertux has no **nursery slope**. We have had uniformly favourable reports on the **ski school**, based at the first stage on the glacier. They have patient native-English-speaking instructors. One school group leader was extremely impressed with the children's classes. The all-day **kindergarten** is at Lanersbach, quarter of an hour away by bus.

Olympic fame

Innsbruck Austria 575m

This historic city at the cross-roads of western Austria, having twice hosted the Olympics, is a thoroughly equipped winter sports town, with an interesting range of skiing within easy commuting range on the (often over-subscribed) free bus services that radiate from it. The city is an excellent base for excursions (notably to Italy), eating and drinking is cheap by skiing standards, and evening entertainment is quite varied. The most challenging skiing is on the steep and often unfriendly south-facing slopes served by the cable-cars from the edge of Innsbruck (Hungerburg), but a greater extent and range is found on the south side of the valley, above small resorts covered by a joint lift pass. Although all are linked by bus, skiers with cars are obviously better placed to make the most of the possibilities, particularly if staying in one outlying resort and wanting to get to another.

Igls (893m) is traditionally the most popular, and even has a Ski Club rep in residence – it is much the smallest resort in the Alps to enjoy that distinction. The village is small, uncommercialized (shops don't take credit cards) and very easy going. It has sedate hotels and tea shops, beautiful walks and the Olympic bob-run, which is open to the public. Recent reporters have been surprised by the number of Italian and French holidaymakers in the resort.

Most of the hotels are in the centre of the village, a bit of a walk from the cable-car station. The Astoria is an 'excellent family hotel' with slightly tatty decor but good facilities, the Sport hotel is more upmarket and expensive, and the Stenn has good rooms and food. One regular visitor recommends the Batzenhäusl, just outside the village – 'good food, good service, nice bar, sauna and jacuzzi'. Après-ski is limited and largely revolves around hotel bars and restaurants (the Sport hotel has a disco). The bar of the Grüberhof is apparently the liveliest and has a games room – Franz, the barman, remembers all his guest's names from one year to the next. The old favourite, the Pfeffer Mühle Pub, is now a pizza place.

The skiing mainly consists of the downhill race-course where Klammer skied himself into legend – a nicely varied north-facing red run beneath the Patscherkofel (2247m), with easier variants. The nursery slope has artificial snow. There are two ski schools, Schigls and Igls 2000. Both are thoroughly recommended – 'well organised, good tuition, attentive instructors' – but apparently it is hard to find any instruction beyond a basic intermediate level. There do not appear to be any specific facilities for children, and several reporters have commented that the resort is best suited to older groups, particularly those wanting a leisurely pace and a variety of non-skiing and excursion possibilities. There are some pleasant cross-country trails in the vicinity.

Axamer Lizum (1600m) is a characterless ski station – a couple of hotels and a huge car park – in the middle of the most interesting local skiing, beneath the neighbouring peaks of Hoadl (2343m) and Pleisen (2236m). Weekend queues for the lifts can be a problem, but the skiing is extensive and varied, mostly above the trees, and includes a splendid long easy black off Pleisen down to the quiet village of Axams (874m). Across the narrow valley, a chair serves a not-too-severe black run and links up with the long, easy, sunny pistes above the charming, unspoilt village of **Mutters** (830m). Expectations of an improved link to form a 'ski circus' here have not so far been met. A recent reporter writes enthusiastically about the village and the conveniently situated Sport hotel, which has a swimming-pool and sauna. There is not much in the way of nightlife, but some hotel bars have piano players.

Slightly further away, with a separate lift pass, the long **Stubaital** has several small, pretty ski areas, each reportedly with its excellent ski school. There are shared lift pass arrangements. Above the small resort of **Fulpmes** (937m), but not directly accessible from it, there is excellent skiing in a sheltered bowl now branded as Schlick 2000 Skizentrum. Lifts include a recently built four-seater chair going up to 2200m and runs include some tough unpisted ones, but the majority are easy and confidence-building, good for near-beginners. There is a small, sunny nursery area. There are two 'moderately priced' mountain restaurants of which the upper one has a 'marvellous terrace with stupendous views'. There is a good sports centre on the edge of the village, well maintained paths along the valley, and Innsbruck can be reached by a scenic train/tram ride. The resort is generally peaceful at night, but there is apparently life to be found. The Stubaierhof hotel is recommended. The jolly village of **Neustift** (993m) is the valley's main community; 20km beyond it is the Stubai glacier, an extensive area of year-round skiing, with lifts from Mutterberg (1750m) up to 3200m ('wonderful views over the Dolomites'). In winter there are long runs, not all of them easy, down to the mid-station at 2300m, and a tough, unpisted route down to the base station. When snow elsewhere is short, queues (to come down as well as to go up) are long and the valley bus service is understandably stretched. New lifts are apparently planned for next season. Reporters agree that Neustift is a picturesque, friendly place with considerable attractions for those unconcerned about après-ski ('take a good selection of books' says one recent reporter). There is an Après Ski bar and a lively restaurant, the Roma, where a resident DJ plays 'an unusual selection of music' and videos on a big screen. The family-run Stubaier Hof hotel is recommended as is the Tyrollerhof, despite indifferent service. The Mutterberg near the main lifts serves 'excellent food' but is rather isolated unless you have a car. There is a ski school ('small groups, reasonable English spoken') and a kindergarten at the top station of the Eisgrat lift.

Tourist offices: Innsbruck ✆ (5222) 25715, Fulpmes ✆ (5225) 2235, Neustift ✆ 5226) 2228, Igls ✆ (5222)77101.

Package holidays Fulpmes: Alpine Tours (hras) Austrian Holidays (h) Austro Tours (h) Crystal (hr) Ski Sutherland (h). Igls: Austrian Holidays (h) Austro Tours (h) Enterprise (h) Inghams (h) Neilson (h) Quest Total Ski (h). Innsbruck: Austro Tours (h) Enterprise (h) Ski Partners (h) Snobiz (h). Mutters: Austrian Holidays (h) Ski Sutherland (h). Neustift: Alpine Tours (hr) Chalets and Hotels Unlimited (h) Crystal (hrs) Inghams (h) Made to Measure (h) Ski Hillwood (ha).

Seefeld Austria 1200m

Good for *Cross-country skiing, not skiing, rail access, easy road access, short airport transfers, family holidays, woodland runs, artificial snow, lift queues*
Bad for *Skiing convenience, tough runs*

To prevent the suspension of diplomatic relations with the tourist office of this popular resort, we no longer flippantly brand Seefeld as 'Bad for downhill skiing'. But let us be clear: if downhill skiing is your main priority, Seefeld is the last major resort in this guide you should think of visiting. The plain fact is that the terrain around Seefeld is admirably suited to the Nordic sport, and less to the Alpine one. There is some pleasant skiing for intermediates who are content with a limited skiing terrain set in attractive scenery. There are a couple of black off-piste runs, but they do not amount to enough to satisfy the adventurous skier. But the resort complements its skiing attractions with a range of non-skiing facilities second to none, and has thus secured its popularity with affluent elderly Germans. For beginners, it has the attraction that there is lots for ski school drop-outs to do instead of skiing.

The resort has been very deliberately developed over recent decades in typically thorough Tyrolean style for a particular purpose, which it meets admirably. Like a number of other Austrian resorts, its chalet-style buildings are too big and too modern to make the place 'good for Alpine charm', but it is easy on the eye. Several reporters have thought prices high by Austrian standards.

The resort is easily reached by car, and the nearby Inn Valley motorway gives speedy access to lots of other Tyrolean resorts. But expeditions can also be organised by rail.

The skiing top 2074m bottom 1180m

There are two quite separate skiing areas. The Rosshütte to the east is for the more serious skier, while the Gschwandtkopf is a low conical peak south of the village centre, used principally by the ski school. The two are connected to each other, and to other points in the village, by a free circular ski-bus service in each direction, starting at 9.30am. Anyone on skis much before 10am is something of an early bird.

The skiing at **Gschwandtkopf** is chiefly concentrated on a broad, north-facing slope which rises for 300m between thick woods, starting from just beyond the sports centre. Chairs and drags serve a single slope on which even the most timid intermediate can happily take a safe course, but on which steeper sections can be found. On one side of the slope you can test your skill on a coin-in-the-slot timed slalom course. There is also a chair-lift from Reith, on the eastern side of the mountain.

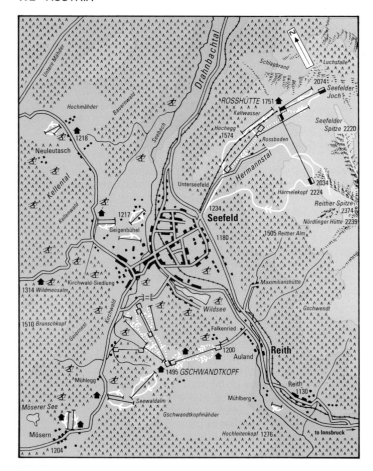

The pleasant run down this side is slightly more demanding.

The starting point for the **Rosshütte** ski area is on the eastern edge of the village beside the by-pass, about 1km from the centre. A funicular railway follows a fairly gentle gradient for about 3km up to the Rosshütte (1750m). There are some easy blue runs served by a couple of drag-lifts on the wide area of piste around Rosshütte, or you can take a short cable-car to the summit of the Seefelder Joch (2074m) with some fine views at the top. A parallel drag-lift also goes almost to the top. A couple of good, though shortish, red runs bring you back to Rosshütte. From here the long path back through the woods to the foot of the railway is an almost flat schuss, but there is now the alternative of a red run down into the Hermannstal, served by a double chair-lift. Adventurous skiers will want to take the small cable-car from Rosshütte which travels high across the Hermannstal to a shoulder of the Harmelekopf at just over 2000m. A short climb to the left then gives access to a couple of steep off-piste runs leading to the flat valley floor, and so back to the railway. The conventional route down from the Harmelekopf descends the shoulder as a nice open red run (watch for worn areas near the top) until at the trees it becomes another schuss.

There are adequate **mountain restaurants** at top and bottom of the main skiing areas, but most people eat lunch in the village. We have had complaints about very slow service at the top of the Gschwandtkopf. There are plenty of sun-terraces, largely for the benefit of non-skiers – though you have to pay for a seat. Rosshütte is particularly popular for basking and views. On the cross-country circuit, one reporter has recommended the Wildmoosalm for 'great schnapps'.

The lift system presents no particular problems with **queues**, even at busy times, though weekend invasions from Munich in good weather can cause delays for the nursery lifts as well as the funicular.

There is **artificial snow** on practically the whole of the Gschwandtkopf, and on most of one long run from Seefelder Joch.

The resort

Seefeld spreads across a broad plateau a few hundred metres above (and a few km to the north of) the Inn valley. There are wooded hills (they can hardly be called mountains) to the south and west, and the more pronounced peaks of the Seefelder Spitze and Reither Spitze to the east. Much of the resort's area is rather suburban-feeling, and the village centre proper is entirely to the south-west of the railway station. The streets forming the central cross-roads are traffic-free, and lined by comfortable, neat hotels and by tourist shops of a kind unseen in more single-minded ski resorts – shoes, jewels, antiques. Because skiing does not rule the lives of visitors, there are always people about – but the place remains calm, with voices never raised above a murmur.

There is all sorts of **accommodation** in abundance. Location should be considered with some care, according to how you plan to spend your time. The central area is convenient for the sports centre, and it's only a short walk out to the ski-bus route. Right on the central crossroads is the friendly old Tiroler Weinstube, more affordable than the Post and the smart Alpenhotel Lamm nearby. There are several hotels between the crossroads and the sports centre. If money is no object, the big Klosterbräu has most of the facilities you could want under one roof. Further along, the Sonneck (B&B only) and next-door Batzenhäusl are a quarter the price. The suburbs to the west are better placed for cross-country than those to the east, between the railway and the by-pass. There is an attractive enclave of exclusive hotels (Astoria, Lärchenhof) to the north of the centre, close to the Geigenbühel nursery slopes. Thoroughly satisfied customers continue to lavish praise on the Astoria – 'outstanding', 'expensive but worth every penny', 'they greeted us like old friends' and 'impossible to fault'. The Philipp is 'extremely friendly', the apartments of the Kaltschmidt 'palatial'.

There's quite a good variety of **après-ski**; tea-dances, bars, discos, a casino, a bowling alley, sleigh rides and plenty of cafés in the pedestrian zone. But it is not a boisterous resort; young Brits who wish it was are to be found making the best of it in a simulated pub called the Britannia.

With thousands of skiers striding along scores of trails, ranging from eight-lane motorways across the plateau to stiff forest tracks, **cross-country** skiing appears to be the major activity in Seefeld. But is it? Quite possibly more people spend their time **not skiing** at all, but skating to Strauss, or curling, or wallowing in the 'fantastic' pool, or lounging on sun beds, or riding in the indoor school, or taking long walks. The resort is well placed for excursions to Innsbruck and further afield (over the Brenner pass to Italy, for example).

There are short beginners' lifts at the foot of the Gschwandtkopf slopes, but the **nursery slopes** proper are on either side of a separate little hill, Geigenbühel, on the north-east fringe of the village. They have a bit more variety of gradient than many, including very gentle bits.

Recent reports of the **ski school** have been fairly unfavourable, with complaints of haphazard allocation to classes, poor tuition and, most recently, middle-aged beginners being pushed too hard and so dropping out. In contrast, the cross-country school has had glowing reports; excellent English-spoken classes for all standards, from the age of four.

Facts on Seefeld   Tirol **Austria**

Prices in schillings

Tourist office
Postcode A-6100
Tel (5212) 2313
Fax (5212) 3355
Tlx 533452

Getting there
By road 989km from Calais. Munich; chains rarely needed.
By rail Main-line station in resort.
By air Munich; transfer 2hr. (Or Innsbruck, transfer abour 1 hr.)

Staying there
Visitor beds 8,500; breakdown: 4,500 in hotels, 2,500 in pensions and private rooms, 1,500 in apartments.
Package holidays Austrian Holidays (h) Austro Tours (h) Crystal (h) Enterprise (h) Horizon (h) Inghams (has) Thomson (h) .
Medical facilities In resort: Doctor, dentist, chemist. Hospital at Innsbruck (20km).

Non-skiing activities
Indoor Swimming, saunas, massage, tennis, squash, bowling.
Outdoor 60km cleared paths, toboggan run, curling, skating, horse-riding, sleigh rides, tube sliding, paragliding.

Kindergartens
Local
Tuition: Yes. Hours: 10.00-4.00. Ages: 4 up. Cost: 1,445.00 per week (with supervision and meals).
Other childcare facilities
All-day care can be arranged by all hotels or at the Tourist Office.

Special skiing facilities
Summer skiing No.
Cross-country Trails totalling 200km, from the Lenerwiese (2.5km, easy) to the Olympia (25km, difficult).

Lift passes
Happy Ski Card
Covers all the lifts in Seefeld, Leutasch, Reith and several other small West Tirol resorts. (17 lifts in total.)
Cost 6 days 1,390.00 (£69.67).
Credit cards accepted No.
Children 990.00 (under 17) saving 29%. Free pass up to age 10.
Beginners Points cards.
Short-term passes Half-day from 12.00pm; individual fares on some lifts.
Other passes Seefelder Hochplateau covers just Seefeld and linked villages (per day 260.00 for adults, 185.00 for children).

Ski school
Local
Classes 10.00-12.00 and 2.00-4.00. Cost: 1,020.00 (5 days).
Lift priority No.
Children's classes Ages: 16. Cost: 1,020.00 (5 days).
Private lessons available 9.00-10.00 and 12.00-1.00. Cost: 350.00 per hour. Each additional person 100.00.

What was new in 91
Installation of snow guns on the north-facing side of the Gschwandtkopf and from half-way down the run from the Seefelder Joch (3km).

Proud relic

Obergurgl Austria 1930m

Good for *Late holidays, Alpine charm, après-ski, ski touring, lift queues, resort-level snow, easy runs, family holidays*
Bad for *Tough runs, easy road access, not skiing, woodland runs*

Obergurgl is a tiny, high village with an awkward, bitty network of chair-lifts and drag-lifts which don't connect properly and don't add up to a large skiing area, even when you count neighbouring Hochgurgl. It became famous in the days when skiing was much closer to what we now call ski touring; for that purpose, the top of the Ötztal, with its 21 glaciers, is (as it has always been) a superlative area.

Not surprisingly, given the altitude, the immediate surroundings of the resort are bleak; but the resort has charm; it has not gone for growth and it is a real, inhabited village, and not merely a mountainside service area for skiers – which is what most resorts at this height are (and exactly what Hochgurgl is). Several reporters have described it as a 'quality resort' – and one, at least, meant by this that it attracts neither lager louts nor Hooray Henrys, but 'British of the better-behaved variety'. A few regular visitors reckon that the village is rapidly becoming too commercialized but practically all reporters agree that it is a very friendly place, with a jolly evening atmosphere; you can't help seeing the same faces around the resort each day, and to a degree each year.

The resort has a reputation for reliable snow which seems largely deserved. Certainly at some times during recent difficult seasons it has had conspicuously better conditions than many lower resorts in Austria or equally high resorts further west. But there are no guarantees; we have found the top slopes bare and unskiable in supposedly safe February, because of wind. At these altitudes, it's not surprising that avalanche danger can also be a problem, closing lifts and, occasionally, the road up to the resort.

Obergurgl is a very remote village at the head of the Ötztal, nearly 50km from the main road west of Innsbruck. This gives it a further attraction: that it does not invite invasion by day-tripping hordes. The combination of snow reliability, village charm and lack of crowds puts Austria's highest parish closer to paradise than other ski resorts in more ways than one.

Only Sölden is within easy reach for a day out (there are buses) and the road up from there is slow and narrow and prone to closure – though less so than it used to be. Readers who have taken their cars have rarely found a use for them, and some have found digging them out of drifts hard work.

We have withdrawn our verdict 'bad for short airport transfers' as most recent reporters have flown to Innsbruck (only 1½ hours away) rather than Munich or Salzburg.

The skiing top 3035m bottom 1910m

The skiing areas of Obergurgl and its satellite Hochgurgl together cover a high, wide, north-west-facing area of the southern end of the Ötztal. The skiing is practically all above the tree-line and intermediate in difficulty (the runs graded black, reporters agree, rarely justify the rating), and consists of three small areas split up by the valleys beneath peaks and glaciers. Hochgurgl's area offers the greatest vertical drop, and adds the variety of a wooded hillside down to Untergurgl. Obergurgl's two sectors have greater off-piste potential and steeper runs (none of them long) near the top of the lifts.

From the middle of Obergurgl, a two-seater chair takes you over gentle slopes to the **Gaisberg** area – attractive short intermediate runs (categorised red, but not difficult) among a scattering of trees, down to the popular Steinmann restaurant, and a couple of short, steeper gullies under the Nederlift. The long single chair-lift to Hohe Mut has an attractive restaurant and sun terrace at the top, and magnificent views out over the glaciers. The only run down from here is officially off-piste but 'only just black', according to one reporter. In good conditions it is not exceedingly difficult, although it is narrow and fairly steep in places; but the terrain is rocky, and poor snow cover may be unannounced.

Access to the **Festkogel** area has been much improved recently, first by the construction of a six-seater gondola from the cluster of hotels at the entrance to Obergurgl, and secondly by the addition of a new two-stage quad chair from the Gaisberg area. The gondola – a long walk from the centre although reachable (with some poling) on skis from the upper part of the village by the ice-rink – climbs in the shade of a steep wall to a plateau with a restaurant and short practice drag-lift and a longer drag up to the highest point of Obergurgl's skiing. Another off-piste marked route of moderate difficulty descends from here, along with a less direct run now marked as a red piste – good long runs down the flank of the beautiful Ferwalltal. There are blue and red pistes of no great difficulty down the long Rosskar chair-lift and an easily manageable run across to Gaisberg. From this run, another short red brings you to the bottom of the new Plattachbahn chair-lift, which ascends to the summit of Festkogel (over 3000m) and serves a new red run, with some variation at the top.

Hochgurgl's skiing is mostly very gentle, on a broad, open mountainside above the resort; there is a short drag-lift on the glacier at the very top (Wurmkogel) with a black run, but it should be graded red. The drag-lift giving access to this slope has been replaced by an impressive new four-seater chair-lift with weather-shields. The slightly less powerful Schermerspitz chair-lift, which goes up from the same point, serves a new red piste which is said to be 'splendid – wide, curving and well prepared'. On the south side of the area is a long drag-lift with a short second section above it, serving another good red – by the standards of this area, long and varied, with moguls on the bottom half in the woods leading down to a car park on the road up to Hochgurgl. The piste map shows a blue variant, which one reporter assures us is marked black on the mountain. There is another good, fast piste through the woods under the chair-lift up from Untergurgl which is the main way into the Hochgurgl skiing for day-visitors.

There are few **mountain restaurants**, and most skiers lunch in the village, where there are hotels with sun terraces. Of the restaurants on-piste David's (at the bottom of the Steinmann lift) is specially recommended for 'home-made pizza and soups'. The Schönwieshütte, a 20-minute ski and walk from the top of the Sattellift, is heartily recommended by several reporters ('another world'). The new Nederhütte at the top of the Gaisberg lift is very popular at the end of the day, when there is often live music and much merriment; the food is said to be excellent, too. At Hochgurgl there are several restaurants near the top of the system – the small Kirchenkar is 'friendly, with stunning views'; the Wurmkogel hut is friendly, attractive and warming, with marvellous views into Italy.

Because Obergurgl is so small and remote, **queues** are hardly ever a problem except at ski school departure time, and when bad weather closes higher lifts. For a small and not very efficiently mechanised ski area, the lift pass is expensive. The checking system has been recently and successfully computerised. In the past we've had complaints that the resort authorities are slow and inefficient in dealing with fresh snowfalls; recent visitors have been completely satisfied, so we take it that piste-grooming efficiency has improved. If heavy snow blocks the road up from Sölden the lift company finds itself short of operators. Several reporters have wished the piste map were larger, more detailed and up to date.

The only **artificial snow** is on the west-facing run from Hochgurgl down to the valley bottom.

The resort

Although traditional in style, Obergurgl is not a picturesque, colourfully painted Tyrolean charmer. A 19th-century guidebook refers to 'a hamlet composed of wretched cowherds' huts, with a church on an eminence'; things have not changed much, except that the hamlet is now composed not of wretched huts but hotels – some comfortable, others simple – offering a not insignificant 3,450 beds. The clientele is predominantly German, with a minority of British visitors – some old faithfuls, others recently attracted by the resort's unusual recipe. There are adequate shops for self-catering. A free and efficient ski-bus runs to and from Untergurgl (for Hochgurgl skiing), and post buses run further afield. Some reporters have wished for a frequent ski-bus service between Ober and Hoch.

The Gurgls are generally very unsuitable for **cross-country** skiers and **non-skiers**, and excursion possibilities are limited. It is possible to organise an outing to Innsbruck by bus, but not many do. One reporter recommends the three-hour return walk through the Zirbelwald – 'superb views'.

For a small village, Obergurgl is not compact, and location of **accommodation** is important. There are basically three clusters of buildings. The first is at the entrance to the village – convenient for the Festkogel gondola, but otherwise unappealing. Clustered above the old village around the skating rink are comfortable, modern and quite expensive hotels – the Austria is the most attractive of them, with sauna, jacuzzi, Turkish bath and massage, but one visitor complains of uncooperative management. These hotels are easy enough to ski back to, but it is a stiff walk up from the village centre – 'exhausting, long and dangerous,' says one report. In the centre there's more of a mixture. The dominant building is the comfortable Edelweiss & Gurgl; some reporters would not stay anywhere else, while others are unimpressed. The new hotel Crystal reportedly 'sticks out like a sore thumb' (locals refer to it as the 'bunker') but guests staying there have been perfectly satisfied. Most UK tour operators use cheaper, smaller places. Recommendations include the friendly, well-placed Wiesental, the new Granat ('good-sized rooms, reasonable prices'), the Hochfirst ('good facilities, cramped rooms'), the family-run Regina, the Jenewien ('convenient, generous portions of good food'), the Fender ('delightful, traditional rooms, best kitchen in Obergurgl'). The Hausfrau is apparently unfriendly. At the lower end of the market is the 'cheap and cheerful' Gletscherblick pension near the Gaisberg lifts.

Hochgurgl, a modern development beside the road over to Italian Merano (closed in winter), does not appeal to us, but does to some, including reporters impressed by the 'superb but expensive' hotel Hochgurgl and the 'exceptional restaurant and friendly staff' of the Angereralm. Most of the hotels in Hochgurgl are not far from the lifts. There is little else going on in the village, though one reporter mentions tea-dances in Toni's Almhutte and discos in the Olymp and Hochgurgl hotels (the latter apparently lacks atmosphere); those in search of lively night-life will need to make the £18 return taxi trip to Obergurgl.

Après-ski is very jolly in a traditional Tyrolean way, and reports are generally enthusiastic. But the dedicated disco piste-basher will soon

---

Facts on Obergurgl   Tirol **Austria**

Prices in schillings
Ski Club represented

Tourist office
Postcode A-6456
Tel (5256) 258/353
Fax (5256) 35377
Tlx 534557

Getting there
By road 1,083km from Calais. Via Ulm, Munich or Basle; chains often necessary.
By rail Ötz (48km); regular buses from station.
By air Munich; transfer 5hr. (Or Innsbruck; transfer about 2hr.)

Staying there
Visitor beds 3,450; breakdown: 2,220 in hotels, 260 in apartments, 970 in private homes.
Package holidays Bladon Lines (hc) Crystal (hr) Horizon (h) Inghams (h) Made to Measure (h) Neilson (h) Supertravel (h) Thomson (h) .
Medical facilities In resort: Doctor and chemist. Hospital: Innsbruck (102km). Dentist: Sölden (15km).

Non-skiing activities
Indoor Public and hotel pools, saunas, whirlpools, steam baths, massage, bowling, pool and billards, squash, table tennis, shooting range.
Outdoor Natural skating rink (open in the evenings), curling, sleigh rides.

Kindergartens
Local
Tuition: Yes. Hours: 9.30-12.30, 1.30-4.30. Ages: from 2. Cost: 1,080.00 per week (lunchtime supervision available 170.00 per day).

Special skiing facilities
Summer skiing No.
Cross-country 13km between Obergurgl and Untergurgl (intermediate). Small loop at Hochgurgl. Instruction available.

Lift passes
Ski pass
Covers all lifts in Obergurgl, Untergurgl and Hochgurgl, and local ski-bus. (22 lifts in total.)
Cost 6 days 1,750.00 (£87.72). Low season: 1,540.00 saving 12%.
Credit cards accepted No.
Senior citizens 1,070.00 (over 60) saving 39%.
Children 1,070.00 (under 15) saving 39%. Free pass up to age 6.
Beginners Lift pass or coupons.
Short-term passes Half-day (from 11.00, 12.00 or 2.00pm).

Ski school
Obergurgl
Classes 10.00-12.00 and 2.00-4.00. Cost: 1,180.00 (6 days).
Lift priority No.
Children's classes Ages: From 5. Cost: 1,080.00 (6 days).
Private lessons available Per hour. Cost: 450.00 per hour. Also available per day 1,850.00 for up to 2 people, or per half-day 1,150.00.
Hochgurgl
Classes 10.00-12.00 and 2.00-4.00. Cost: 1,180.00 (5 days).
Lift priority No.
Children's classes Ages: From 5. Cost: 1,080.00 (5 days).
Private lessons available Per hour. Cost: 450.00 per hour.

What was new in 91
1. New quad chair-lift at Festkogl.
2. Cars now restricted to 2 areas of the village. Private cars may not be used in the village between 11pm and 6am.
3. Child-care over lunch-time at the kindergarten.

tire of the lack of variety. The most popular post-skiing venue is the Nederhütte at the top of the Gaisberg lift, where people congregate at 4.30pm for drinks and tea-dancing (on the tables) and then ski home in the dark. The outdoor umbrella bar of the Edelweiss is also very popular at tea-time; later in the evening it has a lively disco. Other animated bars are the Josl Keller ('the biggest and best', according to one reporter), the café Tirol ('for a quiet night drink') and the bars at the Wiesental and Jenewien hotels. The Krump'n'Stadl is 'a converted barn full of rowdy Germans, great atmosphere, yodelling on alternate nights, expensive drinks'. Most visitors eat in their hotels; recommendations include the Pizzeria at the Madelaine and the independent Pic Nic restaurant. The nouvelle cuisine at the Eidelweiss was not appreciated by all our reporters. The Alpenland hotel has a popular bowling alley (book in advance).

There is a wide, flat **nursery slope** in the village with a small tow beside it, and plenty of scope for easy après-nursery skiing, especially above Hochgurgl, so even beginners may find a lift pass economical.

Of the numerous reports we have had on the **ski school** recently, only a couple have been unfavourable. Most people were delighted with the accurate class allocation, the excellent instruction – 'a good balance of teaching and practicing' – and the good spoken English. Two Aussie instructors have earned especially high praise. High-season classes, however, are on the large side. Impressions of the **ski kindergarten** are also favourable. Many very beautiful and not too arduous day-trip ski tours can be made at any time in the season, and from March onwards tourers can undertake the famous Ötztal Rundtour.

Sölden Austria 1380m

Good for *Après-ski, summer skiing, late holidays*
Bad for *Lift queues, nursery slopes, not skiing, short airport transfers, tough runs*

Linked resort: Hochsölden

Sölden is a long-established, large and lively resort for which we find it hard to work up much enthusiasm, despite its undoubted qualities. The skiing area is extensive and varied, spread along the high (and in places steep) western wall of the Ötztal, and on paper is impressive, with a big gondola going up to over 3000m, and extensive glacier areas. But the skiing served by the top stage of the gondola is limited (at least for most people, most of the time), and the glacier lifts (not normally open until spring) are not connected to the main ski area. The rest of the skiing is not good enough to earn Sölden a place among the top sporty resorts, nor to outweigh the disadvantages of the resort itself – a long, main-road straggle with little charm, redeemed only by vibrant nightlife (in high season, at least). Recent reporters have been more impressed, perhaps partly because they have been grateful to get decent skiing at all when snow has been in short supply.

Hochsölden is a mini-village 700m higher than the mother resort; if isolation above the trees suits you, you may find its ready access to the slopes attractive, but some find it claustrophobic and boring.

Having a car in Sölden is of no great value except for expeditions to Obergurgl, and parking around the resort can be difficult.

The skiing top 3056m bottom 1380m

Sölden's skiing area is in two linked sectors, south and north (often referred to as Hochsölden and Sölden skiing), split by the deep Rettenbachtal (where the road goes up to the glaciers. Both sectors are directly accessible from stations on the edges of Sölden (served by a regular but often busy ski-bus). The skiing is extensive, with a healthy vertical drop of about 1600m from the gondola top station, 1350m from the top above Hochsölden. It is partly open, partly wooded, but less varied in difficulty than the piste map suggests: several of the blues and blacks ought to be red. Most of the slopes are east-facing.

The Gaislachkogel gondola goes up to the **Sölden** skiing area from the southern end of the resort, where there is a large car park. There are open slopes around the middle station with a couple of drag-lifts, one of them taking you to a beautiful, long and usually empty run down to the Gaislachalm (where there are several restaurants) and on down a gentle woodland trail to rejoin the main piste to Sölden at Innerwald. The main run down from the middle station is red, can be icy, and tends to

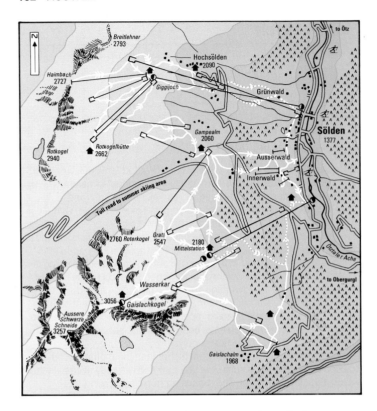

be crowded at the end of the day. Once you get to know the lower slopes it's usually possible to find a route down through the back gardens to most parts of the village. Roads are a hazard.

The top section of the gondola climbs over 850m steeply to the rocky Gaislachkogel peak, where there is a round panoramic restaurant. The bowl underneath the cable-car is very steep and has no marked piste, only a *'wilde abfahrt'* which must be very exciting when conditions are right. The normal run from the top station gives beautiful views, but only at the top does it justify its red grading.

Of the two pistes down into the Rettenbachtal to link up with Hochsölden, the one from the middle gondola station is an easy path and can be pursued as far as Sölden. The run down beside the long Stabele chair-lift is more difficult, and being north-facing often has very good snow. There are some good off-piste possibilities around here, but the underlying terrain is rocky. From the Rettenbachtal there is a more difficult run down to Innerwald and Sölden.

From the northern edge of Sölden a long chair-lift (over 20 minutes) climbs directly to **Hochsölden**, and a gondola (the more popular way in the mornings) goes slightly higher, to the Giggijoch. Above this gondola there is a wide open expanse of gentle mountainside. There is a steeper area between Hochsölden and the Haimbach, but the runs marked black do not deserve the grading. The runs to Hochsölden are graded blue and black, but fairly red in practice – to the discomfort of novices.

From the Rotkogelhütte there are superb views over to the glacier skiing areas and a beautiful, sunny long run down to the Rettenbachtal via the Gampealm restaurant. This run may be a bit much for inexperienced skiers; if so they will not be able to get across to the Sölden skiing, nor down to Sölden, except via the blue to the gondola station. The black next to that blue is another over-graded run.

There are several large, not very attractive **mountain restaurants** in the obvious places, and a few more charming ones, notably the Gampealm and Rotkogelhütte – 'a good gathering point as the lifts close'. Gaislachkogel is 'plush and panoramic', Gaislachalm has great views and good food, but reportedly suffers from disorganised service. Eugen's Obstlerhütte, just below Hochsölden, is 'very jolly'.

At most times during the season, the big gondola has all but eliminated **queues** to get up the Sölden skiing, but in high season there can be problems here and elsewhere – at the gondola to Giggijoch, and on lifts above it, particularly the Silberbrunnl chair-lift. A couple of reporters have been surprised at the cost of the lift pass, considering the limitations of the area.

There is **artificial snow** on the lower parts of the runs to the valley from both ends of the ski area.

The resort

Sölden stretches for miles (literally) along the Ötztal valley floor, and the river and the main road run through the village. Although most buildings are traditional in style, the long, wide main street has no particular character or focus. In high season the resort is extremely busy, with a daily influx from smaller villages in addition to Sölden residents. Visitors come from many countries, the majority being German, many car-borne; traffic is a hazard along the main street. As well as the ski-bus, there are two buses daily between Sölden and Hochsölden, but only expensive taxis in the evening.

Accommodation is nearly all in hotels and guest-houses. Skiers should choose to stay at either end of the town; the northern end is better for inexperienced skiers, for access to Hochsölden skiing. Recommendations include the Tyrolerhof, Parkhotel and the Stefan ('on edge of the piste – snow cannons noisy at night – good food, friendly service'). The central Sonne has received serious criticism. Just above Sölden at the southern end of the town is the hamlet of Innerwald, which has numerous inexpensive pensions, such as Haus Stefanie ('simple, clean, friendly, good breakfasts'). The Hochsölden hotels are traditional and fairly simple. Our regular reporter on the Alpenfriede still likes the food and hot water, but not the atmosphere since it was remodelled.

In season there is a wide variety of lively **après-ski** action – 'Excellent with a capital E' says a 25-year-old reporter. As well as throbbing bars, discos and live music, there are lots of packaged evening outings. After skiing there is a disco at Innerwald in the Café Philip until 6pm, when the chair-lift down to Sölden closes, and popular umbrella bars at either end of the main resort. The most popular organised event is a jeep ride from the Alpenland and Silbertal up to the Gaislachalm for *Glühwein*, dancing and/or dinner, followed by a 6km toboggan ride back. Brits tend to gravitate to the Après Ski bar, of which we have enthusiastic reports.

The main valley is not very attractive for **cross-country** skiing. Although there are some sporting facilities (and good reports of the new leisure centre), it is not really a **non-skier's** resort either, and there are no cleared mountain paths for walkers.

The village **nursery slopes** are not very satisfactory: Innerwald, a short chair-lift ride from Sölden, has a nursery area which goes without sun for much of the day, and often has poor snow conditions. There are much better slopes above the Giggijoch gondola.

Reports suggest that **ski-school** classes are often too large; we also have complaints of language problems, which have also rendered the ski kindergarten useless for at least one family.

Facts on Sölden Tirol **Austria**

Prices in schillings

Tourist office

Postcode A-6450
Tel (5254) 22120
Fax (5254) 221219
Tlx 533247

Getting there

By road 1,000km from Calais. Via Ulm, Munich or Basle; the road from Ötz rarely requires chains.
By rail Ötz (30km); 12 daily buses from station.
By air Munich; transfer 4hr. (Or Innsbruck; transfer about 2hr.)

Staying there

Visitor beds 10,000; breakdown: about 2,600 in hotels, the rest in apartments and private accommodation.
Package holidays Alpine Tours (hr) Crystal (hr) Horizon (h) Inghams (h) Made to Measure (h) Neilson (h) Thomson (h) .
Medical facilities In resort: Doctor, dentist, chemist. Hospital: Innsbruck (87km).

Non-skiing activities

Indoor Freizeit Arena sports complex (swimming, sauna, solarium, gym, bowling, tennis, shooting, cinema).
Outdoor Skating, curling, riding, toboggan run.

Kindergartens

Kindergartens in all centres
Tuition: Yes. Hours: 9.00-4.00. Ages: 3-8. Cost: 1,500.00 per week (with lunch, tuition and baby-lift).
Other childcare facilities
Baby-sitters and day-mothers available from Tourist Office.

Special skiing facilities

Summer skiing Large area up to 3250m, with 10 lifts.
Cross-country 3km and 5km trials along valley floor near Sölden, and at Zwieselstein (6km, easy) and Untergurgl, up the valley.

Lift passes

Ötztal Arena
Covers all lifts in Sölden, Hochsölden and Zwieselstein. (33 lifts in total.)
Cost 6 days 1,640.00 (£82.21). Low season: 1,440.00 saving 12%.
Credit cards accepted No.
Senior citizens 1,370.00 (over 60/65) saving 16%.
Children 950.00 (under 15) saving 42%. Free pass up to age 6.
Notes Cheap half-day pass for OAPs.
Beginners Points tickets, valid on lifts in Innerwald and Hochsölden areas.
Short-term passes Half-day, 'hourly' cards refundable when you hand them in, single ascents for main cable cars and chairlift.
Other passes Separate passes for Vent (6 days 1,190.00 for adults, 820.00 for children) and for the Rettenbach and Tiefenbach glaciers.

Ski school

Local
In all 3 centres.
Classes 10.00-12.00 and 1.30-3.30. Cost: 1,070.00 (6 days).
Lift priority No.
Children's classes Ages: 5 up. Cost: 1,500.00 (6 days). With lunch and use of baby-lifts.
Private lessons available Full day (4 hr). Cost: 450.00 per hour.

Bordering on the ideal

Ischgl Austria 1400m

Good for *Big ski area, après-ski, Alpine charm, beautiful scenery, ski touring, easy runs, sunny slopes*
Bad for *Lift queues, short airport transfers, woodland runs*

Linked resort: Samnaun (Switzerland)
Separate resort: Galtür

Many skiers' recipe for the perfect resort might mix the skiing and snow reliability of Val d'Isère and Tignes with the village charm of Alpbach and après-ski vitality of St Anton – the best aspects of French and Austrian skiing – with the drinks prices of Livigno thrown in for good measure. Ischgl comes closer than most resorts to fitting this recipe. It is an old Tyrolean village, fast developing, high in the remote and beautiful Paznaun valley at the foot of a vast skiing area. And it almost has the good measure thrown in – you can ski over to duty-free Samnaun (in Switzerland) for bargain shopping whenever the drinks cupboard runs dry. These qualities have made the resort highly popular with German and Swedish skiers (and après-skiers). It has not up to now attracted much attention in Britain, but we are now getting very healthy numbers of reports, practically all from satisfied customers.

   Ischgl's skiing contains few severe runs, and we have been tempted to label it 'bad for tough runs'; but there are plenty of satisfyingly long and varied pistes that are difficult enough for most skiers. Equally importantly, there is extensive off-piste skiing – and because Ischgl is not a fashionable resort for experts it does not get 'skied out' in the way that St Anton may do. Many of the lifts are smart and modern, far superior to the Austrian norm, but not free of bottle-necks at times. There are also a fair number of slow, old T-bars and lengthy chair-lifts, prone to stoppages, and a major source of irritation to many of our reporters.

   Galtür is a peaceful and very friendly little village at the head of the valley, long known as an excellent ski touring base and perhaps soon to be better known by those who prefer to ski downhill than up: with the addition of a couple of lifts, Galtür recently doubled the size (and added greatly to the variety) of its small ski area.

   Ischgl is a rather isolated resort, but skiers with cars can make expeditions to St Anton. A car is otherwise of no great advantage. Our 'bad for short transfers' verdict does not apply if you fly via Innsbruck.

The skiing top 2872m bottom 1400m

The skiing consists principally of the splendid slopes above Ischgl; long descents through woods to the village and a series of high, rocky bowls above with plenty of open, easy pistes. A long mountain crest which

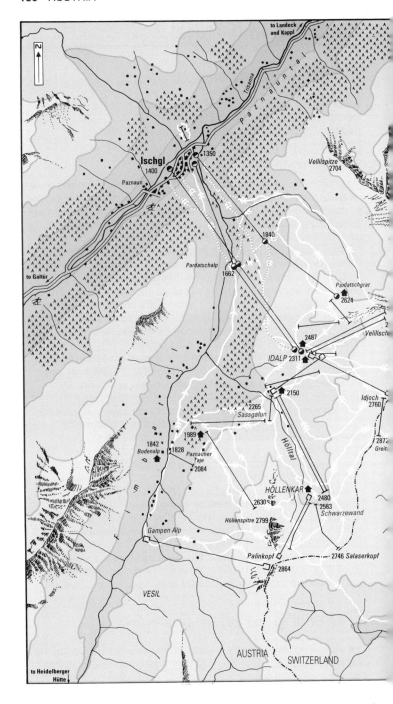

forms the Austro-Swiss border is reached by lift and easily breached on skis in a number of places, opening up a less extensive but no less beautiful Swiss ski area above Samnaun. The slopes on the Ischgl side face north-west and west; on the Samnaun side mainly south and east.

From Ischgl there are lift departures at both ends of the village, to Idalp, a broad, sunny, open plateau with a ski school, restaurants, hotel and nursery slopes, and to the Pardatschgrat above Idalp, with runs back down to Ischgl or an easy connection with the rest of the lift system via Idalp.

The runs down to Ischgl from Pardatschgrat are about the best in the area for good skiers, some of them giving an uninterrupted and demanding 1200m vertical across open slopes and then through woodland. Splendid as these runs are, it is unfortunate that there are none graded easier than red – and one of the reds on the map was deservedly graded black on the mountain when we last visited. In the late afternoon they can get very crowded, and when they are icy the lower parts of these runs can be extremely hazardous.

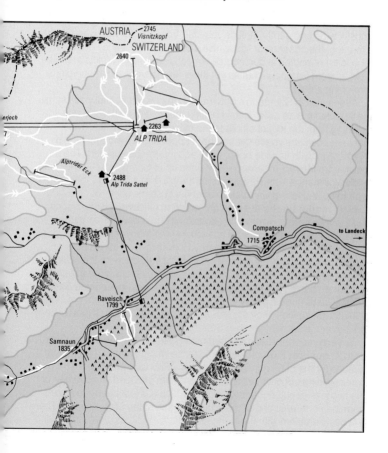

At Idalp there are lots of lifts going all over the place around a fairly shallow, unevenly shelving, rocky bowl with good, easy runs including a few nursery slopes. For better skiers this is not a place to linger, but a staging post with links to other areas. Vellilscharte offers one of the most beautiful and least skied of all the descents to Ischgl, down a valley of its own; it is not always open. From Idjoch, there are easy runs down into the sunny Swiss Alp Trida and a long panoramic traverse to the narrow Hölltal beside Idalp. The lifts up the Hölltal serve a variety of short runs, and also give access to some of the best skiing in the region. Behind Palinkopf (2864m, the high point of the system) is some excellent open skiing with runs marked red and black – scarcely of black steepness but the most challenging of the high runs. As the first step in mechanisation of this beautiful area, a long enclosed chair-lift has been built from Gampen Alp, down in the Fimbatal, back up to Palinkopf; it is still relatively little-used, and its runs – 900m vertical, on- and off-piste – are now an obvious target for good skiers.

The run down a Swiss valley to the scattering of woods around Samnaun can be reached from any of the three lifts near Palinkopf. It is long, and extremely beautiful, but not very interesting skiing, being mostly wide and gentle (unless you start from the Schwarzwand drag). Here too, the absence of lifts, which adds greatly to the joy of the run, is due to be remedied in due course – a cable-car and drag-lifts are to be built up from Samnaun, but as yet there are no signs that these plans are going ahead.

After a visit to Samnaun's duty-free shops (which helpfully sell small backpacks) it is an awkward ski beside the road or a short ski-bus ride (starting from the tourist office) to the cable-car at Raveisch. The cable-car delivers you to the southern upper rim of the beautiful Alp Trida basin, with its wide open, easy and intermediate skiing. The run down from the Alp Trida restaurant ends up at Compatsch, further than walking distance from Raveisch. From Alp Trida, a double T-bar links up with Idalp and Ischgl via Austria's highest customs post.

Most **mountain restaurants** are modern, efficient and impersonal, but there are some worthwhile exceptions. The popular Paznauner Taya, down in the Fimbatal, is a favourite with many reporters; its terrace often has a live band. Nearby Bodenalp is an attractive alternative, as is the 'pleasant small café' at the bottom of the Höllenkar. On the Swiss side, Alp Trida is a huge sun-trap and its large expensive restaurant has an outdoor bar and barbecue, and the Alp Trida Sattel serves 'good quality, pricey food'. The absence of duty is not noticeable in restaurant prices; they are in Swiss francs, but schillings pass. There are several places for lunch in Samnaun itself.

Several reporters have queried our insistence that the area suffers from lift **queues**; they should talk to those who have found 45-minute queues for the main gondola at 8.15 on a February morning. At off-peak times, getting out of the village is no problem provided you use one of the two less popular gondolas, one of which has just been renovated, from the north-east end of the village instead of the Silvrettabahn. There is a basic problem with the Ischgl-Samnaun ski circus: you can travel round it only in one direction, and as nearly all skiers are based in Ischgl

– or, just as important, arrive there in coaches – a large part of the ski area's population finds itself doing the same thing at the same time. Thus, as well as the queues to get out of Ischgl in the morning there are queues to get out of Samnaun in the early afternoon, and to get to the top of the skiing from Alp Trida; there is also congestion on pistes down to Ischgl at the end of the day. Most of these queues can be avoided if you pick your time of day, or time of the season – you do not have to move far from the peak to find much reduced pressure on the system.

Most of the lower pistes back to Ischgl have **artificial snow** on the last few hundred metres; the red run from Idalp has installations all the way down, although reports suggest that there is not much evidence of them.

Facts on Ischgl Tirol **Austria**

Prices in schillings

Tourist office

Postcode A-6561
Tel (5444) 5266/5318
Fax (5444) 5636
Tlx 58148

Getting there

By road 1,017km from Calais. Via Basle or Ulm, then Feldkirch. The road up from Landeck is not difficult, but chains may be needed.
By rail Landeck (30km); frequent buses from station.
By air Munich; transfer 4½hr. (Or Zurich.)

Staying there

Visitor beds 6,600; breakdown: 6,200 in hotels, 400 in apartments.
Package holidays Crystal (hr) Enterprise (h) Inghams (h) Made to Measure (h) Quest Total Ski (h) Quest Travel (schools) (a) Snobiz (h) Thomson (hr) .
Medical facilities In resort: Doctor, chemist. Hospital: Zams (near Landeck).

Non-skiing activities

Indoor In Ischgl: Silvretta Centre (swimming, sauna, steam bath, massage, solarium), skittles, bowling alley, swimming pools in some hotels (open to public), squash at Hotel Solaria. In Galtür: tennis and squash at Galtür sports centre, shooting range. In Mathon: farming museum and pottery displays.
Outdoor 24km cleared walks, skating and curling at Galtür sports centre, sleigh rides, toboggan and mini-bob runs.

Kindergartens

Gastekindergarten
Tuition: No. Hours: 10.00-4.00. Ages: Toddlers. Cost: 900.00 per week (meals 65.00 per day extra). Experienced nurses in recreation room.

Special skiing facilities

Summer skiing No.
Cross-country 20km Ischgl/Galtür/Wirl graded blue. Instruction available.

Lift passes

Silvretta
Covers Ischgl, Kappl, See, Galtür and Samnaun lifts, and local buses. (30 lifts in total.)
Cost 6 days 1,770.00 (£88.72). Low season: 1,485.00 saving 16%.
Credit cards accepted No.
Senior citizens 1,060.00 (over 60) saving 40%.
Children 1,060.00 (under 15) saving 40%. Free pass up to age 6.
Notes Group discounts available.
Beginners Books of tickets, afternoon and 'trial afternoon' passes.
Short-term passes Half-day from 11.30 or 2.00 (Ischgl-Samnaun pass only).
Other passes Ischgl-Samnaun lifts only (6 days 1,750.00 for adults, 1,040.00 for children).
Other periods Passes available for 5 days out of 7, and 10 days out of 14.

Ski school

Ischgl
10% discount in low season.
Classes 10.30-12.30 and 1.30-3.30. Cost: 1,100.00 (6 days).
Lift priority No.
Children's classes Ages: Any. Cost: 1,490.00 (6 days). Price includes lunch.
Private lessons available 2hr or 4hr. Cost: 850.00 per hour. Each additional adult 150.00. Priority in lift queues.

What was new in 91

Despite ambitious plans to connect Samnaun with Zeblasjoch and build two new lifts on the Piz Val Gronda, the only development this year is the renovation of the Pardatschgrat cable-car from Ischgl.

The resort

Ischgl is an old village which has generally developed in a smart and harmonious way with a high standard of new building and accommodation and a generally high price level. Recent building is reportedly less harmonious and many hotels are in danger of losing their 'character' with the addition of charmless modern extensions. The centre is by-passed by the main road and is tightly packed, bustling with activity in the early evening. The rest of the village sprawls along the valley, in the shadow (literally, in January) of the steep, wooded mountainsides which are now the ski slopes. Parts of it are hilly, and there are several staircases and steep paths which can be very hazardous when icy.

A ski-bus service covered by the lift pass links Ischgl, Kappl and Galtür infrequently during the day, and not in the evening. There are also regular buses to Landeck.

Ischgl as a whole is now quite large, but most **accommodation** is conveniently placed for one or other of the two lift departures. The Solaria is about the nicest of the hotels, with a beautiful wooden interior and good facilities for residents (squash, sauna). Recent reports suggest that the management is not quite as slick as it once was. A nearby alternative, run by the versatile Wolf family, is the Olympia. The Post is very central. The Antony, on a hillside opposite the village, is 'very pleasant, with spacious rooms and excellent food'. Other recommendations include the 'excellent but impersonal' Ischglerhof, the 'unpretentious' Alpenrose and the family run Verwall on the western edge of the village.

Après-ski is excellent, starting in mid-afternoon when the outside bar of the hotel Elizabeth starts buzzing. Later on the Tenne is popular. There is a a good choice of traditional music and tea dancing. If you're keen on rowdy singing and dancing the congo on the table-tops, try the Kitzloch. For a quieter tea and cake, reporters recommend the Konditorei Salner and the Dorfcafé. For evening activities, there are sophisticated live music shows and one or two very contemporary discos of the kind to be found wherever young Swedes go. Two of the most popular are the disco beneath the hotel Madlein and the Café Christine. Bar and restaurant recommendations include the Trofana-Alm bar-restaurant ('atmospheric barn-style place where you buy beer by the metre', 'delicious pizza cooked in a wood-burning oven, good salad table'), the ancient painted bar and restaurant of the Goldener Adler, the Nikis Stadl in the Piz Buin hotel and the restaurant at the hotel Tirol. The 'kellar' of the Seespitz has an intriguing nail-hammering game. Popular fondue expeditions to the Heidelberger Hütte (by snow-cat or horse-sleigh) are organised most evenings.

The **cross-country** skiing along the dark valley floor is not very interesting, inconvenient for meeting up with others, and quite often interrupted because of avalanche danger. We saw cross-country activity in the much more attractive upper section of the Fimbatal, reached by gondola or on foot. Ischgl is really a skiers' resort, but there is plenty for

non-skiers to do, with very good fair-weather walks up to the mountain restaurants at Bodenalp and beyond (the mountain restaurants directly accessible by gondola are charmless) and good sports and bathing facilities at the Silvretta centre (and further ones at Galtür). Excursions to Innsbruck are often organised. One reporter recommends a visit to the farming museum at Mathon.

Nursery slopes are at Idalp – open, sunny, with refreshments close at hand. In general though there are much better places than Ischgl for beginners (Galtür is one), especially given the cost, the queues and the awkwardness of runs down to the resort.

Ski school meets at Idalp, with classes starting at the civilised hour of 10.30. We've had contradictory reports of the ski school this year; classes tend to be large but instruction is in reasonable English. The school organises excursions on skins in what is one of the best ski touring areas in the Alps.

Samnaun   1840m

Samnaun is one of those anomalous communities in high, remote, dead-end corners of a country (in this case Switzerland) which has stayed alive thanks to duty-free status. It is not exactly booming – little more than a large cluster of shops and hotels with no more vitality than a supermarket – and it is hardly the place for a winter holiday unless the price of spirits is an all-important consideration. Petrol is also very cheap, but ski equipment, cigarettes and scent are less so. The resort's attraction is that you can ski the Ischgl circus without the rush-hour for lifts and crowds on-piste. There is a 10-km cross-country trail, a ski school which organises ski-tours, and a kindergarten at Alp Trida. Access by car is from the Inn valley south of Landeck, not far from Serfaus and Nauders.

Tourist office ✆ (84) 95154. Tx 854111.

Galtür   1585m

Compared with Ischgl, Galtür is a peaceful little mountain village, although it can muster 3,000 visitor beds. It enjoys a sunnier position at the widening head of the valley but is further away from its ski-lifts, which are at Wirl (1635m), reached by reliable and adequately frequent free ski-bus; you can pole back on skis, given the energy. There are avalanche slopes on both sides of the village, which is quite often cut off from both Ischgl and Wirl. Reporters recommend Galtür for relaxed family holidays. There are hotels and cheerful bars, some with tea-dancing and live music, both in Galtür and beside the lifts at Wirl. The Post hotel has an expensive disco. Galtür is a good base for cross-country skiers (45km of trails, very reliable for snow) and an even better one for ski-tourers, for whom the scope in the Silvretta range is enormous. Heli-skiing can be arranged by the drop or by the week. There are three well-sited hotels in the village, the friendly Rössle, the Post and the Fluchthorn ('food outstanding, free sauna, Turkish baths and fitness facilities'). The Ballunspitze is slightly further out but another good choice, as is the family-run Alpenrose – 'quiet, very welcoming, food excellent'. The hotels at Wirl are isolated, but have their own excellent facilities, and are much used at lunch-time as there is only one ('high quality') mountain restaurant. The Almhof is said to serve good, cheap lunches and has a swimming-pool which is open to non-residents. Two reporters have recommended the Wirlerhof – 'very good with children, excellent facilities, beds a bit hard, fun tea dances'.

There are skating and curling rinks, a floodlit toboggan run and a surprisingly smart sports centre (swimming pool, squash, tennis, bowling) open till midnight, its pool free to holders of a Silvretta lift pass bought in Galtür. There are 'super' walking opportunities. Even after the addition some years ago of lifts on Vorarlberg territory above the Kopssee (1850m), Galtür's ski area is by no means vast. But there are rarely queues (the main access chair-lift is an efficient four-seater with plastic wind-shields, and the drag needed for the return from Kopssee has been recently duplicated). The Kopssee chair-lift added 500m vertical of north-facing slopes (including some off-piste skiing, useful for those preparing for a heli-ski adventure) to the varied east-facing pistes above Wirl, which also has nursery slopes and a well-thought-of ski kindergarten. We've had a glowing report of the ski school – 'certainly the best instruction I've had in seven weeks skiing' – and several enthusiastic comments on the children's classes.

Tourist office ✆ (5443) 204. Telex 58290.
Package holidays Crystal (hr) Enterprise (h) Made to Measure (hs) Thomson (h).

St Anton Austria 1300m

Good for *Tough runs, big ski area, sunny slopes, off-piste skiing, easy road access, rail access, après-ski, chalet holidays, artificial snow*
Bad for *Easy runs, lift queues, nursery slopes, skiing convenience, not skiing, woodland runs*

Linked resorts: St Christoph, Stuben
Separate resort: Pettneu

The Arlberg is not a province or a mountain but a pass, where the waters of western Europe (the Rhine) are divided from those of the eastern Danube. In this century the Arlberg has given its name to a once-revolutionary style of skiing and the ski school which taught it, and to a magnificent ski region spread on both sides of the pass. On the western (Vorarlberg) side are Lech and Zürs, Austria's two most exclusive resorts and the subject of the next chapter. On the Tyrolean side (and separate for practical skiing purposes), St Anton is a teeming thoroughfare with a privileged place in skiing history, and a resort where many a proud skier, flattered by other, gentler ski-fields, discovers that there is more to the sport after all.

Austrian resorts are renowned for village charm and warmth of welcome rather than the extent and challenge of their skiing. St Anton stands out as the main exception – a big-time resort with slopes to rival the best of France and Switzerland. As the home of Hannes Schneider's famous Arlberg ski school, St Anton has the image of a resort for the dedicated technical perfectionist. Its runs offer what is arguably the greatest variety of difficult skiing of any resort. The village has lost most of its charm under the influence of the hordes of young people who swarm in from all over the world. It seems the antithesis of a Tyrolean ski resort. And, although heavy traffic has been reduced by a new road tunnel and lift queues by new lifts, there are still as many who abhor St Anton as adore it. But it should be judged against the places with which it competes for business – Val d'Isère, Verbier and the like. It then emerges as inconvenient in many ways, but full of character, far from unattractive, and very good fun after dark. It does lack very high ski-fields and its slopes get a lot of sun, but it is well known for abundant snowfalls. In 1988 this reputation was reinforced by exceptional depths of snow (in excess of 4 metres) on the upper slopes in the latter part of the season – producing a massive (and fatal) avalanche through the eastern fringe of the village. More recently, it is the resort's very effective snow-making machinery that has underpinned its appeal to skiers.

St Anton has far too many cars, and parking near the centre is always difficult; parking permits are available for those staying in big hotels. A car is handy for après-ski if you aren't staying centrally, and for making the most of the Arlberg skiing. Expeditions further afield are unlikely, but not impossible; Ischgl and (much further away) Sölden and Obergurgl are the most obvious candidates.

St Christoph and Stuben are tiny communities on the Arlberg pass road, linked into the skiing and much used by St Anton residents for lunch, but also worth considering as bases. Pettneu is very different – a quiet valley village a few miles to the east, with its own little ski area.

The skiing   top 2650m bottom 1304m

Skiing at St Anton means skiing in the aura of the Valluga (2811m), a fine peak to the north of the village, and one of skiing's big names. There are many separate slopes of mountain, facing mainly south-east and west, and numerous ridges, bowls and valleys around the subsidiary high-points of Galzig and Kapall. Many of the pistes are steep and challenging, and whereas many resorts have to invent black runs to appeal to good skiers, St Anton has to contrive blue runs in order not to discourage the timid. On the other side of the main road, facing the Valluga, St Anton has a separate ski area – the Rendl, which is sunny and not too difficult. A third area – the Albona, above Stuben on the other side of the Arlberg Pass – is (unlike Rendl) reachable on skis from the Valluga; the slopes are bleak and sunless in midwinter, but often have the best late snow conditions.

St Anton is a connoisseur's area for off-piste skiing, and every descent variant, however rarely skiable, has its name. It is an area which improves as you get to know it (especially since the resort now treats its high, challenging runs as off-piste itineraries – which means no grooming, no patrols and, in many cases, no marking). Many of the main runs above St Anton get a lot of sun, and tend to be icy in the mornings during clear, cold weather; always challenging, they can become treacherous.

The long **Rendl** gondola starts an awkward distance from the resort centre – further than a gentle stroll, but not so far that it really seems worth shoving to get on the village bus, as you often have to. The gondola top station is set on an open west-facing slope below a rocky ridge. Benefiting from sunny afternoons, the Rendl and its restaurant terrace get very full on a fine day. Above and below the gondola station are a few short drags serving intermediate pistes and, further across the slope, two chairs going up to 2650m – the top of the area until the planned second stage of the gondola is built. The more challenging runs served by these chairs are marked as itineraries, which would indicate that they are ungroomed; when snow is sparse, this is not the case. There is only one main run down to St Anton – a long red run, good in the right conditions, but which gets very crowded in the late afternoon, and is often icy and/or worn as well. For good skiers the Rendl offers much more excitement off-piste than on; there is a lot of space on the open shoulder of the ridge below Gampberg, and a very alluring secluded bowl behind it; the awkward woodland path out of the bowl is easy to miss, and crucial.

The main skiing area to the north of St Anton is split in two by the long Steissbachtal, which provides a blue run down to St Anton from each mid-station – daunting in poor snow conditions and often extremely crowded. **Kapall** is the smaller and less crowded area, mostly sunny and south-facing. Most of the runs are intermediate and graded red or blue. The blue runs, for example under the chairs from Kapall to Gampen, may unpleasantly surprise intermediates, and the most direct descent to the resort is the course of the famous Arlberg-Kandahar downhill race. Below Gampen there are some good bump sections down through the trees. The new Gampenbahn quad chair takes you speedily back to the mid-station. The run to the Rodelhütte and Nasserein is one of the most interesting but also one of the first to lose its snow. Beside Kapall, facing east and often keeping better snow than elsewhere, is a short drag-lift with a fairly easy piste beside it, and off-piste runs into the Schöngraben valley – among the most beautiful, least terrifying and most skied in the area.

The major area, and St Anton's most popular one, consists of the rounded knoll of Galzig (now accessible by a fast quad chair, the Zammermoosbahn, from St Anton), and beyond it the peak of the Valluga. Lifts from both St Anton and St Christoph go up to **Galzig** (2185m), with pistes down in all directions and a maze of chairs, cable-cars and tows arriving at different points of the hilltop. There are drag-lifts at the top with easy runs beside them, and an easy but attractively varied run down to St Christoph. The rest of the slopes of Galzig are steep, and provide some very challenging skiing, notably the Osthang – a long, steep mogul-field through trees towards the resort. Remarkably, this is now St Anton's only black run accorded the status of piste. Numerous staple unpisted runs from Galzig include slopes of 30–35° above St Christoph and down into the Steissbachtal (north-facing).

The second section of the cable-car from Galzig takes a spectacular course, high above the Steissbachtal to a first ridge, then across another bowl to the Vallugagrat, a shoulder below the **Valluga** itself. From here a tiny cable-car goes up to the rocky peak (for sightseeing purposes). The direct descents from Vallugagrat are stern, south-facing gullies down into the Steissbachtal, famous unprepared runs with large moguls that seem to go on and on. The Mattun on the far right, a vast bowl with countless variations, is also accessible from Kapall. Schindlerkar, down the next gully, is steeper and narrower with some pitches of 30°. The most exciting descents can be seen below the cable-car, and a glance on the way up will be enough to put most skiers off. These runs get a lot of sun, and timing your runs to avoid morning ice and afternoon slush can be tricky. It is usually possible to avoid the steep part of Schindlergrat by traversing to the Grat chair-lift after the relatively gentle first half of the run.

Less confident skiers, or those not prepared to undertake St Anton's 'high-alpine touring routes', can take a moderate red run (though even this is an unpatrolled 'ski-route') with a single awkward pitch of 25° down to the Ulmerhütte, and from there either easily round to the Steissbachtal and to St Anton, or on to Rauz, over the road and down to Stuben. Rauz is no more than a chair-lift station beside the road, but a very useful back-door-entry to the Valluga, often resorted to by St Anton

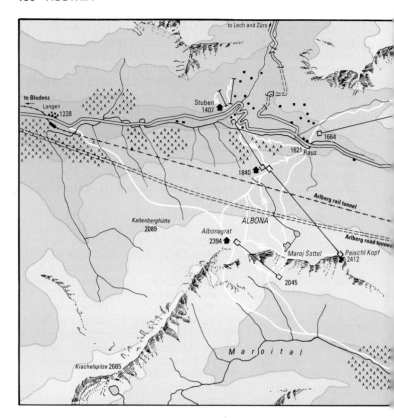

skiers and day-trippers from Lech/Zürs as a Galzig by-pass. It links up
with the Schindlergrat chair-lift, which takes you to much the same
skiing as the Valluga cable-car.

From **Stuben** a long and cold two-stage chair-lift climbs the steep
north-facing slopes of the Albona. Wind often makes it unpleasant, but
in the right conditions there is some exhilarating steep powder and piste
skiing. At the top you can restore circulation in the bar, or beside the
short Sonnleiten south-facing chair-lift. There is one run suitable for
intermediates down to Rauz, and a steeper off-piste descent to St
Christoph. A great excursion is the run down to Langen – unmarked
except by the warning sign at the outset and not easy to follow, but a
beautiful mixture of terrain. Equally beautiful and often more sheltered is
the run via the Maroital (much of it through thick woodlands) ending up
at a restaurant in the Verwalltal, a long walk from St Anton. The first
section requires a steep uphill climb – 'hard work, but worth it for the
beautiful path back down'.

Mountain restaurants are adequately spread around the slopes,
and there are a few memorable ones, notably the Rodelhütte above
Nasserein and the Ulmerhütte – one of the oldest mountain restaurants
in the Alps, and one of the best for sunset panoramas; recent reports

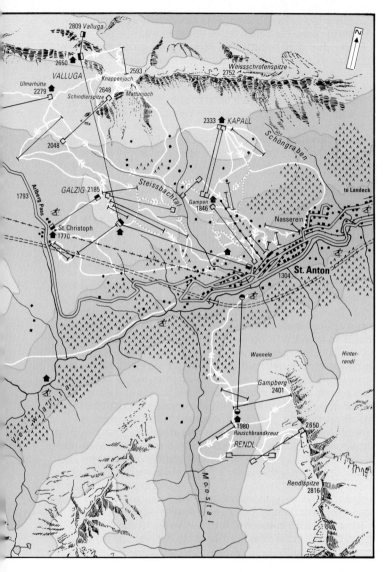

suggest that its standards are slipping. These huts get extremely crowded, and service is often without a smile. The restaurant at the top of the Valluga has panoramic views. The new Rendl Beach is bright and cheerful, and serves good home-made food, including vegetarian dishes. Several reporters have preferred to lunch in St Christoph (Hospitz Alm) or Stuben (Hotel Post or the Berghaus Stuben, at the bottom of the Albona chair – 'best lunch I had in a fortnight'). At the Albona mid-station is a pleasant new restaurant, in a sheltered, sunny spot. Reporters have approved of the aforementioned restaurant on the off-piste run down the Verwalltal, Rasthaus Ferwall.

From a **queueing** point of view, skiing the Valluga is no longer the nightmare it used to be, thanks to the new quad chair from the village to Galzig. Queues can still form at the Valluga cable-car but a ticket-reservation system is in operation which enables you to keep skiing until the number on your ticket comes up. If there are delays in the village, the best way round them is to catch a bus to Rauz. Lifts out of the Steissbachtal get very crowded – quarter-hour waits are common – though the installation of a four-seater chair-lift from the valley up to the Kapall chairs has helped. A great many reporters have complained of dangerously over-crowded pistes – 'often like skiing the M25 at rush hour'.

The resort employs movable guns to apply **artificial snow** on two long pistes down from Galzig, and on the lower slopes of Gampen, and many reporters have remarked on the effectiveness of the installation.

The resort

St Anton is a natural staging post at the bottom of the Arlberg pass road; mountains drop steeply down to the village from both north and south sides. There is room for the village to be by-passed by the main road – but only just, and a number of St Anton's hotels are in effect roadside ones. This main road is not nearly as busy as it used to be, now that the Arlberg tunnel has been constructed, but it is still noisy. Squashed uncomfortably between road and railway is the long, narrow resort centre. Its mixture of hotel buildings old and new, cafés, shops (three good supermarkets, all closing at 6pm) and hot-dog stalls is not the most picturesque in Austria, but the main street is colourful, traffic-free and always bustling. The village has grown into an inconvenient straggle, with chalets and hotels lining the road down to neighbouring villages. Nasserein is a not very convenient suburb where where many UK operators send their clients, not all of whom know where they are bound. St Anton is emphatically a young people's resort and has bars, discos and fast food to cater for their tastes and, to a certain extent, their budgets: it is not a cheap place to stay, but there are ways of living, and living it up, more cheaply than in many Austrian resorts.

There are buses between St Anton centre and St Jakob via Nasserein, and in the other direction to Mooser Kreuz, at the top of the resort. They are often overcrowded, especially between the centre and the Rendl lift station. There is no evening service. Post buses (again, often packed) go to St Christoph, Zürs, Lech, Stuben and Langen. Minibus-style taxis are common, and not expensive if you fill them. Several reporters have commented on the Volks Banc's useful automatic money-changing machine in the main street; you feed in sterling notes and get out Austrian schillings.

Accommodation is varied in comfort, style, cost and desirability of location. The last is important, and skiers lucky enough to stay centrally (in the attractive, expensive Post and Alte Post or the numerous more down-to-earth central B&B hotels such as the Haus Staffler) will be the envy of less privileged skiers stuck half-way between the resort centre and Nasserein, or up above the resort on the steep hill down from the Arlberg pass. Other recommended hotels include the Sporthotel (which houses the lively Stanton bar), the old-fashioned Valluga, the less expensive Kristall and the Grischuna ('fantastic location'). Eastwards along the valley there is ample scope (except in peak season) for skiers with a car to stay within range of St Anton, often very cheaply and

---

Facts on St Anton   Tirol **Austria**

Prices in schillings
Ski Club represented

Tourist office

Postcode A-6580
Tel (5446) 22690
Fax (5446) 253215
Tlx 58335

Getting there

By road 970km from Calais. Via Basle or Ulm, then Feldkirch. The Arlberg Pass is occasionally closed and often requires chains; the toll road-tunnel rarely presents difficulties.
By rail Main-line station in resort.
By air Zurich; transfer 3½hr. (Or Munich.)

Staying there

Visitor beds 8,000; breakdown: 7,000 in hotels and pensions, 1000 in apartments.
Package holidays Activity Travel (hcs) Austro Tours (h) Beach Villas (cs) Bladon Lines (hc) Chalets and Hotels "Unlimited" (hcs) Crystal (hr) Enterprise (h) Inghams (h) Made to Measure (hs) Mark Warner (c) Neilson (hr) Quality Ski Tours (h) Ski Club of GB (h) Ski Equipe (hc) Ski Partners (h) Ski Unique (h) Ski West (hc) Ski Whizz Small World (c) Snobiz (hrc) Supertravel (hc) Thomson (h) .
Medical facilities In resort: Doctors, dentist, chemist. Hospital: Zams (20km).

Non-skiing activities

Indoor Swimming pool (also hotel pools open to the public, with sauna and massage), tennis, squash, bowling, museum.
Outdoor 20km of cleared walks, natural skating rink (skating, curling), sleigh rides, tobogganing, ski-bob.

Kindergartens

Gastekindergarten
Tuition: Yes. Hours: 9.00-4.30. Ages: 3-14. Cost: 1,740.00 per week (with lunch). Free of charge for children between 3 and 4.

Special skiing facilities

Summer skiing No.
Cross-country About 40km along main valley going beyond St Jakob, and in Verwalltal. Marked but not graded.

Lift passes

Arlberg Pass
Covers St Anton, Lech, Zürs and Stuben lifts but not buses between them. (77 lifts in total.)
Cost 6 days 1,750.00 (£87.72). Low season: 1,560.00 saving 11%.
Credit cards accepted No.
Senior citizens 1,350.00 (over 65/60) saving 23%.
Children 1,000.00 (under 15) saving 43%. Free pass up to age 7.
Notes 'Special' Arlberg pass for 6, 7 or 13 days, about 100.00 less than normal price.'Snowman' card for under 7s, 100.00 for season. Available to all visitors staying in the resort.
Beginners Limited pass covering beginners' lifts.
Short-term passes Half-day from 12.00, single and return tickets on certain lifts, also 'Try-out' passes, starting 3pm, and day tickets, refundable when handed in.

Ski school

Arlberg
Classes 4hr: 2hr am and pm. Cost: 1,150.00 (6 days, Sun to Fri).
Lift priority No.
Children's classes Ages: 5-14. Cost: 1,070.00 (6 days, Sun to Fri).
Private lessons available Full- or half-day. Cost: 1,700.00 per hour. Each additional person 150.00.
Special courses One-day ski tour; wedel, powder and firn weeks.
Franz Klimmer
Classes 10.00-12.00 and 1.00-3.00. Cost: 1,050.00 (6 days).
Lift priority No.
Children's classes Ages: 5-14. Cost: 1,000.00 (6 days).
Private lessons available Full- or half-day. Cost: 1,550.00 per hour. Up to 2 people.
Special courses Snowboard course, 1,600 per day.

What was new in 91

1. New 'special' reduced Arlberg pass and 'snowman' card for kids – big savings on 6- and 13-day passes bought in the resort, so not worth buying in advance.
2. Free kindergarten facilities for 3 and 4 year olds.
3. 2 old chairs (the one from the bottom to Gampen and the one from Steissbachtal to Galzig) replaced by new quad chairs.

comfortably. We've had a favourable report on the Haus Hannis Spiss which has rooms and apartments on a B&B basis; 'very attractive, inexpensive, exceptionally friendly'. Chalet accommodation in and (mostly) around St Anton is also easily available. Several reporters found that being able to deposit skis and boots at the bottom of the Galzig lift took a lot of the discomfort out of the daily march to and from skiing.

Après-ski is extremely lively and varied – 'most tastes are catered for, from bop-till-you-drop disco-goers to the tea-and-strudel set'. There are mountain restaurants where skiers linger until dark; bowling; meals around the fire and tobogganing down from the Rodelhütte; lots of bars and tea rooms along the main street, full to bursting from late afternoon onwards (tea-dancing can usually be found, eg in the cosmopolitan Postkeller and in the exceptionally welcoming Sennehütte at the bottom of one of the main runs); lots of restaurants (particularly recommended are the Schwarzer Adler and the Harlequin ('good choice of vegetarian dishes, seafood and pasta'); cheap snack bars (the station bar serves good food and the cheapest beer in town; Hermann's hamburgers are 'something of an experience'; Promodoro has good pizzas); live bands, noisy pick-up joints and discos (the Drop In is reportedly very crowded, the Chick has a karaoke machine). Several reporters have remarked that the legendary Krazy Kangaruh, just above the resort, is overcrowded and over-rated, and that there is better service and better music in the Underground bar and the ever-popular Hazienda. Other recommended bars are Helmuts, Pub 37 and the Piccadilly ('boisterous, plays seventies music, dark and smokey'). Some reporters have commented unfavourably on the presence of large numbers of lively young people and the predominance of loud, bland pop music. Nasserein has a few bars and restaurants; Tom Dooley's is a 'delightful *stube*'; Alt St Anton is 'the best restaurant in town', and particularly attractive upstairs.

Although there are long **cross-country** trails (the Verwalltal is much prettier than the main valley trail beside road and railway), and lots of **non-skiing** activities (one reporter suggests the meditation classes), St Anton is emphatically a resort for keen skiers. The museum is well worth a visit, as are the day-trips to Innsbruck by train.

Despite a couple of recently added lifts, the **nursery slopes** are not very good, and even if they were St Anton would be no place for a beginner. Nasserein is the usual place where learners are confined, and there are small nursery lifts at Galzig and Gampen and on the Rendl.

St Anton's **ski school** has a reputation second to none, and many keen, proficient skiers who would scorn instruction anywhere else come to St Anton for this reason. One such skier was bitterly disappointed by her advanced tuition this year, but she seems to have been the exception rather than the norm; the locals think very highly of the new ski school director, Harald Rofner, and so in general do our reporters. Most reports are complimentary – 'we made amazing progress; within a week we'd skied all areas except Lech' – while only a few are critical ('our instructor spent a lot of time finding himself good powder'). A competing school opened last year, offering smaller classes and a more flexible approach – a welcome stimulus. The school claims to have drawn up a new programme especially for children in their mid-teens, and the **ski kindergarten** has received very favourable reports ('the Fantasyland nursery slope gave fun challenges and the instructors knew every child by name'), but one reporter witnessed several near-misses between children and speeding skiers. There is a youth centre where children can spend lunch-time or await collection at the end of the day.

Stuben 1410m

Stuben is a very small village beside the road on the western side of the Arlberg pass. It is dark, cold and windy, but one of the most convenient places to stay for getting around the Arlberg skiing, especially if you have a car. Rauz is nearby, for queue-free access to St Anton skiing, and Lech and Zürs are also close. There are buses in each direction. Stuben has its own skiing, described above, and also some excellent sunny nursery slopes on the other side of the road from the village (a drawback for toddlers). The village is quiet but does boast some traditional nightlife and has a few friendly hotel bars and restaurants (expensive and over-rated, says one experienced reporter).
Package holidays   Chalets and Hotels Unlimited (hcjas) Ski Miquel (h) Ski Total (hrj).

St Christoph 1780m

A few yards on the Tyrolean side of the Arlberg pass, St Christoph is no more than a few hotels and restaurants beside the road, among them the massive, smartly renovated and pricey old Hospiz. It is a bleak place to be when the blizzards howl, and is not recommended as a holiday base despite access to the Valluga by means of the little cable-car which carries a modest 250 skiers an hour to Galzig. The ski schools is highly regarded, and much in demand as a result.
Package holidays   Inghams (h).

Pettneu 1275m

Two enthusiastic reports from readers prompt us to offer a few words on this traditional Tyrolean village, down the valley from St Anton – both were impressed by its friendly, relaxed and quiet surroundings, and found it an economical base for skiing St Anton (the free ski-bus comes out this far). The local skiing is limited but not negligible – a chair-lift goes up to a beginners' area at Lavenar, and beyond that another up to over 2000m. The ski school operates in St Anton as well as locally, but apparently has some difficulty coping with English-speakers. Haus Matt is an 'excellent, commodious B&B'.
Package holidays   Crystal (hr).

Get stuck in

Lech Austria 1450m

Good for *Easy runs, resort-level snow, Alpine charm, sunny slopes, off-piste skiing, artificial snow, woodland runs, getting marooned*
Bad for *Tough runs, easy road access, mountain restaurants, short airport transfers, lift queues, getting marooned*

Linked resort: Zürs

The deep, steep bowl which divides the Arlberg's two major ski areas could be spanned, but has not been. No doubt this is in order to keep the St Anton riff-raff out of the high seclusion of Lech and Zürs – the smart, expensive, showy winter hideaways of rich and royal, with a national split (for Lech) of 60% German visitors, 20% Austrian, 2% British, and at least 95% swathed in furs. The two resorts share a skiing area which is varied, extensive and open but not well mechanised by modern standards and not as suitable for good piste skiers as for intermediates and beginners. As at St Anton, the more difficult runs are categorised as ski-routes or touring routes; both on and off these routes, the area offers a lot of off-piste skiing, but no great adventures.

Of the two resorts, Lech is the older, larger and more attractive by far – an established village with good cross-country skiing, delightful walks and other sports facilities, and moderately lively in the evenings. Oberlech is a car-free scattering of chalets and hotels in the middle of sunny, gentle ski-fields above Lech and linked to it by cable-car – an attractive base for families with small children. It has more accommodation than Zug, a very picturesque hamlet a mile or two from Lech up a pretty dead-end valley. Zürs is little more than a large group of expensive hotels – mainly modern, although the first hotel was opened over a century ago – above the tree-line along the road to Lech. It is not a French-style eyesore, but it is not attractive, or convenient for skiers – lifts are widely separated.

Lech and Zürs are only a few miles from the major road and rail link between Austria and Switzerland, but they are very awkward miles. Until the turn of the century, the villages could be reached from the Arlberg pass road only by a narrow and hazardous path, and were cut off all winter. Even now there are times when the Flexenpass is blocked for days on end. Parking in the village is restricted and ruthlessly policed; but a car is a great help for good skiers who are likely to be drawn to St Anton – though there are adequate bus services.

The skiing top 2450m bottom 1445m

Lech and Zürs share a skiing area spread over three mountains; you can get around all three on skis, but only clockwise, which means crowds of people all going the same way at the same time. Although the

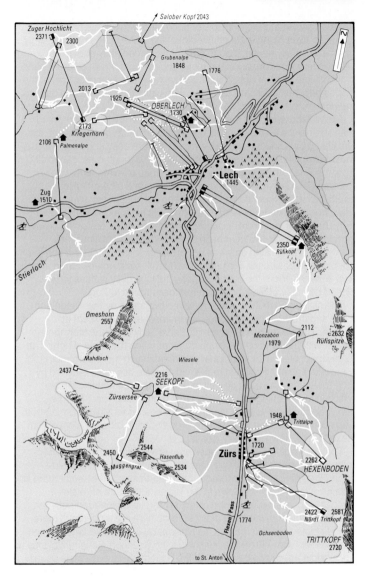

valleys are not wide, the connections across them are not perfect. Zürs is high, with all its skiing above the tree-line, while Lech has a more attractive arrangement of gentle lower slopes among woodland.

The **Rüfikopf** cable-car scales an impressive wall from the centre of Lech, too steep to be skied directly but with long, beautiful and difficult unprepared runs, often closed after heavy snowfall, in several directions – either down to Lech via the Wöster Täli or down the shoulder of the Rüfikopf to the woods by the road from Zürs. Long, beautiful pistes traverse across to Zürs, with lots of good off-piste variants.

Lech's main skiing area, on the other side of the river, is contrastingly open and mostly gentle, though the slopes immediately above the village are uncomfortably steep for near-beginners. From different parts of the village several lifts (including a fast new four-seat chair) serve the slopes between Lech and Oberlech. The cable-car has no piste back to the bottom, only a toboggan run.

Above **Oberlech**, lifts and pistes are spread in a wide, fragmented basin below the peaks of the Kriegerhorn and the Zuger Hochlicht, the two linked by a spectacular cable-car. There are easy and intermediate motorway pistes in all directions, but also some tough runs, especially from the Kriegerhorn – a couple of short, steep off-piste routes down towards Lech and to the Steinmähder chairs, and a beautiful long south-facing ski-route down to Zug, steep but not dauntingly so, where new snow soon deteriorates. Off-piste skiers have a choice of routes from the Zuger Hochlicht, including long traverses before skiing down either to Oberlech or Stubenbach or even Warth; most itineraries involve a lot of walking between bits of skiing. In the other direction the open slopes beside the Steinmähder chair-lift are much favoured after a new snowfall. From the bottom, a beautiful long gully schuss (often closed because of avalanche danger) leads round to Zug.

The skiing above Zürs is also split into two areas by the village and road, and the west-facing slopes are themselves split except at the bottom. The **Hexenboden** chair-lifts serve fairly ordinary intermediate pistes, with plenty of off-piste opportunities when the snow is right. The **Trittkopf** cable-car climbs higher and offers much more demanding runs, with some difficult and renowned off-piste descents reached by long traverses. The most difficult to reach is the run down to Stuben, which involves skiing over a gallery that protects the road. Beside Hexenboden there is a link lift (a fast four-seater) for skiers coming from Lech or for those who have skied the north-facing off-piste slopes from Hexenboden down into the Pazieltal.

The east-facing **Seekopf** slopes are served by a long drag-lift from above the centre of the village near the Zürserhof, and a road-side chair-lift starting below the village. At the north end of the sector there is one long, fairly easy run down to the village with some off-piste descents accessible by a short climb, ending up on the road between Lech and Zürs. On the other side of the lift there are a couple of more difficult pistes, graded red and, as elsewhere, off-piste variants around the hillside. From Zürsersee (just below the Seekopf) a chair-lift climbs a secluded north-facing bowl behind the Hasenfluh; its easy piste usually has good snow. The alternative is to drop over the back into a steep bowl and on to a beautiful out-of-the-way run (a piste, but not well marked) down the Zürser Täli back to Zürs. The other chair-lift from Zürsersee gives access to superb long runs behind the Omeshorn to Lech and Zug, on and off the piste. Both of these lift-free runs are manageable by plucky intermediates.

Mountain restaurants are surprisingly inadequate for such long-established and fashionable resorts. Palmenalpe above Zug is one of the better ones, and gets very crowded. The best places for lunch are

Zug (several restaurants, mostly quite a walk from the pistes), and Oberlech, where there is plenty of choice; the 14th-century Goldener Berg at the top of Oberlech might be captivating were it not so crowded.

The lift system has traditionally suffered from serious **queues** when the resorts are full, as they are for most of the season. Two of the traditional blackspots on the Zürs-Lech circuit, the lifts from below Zürs to Seekopf and from Zug up to Palmenalpe, have been upgraded; the Seekopf lift is now an efficient four-seater chair; sadly, we are still getting reports of serious morning queues, and the Seekopf lifts have priority entrances for local residents and ski school pupils. Other bottle-necks remain – notably the chairs from Zürsersee to Madloch-Joch and up the Zuger Hochlicht. The Trittkopf cable-car continues to be over-subscribed in the afternoon. Helicopter lifts are available.

Reporters are impressed by the piste grooming. Lech has **artificial snow** on all the main lower slopes, and Zürs has it on the bottom of the heavily skied runs from the Seekopf chair-lift.

The resort

Lech is a pleasant, sunny village with a church in the middle, and a covered wooden bridge over the river where sleigh horses take shelter from the elements. There are trees and old buildings, and the modern expansion of the resort has been unobtrusive; chalet-style hotels line the main street, next to the river, and smaller chalets are dotted around. As well as good everyday and ski shops, there are some very chic clothes shops. There are regular but not frequent (and not free) post buses connecting Lech, Zug, Zürs, Stuben, Langen and St Anton.

Accommodation is mostly in comfortable and expensive hotels. The village is fairly compact, and the location of accommodation is not very important, except for the very lazy. To do Lech in style the hotels to choose are the Post, a beautiful traditional hotel in the centre; the Arlberg, modern, plush, central and spacious; or the Tannbergerhof, the centre of Lech's gaudy social life – 'brilliant', says a recent visitor. There are numerous less formal hotels, and some rented chalets, but nowhere is cheap. Rooms are often very hard to come by in high season. Oberlech has several comfortable hotels near the cable-car station, and chalets spread widely around the hillside. The main attraction of staying here is to avoid ski-school crowds on the Schlegelkopf lifts out of Lech itself, and to be away from traffic. One of the most attractive and friendly hotels is the Sporthotel Petersboden, known for its piste-side Red Umbrella bar.

Après-ski is a serious and smart business: Lech après-skiers prefer to put their hair up rather than let it down. The Tannbergerhof has made itself the hub, with a very popular pavement bar in the afternoon, and a disco tea-dance following shortly afterwards; there is live music later on, here and in several other hotels. The Rüfikopf cable-car is turned into a moving cocktail bar at dusk. Dining and dancing out at Zug (by sleigh) and Oberlech (cable-car up, toboggan or walk down if you miss the last cable-car at 1am) are popular. The Goldener Berg at Oberlech does 'excellent' fondue evenings. The Hubertusklause has a cosy, little-known cellar-bar with live music, recommended.

Lech is an attractive place for **cross-country** and **non-skiers**, mainly because it is so pretty. Walks and X-C trails are not remarkably extensive but are well suited to those wanting to meet up with skiers.

The main **nursery slopes** are at Oberlech and are in all respects excellent – there are also very gently slopes above the village on the Rüfikopf side. Once off the nursery slopes, inexperienced skiers will find plenty of scope for building up speed and confidence. We have good reports of teaching standards in the **ski school**, though a recent qualified observer was critical of some instructors ('one pupil skied better than his instructor').

Facts on Lech Vorarlberg **Austria**

Prices in schillings

Tourist office
Postcode A-6764
Tel (5583) 21610
Fax (5583) 3155
Tlx 52680

Getting there
By road 970km from Calais. Via Ulm or Basle, then Feldkirch; chains are routinely needed, and the Flexenpass is liable to closure.
By rail Langen (15km); 12 buses daily from station, buses connect with international trains.
By air Zurich; transfer 3½hr. (Or Munich.)

Staying there
Visitor beds 6,732; breakdown: 6,026 in hotels, 706 in apartments/houses.
Package holidays Austro Tours (h) Crystal (hr) Inghams (h) Made to Measure (hs) Ski Unique (hs) Snobiz (h) Supertravel (hc) .
Medical facilities In resort: Fracture clinic, doctors, chemist. Hospital: Bludenz (40km). Dentist: St Anton (15km).

Non-skiing activities
Indoor Tennis, squash, hotel swimming pools and saunas, cinema, museum, art gallery.
Outdoor 25km of cleared walking paths, toboggan run (from Oberlech), natural skating rink (skating, curling), sleigh rides.

Kindergartens
Ski Kindergarten
Tuition: Yes. Hours: 9.00-4.00. Ages: 2½ up. Cost: 1,070.00 per week (includes meals, ski school supervision and use of baby-lift).

Special skiing facilities
Summer skiing No.
Cross-country 19km of cross-country trails from Stubenbach and to Zug and beyond; graded easy. Instruction available.

Lift passes
Arlberg pass
Covers all St Anton, Lech, Zürs and Stuben lifts, but not the buses between them. (77 lifts in total.)
Cost 6 days 1,750.00 (£87.72). Low season: 1,560.00 saving 11%.
Credit cards accepted No.
Senior citizens 1,350.00 (over 65/60) saving 23%.
Children 1,000.00 (under 15) saving 43%. Free pass up to age 7.
Notes 'Special' Arlberg pass for 6, 7 or 13 days, about 100.00 less than normal pass. 'Snowman' card for under sevens, 100.00 for season. Both available to visitors staying in the resort.
Beginners Limited day passes covering a few lifts.
Short-term passes Half-day and hourly tickets, refundable day tickets, single ascent tickets on some lifts.

Ski school
Lech and Oberlech
Classes 9.00-12.00 or 1.30-5.00. Cost: 1,240.00 (6 days Sun-Fri).
Lift priority No.
Children's classes Ages: 3½-12. Cost: 1,140.00 (6 days Sun-Fri). Children's ski school in Lech and Oberlech, 4hr per day, 10.00-12.00 and 2.00-4.00, lunch provided.
Private lessons available Full day only. Cost: 1,750.00 per hour. Each additional person 100.00.

What was new in 91
1. In Lech, the drag-lift from centre of Lech up to Schlegelkopf has been replaced by an express quad chair-lift.
2. In Zürs, the chair-lift up to Madloch is now a high-speed one and the short chair-lift to Trittalp is a quad.

Montafon multiplier

Schruns, Tschagguns, St Gallenkirch, Gaschurn, Gargellen
Austria

The Montafon is a large skiing region south of Bludenz in the Austrian Vorarlberg, spread along a long and populous valley which is a busy tourist thoroughfare in summer but a dead end in winter. The many villages along the valley (and pretty little Gargellen, tucked away in a secluded side valley) have got together to share a lift pass covering all the ski areas and the fairly frequent buses between them. It adds up to a bitty region of considerable appeal to skiers who want varied intermediate skiing and don't mind taking buses to get to it.

The Montafon is easily reached from southern Germany and, even more than most Austrian areas, is German-dominated; there are weekend coach-party invasions. Gargellen was a great favourite in the early days of package tours to Austria, but there are few British visitors these days and little English is spoken. Our few reporters have recommended the area for its broad, open, well-mechanised intermediate skiing with the chance of long runs down to the valley when the snow is good at these low levels. Reporters also appreciate the friendliness of the villages, by no means the most picturesque in Austria (they all straggle), but less affected by tourism than most. Schruns is the most convenient base for those relying on buses to get around, as the two relevant bus services go from here to Partenen (the end of the road in winter) and Gargellen. Gaschurn and Gargellen are the most charming resorts, and the least subject to the weekend influx.

The main resort in the valley is **Schruns** (700m), a busy little market town and spa beside the river, accessible by train from Bludenz. The skiing is reached by a long two-stage cable-car from near the town centre or a gondola from beside the Montafon road; both go to Kappell (1850m), where a good nursery area is cordoned off from other skiers. Above Kappell a chain of chair-lifts opens up a large area of open easy skiing beneath the rocky crests of Kreuzjoch and Hochjoch – in the view of one reporter, about the best early-intermediate ski area in the Alps. There are some more taxing runs down to Kappell including a possible 11km run for nearly 1700m vertical if snow is good enough to ski down to the village. Slopes face north and north-west. The centre of Schruns is car-free and shopping is attractively varied. There is plenty for non-skiers to do, including skating and curling, squash, a local museum, a reading room, sleigh rides, and indoor tennis and swimming at the large, central Hotel Löwe which is also the focus of Schruns après-ski.

Schruns almost merges with its smaller neighbour **Tschagguns**, on the other side of the valley. There are two small ski areas, neither of them immediately accessible from the village. The larger is Golm (1000m to 2085m), which has some entertaining open and lightly treed intermediate skiing, including a friendly women's downhill course, above the mid-station of its funicular railway – and an 'especially attractive' woodland run down the bottom section.

Higher up the valley, skiing consists of the extensive M-shaped Silvretta Nova system, created by the integration of the north-east-facing slopes above the neighbouring villages of **St Gallenkirch** (880m) and **Gaschurn** (1000m) via the Novatal which divides them. There is lots of space and lots of easy ground to cover on the broad slopes. Lifts reach 2370m above St Gallenkirch and 2200m above Gaschurn, where there are a couple of tougher runs and some good off-piste skiing. Busy lifts have been duplicated in most places, but there are still peak-time queues, especially at weekends. Gaschurn has a long six-seat access gondola with an easy (but over-used and often worn) run down to the valley at Gaschurn. The other access gondola is at the northern end of St Gallenkirch (Galgenul) but the only pistes down to the valley are under the Garfrescha chairs at the southern end. Gaschurn has a tennis hall. The Verwall hotel is 'very comfortable and friendly, with excellent food'.

Gargellen (1430m) is a miniature resort (it has only 750 guest beds) tucked away beneath the Madrisa in a secluded side valley away from the main Montafon thoroughfare. It is an old British family favourite, mainly thanks to the very high standard and the friendliness of the Hotel Madrisa, the main village institution, now expensively modernised but still very handsome. It is the centre of Gargellen après-ski, has a good nursery slope in the back garden, a ski hire shop, swimming pool, fitness room and children's play area. We have favourable reports of the ski school (though English is not widely spoken), and in particular of the excellent ski kindergarten. One reporter could find only one reason for hesitation in recommending Gargellen: the thought that it might be 'discovered', and spoiled. But another was unimpressed by the old-fashioned lift system and high prices. Gargellen's skiing, on the north-east-facing Schafberg, is small but attractively varied. There are easy open slopes at the top of the system between 2000m and 2300m, a beautiful long easy run round the mountain from the top to the Gargellenalp mid-station restaurant (1730m), a short blackish route under the chair-lift to the same point, and some good off-piste skiing nearby. Runs down through the woods to the edge of the straggling village are friendly, and snow at resort level is relatively reliable.

The Montafon has long been famous as an excellent base for ski tours (and, recently, heli-skiing) in the beautiful Silvretta and Rätikon mountains which separate Austria and Switzerland. Tourers strike out from the top of the lifts above Gaschurn, Tschagguns and Gargellen, where the favourite and least arduous excursion is over to Switzerland via Antönierjoch and the beautiful, notoriously avalanche-prone valley of St Antönien. This is only a short bus and train ride away from Klosters whose Madrisa lifts lead back towards Gargellen via the Schlappinerjoch. The skiing is not difficult, the uphill sections are not long, and the resorts honour one another's lift passes. The Silvrettasee (1950m) above Partenen is the best starting point for serious tours in the Silvretta peaks and has high-altitude cross-country skiing.

Tourist offices Gaschurn ✆ (5558) 8201; Schruns ✆ (5556) 2253; Tschagguns ✆ (5556) 2457; St Gallenkirch ✆ (5557) 6234; Gargellen ✆ (5557) 6303.

Ski-running in the old-fashioned way

Davos Switzerland 1560m

Good for *Big ski area, off-piste skiing, ski touring, cross-country skiing, not skiing, sunny slopes, rail access, easy runs*
Bad for *Alpine charm, skiing convenience, freedom from cars*

Klosters Switzerland 1130m

Good for *Big ski area, ski touring, mountain restaurants, sunny slopes, cross-country skiing, easy road access, rail access*
Bad for *Après-ski, skiing convenience*

If skiing has its magic mountain, it is the Parsenn above Davos and Klosters, where the ski pioneers of the 19th century discovered a large range of long and beautiful descents in all directions. These runs have not been bettered: for skiers with a taste for long, leisurely outings involving frequent stops at mountain huts and a train-ride home, the Parsenn is in a league of its own. And it is only one part of the huge range of skiing on offer in this extensive region.

The two resorts which share the Parsenn have little else in common, apart from affluence and long-standing British connections. Davos is one of the big towns of Alpine skiing, and with its square, block buildings it is no beauty; for Swiss Alpine charm, look elsewhere. Already established as a health resort before recreational skiing was invented, it took to the new sport quickly. It was in Davos that a funicular railway was first built especially to carry skiers, and it was here that the first drag-lift was installed.

Thanks largely to the patronage of Prince Charles, Klosters has an exclusive image. It is quite attractive, and smaller and quieter than Davos – a place in which to spend months of the winter, in the seclusion of your chalet. Its local skiing is curious, with exciting and very beautiful runs spread across an enormous north-facing mountain served by hardly any lifts. Until its recent enlargement, the result has been very serious queues for the cable-car out of the village.

A car is helpful in making the most of the separate ski areas – though parking near the lifts is difficult – and (as if the local skiing were not sufficient) for expeditions to St Moritz and Lenzerheide. Arosa and Gargellen (in Austria) are more easily reached on short ski tours. Frequent buses (oversubscribed in high season) link Davos Dorf and Platz from early morning until late in the evening, with more occasional services running elsewhere. In Klosters, day-time buses every half-hour serve Gotschna and Madrisa lifts and points between. There are buses from Serneus about every hour, and frequent trains linking all the ski areas except Pischa. With one or two minor exceptions, all these services are covered by the lift pass.

The skiing top 2844m bottom 813m

The core of the skiing is the Parsenn/Weissfluh area above Davos Dorf, which links up with Strela above Davos Platz and the Gotschna area above Klosters Platz. Most of the lifts are on the Davos side of the mountain, but Klosters has the north-facing slopes and more than its fair share of good skiing. There are four other separate ski areas which offer excellent skiing with much less crowding. The Jakobshorn, the other side of Davos, has excellent challenging runs and very good off-piste skiing when conditions are right. The Rinerhorn, above Glaris, has a good range of skiing giving a drop of over 1000m. The other two areas are not shown on our maps: Madrisa, above Klosters Dorf, is excellent for sunshine, uncomplicated skiing and tours over to Austria and back; Pischa is a little-skied open mountainside with good off-piste potential.

From Davos Platz the **Strela** skiing is reached by a steep funicular to the sunny Schatzalp, where there is a large and comfortable old hotel. From here, there is a toboggan run down to Platz, a path for walkers and skiers down to Dorf and off-piste skiing for adventurers. Above the Schatzalp, the east-facing open bowl below the Strela Pass consists of mainly easy skiing down the middle, and some steeper runs. These lifts are used less for the skiing they serve directly than for access to many famous old ski-tours – both on the Davos/Glaris side of the range and down to Arosa over the other side – and as a back-door way into the Parsenn ski area, via a cable-car and drag-lift.

These lifts take you to **Weissfluhjoch**, the major lift junction above Davos and the point of arrival of the Parsenn funicular railway from Davos Dorf. There are enormous possibilities in three directions: first, back towards Davos Dorf – south-east-facing slopes, gentle on the top half, steeper and often icier lower down. Secondly, the extensive, open, mostly easy motorway pistes behind the Weissfluhjoch, the heart of the **Parsenn** skiing (now with a much enlarged cable-car from Parsennhütte); for good skiers there is an excellent run, steep in places, from the Meierhoftälli drag-lift to the railway at Wolfgang, which can also be reached by a long woodland track, an easy red unless icy, from Parsennhütte. And thirdly, tremendously long runs (10km to 15km), open at first and then wooded, to the villages of Klosters, Serneus, Saas, Küblis and even beyond, to Landquart. Unless you start from the top of the Weissfluh (reached by cable-car) none of the runs is particularly difficult – easiest is a straightforward red via Cavadürli to Klosters, trickiest is a moderate red to Serneus. The mountain is basically north-facing and snow is pretty reliable, though the lower slopes may well be bare or patchy. In between the various runs, there is some tough off-piste skiing in the woods. Recently an extremely long gondola was opened, going from Schifer (1560m) across these previously unmechanised ski-fields to Weissfluhjoch, making it possible to ski the top part of the Serneus run repeatedly. Although this lift diminishes the attractions of the upper part of this area, at least for those who knew it in its virgin state, we're told that there are now fewer skiers on the lower wooded parts (and in the *schwendis* thereon). The runs to Jenaz and Fideris require skins for two uphill sections, before and after the surprising collection of lifts and restaurants at Fideriser Heuberge. These lifts are not covered by the area pass, or so the attendant asserts. The skiing is not steep, but route finding on the lower slopes is not obvious.

The two-stage **Prince of Wales Gotschnagrat** cable-car from near Klosters Platz railway station is the only lift to the Parsenn from Klosters. There are runs of varying difficulty back towards Klosters. The direct run back down to the Gotschnaboden mid-station is the Gotschnawang (or simply Wang) – a slope of awesome steepness, dropping about 500m – which was notorious even before the famous fatal avalanche on an adjacent off-piste slope in 1988. The Wang run itself is categorised as a piste, but is not marked; in practice there are numerous routes down the broad face, ranging from steep to extreme. Mercifully, the slope is often closed either because of too much snow or not enough. Next along the mountainside is Drostobel, a magnificent black run – long, steep, but nothing like as intimidating as the Wang, and safer. On the other side of Gotschnagrat there is an easy traverse across to Parsennhütte and some very easy runs beside the Parsennmeder drag-lift. Underneath the neighbouring Schwarzsee chair-lift is a black run which often consists of formidable moguls. The red run from the bottom of the chair-lift takes you through the woods to a not very convenient fringe of Klosters Platz.

The very sunny, south-west facing **Madrisa** bowl above the Saaseralp (1880m) is reached by gondola from Klosters Dorf. Most of the skiing is above the tree-line, and includes a good nursery area near the Saaseralp and some long runs from the top of the Madrisa lift (2542m), including an unprepared black run to Saaseralp and the beautiful Schlappin run all the way down a wooded valley to the village, marked black but not difficult. This run is joined by a similar black going down directly from Saaseralp, but the wooded lower slopes below Saaseralp are otherwise not skied, and timid intermediates take the lift down. From this area you can make a day-tour round the Madrisa, over to Gargellen in Austria; the skiing is not particularly difficult, but a guide is recommended (as well as a passport). The return route is via the Gargellen lifts (covered by the lift pass) and about an hour on skins, followed by excellent off-piste skiing to St Antönien, a delightful village with buses back to Küblis.

A cable-car serves the whole south-west-facing slope of **Pischa** (1800m to 2485m). There is a simple array of parallel drag-lifts above the tree-line with very sunny, mostly intermediate runs beside them, and some more difficult descents through the trees. There is easy off-piste skiing beside the runs and some much more adventurous possibilities behind the Pischahorn and along the shoulder down to the Klosters road at Laret.

The **Jakobshorn** is the most extensive alternative to the Parsenn/ Weissfluhjoch skiing, and the most handy from Davos, with access from near Platz station. Above the tree-line there is a wide range of long, mostly intermediate runs, facing roughly west, below the peaks of Jakobshorn and Brämabüel. Both are fairly steep at the top. There is

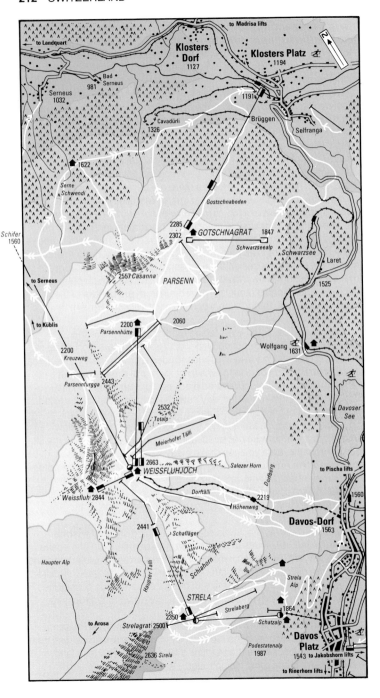

to Madrisa lifts

**Klosters
Dorf**
1127

Klosters Platz
1194

to Landquart

Bad
Serneus

981

Serneus
1032

1191

Brüggen

Selfranga

Cavadürli
1326

1622

Serne
Schwendi

Schifer
1560

Gostschnaboden

2285
2302

GOTSCHNAGRAT 1847

Schwarzseealp

Schwarzsee

Laret

2557 Casanna

PARSENN

1525

to Serneus

to Küblis

2200
Parsennhütte

2060

Wolfgang
1631

2200
Kreuzweg

2443
Parsennfurgga

Davoser
See

2532
Totalp

Meierhofer Tälli

2663
WEISSFLUHJOCH

Salezer Horn

Dorfberg

to Pischa lifts

1560

Weissfluh 2844

Dorftälli

2219

Höhenweg

Davos-Dorf
1563

2441

Schafläger

Haupter Alp

Schiahorn

Haupter Tälli

Strela
Alp

STRELA

Strelaberg

1864

Schatzalp

to Arosa

2350
Strelagrat 2500

Podestatenalp
1987

2636 Sirela

**Davos
Platz**
1543 to Jakobshorn lifts

to Rinerhorn lifts

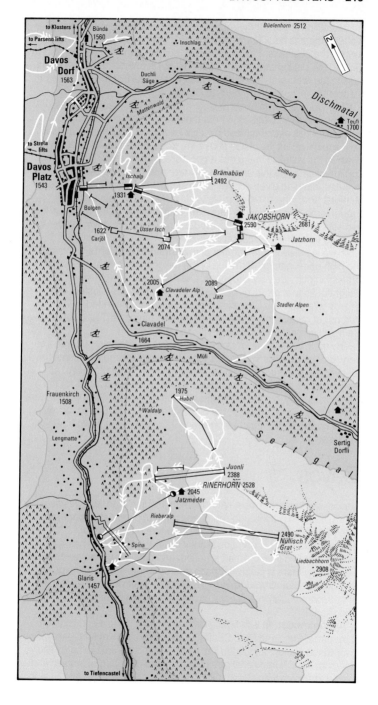

gentler skiing in the sunny, west-facing bowl above Clavadeleralp. The woodland paths back to Davos Platz are not appealing, but there is always the cable-car. The north-facing descent from the Jakobshorn to Teufi in the Dischmatal (nearly 900m below) is one of the best off-piste runs in the area, with a beautiful isolated restaurant at the bottom and an occasional bus service back to Davos.

Rinerhorn is a small area of west-and north-west-facing slopes. Early risers will be pleased to hear that the old, cold chair-lift up to Jatzmeder has been replaced by a six-seat gondola. There is nothing very special about the pistes above the trees, but there are enough runs down to the valley to make this a good area in poor visibility. We cannot confirm claims that this area is a powder-snow paradise. About 20 minutes' climbing gives access to the steep, north-facing side of the Sertigtal from where it is possible to ski down to the train station at Frauenkirch. There is some less extensive off-piste skiing between the two sets of drag-lifts above Jatzmeder, and a long run down to Glaris, reached from the Nüllischgrat drag-lift.

There is an adequate number of **mountain restaurants**, but most of the high ones, notably at the top of the Jakobshorn and at Weissfluhjoch, are very cheerless. Outstandingly attractive are the delightful *schwendis* in the woods on the way down to Klosters and nearby villages – the Contessa is especially recommended – and a number of restaurants in the valleys around Davos (at Teufi, Clavadel, Sertig, Glaris and at the bottom of Pischa).

The main access lifts for both resorts have traditionally suffered from very serious **queues** in high season. The recent lift improvements have relieved the pressure in Klosters ('no problems in March, except at weekends'). From Davos, we have reports of serious queues for the Parsenn railway, but the Strela lifts provide a by-pass. Several reporters have criticised the large number of antiquated T-bars. Davos has no **artificial snow**; Klosters has one snow-gun on the run down from Madrisa.

Davos

Davos is set in a spacious, flat-bottomed junction of valleys beside a lake. The town is a through-route, and often unpleasantly congested with traffic. Buildings are square, grey, concrete and mostly undecorated. Platz is perhaps slightly uglier than Dorf, but has the better shopping (lots of smart jewellers and boutiques) and après-ski. Fortunately there is plenty of space nearby where you can find peace and quiet in beautiful surroundings, and a few outlying hamlets which offer accommodation and easy access to the railway (such as Wolfgang and Glaris).

Accommodation is in hotels large and small, simple and luxurious, throughout Platz and Dorf. Central Platz is more convenient – an easy walk to the station, and to the lifts for Strela and the Jakobshorn. The Belvedere is the traditional grand hotel, these days part of a chain and more expensive than stylish. Of the well-placed hotels, the Alte Post is

Facts on Davos Graubunden **Switzerland**

Prices in francs
Ski Club represented

Tourist office

Promenade 67, Postfach 198
Postcode CH-7270
Tel (81) 435135
Fax (81) 431410
Tlx 853130

Getting there

By road 1,002km from Calais. Via Basle/Zurich.
By rail Station in resort centre.
By air Zurich; transfer 3hr. (Or Basle.)

Staying there

Visitor beds 22,000; breakdown: 6,500 in hotels,
14,000 in apartments, some in others.
Package holidays Crystal (h) Inghams (hs)
Kuoni (h) Made to Measure (hs) Ski Europe (y)
Ski Unique (h) SnowRanger (hs) Supertravel (h)
Swiss-Ski (h) Tailor Made (hs) Thomson (h) .
Medical facilities In resort: Hospital, doctors,
chemists, dentists, oculist.

Non-skiing activities

Indoor Artificial skating rink, fitness centre,
tennis, squash, swimming, sauna, cinema,
museums, galleries.
Outdoor Over 80km of cleared paths (mostly at
valley level), natural skating rink, curling,
toboggan run, horse-riding, hang-gliding, sleigh
rides, paragliding.

Kindergartens

Pinocchio (Davos Dorf)
Tuition: possible with ski school. Hours:
9.00-5.00. Ages: 2½-10. Cost: 149.00 per week
(5 full days with lunch and ski pass).
Mickymaus (Platz)
Tuition: possible with ski school. Hours:
9.00-5.00. Ages: 2½-10. Cost: 149.00 per week
(5 full days with lunch).
Other childcare facilities
Monday morning lessons for mums and kids over
3.

Special skiing facilities

Summer skiing No.
Cross-country About 75km of trails along the
main valley between Glaris and Wolfgang, and up
the Flüela, Dischma and Sertig valleys. Dogs
allowed between Davos Platz and Glaris; small
illuminated loop between Platz and Dorf. Runs
graded easy to medium. Instruction available.

Lift passes

Rega pass
Covers all Davos and Klosters lifts, the railway in
the whole region and buses within the 2 resorts.
(55 lifts in total.)
Cost 6 days 212.00 (£88.33). Low season:
170.00 saving 20%.
Credit cards accepted Yes.
Senior citizens 170.00 (over 70) saving 20%.
Children 127.00 (under 16) saving 40%. Free
pass up to age 6.
Notes Also valid in Gargellen (Austria).
Beginners Books of tickets for nursery lifts;
single and return tickets on main lifts in each area.
Short-term passes Half-day and day passes for
individual areas (eg Jakobshorn).
Other passes A confusing array of passes
covering limited areas (Jakobshorn, Rinerhorn,
Parsenn and Gotschna, Schatzalp and Strela,
Madrisa and other combinations).
Other periods Passes for 8 non-consecutive
days.

Ski school

Swiss Ski School
Special 5-day ski school and lift pass packages
available.
Classes 4hr: 2hr am and pm. Cost: 162.00 (5
days).
Lift priority No.
Children's classes Ages: 4-16. Cost: 130.00 (5
days). Special teenage classes (14-20) during
school holidays.
Private lessons available Half-day, full-day, or
per hour. Cost: 48.00 per hour. Up to 2 people.
Special courses 'Ski sauvage' in certain weeks
of the season; snowboard school, 105.00 for 5
days.

cheerful and reasonable in price. The Meisser is well placed, off the
main road, and less expensive than most of its neighbours. The
Sporthotel at Clavadel is 'excellent, and good value in every respect'.
The Montana, near Dorf station, has received high praise, as have the
Flüela ('excellent service, food and rooms – a first-class establishment')
and the Schweizerhof ('old-fashioned, excellent service'). A slight hike
up the hill behind the town is the Stolzenfels, a quiet family hotel, newly
renovated.

Après-ski is not particularly chic, but there is a variety of bars,
restaurants and well-attended dance spots, though most reporters have
found the place very quiet in the evenings. Some of the most attractive
and least expensive eating places are outside Davos – evenings at Teufi

(reached by car or sleigh) and Schatzalp (last train down at 11pm) are particularly recommended. There is evening skating several times a week at Dorf; Platz has hockey matches, cinemas, and occasional cultural events at the conference centre. Schneider's Café is recommended for tea: 'fabulous cakes'.

Although not a picturesque resort, Davos is large and well equipped with **non-skiing** facilities, including Switzerland's largest natural ice rink – 'the equivalent of several football pitches', according to one reporter – and a popular swimming pool. Gentle walks were the order of the day for the consumptives who first patronised Davos, and it is still an excellent place for walkers – quiet valleys with attractive restaurants, and a few higher paths. **Cross-country** skiing is very popular, with long and attractive valley runs.

Although Davos is not really an ideal place for beginners, the **nursery slopes** beside Davos Platz at the bottom of the Jakobshorn are adequate. Klosters has a good sunny nursery area on the Madrisa at Saaseralp, and a few small lifts beside Klosters Dorf.

Davos is a celebrated area for short ski-tours, and the **ski school** organises group excursions from February onwards. We have good reports, at least of the Rinerhorn branch – video sessions available.

Klosters

In Klosters, Platz and Dorf are separate villages, Platz very much the centre of skiing and social life – a recognisable village centre, with a number of hotels and shops. Both villages are spread along beside the busy through-road and railway, enclosed in a narrowing wooded valley which admits little sunlight in midwinter.

Accommodation consists mostly of private chalets, with some hotels in both villages. Platz is the more convenient base, with a number of comfortable and expensive hotels around the main street near the station and cable-car. One reporter recommends the central, new Silvretta – 'modern and comfortable'. The Alpina Aparthotel is a very smart neo-rustic chalet, the Chesa Grischuna is smaller, older and more desirable. The Kaiser, not far from the cable-car station, is 'excellent and typically Swiss'. The Vereina, just opposite, is also 'traditionally charming', with 'quiet, cosy rooms, and excellent management'; it has a non-ski kindergarten and a large swimming pool. The small Wynegg is a traditional British favourite – warm, welcoming and about as cheap you'll find, though its situation on the road toward Davos is not ideal. Another British favourite is the Steinbock.

Après-ski is quiet. The most attractive places for tea are up the mountain, though in Platz there are several congenial bars and three discos. More sophisticated visitors gravitate to the piano bar below the Chesa Grischuna, or to the Casa Antica. In Dorf the Madrisa Bar is nice for traditional music, dancing and décor, and the Blue Parrot is recommended for 'the young people'. Bowling is available at the Bündnerhof and Chesa Grischuna hotels. For eating out, Chesa Grischuna is the most attractive place, while the Wynegg has the best atmosphere – by appointment to HRH PoW. The Sonne is also recommended.

Klosters does not have the **non-skiing** facilities of Davos, but it is a more attractive place to spend time, and has beautiful walks and **cross-country** skiing trails. The straggling layout along the road is a bit of a drawback – though you can get away up the Vereinatal.

We have one recent and highly favourable report on **ski school** – 'private lessons were profitable and unhurried'. One reporter decided against using the ski kindergarten because the facilities appeared to be minimal – 'a scaled-down version of adult teaching'. Guides are available for ski-tours, including the excursion to Gargellen.

Facts on Klosters   Graubunden **Switzerland**

Prices in francs
Ski Club represented

Tourist office

Promenade 67, Postfach 198
Postcode CH-7250
Tel (81) 691877
Fax (83) 694906
Tlx 853333

Getting there

By road 1,002km from Calais. Via Basle/Zurich; chains may be needed from Klosters.
By rail Station in resort centre.
By air Zurich; transfer 3hr.

Staying there

Visitor beds 8,600; breakdown: 2,000 in hotels, 6,600 in apartments.
Package holidays Crystal (h) Kuoni (h) Made to Measure (hs) Powder Byrne (hc) Ski Club of GB (h) Ski Europe (y) Ski Unique (h) SkiGower (hy) SnowRanger (h) Supertravel (h) Tailor Made (hs) .
Medical facilities In resort: Doctors, chemists, dentist. Hospital: Davos (12km).

Non-skiing activities

Indoor Hotel saunas and swimming pools (open to public), squash/fitness centre, galleries, museum, Küblis tennis centre (10min by car).
Outdoor Natural ice-rink (night skating twice a week, curling, ice hockey), sleigh rides, 3 toboggan runs, 30km of cleared paths (mostly at valley level).

Kindergartens

Madrisa mountain restaurant
Tuition: Yes. Hours: 10.00-12.30 and 1.30–4.00. Ages: 3 up. Cost: 96.00 per week (without lunch).
Hotel Vereina
Tuition: No. Hours: 9.30-4.30, Mon-Fri. Ages: 2-6. Cost: 200.00 per week (with lunch). Baby care on request.
Other childcare facilities
Hotels Steinbock and Vereina do lunches for children in ski school for 12.00.

Special skiing facilities

Summer skiing No.
Cross-country About 40km of trails, between Serneus and Dorf, and in the Vereinatal above Platz. Dogs allowed on small loop near Platz; illuminated two evenings a week. Instruction available.

Lift passes

Rega pass
Covers all the Klosters and Davos lifts, the railway in the whole region and buses within the 2 resorts. (55 lifts in total.)
Cost 6 days 212.00 (£88.33). Low season: 170.00 saving 20%.
Credit cards accepted No.
Children 127.00 (under 16) saving 40%. Free pass up to age 6.
Notes Also valid in Gargellen (Austria).
Beginners Books of tickets for nursery lifts (free nursery lift at Klosters Dorf); single and return tickets on main lifts in each area.
Short-term passes Half-day and day passes for individual areas (eg Jakobshorn).
Other passes A confusing array of passes covering limited areas (Jakobshorn, Rinerhorn, Parsenn and Gotschna, Schatzalp and Strela, Madrisa and other combinations).
Other periods Passes of 8 non-consecutive days.

Ski school

Swiss Ski School
Classes 2hr am or pm. Cost: 105.00 (6 days).
Lift priority No.
Children's classes Ages: 13. Cost: 100.00 (6 days). Lunch for ski school pupils 12.00 per day at Hotel Steinbock.
Private lessons available Half-day, full day and 50 mins (over lunch-time). Cost: 50.00 per hour. 1 to 3 people.
Special courses Ski touring.

What was new in 91

New 4-star Silvretta Park Hotel in centre of Klosters with 280 beds, health centre, swimming pool, beauty salon, sauna, solarium, and hairdresser.

Arosa Switzerland 1775m

Good for *Easy runs, not skiing, cross-country skiing, ski touring, nursery slopes, sunny slopes, resort-level snow, rail access*
Bad for *Tough runs, easy road access, woodland runs*

Of the large, long-established, traditional winter sports centres of Switzerland, Arosa is one of the less widely known in Britain, and for dedicated skiers one of the less interesting. The ski area is high and sunny, but it is not large and most of the runs are not long, and neither the village nor the winter clientele is particularly beautiful. Nevertheless Arosa commands the loyalty of many regular visitors (mostly Swiss and German, but with the British coming third), and it is an excellent place for a varied winter holiday, with some of the most beautiful mountain walks, cross-country trails and sleigh rides in the Alps, and very good ice-rinks; about a third of Arosa's visitors don't ski. Reporters agree that the people are very friendly. But there are drawbacks – principally, the ugliness of Obersee's square grey buildings, and the resort's very awkward layout, in two separate parts – the main centre (Obersee) and the higher old village of Innerarosa – plus development along the steep road linking the two. A further burst of reports this year insisting that Arosa is not 'bad for skiing convenience' has finally persuaded us to change our verdict in that respect; we know the ski-bus is frequent and reliable and that it is possible to ski back to some of the hotels (particularly those in Innerarosa), but don't lose sight of the fact that from some points of the resort access to the ski areas is far from ideal.

The road up to Arosa is tricky, parking and driving in the village is strictly controlled and difficult, and a car isn't much use except for expeditions to Lenzerheide or (more likely) Davos and Klosters.

The skiing top 2653m bottom 1745m

Arosa's ski area largely consists of open slopes above the trees, in two sectors – mainly south-east facing on the Weisshorn and mainly north-east facing below Hörnli. The two sectors are linked by lifts and pistes, and by free (and frequent) buses serving the three bottom stations of the system. An unusual feature of the area is crossing paths with non-skiers. There are runs for toboggans and cleared walking trails across most of the ski area, and sleighs carrying tourists from Maran up to Tschuggen and down to Innerarosa. On a fine day the ski-fields present a rare and attractive picture of a traditional winter sports recreation area.

From Obersee, a two-stage cable-car climbs from near the station and lake to Tschuggen – a broad, sunny plateau above the tree line, also accessible by chair and tow from Innerarosa – and on to the

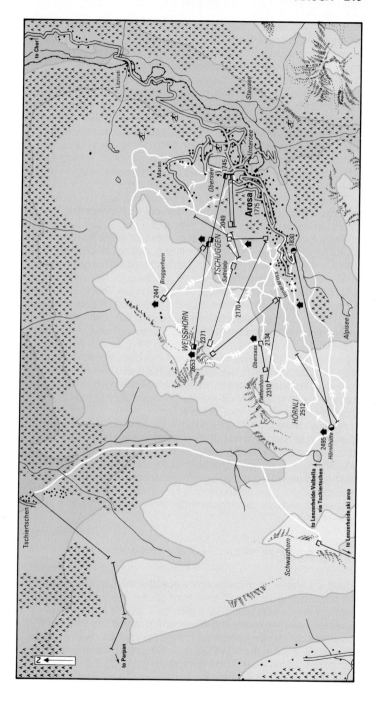

impressive **Weisshorn** (2653m), which has the steepest slopes in the ski area. One run from the top is black, but not very severe except when the south-facing slopes have frozen overnight, and there are some short, steep off-piste pitches between the rocky outcrops down the flanks of the Horn. The other pistes are mostly intermediate and easy. Off-piste skiing is limited to brief forays between the trails except for the steep (and in some cases very difficult) runs off the back and the sides of the Weisshorn, which involve long excursions – to Tschiertschen, Litziruti and Chur. From the top of the Bruggerhorn chair-lift, a long motorway run flanks the mountain and descends to Maran, an uphill suburb of Arosa. Below Tschuggen is the only part of the Arosa ski area which is wooded; there are three runs to Obersee, one under the lift, the other two easier and more roundabout, via Maran.

The slopes of the **Hörnli** are mainly served by a long six-seater gondola which starts an inconvenient distance from Innerarosa. The pistes back down are mostly open, wide and undemanding, but there is one long red run on the south side of the gondola. From the restaurant on the ridge at the top you look down into an inviting bowl and hidden valley. It is a beautiful ski excursion with a marked but not groomed run of no great difficulty down to the woods and along the flank of the mountainside to the little ski village of Tschiertschen. Provided you set out early, you can go from there to Lenzerheide, and ski back either via the Hörnli or down the beautiful, remote off-piste run past Älplisee.

Mountain restaurants are adequate. The sunny restaurant at the top of the Hörnli has a friendly atmosphere, and being accessible on foot is a popular target for non-skiing hikers and their dogs when the weather is fine. Carmennahütte is jolly and atmospheric, and is at present being extended; there are outdoor bars here and at Tschuggen (another good place for meeting up with non-skiers). The Alpenblick, on the fringe of Innerarosa, is a popular spot for lunch.

Although limited, the lift system in general is not prone to serious **queues**. Half-hour waits for the Hörnli gondola are a thing of the past now that its capacity has been improved. Planned improvements to the Weisshorn cable-car should further improve things next season. Contrary to previous disparaging remarks about piste maintenance, reports this year have been uniformly favourable. **Artificial snow** has not been in evidence, but apparently there is a 'useful' moveable snow cannon.

The resort

Arosa is remotely set at the head of a beautiful steep wooded valley at the end of a long, winding 20 miles from Chur. At the bottom, the main centre of the resort is built, in very plain style, around a small lake (Obersee) with the railway and Weisshorn lift station nearby. From here the village climbs along, above and below the road, for about a mile to Innerarosa, which is the old village up in the sunny pastures – pleasant, but with no central focus. There is not much traffic, but the road is often icy and hazardous for walkers. Buses run every 10 minutes between

Innerarosa, Obersee and Maran (the Nightexpress runs every hour).

Accommodation is mostly in hotels varying widely in size and degree of comfort. Obersee is the best location for resort facilities; well-placed hotels include the quiet, comfortable Derby, the large Posthotel, and the very simple, friendly Vetter; the 'quite formal' Eden is widely recommended – 'magnificent but not cheap', 'food outstanding'. Innerarosa (which is more open, sunny and attractive) and Maran are better for access to the skiing. The Hold is very conveniently placed at Innerarosa; simpler and much less expensive than its palatial neighbour the Kulm. The Prätschu and Hof Maran hotels in Maran are both recommended, the latter for 'excellent nouvelle cuisine' and 'beautiful situation'. Lots of hotels are along the road between the two centres, which has little to recommend it. But we have an enthusiastic recommendation of the family-run Hohenfels, above the road near the Catholic church – 'lots of repeat bookings, ski to the door'. The Seehof,

---

Facts on Arosa   Graubunden **Switzerland**

Prices in francs
Ski Club represented

Tourist office
Postcode CH-7050
Tel (81) 311621
Fax (81) 313135
Tlx 851671

Getting there
By road 910km from Calais. Via Basle, Zurich and Chur, the last 30km is narrow, tortuous and difficult; chains often necessary.
By rail Station in resort (Obersee); buses every few minutes.
By air Zurich; transfer 3hr.

Staying there
Visitor beds 11,000; breakdown: 5,700 in hotels, 5,300 in apartments.
Package holidays Kuoni (h) Made to Measure (hs) Powder Byrne (h) Ski Club of GB (h) SkiGower (y) SnowRanger (h) Swiss-Ski (h) .
Medical facilities In resort: Doctors, dentist, chemist, fracture clinic. Hospital: Chur (30km).

Non-skiing activities
Indoor Hotel facilities open to non-residents (swimming, sauna, massage, tennis, squash), indoor golf, bridge, chess, bowling, fitness centre, cinema, concerts, museum.
Outdoor 3 outdoor skating rinks (2 artificial), ice-hockey, skating and curling (weekly beginners' sessions and tournaments), sleigh rides, over 30km of cleared paths, horse-riding, ski-bob, toboggan runs, snow-shoe walks, paragliding, hang-gliding, flying school.

Kindergartens
Skikindergarten
Tuition: Yes. Hours: 9.45-11.45 and 2.15-4.15, Mon- Fri. Ages: 4-6. Cost: 140.00 per week (optional lunch-time supervision).
Other childcare facilities

Day-care available in hotels (Park, Savoy and Hof Maran) from 9.00-6.00 with optional lunch-time supervision.

Special skiing facilities
Summer skiing No.
Cross-country 7½km and 5½km trails at Isla, 8km at Prätschalp plus 6km extension, 2 x 2km loops at Maran, 1km at Obersee; 2km loop floodlit until 9.00. Instruction and off-trail guided excursions.

Lift passes
Arosa pass
Covers entire Arosa ski region. (16 lifts in total.)
Cost 6 days 177.00 (£73.75). Low season: 150.00 saving 15%.
Credit cards accepted No.
Senior citizens 150.00 (over 62/65) saving 15%.
Children 89.00 (under 16) saving 50%. Free pass up to age 6.
Notes Group discounts (13 or more persons).
Beginners Points cards; free baby-lifts at Innerarosa and Obersee.
Short-term passes Half-day (from 12.00); single and return tickets on various lifts.
Other passes Special hiking pass (80.00 for 7 days, covers 4 lifts).

Ski school
Swiss Ski School
Classes 9.45-11.45 and 2.15-4.15. Cost: 160.00 (5 days).
Lift priority No.
Children's classes Ages: 4-12. Cost: 140.00 (5 days).
Private lessons available Half-day, full day or per hour. Cost: 50.00 per hour. 5.00 reduction for pm lessons.
Special courses Surf and telemark courses.

What was new in 91
New panoramic winter walkway from the Sattelhütte down to Pratschli.

between Obersee and the smaller Untersee, is another quiet family hotel, five minutes from the bus route.

Après-ski is varied (floodlit langlauf, evening bus for tobogganers, chess competitions after tea in the Cristallo, ice hockey matches to watch), but far from uproarious. There are about six discos, catering for varying ages and pockets; the Kursaal is among the liveliest. 'The place to be' at tea-time is Kaiser's, on the main street, which has excellent tea and cakes, served on a sunny terrace. The ski instructors congregate in the Rondo for bar billiards practice. Most restaurants are in hotels; a very cheerful exception is the Waldeck – the ice-hockey team's local.

Arosa is very good for **non-skiers**, with an impressive catalogue of other sports facilities and entertainments, and outstanding high-level paths (with benches). A new 'panoramic winterwalking path' was created last season between Sattelhütte and Prätschli. A comprehensive programme of events is published weekly by the highly organised tourist office (one of the most helpful we have come across). The resort is equally good for **cross-country** skiing. Trails are in two areas – the easy runs and longer Prätschalp one starting from the main cross-country centre at Maran, and the more demanding Isel runs in the woods below Obersee, across the railway. Dogs are allowed on the beginners' loop on the lake. There are buses from Obersee to Maran and Isel.

Nursery slopes are adequate. Tschuggen is a broad sunny plateau with refreshment close at hand, and good for meeting up with other skiers. There is another nursery area at Maran.

There is a great variety of day tours to Davos, Klosters and Lenzerheide, which can be arranged through the **ski school** which meets at Tschuggen and Innerarosa. English is widely spoken. Recent reports confirm an earlier view that children are very well looked after in ski school – 'patient and caring instructors seemed dedicated to giving the youngsters a good time'.

Lenzerheide-Valbella Switzerland 1500m

Good for *Easy runs, not skiing, cross-country skiing, big ski area, sunny slopes, woodland runs*
Bad for *Après-ski, tough runs, skiing convenience*

Linked resort: Churwalden

If you haven't heard of Lenzerheide and Valbella, do not fear: you are not alone. Although they share a large skiing area in a famous skiing region, and are popular with the Swiss for family holidays, they have largely escaped international attention. The area has considerable attractions – as well as the extent of the skiing, it can fairly claim excellent cross-country possibilities, no shortage of non-skiing activities, pleasant scenery and a civilised atmosphere. But the extent of the skiing area cannot disguise its lack of variety, for piste skiers at least. And the villages themselves are not particularly attractive or convenient.

The originally distinct villages lie at either end of a lake in a wide, attractively wooded pass running north–south, with high mountains on either side. The road linking them is an important thoroughfare, which in itself reduces the area's appeal for people with small children and has encouraged the two villages to spread along the valley until they have almost merged. Their comfortable chalets sprawl across the valley too. The resulting straggle is surprisingly animated, according to recent reporters, who were generally impressed by the friendliness of the villagers and the resort's genial atmosphere.

Two other smaller villages come into the ski area, both used mainly by weekend visitors. Parpan is hardly more than an old hamlet beside the road up from Chur ('for those who want to spend their evenings playing chess or bridge'), Churwalden a larger village appreciably lower down, with its own little ski area. Hourly buses link them to the major resort area.

Having a car is handy for getting to and from skiing, and for evening entertainment; it also gives the chance of some excellent day-trips – St Moritz, Arosa, Laax-Flims, Davos and Klosters are all within range.

The skiing top 2865m bottom 1230m

The skiing is in separate areas on either side of the inconveniently wide pass. Both have about half woodland and half open skiing terrain; the Danis/ Stätzerhorn area to the west is more extensive, and gets the sun in the morning; the Rothorn to the east is higher, more beautiful, more interesting but more crowded, and gets sun in the afternoon. There are no particularly difficult pistes, although the Rothorn cable-car opens up some off-piste skiing. Runs down to the two villages (or as near to them as they go) are in general gentler than the higher slopes, and suitable

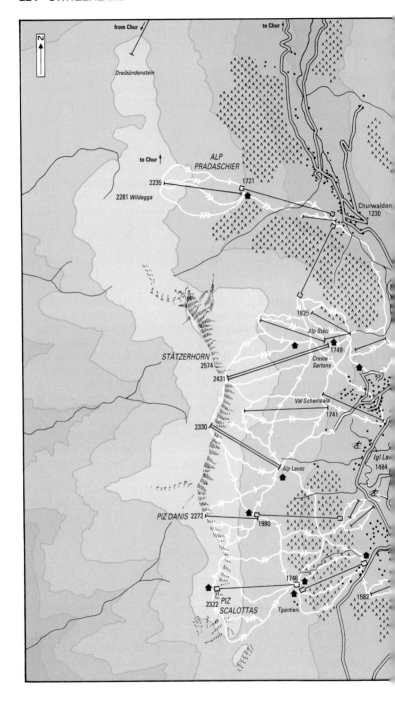

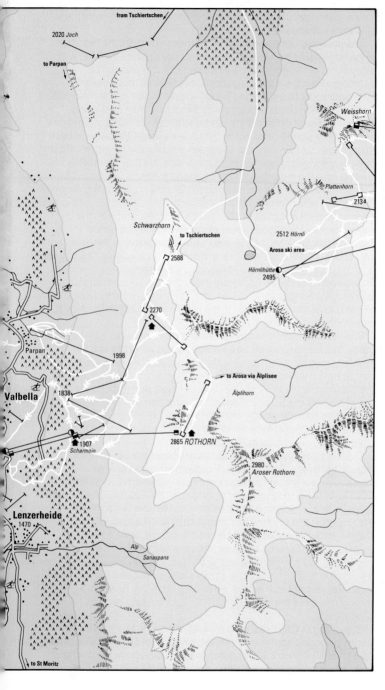

from Tschiertschen

2020 *Joch*

to Parpan

Weisshorn

Plattenhorn

2134

Schwarzhorn

to Tschiertschen

2512 *Hörnli*

Arosa ski area

2588

Hörnlihütte
2495

2270

1998

Parpan

to Arosa via Älplisee

Älplihorn

Valbella

1838

1907
Scharmoin

2865 *ROTHORN*

2980
Aroser Rothorn

Lenzerheide

1470

Alp

Sanaspans

to St Moritz

for inexperienced skiers, except in poor snow conditions – which are said to be not unusual.

The essential components of the **Rothorn** skiing are the two stages of the large cable-car which climbs from a point beside the lake, well away from both villages, to the peak about 1400m above. The panorama from the top is magnificent; the Rothorn drops away in awesome rocky faces, limiting the skiing possibilities to one main piste behind the main crest, through a wooden gallery, then over a ridge giving a choice of descents (red and blue above the Motta chair-lift, red and not-very-severe black below it) to the lifts above Parpan and back to the cable-car mid-station at Scharmoin. In terms of length or difficulty there is nothing very special about these runs, but they do make a change from the local straight-up-and-down pistes.

From Scharmoin there is a choice of several gentle, winding descents through the woods taking you back either to the bottom station or to the edge of Valbella or Lenzerheide. There are several drags on the northern side of Scharmoin, the longest linking with the sunny Schwarzhorn chair-lift, high above Parpan. If tempted by the open, not very steep unpisted hillsides below the chair-lift, be warned that you risk ending up stranded between Parpan and Churwalden.

The best off-piste run goes from the Rothorn to Lenzerheide via the beautiful Alp Sanaspans; it is long and demanding, with no escape once begun except the variant back to the middle station which involves a steep and exposed drop over a rocky ridge.

Various excursions are possible from the Rothorn area into the next valley. You can embark on an enormous circuit via Arosa and Tschiertschen by skiing from the Rothorn via Älplisee (a serious off-piste run) or by first walking round the narrow bowl which divides the top of the Schwarzhorn from Arosa's Hörnli. But most skiers opt for the direct run down from the Schwarzhorn to Tschiertschen – a very beautiful, easily identified and usually easy semi-piste. Lifts bring you back to the slopes above Churwalden. From here you follow paths down to Churwalden, or traverse to Parpan.

Compared with the Rothorn and its neighbour the Lenzerhorn, the **Scalottas/ Danis/ Stätzerhorn/ Pradaschier** peaks are not impressive, but the rather featureless open hillsides below them have been easy to develop for skiers: a long network of parallel lifts – mostly drags, with the exception of the efficient chairs from Lenzerheide up to Piz Scalottas and the new four-seater chair from Lenzerheide to Piz Danis – makes it possible to cover a lot of ground, even if there is precious little difference between one piste and another. Conditions permitting, you can ski just about anywhere – so you can have fun when the snow is fresh. The skiing is mostly intermediate, and the couple of runs categorised black are not particularly terrifying. Runs home through the trees are mostly straightforward, but stop short of Lenzerheide.

The skiing of **Churwalden** is separated from the rest by a steep, densely wooded north-facing hillside, which is not easily skiable. A long, cold chair-lift makes the connection to the slopes above Parpan, and good skiers have fun on the runs under it. The connection in the opposite direction is made by the gentle path which skirts the bottom of the hill beside the road from Parpan to Churwalden. Churwalden's other lifts provide a descent of 1005m back to the village. But from the top the great excursion is to head off northwards along the hill tops for about 2km, to the Dreibundenstein (2174m), at the top of a chain of lifts up from the town of Chur, and then ski down as far as snow permits – providing you can get down to 1170m, you can ride down to Chur (595m) by cable-car.

There is a good range of sunny **mountain restaurants** on the Danis side, all (except the 'beautifully designed, brand new' restaurant at the top of Scalottas) about half-way up, around the tree-line. Among the recommendations are the 'small and attractive' Grischuna (at Tgantieni) and the Café Spoina at Alp Lavoz. On the Rothorn side there are restaurants at half-way and top stations of the cable-car with 'lovely sun terraces'. The Höhe Mut below the Weisshorn is another favourite.

Long **queues** build up for Rothorn lifts, especially at weekends, though the top section of the cable-car has been enlarged, which will help at the mid-station. Queues have also been reported on the nursery slopes, and for the drags out of Parpan. Lift departures are sited to keep weekend visitors out of Lenzerheide, not to make life convenient for Lenzerheiders. A recent reporter was impressed by piste-grooming on the slopes but horrified by the lack of attention paid to over-rutted drag-lift tracks. The piste map can be misleading – the 'black' runs are marked in dark blue. Despite tourist office assertions that there is no **artificial snow**, two reporters have seen snow-guns on lower slopes on the west side of town.

The resort

Lenzerheide is the major centre of development, and consists of a long main street (the main through-road) at the foot of the Rothorn slopes, with some style-less modern development to the west, below the road. On the main street there are some attractive old buildings, but as a whole the place has no particular charm. Valbella has even less identity – it is no more than a large community of hotels and concrete-box holiday homes crammed on to a hillside; but it is in some ways a better base – less of a roadside strip, and giving direct access to the western ski area.

There are free buses effectively linking the villages and lifts, and you need them for crossing from one side of the skiing to the other. The system earns high praise from recent reporters.

Accommodation consists of apartments and hotels in both villages. Location in Lenzerheide is not particularly important as the village is fairly compact and flat, but a reporter warns of getting stuck out in the steep Crapera area on the east side. The most attractive and best-situated of the numerous hotels in the centre of Lenzerheide is the simplest and cheapest – the friendly Danis, where people come to drink and play cards in the evening. From the hotel you can walk up to the Dieschen lift and from there ski down to the Rothorn cable-car station.

Other central hotels include the Sunstar ('excellent friendly hotel, but not cheap', 'ideal for families') and the Schweizerhof ('super food, service and facilities'). Some way out of the resort, the Guarda Val is outstanding – splendid old wooden buildings, expensive and comfortable and with a good restaurant, but remote. La Palanca is attractive and well placed for the Scalottas lifts. The Dieschen is simple and friendly, with a good restaurant; you can ski down to the Rothorn lift

Facts on Lenzerheide   Graubunden **Switzerland**

Prices in francs

Tourist office
Postcode CH-7078
Tel (81) 343434
Fax (81) 345383
Tlx 851700

Getting there
By road 989km from Calais. Via Zurich; chains may be required.
By rail Chur; hourly buses from station.
By air Zurich; transfer 3hr.

Staying there
Visitor beds 13,700; breakdown: 2,700 in hotels, 11,000 in apartments.
Package holidays Inghams (hs) Kuoni (ha) Made to Measure (hs) Ski Unique (h) SnowRanger (hs) Swiss-Ski (h) Tailor Made (hs) .
Medical facilities In resort: Doctors, dentist, chemists, fracture clinic. Hospital: Chur (17km).

Non-skiing activities
Indoor Dieschen sports centre (swimming, sauna, jacuzzi, solarium, curling, skating), fitness centre, cinema, tennis, squash and bowling at Hotel Schweizerhof (open to public).
Outdoor Natural skating rink (skating, curling), 35km cleared paths, toboggan runs (one floodlit), sleigh rides, ski-bob pistes.

Kindergartens
Hotel Valbella
Tuition: No. Hours: 9.00-5.00. Ages: 3-7. Cost: 252.00 per week (with meals).
Hotel Schweizerhof (Lenzerheide)
Tuition: No. Hours: 8.00-12.00. Ages: 3-7. Cost: 84.00 per week (6 half-days, with meals).
Other childcare facilities
Baby-sitting available from Tourist Office.

Special skiing facilities
Summer skiing No.
Cross-country 42km of trails of all grades including those at Lantsch and Parpan. The Luziuswiese and Heidsee at Lenzerheide are floodlit from 7.00–9.30. Tours and instruction at all three centres.

Lift passes
Area pass
Covers lifts in Lenzerheide, Valbella, Parpan and Churwalden and the sportbus. (38 lifts in total.)
Cost 6 days 176.00 (£73.33).
Credit cards accepted Yes.
Senior citizens 141.00 (over 65/62) saving 20%.
Children 106.00 (under 16) saving 40%. Free pass up to age 6.
Notes Discounts for students (ages 16-20).
Beginners Points cards.
Short-term passes Half-day (from 12.00); single and return tickets on some lifts.
Other periods Passes available for 5 days out of 10, and 10 days out of 30.

Ski school
Swiss Ski School (Lenzerheide)
Classes 4hr: 10.00-3.00, with 1hr lunch. Cost: 160.00 (5½ days). 5½ days ski school with 7-day lift pass costs 280.00 for adults and 240.00 for children).
Lift priority No.
Children's classes Ages: 4 up. Cost: 110.00 (5½ days).
Private lessons available Hourly. Cost: 60.00 per hour.
Special courses Snowboard and telemark courses.
Swiss Ski School (Valbella)
Classes 2hr am. Cost: 110.00 (6 half-days).
Lift priority No.
Children's classes Ages: 4-7 or 7-16. Cost: 110.00 (6 half-days).
Private lessons available Hourly. Cost: 60.00 per hour.
Caselva (Valbella)
Classes 9.45-11.45 and 2.00-4.00. Cost: 110.00 (6 half-days, Mon-Sat).
Lift priority No.
Children's classes Ages: 4 up. Cost: 110.00 (6 half-days, Mon-Sat). Lunch extra 14.00.
Private lessons available Hourly. Cost: 60.00 per hour.

What was new in 91
1. New 4-seater chair (Pedra Grossa) from edge of Lenzerheide up the Piz Danis, replacing old drag-lift.
2. New mountain restaurant at top of Pedra Grossa lift called Alp Nova.

station directly from the hotel. In Valbella the best choice is the Chesa Rustica, close to the Danis lifts. A recent reporter commends its efficiency, friendliness and food, but was disappointed to find no guests' lounge.

Après-ski is fairly quiet, even in Lenzerheide – a couple of tea-rooms (the Aurora café is recommended 'for tea overlooking the ice rink') – a few restaurants, a disco and some cheek-to-cheek live music hotels. Nino's, on the main street, seems to be where the locals gather. The sedate hotel Postli is the place to have a quiet draught beer with your evening newspaper. The Schweizerhof has a nightclub, and there is live music and dancing ('not disco-style') in the Sunstar. There is a fair selection of restaurants including a good pizzeria near the ice-rink and a Chinese at the hotel Ratia.

Non-skiers (or active ones, at least) are well provided for, especially for skating, curling (a free lesson is offered) and tobogganing (there are three runs). There is a smart sports centre at Dieschen, and an extensive and well-used network of cleared walks, particularly around the lake. **Cross-country** trails are very good – long, mostly fairly easy, in linked sectors along the pass, through attractive woods and round the lake; and there is excellent scope for more adventurous excursions on wide open slopes above Parpan and Churwalden on the eastern side, and in the Danis Alpine skiing area – good for restaurant access.

There are several adequate **nursery slopes**, all at the bottom of the mountains (except for two baby lifts beside the Rothorn middle station). The best area is the gentle lower slope at Churwalden.

The Lenzerheide **ski school** is reportedly well organised, with small classes; there are English-speaking instructors, but not enough to guarantee English classes. The Valbella branch is 'friendly but sloppily run; for all that, instruction was good and progress fast'.

In with the Inn crowd

St Moritz Switzerland 1800m

Good for *Beautiful scenery, big ski area, resort-level snow, not skiing, cross-country skiing, après-ski, mountain restaurants, artificial snow, rail access, sunny slopes, late holidays*
Bad for *Skiing convenience, nursery slopes, easy road access, short airport transfers, lift queues, woodland runs*

Linked resort: Celerina
Separate resort: Pontresina

The official line is that you don't have to be rich to enjoy St Moritz. You certainly don't have to be much richer than you need be to enjoy other large, fashionable Swiss resorts, and many skiers who never give St Moritz consideration are making a mistake. The scenery is wonderful – the infant river Inn fills a succession of beautiful lakes against a backdrop of 4000-metre peaks with glaciers draped on their shoulders; the non-skier and cross-country skier are better catered for than almost anywhere else in the Alps; and, for a resort which became fashionable because of its scenery and climate, the skiing is surprisingly good, provided there is snow in this dry and sunny corner of the Alps. Its main drawback is the resort itself – more of a town than a village, disappointingly ugly and inconvenient. Skiers keener on sport and mountain (as opposed to human) scenery may prefer to stay in Celerina, a quiet village nearby with good skiing access.

The British began wintering in St Moritz before skiing became a sport, and the resort still revolves as much round tobogganing and riding on the frozen lake as it does around skiing – despite being among the highest of Alpine resorts, with excellent late-winter skiing, its real season ends early because the ice starts to thin and the toboggan runs close in late February or early March. St Moritz now fills only five per cent of its beds with British occupants, and old hands say that the place has lost its style, as the original core of well-to-do British has been replaced by Continentals and Americans, trying to behave in the same way but succeeding only in behaving wealthily. Certainly the Palace, most expensive of the luxury hotels, seems flashy and cosmopolitan. But the Carlton and the Kulm still have the quiet formality, the card tables, the worn leather and the heavy jowls of London clubs, and under Col. Digby Willoughby the St Moritz Tobogganing Club remains defiantly British.

All approaches except that from Austria involve high passes – the Julier pass (from Chur) is kept open but is often snowy. But a car is very valuable for getting around the ski areas, and for après-ski if not staying centrally. The past lives on in the special train service from London, and rail is the best means of access (apart from flying to nearby Samedan). St Moritz is also one terminus of the Glacier Express, which runs to and from Zermatt via Andermatt – a spectacular journey, 'not to be missed' according to a recent passenger.

The skiing top 3300m bottom 1720m

There are wide open sunny slopes to flatter tan-conscious
intermediates; steep and gentle descents through woods; long, steep
pitches with walls and bumps; excellent glacier skiing with superb
views; and lots of scope for long off-piste excursions which few skiers
exploit. But these different kinds of skiing are found on mountains
spread widely around the two valleys which meet at Celerina, just below
St Moritz. Some reporters have found the ski-bus service unreliable, but
in general it works well. Several reporters have felt that some runs are
over-graded, particularly on Corvatsch.

Corviglia is the sunny south-facing mountain immediately above St
Moritz. The funicular railway from the top of Dorf and the cable-car from
the edge of Bad give access to wide open slopes with a series of
drag-lifts serving not very varied intermediate runs, few challenging
enough to distract from the panorama. The cable-car up to Piz Nair
gives access to off-piste runs down the Suvretta valley towards Bad,
and to long and beautiful pistes down to Marguns. This bowl, reached
more directly from Corviglia, offers long runs both easy and challenging
down from Trais Fluors and Glüna. The fast chair-lift recently installed
on Piz Grisch has widened the possibilities from the latter and provided
an alternative route to the off-piste Val Silvretta run. Now, the only skiing
exclusively served by the cable-car is the short, steep, front face, often
unskiable. From Marguns there is an occasionally narrow and awkward
run down to Celerina, whence a gondola goes back up to Marguns.

The **Corvatsch** area, similarly, is accessible from both ends at valley
level and consists of a band of connected drag-lifts above the tree-line
serving intermediate skiing, with a single cable-car climbing much
higher. But the skiing is more varied and challenging – especially from
the top station, where the snow is nearly always excellent and the
views, across to the glaciers of Piz Bernina, even better. The direct piste
is an exhilarating sustained slope, either bumpy or hard and very fast.
The less direct route is manageable by most intermediates. Another
great joy is the beautiful long Hahnensee run through the woods to St
Moritz Bad, via a secluded mountain hut. There is good off-piste skiing;
one reporter was pleased to find the various runs down to Champfér,
Surlej and (more adventurously) into the Roseg valley so little used.

A piste down from Corvatsch mid-station connects with the
Furtschellas skiing above Sils Maria via a long chain of lifts stretching
across rocky mountainsides. At the other end there are some excellent
long runs from Furtschellas itself to the isolated base station. Although
not precipitous, none of the lower runs is easy.

A single long cable-car goes up from the Bernina pass road to the
magnificently situated hotel, restaurant and sun-terrace of **Diavolezza**,
amid marvellous glacier scenery. There is an easy open slope beside
the drag-lifts at the top, and a splendid long intermediate run back down
under the lift, but the great attraction is the much-skied off-piste run over
the back, across the glacier and through woods to Morteratsch. It
involves some walking, and there are narrow passages between big

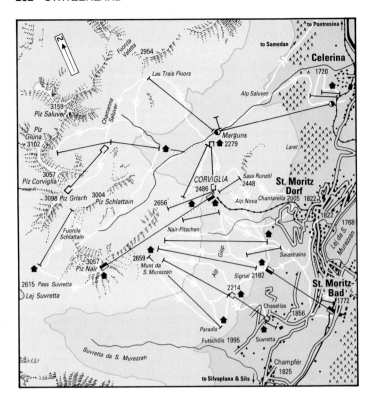

holes and an awkward icy drop to negotiate at the end of the glacier; these should not deter reasonably competent skiers ('an enjoyable slog', says a reporter).

Lagalb is a consistently steep conical mountain opposite Diavolezza which presents long runs from top to bottom – ranging from very challenging (the direct route, initially steep and usually very bumpy) to the moderately easy. A run from the top station links up with a couple of drag-lifts at the Bernina pass.

Reporters tell us that **Muottas Muragl**, between Celerina and Pontresina, is worth a visit for beautiful views and a good lunch. There are a few short, sunny, easy runs near the top of a funicular and one run down through the woods, intermediate except for one steep section. **Alp Languard** is directly accessible from Pontresina; it has a nursery area and a long T-bar serving a red run.

Mountain restaurants on Corviglia are plentiful and varied, from anonymous self-service cafeterias to very attractive chalets. On the Corvatsch side, Fuorcla Surlej, Hahnensee (Lej dals Chöds) and the cosy restaurant behind the top-station self-service have charm. There is a good new restaurant (with a big log fire) on the Crap Nair run below the Murtel cable-car station. In the Corviglia sector, recommendations include the small new restaurant in the Piz Nair bowl, the Alpina Hütte

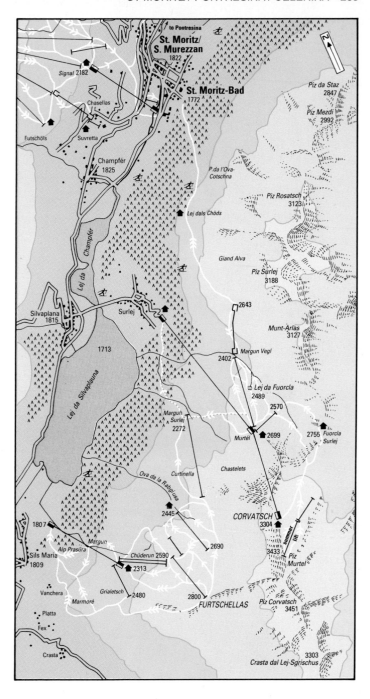

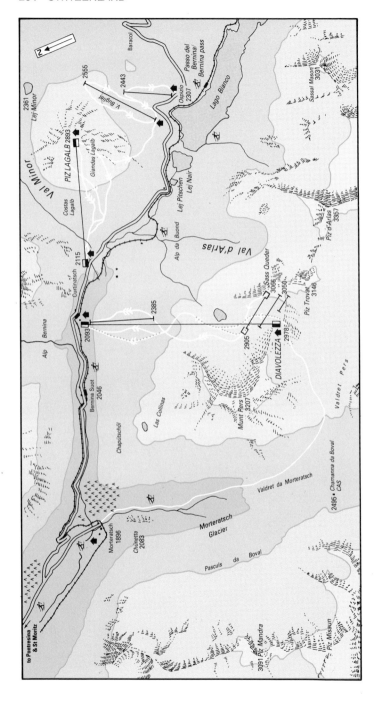

and the Marmite (booking necessary). The restaurants at several of the top stations have splendid views. Prices are high.

Large areas of skiing depend on few lifts, especially the cable-cars, where there are often long **queues** (especially at weekends) despite the high proportion of non-skiers in the resort. A system of stamping numbers on skis has reportedly been introduced, so that you don't have to stand in line while waiting for your number to come up. The Sils Maria cable-car on the Corvatsch side is reported to be queue-free – unlike the more direct and easily accessible Surlej one ('long queues until nearly mid-day'). There may be half-hour queues for Piz Nair above Corviglia even in January (which is busy by Swiss standards). Easter is another peak. There can be irritating queues for chair and drag-lifts which several reporters felt could be done away with if people were discouraged from riding alone.

In recent winters the skiing in St Moritz has depended heavily on the very extensive **artificial snow** installation. There are guns on a long lower piste on Corvatsch; several shorter pistes on Corviglia; and from top to bottom of Diavolezza.

The resort

St Moritz is a resort of parts. **St Moritz Bad**, the spa part, is spread out beside the lake on the valley floor without shape, style or animation. There are good although not especially smart shopping facilities. The cross-country track passes through, and there is direct access to Corviglia. **St Moritz Dorf** is tightly packed on the steep hillside to the north of the lake, beneath the ski slopes of Corviglia. This is fashionable St Moritz, more like a town centre than a village. Bulky Victorian hotels loom over the lake – exclusive worlds of their own, at the heart of high society; outside them and the expensive shopping precincts, St Moritz is not particularly smart or attractive. Nor is it convenient – distances on foot are considerable and parking is difficult. From the top of the resort a road winds down an attractive wooded slope, following the course of the Cresta and Bob runs to the edge of the quiet, spacious village of Celerina. Trains and buses between ski stations are reliable but not frequent – and the bus service between Bad and Dorf is often oversubscribed. There are no evening buses, and trains stop at about 11pm. Parking is difficult in Dorf – there is a multi-storey park.

Accommodation is spread out around the two component parts of town. Most of St Moritz's hotel beds are in four-and five-star hotels. For ski-lift convenience the best locations are on the edge of Bad near the Signal lift – where the secluded Chesa Sur L'En is a luxurious old chalet, beautifully decorated and furnished – or high up in the centre of Dorf. The Steffani is one of the most attractive of the smaller hotels, with a pool; simpler, but still comfortable, B&B hotels in the centre are the Eden and the Languard. Centrally positioned in Dorf, the Schweizerhof is 'very gracious, with excellent food and service'. The Parkhotel Kurhaus on the far side of Bad is 'wonderfully located for cross-country skiing, and getting away from it all'. The Crystal is recommended for its

Facts on St Moritz Graubunden **Switzerland**

Prices in francs
Ski Club represented

Tourist office

Postcode CH-7500
Tel (82) 33147/48
Fax (82) 32952
Tlx 852129

Getting there

By road 1,047km from Calais. Via Zurich, Chur; chains often needed on Julierpass.
By rail Main-line station in resort. Post buses every half-hour from station.
By air Zurich; transfer 4hr. (Or 3 flights daily Zurich–Samedan.)

Staying there

Visitor beds 12,550; breakdown: about 5,600 in hotels, 5,750 in apartments.
Package holidays Club Med (h) Inghams (hs) Kuoni (h) Made to Measure (hs) Powder Byrne (h) Ski Alternatives (h) SkiGower (y) SnowRanger (hs) Supertravel (h) Swiss-Ski (h) Tailor Made (hs) Thomson (h) .
Medical facilities In resort: Doctor, dentist, chemist, fracture clinic. Hospital: Samedan (6km).

Non-skiing activities

Indoor Ice-rink, curling, swimming, sauna, solarium, tennis, squash, museum, spa cures, cinema (English films), aerobics.
Outdoor Sleigh rides, toboggan run, hang-gliding, golf on frozen lake, Cresta run, 120km cleared paths, joy-rides, horse-riding and racing, polo tournaments, cricket tournaments.

Kindergartens

Parkhotel Kurhaus
Tuition: Yes. Hours: 9.00-4.30, Mon-Fri. Ages: 3-12. Cost: 140.00 per week (with lunch).
Carlton Hotel
Tuition: Yes. Hours: 9.00-5.00, Mon-Fri. Ages: 3-12. Cost: 150.00 per week (with lunch).
Hotel Schweizerhof
Tuition: Yes. Hours: 9.00-5.00. Ages: 3-12. Cost: 170.00 per week (with lunch).

Special skiing facilities

Summer skiing Small area around 3300m on Corvatsch (2 lifts). Small area around 3000m on Diavolezza (2 lifts).
Cross-country 150km in Engadine; 30% easy, 50% middling, 20% difficult. 1.6km easy floodlit trail at Bad.

Lift passes

General
Covers all lifts and public transport in the Engadine area and swimming pools. (59 lifts in total.)
Cost 6 days 212.00 (£88.33).
Credit cards accepted Yes.
Children 156.00 (under 16) saving 26%. Free pass up to age 6.
Beginners 2 nursery lifts included in ski school cost; points tickets.
Short-term passes Half-day (from 11.45am) and day-passes in each area; single or return tickets for some lifts in each area.
Other passes Limited passes for each area (eg St Moritz and Celerina lifts only); new Engadine pass covers the Engadine area and Livigno and the Altavaltellina.
Other periods 5 or 10 non-consecutive days available.

Ski school

St Moritz
Classes 10.00-12.00 and/or 1.30-3.30. Cost: 185.00 (6 days, Sun-Fri).
Lift priority No.
Children's classes Ages: up to 12. Cost: 185.00 (6 days, Sun-Fri). Lunchtime supervision available for 15.00 per day.
Private lessons available Any time between 10.00-4.00, minimum 1½hr. Cost: 70.00 per hour. Each additional person 10.00.
Special courses Surf courses (220.00 per day).
Suvretta
Classes 2hr am or pm. Cost: 170.00 (6 days).
Lift priority No.
Children's classes Ages: up to 12. Cost: 210.00 (6 days). Courses run from Sun-Fri, 10.00-3.30. Lunch costs 11.00 per day.
Private lessons available Full day, half-day or hourly. Cost: 65.00 per hour. 1-3 people. Instruction also available for private groups.
Special courses Surf courses (220.00 per day).

What was new in 91

Gletscher drag-lift on glacier at Diavolezza replaced by new chair-lift.

What is new for 92

1. Corvatsch: drag-lift at Marguns to be replaced by chair-lift Gluna; new restaurant at Murtel.
2. Corviglia: 2 new chair-lifts, a drag-lift and restaurant.
3. Celerina to Marguns new 6-seat cable-car.

'good location and incredibly attentive service'.

A recent reporter found Celerina a convenient base, and recommends the English-owned Chesa Rosatsch hotel.

Most of the stylish **après-ski** is hotel-based, with formal dress requirements in several establishments – including the Palace Hotel's King's Club disco, where photographers and bouncers crowd the door, and Dracula's (members only). The bar of the Steffani – watering-hole of the Cresta riders – is a popular, rather more casual and less expensive venue for drinking and dancing. The Schweizerhof has one bar 'packed with youth' and another, quieter piano bar – 'a little more genteel'. There is tea-dancing at the Zuber Hütte and at the Chantarella on the way down from Corviglia. For tea without the dancing, recommendations include Hanselmann's and Glattfelders ('for caviar, tea and coffee'). There are a few simple, honest restaurants on the main square in Dorf, and in Bad. Restaurant recommendations include the Cascade – a large bar with good restaurant attached – and the Chesa Veglia. The Casino is apparently a strip-joint.

The frozen lakes and side-valleys make up one of the most famous and beautiful **cross-country** areas in Europe, and the annual 42km marathon attracts over 10,000 entrants. St Moritz is also a spectacular destination for **non-skiers** both active and inactive. There are long and beautiful walks to restaurants in the skiing area (Corviglia) and up the Roseg, Morteratsch and Fex valleys, with only cross-country skiers and chamois for company. In season, (until the end of February) there are lots of spectator sports.

Nursery slopes are not very satisfactory, there being very little available space on the valley floor except at Celerina at the foot of the Marguns gondola. Most St Moritz beginners start on slopes at Corviglia around Chantarella and Salastrains where there is a beginners' merry-go-round; when snow conditions are good they can progress to long easy runs in this sector, but often the transition is an awkward one.

Reports of the St Moritz **ski school** are generally favourable – 'good English, took a lot of trouble' – though we have also heard of large classes. Many hotels have their own private instructors.

Pontresina   1800m

Pontresina is much more developed than the other villages around St Moritz – it feels and looks like a self-sufficient resort, albeit a sedate one. Although it is closer than St Moritz to some of the best skiing (Diavolezza and Lagalb) there is no significant skiing from the village itself. Many traditionalists return annually to the great comfort and considerable charm of Pontresina hotels, and appreciate being at a distance from the glitter and hubbub of St Moritz. The Steinbock and Engadinerhof ('friendly staff, excellent food') are very comfortable and attractively traditional hotels on the single main street. It is one of the best locations in the region for cross-country skiers, and also has a good skating/curling rink and pool (covered by the lift pass). One report complains of little English spoken in the ski school.
Tourist office ✆ (82) 66488.
Package holidays Club Med (h) Made to Measure (hs) SkiGower (y) SnowRanger (h) Swiss-Ski (h).

New in to the arena

Flims Switzerland 1100m

Good for *Big ski area, sunny slopes, cross-country skiing , woodland runs*
Bad for *Tough runs, skiing convenience, late holidays, après-ski, resort-level snow*

Linked resorts: Laax, Falera

Take a long-established, sedate, year-round resort, better known for its sunshine and woodland walks than for its skiing (and little known at all in Britain), and graft on to its modest lift system a huge new network of mechanisation opening up a vast interconnected ski area, and you have the strange hybrid phenomenon that is Flims and Laax and the White Arena ski area which they share – extensive, varied, beautiful, intelligently conceived and smartly equipped. The resorts aren't ideal bases for skiers, and don't fit in with the brave new image of the modern ski-circus. But in other ways Flims and Laax have a lot to offer.

Flims lies on a wooded hillside near the foot of the mountains which form the northern wall of the Vorderrhein valley. Hundreds of metres beneath the wooded shelf on which the resorts stand, the river cuts through a rocky gorge. The railway follows it, but the main road runs through Flims (and is busy at weekends). Although the mountains climb high they are not steep, and the valley is so wide that the setting is open and sunny. Flims is split into two parts – Dorf and Waldhaus.

Laax, 5km away, is smaller and more attractive, with a modern purpose-built satellite at Murschetg. The rustic farming hamlet of Falera adds yet another alternative style of base.

There are no other major resorts very close to Flims, but with a car day-trips to Arosa and Lenzerheide are possible. A car can be useful around the resort, too, depending on where you are staying.

The skiing top 2980m bottom 1080m

The skiing area extends over a very broad section of the northern wall of the valley. It faces mainly south-east, but is broken up by a number of deep gullies and tributary valleys whose flanks face south-west and north-east – and links between the sectors can be interrupted by bad weather. Most of the ski area is very sunny, and the runs down to the resorts cannot be relied upon late in the season. The terrain is varied, with long woodland runs on the lower slopes, open ground above and a small area of glacier skiing at the top. There are few very steep slopes.

The Flims entrance to the ski area is on the edge of Flims Dorf. Of the two main lifts, the more important for Flims's pistes is the three-seater chair. The runs beneath this lift and the gondola to Startgels are mostly easy, and the red runs from Naraus hold no terrors, apart from frequently inadequate snow cover. There are usually a lot of people around though, because the cheaper restricted Flims day-pass covers only this area.

For good skiers, the main attraction of Flims's skiing is the descent from **Cassons**, reached by cable car from Naraus up over the cliffs of the Flimserstein. There is an annoying walk up behind the top station, but the view is splendid, as is the direct black descent back to Naraus – a fairly steep, wide open 800m face, paradise in good fresh or spring snow conditions. Only the gentler bottom half ever has a prepared piste. The alternative semi-piste is less satisfactory, with one rather steep section near the beginning followed by a walk up to the Segnes-Hütte.

Flims' skiing is connected to the **La Siala** area, between Flims and Laax, by a cable-car from Startgels to Grauberg and a triple chair-lift to Nagens. The runs back down to Startgels are good, challenging ones. Most of the skiing on La Siala consists of long, open, featureless pistes, but the top chair-lift serves long, beautiful runs, mixing motorway with moguls, down to Grauberg.

From La Siala there are connections with Laax skiing either by traversing to (or from) the Vorab glacier restaurant, or via Plaun at the bottom of a steep-sided valley with lifts up either side. The awkward bumpy paths down to Plaun are categorised black, and lots of skiers take the chair down. The other side of the valley is much more satisfactory, with longer runs down from Crap Sogn Gion to Plaun.

Crap Sogn Gion (St John's Hill) is where the vast but still inadequate cable-car from Murschetg arrives. A series of three chair-lifts (the top one a four-seater) make the same journey without queues, but more slowly. The run under the cable-car from Crap Sogn Gion is the downhill course – a magnificent trail, cutting a broad swathe through the woods, with a vertical drop of over 1000m. There are other gentler descents, through Curnius under the chairs, and down to Falera, a useful back-door way into the lift system.

The cable-car to **Crap Masegn** doesn't climb much but gives access to good, long, open runs down to Alp Ruschein, which are usually deserted and often good for off-but-near-the-piste skiing. In the other direction a gondola goes down into a gully then up again to the bottom of the **Vorab** glacier, which offers gentle skiing with reliably flattering snow, accessible to all. The great attraction of the Vorab is the run which drops over a saddle near the top down into an empty and beautiful valley. The run is marked black, but the short steep beginning is not as steep as all that, and the rest is mostly glorious, wide-open, fast cruising for over 1000m vertical to Alp Ruschein.

The old part of the ski area, above Flims, is well provided with attractive old **mountain restaurants**, many of them accessible to walkers. Runcahöhe, off the pistes below Startgels, is among them, and 'worth a visit for the *rösti* alone'. On the Laax side there are just a few large, functional service areas, at obvious points. A happy exception is the piste-side chalet at Larnags. The glacier restaurant has stupendous views from its sun terrace, but you have to pay for deck chairs. The Berghaus Nagens is recommended for its food.

Latest reports suggest that **queues** are not generally a problem. The

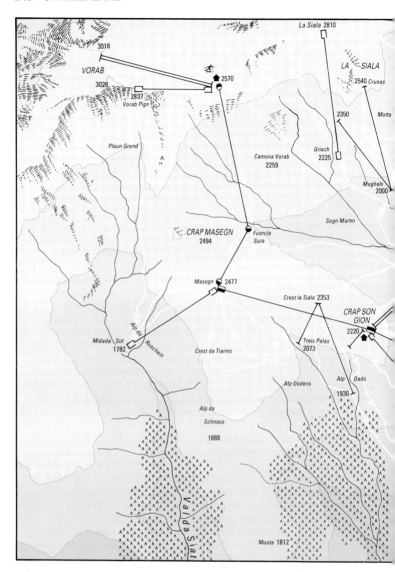

exceptions are the Laax cable-car during the morning rush and many lifts on fine weekends, when there is a car-borne invasion – especially the access lifts out of Flims and the drags toward La Siala from Mughels. Even in January there may be queues for the Treis Palas drag, and sometimes for the Startgels gondola from Flims. There is no **artificial snow**.

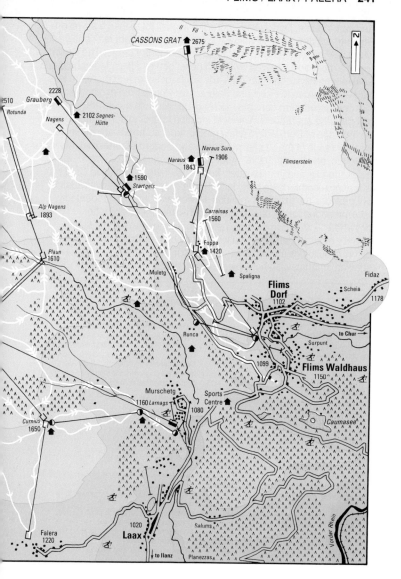

The resort

Flims Dorf is the original village, long and spread out along a busy main road in a rather characterless way. The base lift station is at the western edge of the village. Half a mile or so further south, Waldhaus, with no ski-lifts of its own, is the traditional resort – a large pleasant cluster of hotels among the trees and beside the main road. Waldhaus is quiet and comfortable, Dorf livelier, more like a small town than a ski resort. Both stretch down the hill below the road in a suburban, residential way with a few hotels mainly of interest to cross-country skiers. The daytime regional post bus (covered by the lift pass) serves Flims, Murschetg and Laax punctually but neither regularly nor frequently; and there are less frequent services to Fidaz and Falera. Many hotels run minibuses.

Accommodation consists mainly of comfortable hotels and self-catering apartments. The best location for skiing accommodation is on the edge of Dorf, where a few medium-priced hotels are within easy walking range of the lift station – the lively, modern Albanasport, Meiler, Bellevue, and the attractive, modern chalet-style Garni Curtgin – small, quiet, friendly, and immaculately kept. The newly refurbished Crap Ner is the most comfortable hotel in Dorf; it is very inconveniently situated, but provides an 'excellent' minibus service and has been repeatedly recommended for its 'outstanding' food – 'seldom eaten better, anywhere' – and its 'extremely helpful' manager. In Waldhaus, the 'slightly gloomy' Parkhotel is a world of its own, with a number of different buildings spread around the grounds. The Waldeck is a smaller, smart newish hotel by the main road, with neat and tidy rooms

Facts on Flims   Graubunden **Switzerland**

Prices in francs

Tourist office
Postcode CH-7018
Tel (81) 391022
Fax (81) 394308
Tlx 851919

Getting there
By road 994km from Calais. Via Basle/Zurich; chains rarely necessary.
By rail Chur (17km); buses every hour from station.
By air Zurich; transfer 3hr.

Staying there
Visitor beds 19,000; breakdown: 4,000 in hotels, 15,000 in apartments.
Package holidays Kuoni (h) Made to Measure (hs) Powder Byrne (hc) Ski Unique (h) SnowRanger (hs) Swiss-Ski (h) .
Medical facilities In resort: Doctor, chemist, dentist. Hospital: Ilanz (11km).

Non-skiing activities
Indoor 5 hotel swimming pools open to public, saunas, 2 tennis courts, covered hall with 4 skating rinks, bowling, fitness centres.
Outdoor 60km of cleared paths, natural skating rinks, curling, sleigh rides, toboggan runs, ski-bob.

Kindergartens
Swiss Ski School
Tuition: Yes. Hours: 9.00-5.00. Ages: from 4. Cost: 135.00 per week (5 days, without lunch).
Day nursery
Tuition: No. Hours: 9.00-5.00. Ages: from 3. Cost: 135.00 per week (5 days, lunch available).

Special skiing facilities
Summer skiing Small area of about 400m vertical on Vorab glacier (3 lifts); small summer cross-country piste.
Cross-country Total length of trails 60km, from 3km to 20km; 3km floodlit trail; cross-country centre and school at Flims-Unter-Wildhaus.

Lift passes
White Arena pass
Covers all lifts and buses between Flims, Laax and Falera. (33 lifts in total.)
Cost 6 days 218.00 (£90.83).
Credit cards accepted Yes.
Children 109.00 (under 16) saving 50%. Free pass up to age 6.
Notes Day passes for Vorab glacier available in April and May.
Beginners Half-day and day passes for 'mini regions' in both Laax and Flims (covering a handful of lifts); single ascents on most lifts in Laax and Flims; points tickets.
Short-term passes Half-day (from 11.00 or 12.30) and day pass.
Other periods Passes for 8 non-consecutive days.

Ski school
Swiss Ski School
Classes 2hr am and/or pm. Cost: 160.00 (5 days, Mon-Fri).
Lift priority No.
Children's classes Ages: 12. Cost: 135.00 (5 days, Mon-Fri).
Private lessons available Full- or half-day. Cost: 200.00 per hour. 110.00 for half-day.
Special courses 3-day surf course 130.00.

and a comfortable restaurant that prides itself on its fish. The Cresta is 'thoroughly recommended'. The owner/chef and staff of the National are 'delightful', and the hotel runs a minibus. One vegetarian reporter was very enthusiastic about the Hotel des Alpes, which has fully equipped kitchenettes in its rooms. The Surpunt is outstandingly well-placed for cross-country skiers. The Fidazerhof is remote (in a little community of chalets above Dorf), restful and comfortable.

Après-ski is generally muted. In Flims Dorf the meeting place for young people is the Albana pub (with disco – there is also one in Waldhaus). Most restaurants and bars are in hotels. There is tea-dancing at the Meiler, near the Dorf lifts. A recent report goes: 'Top range food at the Barga (Hotel Adula), Parkhaus and Schweizerhof. Good wholesome stuff at Alpina (pizza, pasta), Cabana and Chesa (grills)'. The Foppa chair-lift facilitates fondue evenings up the mountain, and toboggan rides home.

Both Flims and Laax cater very well for **cross-country** skiers and **non-skiers**, with long well-marked walks and trails through beautiful woodland scenery and up into the skiing area – 'a most interesting selection of beautiful trails, and an excellent training school'. Flims has more scope than Laax. A sports centre has been opened between the two resort centres.

There are good wide **nursery slopes** beside Flims Dorf, and another nursery lift at the top of the Startgels gondola. There is a small nursery slope at Murschetg, and an easy open slope high up at Crap Sogn Gion. Skiers with a few days' experience will find plenty of scope. Recent reports speak well of the **ski school** – 'good English, good/reasonable classes, very good private tuition' and 'good organisation, classes well balanced and fun'.

Laax 1020m

Laax has been unaffected by the development of the ski area, mainly because the lifts are further than a walk away. Much the nicest hotel is the Posta Veglia; old, charming, with a warm and lively atmosphere and reasonable prices – for rooms and in the restaurant, the *stübli* and the piano bar. Murschetg is a big new resort complex, most of which is at least convenient for the slopes (although a major element of it, the Happy Rancho complex, is a tiresome walk down the hill). At the foot of the pistes is the expensively neo-rustic Signina. Like Flims, Laax is a good resort for walkers and cross-country skiers (Murschetg is linked to Flims by cross-country trail), and offers free skating on the village pond.

Of the other communities dotted around the sunny hillsides, **Falera** is the most important; it is a sleepy old village with farming smells and noises and just a couple of hotels, reached by narrow road. Falera has the great advantage of direct access to the main lift system; the Encarna is a central, simple hotel.

For skiing convenience and queue avoidance you can stay up the mountain in the modern and very well appointed Crap Sogn Gion Berghotel; panoramic views, pool/sauna, bowling).

Tourist offices Laax ✆ (86) 34343. Tx 856111. Falera ✆ (86) 33030.
Package holidays Made to Measure (hs) SnowRanger (h).

Gemsstock gem

Andermatt Switzerland 1445m

Good for *Tough runs, Alpine charm, off-piste skiing, rail access, resort-level snow, ski touring*
Bad for *Easy runs, nursery slopes, skiing convenience, lift queues, mountain restaurants, not skiing, après-ski, woodland runs*

'No packaged tourists; peaceful, relaxed atmosphere; vast off-piste opportunities' – a recent reporter's summary of Andermatt – is a rare and alluring prospect for a dedicated skiing minority, especially when you add the resort's reputation for heavy snowfalls. Once much favoured by British skiers, Andermatt is now neglected by all but a faithful few – good skiers, for whom it is something of a retreat. Many of them are lured to the resort by the presence of two specialist off-piste ski schools. Over fine weekends and at Christmas and Easter it is very full of local Swiss and Italians, but most of the time the resort ticks over very slowly and threatens to stall.

Andermatt is a substantial village; it was one of the busiest Swiss resorts for tourists of earlier generations, for whom the Gotthard pass was a major transalpine thoroughfare. Now the high, flat-bottomed Urseren valley, of which Andermatt is the main settlement, is under-passed by the Gotthard road and rail tunnels. It sees only modest through-traffic in summer and in winter is almost a dead-end. Its livelihood depends on its being one of the most important places in Switzerland for mountain military service. Although initial impressions of grim barracks, stony-faced guards and steep bare hillsides may be off-putting, closer inspection reveals that Andermatt is a very attractive village; its cobbled streets have a slightly towny air, but the place still retains a lot of simple Alpine charm.

The skiing on the mighty Gemsstock can be as exciting and challenging as anywhere. There is also some good skiing for near-beginners, but there is not a large network of lifts, and bad weather or heavy weekend queues can make skiing practically impossible. It is a celebrated centre for ski touring.

The Oberalppass leading from Andermatt eastward towards Flims and the Furkapass leading westward to the resorts of the Valais are closed in winter, but car-carrying trains keep the links open.

The skiing top 2965m bottom 1445m

There are four ski areas along the flanks of the Urseren valley, between the Furka and Oberalp passes. The two main ones lie at either end of Andermatt, the two smaller and less popular areas south-west of Andermatt at the villages of Hospental and Realp.

The **Gemsstock** is Andermatt's big hill, climbing steeply from the

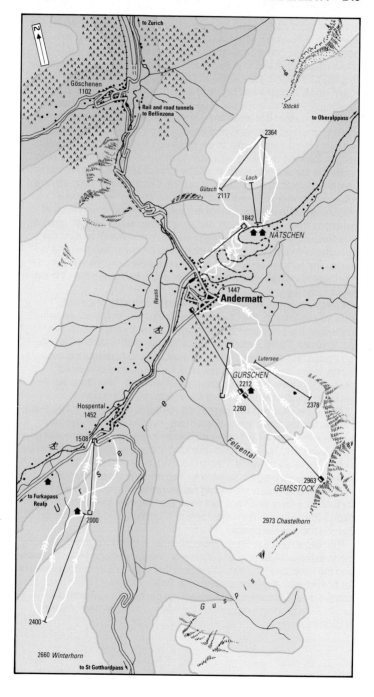

N

to Zurich

Göschenen
1102

Rail and road tunnels
to Bellinzona

Stöckli

to Oberalppass

2364

Loch

Gütsch
2117

1842

NÄTSCHEN

Reuss

1447
Andermatt

Lutersee

GURSCHEN
2212

2260

2378

Felsental

Hospental
1452

Urseren

1508

2963
GEMSSTOCK

2973 Chastelhorn

to Furkapass
Realp

2000

Guspis

2400

2660 Winterhorn

to St Gotthardpass

south-western edge of the village to a peak over 1500m higher. The lift system is simple and incapable of accommodating large numbers of people, despite current improvements: there is a two-stage cable-car and a couple of lifts around the middle station (at Gurschen) where the mountainside flattens out a little to provide a small area suitable for intermediates. Above and below this the runs are moderately or very demanding. The steep slopes face north and keep their snow well; but avalanche danger can close large areas after snowfalls. From the top station, which gives magnificent views, you can traverse to a beautiful red run around the shoulder of the mountain, with a moderately steep section followed by a long path back to the middle station. Or you can tackle the various runs down the sunless front of the Gemsstock which offer 800m vertical, almost all of it severe. The top half is rugged terrain – some glacier, a lot of rocks, no trees. Apart from the hazardous off-piste skiing in this bowl, there are very long off-piste runs in other directions from the top station, ending up either at the St Gotthard pass (the Guspis run), near Hospental (Felsental) or at Andermatt via the beautiful Unteralptal. None of these should be undertaken without a guide. The bottom half of the main face is hardly more friendly than the top; there is a single long and challenging run, less steep than the top section, but a genuine black with pitches of nearly 30˚.

From Andermatt, a chair-lift from near the barracks or a short train-ride up towards the Oberalp Pass brings you to **Nätschen**, where three drag-lifts serve a small sunny area of mostly easy, south-west-facing pistes. There is plenty of space for skiing off-piste between the top station and the railway line. The main piste to Andermatt is easy, mostly following the road (closed in winter); there is also a direct descent (not pisted) more or less under the chairs. This starts gently, but becomes much steeper towards the village.

Above the village at **Hospental**, on the south side of the valley, there are just two lifts towards the Winterhorn – a chair over the steeper, scrub-covered lower half of the mountain, followed by a drag serving open blue runs. The lifts, which are long enough to give very worthwhile skiing, are rarely crowded. **Realp** (1538m), several miles further away, has a little-used drag-lift, suitable for beginners and near-beginners.

There are not many **mountain restaurants** to tempt you to stay high for lunch – a fairly basic one (waitress service) near the Gemsstock mid-station, two sunnier restaurants at Nätschen, and one at the top of the chair above Hospental.

The capacity of the Gemsstock cable-car is being roughly doubled by the installation of 80-person cabins – on the upper stage for last season and the lower one for 1992. In the past there have been serious **queues** for both stages at weekends and peak holiday times. At other times the cable-car runs according to demand and the bottom half closes for lunch. Piste grading exaggerates the variety of the Winterhorn and Nätschen skiing.

The resort

Andermatt stretches along a single, sharply bent main street between the two ski areas; the old compact heart of the village (which gets little sun) has little traffic and a mixture of buildings, some dilapidated hotels of faded grandeur, others garishly colourful, and some attractive old chalets. There is no public transport within the resort, and none is necessary. Having a car is no more than a luxury, saving some walking and a few train rides.

Accommodation is nearly all in hotels (or barracks). Nowhere is ideal for all the skiing. For the Gemsstock, the Aurora is most convenient. The central Gasthaus zum Sternen (run by an English lady) is the most attractive old wooden chalet in Andermatt – cheap, fun, and a popular meeting and eating place. The Ochsen also does inexpensive B&B. The Bergidyll is a comfortable chalet-style hotel near the station; friendly, with good breakfasts, and popular with the British. The Sonne is comfortably traditional, run by two charming English-speaking ladies and well placed between the village centre and the cable-car.

Facts on Andermatt Zentralschweiz **Switzerland**

Prices in francs

Tourist office
Postcode CH-6490
Tel (44) 67454
Fax (44) 68185
Tlx 868604

Getting there
By road 806km from Calais. Via Zurich; chains may be needed.
By rail Station in resort.
By air Zurich; transfer 3hr. (Or Geneva/Lugano.)

Staying there
Visitor beds 1,450; breakdown: 650 in hotels, 800 in apartments.
Package holidays Made to Measure (hs) Ski Club of GB (h) Ski Unique (h) SnowRanger (h) .
Medical facilities In resort: Military hospital, doctor, dentist, chemist.

Non-skiing activities
Indoor Fitness centre with sauna and solarium.
Outdoor Natural skating rink, skating, curling, paragliding, mountaineering (2 mountaineering schools), 4km sledge run.

Special skiing facilities
Summer skiing No.
Cross-country 20km of easy and medium trails along valley floor, and as far as Realp.

Lift passes
Area
Covers all Urseren valley lifts and the train. (12 lifts in total.)
Cost 6 days 160.00 (£66.67).
Credit cards accepted Only at Gemsstock and railway.
Children 107.00 (under 16) saving 33%. Free pass up to age 6.
Beginners Coupons or single tickets.
Short-term passes Half-day pass (from 12.30pm); single and return tickets on some lifts.
Other passes Passes for 6 different areas available. Weekly Oberalp pass gives seven separate day-passes for local areas, including Disentis (not covered by Urseren valley pass) and 50% reduction on trains from Realp to Disentis, and Andermatt to Göschenen.

Ski school
Swiss Ski School Andermatt
Classes 4hr: 2hr am and pm. Cost: 153.00 (6 days, Mon-Sat).
Lift priority Yes.
Children's classes Ages: 4½-12. Cost: 128.00 (6 days, Mon-Sat). Usually no lunch-time arrangements possible.
Private lessons available Daily, or hourly outside ski school hours. Cost: 45.00 per hour. 1-3 people.
Special courses Ski-touring.

What was new in 91
1. Capacity of the Gemsstock cable-car has nearly doubled.
2. New black runs down drag and chair to Hospental.

Après-ski revolves mainly around bars; some, like the Tell and the Adler, are packed with locals and soldiers. Others, like the Sternen and the cosy Ochsen pub (hosted by a Swiss-American powder freak), are popular with skiers. The Postillion and Spycher are popular with younger locals and the army. There is one disco. Restaurants, apart from the friendly Tell, are in hotels. The Sternen and the lovely old Hotel St Gotthard at Hospental are recommended.

The wide, flat valley makes an ideal easy **cross-country** track which rises less than 100m over 10km. The trail is graded into green, blue and red loops – referring more to length than difficulty. Andermatt is not devoid of **non-skiing** activities, but cannot safely be recommended for the inactive.

Andermatt has little in the way of **nursery slopes**, but there are some easy runs at Hospental, and for near-beginners the long run down from Nätschen to Andermatt is excellent.

The main **ski school** has a few native-English-speaking instructors. Children's classes 'looked lots of fun, with good, challenging exercises'. The well-known local guide Martin Epp is now more often to be seen in Wengen. Another local skier and climber, Alex Clapasson, runs weekly off-piste and touring courses (under the name Mountain Reality) in competition with Canadian guide John Hogg (Alpine Adventures).

Wengen Switzerland 1270m

Good for *Beautiful scenery, nursery slopes, easy runs, big ski area, not skiing, family holidays, Alpine charm, woodland runs, rail access, chalet holidays, ski touring, freedom from cars*
Bad for *Tough runs, late holidays, skiing convenience*

Linked resort: Grindelwald

According to the authorised (British) version of skiing history, the Jungfrau region is the cradle of the recreational and competitive sport of today. It was at Wengen that British skiers hit on the idea of using the railway to turn skiing into a 'downhill only' pastime, and at Mürren (across the valley) that Arnold Lunn organised the first slalom race. Wengen has changed less than most of the famous early resorts. It is still small and almost car-free, and life still revolves around the railway. It is very welcoming to British skiers, who still dominate the place despite the conspicuous arrival of Club Med. Families return year after year to the same hotels, chalets and drinks parties, and treat the resort as a second home. Not surprisingly, some other visitors find this off-putting.

The regulars do not return purely out of nostalgia. The village is among the most picturesque of Alpine resorts, and the surrounding peaks are majestic, including the famous ascending trio of Eiger, Mönch and Jungfrau (4158m). The skiing, shared with neighbouring Grindelwald, is extensive and scenic; and the lack of cars, the good sunny village nursery slopes and guaranteed English-speaking instruction make Wengen attractive to beginners and children. Good skiers come hoping to find good snow off-piste beneath the Eiger.

Grindelwald, the original climbing resort, is overshadowed by the mountains (it gets one hour of sun a day in mid-winter) and by the special qualities of Wengen. It is larger, and the obvious access point to the skiing for motorists, local weekenders and commuters from cheap hotels in Interlaken and Wilderswil. But it enjoys superb views, is not full of British visitors and has more to offer in the evening.

Taking a car to Wengen seems pointless – you have to leave it at Lauterbrunnen, and you are unlikely to make expeditions further afield than Mürren. (A shared lift pass is available; if you go, it's quicker and easier to take the bus/cable-car route from Lauterbrunnen rather than the funicular/railway route.) Convenient parking is in short supply, but spaces can be reserved in the multi-storey car park at Lauterbrunnen.

The skiing top 2971m bottom 943m

The skiing shared by Wengen and Grindelwald falls into two areas. The main one, Kleine Scheidegg/Männlichen, is a rolling, partly wooded area of predominantly easy and intermediate pistes. The slopes above

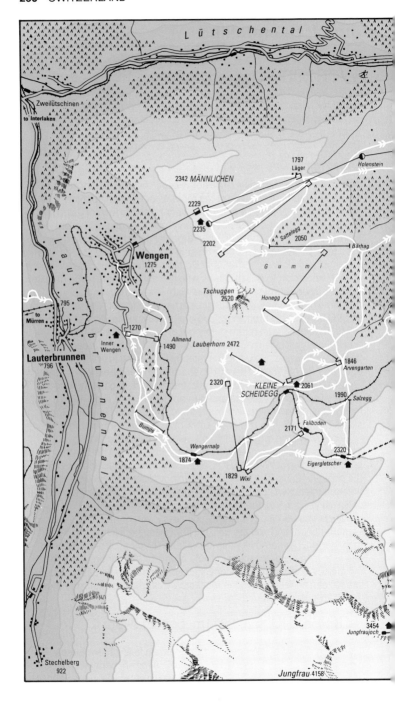

Lütschental

Zweilütschinen
to Interlaken

1797
Läger

Holenstein

2342 MÄNNLICHEN

2229
2235

2202

Sattelegg
2050

Bärhag

Gummi

Wengen
1275

Tschuggen
2520

Honegg

795

to
Mürren

1270

Inner
Wengen

Allmend
1490

Lauberhorn 2472

1846
Arvengarten

Lauterbrunnen
796

Lauterbrunnental

2320

KLEINE
SCHEIDEGG

2061

1990   Salzegg

Bumps

Wengernalp
1874

Falboden

2171

2320
Eigergletscher

1829 Wixi

3454
Jungfraujoch

Stechelberg
922

Jungfrau 4158

First ski area

Grindelwald
1034

1061

986

959

Grund
943

Aspen

1391
Pfingstegg
(summer only)

1332
Brandegg

1615
Alpiglen

Hörnli

2865 Eigerwand

3970
Eiger

Kl. Eiger
3472

3160 Eismeer

Eigerjoch 3614

(underground railway)

Mönch
4099

3299
Berglihütte

3692
Walcherhorn

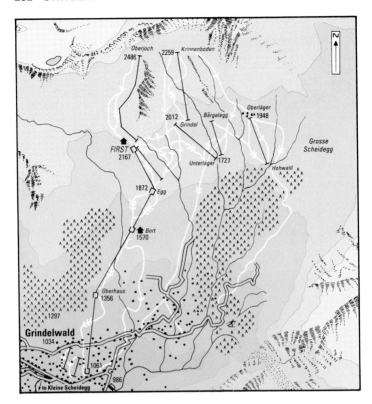

Wengen face west, those above Grindelwald mostly east. On the opposite side of Grindelwald is First, a smaller sunny area.

A cog railway links both Wengen and Grindelwald with the col of **Kleine Scheidegg**; another climbs from there to Eigergletscher and on, by a tunnel through the Eiger, to Jungfraujoch, the highest railway station in Europe. From here various excursions can be undertaken (with a guide), the easiest of them leading down the Aletsch glacier, the longest in the Alps, towards Brig. In good weather this makes a superb day trip; the skiing is easy throughout, but there is normally a hard climb out at the end (skins needed). The Black Rock run from Eigergletscher is not genuinely steep, but is the most challenging piste in this area; the north-facing red down the Salzegg drag often has the best snow around. There is also some good off-piste skiing – notably under the north face of the Eiger ('White Hare') and down to Wixi by 'Oh God!'. This is not really an area for the novice, although the run from Fallboden to Wixi is popular with inexperienced skiers.

On the opposite side of Kleine Scheidegg is the Lauberhorn, a good intermediate and off-piste area, with many possible variants of the run back to the bottom of the drag-lift or on down to Wengen – a mixture of open piste and path, the latter often very crowded and worn. Most of it can be avoided by skiing down to the Innerwengen chair. The Bumps

The Wengen Downhill: Bell's view

Wengen has a very special atmosphere – and its race, the Lauberhorn, is one of the two great classics (the other being Kitzbühel's Hahnenkamm). The main thing about it is the length of the course – about half a minute longer than most of the others. It doesn't have a lot more turns, but there are long straight sections between them so if you mess up a turn and carry less speed into the straight you really pay for your mistake. The course includes some weird things that wouldn't be allowed in a new course, like going under the railway bridge.

From the start you pick up a lot of speed on long sweeping sections before coming to a 180° turn where you slow down (fortunately!) from about 80mph to about 30mph before going over the Hundschopf, which must be one of the most dramatic sections on any course: a 20m vertical drop between two cliff faces. Then comes Canadian Corner, where a lot of Canadians crashed one year, then the bridge, then Austrian Hole, named after another national débâcle, and finally the S-bends and a jump into the finish, site of Peter's Müller's famous crash. Müller was risking a lot through the S-bends, using the full width of the piste like a Grand Prix driver using the curb stones – letting it run out, we call it. But if you only just squeeze through the gate before the jump you don't have time to squash it, so he flew a long way, landed hard and his legs just gave way and he sat down. They still had hay bales in those days, and Müller ended up in one.

drag, very popular with the ski school, serves an easy slope with steeper options at the finish.

On the Grindelwald side of Kleine Scheidegg, a series of lifts link up with the **Männlichen**, which can also be reached by cable-car from Wengen and gondola from Grund, on the fringes of Grindelwald. There are good intermediate pistes here, and some interesting off-piste skiing, particularly around the Gummi chair. The Arvengarten chair to Kleine Scheidegg and drag to Honegg give access to a lot of skiing, but the chair suffers from being the only link back to Scheidegg. The Männlichen is mostly open and easy, with a few more challenging runs and open off-piste slopes below the summit, to the north.

There are several routes down towards Grindelwald from both Männlichen and Kleine Scheidegg, with open pistes on top and wooded areas further down. The piste gradings overstate difficulty and, provided snow is good enough, these very long, beautiful and easy runs to Grund (including a blue of 8.5km) are a leisurely skier's paradise.

On the other side of Grindelwald, a bus-ride from the centre, the south-facing **First** area has until now been reached by a very slow chair-lift, being replaced this year by a gondola; a drag beyond it on Oberjoch serves easy open skiing (and often good spring snow) on the upper slopes, and there are touring possibilities for the adventurer. The area to the east of First has now been extended by the addition of two drags to make a total of four, serving open, easy runs. From the top of the Schilt drag (2260m) there is a long, scenic run to the valley ending at the hotel Wetterhorn, whence frequent buses go to the village. The black run down from First, under the chairs, is nowhere very steep.

Mountain restaurants are inadequate in number, and poorly distributed, but some are very attractive. Reporters' favourite is Brandegg – 'friendly staff', 'cheaper than most', 'wonderful apple fritters'. The pricey Jungfrau hotel at Wengernalp divides reporters: is it 'the best', or 'over-rated and over-priced'? Other recommendations: Grindelwald Blick at Kleine Scheidegg and Bort at First.

Both the gondola and the train at Grund can generate horrendous **queues** in high season and at weekends. There are various peak-time bottle-necks where ten-minute waits are not unusual – though the Männlichen drag-lift has been replaced by an efficient chair and the Lauberhorn drag is to be so replaced this season. The railway has some new trains taking more people; unfortunately for non-skiers, skis on these trains are carried inside, not in a separate truck. Several reporters have commented wearily on the amount of poling needed to get from lift to lift (and along the pistes), but routes can usually be planned to avoid awkward links. Several skiers have felt that piste gradings overstate difficulty. There is **artificial snow** only on the short piste served by the Aspen drag at Grindelwald.

The resort

Set on an open shelf above the Lauterbrunnen valley and overlooked by the Jungfrau, Wengen is one of the most beautifully situated of Alpine resorts, surpassed for drama and views only by Mürren. Lots of chalets are dotted about the shelf, and the compact centre consists of large, comfortable, traditional hotels. The train from Lauterbrunnen to Kleine Scheidegg runs through the resort, and the station is the natural focus. All the activity is on or close to the main street, which is lined with hotels and shops (limited in range). There is an English church.

There is now a taxi service in the resort. The main access problem is the risk of missing the last train from Lauterbrunnen (about 11pm).

Accommodation offered by UK tour operators consists mainly of hotels, with some staffed chalets; but there is also self-catering accommodation available locally. Although not a large resort, Wengen is quite spread out and hilly, and skiers not staying centrally can face long walks to the cable-car or station. Hotel standards are high, and complaints few. Among recent recommendations, only the Regina is central, just up from the station; the highly idiosyncratic Falken is up the hill behind it; the five-star Park Beausite is at the top of the village, by the cable-car; the Belvédère and Bellevue are at the north end of the village; the Brunner is to the south, up the railway; the Alpenrose down the hill below the station. Other convenient hotels include the rebuilt Eiger and the luxurious but staid Victoria-Lauberhorn, by the station. In the main street, the Bernerhof is traditional and good value, but is said to have an unhelpful manager; the smart Sunstar has a good pool.

Après-ski is fairly quiet and unsophisticated. Wengernalp is a favourite place for a last drink on the mountain; Café Oberland and Mary's Café are closer to home. In the village, the obvious meeting place is the *stube* of the Hotel Eiger, by the station ('great snails, *rösti*, fondue, gargantuan pastries'), not to be confused with the smaller Eiger Bar (aka the Pickle) on the main street – also packed after skiing. Other favourite tea-time spots include the Tanne bar and the 'quiet' Monica's bar in the hotel Silberhorn. At night there is live music in a couple of bars, a night-club and a couple of discos – the Carousel in the Regina is popular with all ages, thanks to its eccentric over-60 DJ, Lord Henry. There are ice-hockey and curling matches, and occasional ski-jump and parallel slalom competitions; a splendid toboggan run down to

Facts on Wengen   Berner Oberland **Switzerland**

Prices in francs
Ski Club represented

Tourist office

Postcode CH-3823
Tel (36) 551414
Fax (36) 553060
Tlx 923271

Getting there

By road 835km from Calais. Cars must be left at parks in Interlaken or Lauterbrunnen. Access via Basle; chains rarely needed.
By rail Station in resort.
By air Zurich; transfer 3½hr. (Or Berne is closest. Also Geneva.)

Staying there

Visitor beds 5,800; breakdown: 2,300 in hotels; 3,500 in apartments.
Package holidays Club Med (h) Crystal (h) Hoverspeed Ski-Drive (h) Inghams (hs) Kuoni (h) Made to Measure (hs) PR Christian Holidays (h) Ski Club of GB (h) Ski Sutherland (h) Ski Unique (h) SnowRanger (h) Supertravel (hc) Swiss-Ski (h) Thomson (h) .
Medical facilities In resort: Doctor, chemist. Dentist: Lauterbrunnen. Hospital: Interlaken (12km from Lauterbrunnen).

Non-skiing activities

Indoor Curling, swimming pool (in Park Hotel), sauna, solarium (in hotels), cinema (English films), bowling, billiards.
Outdoor Skating, curling, 20km cleared paths, toboggan runs, ski-bobs, sleigh rides, paragliding, hang-gliding.

Kindergartens

Gastekindergarten
Tuition: Yes. Hours: 8.45-4.30 from Mon-Fri, 8.45-12.30 on Sat. Ages: 3-7. Cost: 95.00 per week (with lunch; price assumes Visitor's Card – it is substantially more without one). On second floor of Sport Pavilion. Transport to and from ski school can be arranged with kindergarten.

Special skiing facilities

Summer skiing One small lift on the Jungfrau (tourist attraction) open Jun-Sep.
Cross-country None in Wengen, but 18km in Lauterbrunnen valley.

Lift passes

Jungfrau pass
Covers all lifts in Wengen, Mürren and Grindelwald, and trains between them, also Grindelwald ski-bus. (35 lifts in total.)
Cost 6 days 212.00 (£88.33).
Credit cards accepted Yes.
Children 142.00 (under 16) saving 33%. Free pass up to age 6.
Notes Trains between Eigergletscher and Jungfraujoch not covered by any pass.
Beginners Coupons.
Short-term passes Half-day for Kleine Scheidegg/Männlichen; single and return tickets on most lifts.
Other passes Kleine Scheidegg/Männlichen pass covers all lifts from Wengen to Grindelwald (6 days 179.00 for adults, 120.00 for children). One day extension available to cover another area (32.00).

Ski school

Swiss Ski School
Classes 4hr: 2hr am and pm. Cost: 166.00 (6 days, Mon to Sat).
Lift priority No.
Children's classes Ages: 4-12. Cost: 166.00 (6 days, Mon to Sat).
Private lessons available Full day or half-day. Cost: 55.00 per hour. 1-4 people.
Special courses Heli-skiing and glacier touring.

What was new in 91

New 4-seater chair-lift to replace Männlichen drag-lift.

What is new for 92

New 4-seater chair-lift to replace Lauberhorn drag-lift.

Lauterbrunnen (when conditions permit); evening skating once or twice a week (hire skates in the afternoon). Dinner at Kleine Scheidegg or Wengernalp, followed by moonlit skiing, is often arranged.

Wengen is a splendid resort for **non-skiers** who are content to potter about the village and the mountains, provided the weather is kind. Long, beautiful mountain walks and the train make it possible to meet up with skiing companions; there's plenty of scope for longer excursions, including the 'unmissable' train trip up to Jungfraujoch, on which lift pass holders get a discount. But the continued lack of sports facilities is disappointing; access to the Park hotel's pool is restricted and pricey. It is no place for **cross-country** skiers.

Wengen's central and sunny **nursery slope** is friendly and gentle, though one reporter is critical of its lift (and more than one have been surprised to find that it is not covered by the lift pass). Provided snow is good the transition to the large expanses of easy piste skiing accessible by train is not too traumatic, but the path down to Wengen gets uncomfortably crowded. Reports on **ski school** are mostly good, with English widely spoken and the timetable compensating for long train rides, but classes may be large (up to a 'disgraceful' 24), and some instructors are 'old and impatient'. A good video system helps you select your class. There are several freelance instructors, most bookable through Molitor Sports. Heli-skiing is organised by the school and by Andreas Cova (hotel Falken).

Grindelwald   1040m

Grindelwald is a large and busy year-round resort spread along the valley floor between the magnificent peaks of Wetterhorn and Eiger on the one side and the gentler wooded slopes of First on the other. The resort has lots of accommodation and leisure facilities including an 'excellent' sports centre (skating, curling, swimming, sauna), long and beautiful walks high above the valley floor and (unlike the other Jungfrau resorts) long cross-country trails, totalling 45km. For skiers the place to stay is Grund, at the bottom of the main ski area, or near Grindelwald station, for easy access to Grund by train. Several reporters have recommended the 'unsophisticated' hotel Derby, right on the station – 'excellent value, good varied food, noise not a problem' – but one case of overbooking has been reported. Our only recent recommendation is of the Schönegg, which sounds excellent in every respect except the nocturnal noise of the proprietor's Huskies.

Après-ski is more varied than in the other local resorts – live music of various kinds in many hotel bars – but even here there is not much going on into the small hours. There is a good daytime bus service linking Grund, Grindelwald centre and the First lift. Our one recent report on the ski school is favourable. The sunny Bodmi nursery slopes are next to the village; a reporter was (to say the least) disappointed to find that when lack of snow put the slopes out of action the non-ski kindergarten was also closed.

Tourist office ✆ (36) 531212. Tx 923217. **Package holidays** Crystal (h) Hoverspeed Ski-Drive (h) Inghams (h) Kuoni (h) Made to Measure (hs) Neilson (h) Powder Byrne (hca) SnowRanger (hs) Supertravel (h) Swiss-Ski (h) Thomson (h).

Towering inferno

Mürren Switzerland 1640m

Good for *Beautiful scenery, resort-level snow, family holidays, Alpine charm, freedom from cars, rail access*
Bad for *Easy runs, après-ski*

Like neighbouring Wengen, Mürren is one of the original and most fiercely traditional of ski resorts, with strong British connections based on a racing club for youngsters (the Kandahar) and the undying loyalty of many of its alumni, who include the Lunn family. It was Henry Lunn (a non-skier) who persuaded the locals to run their mountain railway in winter (which they did for the first time in December 1910), and his son Arnold who organised at Mürren the first slalom race (in 1922) and the first World Championships in downhill and slalom racing (in 1931). Arnold's son Peter has been skiing in Mürren for 75 years and still spends much of the winter there, visited by his son Stephen and the fifth generation of Lunns.

Nearer to traffic-free than any other resort, Mürren has no serious rivals as a peaceful and idyllic winter hideaway: old chalets line snowy paths on a high cliff-top shelf (reached by funicular or cable-car) which is itself quite steeply sloping, so that most of the village shares the same glorious view across to the Eiger and Jungfrau. The skiing is similarly spectacular, and the long run down from the famous revolving restaurant at the top of the Schilthorn is something no competent skier in the region should miss, weather permitting. There are a few other interesting runs on the slopes immediately above Mürren but not much of the skiing is easy and, for piste skiers at least, it is rather a one-run resort.

The skiing top 2970m bottom 800m

The original lift in Mürren, opened in 1912, is the old funicular from the top of the village to the Allmendhubel. It still serves moderately easy runs down to the village and connections with the skiing on either side. Mürren's best gentle skiing is down to the woods above Winteregg, where the middle station on the railway line provides Wengen-based skiers with a direct way into and out of the skiing. When snow is good it is possible to ski down to Lauterbrunnen via a long, tortuous and not particularly interesting path through the steep woods. This is the last leg of the famous Inferno course from the top of the Schilthorn (15.8km long, 2144m vertical). The race is run every January by over 1,000 skiers; the record time for the course is about 15½ minutes, including some uphill skiing which holiday skiers can avoid by using the Maulerhubel drag. On the other side of the village, the steep Schiltgrat drag-lifts serve a serious black run of about 1.5km for 500m vertical,

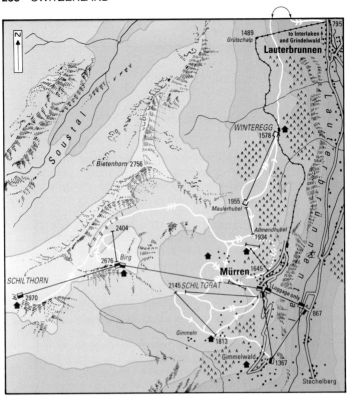

often huge moguls all the way, and some easier, sunny skiing down to Gimmeln.

The two-stage cable-car to Schilthorn climbs more than 1300m up the cliff face to Birg and onward over a deep bowl to the famous round (and revolving) restaurant which crowns Piz Gloria, as seen in the film *On Her Majesty's Secret Service*. The 360° views from the top are wonderful, and the run down is no less exciting. The first section is not fearsomely steep, but usually very bumpy or wind-blown, and may be bare at the very top (there is now dry-slope matting, which helps). The run opens out into a beautiful, gentle, open bowl (the Engetal); from here a short, steep drag-lift goes up to Birg, permitting repeated skiing of the top half of the Schilthorn run and serving open blue and red runs of its own. Beneath the Engetal the run provides stunning views across to the Jungfrau massif before entering the Kanonenrohr (gunbarrel); the run then presents an unnerving mixture of narrowness, rocks, moguls and a precipitous drop protected by nets, before running out gently towards Allmendhubel. Deplorably, descent by the cable-car is not covered by any lift pass, encouraging incompetent skiers to risk their necks rather than pay the fare.

The **mountain restaurants** at Birg and Piz Gloria have little to commend them apart from their superlative views, enjoyable from a terrace at the former but not the latter. Lower down, the Suppenalp and the Sonnenberg (both in the Blumental, between Allmendhubel and Schiltgrat) are 'excellent and friendly'; the Sonnenberg is particularly recommended for 'excellent pasta'. The Gimmeln is also recommended.

In general there are no serious lift **queues** except for the cable-car at peak times and when Wengen and Grindelwald are short of snow. The Engetal drag can produce queues, particularly when the lower part of the Schilthorn run is closed. There are plans for new lifts between Engetal and the Kanonenrohr, which will be very welcome. Piste grooming apparently does not take place while snow is falling, which leaves a lot to be done when it stops. There is **artificial snow** on one short run above the village.

The resort

The train which winds along the mountain shelf from the top of the funicular up from Lauterbrunnen arrives at one end of the village, and at the other end is the cable-car station – point of arrival from Stechelberg and departure for Piz Gloria. Between the two is the tightly-packed village.

Most of the **accommodation** is in hotels. There are a couple of large, expensive ones (the Mürren and the Eiger) by the railway station; they are not well placed for skiing but each has its devotees. The sunny terrace of the Bellevue near the Allmendhubel lives up to its name. About the cheapest accommodation is in the large, central Regina. The Alpenruh is an attractive chalet hotel right next to the cable-car station. The Belmont offers 'good value'. You can stay on-piste above the village at the Sonnenberg or Suppenalp.

Mürren's **après-ski** is very quiet. Fondue/toboggan evenings at Suppenalp are regularly organised. Recommended places to eat include the Tächi-Bar in the hotel Eiger ('romantic candle-lit dinners, and a live band') and the restaurant in the Alpenruh ('excellent nouvelle cuisine'). Locals tend to congregate in the Stägerstübli ('good and cheap'). The Bliemlichäller is a livelier spot 'for the young'. One reporter found the Ibex pub in the hotel Belmont to be the hub of the après-ski scene.

A village which is so small and quiet is difficult to recommend to **non-skiers**, despite the extremely impressive sports centre (with a 'super' pool, jacuzzi and squash courts), the very pretty walks, beautifully positioned skating rink, expensive sleigh rides and the absence of traffic. The local **cross-country** skiing trail is too short to be of much interest and the alternative is the indignity of taking a lift down to the valley trails.

The small **nursery slope** on the Allmendhubel is gentle, sunny and snow-sure, which would be the envy of many a sizeable resort; there is another behind the hotel Jungfrau. The **ski school** has been in a state of flux for some time, with repeated changes of management. According to one report, instruction concentrates heavily on technique. We have had an enthusiastic report on the children's classes – 'good,

Facts on Mürren   Berner Oberland **Switzerland**

Prices in francs
Ski Club represented

Tourist office
Postcode CH-3825
Tel (36) 551616
Fax (36) 553769
Tlx 923212

Getting there
By road 940km from Calais. Cars must be left at parks in Interlaken or Lauterbrunnen. Access via Basle; chains rarely needed.
By rail Station in resort.
By air Zurich; transfer 3½hr. (Or Berne is closest. Also Geneva.)

Staying there
Visitor beds 2,000; breakdown: 800 in hotels and guest-houses, 1,200 in chalets and apartments.
Package holidays Kuoni (h) Made to Measure (hs) Ski Unique (h) Supertravel (hc) Swiss-Ski (h)
.
Medical facilities In resort: Doctor, chemist. Dentist: Lauterbrunnen. Hospital: Interlaken (12km from Lauterbrunnen).

Non-skiing activities
Indoor 'Alpine Sports Centre Mürren' (swimming pool, whirl-pool and children's pool, library, children's playroom, gymnasium, squash, sauna, solarium, judo, massage); private sauna at Chalet uf em Bort.
Outdoor Artificial ice-rink (curling, skating, tuition available – free with Visitor's card); toboggan run to Gimmelwald, 15km walks.

Kindergartens
Chalet Louise
Tuition: Possible from 3yr. Hours: 9.30-4.00. Ages: from 4mths (mornings only), from 3yr (full day). Cost: 150.00 per week (with lunch). Price assumes you have a Visitor's card – considerably more expensive without.

Other childcare facilities
2 children's playgrounds and playroom in Sports Centre.

Special skiing facilities
Summer skiing No.
Cross-country 2km loop, and 12km in Lauterbrunnen valley. Instruction available.

Lift passes
Jungfrau pass
Covers all lifts in Wengen, Mürren and Grindelwald and trains between them. (35 lifts in total.)
Cost 6 days 212.00 (£88.33).
Credit cards accepted Yes.
Children 142.00 (under 17) saving 33%. Free pass up to age 6.
Notes Low season price with packages only.
Beginners Coupons.
Short-term passes Half-day (from 12 noon) for Mürren/Schilthorn; single and return tickets on some lifts.
Other passes Mürren/Schilthorn pass covering just Mürren lifts (6 days 158.00 for adults, 106.00 for children); extensions possible to cover other areas.

Ski school
Local
Classes 10.00-12.00am, Mon-Sat. Cost: 95.00 (6 days).
Lift priority No.
Children's classes Ages: 4-14. Cost: 85.00 (6 days).
Private lessons available Full- or half-day. Cost: 90.00 per morning, 80.00 per afternoon.
Special courses Heli-skiing.

What was new in 91
Nothing.

What is new for 92
New cable-car and 2 chair-lifts planned.

---

confidence-building instruction'. But we have also had a comprehensively damning report on the kindergarten at the sports centre, which is said to be inadequately equipped and staffed – 'one small and overheated room, with only one untrained assistant, very few books or toys at all and hardly any suitable for the under-3s'.

Speed skiing for beginners

Cervinia Italy 2050m

Good for *Nursery slopes, easy runs, big ski area, sunny slopes, resort-level snow, late holidays, summer skiing*
Bad for *Alpine charm, not skiing, lift queues, tough runs, mountain restaurants, freedom from cars, woodland runs*

Cervinia was once the showpiece of Italian ski resort development. Half a century ago the old climbing base of Breuil, set very high in a bleak, open setting on the sunny side of the Matterhorn, became new Cervinia. Cable-cars were built spanning vast glacial wastelands up to the unprecedented height of 3500m, opening up enormously long, very sunny ski runs and bringing the smart set to Cervinia's new grand hotels. More recently, Cervinia has been eclipsed by developments elsewhere. Its lift system, which had fallen way behind the times, has recently been improved by the addition of a smart new gondola to Plateau Rosa and several speedy chair-lifts, but the resort still has a lot of catching up to do. And no amount of investment can alter the basic nature of Cervinia's skiing, which is lacking in challenge. The fact that the skiing links with that of Zermatt does not provide a solution, either: on day-trips it is not possible to get more than a taste of Zermatt's skiing (and the link is notoriously windy and often closed).

As a village, too, Cervinia has drawbacks. Its pre-War architecture has not aged well, so it cannot sell on charm; but the resort was not purpose-designed, as more modern high-altitude resorts have been – so it cannot sell on convenience either. The smart set decamped long ago and is unlikely to return.

But Cervinia is still a lively and popular international resort, with plenty of British visitors 'of neither the yuppie nor the lager lout variety', reports one satisfied visitor. The skiing is still sunny and pretty reliable for snow, and this in particular has worked to the resort's advantage recently. Of more permanent value is the fact that there is nowhere else in the world where beginners and timid but enthusiastic skiers can with complete confidence cover so much ground in scenery of such grandeur (even if the Matterhorn was designed to be seen from Switzerland). Several of our most enthusiastic reporters are elderly: 'Such marvellous geriatric skiing!' explained one. The few reporters who have regretted choosing the resort were mainly disappointed by the lack of challenge in the skiing – 'the few blacks were flatteringly easy'. But many more reporters have expressed the reservation that it is a more expensive place than they had expected. We even have reports of skiers crossing over into Switzerland to keep lunch costs down.

A car is of no advantage in the resort, which suffers from too much traffic and inadequate parking provision; some hotels have garages, but charge handsomely for the use of them. But expeditions are possible to La Thuile or Courmayeur, or even into France (the Chamonix valley).

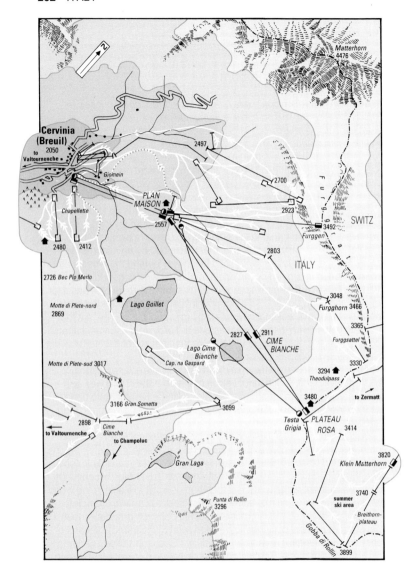

The skiing top 3490m bottom 1620m

The terrain is rocky and only a section of the horseshoe surrounding Cervinia is skiable, with slopes facing south and west. It is a remarkably open, sunny skiing area between 2000m and 3500m, shelving gently in steps, and broken up by clefts and lakes.

The main lifts from the resort are the cable-car and gondola up to

Plan Maison, and the Cretaz drag-lifts from the lower part of the village to the northern edge of this area – a vast nursery and sunbathing plateau. From Plan Maison, another chain of drag-lifts continues on up to the Theodulpass, where an awkward walk leads to the run down to Zermatt. On the Cervinia side there are long, easy motorways back down to Plan Maison, and from there a very gentle, roundabout blue run goes back to the resort. On the lower slopes above Cervinia are more direct runs: blacks under the gondola and red 3 to the side of it, on which snow cannon have been recently installed.

From Plan Maison a little cable-car with a big build-up of warnings climbs nearly 1000m over an awesome cliff to Furggen, at the shoulder of the Matterhorn. A tedious walk down an internal staircase of nearly 300 steps brings you to the broad ledge at the top of the cliff. It is a beautiful, isolated, long run, graded black – mainly easy but with a couple of short, 'nerve tingling' sections near the beginning. There are some adventurous off-piste variants, not obvious to the uninitiated. A short black run from the new Pancheron chair-lift meets the Furggen run; from here it is possible to continue on to the lower part of the village on various reds and blues.

The parallel cable-cars up to Plateau Rosa give direct and easy skiing access to Zermatt. The main run back to Cervinia is the famous Ventina, an uninterrupted run of nearly 8km for 1500m vertical. There is no great difficulty involved, apart from keeping up your momentum on the flat bits. The chair-lift at Lago Goillet has made it possible to ski the middle section of the run repeatedly. This area has been made directly accessible from Plan Maison by a new 12-person gondola to Plateau Rosa, with a mid-station at Laghi Cime Bianche. It is, by all accounts, an impressive ride and has greatly improved access (and relieved queues) to the glacier.

The top of the Lago Goillet chair-lift meets the Gran Sometta drag, the highest of the lifts up from Valtournenche. The run down those lifts is sometimes claimed as the longest piste in the Alps (starting at the Klein Matterhorn) but is actually punctuated by a short drag-lift ride at Cime Bianche and by a couple of tedious uphill stretches. The Gran Sommetta drag is at the head of the Val d'Ayas: tracks leading off from the bottom of the lift end up at Champoluc.

To the south-east of Cervinia are the **Carosello** lifts – little-used chairs and drags starting from the high part of the resort (each of the two luxury hotels has a lift outside the front door), accessible from the Ventina run. The slopes face west and north-west, are fairly steep and often unprepared, with scope for exploring between the pistes.

Cervinia's **mountain restaurants** are inadequate in number, very expensive by Italian standards, and in general extremely insanitary. One exception is the English-run Igloo, at the top of the Bardoney chair. One reporter says that the best value is to be found at the pretty little bar on the blue home run from Plan Maison. There is a picnic area at Plan Maison. The restaurant at Salette, on the way down to Valtournenche, is also recommended 'for generous pizzas and good cappuccinos'.

Cervinia's lift system is antiquated and inadequate. Despite doubling up of some key lifts there are still very long **queues** to get up the mountain at weekends and at peak holiday times. Queues at Plan Maison have been partly relieved by the new gondola. At quiet times lifts run infrequently, and at any time lifts are liable to be closed for no apparent reason. The cable-cars (notably Furggen) are often closed quite legitimately by wind, at very short notice. There are also irritating walks between lifts.

Having won a fierce battle against the environmentalists, the authorities have finally been able to install **artificial snow** on two main runs back to the village; red 3 (from Plan Maison) and the bottom section of the Ventina, beside the Bardoney chair-lift.

The resort

In the centre at the foot of the slopes is a small area of lively bars and shops at the foot of the slopes. Some of it is reserved for pedestrians, the rest a one-way circuit, plagued with weekend traffic. One particularly unimpressed reporter complains of litter-strewn streets and rude residents.

Above the cable-car station, buildings (mostly the smarter hotels) stretch on up the hill towards the Carosello lifts. Apart from this upper part, it is a compact resort, easily enough negotiated on foot, although the climb up to the main lift station is tiresome. The more remote hotels tend to have courtesy minibuses. Shopping is adequate.

Except for some new apartment development on the lower slopes near the cable-car (not rated highly), most **accommodation** is in simple hotels. Most of the hotels used by UK operators are in the main centre, within walking distance of the Cretaz drag-lifts. We have had few enthusiastic reports and several very unenthusiastic ones – notably on the Rosà. The more comfortable hotels are more spaciously set above the cable-car station, beneath the Carosello lifts. Only the smartly modernised, expensive Grand Cristallo is at all luxurious and cosmopolitan. Of the central hotels, one regular visitor recommends the Fosson – 'simple, friendly, popular with Italians'. We've also had good reports of the nearby Perruquet ('well furnished, lively bar'), the Bucaneve and its neighbour the Jumeaux (both spacious, comfortable and cheerful) and the Joly ('a recently refurbished B&B, can ski to the door, overlooks noisy pub'). Just above the centre, behind the cable-car station, are the 'relatively attractive' Al Piolet and the 'smallish, smart' Edelweiss.

Après-ski is expensive by Italian standards. Bars are mainly in hotels, without much character. Exceptions are the Dragon Pub in the hotel Pelissier (a favourite British haunt with Guinness and karaoke), the lively Lino's bar by the ice-rink, the touristy Yeti and the Gran Becca. Most of them show videos or Sky TV. There are two main discos: the Chimera, popular with the British and, according to one reporter, with single Italian men; and the Blow-Up, which has free transport (it's up the hill from the village). Restaurant recommendations include the Matterhorn ('high-quality food, with prices to match'), the Copa Pan ('quirkily amusing, thanks to the comic waiter') and Le Dau ('basic but

Facts on Cervinia   Val d'Aosta **Italy**

Prices in lire
Ski Club represented

Tourist office

Via J A Carrel
Postcode 11021
Tel (166) 949136
Fax (166) 949731
Tlx 211822

Getting there

By road 1,001km from Calais. Via
Macon/Geneva and Mont Blanc tunnel; chains
may be needed.
By rail Châtillon (27km); 4 daily buses from
station.
By air Turin; transfer 2½hr. (Or Milan, Geneva.)

Staying there

Visitor beds 5,150; breakdown: 2,150 in hotels,
3,000 in apartments.
Package holidays Citalia (hs) Crystal (hs)
Enterprise (h) Inghams (hs) Neilson (hs)
SnowRanger (hs) Thomson (h) .
Medical facilities In resort: Fracture clinic,
doctors, chemist. Hospital: Aosta (52km).

Non-skiing activities

Indoor Hotel pools/sauna, bowling, casino,
fitness centre.
Outdoor Natural ice-rink (until March), bob-sleigh
run, horse-riding, tennis, paragliding and
hang-gliding, mountaineering, walks, heli-skiing.

Kindergartens

Other childcare facilities
Baby-sitters can be arranged at the Tourist Office.

Special skiing facilities

Summer skiing Extensive; 8 lifts, 2935m to
3899m, 30km of runs, all on Swiss territory.
Cross-country 5km intermediate track on the
golf course in the village, and another at
Crête-Pérrères. Equipment available.

Lift passes

Cervinia pass
Covers all lifts on the Italian side of the border. (27
lifts in total.)
Cost 6 days 165,000.00 (£77.10).
Credit cards accepted Yes.
Notes Passes of 6 days or more allow one day in
Courmayeur. Daily extension for Zermatt lifts
around Klein Matterhorn and Schwarzsee
(25,000.00).
Beginners Free nursery lift at Plan Maison;
points tickets; passes for Cretaz only.
Short-term passes Half-day (morning and
afternoon for Cretaz, afternoon only for Cervinia);
single and return tickets on 8 main lifts.
Other passes Carosello lifts only (23,000.00 per
day), Cretaz lifts only (23,000.00 per day),
Valtournenche only (25,000.00 per day).
International day pass for Zermatt (50,000.00),
take passport.

Ski school

Cervinia Ski School
Classes 9.00-12.30. Cost: 140,000.00 (6 days).
Video sessions possible at extra cost.
Lift priority No.
Children's classes Ages: Any. Cost: 140,000.00
(6 days).
Private lessons available Hourly. Cost:
35,000.00 per hour. 1-2 people.
Special courses Heli-skiing and mono courses.

What was new in 91

Artificial snow-guns installed on run 3 back to
Cervinia.

What is new for 92

1. Plans to replace 3 lifts, the Plan Maison, Fornet
and Bontadini, with modern installations.
2. Opening Dec 1991 the second section of
Plateau Rosa 6-man gondola from the Laghi
Cime Blanche.

---

good food, reasonably priced for Cervinia').

Cervinia is not recommended for **cross-country** skiers or
non-skiers, although there are several sports facilities, including three
reasonable hotel pools, open to the public. There is a natural bob-sleigh
run.

The **nursery slopes** on the edge of the village get very crowded, but
there are better ones at Plan Maison. Sporty beginners can be roaring
down very long nursery-ish runs at the end of a week.

Reports on the **ski school** are generally favourable; one recent
reporter was impressed by her instructor – 'wise, kind and unfailingly
cheery' – and by his good command of English. Classes tend to be on
the large side. There is no **kindergarten**.

The tills are alive....

Zermatt Switzerland 1620m

Good for *Beautiful scenery, mountain restaurants, big ski area, rail access, Alpine charm, après-ski, tough runs, off-piste skiing, ski touring, late holidays, chalet holidays, resort-level snow, summer skiing, not skiing, woodland runs, artificial snow*
Bad for *Skiing convenience, easy road access, short airport transfers, nursery slopes*

Few resorts can rival Zermatt for picturesque village charm, exciting skiing or beautiful scenery. For a combination of the three it is way out in front, and it can also boast plenty of nightlife, the best mountain restaurants in the Alps, luxury hotels and history. Zermatt regulars fail to understand how anyone can want to go anywhere else, and it is hard to deny that on any objective assessment this is quite simply the best resort there is – particularly now that a formidable campaign of modernisation has made the resort and its lift system run more smoothly. Yet a number of reports sent to us confirm that it is possible to visit Zermatt and come away uncaptivated.

Zermatt is a large, close-knit village which has grown to fill the limited space available at the foot of a steep ring of very high mountains, the Matterhorn outstandingly beautiful among them. It is a world of its own, naturally cut off from Täsch and the valley below by a narrow, steep-sided gorge which is prone to avalanche blockage. Visitors have to leave their cars at Täsch (or Visp), and travel by train or auto-taxi up to Zermatt, where the only transport is powered by horse or battery.

The village became a busy climbing resort in the 19th century. Like Chamonix, it does as much summer as winter business and is a fascinating place for anyone with an interest in Alpine history (a visit to the graveyard is a must). In the early days, the British were prominent, and there is still a sizeable contingent of traditionalists to attend the English church, and a new generation of keen young skiers and après-skiers. But there are more American visitors than British, and more Germans than Americans. The tourist office has a person devoted to handling Japanese enquiries. The style of the village is increasingly plush and expensive, and the American influence is more obvious than anywhere else in the Alps except St Moritz.

So do not expect a small unspoilt Alpine village full of friendly rustic folk. Zermatt is big business. The village is large and has areas (including the main shopping streets) of fairly anonymous modern buildings, albeit traditional in style. Although car-free it is by no means traffic-free: electric taxis, rushing around at hazardous speed, detract significantly from Zermatt's appeal as a remote mountain hideaway. It is easy to get the impression (which the locals do not try very hard to dispel) that Zermatt is a very artfully laid, very beautiful trap.

The skiing is beautiful and enormous in both extent and variety, but has drawbacks. It can be awkward for inexperienced skiers (reporters are unanimous in warning beginners to stay away), and is served by a lift system which does not impress keen piste-bashers. For good cover the rocky slopes need heavy snowfalls and often do not get them. The ski areas are not well connected, and in the town long and icy walks are avoidable only by paying. 'Many a boot blister resulted,' reports one sore skier. So has many a bruised coccyx. The skiing links with that of Cervinia, but the attractions of crossing the border are limited, except when snow is better on the Italian side, as it was for much of last season.

Zermatt is one terminus of the spectacular Glacier Express, which runs to St Moritz via Andermatt. It is one of the few resorts which from Britain is still most conveniently reached by train.

The skiing top 3900m bottom 1620m

Zermatt's skiing divides naturally into three sectors. On the eastern side of the deep horseshoe of mountains surrounding the village are the two linked sectors of Blauherd/Sunnegga and Gornergrat/Stockhorn, both providing a mix of easy intermediate and steep skiing, much of it north-facing. To the south of the resort the Schwarzsee and Trockener Steg lifts climb over steep north-facing slopes (valuable to good skiers when the weather is bad higher up) to glaciers, where Europe's highest lifts provide a huge area of easy skiing. It takes a long time to travel around the ski area and especially to reach Stockhorn (usually quicker via Sunnegga than Gornergrat). The best way to enjoy Zermatt's skiing is to settle for one sector and spend the day there.

Last winter, a large proportion of the resort's black pistes and some of its reds lost their piste status and became 'Downhill routes'; these are marked in yellow on the resort piste map, which does not explain the meaning of the new designation.

The **Gornergrat/Stockhorn** skiing starts with a 40-minute train ride to Gornergrat, passing an area of excellent, easy runs above Riffelberg – Zermatt's best nursery area, with plenty of sun and beautiful views of the Matterhorn. The run down to Zermatt has some steep sections but in good conditions is not difficult. There is a tough and scenic intermediate run towards Gant and Findeln, and some steep off-piste slopes. Beyond Gornergrat cable-cars stretch along a narrow, rocky crest, not climbing much but serving the wide, north-facing slopes above the Findeln glacier. This area, rarely open before February, is one of the premier tough skiing areas in the Alps, with huge mogul fields and late powder (beware crevasse and rock danger off-piste). From the top of the first stage (Hohtälli) there are long, testing runs to Gant and Riffelalp. The original second stage climbs gently to Stockhorn. More popular now is the new single-car hop across to the lower point of Rote Nase. This is the top of the Triftji drag, which is where many good skiers like to spend their time: the black piste down it is steep, but you can to an extent pick your gradient – 34° in the steepest parts. The new cable-car cuts out what was an unpleasant ridge walk back to Hohtälli.

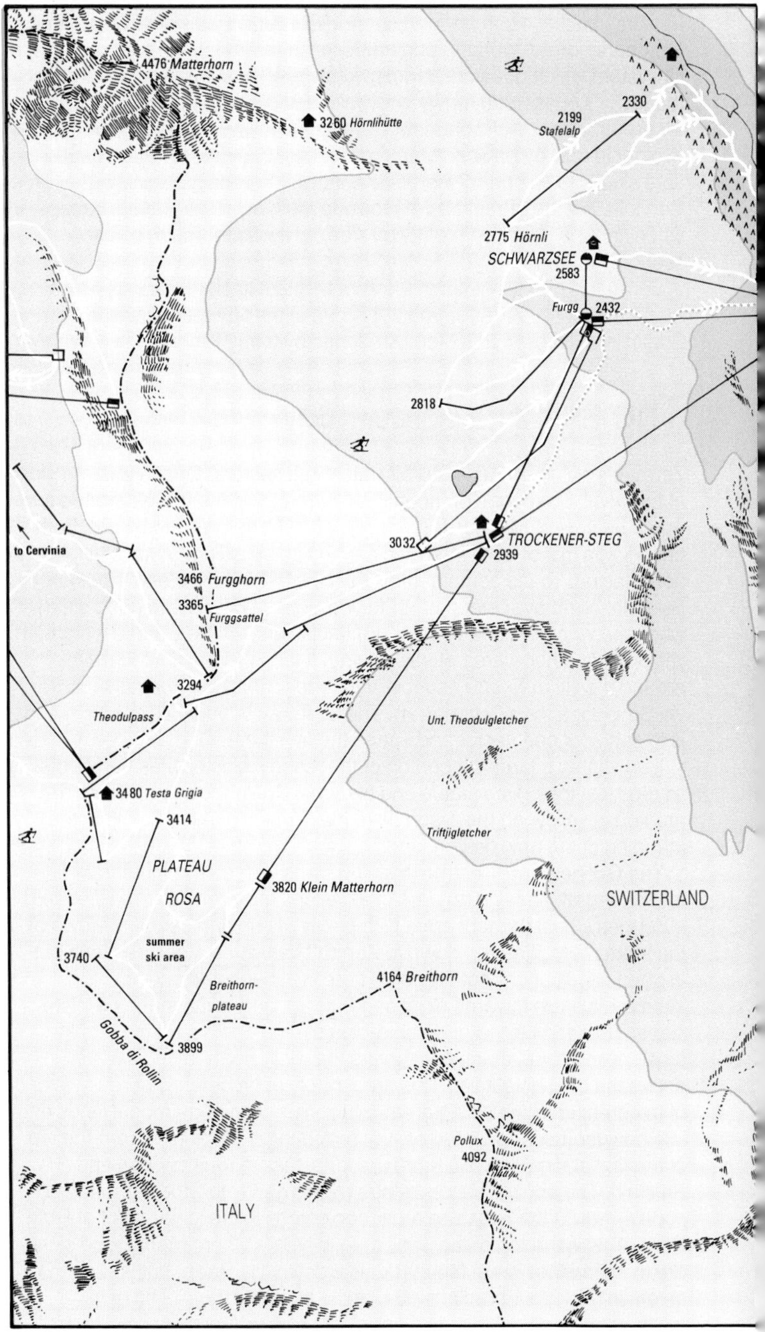

4476 Matterhorn

3260 Hörnlihütte

2330

2199 Stafelalp

2775 Hörnli

SCHWARZSEE

2583

Furgg 2432

2818

to Cervinia

3032

TROCKENER-STEG

2939

3466 Furgghorn

3365 Furggsattel

3294

Theodulpass

34 80 Testa Grigia

3414

PLATEAU

ROSA

Unt. Theodulgletscher

Triftjigletscher

SWITZERLAND

3820 Klein Matterhorn

summer ski area

3740

Breithorn- plateau

4164 Breithorn

Gobba di Rollin

3899

Pollux 4092

ITALY

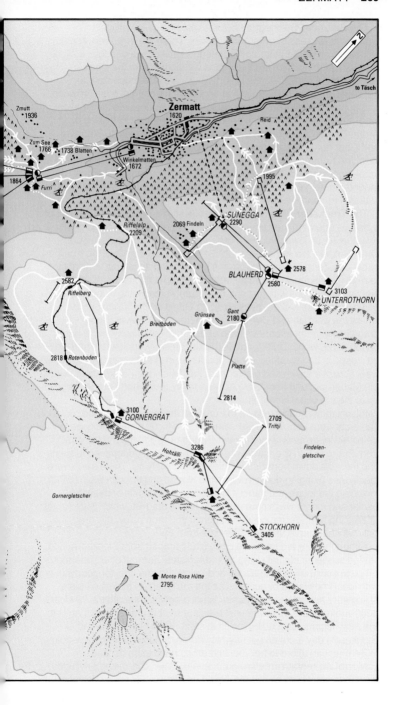

Zmutt
•1936

Zum See
1766
1738 Blatten •
Winkelmatten
1672

1864

Furri

Zermatt
1620

Reid

to Täsch

1995

Riffelalp
2209

2069 Findeln

SUNEGGA
2290

BLAUHERD
2580

2578

3103

UNTERROTHORN

2582

Riffelberg

Breitboden

Grünsee

Gant
2180

Platte

2814

2818 Rotenboden

3100
GORNERGRAT

Hohtälli

3286

2709
Triftji

Findelen-
gletscher

Gornergletscher

STOCKHORN
3405

Monte Rosa Hütte
2795

The **Blauherd/Sunnegga** sector is reached by the efficient Sunnegga Express underground railway. There are easy, very sunny slopes between Blauherd and Sunnegga served by a gondola; a slightly steeper run to Findeln; and easy runs winding around the steep, wooded mountainside to the resort. There are also much steeper descents, notably the famous National downhill course, often crowded and bumpy. The **Unterrothorn** cable-car gives access to an excellent, long, steep, open face which needs very good snow to be skiable. Around the back of the peak, intermediate runs go down to Blauherd and Gant (for access to the Triftji drag on the Stockhorn). On the north face, the Kumme chair-lift serves entertaining intermediate pistes and some popular off-piste slopes, and excellent long runs (red around the mountain and genuinely black down the front) down to the bottom of the National run and lift (now a very efficient chair-lift).

The **Trockener Steg/Schwarzsee** lifts start a brisk 15-minute walk or a ski-bus ride from the centre. A cable-car and a gondola climb gently over the lumpy lower slopes to Furi, where three cable-cars fan out. One climbs to Trockener Steg, above which the Klein Matterhorn cable-car, Zermatt's flagship, spans ice falls and an almost vertical face to reach the highest cable-car station in Europe. A long tunnel leads to easy glacier slopes with just one moderately steep pitch in the long run down to Trockener Steg, passing Testa Grigia on the Italian border, where the Zermatt and Cervinia lift systems meet. Several long drag-lifts serve an enormous area of uncomplicated easy skiing here, on top of the world. Unfortunately the lifts are very unpleasant and may be closed in bad weather. A very beautiful run in this sector heads gently west across a crevassed glacier from just below the Furggsattel towards the Matterhorn and from there either sharply round and back to Furgg or up to the top of the Hörnli lift.

Intermediates can ski down to Furgg, to the top of the second cable-car from Furi. There are some more difficult pistes and good off-piste slopes served by the bent Garten drag-lift, and the run down from Furgg to Furi is an awkward reddish-black. In general, good skiers find the runs down from Schwarzsee more satisfying. There are several black ones plunging down towards the woods and through them to Furi, including the tough and narrow Tiefbach, and a couple of beautiful easier and longer ways down past the Hörnli drag-lift, which itself serves interesting north-facing gullies. But once you drop below this drag, the only way back up is via the cable-cars from Furi.

Although there are few wide open slopes (apart from Stockhorn) and limited scope for casual skiing near the pistes, Zermatt offers enormous off-piste possibilities both above and below the tree-line, for good skiers with local knowledge or guides. But the rocky terrain makes off-piste skiing very hazardous when snow is not plentiful. Beneath the 29 local 4000-metre peaks there are vast areas of skiable glacier, and thanks to the new heights reached by the lift system (Klein Matterhorn and Stockhorn) day tours do not have to be very arduous. Plenty of people in Zermatt can afford to heli-ski, and drops need to be booked.

Mountain restaurants are greater in number, charm and privileged view than anywhere else in the Alps. Lunching is a serious business: the indicator board at the Sunnegga lift station shows which restaurants are open, as well as which lifts and pistes. As well as the smart, characterless new restaurants at the main lift stations (recommended for loo stops), there are many delightful little huts spread around the wooded lower slopes – skiing home at the end of the day can be a protracted business. Enzo's and Chalet Vroni at Findeln, Otmar's above Ried and those below Furi at Zum See and Blatten are outstanding. New recommendations include Gandegghütte, Flühalp, Aroleid, Toni's Grotta at Riffelalp, the Alm near Furi (fresh trout) and the Farmer Haus at Furi (for good Swiss food). When snow conditions are poor, most of the good restaurants may be inaccessible on skis.

Zermatt is not a weekend resort (Saturday is one of the least busy days on the slopes) and from February to April **queues** do not vary greatly, except when weather or poor snow limits the skiing. The main problem is the lifts up to the Klein Matterhorn area, which are often crowded in normal snow conditions but become very much so when other areas are short of snow. Lift passes are scrupulously inspected, and plain-clothes policemen patrol the pistes to keep order. The new Rote Nase cable-car is a distinct improvement, as is the new National chair-lift. The new chair from Furgg to above Trockener Steg relieves an important bottleneck, but is reported to have generated queues. Zermatt has introduced a new category of 'yellow' runs (some previously black, others off-piste). Last winter's piste map gave no explanation for the status of these runs beyond identifying them as *abfahrtsfoute*. We understand they are marked, made safe, but not bashed or patrolled.

The link with Cervinia involves no difficult skiing, but is very high: closure because of bad weather is frequent and unpredictable and the 'international' lift pass supplements may be on sale when the link is closed. A lot of time is needed for the return journey, but from Zermatt it is possible to do most of Cervinia's skiing in a day (in low season). Cervinia is widely advertised as a delightful place for a cheap lunch. It isn't. Take loo paper, a passport and money (in case you get stranded for the night). The skiing link is more enjoyable via Testa Grigia than Theodulpass.

The resort

The village is a delightful maze of snowy paths, and all the buildings are in traditional chalet style except for the large luxury hotels, old and new, in the centre. There are picturesque old quarters above and below the church, but most of the resort is new. The busy main street is lined with new hotels, expensive shops (countless jewellers) and banks. The centre is flat, and walking around is not difficult, apart from the considerable hazards of taxis and icy paths. The bus from the station to the bottom of the Matterhorn lifts cost SF2 a ride, is not covered by the lift pass and is often full after the first stop; taxis cost not much more if you fill them; the walk takes about 15 minutes. When there's enough snow, people ski along the village streets, although they're not supposed to.

Accommodation is mostly in hotels, new, luxurious and very expensive or simple and slightly less expensive. A few companies offer staffed chalet holidays and self-catering in chalet apartments which tend to be less cramped than flats in modern French resorts. The least inconvenient location is probably in the middle near the river, the most inconvenient up in the old village. For up-to-the-minute facilities the luxury hotels to choose are the Zermatterhof, the Schweizerhof, the widely recommended Alex ('extensive facilities, lively bar, six-course dinners, helpful management') or the Mont Cervin ('one of the best hotels in Europe'), but for style there is no beating the elegantly modernised Monte Rosa, the original Zermatt hotel, with its Alpine club

Facts on Zermatt Valais **Switzerland**

Prices in francs
Ski Club represented

Tourist office
Postcode CH-3920
Tel (28) 661181
Fax (28) 661185
Tlx 472130

Getting there
By road 1,076km from Calais. Visitors' cars not allowed beyond Täsch (5km); chains may be needed.
By rail Station in resort.
By air Geneva; transfer 4½hr. (Or quicker by train.)

Staying there
Visitor beds 18,300; breakdown: 6,300 in hotels, 12,000 in apartments.
Package holidays Activity Travel (hc) Bladon Lines (hc) Chalets and Hotels "Unlimited" (hcs) Enterprise (h) Fresh Tracks (h) Inghams (hs) Kuoni (h) Made to Measure (hs) Mark Warner (c) Neilson (hs) Powder Byrne (h) Ski Alternatives (h) Ski Club of GB (h) Ski Scott Dunn (hc) Ski Unique (h) Ski Whizz Small World (c) SkiGower (y) SnowRanger (hs) Supertravel (hc) Swiss-Ski (h) Tailor Made (hs) Thomson (hs) .
Medical facilities In resort: Fracture clinic, dentist, doctors, chemists. Hospital: Visp.

Non-skiing activities
Indoor Sauna, tennis, hotel swimming pools (some open to public) and a salt water pool, keep-fit centre, squash, billiards, gallery and museum.
Outdoor Curling, skating, horse-riding, sleigh rides, 30km cleared paths.

Kindergartens
Ginabelle
Tuition: Yes. Hours: 9.00-5.00. Ages: 2-8. Cost: 400.00 per week (with lunch and tuition).
Nicoletta
Tuition: No. Hours: 9.00-5.00, Mon to Fri. Ages: 2-8. Cost: 210.00 per week (with lunch).

Special skiing facilities
Summer skiing Extensive area on Klein Matterhorn; 8 lifts, 2935m to 3899m.
Cross-country Winkelmatten to Tuftra (3km), Furri to Schweigmatten (4km). More extensive trails (up to 15km) at Täsch. 'Ski walking' trails at altitude (50km). Instruction available.

Lift passes
Area Pass
Covers all lifts on the Swiss side of the border. (36 lifts in total.)
Cost 6 days 238.00 (£99.17).
Credit cards accepted No.
Senior citizens 178.00 (over 62/65) saving 25%.
Notes Daily supplement available for Cervinia (25.00) although not valid on all Cervinia lifts. Day pass for Cervinia (50.00).
Beginners Coupons or payment by the ride.
Other passes Gornergrat lifts only (per day 46.00); Sunnegga lifts only (per day 44.00).

Ski school
Swiss Ski School
'Maxi-mini-classes' available – guarantees no more than 6 pupils per class, costs 285.00 for 5 days.
Classes 4hr: 2hr am and pm. Cost: 165.00 (6 days).
Lift priority No.
Children's classes Ages: 6-12. Cost: 190.00 (6 days). Price includes lunch and drink; children from 12-16yr cost 150.00.
Private lessons available Full- or half-day. Cost: 220.00 per day (each additional person 10.00). Half-day 120.00 (each additional person 5.00).
Special courses Wedel-skiing course 360.00 per week; 'Ski-total' course, includes surf, mono and paraskiing; heli-skiing weeks from 2,150.00 (includes accommodation); Ski Sauvage (deep powder) from 1,430.00 per week (includes accommodation); ski-touring from 900.00.

What was new in 91
1. New quad chair-lift from Furgg to above Trockener Steg, to replace old drag.
2. New drag-lift on the glacier, Plateau Rosa 2.
3. New public library.

mementoes and its Whymperstube bar. Most of the simpler hotels are clean and comfortable in a typically Swiss way: reporters have been pleased with the Gornergrat, near the stations, though some of the rooms are noisy. Also recommended are the Nicoletta, which has an excellent kindergarten, the Ambassador, near the Gornegrat train; the Schönegg, convenient for Sunnegga; and the Riffelalp, a mile from the resort up the railway line – 'comfortable, friendly, peaceful, panoramic, excellent food'.

Après-ski is very varied, with bars, restaurants and dance spots to cater for most tastes and full pockets. Youth gathers in the Papperla Pub, the Castle night-club ('great DJ and free entry'), the disco in the Pollux hotel (some live bands) and Tschuggi's Bar (videos and music). The plastic neo-ranch-style Broken Bar/Brown Cow complex is popular for drinking, pasta and disco (in separate rooms). The North Wall bar is British, cheap and lively. The Pink Elephant in the hotel Post is popular for late-night jazz. For a more civilised atmosphere, there is Elsie's bar for oysters or snails and hock, or the Otto-Fürrer for fondue and raclette. Reporters recommend Le Mazot for expensive meals, the Whymperstube for cheaper Swiss food, Chez Heini for fondu chinoise, the Stockhorn for meat fondue (restaurant tables should be reserved). The Alex has a smart disco for grown-ups, and there is also dancing at the Bristol – 'a jolly mix of 7- to 70-year-olds cavorting'. Curling evenings are organised by tour operators, and very popular.

Summer is probably the best time for a **non-skiing** visit to Zermatt, but there are beautiful winter walks around the village and the lower reaches of the ski area (to Zmutt, Riffelalp and Findeln restaurants), beautiful bu expensive lift rides, an interesting museum and various sports facilities in the village. Zermatt has plenty of short **cross-country** trails, in all three main downhill ski areas, but nothing for the competent practitioner, who must descend by train to the long trails around Täsch.

The main ski school **nursery slope** is at Sunnegga, set apart but small. Riffelberg also has a nursery lift and a much larger area of easy skiing beside the railway. Both these areas are sunny and panoramic but reporters (including beginners) unanimously declare the resort unsuitable for first-timers. The **ski school**, long a source of readers' complaints, has now been under dynamic new management long enough for results to be evident; and we are happy to report that the flow of negative reports is drying up while the trickle of positive ones is swelling.

Pearl or plain?

Saas Fee Switzerland 1800m

Good for *Alpine charm, late holidays, family holidays, nursery slopes, beautiful scenery, freedom from cars, resort-level snow, ski-touring, summer skiing*
Bad for *Short airport transfers, skiing convenience, lift queues, easy road access, woodland runs*

Separate resort: Saas Grund

Saas Fee calls itself the pearl of the Alps. It certainly has a pearl-like setting, in the pit of a tight, deep horseshoe of mountains; and in some eyes at least it is what might be called a pearl of a ski resort. Like neighbouring Zermatt, it is one of the very few resorts to be both long-established and car-free. Unlike Zermatt, it has not developed into a glamorous, noisy international resort; but its size surprises some visitors, and others report that the electric carts and taxis that whirr along between its beautiful old log cabins are becoming hazardous here, as they have long been in Zermatt. The setting is dramatic and beautiful, though oppressive in mid-winter when little sunshine reaches the village. The skiing has in the past disappointed some visitors, and the considerable extra skiing opened up by the Metro Alpin underground railway only partly answers the critics. Although there are excellent nursery slopes beside the resort, and splendid, open, easy glacier slopes up the mountain, much of the skiing is on the steep side (there is no blue to the village from the main areas) – but there is not enough of it to keep eager piste-bashers happy for long, and experts are frustrated by the lack of off-piste skiing (limited by glacier danger). On the other hand, Saas Fee is a major point of departure for ski-tours.

The resort is inconvenient for weekenders, but the skiing reached via the main cable-car is sufficiently attractive to generate very long queues, especially late in the season. Happily, this problem is being tackled vigorously: this season should see the opening of a very powerful gondola up to Maste 4, at the foot of the main Felskinn ski area. This will be particularly welcomed by day visitors, since it will start from the car parks at the edge of the village, where all cars must be left. For those based in Saas Fee, a car is handy for day-trips around the mountain to Zermatt; but parking is expensive. Crans-Montana is also within reach.

Saas Grund is a valley village, 250m and a ten-minute drive down the mountain. It has none of the appeal of Saas Fee as a village, and at weekends is plagued by traffic. But its skiing is high and sunny, and not without interest for intermediate and off-piste skiers.

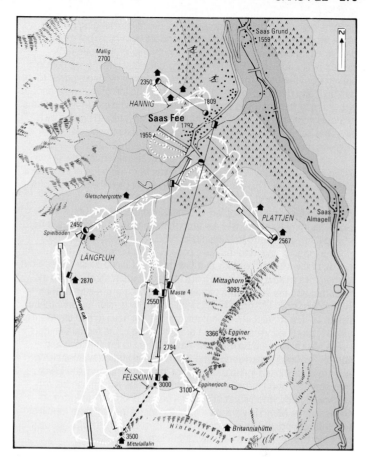

The skiing top 3500m bottom 1800m

Saas Fee has skiing all year round thanks to the Feegletscher, hanging impressively on the mountainside south of the village. But at lower altitudes the glacier is a nuisance, dividing the north-facing skiing into two areas. Most obvious from the terraces of the village hotels are the mogul-fields of the Längfluh, on banks of moraine between two arms of the glacier. There are links (just) at the top of this area to the major Felskinn sector. The Plattjen area is a north-east facing slope, closer to the village and much used by the ski-school. Last, and distinctly least, is the Hannig on the opposite side of the village – low, little and sunny.

The **Längfluh** area is consistently fairly steep, and well suited to intermediate skiers wanting a bit of a challenge. The gondola from the extreme edge of the village to Spielboden is surmounted not only by a short cable-car (to 2870m) but also by a steep drag serving the shortest genuine black run we have encountered. Good, challenging red and black mogul runs go down under the gondola from here, but most people go up the cable-car to play on the middle-of-the-road reds served by the top chair-lift. The only way back down to the top gondola station from the bottom of this chair is black, so many skiers prefer to ride up it and descend in the cable-car. From the top of the cable-car, you can pay four francs to take the Fee-Chatz 'snow-cat' (riding inside a hideously cramped tracked bus or trailer, or being towed on skis by a piste-basher) gently uphill beside a blue run across the glacier to the Felskinn area.

The **Felskinn** skiing, normally reached by an inadequate cable-car which starts an annoying drag-lift-ride away from the edge of the resort, is more extensive. There is some very easy skiing on the top half (between 3000m and 2500m) served by drag-lifts; lower down it becomes steeper and bumpier, and inexperienced skiers can join the cable-car in mid-air at Maste 4 – though the easiest runs down are not intimidating. The Metro to Mittelallalin (3500m) has opened up more glorious open skiing, and makes it possible to ski across to Längfluh. At the top of the Metro, those up to a few metres of steep black run can put on their skis almost immediately, but the red starts a short hike up the mountain and the blue starts higher still, involving a 'ghastly' 15-minute trudge. Two drag-lifts have been installed on the glacier to serve these pistes, so that to ski them repeatedly you do not have to use the Metro, which is regained via a third short drag to a hole in the mountainside.

The Metro can also be reached via the drags to Egginerjoch and Kamel (3250m). These serve what was the pre-Metro summer skiing, and are often closed in the early part of the winter season; the lower drag serves a good, broad red run, the upper one (which can be very awkward to ride when short of snow) a pair of short but steep blacks. Access to the Metro is via a path from the top of the first drag (uphill at first, then poling, then a schuss) or the Kamel black run from the top of the second one; this involves a walk but is nowhere steep.

The Metro has a mid-station, with a tunnel leading out to the far side of the mountain. The lift normally does not stop here, but may when conditions are right for the off-piste runs to which the tunnel gives access. On one visit several years ago we found a piste down to a short lift up to Britanniahütte, but we understand that this is unlikely to recur.

The **Plattjen** gondola runs (from the same building as that for Längfluh) up to 2567m. Its skiing is of easy-intermediate difficulty, with a slightly awkward start at the top. The main slope, above the trees, is served by a chair where moderate queues tend to form; there are easy and more difficult runs down from there through woods to the village – the black justifying its grading because of lumpy terrain, the blue a long, narrow path which is tricky when icy.

The gondola to **Hannig** (2350m) serves short runs which are little skied except early in the season when other areas are cold or closed; later on they are often bare.

All the main lift stations have **mountain restaurants** which are adequate but rarely charming; that at the top of Plattjen is particularly dire, but there is an atmospheric Berghaus half-way down the hill (with 'excellent *rösti*) which compensates. The Gletschergrotte, hidden among trees off the piste down from Spielboden, is worth seeking out for good food ('excellent *rösti* again) as well as charm; service can be slow. The sheltered terrace at Spielboden is entertaining, giving a good view of the short, sharp black run above it. There are superb close-up views of the glacier from Längfluh – worth a trip for non-skiers. The Metro takes you to the highest revolving restaurant in the world; it does not take you higher than the surrounding peaks, which means that the views are limited. There is a stationary lower level, self-service. From Egginerjoch it is a few minutes' appetising plod to the atmospheric old mountain refuge and excellent views of Britanniahütte.

For some time Saas Fee's skiing has been too attractive for the access lifts, particularly in late season; the snow shortages of recent seasons have aggravated the problem. Huge (and very nastily behaved) **queues** have built up for the Felskinn cable-car (and non-trivial ones for the Spielboden gondola), morning and afternoon, forcing skiers to set out very early or accept serious delays. At the end of the day there have also been queues to get the cable-car down from Maste 4. Both problems should be solved by the big new gondola up to Maste 4 (employing three cables to carry 30-person cabins) which is being built for 1992. An additional drag is also being built above Maste 4. When snow low down is poor, there can be long queues for the high glacier drags and for the Längfluh chair.

There is **artificial snow** on the nursery slopes, though it has not always been used when reporters wished for it.

The resort

Although a small resort in a confined setting, Saas Fee is by no means compact enough to suit idle or weary ski-booted pedestrians: it spreads for over half a mile along a couple of narrow, car-free, occasionally hilly streets, through something like a resort centre where streets converge, along over a river to the bottom of the north-facing ski slopes, where skiers' hotels have grown up. There are depots here where you can leave your skis and boots at not exorbitant cost; remote hotels may have free lockers for guests. Shopping facilities are adequate, with food shops at various points in the village. Within the village there are pricey electric carts and taxis to help you get around.

Accommodation is mostly in traditional-looking hotels, comfortable but not luxurious, and self-catering chalets. The bulk of the resort is near the entrance car parks. Hotels over the river at the far end are much more convenient for skiers, and this is the main consideration. (Tour operator brochures may stress proximity to the Hannig lifts, but this is of very little value). Two typical chalet-style hotels which are ideally placed for the lifts are the Waldesruh and the Derby – both medium-sized, comfortable but slightly dull. The adjacent Belmont is smarter. Further away from the lifts, the Dom is friendly, with a jolly restaurant specialising in *rösti*, but too close to the church bells for one reporter's comfort. The Marmotte serves 'superb' six-course dinners. The

Beau-Site is recommended for its 'good food and engaging proprietors', as is the Aparthotel Zurbriggen. The Tenne is 'cosy, with good bar and restaurant, ample space'. A regular visitor recommends the swish Walliserhof for its 'absolutely outstanding nouvelle cuisine, service, swimming pool and excellent nightclub'. The Alphubel is at the 'wrong' end of town, but recommended for children. In a league and location of its own is the Waldhotel Fletschhorn, a 20-minute walk through woods (along a track negotiable by electric taxis) to the north of the resort, overlooking Saas Grund – quiet, comfortable, charmingly run, with excellent nouvelle cuisine.

Après-ski is limited. Tea-time recommendations include the Ski Hütte ('great cakes on a sunny terrace') and the hotel Belmont. There are live bands in a couple of hotels; the tiny bar of the Christiania gets packed, the Sissy bar of the Tenne is 'cosy and friendly, best between 10pm and

Facts on Saas Fee Valais **Switzerland**

Prices in francs
Ski Club represented

Tourist office
Postcode CH-3906
Tel (28) 571457
Fax (28) 571860
Tlx 472230

Getting there
By road 1,072km from Calais. Via Geneva or Basle/Berne. The 26km drive from the main road near Visp is slow and may require snow chains.
By rail Brig; 15 daily buses from station.
By air Geneva; transfer 4hr.

Staying there
Visitor beds 8,500; breakdown: 2,500 in hotels, 6,000 in apartments.
Package holidays Bladon Lines (hcs) Chalets and Hotels "Unlimited" (h) Crystal (hrs) Enterprise (h) Horizon (h) Inghams (hs) Kuoni (h) Made to Measure (hs) Ski Alternatives (h) Ski Unique (h) SkiGower (y) SnowRanger (hs) Supertravel (h) Swiss-Ski (hs) Thomson (hs) .
Medical facilities In resort: Doctor, chemist, dentist. Hospital: Visp (26km).

Non-skiing activities
Indoor Bielen Leisure centre (swimming, jacuzzi, steam bath, solaria, sauna, massage, tennis, gym), cinema, museum, cultural centre at Steinmatte, concerts.
Outdoor 20km cleared paths, natural ice-rink (skating, curling, ice-hockey), ski-bob runs, toboggan run.

Kindergartens
Snowland
Tuition: Yes. Hours: 9.00-4.30, Sun-Fri. Ages: 3-6. Cost: 144.00 per week (with lunch and lunch-time supervision).

Special skiing facilities
Summer skiing Extensive runs from 3600m

(Mitelallalin) and 3250m (Kamel) to Felskinn mid-station (2550m). 15km of piste.
Cross-country 8km loop through woods starts at Wildi, near entrance to village; further trails (25km) in Saas valley. Instruction available.

Lift passes
Area Pass
Covers all lifts but not the Längfluh snow-cat (per ride 4.00 for adults, 1.00 for children). (26 lifts in total.)
Cost 6 days 200.00 (£83.33).
Credit cards accepted Yes.
Senior citizens 180.00 (over 62) saving 10%.
Children 120.00 (under 16) saving 40%. Free pass up to age 6.
Beginners Single tickets on nursery lifts; 'Pleasure' day ticket covers lifts in village.
Short-term passes Half-day (from 12.00pm) and day pass; single and return tickets on all main lifts.
Other passes Limited passes for Hannig and Plattjen only.

Ski school
Swiss Ski School
Classes 9.45-11.45 and 1.30-3.30. Cost: 152.00 (5 days, Mon-Fri).
Lift priority No.
Children's classes Ages: 5-12. Cost: 135.00 (5 days, Mon-Fri). Lunch and supervision 18.00.
Private lessons available Full- or half-day or hourly. Cost: 45.00 per hour for 1-2 people, 55.00 for 3-4 people.
Special courses Touring weeks, particularly the Haute Route from Saas Fee to Chamonix.

What was new in 91
1. New drag-lift parallel to Mittelallalin 1.
2. New kindergarten called Snowland.

What is new for 92
New Alpine-Express cable-car from bottom of village to Maste at 2550m.

1am'. Among other bars, the 'reasonably priced' Go Inn is a favourite with tour operator reps, and the Fee pub is recommended. The restaurant at the Tenne does 'excellent charcoal grills'. The Alp Hitta is recommended for traditional Swiss food, Zur Mühle for fondue Chinoise. The out-of-town Fletschhorn caters for gastronomes. There are three or four discos.

Saas Fee is not a particularly good resort for **cross-country** skiers, though there are local trails and it is not far by bus down to the extensive trails along the valley between Saas Almagell and Saas Grund, and beyond. **Non-skiers** should enjoy the attractive walks, and the village itself, but it is a bit claustrophobic, particularly in mid-winter. The leisure/sports centre is a great asset – very well equipped and civilised (but expensive if you want just a quick swim). The skating rink is not always in operation.

The **nursery slopes** are excellent – broad, gentle and well-placed for lunches and meeting up with other skiers; but the bottom, flat parts are not very sunny in mid-winter.

The **ski school** has generally not received favourable reports; class sizes are too big at busy times, organisation is lacking and English is far from universally spoken; more seriously, we have a report of very poor treatment of young children. Touring weeks involve several nights spent in refuges and a trip to Zermatt. Monte Rosa, Europe's second-highest peak (4634m), is nearby, and a ski-touring proposition.

Saas Grund 1560m

Saas Grund is strung out along the valley road up to Saas Almagell, with the junction for Saas Fee forming a vague centre. There are a great many chalets and apartments to rent, and a wide choice of modest hotels, two or three of which have swimming pools. The skiing is centred on the high sunny shelf of Kreuzboden (2400m), reached by gondola. The only runs back to the valley are an off-piste itinerary and a long narrow path with unpleasantly exposed drops at the side. A popular and harmless red run from the top of the gondola is served by a chair-lift, while above Kreuzboden a pair of longish drag-lifts serve broad, gentle red and blue pistes. The top section of the gondola goes up to Hohsaas (3098m), serving a long and varied red piste; on the occasion of our March visit both piste and lift were blissfully uncrowded – in marked contrast to Saas Fee. There is also plenty of opportunity to venture off-piste – another difference from Saas Fee. There is a big restaurant at Kreuzboden, and a little hut at Hohsaas with a glorious view from its sun-terrace across to Saas Fee, and 'excellent' food. Saas Grund has adequate nursery slopes as well as the gentle runs at Kreuzboden, a natural ice rink and long cross-country trails along the valley, climbing gently towards Saas Almagell and descending equally gently towards Saas Balen.

Tourist office ✆ (28)572403.
Package holidays Ski Europe (h) Snowranger (hs).

Crans-Montana Switzerland 1500m

Good for *Sunny slopes, beautiful scenery, big ski area, easy runs, not skiing, cross-country skiing, rail access, easy road access, woodland runs*
Bad for *Tough runs, Alpine charm, skiing convenience, late holidays, freedom from cars*

Separate resort: Anzère

Crans and Montana, once separate, have now merged to form the largest resort in Switzerland – a vast suburban sprawl whose main quality is a splendid south-facing balcony setting, high above the Rhône valley on a wooded ledge broad enough to accommodate two golf courses, one of which hosts the Swiss Open. Arnold Lunn, who had seen a few, rated the view across the valley as one of the seven finest panoramas in the Alps. On a fine day in December the resort gets eight hours of sun, when Grindelwald gets one. This may be welcome in December, but sunshine tends to have dire effects on the snow conditions later in the season, as many March reporters know.

As they have grown together the distinction between simple Montana for skiers and smart Crans for furs, bridge and golf has become less and less noticeable. Both parts of the resort lack village atmosphere, with residential outskirts, traffic jams and one-way systems, parking meters, and concrete shopping precincts not obviously geared to winter sports. The resort has the characterless comfort and multiple amenities of a conference town, with little of the charm of Switzerland at its best. The building style is mostly urban and undistinguished, although softened by the trees (of which there are many). Despite the many smart shops in Crans (Cartier, Gucci, caviar, furs), the resort as a whole is more expensive than stylish; and its skiing, although extensive, lacks variety – specifically, it lacks challenge.

Yet we have reports from satisfied customers. What they like about the resort is not so much the comfortable hotels and the outstanding range of off-slope facilities (including beautiful walks and cross-country trails) as the views, the sunshine, and the comfortable air of affluence.

Day trips to several major resorts on the south side of the Rhône trench are possible for skiers with a car – Zermatt and Saas Fee to the east, Verbier (via Siviez) to the west. The resort is easy to reach by car, and having a car is a considerable asset, given the extent of the resort.

The skiing top 3000m bottom 1500m

There are three well-linked areas accessible from four base stations along the broad south-facing mountainside. There are one or two difficult runs and plenty of space, especially at the eastern end, for

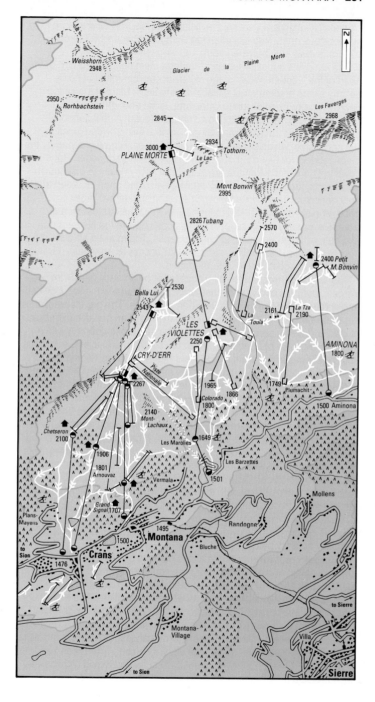

off-piste skiing; but in general the skiing suits leisurely skiers more than adventurous ones. Virtually all of the skiing is between 1500m and 2500m, evenly split between open and wooded terrain.

The main lifts out of Crans and Montana meet up at **Cry-d'Err**, at the heart of the western sector of the ski area – the one most used by holiday skiers and the most suitable for the timid. Most of the skiing nearby is easy, and the run to Chetseron is flat enough for near-beginners; two drag-lifts now serve this piste. A new gondola station has been built at Grand Signal, so that this crowded junction of lifts and pistes, which serves as the nursery area, is now reached by the main gondola for Cry-d'Err, rather than its own short gondola. Runs down to Crans and Montana are paths, not always easy to distinguish from roads, footpaths and cross-country trails, and often crowded and in poor condition. The woods below Chetseron sometimes provide some good off-piste skiing. There is tougher skiing on the eastern side of Cry-d'Err, notably the excellent racing slopes beside the Nationale lift and below it, past Vermala, to Les Barzettes. The marked off-piste run from Bella Lui to Les Violettes is useful for access to Aminona – largely a traverse, but good fun for intermediates.

The **Les Violettes** sector, also accessible by an easy path from Les Verdets, consists of a web of criss-crossing red runs, with mogul-fields and some scope for exploring between the pistes. The great attraction is the **Plaine Morte** cable-car, climbing to the rim of an oceanic expanse of glacier (used in summer and poor winters for cross-country) with a breathtaking view of famous peaks to the south. The glacier is a famous and excellent starting point for ski tours (short climbs to Wildhorn and Wildstrubel and long descents over the other side towards Gstaad, Lenk and Adelboden) but the glacier itself is too flat to be of much interest and descents from it are strictly limited. Apart from the occasional, hazardous off-piste route beneath Les Faverges to Aminona, there is only one run down to the resort – a red piste that is wide and nowhere steep. It drops into a steep-sided valley which has some off-piste skiing and the resort's only black run, served by the Toula chair and drag. This is neither long nor steep, but the lifts offer an alternative way into the pleasantly uncrowded **Aminona** sector of the ski area, otherwise reached by a long, pretty path through the woods to Plumachit. There is lots of easy, wide-open skiing on the slopes below Petit Bonvin, served by several short drag-lifts, and some more challenging runs (including good off-piste skiing) below the tree-line. The run down to Aminona itself is mostly an easy path.

Mountain restaurants are in all the obvious places, but the majority are convenient and efficient rather than captivating, and there are few in the Violettes and Aminona sectors. Many are easily accessible to walkers and cross-country skiers as well as downhillers. The most attractive is Merbé, at the mid-station of the Crans-Cry-d'Err gondola ('magnificent panoramic views'). Other recommendations are Les Violettes ('excellent salad bar, quiet surroundings'), Chetseron and Bella Lui ('both excellent waitress-service places with sunny terraces') and Petit Bonvin. One reporter was pleasantly surprised to find picnic areas outside some restaurants.

Recent reporters have found very few **queues**, except for access to Plaine Morte, where they have waited for up to 1½ hours. The problem should be alleviated in the near future by a new system up to the glacier.

There is **artificial snow** on the lower slopes of the Les Violettes and Cry-d'Err sectors. Crans-Montana was one of the first Swiss resorts to open (at Aminona) a half-pipe. There is a ski-bob run on Chetseron.

The resort

Crans stretches up through the woods to Plans Mayens (1620m). Montana's upper suburb is Vermala (1600m), a string of residential chalets and a couple of tall hotel blocks. East of Montana the road along the mountainside is built up as far as Les Barzettes, a convenient skiing access point with some hotels but no resort life. Aminona is a self-contained apartment-based satellite.

The resort is very spread-out and the free ski-bus is an invaluable complement to the lift system (essential when snow is short, and the skiing breaks down into separate areas), running reliably to a timetable between Crans and Aminona, serving all the main lift departures. There are less frequent evening buses, not covered by the lift pass. Parking anywhere in the centre of the resort is difficult and restricted, though all the main access lifts now have free garages.

Accommodation is mostly in apartments and comfortable hotels, some of them modern and very expensive, others long-established and old-fashioned. In Montana, the Hauts de Crans is a luxury chalet-style development in the woods above the village , well placed for skiers and walkers; the Mont-Paisible is close to the Violettes lifts and is 'quiet, with lots of charm'; the central Olympic is recommended as good value, but is in a noisy area; the Quatre Canetons offers 'superb accommodation'; and the Curling is 'quiet and friendly, and has excellent food'. In Crans, the Etoile and National are popular choices within easy walking distance of the lifts; and the very friendly old Mont Blanc is particularly beautifully set above Plans Mayens, a long way from the resort but beside the pistes down from Chetseron and excellent for walks and cross-country.

Après-ski includes discos, lots of tea-rooms and bars (including a 'very pleasant' piano bar), a cinema and a casino in Crans. The George and Dragon in Crans is popular with the Brits but tends to get too noisy for conversation, as does Valentino's (where resort staff congregate). The best choice of the bars in Montana is the Grange. Recommended night-clubs include Jack and Lucy's in Crans and Number One in Montana. There is no shortage of expensive restaurants, with much more variety than in most Swiss resorts; the Bistro is recommended.

Crans-Montana is an excellent resort for **cross-country** ('especially for those who like to explore and do not want to go round and round the same loop every day') and **non-skiers**. There are long, sunny and beautiful walks, many of them beside the cross-country tracks, punctuated by restaurants with sun terraces, on the lower slopes of the Alpine skiing area. The Hotel Aïda Castel in Montana has weekly bridge tournaments, there are frequent curling tournaments, hot-air balloon rides, and golf on snow at New Year and in mid-February. Excursions to the valley by bus or funicular are possible, and from there joy-rides around the Matterhorn.

Nursery slopes are excellent at Crans. There is flat skiing, with baby-lifts, on the golf course, and easy runs around Cry-d'Err. Montana's Grand Signal area is crowded and a bit steep, but has the advantage of being part of the main ski area.

Crans and Montana have separate **ski schools**, with various meeting places around the slopes for different classes. Enthusiasm for them seems to vary; our most recent reporter complained of 'only French instruction, classes of up to 18 pupils'. The Friday lunch-time parties are a highlight of the week. We have had no recent reports on the **kindergarten** facilities.

Facts on Crans-Montana   Valais **Switzerland**

Prices in francs
Ski Club represented

Tourist office
Postcode CH-3963 CRANS
Tel (27) 412132
Fax (27) 411794
Tlx 473173

Getting there
By road 1,012km from Calais. Via Pontarlier, Lausanne; chains may be needed.
By rail Sierre (5km); funicular or bus to resort every 20 mins.
By air Geneva; transfer 3hr. (Or Sion.)

Staying there
Visitor beds 40,000; breakdown: 5,000 in hotels, 35,000 in apartments.
Package holidays Bladon Lines (hcs) Hoverspeed Ski-Drive (hs) Inghams (hs) Kuoni (h) Made to Measure (hs) Quest Total Ski (h) Quest Travel (schools) (h) Ski Alternatives (h) Ski Europe (h) SnowRanger (hs) Swiss-Ski (h) .
Medical facilities In resort: Fracture clinic, doctors, dentists, chemists. Hospital: Sierre (15km).

Non-skiing activities
Indoor Hotel swimming pools, tennis, fitness centre, bowling, bridge, squash, concerts.
Outdoor Skating, curling, toboggan run, ski-bob, husky sled rides, horse-riding.

Kindergartens
Bibiland
Tuition: Yes. Hours: 8.00-6.00, Mon to Fri. Ages: 3-6. Cost: 115.00 per week (lunch 10.00 per day). Transport possible. Also nursery facilities.
Fleurs des Champs
Tuition: No. Hours: 8.00-6.00. Ages: 2mths-12 yrs. Cost: 180.00 per week (lunch 5.00).
Other childcare facilities
Les Coccinelles: ski camps for children aged 3-16

(kindergarten for babies over 18mths).

Special skiing facilities
Summer skiing Small area on Plaine Morte, from 2800m to 3000m (2 lifts).
Cross-country 52km in 3 areas. 15km (easy) around Crans, 22km (more difficult) across mountain between Plans Mayens and Aminona via Grand Signal, 15km on Plaine Morte, also open in summer.

Lift passes
Crans-Montana Aminona
Covers all lifts in Crans-Montana and Aminona and ski-bus. (42 lifts in total.)
Cost 6 days 179.00 (£74.58).
Credit cards accepted Yes.
Senior citizens 90.00 (over 62/65) saving 50%.
Children 107.00 (under 16) saving 40%. Free pass up to age 6.
Notes 30% discount for families of four or more.
Beginners Coupons.
Short-term passes 'Hourly' passes, refund when handed in early; single ascent tickets for some lifts.
Other passes Passes for non-skiers available.
Other periods Passes for 8 non-consecutive days available.

Ski school
Swiss Ski School
in both Crans and Montana.
Classes 9.30-12.30. Cost: 140.00 (6 days). Raclette lunch on Thursdays.
Lift priority No.
Children's classes Ages: 6 up. Cost: 140.00 (6 days).
Private lessons available Hourly. Cost: 45.00 per hour.

What was new in 91
New Pas de Loup drag-lift next to gondola up to Cry d'Err plateau.

Anzère Switzerland 1430m

Anzère is a small, modern resort just along the hill from Crans-Montana but with a quite separate, equally beautiful ski area. It is not the ultimate convenience resort, but neither is it the soulless monstrosity that many such resorts are. It consists mainly of apartment buildings, disguised as giant chalets, with a car-free commercial precinct in the centre, where there are two hotels. A reporter recommends the Eden. In general the self-catering accommodation is of a high standard, and it includes some individual small chalets on the edges of the main complex. The village is built on a slope (1430m to 1550m) and extends a long way across the mountainside, but there are lift departures from each end, so location is not critical – except in mid-winter, when the westerly gondola is naturally to be preferred to the easterly chair-lift. One reporter has pronounced Anzère 'a friendly place where everyone got on easily. Despite its being new, you feel you're in a village.' Other recent reporters agree.

The ski area (up to 2420m) is small and very sunny, with magnificent views across the Rhône valley. It consists mostly of easy and intermediate skiing above the tree-line; it is not a place for experts, and is far from ideal for beginners; the main small nursery area is at the top of the mountain (which means paying for lifts from the start), and the terrain does not provide confidence-building runs to progress to – the piste map shows only one short blue run, and that is reached via a red. There are longer runs through the woods to the village offering more variety and challenge – but changing snow conditions through the day can create treacherously icy mogul-fields which may prompt even the most accomplished skiers to go down by lift. At the bottom of the long, gentle, east-facing Combe de Serin run down to Les Rousses (1780m) you can grill your own lunch at the restaurant ('superb'). The large, self-service Tsalan restaurant (at the top of the Pralan chair) is also an excellent lunch-stop. Lifts hardly ever suffer from serious crowds. A lift pass for seven non-consecutive days is available – attractive for car-borne visitors interested in excursions.

The resort is quiet after dark, but there are a couple of low-key discos and some good restaurants (the Premiers Pas is recommended). There are two cross-country skiing trails (total 18km), a toboggan run, and marked walking paths through the woods at resort level. Other facilities include an artificial skating and curling rink, a fitness room, a swimming pool and several saunas. There is also a 'very active' parapenting school with three instructors and tuition at all levels. The ski school is reported to be 'cheerful and well run', though spoken English is 'variable'. There are skiing and non-skiing kindergartens. The two supermarkets are well stocked and supplemented by an 'excellent but pricey butcher/deli' and a patisserie. The valley town of Sion is easily reached by car or bus, for a change of scene.

Tourist office ✆ (27) 382519. **Package holidays** Made to Measure (hs).

Skiing for achievers

Verbier Switzerland 1500m

Good for *Off-piste skiing, tough runs, big ski area, ski touring, après-ski, easy road access, beautiful scenery, sunny slopes, chalet holidays, rail access*
Bad for *Skiing convenience, lift queues, easy runs*

Linked resorts: Nendaz, Thyon 2000, Veysonnaz, La Tzoumaz, Le Châble

Separate resort: Bruson

Lots of smart young Britons go to Verbier for social reasons. It offers an unmatched range of chalet accommodation, which means lots of winter job opportunities (for those with work permits, emphasises the tourist office) and a good social life for the seasonal immigrants and, up to a point, their house guests. It has become the prime target for the yuppy generation of British weekend skiers.

Lots of keen skiers choose Verbier for the skiing – a big, beautiful and mostly challenging ski area with some formidable black runs and tremendous off-piste skiing. But it also has important drawbacks, particularly for non-experts. There are lift bottle-necks, despite improvements; the main ski area around Les Attelas and Les Ruinettes is too congested for the good of the pistes or of skiers; the main run out of this area is a steep mogul-field; and the lift pass is the most expensive in Europe (except for families and pensioners). The building of a big cable-car providing an alternative route to the top of the skiing (Mont-Fort) has provided some relief for the first three problems, and helps to explain the fourth.

The resort is a vast sprawl of chalets and chalet-style hotels and apartments. Most of its development has been post-War and, despite the pitched roofs, by Swiss standards the village does not have much character. Although fashionable (with some of the Swiss, as well as the British), it has little of the glitter of traditionally grand resorts. The après-ski is lively but casual, and there are no notably sumptuous hotels – though the Rosalp is a temple of gastronomy. There has been a noticeable increase over recent years in the number of fashion-filled shop windows.

Nendaz (the name we are now encouraged to use for Haute-Nendaz and its satellite Nendaz-Station combined) is a large and amorphous apartment resort, better placed than Verbier for skiers who want to explore the whole region. Its queues and layout make it best suited to skiers with a car. Veysonnaz and Thyon 2000 are much smaller, modern self-catering resorts at the eastern end of the ski area. Thyon (above the more traditional-style Les Collons) is high, open and convenience-oriented, and well suited to families. Veysonnaz is below it, at the bottom of some splendid woodland runs.

Le Châble is the valley village (with railway station) at the foot of the winding road and gondola up to Verbier, mainly of interest as a way into the skiing for day-trippers. Across the valley is the worthwhile little ski area of Bruson, at present reached by ski-bus and refreshingly free of development and crowds. This and other outlying ski areas are covered by the Verbier ski pass.

Verbier is not far from the Alpine crossroads of Martigny, from which point there are other resorts within day-trip range in all directions – including the Chamonix valley in France, over the Col des Montets. A car is useful for getting around Verbier in the evening – and for other purposes if you are in a backwater chalet.

The skiing top 3328m bottom 820m

Verbier's local skiing takes place in two separate areas, with lift departures at opposite ends of the resort. The two are linked by gentle off-piste runs which are often skied into a piste-like state, and by regular but not very frequent ski-buses. The larger area links with the skiing of Nendaz, Thyon 2000 and Veysonnaz; these resorts are not far away as the crow flies, but skiers who miss the last lifts back face a hugely expensive taxi-ride home via Martigny.

The smaller area is **Savoleyres**, nearly always pleasantly quiet, and reached by lifts starting high above the centre. The runs down on the sunny Verbier side of the mountain are mostly open and intermediate, but steep enough to accommodate the resort's slalom race-course; off-piste, there can be good spring snow skiing here, but snow on the lower pistes is unreliable and conditions often difficult. On the north-facing side (where there is a Super-G course) there are long trails, the lower parts through woods, to La Tzoumaz – little skied, and usually with good snow even when the front of the mountain is spring-like. The dog-leg drag to the top station is steep, and there are tough bits of skiing to be found – deep snow or big moguls, according to conditions. Beside the Taillay chair-lift is a speed-skiing course which is open to all comers; we're told that, even with flapping salopettes and run-of-the-mill 205cm skis, speeds in excess of 120km/hr can be achieved.

At the other end of the village, various alternative lifts go up from Medran to the heart of Verbier's skiing on the slopes around Les Ruinettes, beneath the ridge of **Les Attelas**. The slower four-seat gondola is the more popular because it goes all the way to the top; the more modern six-seat one terminates at the mid-station of Ruinettes, whence a small cable-car offers an alternative route to Attelas. The chair-lift route up the mountain is under-used.

East of the Attelas ridge, the skiing in the sheltered bowl of Lac des Vaux is limited in extent, but covers a wide range of intermediate difficulty, and the area is popular with ski school classes graduating from the nursery slopes. West of the ridge, the skiing down past Ruinettes is tougher and more extensive. For many competent but not expert piste skiers, this curving coomb, served by a series of three chair-lifts, is the heart of Verbier's skiing; it is a good, varied, testing intermediate area

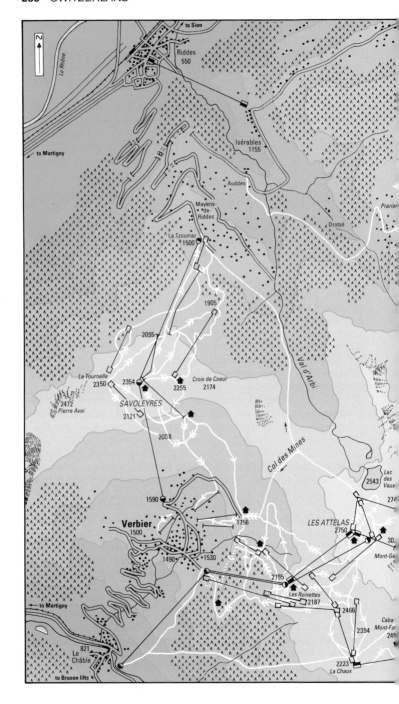

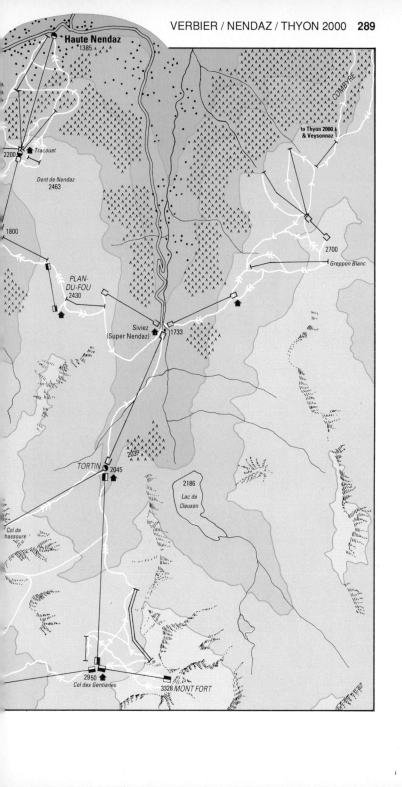

Haute Nendaz
1385

2200 Tracouet

Dent de Nendaz
2463

1800

PLAN-
DU-FOU
2430

COMBYRE

to Thyon 2000
& Veysonnaz

2700

Greppon Blanc

Siviez
(Super Nendaz) 1733

2039

TORTIN 2045

2186
Lac de
Cleuson

Col de
Chassoure

2950
Col des Gentianes

3328 MONT FORT

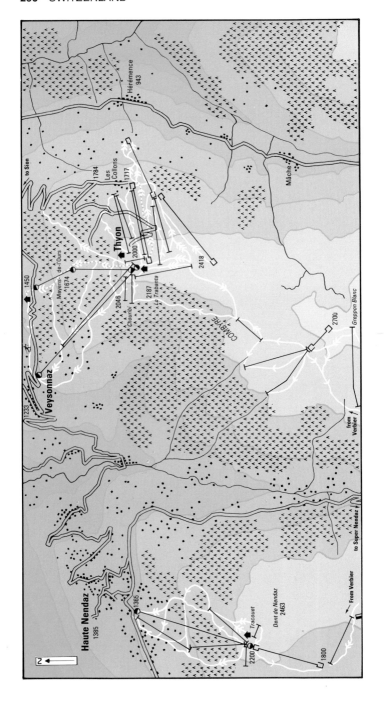

with no easy way down and nothing of intimidating steepness even on the black variant – but at peak times it becomes very crowded. From Ruinettes to Verbier there is a good variety of other runs, with a blue path winding down to Verbier as well as tough mogul runs directly down through the trees towards the hamlet of Clambin. These wooded slopes are very useful in bad weather, at least for good skiers.

An attractive way home from Lac des Vaux is the Col des Mines route, which runs around from the bottom of the lifts before crossing over the ridge to the south-facing slopes above the nursery lifts. These slopes are often unsafe, and the run is emphatically off-piste; but it is not difficult to ski, and is understandably popular. An alternative off-piste run is the Val d'Arbi, prettily down through the woods to La Tzoumaz.

By keeping left on the way down from Attelas to Ruinettes, you can make your way over to the sunny, open bowl of La Chaux, where various intermediate pistes go down to the bottom station of the cable-car up to the Col des Gentianes and the glacier skiing of Mont-Fort. These pistes (and thus the cable-car) can also be reached by chair-lift from Ruinettes and Verbier.

The cable-car from Attelas to Mont-Gelé is small and short, and unlikely to be replaced when it reaches the end of its working life in a couple of years' time. But for the moment it still serves some of Verbier's most famous skiing – all of it off-piste. There are very extreme couloirs down to Attelas which are occasionally skied, but the main runs are the longer, less severe (but still steep) ones behind Mont-Gelé, ending up at Tortin or La Chaux. These slopes are rocky and exposed, and require good snow cover for safety; they have rarely had it in recent years.

The main link with the eastern half of the skiing is the chair-lift from Lac des Vaux to Col de Chassoure at the top of a dauntingly long, wide and steep mogul-field – a splendid run for skiers who like that kind of thing, but often congested by skiers who don't. The run (or gondola-ride down) ends at the plateau of Tortin, and is usually known by that name. From the bottom, a cable-car climbs to the Col des Gentianes.

From the Col, a cable-car climbs over the glacier to **Mont-Fort**. From the top (which gives spectacular views, ranging from the Matterhorn to Mont Blanc) there is a roundabout alternative to the very steep direct run under the cable-car (over 35°), but even this presents a slope of 33° and should be graded black rather than red. Below the Col des Gentianes there are some splendid open runs served by drag-lifts, mainly easy but with moguls towards the bottom. There are plentiful opportunities to go off-piste throughout this area, but the dangers of avalanches and crevasses should not be underestimated.

The long north-facing run down from Col des Gentianes to Tortin is a splendid black, testing more because of popularity and occasional narrowness than because of steepness, with some excellent off-piste variants. The run down from Col des Gentianes to La Chaux, under the cable-car, is much less difficult but also much less interesting – the top part of it is zig-zag path, except when good snow permits corner-cutting; it provides splendid views of the Grand Combin and neighbouring glaciers. In good snow it is possible to ski off-piste to Le Châble, across vineyard terraces; from Mont-Fort the run is said to be 18km for the enormous 2500m drop.

From Tortin there are easy runs down to the skiing service station of Siviez (formerly known as Super-Nendaz), where lifts branch east for Thyon 2000 and Veysonnaz, and west for Nendaz. A long chain of short lifts and easy runs along the upper slopes of the mountainside leads to the high modern resort of **Thyon 2000**, where there are broad nursery slopes and some excellent long runs down through the woods to Veysonnaz and Mayens-de-l'Ours. On the other side of Siviez, a steep drag-lift and a chair-lift to Plan-du-Fou give access to an off-piste run (not difficult) to Prarion and on down through woods to Auddes, where a special bus links up with lifts from La Tzoumaz up to Savoleyres.

The skiing of **Nendaz** is a simple arrangement of long intermediate north-facing runs above the resort, served by the long Tracouet gondola or alternative drags, and shorter south-facing slopes behind Tracouet down to Prarion. The Plan-du-Fou cable-car above Prarion makes it possible to get to Siviez on skis, for access to Tortin and Mont-Fort.

Mountain restaurants are not very plentiful, not generally very appealing, and in some reporters' view expensive. The Carrefour at the top of the nursery slopes and the bottom of the pistes down to the resort is friendly, and popular throughout the day and evening. Attractive, out-of-the-way restaurants are Chez Dany at Clambin (on one of the indirect runs from Ruinettes), Cabane de Mont-Fort (between Gentianes and La Chaux), Au Mayens (at the foot of the La Combe chair-lifts) and Les Marmottes (at the bottom of Savoleyres Sud drag-lift). Chez Simon, also in the Savoleyres sector, is singled out by several reporters – 'simple, friendly, and half the price of grander places'. The Violon d'Ingres (upstairs) at Ruinettes is excellent. The new octagonal restaurant at Plan-du-Fou (between Siviez and Nendaz) is recommended. Queues at Col des Gentianes are a reported problem.

Verbier has an unenviable reputation for lift **queues**, which the tourist office and some reporters insist is now groundless. Certainly, new lifts have improved the flow from the resort into the ski area – at the cost of ever-increasing piste congestion. But we and many other reporters encountered serious bottle-necks in many places at different stages of last season: the Medran lifts out of Verbier, both lifts out of Tortin, the lifts from Siviez towards Tortin and towards Greppon Blanc (for Thyon), the glacier drags and the top Mont-Fort cable-car. So Verbier remains 'bad for lift queues'.

The big cable-car to Col des Gentianes is not open to skiers without the Mont-Fort **lift pass**. There are spot checks for passes on the mountain, and substantial fines for cheating. Four Valleys lift passes do not cover all lifts of Thyon 2000. The lift pass is the most expensive in Europe; in order to soften the impact of the price on family visitors, special reductions are available for them (and for senior citizens). The resort piste map is extremely confusing in places. There is an alternative, in the form of a *Ski Guide* to the Four Valleys – a piste-per-page booklet showing each run in detail.

Verbier has mobile guns for the application of **artificial snow** to the final woodland path piste to the village, though they were not much in evidence last season; more are planned for 1992. Many reporters have judged piste maintenance to be slack. Thyon 2000 and Veysonnaz both have snow-guns on the full length of a major piste, and Nendaz has a short stretch.

The resort

Verbier is splendidly set on a wide, sloping, sunny ledge high above Le Châble, with beautiful views of the mountains that separate Switzerland,

Facts on Verbier   Valais **Switzerland**

Prices in francs
Ski Club represented

Tourist office
Postcode CH-1936
Tel (26) 316222
Fax (26) 313272
Tlx 473247

Getting there
By road 998km from Calais. Via Pontarlier, Lausanne; chains may be needed.
By rail Le Châble (7km); 11 daily buses to resort or gondola.
By air Geneva; transfer 2½hr.

Staying there
Visitor beds 23,700; breakdown: 1,500 in hotels, 22,000 in chalets and apartments.
Package holidays Activity Travel (hcs) Beach Villas (hcas) Bladon Lines (hcjs) Chalets and Hotels "Unlimited" (hcs) Crystal (h) Kuoni (h) Made to Measure (hs) Mark Warner (cj) Neilson (h) Silver Ski (c) Ski Alternatives (ha) Ski Club of GB (hcj) Ski Equipe (hcs) Ski Esprit (c) Ski Jeannie (hcas) Ski West (cs) Ski Whizz Small World (c) SnowRanger (hs) Supertravel (hcjs) Thomson (c) Vacances Elite (hcs) .
Medical facilities In resort: Clinic, doctor, dentist, chemist. Hospital: Martigny (25km).

Non-skiing activities
Indoor Sports centre (swimming, skating, curling, squash, sauna, solarium, jacuzzi), tennis, fitness centre, cinema.
Outdoor Ski-bob, 15km cleared paths, paragliding, hang-gliding, toboggan run, mountaineering.

Kindergartens
Mini Champions (Swiss Ski School)
Tuition: Yes. Hours: 9.00-4.30. Ages: 3-10. Cost: 220.00 per week (with lunch).
The Smurfs
Tuition: No. Hours: 8.30-5.30. Ages: 1½ up. Cost: 210.00 per week (with lunch).
Other childcare facilities
Private baby-sitters available, information from Tourist Office.

Special skiing facilities
Summer skiing Small area at Mont-Fort, 2700m

to 3300m.
Cross-country 4km trail at Verbier, 30km at Le Châble, 4km at Bruson.

Lift passes
Four Valley pass
Covers all lifts and ski buses in the Four Valley area except Mont-Fort and top lifts at Thyon 2000; also covers several other areas nearby (Bruson, Val Ferret, Champex and Vichères). (86 lifts in total.)
Cost 6 days 228.00 (£95.00).
Credit cards accepted Yes.
Senior citizens 114.00 (over 65) saving 50%.
Children 114.00 (under 16) saving 50%. Free pass up to age 6.
Notes Day extensions for Mont-Fort. Reductions for families.
Beginners Day and half-day passes for nursery lifts.
Short-term passes Half-day.
Other passes Limited passes for Savoleyres (36.00 per day).
Other periods Passes for 10 non-consecutive days.

Ski school
Swiss Ski School
Classes 9.15-11.15 or 2.10-4.30. Cost: 90.00 (6 half-days). Sun 10.00-12.15.
Lift priority Yes.
Children's classes Ages: 3-12. Cost: 90.00 (6 half-days – full-day classes available during the school holidays). Lunch for children 20.00 per day.
Private lessons available Full day, half-day, hourly. Cost: 45.00 per hour.
Special courses Competition courses in school holidays, 6 days cost 140.00; Alpine touring; heli-skiing with Ecole du Ski Fantastique, between 200.00-300.00 per lift.

What was new in 91
1. Speed skiing course developed on Savoleyres, next to the Taillay chair.
2. Pasay chair-lift replaced the drag-lift above Mayens-de-Brusons.

What is new for 92
Les Clérondes chair-lift to be installed, serving slopes below the bottom cable-car station at La Chaux.

Italy and France. A central square is the focal point of the resort, surrounded by a complicated one-way system of busy streets, often congested at weekends, when all the second-home owners pour into town. Most of the shops, bars and hotels are on, or close to, the square and the street up to the Medran lifts. Below it there is still a bit of an old village backwater, but most of Verbier's continuing expansion has taken place across the broad slopes between Ruinettes and Savoleyres, where it is very easy to get lost among so many identical chalets. Shopping is good, and less expensive than some reporters expected.

Regular free ski-buses link Savoleyres and Medran lifts with the Place Centrale from about 8.30am to 7.30pm. They get very crowded at peak times, and follow a variety of routes, not all of them frequently. Parking centrally is difficult and vigorously policed. There is a multi-storey car park at the entrance to the resort.

Verbier is not generally suitable for **cross-country** skiers, and is unlikely to appeal to **non-skiers**, but the facilities of the smart sports centre (squash, swimming, artificial ice rink) are impressive and excursions are easily organised. Ski-bobbing is popular on Savoleyres (instruction is available), and once again permitted on pistes and some lifts between Verbier and Attelas. Paragliding is popular.

Accommodation offered by British operators is mostly in chalets, of which there is a huge variety. Location matters: the top of the resort is good for skiing but very tiring for après-ski and especially inconvenient for self-caterers, who face long walks to and from shops. Most of the hotels are central – none more so than the comfortably traditional Hôtel de Verbier: late-night noise from the square is the only complaint from our recent reporter. The Mazot, just off the main square, is 'exceptionally friendly, with excellent food'. The Parc, again not far away, has impressed a recent visitor.

Après-ski is livelier than in many chalet resorts. As well as all the chalet-party parties there are loud and popular bars, notably the teeming Pub Montfort in a Mark Warner chalet ('full of drunken Scans') and the Nelson, a typical plush Continental 'pub' with draught bitter. Of the discos, the Farm Club is the smartest, and very expensive (popular with sophisticated chalet girls), the Scotch cheapest – 'terribly overcrowded', 'very smoky' 'just horrible' (not popular with sophisticated chalet girls). Several reporters have preferred Marshall's – 'great lively atmosphere, excellent music' – and the New Club, which has a jazz piano bar ('loads of fun'). There are plenty of quieter places for a drink, too. There is a wide range of restaurants, from the very expensive and highly regarded Hotel Rosalp (Roland Pierroz is one of Switzerland's top chefs, and he keeps a remarkable cellar) via excellent steaks at La Luge to simple pizzas at the ever-popular Fer à Cheval (and more impressive ones at Borsalino). Reporters recommend Robinsons and Le Caveau (fondue and raclette); La Crêperie ('brilliant and very cheap'); L'Ecurie ('pricey but worth it'). The trendy places at tea-time are milk bars – the Milk Bar (especially late in the season, when its terrace comes into its own) and the Offshore at the Medran lift station.

Verbier's **nursery slopes**, between Ruinettes and Savoleyres, are sunny and gentle, but they have been encroached upon by the growth of the resort, are not very reliable for snow, and suffer from skiers in transit at the beginning and end of the day. The ski area is far from ideal for skiers progressing from nursery to piste.

Reports on the main **ski school** continue to suggest that instructors do an admirable job of coping with chaotically organised classes – 'large groups of constantly changing pupils of variable standards, speaking several different languages'. A second ski school, L'Ecole du Ski Fantastique, specialises in off-piste skiing, heli-skiing, and tours. Verbier is on the Haute Route, so tourers can find plenty to do.

Nendaz   1350m

High up on the steep southern wall of the Rhône Valley, Nendaz-Station and Haute-Nendaz have merged to form a long, hilly hairpin resort without much village atmosphere, with most of its self-catering a 15-minute walk below the lifts. Unfortunately its lift system is inadequate and inconvenient, and for many skiers the day starts with a queue for the bus up to Siviez, no more than a cluster of service buildings at the foot of lifts up to Tortin, but genuinely convenient, at the centre of the linked ski area and ideal for early access to Mont-Fort – keen skiers who don't mind evening isolation should consider the hotel Siviez. There are a few hotels in the main resort. There are 20km of cross-country trails, an artificial ice rink, swimming, squash, long walks and a kindergarten.
Tourist office ℂ (27) 881444. Tx 38643.
Package holidays Inghams (hs) Ski Party Snow World (hs) SnowRanger (s).

Bruson   1100m

Although there are medium-term plans to build a lift up from Le Châble to Bruson, thus linking it to Verbier, this quiet mountainside community is at present reached by infrequent free ski-buses from Le Châble station.

From the hamlet of Bruson a chair-lift goes up over gentle slopes to Mayens-de-Bruson (aka Bruson-les-Forêts) – no more than a scattering of chalets at present, but destined for development if and when the lift-builders overcome green objections to projected chairs on the north-facing slopes of Six Blanc. A short drag and a path across the mountainside (via a welcoming and reasonably priced restaurant) take you to the new Pasay chair, which goes up over a broad piste through the forest, graded black on the piste map but of red steepness except at the very top. Over on the western side of the ridge reached by this chair, a short run southwards across the mountainside takes you to the Grand-Tsai drag. This serves a splendid little bowl on the western side of the ridge, with an easy piste and abundant off-piste areas, and gives access to routes on- and off-piste on the eastern side of the ridge, back to Mayens. When snow is good you can ski down from Mayens to Le Châble; direction-finding is not always easy, and some of the paths involved are unpleasantly narrow, but with luck you'll encounter some entertainingly powdery pastures, too.
Tourist office ℂ (26) 361681. Fax (26) 361541.

United we stand

Adelboden Switzerland 1400m

Good for *Sunny slopes, cross-country skiing, Alpine charm, family holidays, woodland runs*
Bad for *Tough runs, late holidays*

Linked resort: Lenk

Adelboden and Lenk are widely differing but connected resorts a couple of valleys to the west of the famous Jungfrau region. Adelboden is a charming old village, its long main street lined with overhanging wooden buildings, which has around it a considerable quantity and variety of skiing. That skiing is split into five areas, of which only one has in the past been directly accessible from the village. But Adelboden's ambitious plans to link the village to two other areas have at last been realised. It has not been transformed into a convenience resort, but its combination of quiet village charm and moderately extensive intermediate skiing is now an attractive one, and it has pleased all our recent reporters.

Lenk is more modern and less appealing as a village, and less convenient as a skiers' base: its two ski areas (one linking with Adelboden) remain widely separated.

A car is still be useful for getting to the outlying ski areas, and might be used for excursions to the Jungfrau region (Wengen, Mürren). But the road up to the major lift station at Geils is not open to cars.

The skiing top 2330m bottom 1330m

Adelboden's main ski areas are the Schwandfeldspitz, immediately above the village on the west side; Fleckli, across the valley on the east; Höchsthorn, to the south; Engstligenalp, 6km away to the south; and Geils, to the south-west, which links with Lenk. Until last season, only the first of these was directly accessible by lift from the village, the others being reached by free ski-buses. The ski-buses still run (and are reportedly reliable and adequately capacious), but now a long gondola from the village to Sillerenbühl provides access to Höchsthorn and Geils.

The skiing on **Schwandfeldspitz** starts from a chair-lift close to the main street, going up to 1938m; there is a justifiably black run back to the village, but most of the skiing is open intermediate runs on the wide flank of the mountain facing north-east – shortish pistes served by a drag, and a fine long red to Möser with a chair-lift return. Those not up to the black to the village can take a long roundabout blue run. A new red run has been created on the south side, going down through woods to a short lift giving access to Höchsthorn and the gondola.

In the rural suburb of Boden, there are nursery lifts and a drag-lift above them going up to Kuonisbergli (1730m) and on to **Höchsthorn**

(1903m). You can travel to and from this area via the new gondola, but not directly; you must also take a down-then-up chair-lift between the village and the base station. The spectrum of gradings of the runs on the lower part of the mountain exaggerates the variety of pistes – all the skiing is of easy to moderate difficulty. Across the valley, the drag-lift to **Fleckli** (1862m) serves runs marked red and black which again hold no terrors.

A minibus takes you to the cable-car which climbs steeply over 500m to **Engstligenalp** (1964m). Beyond the cluster of hotels and houses is an extraordinary flat-bottomed bowl of mountains; it has a double drag-lift on the far side, serving pistes of moderate length and steepness and giving access to off-piste skiing in the bowl and ski-tours outside it. There's a flat tow-drag across the bowl, but still a lot of plodding.

The new gondola gives access to the extensive and varied skiing at **Geils**; but it has also added to that skiing. North-facing open slopes below its terminus at Sillerenbühl (1975m) have been equipped with drag lifts and red and black pistes, the longest descending over 500m from the nearby high-point of Stand (2076m) to Aebi. There are pistes from both Stand and Sillerenbühl to the original lift station at Geils. From here, chairs up each side of a wide, open bowl to Luegli (2080m) and Laveygrat (2200m) serve intermediate and genuinely black runs back to Geils, but there are also links to the easier runs towards the centre. The run from Luegli marked black on the map was more accurately marked red on the mountain when we visited. The triple chair to Laveygrat (the high point of the area) serves a challenging, genuinely steep run back to Geils of almost 500m vertical (with big moguls at the top), and to a red down to Stand, for access to Sillerenbühl. There is also an off-piste descent off the back of the hill to Lenk.

The normal access to **Lenk** is via the gondola to Hahnenmoos, a broad col only 250m higher than Geils. The blue run underneath the lift is easy and attractive, and very popular with near-beginners. In the Lenk direction, an easy piste goes down only as far as Bühlberg – though there are off-piste ways down when snow permits. The more interesting skiing on this side of Lenk is the broad, open expanse of mountain above Metsch, served by two double drag-lifts up to Metschstand (2098m) giving long, easy and intermediate west-facing runs of 600m vertical. Metsch is reached from Lenk by bus and cable-car, and again there are only off-piste ways back.

The Betelberg area starts a short bus-ride to the far side of Lenk. The main gondola gives access to all the skiing, though there are supplementary drags and chair-lifts as alternatives. The runs are broad, partly above the trees and partly cut through them, and almost entirely gentle. The blues can be schussed (and are often used by cross-country skiers), the reds rarely form moguls. The one black run, down the lower half of the gondola, has a mogul-field at the bottom.

There is no shortage of **mountain restaurants**, which are 'friendly, warm and roomy, with good toilet facilities'; most also have sunny terraces, and Metschstand is said to be appealingly atmospheric. There may be **queues** for the new gondola and for the Engstligenalp cable-car when snow in the lower areas is in short supply. There is **artificial snow**

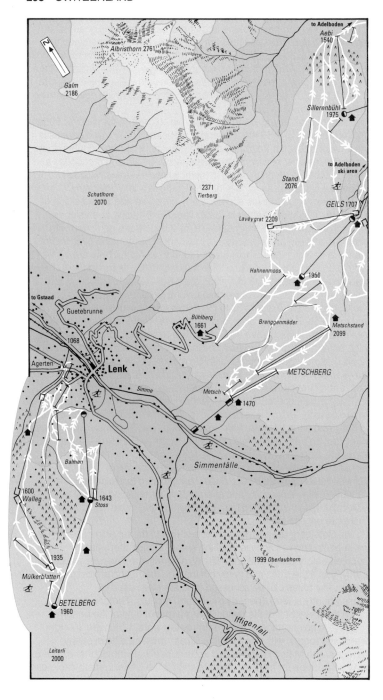

N

Albristhorn 2761

Galm
2186

to Adelboden

Aebi
1540

Sillerenbühl
1975

to Adelboden
ski area

Schatlhore
2070

2371
Tierberg

Stand
2076

GEILS 1707

Laveygrat 2209

to Gstaad

Guetebrunne

Hahnenmoos   1956

1068

Bühlberg
1661

Brenggenmäder

Metschstand
2099

Agerten

Lenk

Simme

METSCHBERG

Metsch   1470

Balmen

Simmentälle

1600
Walleg

1643
Stoss

1999 Oberlaubhorn

1935

Mülkerblatten

BETELBERG
1960

Iffigenfall

Leiterli
2000

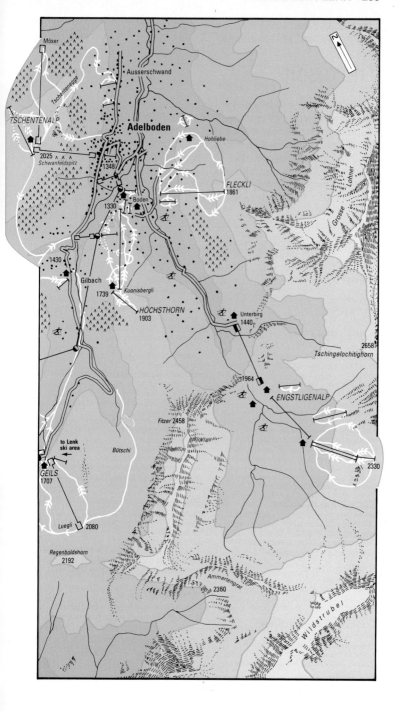

on the bottom half of Höchsthorn and of two runs from
Schwandfeldspitz to Tschentenalp.

The resort

Adelboden sits in a slightly elevated position to one side of a broad
valley which is split by the course of the swift-flowing Allebach. The
village spreads down to the river from the main street running across
the hillside, with the nursery slopes and sports centre between the two.

Most of the **accommodation** is in chalets and apartments, but there
are numerous hotels and guest-houses; three smart new hotels have
been built recently. Among the most welcoming of the older hotels is the
modest Kreuz 'thoroughly recommended' by a recent visitor who

---

Facts on Adelboden   Berner Oberland **Switzerland**

Prices in francs

Tourist office
Postcode CH-3715
Tel (33) 732252
Fax (33) 734252
Tlx 922121

Getting there
By road 837km from Calais. Via Basle and
Berne; chains may be needed.
By rail Frutigen (16km); 15 daily buses from
station.
By air Basle; transfer 3hr. (Or Zurich, Geneva.)

Staying there
Visitor beds 9,800; breakdown: 1,300 in hotels
and pensions, 7,000 in chalets and apartments,
1,500 in group accommodation facilities.
Package holidays Inghams (hs) Made to
Measure (hs) PR Christian Holidays (h) Ski Club
of GB (h) Ski Unique (h) SnowRanger (h)
Swiss-Ski (h) .
Medical facilities In resort: Doctors, chemist,
dentist. Hospital: Frutigen (16km).

Non-skiing activities
Indoor Artificial skating rink, curling, hotel
swimming pool (open to non-residents), museum,
skittles, cinema, concerts.
Outdoor Curling, 40km cleared paths,
hang-gliding, sleigh rides, ski-bobs.

Kindergartens
Tennis Center
Tuition: possible. Hours: 9.00-5.00, Mon-Fri.
Ages: 2-6. Cost: 60.00 per week (lunch 10.00 per
day). Substantial reductions with Visitor's card.

Special skiing facilities
Summer skiing No.
Cross-country Total 40km easy trails at
Ausserschwand and Engstligenalp (at almost
2000m), easy and intermediate trails at Boden,

Stiegelschwand and Geils. Instruction available.

Lift passes
Poolskipass
Covers all Adelboden and Lenk lifts, and buses
during the skiing day. Also gives reductions on
Lenk swimming pool. (45 lifts in total.)
Cost 6 days 170.00 (£70.83).
Credit cards accepted Yes.
Senior citizens 136.00 (over 62/65) saving 20%.
Children 102.00 (under 16) saving 40%. Free
pass up to age 6.
Notes 10% reduction for families of 4 or more
and for people between 16 and 19 years. Passes
for 6 days or more allow one day in the Gstaad
area. Reductions available at Lenk swimming
pool with Poolskipass.
Beginners Electronic points card.
Short-term passes Half-day (from 12.00pm) for
Poolskipass and limited area passes.
Other passes Various limited area passes
available (Schwandfeldspit, Boden,
Engstligenalp, Silleren); Combined lift pass and
ski school package (6 days) costs 283.00 for
adults, 232.00 for children.

Ski school
Swiss Ski School
Classes 9.30-11.30 and 2.00-4.00. Cost: 147.00
(6 days, Mon-Sat).
Lift priority No.
Children's classes Ages: 4-16. Cost: 147.00 (6
days, Mon-Sat). Lunch available, 10.00 per day.
Private lessons available Hourly. Cost: 45.00
per hour.

What was new in 91
1. New Grand Hotel Regina, 4 star, 180 beds.
2. New lift pass reductions for families of 4 or
more.

What is new for 92
New 120-bed 4-star hotel, the Steinmatti.

appreciated the 'tasty and tempting' food. The Huldi lacks atmosphere but is recommended for 'good food and friendly owners'. The Parkhotel Bellevue is 'very comfortable and friendly'. **Après-ski** is quiet and traditional, revolving more around tea-time cakes than all-night revels. The liveliest bar is said to be Alfredo, with one-man-band. There are extensive **cross-country** skiing trails of easy and medium grades at Boden, Engstligenalp and Geils. The resort has considerable appeal for **non-skiers**, too – quite good sports facilities, and good excursions.

There are good **nursery slopes** in the heart of the village (admirably gentle), on the northern fringes, and at Boden (at the foot of the Höchsthorn). Our several recent reports on **ski school** are all positive, and include approval of conventional and snowboard classes; English is spoken, though there is little demand for it. The kindergarten is 'adequate and safe, but not dynamic'; English is not spoken.

Lenk   1070m

Lenk has been greatly expanded in recent years, mainly in chalet style. It is spacious and not unpleasant, but does not add up to a particularly appealing whole. It attracts many middle-aged German cross-country skiers and walkers (for both of whom there are abundant opportunities), offering spa treatments as well as good non-skiing sports facilities.

Tourist office ✆ (33) 732252. Tx 922121.

Package holidays Made to Measure (hs) SnowRanger (h) Swiss-Ski (h).

Where eaglets dare

Villars Switzerland 1300m

Good for *Easy runs, beautiful scenery, sunny slopes, cross-country skiing, not skiing, short airport transfers, easy road access, rail access, family holidays*
Bad for *Tough runs, freedom from cars*

Linked resort: Les Diablerets

Villars is a long-established all-round resort (complete with mountain railway from the valley and up into the skiing) in a beautiful, sunny balcony setting, facing south-west across the Rhône valley. A former British favourite, after a period of neglect it is now enjoying something of a revival of interest, particularly among families. The resort does not have the charm of some of its traditional Swiss competitors – in particular, it suffers slightly from traffic in the main street (although a reporter rightly points out that it is scarcely in the same league as a valley town). But most of the buildings are in chalet style, and the fringes of the village are pleasantly rustic. There are several boarding schools in the locality, Aiglon College the most prominent.

The ski area is not large, does not reach very high, and contains little to challenge the expert; but it is attractive and varied – well suited to intermediate skiers who have not been spoilt by the vast networks of French mega-resorts, and to beginners. The skiing link opened a few years ago with Les Diablerets – another friendly, intermediate's resort with the additional feature of glacier skiing on the mountain of the same name – certainly adds to the appeal for adventurous skiers, but it is a pity that the connections are not more easily skiable.

A car could be useful for visits to the Diablerets glacier, or for exploring other resorts off the Rhône valley, and some people find one helpful for getting around the resort.

The skiing top 2970m bottom 800m

The mountain railway from the west side of the resort centre goes up to **Bretaye** (1800m) – a col with a couple of hotel-restaurants at the heart of the main ski area, with drags and chair-lifts going up the slopes on either side, and runs converging (with resultant congestion). The east-facing runs from Grand and Petit Chamossaire are open red slopes, very exposed at the top, steep enough to be satisfying, but not long. Roc d'Orsay, on the flank of Grand Chamossaire, can be reached by a gondola from the northern fringes of the resort as well as a drag from Bretaye, and has a couple of entertaining runs served by a short drag on the back of the hill. The west-facing runs from Chaux Ronde to Bretaye cover an open slope which is steep enough to provide a slalom course directly above the col, with easier blue routes available. The

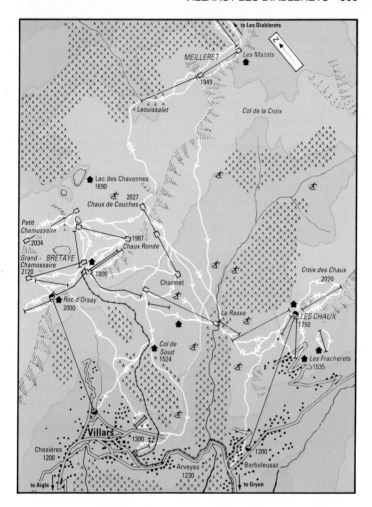

black run from Chaux Ronde served by a chair-lift is pretty and uncrowded, but of nothing like black steepness and easily skied by intermediates (it is unprepared, but gets skied into a piste-like state).

There are pistes from Roc d'Orsay and Bretaye to the village, the latter linking with extensive, open, easy, sunny slopes going down to La Rasse. The chair-lift to Chaux de Conches from this area serves a range of amiable blue and red runs across the mountainside from its middle station, and below the top section is a bumpy black run which is reportedly 'very steep, very worthwhile'.

Drag-lifts from La Rasse link with the otherwise separate skiing on the open flanks of **Les Chaux** – further easy-intermediate skiing of modest extent. The run to the hamlet of Les Fracherets gets a lot of sun and suffers accordingly. A long gondola from Barboleusaz (where there are big car parks) offers an alternative way into the skiing. The run down the gondola poses no difficulties except that it gets too much sun.

The Chaux de Conches chair-lift also gives access to Les Diablerets – though there are snags with the link. The run is rightly graded black because of an unprepared and steep mogul-field near the top, but only a keen student of the piste map would be prepared for this. When last we skied it, only at the point of departure from the Villars lifts did we encounter a sign announcing that the run was effectively off-piste, which seems irresponsible. This is all rather a pity, because most of the run is lovely motorway cruising, and the skiing of Les Diablerets is not difficult. The Laouissalet drag delivers you to the Tête du Meilleret, the top of Les Diablerets' skiing (excluding the glacier). On your return you are delivered to this same point by a chair-lift, and then face an exhausting plod along the ridge before embarking on another splendid easy run, across an open mountainside dotted with chalets, back towards Villars.

The skiing on the Villars side of **Les Diablerets** is nicely varied easy-intermediate stuff, on north-facing trails sweeping through the forest, down to the resort and to the slightly lower village of Vers l'Eglise. The runs are not graded on the piste map, but are in practice all easy reds or interesting blues. On the far side of the village, a gondola goes up to the sunny, open slopes of Isenau – a consistently gentle area apart from one moderately steep drag at the top.

The Glacier des Diablerets

The glacier is part of the Gstaad ski area, but is much closer to the village of Les Diablerets. It is accessed via a series of three lifts whether you start from the Col du Pillon or from Reusch, closer to Gstaad. The final stage in either case is a cable-car across the deep bowl separating Cabane des Diablerets from the higher Sex Rouge; instead of taking this lift you can ski down the middle cable-car of the ascent from Reusch, to reach Oldenegg – a satisfying and scenically impressive intermediate run with a real high-mountain flavour. At about 3000m, the Sex Rouge top station is not very high by glacier standards, but it gives access to some worthwhile skiing (both on and off the glacier) as well as wide views of the Valais mountains to the south. The skiing on the glacier consists of broad pistes down either side of two long drag-lifts – one pair easy, the other very easy – plus long linking trails. But the area's ace is the run from the glacier down the dramatic Combe d'Audon round the back of the Audon (Oldenhorn). This is one of the great intermediate runs of the Alps, a fast, sweeping groomed piste after a short patch of moguls and a comfortable ledge at the top of the valley. The precipices on the south side keep much of the run in the shade, even late in the season, and the snow may be excellent even when Gstaad is bare. A short drag or a chair take you up to Oldenegg, whence a pretty and interesting run goes down (eventually through woods) to Reusch via a short final drag. Post buses connect the valley lift stations at around hourly intervals.

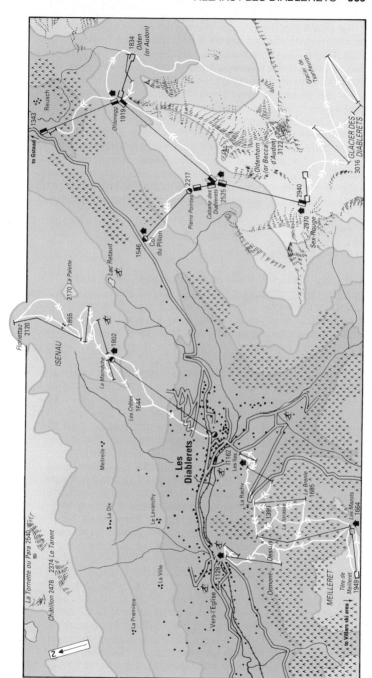

For a traditional Swiss resort, Villars is not well equipped with **mountain restaurants**; there are quite a few of them, several accessible to non-skiers, but few are notably attractive. The main one at Bretaye, the Col, has reportedly been smartened up but is often crowded; there are more attractive chalets beyond it, and the restaurant at Lac des Chavonnes (beyond the lifts, and 'a bit of a trek' unless you take a snow-cat) is widely reported to be excellent. For cross-country skiers, Chez Mic's is apparently 'a haven'.

Lift **queues** are rarely very serious, but the main lifts up from Bretaye can be bottle-necks (especially in the afternoon) and the trains can be unpleasantly crowded at peak times. The Barboleusaz gondola has recently been upgraded. The piste map looks clear but misrepresents some runs and invents others. And piste marking and direction signing is casual. There is no **artificial snow**, although the resort could do with some.

The resort

The village is a slightly diffuse affair, spread along a road which descends to the valley in both directions; there is one village focus at the junction of the road up to the Col de la Croix (closed in winter) and another along the hillside at the station. The road in one direction passes through the satellite village of Chesières; in the other, through the spread-out community of Arveyes. A free ski-bus circles the resort, serving both lift stations. There is no shortage of shops, but a car-borne self-catering reporter found trips to valley supermarkets worthwhile.

Most of the **accommodation** is in apartments and private chalets, but there are also numerous hotels, many of them above the centre of the village in quiet wooded suburbs leading to the Roc d'Orsay gondola and accessible on skis from Bretaye when snow conditions are good. One such is the pleasant Renardière, occupying three large chalets ('very acceptable without being over-luxurious'). Several reporters have spoken highly of the big, modern Eurotel, nearby – 'good food, good service, quiet rooms'. Directly opposite the station is the chalet-style Alpe-Fleurie – friendly, but reported to have small rooms. The Golf et Marie-Louise is also convenient, and recommended – 'nice room, excellent food and service'. Other recommendations include two four-star hotels, the Bristol ('very comfortable') and the Panorama ('excellent Chinese restaurant'). The Montesano, out of the resort at Arveyes, is reportedly very jolly. The monstrous Palace hotel, which dominates the resort from a distance, is now a Club Med.

On our own January visits we have not been surprised to find the **après-ski** scene quiet. But a February visitor also reports that 'the town seemed to stop in the evenings; everyone disappeared – the streets became deserted'. There are tea-rooms (La Chaumière is about the best), bars, one or two discos and a reasonable range of restaurants, from a pizzeria ('poor service, excellent pizzas') to the determinedly rustic Vieux Villars. A reporter enthusiastically recommends the Café de la Gare (aka Chez Jo) for its warm evening ambience, with live music

Facts on Villars Vaud **Switzerland**

Prices in francs
Ski Club represented

Tourist office
Postcode CH-1884
Tel (25) 353232
Fax (25) 352794
Tlx 456200

Getting there
By road 952km from Calais. Via Lausanne or Berne (longer but not simpler); chains may be needed.
By rail Mountain railway in village, connects with main line at Aigle or Bex, 12 daily buses from station.
By air Geneva; transfer 2hr.

Staying there
Visitor beds 6,700; breakdown: 1,700 in hotels, 5,000 in chalets and apartments.
Package holidays Club Med (h) Collineige Ski (ha) Crystal (h) Hoverspeed Ski-Drive (s) Inghams (hs) Kuoni (h) Made to Measure (hs) Neilson (hs) Ski Esprit (c) Ski Weekend (h) SnowRanger (hs) Swiss-Ski (hs) Winterworld (hcs) .
Medical facilities In resort: Doctors, dentist, physiotherapist, chemists. Hospital: Aigle (13km).

Non-skiing activities
Indoor Tennis (6 courts), skating, curling, swimming pool, bowling, riding school, fitness centre, squash, cinema.
Outdoor Horse-riding, ski-bob runs, 25km signed walks.

Kindergartens
Swiss Ski School
Tuition: Yes. Hours: 9.00-4.30, Mon-Sat. Ages: 3-12. Cost: 250.00 per week (with meals, supervision and lifts).
Other childcare facilities
List of baby-sitters available from Tourist Office for day and evening.

Special skiing facilities
Summer skiing Glacier des Diablerets.

Cross-country 39km in total, mainly up the valley which splits the Alpine ski area, towards the Col de la Croix; shorter loops at Bretaye. Instruction available.

Lift passes
Villars-Les Diablerets
Covers the Villars and Les Diablerets lifts. (45 lifts in total.)
Cost 6 days 167.00 (£69.58).
Credit cards accepted No.
Senior citizens 117.00 (over 65) saving 30%.
Children 117.00 (under 16) saving 30%. Free pass up to age 6.
Notes Family rates available for 3 or more people.
Beginners Limited lift pass for beginners included in ski school rate.
Short-term passes Half-day (morning and afternoon).
Other passes Alpes de la Riviera pass covering Villars, Les Diablerets, Leysin and Chateau d'Oex but not transport between them.

Ski school
Swiss Ski School
Classes 10.15-12.00. Cost: 100.00 (6 half-days, Mon-Sat).
Lift priority No.
Children's classes Ages: up to 12. Cost: 100.00 (6 half-days, Mon-Sat). Accompanied skiing from 10.15 to 4.00 for intermediate children, 420.00 for 6 days including ski pass.
Private lessons available Hourly. Cost: 45.00 per hour. Priority in lift queues.
Special courses Mono and telemark courses, 6 half-days 165.00.
Ecole de Ski Moderne
Classes 10.30-12.00. Cost: 95.00 (6 half-days, Mon-Sat). Classes limited to 10 pupils.
Lift priority No.
Children's classes Ages: 3-12. Cost: 95.00 (6 half-days, Mon-Sat).
Private lessons available Hourly. Cost: 45.00 per hour. Priority in lift queues.
Special courses Mono, snowboard and telemark courses available.

---

and plenty of local customers. Other recommendations include the Refuge de France, the new basement restaurant in the hotel Golf et Marie-Louise (for raclette) and Pepino's in the Eurotel ('excellent salad bowl'). Villars is an excellent resort for **non-skiers**. The mountain railway gives dignified access to Bretaye for meeting up with skiers, the village is an attractive place to while away time, the sports facilities are good (though the smart tennis/squash centre is extremely expensive), there a plenty of well marked scenic walks, and excursions to Montreux, Lausanne or even Geneva are possible. The **cross-country** skiing trails are attractive.

The **nursery slopes** immediately above the railway station are gentle, open and sunny and there are very easy (though sometimes crowded) pistes up the mountain at Bretaye.

Most **ski school** classes meet at Bretaye, though the beginners classes meet at the Palace nursery lift above the village. Our recent reports on the main school are uniformly favourable: 'One slow learner in our group had a free afternoon lesson, as the instructor thought he had neglected her'. A recent reporter was also impressed with his cross-country lesson. There are guides available for ski tours, including the Haute Route, a few miles away to the south. We have also heard good things about the **ski kindergarten**; 'Outstanding' says one reporter, whose two small children learned to ski in three days and had tremendous fun in the process.

Les Diablerets   1160m

Les Diablerets (the village) is a relaxed, spacious sprawl of chalets at the bottom of a broad U-shaped valley with the craggy crest of Les Diablerets (the mountain) at its head. There are adequate non-skiing amusements – swimming, 20km of cross-country trails, indoor and outdoor skating and curling, toboggan descents from the Col de la Croix, and riding. There are only a few hotels, mostly modern and anonymous, and a couple of them conspicuously at odds with the general chalet style of the resort. The modest old Auberge de la Poste is a cheap and cheerful exception, in a good central position slightly closer to the Isenau lift than to the Meilleret ones. Après-ski is not riotous, but the resort works hard to lay on musical and other events. As well as a branch of the Swiss Ski School, there is a group of mountain guides operating under the name Ski Total. There is an kindergarten offering all-day care with lunch.

Tourist office ✆ (25) 531358. Tx 456175. **Package holidays** Bladon Lines (hc) Crystal (h) Made to Measure (hs) Ski La Vie (hcas) SkiGower (y) SnowRanger (h).

Portes du Soleil: open invitation

Avoriaz France 1800m

Good for *Big ski area, nursery slopes, skiing convenience, family holidays, freedom from cars, short airport transfers, resort-level snow*
Bad for *Not skiing, Alpine charm, lift queues, late holidays*

Linked resorts: Châtel, Champéry, Les Crosets, Champoussin, Morgins (and others)

If 'Portes du Soleil' doesn't tempt you, the promoters of this huge Franco-Swiss ski area have a ready supply of other slogans. How about 'Ski sans frontière'? Or 'Le plus grand domaine skiable du monde'? This last may sound familiar; the rival French ski area of the Trois Vallées has for years been awarding itself the same distinction. The fact that neither area has established its superiority over the other should not be taken to mean that they are indistinguishable. Whereas the Trois Vallées is four adjacent, densely mechanised ski areas efficiently linked together, the Portes du Soleil is a looser network of skiing in as many as 15 resorts, some of them linked up in only twos and threes. But there is a core circuit of skiing linking the resorts of Avoriaz and Châtel in France with Morgins and Champéry in Switzerland, and it is the linked skiing of these resorts (and one or two smaller Swiss ones) which draws people back. The circuit can be done by early intermediates with a sense of adventure. There is now also a linear link between Avoriaz and the otherwise separate Morzine/Les Gets area (see next chapter).

For keen skiers, Avoriaz is the best-placed resort in the Portes du Soleil area. It is one of the most individual of French purpose-built resorts, built on a steep slope in a bold architectural style which fits in with the craggy surroundings better than most such developments. It has adopted neither the monolith approach nor the multiple hamlet approach, but is basically a village made up of apartment blocks. There is skiing below it, above it, beside it, through it; but it is not quite as convenient as it sounds, because most of the skiing ends up at the foot of the steep village slope and you often need to take a lift home. It is very much a self-catering resort, and is not fashionable or smart, but has more après-ski life than many such places. The apartments wherein you cater for yourself are unlikely to add much to your holiday pleasure.

The main alternative base in the Portes du Soleil for British skiers is Châtel – a much-developed old French village, friendly and quite lively, with a lot of modest hotel accommodation and access to about the most interesting sector of the skiing circuit. The main resorts in Switzerland are Morgins – a pleasant, spacious, chalet-style village, mainly of recent development – and Champéry, an atmospheric old Swiss mountain village, its long main street lined by wooden chalets; it is not ideally placed for skiing. Between the two are the small isolated ski stations of Les Crosets and Champoussin.

You are unlikely to make any use of a car while in Avoriaz, and you may worry about whether it will start after sitting on an exposed col at 1800m for a week or two (though there is covered parking). The road up from Morzine is long, tortuous and snowy, and expeditions are better organised around the cable-car to the valley. The shuttle bus between there and Morzine is free, but reported to be infrequent and erratic. In most other Portes du Soleil resorts, a car is well worth having – particularly in case of interruptions to the ski circuit.

The skiing top2275m bottom 1100m

The skiing covered by the Portes du Soleil lift pass embraces hundreds of miles of piste. We are limiting ourselves here to the main circuit, where most British visitors spend their time. (The skiing of Morzine and Les Gets, covered by the pass but an offshoot of this circuit, is described in a separate chapter.) The Portes du Soleil piste maps were substantially revised last season (or at least some of them were); the new style conveys the circuit links more clearly, but skiers who want to do more than the circuit still have to obtain separate piste maps on arrival in each resort in which they plan to ski – an infuriating waste of time. Navigation would be greatly aided by improved direction signing, too. There are no passport controls, but skiers are advised to carry identification in case of difficulties. Although some resorts in the area are linked directly by road, most are not, so it pays to set off home in good time. The two currencies are used everywhere, but exchange rates are poor, so carry both.

Avoriaz The skiing around Avoriaz itself can be divided into four areas. Above the village is an upward extension of the main nursery slopes, Le Plateau, with a variety of drags serving runs from green to very green – a splendid though rather exposed area for confidence-building, which links with the series of lifts coming up from Morzine. The pistes down the top lifts in this chain are again excellent for novices. In the opposite direction are pistes down to Les Marmottes, whence lifts go off towards Châtel; these runs are not trivially easy, and are often crowded. From Les Marmottes a harmless and scenic red run goes on down to Ardent, from where a ten-person gondola goes back up (and provides a good way into the skiing for skiers based in lower villages).

At the bottom of the village there are essentially three alternative directions that you can take.

Directly south of the village is the main **Arare** sector, which from Avoriaz looks steeper than it is. There are some trees towards the bottom, but the skiing is mainly above the tree-line; there are several marked pistes, but the whole face becomes a piste as skiers stray all over it. The runs are all easy, getting a little more difficult towards the bottom. Unfortunately, they get very crowded; the ski school comes up here and so do the fledgling racers, who occasionally close off part of the piste for practice.

A long chair starting on the left but veering right from the same area at the bottom of the village takes you to **Hauts Forts**, the most challenging skiing in Avoriaz and an excellent area for good skiers. There are several routes descending all or part of the way towards Prodain, 650m below Avoriaz and over 1300m below Les Hauts Forts. The mogulled pistes become narrower as you descend into the trees; the blacks are genuinely black, and even the red run into this area from the Arare sector has an absolutely black pitch which unprepared intermediates find very problematic. The lower runs are crowded in the late afternoon, and dodgy for snow, but very valuable in bad weather.

The third direction is by chair and drag to the north-west-facing bowl between Pas de Chavanette and Col du Fornet – the Chavanette sector. Here there are several marked runs but it is another area of wide open, intermediate skiing above the tree-line where you can ski virtually wherever you want – an excellent area for initial adventures off-piste; there is an easy trail back to the bottom of the village. An alternative way back from Chavanette for adventurous intermediates is over into the next valley – a lovely, easy run after the top mogul-field – down to Les Marmottes.

Champéry/Les Crosets/Champoussin Chavanette is where the skiing of Avoriaz meets the big, open, sunny ski-fields of these three Swiss resorts. It starts with the notorious 'Swiss Wall' – a long, broad mogul slope of about 300m vertical, easily covered in a single fall when the snow is hard. It is not exceptionally steep, but does maintain a gradient of about 34° for a good part of its length. The severity and danger depend critically on the very variable snow conditions – the slope gets a lot of sun – and on the state of the very top section, which is much narrower than the slope as a whole and often presents difficulties; last season we encountered moguls the size of cars. There is reportedly an alternative, easier black to the left side, or you can take the chair-lift down instead. Below the Wall there is acres of open easy skiing served by the lifts either side of the Chavanette chair, connecting with the Planachaux slopes above Champéry, and with the adjacent bowl of Les Crosets. Planachaux is now reached from Champéry by a big cable-car, or by chair-lift from Grand Paradis. The pistes down to the valley end at this point, having wound their way through hamlets and across the river – an interesting route, and not difficult, but hard work. There are minibuses between Grand Paradis and Champéry.

Les Crosets sits above the tree-line surrounded by abundant, wide open pistes – good, easy to intermediate skiing, some of it north-facing but most of It sunny. There are lifts up to points on the French border, that to Cubore serving a steep unprepared (and often uncovered) black slope at the top which mellows as it descends. Via the Pointe de l'Au, a series of linked drags and easy-intermediate pistes makes the connection first with Champoussin and then with Morgins. The mountainside above Champoussin is broad and sunny, with little variety of terrain; but the skiing possibilities have been widened recently by a four-seater chair-lift going up from above Champoussin to the ridge. This whole area is ideally suited to the timid intermediate skier; for good skiers the main interest will be in the extensive opportunity to venture off-piste.

Morgins/Châtel Morgins does not have much skiing on the side reached from Champoussin, but it includes a splendid north-facing intermediate trail through tall pine forests to the village. Skiers bent on the Soleil circuit then face a short walk across the village to the nursery slopes and the lifts for Châtel. The area between Morgins and Châtel is a pleasant contrast to the bleak ski-fields of Avoriaz and Planachaux – a series of short drags and winding pistes, largely among thin woods, eventually takes you over the border to the open slopes of Super-Châtel, in France. The Morclan chair-lift from Super-Châtel up to 1970m serves the most challenging slope – basically a moderate red mogul-field. There is also a black piste down towards the village, which proved elusive when we visited. The top of this chair is the point of departure for Torgon, one of the furthest extremities of the Portes du Soleil network. The rest of Super-Châtel's skiing is mostly easy-

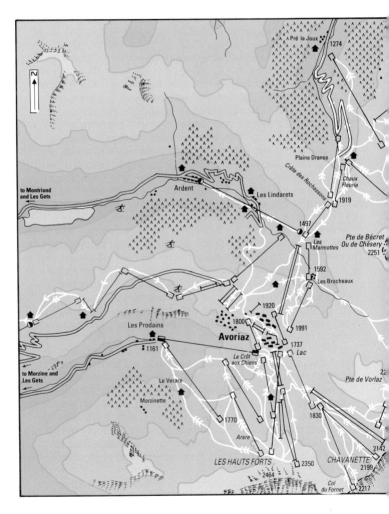

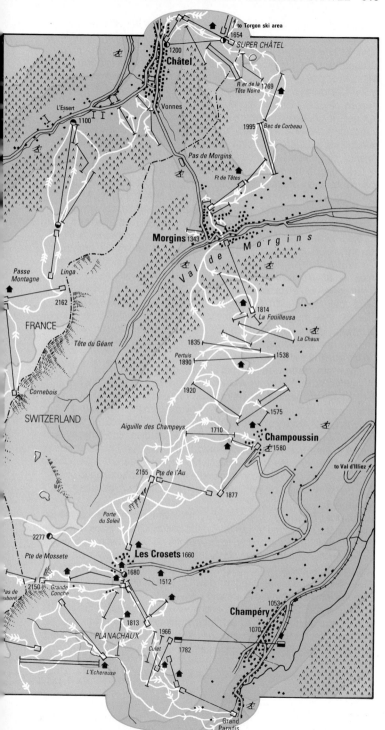

to Torgon ski area
1654
SUPER CHÂTEL
1200
Châtel
R. er de la
Tête Noire   1769
Vonnes
1995   Bec de Corbeau
L'Essert
1100
Pas de Morgins
Ft de Têtes
Morgins 1343
M o r g i n s
V a l   d e
Passe
Montagne   Linga
1814
2162   La Fouilleusa
FRANCE   La Chaux
Tête du Géant
1835
1538
Pertuis
1890
Cornebois
1920
SWITZERLAND
1575
Aiguille des Champeys   1710
Champoussin
1580
to Val d'Illiez
2155   Pte de l'Au
1877
Porte
du Soleil
2277
Pte de Mossete
Les Crosets 1660
2150   Grande
as de   Conche
uboré   1680
1512
1053
1813   **Champéry**
1070
PLANACHAUX   1966
1782
Culet
L'Echereuse
Grand
Paradis

intermediate stuff, on wide areas above and below the big restaurant and lift station; the runs to the valley can be tricky in poor snow, which is not infrequent (they get the afternoon sun).

Châtel/Avoriaz It is at Châtel that the Soleil circuit breaks down. Whichever way you are travelling, the link cannot be made on skis; if going clockwise, a green traverse from the Linga lifts delivers you to the nursery slopes of Châtel, leaving a walk across the village to the ten-person gondola for Super-Châtel; if going anti-clockwise, a substantial bus-ride is needed from downtown Châtel to the ten-person gondola up to Linga, the first of a long chain of lifts and pistes towards Avoriaz, or further along the valley to the chair up from Pré-la-Joux.

The skiing in this sector offers more variety than other major legs of the circuit, and includes a long, challenging but not severe black beside the Linga gondola (for skiers going clockwise or with the time to play about en route). The steepish slope above the gondola, served by a chair-lift, now has a blue traverse cut in to it as well as the red and black routes shown on the piste map. The run down the Combes chair-lift towards Avoriaz is a satisfying and attractive red, and the recently built Cornebois chair-lift which goes up from the same point now has good intermediate pistes of its own as well as connecting with the top of the Chaux des Rosées chair up from Plaine Dranse. The runs down this latter chair are quite challenging, the black offering a choice of routes down its wide mogul-field, with the steepest approaching 35° over a short pitch, the red taking a scenic roundabout route. One more lift and an easy run down brings you to Les Marmottes, along with a lot of other skiers wanting a lift up to Avoriaz.

Mountain restaurants are not a strong point of the area as a whole, though we no longer award a black mark in this respect. There is a remarkable concentration of attractively rustic places with sunny terraces at Les Lindarets, just north of Avoriaz, on the way down to Ardent. Other more than averagely charming places are Chez Marius (or Les Clavets) on the way down to Grand Paradis from Planachaux, and at Plaine Dranse between Avoriaz and Châtel. Last winter we had our worst-ever Alpine lunch at Passe Montagne. The Perdrix Blanche down at Pré-la-Joux is recommended – 'nice atmosphere, good value'. Pas de Chavanette, on the Swiss border, is said to be particularly expensive.

Despite PR protests to the contrary, reporters confirm our experience that Avoriaz is plagued by **queues** at the bottom of the village for lifts up to the top of the village and up to the various ski areas facing it. Skiers bound for Switzerland can avoid the queue for the seriously inadequate lift up to Chavanette by going up to Tête aux Boeufs, at the base of the Arare sector, and taking a red run down to the Chavanette drags. Queues for lifts within the Arare and Chavanette sectors may be non-trivial, too. Geneva is close, and weekend skiers add to the crowds.

We understand there is no **artificial snow** except at Morzine (see separate chapter). A large half-pipe (100m long, 15m across) has been built near the cable-car station for surfing purposes.

The resort

Avoriaz is reached from the valley either by a narrow, winding road or cable-car from Prodain, near Morzine. It is set on a long south-facing slope which steepens towards the bottom. Cars must be left in parks at the top of the slope; you have to take a horse-drawn sleigh or ratrac to get you and your luggage to your accommodation. The combined cost of covered parking and carriage (twice) can exceed £50 a week. There are also public lifts within buildings to help you get about without too much effort when you're not on skis. The busiest part of the resort is the middle section, around the foot of the nursery slopes; there are lots of bars and restaurants lining the slopes, and shops for ski gear, clothes and food. The shopping is more varied than in some modern resorts; the consensus among reporters is that the three supermarkets carry good stocks and are not overpriced. What used to be an entirely open

Facts on Avoriaz   Haute-Savoie **France**

Prices in francs

Tourist office
Postcode 74110
Tel 50740211
Fax 50741825
Tlx 385578

Getting there
By road 889km from Calais. Via Macon/Geneva; chains may be needed. Cars must be left in open or covered parks just outside the resort.
By rail Cluses (40km); bus and cable-car to resort. Thonon (45km); bus and cable-car to resort.
By air Geneva; transfer 2½hr. (Or Annecy.)

Staying there
Visitor beds 12,120; breakdown: mainly in apartments.
Package holidays Bladon Lines (hs) Brittany Ferries (s) Chalet Morzine (hcs) Chalets and Hotels "Unlimited" (cs) Club Med (h) Enterprise (hs) French Impressions (s) Horizon (hs) Hoverspeed Ski-Drive (hs) Inghams (hs) Made to Measure (hs) Neilson (hs) Ski Global (hs) Ski Party Snow World (hs) Ski West (hs) SnowRanger (s) Supertravel (c) Thomson (hs) Vacations (hs) .
Medical facilities In resort: Medical centre, dentist, chemist. Hospital: Thonon (45km).

Non-skiing activities
Indoor Health centre 'Altiform' (sauna, massage, solarium, gym, aerobics), squash, cinema.
Outdoor Sledge excursions, hang-gliding, delta planes, cleared paths, snow motorcycles, paragliding, snow-shoe walks, reindeer sleighs, helicopter flights.

Kindergartens
Annie Famose children's village
Tuition: Yes. Hours: 9.00-5.30. Ages: 3-16. Cost:

950.00 per week (with lunch). Accommodation also available for 7-16 year olds.
Les P'tits Loups
Tuition: No. Hours: 9.00-6.00. Ages: 3mth-3yr. Cost: 1,020.00 per week (with lunch). Baby-sitting also possible.

Special skiing facilities
Summer skiing No.
Cross-country 4 circuits totalling 40km, on the way into the resort, of which one km is for beginners. Instruction available.

Lift passes
Portes du Soleil pass
Covers all lifts in all 12 resorts, and shuttle buses. (70 lifts in total.)
Cost 6 days 735.00 (£75.77).
Credit cards accepted Yes.
Senior citizens 576.00 (over 60) saving 22%.
Children 482.00 (under 12) saving 34%.
Beginners Special beginners' prices on half-day and day passes for Avoriaz only (60.00 half-day, 73.00 day pass).
Short-term passes Half-day pass (from 12.00); tickets for téléphérique.
Other passes Pass covering Avoriaz lifts only (per day 120.00 for adults, 90.00 for children).

Ski school
ESF
Classes 9.30-11.30 or 10.00-12.00 am and 2.00-5.00 pm. Cost: 680.00 (6 full days).
Lift priority Yes.
Children's classes Ages: 5-12. Cost: 530.00 (6 full days).
Private lessons available Hourly or 2-hourly. Cost: 140.00 per hour. 1-3 people.
Special courses Race-training 6 days 1,030.00; one day 'discovery' tours 230.00; half-day surf and mono courses 148.00.

area beside the children's nursery slopes has been built on, rather spoiling the view from the chairs which appear outside the cafés on a sunny day. The lack of cars and the specially enclosed nursery area suits children well, but with skiers and sleighs cutting through the resort it is hardly hazard-free.

Nearly all **accommodation** is in apartments; there are a couple of hotels, too, but they're indistinguishable from the apartment blocks. Some of the apartments are now getting tatty, and reports suggest that newer buildings are the best bet. In all of them, it seems prudent to halve the number of advertised bed spaces. The Snow apartments are reportedly well placed and designed, but poorly maintained and exposed to noise from two nearby bars. Saskia 3 is 'well equipped and comfortable'. The Pierre et Vacances apartments at Falaise are 'quiet, reasonably spacious, but in need of refurbishment'; those at Alpage I have had a recent favourable report. The Sirius apartments, right at the top of the resort, have 'excellent views from south-facing balconies'.

Location in the resort is not very important for skiing purposes, although some of the village pistes are tricky for novices; but location matters more for access to shops and après-ski – if you stay right at the top it can be rather a hike back after a night out.

Après-ski is fairly lively and varied by the standards of purpose-built resorts. There are lots of bars and all are fairly crowded in the evening; reporters felt they were generally expensive. Le Choucas is recommended for 'live bands, with no entry charge'. There are several more relaxed cocktail and piano bars with even higher prices, and two discos. There are almost 30 restaurants, including pizzerias and several Asian/ Oriental ones as well those doing serious French food, and reporters generally enjoyed their eating out. A recent reporter is particularly enthusiastic about the central Bistro for 'substantial nouvelle cuisine, or pierrade'. Other recommendations include La Falaise, at the top of the resort ('service laid back but good, UK prices'), La Tanière near the top of the cable-car and L'Ortolan (lunchtime barbecues). La Mammaz, at the lower end of the resort, is a popular restaurant/ nightclub with cabaret, appealing to all ages (staff in fancy dress).

We lack informed reports on the rewards of the **cross-country** trails, but they are quite lengthy and at high altitude – beside the approach road up from Morzine – and range from green to black in difficulty. The resort cannot be recommended for **non-skiers**, although the cable-car offers an escape route to less hostile surroundings in Morzine, and thence further afield. There is not much to do apart from skiing.

At Avoriaz the **nursery slopes** run alongside the top half of the village to Le Plateau; it is an excellent area, convenient for the bars and restaurants of the village, high and sunny, and connecting with longer runs which are also gentle. We lack recent reports on the **ski school**; earlier ones were divided, with some highly complimentary comments and some quite scathing. Opinions have been divided about the **ski kindergarten**, the Annie Famose Children's Village; in principle, it seems a splendid facility, with games rooms as well as specially contrived slopes – and we have had favourable reports. But other reports suggest that there is a lack of sympathy towards children who don't like wearing ski boots all day, and perhaps towards non-French children. The non-ski kindergarten, Les Marmots, left one family very unimpressed, especially with the icy steps up to the door.

Minor resorts

Châtel France 1200m

Châtel is an old village which has been thoroughly overwhelmed by its recent development as a ski resort – though a reporter notes that cow-sheds are still allowed to occupy prime sites. It now extends for some way along the road running through towards Morgins, down the hillside and along the valley towards the Linga lift which is its connection with the skiing of Avoriaz. In the opposite direction, taking the Portes du Soleil clockwise, is Morgins, reached via Super-Châtel (1650m). This skiing service station is the heart of Châtel's own skiing, directly above the village. The valley lift departures are linked by free *navettes* (crowded at the end of the day), which have to fight their way through a village centre which at busy times is choked with cars and buses – particularly at weekends. Despite this, there is something to be said for having a car, for shopping if you are self-catering and for flexible access to the out-of-town lift stations and other resorts. There is a new covered car park. There are lots of hotels, the great majority being modest chalets offering good value – the Amethyste is 'excellent and cheap – and hundreds of private chalets and apartments to rent. There are 20 ski shops and a dozen restaurants – all buzzing when the French are in town. The Vieux Four is highly regarded and has a warm woody interior; the Fleur de Neige probably does the best food; Tick's Blues is an excellent pizzeria-grill with jazz. Le Kitchen, out of town, is recommended for raclette ('great atmosphere, log fire'). There are lively bars of various species; L'Isba is about the most popular, especially later on (with video); the Slalom is British-owned; the Godille is a plain locals' place. The cinema shows English films three times a week. A reporter claims that the discos are full of teenies. The skating rink is a 'poor little affair', but there is a modern bowling alley. Long walks and cross-country trails go up and down the valley, and there is a short loop at Super-Châtel and a floodlit 'nursery' loop close to the resort. Châtel has large nursery slopes inconveniently located outside the village, and big open easy areas up the mountain at Super-Châtel. There are two local ski schools – Portes du Soleil as well as ESF; reports suggest that the PdS is the better bet – it makes use of video. There is also the unique British Alpine Ski School, which has greatly impressed the reporters who have used it. We have had critical reports on the Marmottons ski kindergarten – a very rigid regime, to which British children (and parents) don't adapt easily.

Tourist office ✆ 50732244. Tx 385856.

Package holidays Chalets and Hotels Unlimited (hcs) Enterprise (hs) Freedom Holidays (hcas) French Impressions (hs) Made to Measure (h) Mogul Ski Holidays (hs) Ski Club of GB (c) Ski Total (js) Ski Weekend (h) SnowRanger (s) Snowline (c) Thomson (hcs) Winter Adventure Holidays (hs).

Morgins Switzerland 1350m

Morgins is a spacious residential resort spreading across its broad valley just below the low pass separating it from French Châtel. It is not the ideal base for keen skiers; most of the best Portes du Soleil skiing is elsewhere, and the Pointe de l'Au chair-lift towards Champoussin and Champéry is prone to closure by wind. A car is helpful in such circumstances. Almost all the accommodation is in chalets and apartments, and the resort is fairly quiet and relaxed, without much life or character. The broad, sunny nursery slopes, of which there are two, are 'excellent, but prone to invasion by other skiers.' There are a handful of hotels; most hotel-based reporters have stayed in the token-chalet-style Bellevue which looks over the resort from its hillside, and have generally approved – 'staff very friendly and helpful', 'comfortable room, good although unadventurous food'. There is a reasonable range of shops, two discos and a few bar-restaurants, but it is not a resort for keen après-skiers. The Crystal is said to be the new 'in' bar. There is indoor tennis and a natural ice-rink which is not reliably available; the small swimming pool at the Bellevue is open to the public. Several reporters have enjoyed the thermal baths of Val d'Illiez. The three cross-country loops amount to 15km, and there is a long marked but not prepared route to Champoussin.

Tourist office ✆ (25) 772361. Tx 456261.
Package holidays Chalets and Hotels Unlimited (hcs) Kuoni (h) Ski M & M (hrcs) Ski Morgins (hcs) Summit (hc).

Champéry Switzerland 1050m

Champéry is a pretty and rather sleepy traditional Alpine village set in attractive surroundings on the side of a valley facing the savage peaks of the Dents du Midi. The one-way main street, lined with wooden chalets, runs the length of the village, with most of the hotels, restaurants and shops along its length. But the focus of development has moved down the hill to the valley road which skirts the village. The sports centre is down here, with excellent facilities for skating, curling, swimming and bowling. So is the bottom station of the new 125-person cable-car to Planachaux – less convenient for many hotels than the old station at the end of the main street, but better able to cope with non-residents. It is served by a free minibus which does a circuit of the village. Last season the railway was extended from its original terminus at the entrance to the village to a new station right next to the cable-car.

Skiers normally return to the village via the cable-car or by skiing down to Grand Paradis, higher up the valley, and getting a bus from there; but we are told it is possible to ski to the village. Champéry's main nursery slopes are up at Planachaux, involving novices in payment for rides up the cable-car; they are also a bit on the steep side. When snow permits, children are taught on a small slope in the village – but it does not get much sun in mid-winter. The ski school (which reportedly has several native English-speakers) runs a kindergarten offering lunchtime care, and among other things advertises heli-skiing. There are cleared walks, and a short cross-country course up the valley at Grand Paradis which two recent reporters describe as 'inadequately signed and prepared, with impossible gradients'. Food shopping in the village is good – in addition to the supermarkets there are small specialist shops; there are also shops selling clothes and souvenirs as well as ski equipment (a clue to the village's summer popularity). There is not much après-ski – a couple of discos (Le Levant is 'youngish, but not too trendy') and some live music, and several bars and restaurants, none of them notable. The dozen hotels range from the fairly simple to the moderately plush.

Tourist office ✆ (25) 791141. Tx 456263.
Package holidays Chalets & Hotels Unlimited (h) Kuoni (h) Made to Measure (h) Piste Artistes (hc) Ski La Vie (hcas) Ski Scott Dunn (hcjs) Ski Total (cas) Ski Unique (h) Ski Weekend (h).

Les Crosets Switzerland 1660m

Les Crosets is a ski station in the heart of the open slopes on the Swiss side of the Portes du Soleil circuit. It is a tiny place, with a couple of hotels and a handful of restaurants, all fairly functional and with no obvious appeal – though one visitor found it 'blissful – absolutely *no* nightlife'. For sporting facilities or a bit more life, it's a two-hour walk into Champéry according to another reporter, who 'didn't see a bus all week'.

Tourist office ✆ (25) 791423.

Champoussin Switzerland 1580m

Champoussin represents more of an attempt to create a mini-resort than Les Crosets. Its new buildings, in rustic style, are almost all apartments under the skin, but most of our reporters have stayed in the main hotel, the Alpage, and have been impressed. It also has a sauna, table-tennis, a pool with a superb view of the Dents du Midi and a disco – but the resort is 'death to après-skiers'. The Alpage Ambassador apartments are highly recommended by one reporter. The ski school is recommended – 'small groups, good allocation, good English'. There is a skating rink, and a para-gliding school. The one supermarket is 'inadequate'.

Tourist office ✆ (25) 772727.
Package holidays Hoverspeed Ski-Drive (h) Ski Global (has) SnowRanger (hs) Snowline (hcas).

Morzine France 1000m

Good for *Beautiful scenery, big ski area, easy runs, short airport transfers, easy road access, cross-country skiing, not skiing, mountain restaurants, woodland runs*
Bad for *Tough runs, late holidays, resort-level snow, skiing convenience, freedom from cars*

Linked resort: Les Gets

Morzine is a long-established resort at the foot of the road up to Avoriaz, and now linked to it (and so to the main circuit of the Portes du Soleil ski area) by a series of lifts and pistes. Like La Clusaz and Megève, distant neighbours in Haute Savoie, Morzine combines the traditional all-round appeal of an old chalet-style resort (though in this case a rather towny one), a prettily wooded landscape, a very French atmosphere, family hotels in the best Gallic tradition, and a large, attractive ski area. What more could any francophile skier ask for?

In a word, altitude. This is skiing as you find it in the lower resorts of Austria, nearly all below the tree-line and with only two lifts reaching 2000m. As any Kitzbühel regular will tell you, at this height you take the rough (or rather the ice and slush) with the smooth – snow guns or no snow guns. It is when snow is in short supply, as several of our reporters have found, that nearby Avoriaz can prove invaluable (though even there the top height of the skiing is not high by French standards).

The linked resort of Les Gets is smaller, slightly higher and similarly long-established. The village has no great character (and no discernible centre) and suffers a little from through traffic over the pass around which is it spread; but it is sunny (which in January Morzine is not), spacious and architecturally unobjectionable (mainly in chalet style), and the many reporters we have heard from this year have liked its friendly village atmosphere and Frenchness. Since the resort is now beginning to attract noticeable numbers of British skiers, this last quality may not persist for long.

If you have a car you do not have to start your exploration of the main Portes du Soleil area at Avoriaz: it is a beautiful hour's drive to Châtel, and the low pass from there to Morgins in Switzerland is kept open. Flaine and the resorts of the Chamonix valley are within reach.

The skiing top 2000m bottom 975m

A gondola and a cable-car climb steeply from the edge of the village to **Le Pleney** (1500m), less of a peak than a sunny ridge, with a path/cross-country trail along it. From the lifts you look down on the less enticing sections of the direct black run down from Le Pleney, fairly steep and often scraped. There is easy skiing on the north-west side of

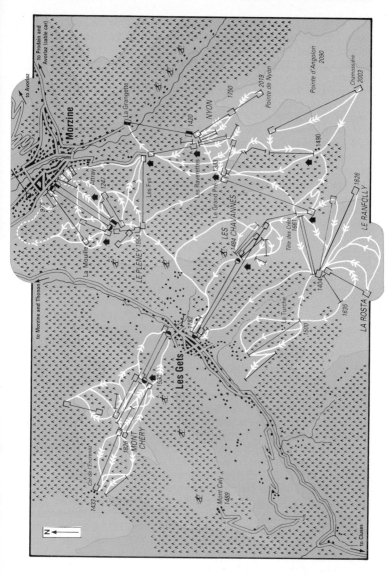

the hill, including a long blue down to the resort with snow machines
near the bottom; and on the eastern side is an attractive area of
intermediate runs, mostly red and complicated only by piste
cross-roads. From the eastern extremity of this area (Les Fys, 1150m) a
four-seater chair gives direct access to Plateau de Nyon; the Fys chair
climbs back to the top of the ridge (Belvedere), from where easy link
runs go down both wooded flanks of the ridge – south-west to the village
of Les Gets, and south-east to the junction of Le Grand Pré, where a

chair-lift and a drag link with Nyon and a long chair (Charniaz) climbing gently and very prettily to the Tête des Crêts. This lift is the usual access route to the Les Gets ski area, and the runs beneath it – a red which is mostly a schuss, then a green along a road – are the only ways back to Morzine.

Plateau de Nyon can be reached by cable-car from outside Morzine. Its main appeal is to good skiers: the Pointe and Chamossière chair-lifts reach the high points of the system and serve its most challenging skiing – shadowy north-facing coombs beneath the beautiful sharp peaks which dominate Morzine's ski area and keep the early sun off much of it. Of the two black runs, Aigle (from the Pointe) is narrower and steeper. The wide bowl below the Chamossière lift offers more space for skiing off-piste; extremists sometimes tackle the steep slopes between the two lifts (Nant Golon). Behind Chamossière, a splendid sunny red also has some good off-piste variations before following a summer road through the woods to Le Grand Pré. From the Plateau de Nyon you can ski down either to the bottom of the cable-car or, via a flimsy-looking but well protected bridge over a gaping river gorge, directly back to Morzine – apparently 11.5km from Chamossière.

The Tête des Crêts (1660m) is near the top of the north-facing half of Les Gets' skiing. This is gentle and pleasantly pastoral, with long easy runs over lightly wooded slopes to the resort, passing through **Les Chavannes** – a cluster of restaurant and hotel buildings with an area of nursery slopes, paths and cross-country trails (linking up with Le Pleney), accessible by road as well as by lift from Les Gets. Only one of the Les Chavannes drags climbs to Tête des Crêts, for access not only to Morzine but also to a broad upper bowl where a fan of six lifts offers a variety of short intermediate runs and one moderate black. The direct blue run to Les Gets from here is not obvious; the piste down the La Turche drag to the edge of the village is an equally gentle alternative.

The south-facing skiing of Les Gets is on **Mont Chéry**, reached by a six-seater gondola, its bottom station a short walk across road and resort from the Les Chavannes lifts and runs. Good snow on the lower runs (red and black) must be short-lived. The black has some steep moguls just below the mid-station, distinctly tricky on a cold morning. The top half of the mountain has easier open skiing (the black is not all difficult above mid-station), with magnificent views of the Mont Blanc massif to the south. The fairly steep open slope behind Mont Chéry has good black and red runs of about 400m vertical down to the Col de l'Encrenaz, quite deserted when we came upon them, and well worth the journey from Morzine. Alone on the dark north side of the mountain, Bouquetin is a short sharp run which tempts even fewer skiers. The bowl at the top is genuinely steep.

Mountain restaurants are in most of the obvious places, mostly reasonably attractive and reasonably priced. The little restaurant at the foot of the Attray chair-lift is particularly welcoming and well adapted for all conditions, with a warming stove inside and a sun terrace. We have had very enthusiastic reports on the Soleray at the top of Mont Chéry, both for food and atmosphere, and on the Griffon at Les Chavannes.

In the past we have found **queues** for the Avoriaz cable-car at Les

Prodains and crowds on the buses from (and especially to) Morzine at peak times, particularly when snow is poor. But to judge by recent reports the ski-lifts up to Avoriaz – a long series of lifts starting at the bottom of Morzine near the sports centre – have solved the problem. The only report we have of queues in Morzine's own ski area concerns short but inescapable waits for the lifts around the summit of the Pleney area.

There is a fair-sized **artificial snow** installation, covering runs to the valley from Le Pleney and Nyon.

The resort

Morzine is a confusing town covering a large area on both sides of a river gorge and on several levels. It is a thoroughfare with a significant traffic problem, but a high foot-bridge over the river makes getting around less tortuous for pedestrians than motorists. A single congested shopping street climbs from the old village centre beside the river to the more open ground where the resort has developed, with hotels and shops around the tourist office at the foot of Le Pleney. There is a bus service around the western side of the resort, and also several buses a day to Les Gets (not covered by the lift pass), Avoriaz and the Avoriaz cable-car at Les Prodains.

Accommodation consists of chalets and some 70 hotels, widely scattered around the resort and varying in convenience from very to not at all. Most of the hotels are chalet-style buildings, none is luxurious and many are simple and inexpensive. In the central area around the tourist office, the big Airelles is one of the more comfortable (pool and sauna) though less personal hotels. The Tremplin is also comfortable, and right at the foot of the slopes. The very attractive Chamois d'Or, also well placed, is smaller, cheaper and very friendly. The Dahu is out of the way, but highly recommended: comfortable, quiet, welcoming, sunny and panoramic, with good food – 'the best hotel we have ever stayed at', says a report. A second-time visitor to the Fleur de Neige confirms her liking for its 'friendly family atmosphere and good food'.

The resort's **après-ski** lacks the glitter of Megève, its most direct competitor, but there is no shortage of bars, tea-rooms, restaurants or discos, or of British companions. La Chamade is a 'renowned and pricey' restaurant. Young people crowd into the Wallington – bowling alley, pool hall, bar and video disco. Le Pacha is popular disco, described by a reporter as 'somewhat naughty'.

There is plenty for **non-skiers**: a good sports centre with ice rinks, enormous scope for walking and riding in beautiful surroundings (both in the ski area and away from it in quiet valleys), and sleigh rides.

There are very extensive **cross-country** trails in several different sectors served by morning and afternoon buses. The beautiful Vallée de la Manche has varied runs along the valley floor and long itineraries for experts. The Supermorzine trails are higher and sunnier than others. Access to the trails between Le Pleney and Les Chavannes (above Les Gets) is by cable-car; there is a 7km itinerary for the return via the old

Facts on Morzine Haute-Savoie **France**

Prices in francs

Tourist office

Postcode 74110
Tel 50790345
Fax 50790348
Tlx 385620

Getting there

By road 881km from Calais. Via Macon/Geneva; chains may be needed.
By rail Cluses or Thonon (30km). Bus connections to resort.
By air Geneva; transfer 1½hr. (Or Lyon Airport (200 km).)

Staying there

Visitor beds 16,000; breakdown: 4,000 in hotels, 12,000 in apartments and chalets.
Package holidays Chalet Morzine (hcs) Chalets and Hotels "Unlimited" (hcj) Enterprise (h) French Impressions (hs) Hoverspeed Ski-Drive (h) Kings Ski Club (js) Made to Measure (hcs) Neilson (h) Quest Total Ski (h) Ski Chamois (j) Ski Esprit (cj) Ski Global (hs) Ski Jeannie (hcjas) Ski Red Guide (hcs) Ski Tips (hcj) Ski Valkyrie (hs) Ski Weekend (hcs) SnowRanger (s) Tracer Holidays (cj) White Roc Ski (hc) .
Medical facilities In resort: Doctor, dentist, chemist. Hospital: Cluses and Thonon (30km).

Non-skiing activities

Indoor Skating, curling, bowling, cinemas, sauna, massage, gym, table tennis.
Outdoor Horse-riding, sleigh rides, paragliding.

Kindergartens

Outa crèche
Tuition: Yes, from 4. Hours: 8.30-6.00. Ages: 2mth-6.00. Cost: 750.00 per week (meals extra 30.00). Lessons taken with ESF.
Leisure Centre
Tuition: Yes. Hours: 8.30-6.00. Ages: 2-12. Cost: 800.00 per week (meals extra 35.00).

Special skiing facilities

Summer skiing No.
Cross-country 6km beside river in resort centre, easy; 25km in Vallée de la Manche, all grades; 30km Super-Morzine/Avoriaz, all grades; 10km around Lac de Montriond, easy; 8.5km Le Plénay/Les Chavannes, easy/moderate.

Lift passes

Portes du Soleil pass
Covers all lifts in all 12 resorts, and shuttle buses. (70 lifts in total.)
Cost 6 days 735.00 (£75.77).
Credit cards accepted Yes.
Children 482.00 (under 12) saving 34%. Free pass up to age 3.
Notes Discounts for large groups.
Beginners Limited area pass.
Short-term passes Half-day pass for Plénay/Nyon/Les Gets lifts (from 12.00).
Other passes Plénay/Nyon/Les Gets pass covers all lifts in vicinity of Morzine and Les Gets (6 days 550.00 for adults, 413.00 for children); Sports Pass (6 days of ski lifts Portes du Soleil, Carte Niege, 6 lessons, ice skating costs 1,170.00 for adults, 870.00 for children).

Ski school

ESF Morzine
Classes 5hr: 2½hr am and pm (Sat am only). Cost: 660.00 (5½ days).
Lift priority Yes.
Children's classes Ages: Under 12. Cost: 540.00 (5½ days).
Private lessons available Per hour. Cost: 135.00 per hour.
Special courses 'Multiski' and competition courses.

What was new in 91

New two-star hotel in town centre, the Frond Neige.

What is new for 92

Not known.

hamlet of Les Nants, where a farm offers tastings of Savoyard produce.

The village **nursery slopes** are at the foot of Le Pleney, with plenty of bars and restaurants close at hand, and a slalom practice slope for precocious beginners. Although wide and gentle, the area suffers from through-traffic. Nyon has a higher area accessible by cable-car.

Ski school usually meets at the foot of Le Pleney. We lack recent reports, but in the past there have been some problems. The kindergarten L'Outa is 'excellent – plenty of facilities and entertainments'.

Les Gets 1175m

Les Gets is strung out along a low pass 6km from Morzine, with lifts and pistes on both sides, and good nursery slopes on the edge of the village and at Les Chavannes (1490m), reached by road or gondola. There is a

large and under-used floodlit piste. Large parts of the ski area, and many of the restaurants within it, are accessible on foot: there are 50km of walks on minor roads and cleared paths, and 25km of cross-country trails around the half-way stations on both sides of the resort. There is a bus service to Morzine for access to Avoriaz, but it starts late in the morning and is not frequent. Les Gets has three ski schools (on which reports have been generally favourable – Ski Plus specialises in 'excellent private tuition, in good English'), various kindergartens (the Ski Espace one – 'lots of fun games', 'well organised' – gets better reports than the ESF ski kindergarten), a pool in the hotel Marmottes, a new open-air artificial ice-rink in the centre of the resort, a circuit for motor tricycles, a mechanical museum, and tourist 'train', two cinemas, three discos, and bars and restaurants in most of the hotels. There are about 20 of these, mostly simple and nearly all attractive-looking chalet buildings. The Régina is in the middle of the price range, and well placed on the quieter of the main streets. We have good reports of the hotel L'Ours Blanc ('central and excellent'). Reporters have mainly stayed in catered chalets and self-catering apartments, and have generally been well satisfied; the Soleil and La Bouillandire apartments are recommended. Recommended restaurants include Le Tyrol ('good pizzas, friendly, not expensive'), the Magnetic ('one of the best, with prices to match'), and Le Gallichou ('excellent cider and crêpes'). The English-run Pring's and the piano bar in the Régina are lively at night.
Tourist office ✆ 50797555. Tx 385026.
Package holidays Enterprise (hs) French Impressions (hs) Made to Measure (s) Ski Chamois (s) Ski M & M (hcas) Ski Total (hcjs) Ski-Tal (cs) Supersports Ski Chalets (cjs) Tracer Holidays (cj).

Massif face-lift

Flaine France 1600m

Good for *Family holidays, nursery slopes, big ski area, skiing convenience, lift queues, short airport transfers, freedom from cars, late holidays, easy runs, resort-level snow*
Bad for *Alpine charm, not skiing, mountain restaurants, après-ski, woodland runs*

Linked resorts: Les Carroz, Morillon, Samoëns

Le Grand Massif is a loosely linked ski area spread over what is indeed a large, although not outstandingly high, group of mountains. At its heart is Flaine, a modern resort created by Eric Boissonnas, who discovered the bowl in which it lies on an exploratory ski-tour in 1959. The resort he built – like most other French resorts of its generation – was entirely functional, providing convenient and affordable access to high-altitude skiing with no regard for appearance and very little for the other qualities that give traditional resorts a much broader appeal. The Boissonnas family have recently sold the resort, and the new owners – again, conforming to a pattern recognisable elsewhere in the French Alps – have plans to 'smarten up' Flaine, and give it a more upmarket image. They are already putting some of their ambitious projects into practice.

Flaine's virtues are as clear-cut as its vices, and obviously more important to those who go there. It is ideal for what the tourist office calls careless skiing: hardly any foot-slogging, hardly any cars, excellent nursery slopes and facilities, a wide range of intermediate runs, reliable snow, not much queuing. Add very short transfers from Geneva airport, and the resort's popularity with British families is explained. It is also becoming increasingly popular with other groups; BASI have used Flaine for their training weeks, the 'Over the Hill' club find it an ideal place for the over forties, and the budget-conscious are drawn by the self-catering facilities.

The skiing within Flaine's high bowl links with that of three other villages outside it – Samoëns, Morillon and Les Carroz. These areas extend Flaine's skiing greatly, and add otherwise missing ingredients – long runs through a wooded, inhabited landscape. Unfortunately, the exposed link lifts are often closed in bad weather or poor snow, when these sheltered slopes are at their most appealing. For skiers who don't appreciate the uncompromising modernity of Flaine, the lower village of Les Carroz provides an attractive alternative base (especially for cross-country skiers). It is a sharp contrast to Flaine – inconveniently arranged on the road up, in a beautiful setting. Samoëns and Morillon are valley communities. Morillon has a few hotels, and at the top of the first lift out of the village a new resort has been taking shape since 1986 – Morillon-Grand-Massif, where eventually 5,000 skiers will be accommodated behind 'omnipresent wooden façades'.

The climb up from the valley to Flaine is a slow, tortuous 30km, and often snowy beyond Les Carroz. Cars are banished to become snow-drifts in peripheral car parks and useful only for day-trips to other resorts (Morzine/Avoriaz and Chamonix/Argentière, for example).

The skiing top 2480m bottom 690m

The Grand Massif skiing divides into several sectors, each linked to the next at only one or two points. Most of **Flaine's** skiing is spread around the north-facing half of the basin in which the resort lies, with several lifts climbing to different points around the rim at nearly 2500m, giving a vertical range of some 900m. Most of the skiing is above the tree-line. The main lift is a massive gondola to **Grandes Platières**, a broad, high plateau, flat enough for walking and cross-country, too flat for lazy downhill skiers. This top section gives you plenty of time to admire the magnificent spikes, glaciers and domes of Mont Blanc. From here a large number of intersecting runs go down to the resort, most of them easy red or stiff blue. For timid skiers there are less direct, open blue runs on the sunny west-facing slopes of the bowl – great for confidence-building. They are served by a series of drag and chair-lifts (whose capacity is to be increased next season). The most difficult descents are in the middle of the bowl, where the terrain is very fragmented and off-piste skiing unwise unless you know the area – exploration in search of virgin snow may end abruptly at the brink of a cliff or a pot-hole. Tricky sections in the middle of otherwise uncomplicated runs explain the gradings – black under the gondola and red either side. The black Diamond Noir attracts bump freaks and provides good entertainment for the skiers in the lift above. A new and exciting skiing area down the back of the bowl towards Charbonnière is planned, but will have to overcome almighty planning problems. For those in search of good off-piste skiing, there is an interesting area in the Combe de Gers, reached with some difficulty from Grandes Platières. It is a steep, deep coomb, prone to avalanche; the long drag that serves it opens late in the season, and closes early in the afternoon. The much shorter Véret lift serves a similar, fairly steep, often dangerous bowl, reached from the Grands Vans chair. The blue Serpentine run from the top of Grands Vans to Le Fôret was vastly improved last season to hold the snow better.

The **Aujon** skiing on the east-facing slopes of the bowl is reached by gondola from the resort or a run down from Grandes Platières. It is an interesting area of straightforward intermediate runs above and below the tree line, with a bumps course, and several competition pistes descending to the valley. A chair-lift takes you up to the highest point – Tête des Lindars (2561m) – from where a red run round the shoulder or a more direct black down the face provide more challenging skiing. One reporter warns of the particularly vicious drag-lift in Aujon which propels its passengers off the ground.

The rest of the Grand Massif skiing is reached via the valley of the Lac de Vernant, often crowded with commuting skiers. The Tête du Pré des Saix on the far side is the central point of the whole Grand Massif

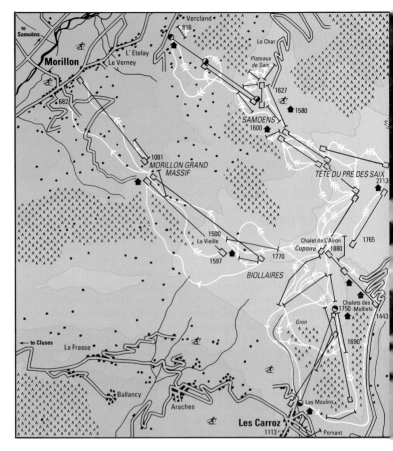

system. North-facing runs descend steeply down towards **Samoëns** far below. The top section offers some of the best, albeit short, tough runs in the area (bumpy piste and off-piste). The descent is interrupted by the Plateau des Saix, where lifts go up the short rise to an outpost of Samoëns, called Samoëns 1600. Then there's a further 800m vertical down to the outskirts of Samoëns itself; the steeper black option is a splendid sweeping course through the woods, but is soon scraped bare. On the other side of a wide valley, the pistes towards **Morillon** run in parallel: long, gentle, woodland trails – less varied than the piste map suggests – punctuated by clearings with restaurants. The lift up from Morillon-Villages to Morillon-Grand-Massif is an efficient new gondola, not yet shown on our map. The runs down to **Les Carroz** are shorter than those to the other low villages, but offer a broader network and greater variety of trails (mainly below the tree-line), with distinctly blackish sections at the top of some of the red runs, and some good off-piste slopes. There are gentle runs around the top of the gondola, but the blue run to the village is often in poor condition and crowded.

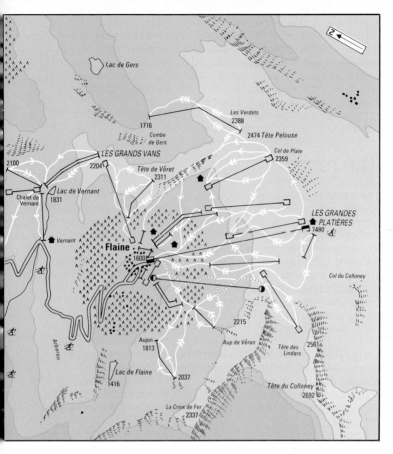

Flaine's **mountain restaurants** are few and far between, especially in the Aujon area. The restaurant at the top of the cable-car serves as one of the most spectacular sunbathing and picnic spots in the Alps – some reports suggest that the service does not match the view. We've had positive reports of the Cascade restaurant above the village and of several other attractive places on the runs down to the village on the Platières side including Le Blanchot ('delicious soup, sunny terrace') and Le Bissac ('quick, excellent food and generous helpings, often crowded'), though many people return to their hotels for lunch. One reporter recommends the Igloo at Morillon 'on sunny days' and several others suggest the l'Oréade restaurant at the top of the Samoëns gondola for 'good value and a splendid terrace'. Pick of the mountain restaurants according to one reporter is the Chariande near Samoëns 1600 – 'delightful location, reasonable prices, filling food'.

Since the installation of the Grand Platières gondola, we have had very few complaints about **queues**. The Grands Vans and Lac de Vernant drag-lifts are reportedly bottle-necks at peak times. Piste signing is adequate, and several reporters have remarked on the efficient piste grooming. Most reporters agree that piste gradings are generally reliable, though some easy runs have difficult sections. The local Flaine pass may be a better buy if bad weather or poor snow looks likely to limit your use of the Grand Massif area, though the difference in price is not great. Beginners should not buy any pass in advance, as they may not progress beyond the free nursery lifts.

Flaine has **artificial snow** on one long piste beneath the Aujon gondola, and one shorter one to the south of it.

The resort

The access road to Flaine winds up the mountain through the villages of Arâches and Les Carroz to the rim of a wide natural bowl – and your first glimpse of the resort, a collection of early 1970s blocks on one side of the bowl, a couple of hundred metres below. The resort is built on two levels; Flaine Forum (the main square on the lower level) is the heart of the resort, with most of the bars, restaurants, shops and hotels; Flaine Forêt (on a shelf above it) is the self-catering ghetto, with its own supply of shops and cafés, and the famous auditorium where Flaine holds a huge music festival in the summer months. Two free shuttle lifts, the 'red devils', go backwards and forwards between the two levels, day and night. Cars are supposedly left outside the village except when unloading luggage, but two recent reports suggest that the rule is not being as strictly maintained as it used to be and that a large number of cars are being left outside apartments all week. The resort is so compact that you can get to everywhere on foot. There is a new under-used bus service connecting Le Hameau with the ski slopes via Fôret, saving people staying at the far end of Fôret a ten-minute hike to the slopes.

Throughout the village you come across modern art; in the streets, in the hotels and apartments and in the galleries. Over the years, Flaine's original owners, Eric and Sylvie Boissonnas, have collected many avant-garde works – both famous and unknown. The Forum is dominated by Dubuffet's polystyrene 'Trees' and Vaserly's 'Hexagons', the auditorium has a spectacular Bury fountain, and hopefully Picasso's Totem will soon stand outside the hotel of the same name.

Flaine's **accommodation** is in either hotels (mostly in Forum) or self-catering flats (mostly in Forêt). A new development of smart 'Scandinavian' chalets – Hameau de Flaine – has been built west of the resort, overlooking the Lac de Flaine. It will eventually be linked by lifts to the main skiing area. We have favourable reports of all the central hotels, especially Les Lindars ('unbeatable family hotel with superb facilities for children'), and the Totem, which has recently incorporated its neighbour, the Gradins Gris, and has been satisfactorily upgraded. Reporters have commented on the high standard of the nouvelle cuisine. The two-star Aujon has 'small but adequate rooms, exceptional brunches, tasty four-course dinners (no choice)'. On the upper level, most of our reporters have stayed in the massive Residence de la Forêt (ask for a south-facing apartment). There are no signs of the proposed refurbishments to the apartments and dining-room that were supposed to take place last season. Just up the road is a brand new block of apartments, Residence du Grand Massif, under the same management as the Residence de la Forêt; much thought has gone into creating 'perfect apartments', and they are spacious and comfortable, with American-style conveniences such as microwaves and infra-red ovens.

Facts on Flaine Haute-Savoie **France**

Prices in francs
Ski Club represented

Tourist office
Postcode 74300
Tel 50908001
Fax 50908626
Tlx 385662
This resort is represented in Britain by Erna Low Consultants Ltd, 9 Reece Mews, London, SW7 3HE. Tel 071-584 2841

Getting there
By road 877km from Calais. Via Macon/Geneva, autoroute blanche; chains often needed.
By rail Cluses (30km); 2 buses daily (Alpbus).
By air Geneva; transfer 2hr. (Or Lyon.)

Staying there
Visitor beds 9,000; breakdown: mainly apartments.
Package holidays Bladon Lines (hs) Chalets and Hotels "Unlimited" (hcs) Enterprise (hs) Falcon (hs) Horizon (hs) Hoverspeed Ski-Drive (hs) Inghams (hs) Made to Measure (hs) Neilson (hs) Over the Hill (h) Ski Alternatives (h) Ski Club of GB (h) Ski Global (hs) Ski Red Guide (hs) Ski Valkyrie (hs) Ski West (hs) Thomson (hs) .
Medical facilities In resort: Doctor, chemist. Hospital: Sallanches (40km). Dentist: Cluses (30km).

Non-skiing activities
Indoor Top Form centre (swimming pool complex with sauna, solarium, gymnasium, massage), arts/crafts gallery, cinema, auditorium.
Outdoor Ice-rink, snow-shoe excursions, hang-gliding, paraskiing, helicopter rides, snowmobiles, snow scooters, high mountain outings, ice-driving car circuit, ATC motorbikes (In spring).

Kindergartens
ESF Rabbit Club
Tuition: Yes with Fantaski. Hours: 9.00-5.30. Ages: 7-12. Cost: 700.00 per week (with meals).
SEI Ski Junior
Tuition: Yes, 1 to 2 hr sessions. Hours: 9.00-5.00. Ages: 3-12. Cost: 890.00 per week (with meals).
Flaine Junior
Tuition: Yes, 2 to 4 hr with ESF or SEI. Hours: Full day; evening baby-sitting service 7.00-11.00. Ages: 2-7; nursery for under 2. Cost: 890.00 per week (but cost depends on age and whether resident; meals included in price). Based at Hotel Les Lindars; residents get priority.

Special skiing facilities
Summer skiing No.
Cross-country 700m loop on La Cascade Plateau; 8km off-piste trail at Grandes Platières (gondola up from Flaine); 8km of trails at Vernant and Col de Pierre Carrée (bus from Flaine). Longer trails near Les Carroz. Instruction available.

Lift passes
Grand Massif
Covers all the lifts in Flaine, Les Carroz, Morillon, Samoens and Sixt. (81 lifts in total.)
Cost 6 days 665.00 (£68.56). Low season: 565.00 saving 15%.
Credit cards accepted Yes.
Senior citizens 540.00 (over 65) saving 19%.
Children 540.00 (under 12) saving 19%.
Beginners Five free lifts. Ski pass for beginners covers the Poma and Petit Balacha lifts.
Short-term passes Half-day (from 12.00pm).
Other passes Flaine area only (6 days 600.00 for adults, 475.00 for children); Flaine pass can be extended one day to cover Grand Massif lifts.

Ski school
ESF
Classes 2hr am or pm. Cost: 370.00 (6 half-days).
Lift priority Yes.
Children's classes Ages: 12. Cost: 290.00 (6 half-days).
Private lessons available Hourly. Cost: 150.00 per hour for 1-2 people, 370.00 for 3-4 people.
Special courses Race-training; 6 days with 2 tests 990.00.
Ski Ecole International
Classes 9.30-11.30 and 2.30-4.30. Cost: 540.00 (6 days, Sun or Mon to Fri).
Lift priority Yes.
Children's classes Ages: 12. Cost: 400.00 (6 days, Sun or Mon to Fri).
Private lessons available Hourly. Cost: 140.00 per hour. 1-2 people.
Special courses Surf and mono courses; day-trips round Grand Massif area.
Flaine Super Ski
Classes 9.15-12.00 and 2.00-4.30. Cost: 1,620.00 (6 days, Mon-Sat). Price includes lift pass; advanced skiers only.
Lift priority Yes.
Children's classes Ages: 8-15. Cost: 1,620.00 (6 days, Mon-Sat).
Special courses On request.

There is a new shopping complex opposite, with food shops, boutiques, and restaurants.

Après-ski is notably expensive, and not very extensive (though 'just about enough for a week's holiday' according to two reporters). The liveliest night-spot is the very British White Grouse Pub, with its darts, bitter and sports videos. There are two discos, of which the pricey Shelby seems the more popular. Most visitors confine themselves to hotel bars and restaurants. Recommendations include Eve's Pub (for 'ice-creams and pop videos' after skiing), Chez Daniel (for 'authentic French atmosphere and excellent pierrade'), and the rustic Les Chalets du Michet – one of the few original buildings in the valley, converted from a cow shed to an excellent fondue/raclette restaurant. On the upper level of the resort, reporters recommend the Perdrix Noir ('undoubtedly the best restaurant in Flaine'). The Diamont-Noir Chinese restaurant has been replaced by the Aquarium, serving fondues. There are torchlit descents from Le Blanchot every Thursday.

Flaine is far from ideal for **non-skiers**, but more effort is being made to accommodate them; there is a swimming pool complex in Forum (open only from 4.00pm), and a cinema and auditorium (jazz and classical concerts) in Fôret. One reporter found a good library with English books and an interesting video of Flaine's construction. Several reporters recommend skidoo rides and ice-motorbikes ('for keeping the kids quiet for ten minutes'). Towards the end of the season, the ice-rink is turned into a volleyball court. For **cross-country** skiing you have to be prepared to take buses or lifts to the trails, which is hardly ideal; Les Carroz is a much more suitable base.

The **nursery slopes** are excellent – spacious and absolutely central, ranging from the gentle to the flat, and served by several free lifts; but the slopes and lifts are used by lots of other skiers on their way to and from the main runs.

We have had predominantly favourable reports on both of the main **ski schools**. The Ski Ecole Internationale (started here 15 years ago to shake up the ESF) aims to offer smaller classes and better spoken English, but the Ecole du Ski Français now enjoys an equal reputation and most instructors speak some English. There is another school, Flaine Super Ski, for advanced skiers and race-training, and a surf school called Black Slide. The children's classes and **ski kindergarten** have been described as 'excellent', although class-sizes are 'far from ideal in high season'. Two reporters have commented on the helpful, caring attitude of the lift operators towards small children. The non-ski kindergarten at the hotel Les Lindars (open to non-residents) has also impressed – 'our children seemed very happy under the supervision of two English nannies'. The hotel provides a children's dining-room and meals, and an evening baby-sitting service. Children's' facilities around the resort, such as swings and slides in the Forum and Children's' films at the cinema, have impressed reporting parents.

Les Carroz 1160m

Last outpost of civilisation on the road to Flaine, Les Carroz is an attractive, spacious village, spread broadly across a sunny, sloping shelf. It attracts lots of families and weekend day-trippers whose cars strangle the resort. The gondola and chair-lift are a steep walk above the centre of the village, but within easy reach of some attractive, simple old hotels such as the Airelles and the charming Croix de Savoie. The Belles Pistes has been recently taken over by an English couple and totally refurbished. Rooms are reportedly clean, comfortable and reasonably priced; all have en-suite bathrooms. The Front de Neige, a long walk up from the village, is said to cope well with children. Most of the self-catering accommodation is much less conveniently placed. Cross-country skiing is very good; the trails (64km) are not immediately by the village – the ski-bus serves them as well as the lift station. The bus is not included on the lift pass and there are only three services a day to Flaine. Reporters have had problems getting taxis back to Les Carroz after about 10.00pm.

Les Carroz is quiet in the evenings except during school holidays – there are several friendly bars (Musketeers has a good choice of beers), tea-time cafés and cosy restaurants, and a couple of discos, one fronted by a red London bus. Non-skiing activities include parapenting, hang-gliding and, towards the end of the season, horse-riding and mountain biking in the beautiful surrounding countryside. We have had favourable reports of the three ski schools, particularly Skinori which offers private lessons 'almost as cheaply as group tuition' and caters well for youngsters. There is a baby club (La souris verte) in the town.
Tourist office ✆ 50900004. Tx 385281.
Package holidays Brittany Ferries (s) Enterprise (hs) Quest Total Ski (h) Ski-Tal (hcas).

Samoëns 720m

The beautiful old town of Samoëns in the Giffre Valley is the only ski resort in France to be listed as a historical site. It was once a thriving stone-cutting centre and twice a week the tourist office organises guided tours around the town's architectural sites. In the centre of town is a botanical alpine garden with over 4,000 species of mountain plants from all around the world. There are plenty of traditional-style bars and restaurants; food is typically Savoyard. The resort is virtually unknown on the British market and a recent reporter was delighted to discover this truly French enclave with its 'charming and friendly inhabitants'. She recommends the central 7 Monts hotel. Another reporter suggests the Drugeres whose owner is 'a perfect host'; food is excellent.

Samoëns is connected to the Grand Massif ski area by a gondola which climbs from the hamlet of Vercland to Samoëns 1600. Regular free ski-buses connect the main town with Vercland. The runs back down are north-facing and retain good snow but are not easy. Samoëns has a ski school and ski kindergarten, and a cross-country school. There are easy and intermediate trails just north of the town and around Samoëns 1600, and more extensive routes higher up the Giffre valley at the tiny resort of Sixt.
Tourist office ✆ 50344028. Fax 50349582. Tx 384924.
Package holidays Quest Total Ski (h) Quest Travel (schools) (h) SnowRanger (s)

La Clusaz France 1100m

Good for *Cross-country skiing, easy road access, short airport transfers, beautiful scenery, mountain restaurants, woodland runs*
Bad for *Skiing convenience, late holidays, freedom from cars, resort-level snow*

La Clusaz is a large, long-established summer and winter resort just up the road from Annecy – in style, as in location, mid-way between the small, old-fashioned family resorts of the Mont Blanc area and the big, modern sporty ones of the Tarentaise. The layout of the resort is messy and inconvenient, but its atmosphere is very French and unfussy and, for a resort that only recently attracted the attention of the international package industry, it has a lot of skiing. Much of the skiing is below 2000m and consists of broad runs through woodland, but there is also some high, open skiing with good off-piste runs – making it a flexible resort, capable of amusing most categories of skier in most weather conditions. Its all-round appeal is like that of nearby Megève, but with a difference of emphasis: La Clusaz is less self-consciously fashionable and its skiing is less extensive but more challenging, more varied and slightly less inconveniently arranged. The village fills up with local youth at weekends and holiday times, when it is very lively; out of season it is quiet – too quiet for some, but pleasantly relaxing for others.

The only resort within practical reach for day trips is Le Grand-Bornand, where La Clusaz skiers can ski for one day a week. A car does not offer much advantage, though it would allow determined explorers to venture further afield – over the snowy Col des Aravis to Megève. Having a car in the resort is handy – very handy when poor snow interferes with links between areas.

The skiing top 2490m bottom 1100m

La Clusaz now gives access to five more-or-less distinct ski areas, spread round the sides of several valleys and facing north, east and west. Two – Beauregard and L'Aiguille – are reached by lifts from the resort centre, the other three from points along the valleys. Despite roads and rivers, all five areas are linked by lift or piste – though some of the links are long green pistes involving some walking, and another is a cross-valley cable-car shuttle.

Beauregard, served by a single cable-car from the bottom of the resort, is a flat-topped wooded mountain with very attractive easy skiing in pastoral surroundings at the top (1650m) – good for beginners, walkers and cross-country skiers – and a couple of longer runs back down to the resort. The black starts gently but becomes genuinely steep, with an awkward link between two pitches, the first a short but

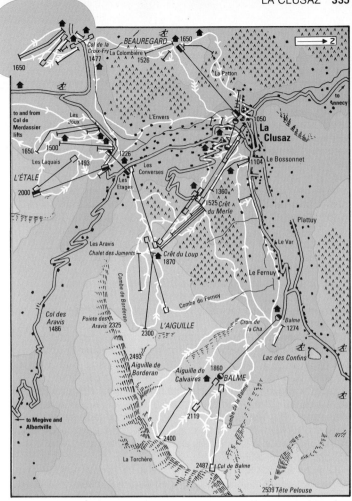

impressive mogul-field of nearly 35˚. The blue on the other side of the cable-car is a splendid varied run, not all of it easy. The green run round the mountain is very gentle for most of its length.

A chair-lift beside the run down from Beauregard to the foot of L'Etale has created a link with the enjoyable area of short, gentle woodland runs spread over a knoll between the cols of **La Croix-Fry** and **Merdassier**. The most westerly runs at La Croix-Fry, including a red which is not at all steep but fairly narrow, face almost north and are shaded by trees, and so keep their snow well. There are some steeper and more open runs on the other side of Merdassier (off our map), and a very gentle run across to L'Etale providing the return link. Apart from the attraction of the extra skiing, the area is well provided with restaurants beside the two cols.

L'Etale, like Beauregard, is mainly served by a single cable-car from bottom (1250m) to top (1960m). Skiing is limited to one flank of the mountain (facing north-west), open and fairly steep at the top, with several drag-lifts serving the gentler and more spacious slopes at the bottom, and giving access to an easy run across to Merdassier. From the bottom station, the Transval cable-car shuttles skiers to and from the Aiguille area.

L'Aiguille is the largest area, directly accessible from the village by efficient chair- and drag-lifts. There are several sections. The Crêt du Merle is a half-way station with a small nursery area, ski school assembly point and restaurants. None of the several ways back down to the village is particularly difficult. Above Crêt du Merle there is a fairly stiff red run from Crêt du Loup, with plenty of room for a gentler course to be taken. The west-facing run from Crêt du Loup to the valley is marked blue, but is long (over 600m vertical) and in places fairly steep. In deep snow, off-piste skiers can have fun under the chairs. The bowl above Crêt du Loup is mostly fairly gentle, but the lifts give access to some interesting off-piste skiing – the Combe de Borderan and the Combe du Fernuy, the first of about a dozen long, steep gullies in the wall of the Chaîne des Aravis.

The north-west-facing **Balme** and Torchère slopes provide La Clusaz's highest and most challenging pistes, with fine, long runs down two more of the Aravis coombs giving skiing of over 1200m vertical. The main black run is steep enough to serve as a speed-skiing course. There are moderate reds from both top stations (one is very poorly marked) and a long blue down from the top of the Bergerie chair-lift. Two green runs go back to the resort; the lower one, from the bottom of the gondola, is reportedly 'mostly uphill – an absolute disgrace'.

Except in the Balme area, **mountain restaurants** are plentiful, attractively old-fashioned and inexpensive (especially at La Croix-Fry/ Merdassier). The Vieux Ferme at Merdassier is reportedly 'excellent value and very charming'. The Vieux Chalet beside the piste and road at the top of the Patinoire gondola is expensive and very good. The Crêt du Loup is recommended.

Queues are long for the Beauregard cable-car at peak times, but not bad elsewhere – though there is a pronounced and problematic influx of local weekenders when conditions are good. Access to Balme has been much improved by the recently built stand-up gondola. There is no **artificial snow**. The relatively high Balme area keeps its snow better than the other sectors.

The resort

The setting of La Clusaz is a rather enclosed one beside a river at the meeting point of several steep-sided wooded valleys. The village has grown and no longer fits comfortably into its narrow slot, and the sprawl of buildings along the valley and up its sides is complicated by a series of road junctions and roundabouts; it is a somewhat confusing and traffic-ridden place, especially at weekends, when parking can be a problem (though there is an underground car park). Downtown La

Clusaz, or La Clusaz Sud as it is signposted, is pleasantly traditional, built around a large bulbous-towered church, with a stylish modern shopping precinct beside it and a fast-flowing stream below. Shopping is attractively varied, and there are the very ordinary cafés you find in every French village but in few French ski resorts. A daytime bus service (covered by the lift pass) links the various ski areas with the resort centre. The service has not impressed most reporters, who variously found it unreliable, insufficiently frequent, overcrowded and over-complex.

La Clusaz is very much a weekend resort for inhabitants of Annecy and Geneva, and most of the **accommodation** is in private chalets dotted around the hillsides, many of which are available for rent. If you don't have a car, make sure your chalet is near a bus stop. In the centre of the resort there are lots of simple, reasonably priced hotels. The

Facts on La Clusaz   Haute-Savoie **France**

Prices in francs

Tourist office
Postcode 74220
Tel 50026092
Fax 50025982
Tlx 385125

Getting there
By road 862km from Calais. Via Macon/Annecy; chains rarely needed.
By rail Annecy (32km); 8 daily buses from station.
By air Geneva; transfer 2hr.

Staying there
Visitor beds 9,400; breakdown: 2,200 in hotels, about 7,200 in apartments.
Package holidays Activity Travel (hcs) Chalets and Hotels "Unlimited" (hcs) Crystal (hs) Enterprise (hcs) French Impressions (hs) Made to Measure (hs) Neilson (hs) Quality Ski Tours (h) Quest Total Ski (h) Quest Travel (schools) (h) Silver Ski (c) Ski Esprit (c) Ski Party Snow World (h) Ski Total (cjs) Ski Valkyrie (hcs) SkiBound (h) SnowRanger (s) Snowbugs (hcs) Thomson (s) .
Medical facilities In resort: Doctors, dentist, chemist. Hospital: Annecy (32km).

Non-skiing activities
Indoor Vitahotel Fitness Centre (swimming pool), Californian Fitness Centre (sauna, massage etc), cinema.
Outdoor Walks (with or without snow-shoes), snowmobile rides, artificial ice-rink (curling, skating), hang-gliding, paragliding, flying, motor bike circuit, sleigh rides.

Kindergartens
Club de Champions
Tuition: Yes (under 5 yrs 1hr per day, over 5 yrs 2½hr per day). Hours: 8.30-6.00. Ages: 3½-6. Cost: 796.00 per week (with lunch).
Club de Mouflets
Tuition: No. Hours: 8.30-6.00. Ages: 8mth-4½yr. Cost: 520.00 per week (with lunch).

Other childcare facilities
Baby-sitters available from Tourist Office; baby-changing facilities in Tourist Office.

Special skiing facilities
Summer skiing No.
Cross-country 4km green, 8km blue, 9km red, 20km black in Les Confins valley, and link with Le Grand Bornand trails; 4km green, 3km blue, 6km red, 13km black at Beauregard. Ski school in each sector.

Lift passes
Area pass
Covers all La Clusaz and Croix-Fry/Merdassier lifts. (56 lifts in total.)
Cost 6 days 630.00 (£64.95). Low season: 570.00 saving 10%.
Credit cards accepted Yes.
Senior citizens 500.00 (over 60) saving 21%.
Children 500.00 (under 13) saving 21%. Free pass up to age 7.
Notes Area pass for four days or more covers ski-bus; weekly pass allows one day in Le Grand-Bornand.
Beginners Points cards.
Short-term passes Half-day (from 11.00am or 1.00pm); points cards.
Other passes New Aravis pass covers all La Clusaz and Le Grand-Bornand lifts (6 days 660.00 for adults, 530.00 for children).

Ski school
ESF
7% off prices in low season.
Classes 9.30-11.30 and 2.30-4.30. Cost: 640.00 (6 days). Reductions on price with Visitor's card.
Lift priority Yes.
Children's classes Ages: 12. Cost: 499.00 (6 days).
Private lessons available Hourly. Cost: 139.00 per hour. 1-3 people.
Special courses Intensive race training, 6 hours per day, Mon-Sat.

Christiania, the Aravis-Village and the Montagne are all centrally placed, quiet family hotels. The very welcoming Lac des Confins is in a remote and beautiful but not particularly inconvenient setting, ideal for cross-country skiers and escapists. We have good reports of the Vieux Chalet, a smart restaurant with a few bedrooms, beside the piste and road below Crêt du Merle, and of the Hotel les Sapins. The resort has enterprisingly opened a UK booking office.

Après-ski is lively at weekends and peak holiday period, otherwise quiet. The ice rink (recently enlarged) is open every evening, snow-shoe excursions to mountain restaurants for a fondue are organised once a week and there are four discos. Recommended bars include Chez George and Le Pressoire ('draught Guinness and videos'). There are lots of restaurants, both in the resort centre and dotted around the valleys – they get booked up, and close early. Recommendations include L'Outa for pizzas and the hotel de Savoie ('good food, good value'). St Jacques is a recommended traditional Savoyard restaurant. Le Foly is a particularly attractive (but expensive) log cabin up in the Confins valley.

Cross-country trails are varied and beautiful although not immediately accessible from the resort – most are up the Confins valley. For access to Beauregard, there is no alternative to paying for the cable-car trip by trip. For **non-skiers** there are good walks, and worthwhile excursions for sightseeing and shopping to Annecy and Thônes (where there is also tennis). There is an ice-rink and swimming pool.

There are small **nursery slopes** beside the resort and at the bottom of each sector. The best nursery areas are at the Crêt du Merle and on the top of Beauregard, which is delightful – though that at the bottom of Balme is also recommended. Reports on **ski school** are generally very favourable, though we have reports of large classes and an instructor starting late and finishing early. Three enthusiastic reporters this year highly recommend courses run by The Ski Company, who offer holidays with tuition in La Clusaz. The Club Mouflets **kindergarten** is highly recommended.

French skiing with a human face

Megève France 1100m

Good for *Easy runs, big ski area, mountain restaurants, beautiful scenery, cross-country skiing, not skiing, après-ski, short airport transfers, easy road access, sunny slopes, woodland runs*
Bad for *Tough runs, skiing convenience, late holidays, resort-level snow, freedom from cars*

Linked resorts: St-Gervais, St-Nicolas-de-Véroce, Combloux
Separate resorts: Praz-sur-Arly, Nôtre-Dame-de-Bellecombe

Megève, an old village in a beautiful, sunny setting at medium altitude, became France's fashionable ski resort in the early days of the sport. Many keen skiers have come to demand more of a challenge than the gentle surroundings of Megève can supply, but the resort has not lost its popularity. It has the traditional charm of a village where, in the words of the tourist office, wood has not given way to concrete, and where the variety of wintersports has been maintained. Horses and (wheeled) sleighs wait in the square, before a fine old church; carefully restored old buildings and an open-air ice rink add to the scene. The narrow central streets are car-free most of the time, and lined by attractive and expensive shop windows. Unfortunately there is a lot of Megève between the centre and the ski areas; the inconvenience and the often heavy traffic and pollution ('verging on LA smog at times') around town do a lot to mar the general effect.

Megève's skiing is not enormously varied, but there is a lot of it. It is friendly skiing, mostly below the tree-line but with open pastures giving long, gentle runs for near-beginners and intermediate skiers, lots of sun and superb views. Old restaurants and even hotels are spread round the ridges at the top of the lifts, and much of the area is as easily enjoyed by walkers and cross-country skiers as by downhillers. It is not super-reliable for snow, and queues can be a problem; but Megève has recently spent heavily to improve its lift system, which no longer seems hopelessly old-fashioned.

Cross-country and downhill runs link up with St-Gervais, a large and old-fashioned spa on the western flanks of the Mont Blanc massif boasting the largest vertical range of any commune in France – 4222 metres from the summit of Mont Blanc to Le Fayet. In winter its main attraction is as a base for exploring a large number of other resorts.

Along the valley from Megève is the small but growing resort of Praz-sur-Arly – a friendly village with easy access to an interesting skiing area on the north-facing slopes of the Crêt du Midi and links with Nôtre-Dame-de-Bellecombe.

A car is handy for making the most of the Megève skiing, and more-or-less essential if you want to explore the whole of the Mont Blanc ski pass area (ie the Chamonix valley). But the resort is not easy to negotiate by car, and is often jammed with traffic.

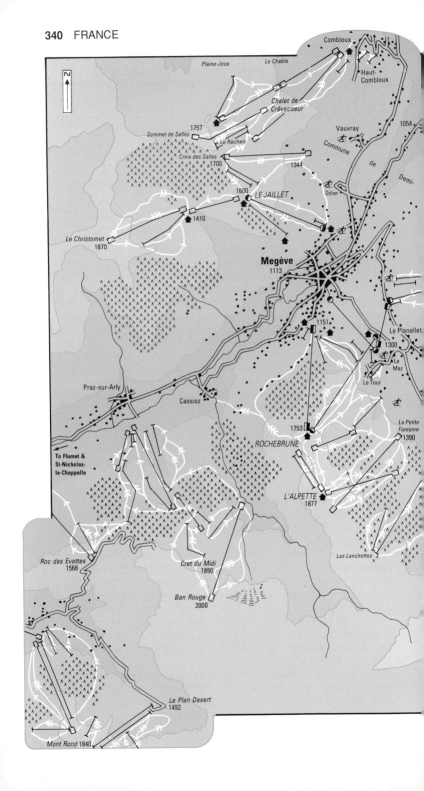

Plaine-Joux   Le Chable

Combloux

Haut-Combloux

Chalet de Crévecoeur

1757

Sommet de Salles

Le Rachais

Vauvray

Commune

Odier

1054

de

Demi-

Croix des Salles
1700

1344

1600   *LE JAILLET*

1410

Le Christomet
1870

Megève
1113

1151

Le Planellet

1300

Le Maz

Le Tour

Praz-sur-Arly

Cassioz

1753

ROCHEBRUNE

La Petite Fontaine
1390

To Flumet & St-Nicholas-la-Chappelle

L'ALPETTE
1877

Roc des Evettes
1566

Cret du Midi
1890

Les Lanchettes

Ban Rouge
2000

Le Plan Desert
1492

Mont Rond 1840

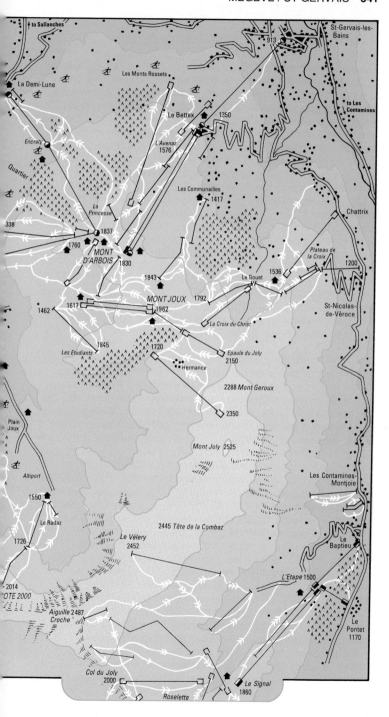

to Sallanches

St-Gervais-les-Bains
913

La Demi-Lune

Les Monts Rossets

Le Bettex 1350

to Les Contamines

Encraty

L'Avenaz 1576

Quartier

Les Communailles 1417

Chattrix

La Princesse

338

1837
1760
1830
MONT D'ARBOIS

Plateau de la Croix
1200

1536
Le Gouet

1843

1462
1617

MONT JOUX 1792

St-Nicolas-de-Vèroce

1962

La Croix du Christ

1845
Les Etudiants

1720

Epaule du Joly 2150

Hermance

2288 Mont Geroux

2350

Mont Joly 2525

Les Contamines-Montjoie

Plain Joux

Altiport

1550

Le Radaz

1726

2445 Tête de la Combaz

Le Vélery 2452

Le Baptieu

L'Etape 1500

2014
OTE 2000

Aiguille 2487 Croche

Le Pontet 1170

Col du Joly 2000

Le Signal 1860

Roselette

The skiing top 2350m bottom 900m

The skiing is in three widely separated areas. The least busy is reached by gondola starting some way north of the town and going over open slopes to the sunny, wooded knoll of **Le Jaillet**. To the west, beyond a dip, is the bald high-point of Le Christomet. To the north, easy pistes and lifts take you into the skiing above Combloux. The skiing in this area as a whole is friendly and easy, though there are more challenging runs under both the gondola and the Christomet chair, and on the upper slopes above Combloux. On the other side of the resort there is much more skiing, mostly facing west and north, on the two sides of the wide horseshoe of slopes beneath the elegant peak of Mont Joly.

Megève's original cable-car, to the plateau of **Rochebrune**, starts a long way from the centre, but is now duplicated by a dog-leg gondola from the centre of town. There are then parallel drag- and chair-lifts up to the Alpette, the top of the sector and of Megève's famous downhill course, rarely used as a recreational piste. None of the other runs is particularly difficult, and intermediate and inexperienced skiers will particularly enjoy the length of them (up to 760m vertical). A series of enjoyable pistes, now served by new quad chair-lifts, make a link across the wide mountainside to **Côte 2000**, where two 'unreliable old drags' serve fairly challenging skiing, including the women's downhill course and some good off-piste slopes. The area is shaded, and usually holds its snow well.

Megève's most famous skiing mountain is the rounded end of the easterly arm of the horseshoe. A cross-valley cable-car gives access from Rochebrune to the main gondola for the **Mont d'Arbois**, starting high above the resort. On the crest where these lifts meet the cable-car and gondola from Le Bettex (an outpost of St-Gervais), there are lots of little link runs, a few hotels and restaurants, and panoramic walking paths. The runs down to Megève are mostly open and easy, and include a long green. There is some more challenging skiing around Mont Joux, the next peak along from Mont d'Arbois on the ridge which climbs towards Mont Joly, with increasingly steep slopes around the bowl. The scope here has been greatly increased by the chair-lift going up over an impressive open slope of about 33° in places to the area's high-point (2350m). The nearby Epaule also serves short, challenging pistes and gives access to some splendid gentler runs and wide, little-used off-piste slopes over the mountain above St-Nicolas-de-Véroce (1200m). For good skiers this is some of the best terrain in the whole area. From Mont Joux there are also long easy runs, mixed open and woodland terrain, down to Les Communailles near Le Bettex, with drag-lifts back up to the ridge. The once-laborious route from Croix du Christ to the top of Mont Joux has been vastly improved by the installation of a short new drag-lift, eliminating ten minutes' tedious poling. From Mont Joux, you can ski straight back to Megève.

The slopes on the north-facing Princesse side of the mountain (served by a long, two-stage gondola starting out of town at Demi-Lune) are wooded and more challenging than the runs down to Megève, but the black labels overstate the difficulty. There is often some good off-piste skiing among the trees underneath the top half of the gondola.

Mountain restaurants are one of the great attractions of skiing in Megève: numerous, mostly attractive and panoramic, but expensive. Old restaurants and hotels, easily accessible to skiers and non-skiers alike, stand at the top of the Mont d'Arbois. The Côte 2000 is a smart and civilised chalet restaurant ('for poseurs in fur'); the Le Rosay self-service cafeteria 'has a pro-British *patron*' and offers the best value locally; La Caboche on Rochebrune is a favourite, recommended for value; the wooden chalet at Alpette offers 'excellent quality, at a price'; the big Igloo on Mont d'Arbois has 'somewhat bland self-service' but is good for views and lack of crowds; the family-run Chez Tartine, part-way down the Princesse gondola, apparently operates a free kindergarten over lunch. One reporter recommends the Alpage at Comunailles – 'frequented by seafood gourmets'.

Queues have diminished thanks to new lifts, but they can still be a problem in French holiday periods and at weekends. The Petite Fontaine drag-lift is used by skiers travelling in both directions between Rochebrune and Côte 2000, and is a bottle-neck; the next-door Lanchettes drag also gets busy in the afternoon. Surprisingly, the quad chairs up Mont Joux and Mont d'Arbois are reportedly queue-prone. The run down to St-Gervais is often unskiable (and always awkward, with road crossings), generating long queues for the gondola down from Le Bettex, especially at weekends. Reporters have been impressed by the booklet-style piste map, which shows the different areas very clearly. The area has no **artificial snow.**

The resort

As Megève has grown to become one of the largest resorts in France, it has spread far in all directions from the centre, with a complicated system of roads radiating from the hub. A main road runs through the resort but bypasses the centre. There are expensive indoor car parks. Daytime ski-buses link the centre with the access lifts, and coaches run to other resorts (both services covered by the Mont Blanc lift pass). Sleighs form an effective (and expensive) transport system. Shopping is varied, but not cheap; there are some 'superb' food shops. Visitors with cars can investigate the larger, cheaper supermarkets down the road to Sallanches.

Accommodation is in a wide range of hotels and private chalets let out for self-catering holidays. For those without a car, the resort centre is the best compromise location. Outstanding luxury hotels are the central Mont Blanc, murals by Jean Cocteau, and the Chalet du Mont d'Arbois near the cable-car. The comfortable Ferme Hotel Duvillard is very convenient for the Mont d'Arbois lift but a fair walk from the town centre. We have two enthusiastic reports on the Fer à Cheval ('gorgeous – terrific ambience'). More central and more basic is Mon Idéal; it has no restaurant. On the other side of town (Le Jaillet), a reporter recommends L'Auguille – 'very comfortable, with a motherly *patronne*'.

The Mont Blanc Voyages apartments are clean but very basic.

Après-ski is lively and smart, at least until the end of February. There are scores of restaurants in a great variety of styles but, according to one reporter, 'all delightfully French' – recommendations include La Conga ('excellent, small, irresistible chocolate fondue'), the Cintra

Facts on Megève Haute-Savoie **France**

Prices in francs
Ski Club represented

Tourist office
Postcode 74120
Tel 50212728
Fax 50930309
Tlx 385532

Getting there
By road 890km from Calais. Via Macon/Geneva; chains rarely needed.
By rail Sallanches (13km); 10 daily buses from station.
By air Geneva; transfer 1½hr. (Or Lyon; transfer about 3hr.)

Staying there
Visitor beds 41,660; breakdown: 3,500 in hotels, 10,650 in apartments.
Package holidays Brittany Ferries (s) Chalets and Hotels "Unlimited" (hcs) French Impressions (hs) Made to Measure (hs) Quest Travel (schools) (h) Ski Esprit (c) Ski Whizz Small World (cj) SnowRanger (s) Supertravel (h) White Roc Ski (hcs) .
Medical facilities In resort: Doctors, dentists, chemists, optician. Hospital: Sallaches (12km).

Non-skiing activities
Indoor 'Palais des Sports' (climbing wall, swimming pool, sauna, solarium, skating, gym, and golf driving); judo, classical and contemporary dance classes, bridge, tennis, yoga, archery, language classes, museum, library, cinemas, pottery, casino, concert and play hall.
Outdoor 50km cleared paths, skating rink, horse-riding, sleigh rides, plane and helicopter trips, paragliding.

Kindergartens
Alpage
Tuition: Yes. Hours: 9.15-5.30. Ages: 3-6. Cost: 1,860.00 per week (with tuition and lifts; ski hire possible). Next to Mt d'Arbois cable-car.
Princesse
Tuition: Yes. Hours: 9.00-5.00. Ages: 3-12. Cost: 1,140.00 per week (with tuition and lifts). Next to Princesse cable-car.
Chalet St Michael
Tuition: No. Hours: 9.00-6.00. Ages: 4-12. Cost: 960.00 per week.
Baby Club
Tuition: Possible. Hours: 9.00-5.30. Ages: 1-6. Cost: 960.00 per week (with lifts).
Montjoie
Tuition: Possible. Hours: 9.00-5.30. Ages: 3-13.

Cost: 1,020.00 per week (lessons with ESF).

Special skiing facilities
Summer skiing No.
Cross-country 3 areas, each with green, blue and red loops: bottom of Jaillet (total 16km); bottom of the Mont d'Arbois cable-car to Princesse mid-station (total 9km); beyond Le Maz in valley between bottom of Rochebrune and Côte 2000 lifts (total 31km). Instruction available.

Lift passes
Mont-Blanc pass
Covers all lifts in the 13 ski resorts in the Mont Blanc region, and bus and coach shuttles between them. (207 lifts in total.)
Cost 6 days 765.00 (£78.87). Low season: 690.00 saving 10%.
Credit cards accepted Yes.
Senior citizens 610.00 (over 60) saving 20%.
Children 610.00 (under 13) saving 20%.
Beginners Pay by the ride.
Short-term passes Individual tariffs for the massif du Mont Arbois/Princesse, the massif de Rochebrune/côte 2000 and the massif du Jaillet.
Other passes Mont-Blanc Evasion pass covers all lifts in the Megève, St Gervais, St Nicolas and Combloux areas, (6 days cost 708.00 for adults, 598.00 for children).

Ski school
Ecole de Ski Megève
Classes 4hr: 2hr am and pm. Cost: 540.00 (6 days).
Lift priority Yes.
Children's classes Ages: Under 12. Cost: 450.00 (6 days).
Private lessons available Hourly. Cost: 155.00 per hour, up to 2 people; 185.00 3-5 people.
Special courses Surf – 6 x 3hr lessons 900.00.
SEI
Classes 4hr: 2hr am and pm. Cost: 495.00 (6 days). 3½ hour classes available in Feb.
Lift priority Yes.
Children's classes Ages: 12. Cost: 420.00 (6 days).
Private lessons available Hourly. Cost: 160.00 per hour. Up to 3 people.
Special courses Ski-Adventure – 6-day guided tour 1250.00 per person.

What was new in 91
1. 2 new quad in the Alpette region, the Petite Fontaine and the Jardins.
2. New drag-lift from bottom of Epaule du Joly to top of Mont Joux.

Bistrot ('mindblowingly-big seafood platters'), the restaurant of the Mont-Joly hotel, and the informal Le Sapinière – some smart nightlife in the disco/cabaret/casino and the Club des Cinque Rues (a jazz club – 'good music, expensive drinks'). But there is not much cheap, informal après-ski apart from a bowling alley ('best-value entertainment we found') and ice hockey matches; the Megève/St-Gervais team are among the best in France. The rink's Puck bar attracts crowds, including families and 'rowdy Brits'. The Cocoon bar (new last season, with a happy hour) is also very popular with the British and now has a karaoke machine; the Bar du Chamois is small, very French and popular with locals; the Rols Club is expensively exclusive.

The resort is very large, and no tranquil Alpine backwater, but **cross-country** trails are in varied and attractive surroundings, including some at altitude. The Mont d'Arbois/Princesse trails link up with the St-Gervais ones. There is plenty for **non-skiers** to do, with a big sports/conference centre and particularly good walks in the ski areas, all of which give marvellous views. Walks are graded from easy to off-piste (there are no 'black' walks) and the tourist office produces excellent maps to follow. One reporter recommends the Route de Calvaire from Le Planellet to the centre, which has a farm restaurant en route. Annecy makes an attractive excursion, as does Chamonix.

Nursery slopes at the bottom of the major lifts are good but not very reliable for snow. In good conditions most novices will soon be able to handle Le Jaillet. The **ski school** becomes ridiculously overcrowded in French holiday periods, and English is not reliably spoken. One regular visitor recommends taking lessons with BASI-qualified instructor Mike Butler. We have an enthusiastic report on the new Garderie de la Caboche **kindergarten** (not listed by the tourist office); 'the staff were very kind and helpful but lacked English, facilities were clean and modern, the snow garden was pleasant and full of play things, meals were varied and nutritious'. Book in advance.

Praz-sur-Arly 1036m

Praz has a couple of cross-country trails, graded green and red, and fifteen kilometres of cleared paths, ('flora and fauna' walks with local guides are possible). Accommodation is mainly in hotels and chalets, and there are restaurants, bars, a sports club, a library, a ski school and a *Jardin des Neiges* (for children from 18 months) in the village.

Two chair-lifts from the village take you up to the main skiing area below the Crêt du Midi (1900m) where several drags serve mainly blue runs just above the tree-line. The addition of a new chair last season up to Ban Rouge at 2000m has opened up a larger area with some more taxing runs (including a short black) and panoramic views. From the nursery slopes a chair and drag-lift provide the connection with the Roc des Evettes and Mont Reguet skiing – mainly wooded and easy, with the exception of one black run beside the Seigneurs drag lift. A chair-lift links Mont Reguet with the Mont Rond skiing (also accessible by road), where several lifts, serving a variety of pistes on all flanks of the mountain, converge at the peak (1840m).

Tourist office ✆ 50219057. **Package holidays** Quest Travel (schools) (h)

Nôtre-Dame-de-Bellecombe 1130m

At the base of Mont Reguet is another pleasant village yet to feature prominently on the British ski market. The main Flumet/Les Saisies road skirts the village, making it unpleasantly busy at times. Accommodation is mainly in apartments, but these are 'not of the mega concrete block variety'. Those in the Equipe are very spacious. There are half a dozen two-star hotels, several bars and at least two decent restaurants, the Equipe (apparently the resort favourite, 'excellent food, very busy, good value') and Le Slalom. A car is useful for excursions and essential for those staying in the nearby hamlet of Le Planay (at the base of the Mont Rond skiing area).

The skiing is in two main sectors, the west-facing slopes of Mont Reguet and a more extensive area on Mont Rond. The Mont Rond skiing is most easily accessible from Le Planay, reached by car or free ski bus from Nôtre-Dame. Le Planay can also be skied to, via Mont Reguet. From here the main lift up Mont Rond is a long chair, ascending to 2010m, serving a long blue and more direct red and black runs back down. The top section connects with a drag-lift on the west-facing slopes above the village of Les Frasses. On the other side of Mont Rond, more challenging pistes, served by a drags, descend to Plan Dessert. The lengthiest runs in this area are from the top of the Vorès dog-leg drag back to Plan Dessert; there are blue and red alternatives. A recent reporter praised the piste grooming, but found the pistes more severely graded than in other French resorts. There are no restaurants on the slopes but pleasant places to eat in the surrounding villages. The ski school is well thought of, but lacks English-speaking instructors.
Tourist office ✆ 79316140. **Package holidays** Quest Total Ski (h) Quest Travel (schools) (h).

St-Gervais 850m

St-Gervais is inconveniently arranged in a cramped setting on both sides of an impressive river gorge; the main street is a busy road. There is a large indoor ice-rink and a kindergarten. The main ski area is on the Megève side, reached by a fast 20-person gondola from the edge of the resort to Le Bettex, which has some accommodation, including the comfortable hotels Arbois/Bettex and Carlina, but is reportedly 'very quiet'. Le Bettex is accessible by car and has good cross-country trails and walks around the mountain (Megève and Le Bettex trails link up). The second stage of the lift goes up to Mont d'Arbois, known on this side of the hill as St-Gervais 1850. This is a popular way into the Megève ski area for day-trippers, and often crowded.

Skiing on the Mont Blanc side of St-Gervais is served by the Tramway – a funicular which climbs occasionally and very slowly to the Col de Voza (1653m) where it links up the skiing above Les Houches. There are a few short runs and lifts on the St-Gervais side of the col, but the only run down back to St-Gervais is off-piste and often unskiable. A daytime bus service runs between the lift stations, via the resort centre.
Tourist office ✆ 50782243. Tx 385607. **Package holidays** Brittany Ferries (s) Hoverspeed Ski-Drive (s) Quality Ski Tours (h).

Les Contamines France 1164m

This small village near the head of the quiet, narrow Montjoie valley, over the hill from Megève, could serve as a model of poor ski resort planning. The long village is on one side of the river and the ski area on the other, its bottom station at Le Lay a long uphill walk from the centre. Two access lifts (both now efficient gondolas) converge on a narrow plateau (1500m) where queues form for the further gondola to Le Signal (1900m), the start of the real skiing. There is a short nursery lift by Le Signal which is often very busy ('20-minute queues') when there is little snow lower down. Runs back from Le Signal are often crowded, particularly in bad weather, when they provide the only woodland skiing in the resort. It is rarely possible to ski right down to the valley, although there are marked blue runs. This apart, there is little challenging skiing, and little that is very easy. But more than a few people like Les Contamines. They like it because it is just a quiet, unspoilt Savoyard village (English is not widely spoken) with simple accommodation and modest prices; and because once you get to the ski area it gives 'outstandingly beautiful' views and a fair amount of open intermediate skiing, much of which is now shown on our Megève map. It has also developed a reputation for reliable snow.

A large number of short runs are spread around a vast bowl (mainly north-east facing) behind Le Signal, between 2500m and about 1700m, with plenty of space for off-piste skiing. The Col du Joly (2000m) separates this main bowl from a smaller, less popular but equally open area of south-west-facing intermediate runs, and has a splendid restaurant. The 'very average' restaurant at Le Signal has a picnic room.

The village runs along a single long street (now bypassed by traffic up the valley to the ski-lifts), with an old church, a row of old-fashioned hotels and a few shops and cafés. Near the main access gondola at Le Lay, Le Chemenaz is an ideally placed, attractive and comfortable modern hotel. The central Chamois is recommended for 'excellent five-course dinners'. One self-catering reporter recommends the Marmottes residence, a chalet-style complex near the village centre. For families, Residence Le Lay, a pleasant quiet block on the edge of the village, is a better bet. The resort has very limited nightlife (the discos often lack support) and not much to offer non-skiers apart from a natural ice-rink. A reporter recommends the menus at Le Husky, and 'huge crêpes and pizzas' at La Cressoua. At Le Lay, the Tetras is a friendly and popular 'pub'. Cross-country trails are reasonably extensive and the ski school advertises off-piste excursions into Italy for advanced *fondeurs*. Reports on the ski school are generally encouraging, and the local guides run well organised Vallée Blanche outings. There is a ski-bus, but having a car is extremely useful for exploration.

Tourist office ✆ 50470158. Tx 385730. **Package holidays** Chalets and Hotels Unlimited (hc) Enterprise (hs) Quest Total Ski (h) Ski Total (cjs) SnowRanger (s).

Chamonix France 1040m

Good for *Beautiful scenery, tough runs, ski touring, off-piste skiing, après-ski, cross-country skiing, late holidays, rail access, easy road access, short transfers*
Bad for *Skiing convenience, nursery slopes, resort-level snow, lift queues, easy runs, mountain restaurants, freedom from cars, woodland runs*

Separate resorts Argentière, Les Houches, Le Tour

Chamonix grew up with the fashion for climbing and mountain sightseeing in the 19th century, and remains a town of mountain guides and hoteliers. Although not pretty, it has great character and a history that dominates the town in the form of the mountains and glaciers of Mont Blanc. Its population is diverse and colourful, and to its resident colony of Real Mountain Men from all over the world is added a large winter influx of young adventurers and groupies. After going through its dark age as a winter resort, the home of the first Winter Olympics is now in full renaissance as more skiers develop a taste for the excitement these mountains can offer. The number of British visitors has grown rapidly (we now account for about 20% of winter tourists). To judge from our reports, most go for the right reasons, but many skiers would undoubtedly find the local skiing not greatly to their liking, and be equally put off by the macho-chic atmosphere.

The drawbacks of the skiing are clear: the areas are not linked and only one is immediately accessible from the centre of Chamonix; there is not much gentle skiing; runs down to the valley on the south-facing side are difficult and often closed; skiing on the Grands Montets at Argentière is extremely expensive and queues are often long. But, for skiers fit enough for long challenging runs and with an eye for the grandest of all Alpine scenery, it is intensely enjoyable, and makes skiing in most other resorts seem a bit predictable. To make the most of it you need luck (with the conditions) and the services of a mountain guide. 'Packaged adventure' may seem a contradiction in terms, but that is what the Chamonix valley has to offer, and its high tourist mortality rate is a reminder that these mountains have not been tamed.

The main alternative to Chamonix for skiing or accommodation is the old village of Argentière, five miles up the valley at the foot of the Grands Montets, perhaps the most impressive ski hill of them all. At the head of the valley, little Le Tour claims to be the snowiest village in France; it is old, picturesquely set at the foot of its glacier, and has some open, easy skiing. Below Chamonix is Les Houches, an old farming village that has become a sprawling resort suburb; its skiing area is low (useful in bad weather), but its nursery slopes are surprisingly high and snow-sure.

Despite the frequency of rain in the valley, Chamonix is usually at its best late in the season when the high glacier runs are accessible to

skiers and ski tourers. A car is very useful both in the valley and for
excursions outside it – many reporters rate it essential. Courmayeur and
Megève are within easy reach and offer good skiing in bad weather, and
it is now usually possible to drive to Verbier even when the Col des
Montets is closed – the rail tunnel is opened to one-way road traffic.

The skiing top 3790m bottom 1035m

The Chamonix valley skiing is split up into six separate areas. The best
of the scenery and skiing is on the enormous, steep, mostly north-facing
slopes of the mountains at the shoulder of Mont Blanc, served by
cable-cars from Argentière to the Grands Montets and from Chamonix
to the Aiguille du Midi – Europe's most spectacular cable-car, newly
renovated and giving access to the famous Vallée Blanche run.

Chamonix's original skiing fame was based on **Brévent**, now served
by a six-seater gondola starting a steep walk from the centre (also
reachable on skis from the nursery slopes) followed by an exciting
cable-car over an abyss to the top station, which gives marvellous views
of Mont Blanc. Apart from a few short lifts serving easy runs near
mid-station, and a chair-lift up to the Col Cornu, Brévent has basically
one run. It is quite a run: the top section to Planpraz (served by a
cable-car whose capacity is now much improved) is an impressive
descent with an exposed, bumpy wall, although not tough enough for its
black grading, say reporters; the much longer bottom section (no longer
a piste) is even more demanding – a long, narrow gully followed by a
wider, bumpy section, which seems to go on for ever. All in all, a
relentless 1500m vertical. A black run has been cleared through the
woods, from the bottom of the Combe de Vioz chair-lift.

The **Flégère** skiing, a few ridges along from Brévent, is similar in
many ways. The top section, served by an enclosed chair-lift, is less
awesome but has a greater variety of runs, mostly tough blue to tough
red. There is only one run to the valley, and that is difficult and often
closed. Snow permitting, La Flégère has better off-piste possibilities; it is
especially good for spring snow. Rumours persist about a
Flégère–Brévent link. It should be in place for this season.

The notoriously queue-plagued cable-car from **Argentière** to Croix
de Lognan has at last been relieved by the installation of an efficient
chair-lift up to the slightly lower point of Plan Joran. Lognan is the
bottom of the main skiing area – there is only one run down the steep,
wooded slope to the valley, a long and tiring red, not in itself particularly
difficult, but often in poor condition, and crowded in the late afternoon.
The area above Lognan may seem limited, but, with the right conditions
and the right guidance, good skiers can find more satisfaction and even
more variety here than in far more extensive ski areas – and it attracts
an unrivalled congregation of rubber-legged experts and bone-headed
maniacs. Crevasse and avalanche danger is considerable.

Most of the main face of the mountain between about 2000m and
2600m is a wide open area of ridges and bowls, mogul-fields and gullies
where the distinction between piste and off-piste means little more than

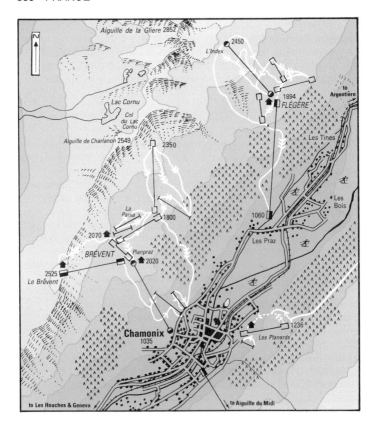

a line of poles to follow in bad visibility. The chair-lift under the top
section of the cable-car alone offers at least half a dozen different
descents, all involving stiff mogul-fields. Recent development has added
some good new runs and a very welcome new restaurant, but there are
still no really easy runs, and few runs that are prepared. One of the few
is a long and often crowded red served by a hybrid gondola/chair-lift
which also gives access to the Combe de la Pendant, a magnificent
wide bowl leading to steep wooded slopes above the hamlet of Le
Lavancher. Although the bowl is now served by a chair-lift and has been
staked out with a long unbashed run (1000m vertical), there is still
masses of room off-piste. The Arolles run under this lift has a seriously
steep wall. The off-piste run through the woods to Le Lavancher has
several steep sections, and snow conditions are usually difficult. There
is a free bus back from the bottom to Argentière.

   The top cable-car is followed by an exposed 200-step metal staircase
down to the pistes, or a shorter staircase up to a viewing platform which
is also the point of departure of a vertiginous off-piste alternative start.
The views from here are stupendous, and the runs long and
consistently challenging – 4km and 5km for the 1260m vertical to the

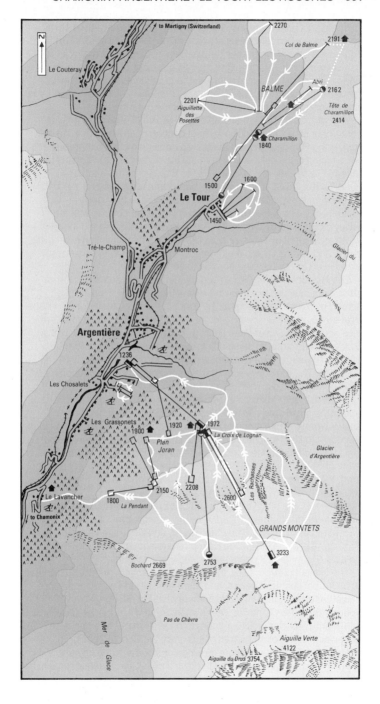

mid-station. Of the two runs, the longer Pointe de Vue is more scenic, giving some awesome views of some of the choppiest sections of the Argentière glacier; no part of it is particularly steep – the main qualities it asks of a skier are stamina (the moguls are more or less continuous) and in particular a resilient right leg (the run proceeds anti-clockwise around the mountain). The Pylones run branches left from Point de Vue and descends the main northerly face of the mountain.

The various off-piste descents offer a choice of grandiose glacier scenery or steep, open slopes. The most notorious of all Argentière's runs is the Pas de Chèvre (Goat's Hop), down an often dangerous west-facing slope, all the way from the top of the Grands Montets to the Mer de Glace, where it joins the Vallée Blanche run to Chamonix.

Le Tour's skiing is open, gentle, sunny and uncomplicated. As well as the long, easy intermediate runs (easier above the gondola mid-station), there are a couple of drag-lifts at the bottom, with the valley's best nursery slopes. The upper slopes (last year extended in width and height by two new drag lifts) are ideal for initiation in off-piste skiing and surfing. There are more advanced off-piste excursions to stations on the railway line from Switzerland.

Les Houches' skiing would seem a perfectly agreeable little area were it not overshadowed by the rest of the Chamonix valley. It is served by a small cable-car and a gondola from either end of the village over steep, wooded slopes to either side of the Col de Voza (1653m) – also accessible, two or three times a day, by railway from Le Fayet and St-Gervais. From both these points (Bellevue, 1812m, and Prarion, 1966m) there are splendid long, wide trails through the woods to Les Houches. The run down from Prarion is the official downhill course and is categorised black. There is a small network of drag-lifts between the Col de Voza and Prarion, serving an open slope of about 300m vertical, and some small drag-lifts with slopes suitable for beginners, often snowy when Le Tour's nursery slopes are not. There is also a wide blue run down to Les Houches. Behind the Col de Voza a good, wide red piste beside the Plancerts drag turns into an off-piste run down to the edge of St-Gervais, not far from the station. After a deceptively pleasant start, the run becomes obscure, and there are only two or three trains a day (not covered by day passes) back up to the col.

Chamonix is a place for off-piste picnics rather than leisurely lunches, and **mountain restaurants** are few, uninteresting and expensive, except at Les Houches. The Plan Roujon and Chavanne restaurants at Argentière and the old Col de Balme refuge above Le Tour's lifts are notable exceptions. Flégère is reportedly good value.

The lifts out of Argentière, though much improved, are not guaranteed to be free of serious **queues**, and there are still long waits for the top cable-car despite the hefty supplement of 25F a ride (payable before you join the queue) and last year's improvement in capacity. One late-March reporter took four hours to do two runs. There may also be long waits for the other high lift in this area, the Bochard chair. The run to the valley is now even more crowded at the end of the day (if it is skiable – expect queues for a ride down if not). Other queues remain: to get down from Flégère or Brévent when the valley runs are closed; in bad weather at Les Houches (although a new chair-lift has improved matters); and in all probability for the new Aiguile du Midi lift in fine weather. Because of the risk of lift closures in bad weather, many skiers prefer the coupon-for-day-pass formula, although the new arrangement with Courmayeur adds to the attraction of the area pass. The single-sheet piste map covering the whole valley is unreliable, but there is a much better alternative in booklet form, entitled *Cham'ski*, incorporating descriptions of pistes as well as individual maps of each area. The Argentière map, at least, is also distributed locally as a leaflet.

The resort

Traditional and old-fashioned though its centre is, Chamonix is no longer pretty. The centre is crowded, noisy and full of traffic. Modern blocks stand around the edge of town, and Chamonix merges with neighbouring hamlets and villages. Bus services (covered by the area lift pass but otherwise expensive – books of tickets bought in advance offer a saving) link the town centre with Argentière, Le Tour and Les Houches. They are just about adequate for skiing purposes but in the afternoon may be full of Argentière skiers when they get to Flégère. They stop at about 7pm. There is also a small railway from Le Fayet (below St-Gervais) to Martigny in Switzerland via Chamonix and Argentière, and linking up with main-line services at both ends. There is a good open market on Saturdays.

   Most of the **accommodation** offered by British operators is in or near Chamonix. There are a few expensive comfortable hotels, many simple old cheap ones, a few hostels with very cheap beds, and plenty of self-catering accommodation in new complexes (the main one is Chamonix Sud, near the Aiguille du Midi cable-car, and convenient for buses) and chalets around the valley. There is no ideal location, except perhaps near the bus terminal. Unless taking a car, avoid accommodation downstream of Chamonix, which means a change of buses to reach Flégère and Argentière. The Bois Prin is the most expensive and desirable hotel in town, a luxury chalet in a magnificent but very inconvenient position not far from the Brévent lift. The Mont Blanc is large and absolutely central, has a heated outdoor pool and is also expensive. The Albert Premier is large, comfortable and fairly convenient, with a bus stop nearby. All these hotels (especially the Albert) have excellent restaurants. The Sapinière is one of Chamonix's most handsomely traditional large hotels, in a beautiful, peaceful but not inconvenient position near the nursery slopes. A town-centre hotel without a restaurant is an attractive formula; we have good reports of the inexpensive Vallée Blanche. Other recommendations are the Hermitage and the Croix Blanche, near the centre.

   Après-ski is varied and very lively, at least so far as bars (with and without music, videos and karaoke) and restaurants go. The most popular places to hang out and pick up something young and virulent are Chambre 9, Choucas, Jean's Bar, Driver's and the Brévent. All these are usually full far past the gunwhales, unlike the National, a good quiet place for good French food and drink. There are dozens of restaurants, including cheap pizzerias and crêperies. The best restaurants are in the hotels mentioned above, the Eden at Les Praz (near La Flégère) and the more informal Le Sarpé, at Les Bois (near Les Praz). There is a casino, a jazz club and a few discos.

The valley is too built-up near Chamonix for **cross-country** skiing, but interlinked woodland loops of different grades further up the valley, between Les Praz and Argentière, offer lots of scope. Accomplished *fondeurs* may be tempted to join the small but growing community of

---

Facts on Chamonix   Haute-Savoie **France**

Prices in francs
Ski Club represented

Tourist office
Postcode 74400
Tel 50530024
Fax 50535890
Tlx 385022

Getting there
By road 899km from Calais. Via Macon/Geneva; chains rarely necessary, except higher up the valley.
By rail Station in resort.
By air Geneva; transfer 1½hr. (Or Lyon.)

Staying there
Visitor beds 14,100; breakdown: 4,900 in hotels, 9,200 in apartments and chalets.
Package holidays Abercrombie and Kent Travel (c) Adventure Unlimited (c) Allez France (h) Brittany Ferries (s) Chalets and Hotels "Unlimited" (hcs) Club Med (h) Collineige Ski (hcs) Crystal (hs) Enterprise (hs) French Impressions (s) Fresh Tracks (h) Hoverspeed Ski-Drive (hs) HuSki (cs) Inghams (hcs) Made to Measure (hcs) Neilson (hs) Quest Travel (schools) (h) Sally Holidays (s) Ski Alternatives (h) Ski Oui (hcs) Ski Valkyrie (hcs) Ski Weekend (hcs) Ski Whizz Small World (c) SnowRanger (s) The Ski Company Ltd (c) Vacations (hs) White Roc Ski (h) .
Medical facilities In resort: Hospital, chemists, doctors and dentists.

Non-skiing activities
Indoor Sports complex (sports hall, weight training, table tennis), skating and curling rinks, speed skating, ice hockey, swimming pool with giant water slide, saunas, 2 tennis courts, 2 squash courts, archery, fitness centre, Alpine museum (open school holidays), classical and ballet dancing, casino, 3 cinemas.
Outdoor Toboggan runs, ski-jumps, snow-shoe outings, ice-driving circuit, horse-riding school, mountain biking, hang-gliding, paragliding.

Kindergartens
Panda Club
Tuition: Yes. Hours: 8.30-5.30, Mon-Fri. Ages: 3mths-2½yrs, 2½-12. Cost: 1,100.00 per week (with meals and tuition).

Special skiing facilities
Summer skiing No.
Cross-country Two main networks, with 2km (black) trail linking the two. Chamonix (from Les Praz): 10km green, 6km blue, 4km red. Argentière: 3km green, 3km blue, 4km red. Also 14km trails at Les Houches.

Lift passes
Mont Blanc area pass
Covers lifts in 13 resorts in the Mont Blanc region and ski buses in each resort. (180 lifts in total.)
Cost 6 days 765.00 (£78.87). Low season: 690.00 saving 10%.
Credit cards accepted Yes.
Senior citizens 610.00 (over 60) saving 20%.
Children 610.00 (under 11) saving 20%. Free pass up to age 4.
Notes Passes of 5 days or more allow one day in Courmayeur.
Beginners Coupons or pay by the ride on nursery lifts.
Short-term passes Half-day passes for limited areas; single and return tickets on most lifts.
Other passes Passes available for all the individual areas (Brévent, La Flégère, Balme, Les Houches, Grands Montets, Argentière and Le Tour).

Ski school
ESF
in both Chamonix and Argentière.
Classes 4hr: 2hr am and pm. Cost: 540.00 (6 days).
Lift priority Yes.
Children's classes Ages: 4-12. Cost: 690.00 (6 days).
Private lessons available Hourly. Cost: 150.00 per hour. 1-2 people.
Special courses Variety of courses available. Mountain guides costs about 1,150.00 per day.

What was new in 91
2 new drag-lifts in the Le Tour sector – one up to the Aiguillette des Posettes at 2201m, one up to 2270m between the Aiguillette and the Col de Balme.

What is new for 92
Plans to link Brevent and Flégère.

telemark skiers. Instruction can be arranged.

In winter, the valley is no place for mountain walkers, but there is plenty for **non-skiers** to do: beautiful cable-car excursions, an excellent sports centre, an Alpine museum (fascinating provided you can read French) and plenty of organised coach trips.

Chamonix is hardly the place for beginners but there are **nursery slopes** at various points along the valley, the best of them at Le Tour and the Col de Vosa – open, sunny and reliable for snow. Chamonix has a sunny nursery area near the bottom of the Brévent lift, and the gentle slopes of Les Planards (at the bottom of the Vallée Blanche run) now have **artificial snow**. There are small areas of sunny easy skiing around the half-way stations of Brévent and Flégère.

Chamonix is the HQ of French ski teaching. The local branches of **ski school** have tried hard to keep up with the times, and offer a variety of inclusive courses designed to appeal to the skiing adventurer. We have no reports on these or the quality of instruction in basic ski school. The valley is one of the most famous ski touring areas in the Alps, and Chamonix has two associations of mountain guides. You can hire a guide individually or join an organised tour: there are daily excursions (including the Vallée Blanche) and weekly departures in April and May for the famous Haute Route from Argentière to Saas Fee. We have good reports of the Panda Club kindergartens in Chamonix and Argentière, organised by a Chinese American – 'an excellent set-up'.

Argentière 1240m

Argentière is a small but strung-out village, beautifully set beneath the local glacier, its church's bulbous belfry outlined against the ice-falls and jagged peaks in a natural postcard scene. Chalet development and some ugly modern blocks are spread up and down the valley on either side of the old village centre. The main street is the Chamonix to Martigny road; although no major route, this sees quite a lot of traffic. A further hazard to pedestrians is the large and unruly dog population.

In the evening you can eat and drink in congenial surroundings, and occasionally dance; during high season the few establishments are very crowded. Reporters recommend the family-run Dahu for good-value food, the Piano Bar for 'entertainment and non-outrageous prices', the Stone bar for hangovers. To sample the much brighter lights of Chamonix, a car is more-or-less essential; taxis are reportedly hard to come by late at night. Hotels are mostly simple. The secluded Grands Montets, now with restaurant, is convenient for the cable-car, 'comfortable and friendly', and full of Brits. The Savoie, now without restaurant, is cheap, cheerful, and a perfectly manageable walk from the cable-car. The Montana is recommended – 'pleasant rooms but limited menu'. Argentière has a small playground/nursery area near the bottom of the cable-car, a kindergarten and a ski school with guides and off-piste skiing tuition aimed at very strong skiers ('positive tuition').
Tourist office ✆ 50540214.
Package holidays Alpine Life (cas) Chalets and Hotels Unlimited (hcs) Collineige Ski (hcs) Enterprise (hs) Inghams (h) Poles Apart (cs) Ski Alternatives (h) Ski Club of GB (h) Ski Esprit (c) Ski Jeannie (c) Ski Oui (hcas) Ski Valkyrie (hcs) Ski Whizz Small World (c) Supertravel (h) White Roc Ski (c).

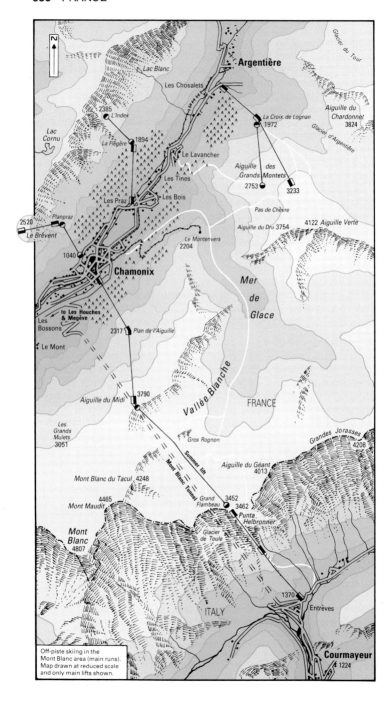

N

Argentière

Lac Blanc

Les Chosalets

Aiguille du Chardonnet 3824

La Croix de Lognan 1972

2385
L'Index

Glacier d'Argentière

La Flégère 1894

Le Lavancher

Lac Cornu

Aiguille des Grands Montets 2753

3233

Les Tines

Les Praz

Les Bois

Pas de Chèvre

Planpraz

2520
Le Brévent

Aiguille du Dru 3754

4122 Aiguille Verte

1040

Le Montenvers 2204

Chamonix

Mer de Glace

to Les Houches & Megève

Les Bossons

Le Mont

2317   Plan de l'Aiguille

Vallée Blanche

FRANCE

Aiguille du Midi   3790

Les Grands Mulets 3051

Gros Rognon

Grandes Jorasses 4208

Summer lift

Aiguille du Géant 4013

Mont Blanc du Tacul 4248

Mont Blanc Tunnel

4465
Mont Maudit

Grand Flambeau   3452

3462
Punta Helbronner

Mont Blanc 4807

Glacier de Toule

1370   Entrèves

ITALY

Courmayeur

1224

Off-piste skiing in the Mont Blanc area (main runs). Map drawn at reduced scale and only main lifts shown.

The Vallée Blanche

The Vallée Blanche may no longer be the most famous ski run in the world, but it remains the longest and one of the most alluring. Estimates of its length range up to 24km, with a vertical drop of 2770m – impressive statistics which immediately suggest one of its characteristics: that it is not at all steep. Many good skiers expect a technical challenge, and are disappointed – all you need is control over your speed and direction on a moderate slope. If fresh snow has fallen, there may be some poling, or even walking. The run gives intermediate skiers the chance to enjoy grandiose glacier scenery normally reserved for a hardy minority of adventurous off-piste skiers and ski tourers. It is a sightseeing excursion on skis, to be done on a good day and at a gentle pace. Naturally, the run is extremely popular, and on a fine day there can be enormous queues for the lift and at bottlenecks on the run. Although usually easy to follow, the Vallée Blanche is not a piste, and it makes sense to ski it in a group with a guide; apart from the obvious benefits, a guide can queue for your lift tickets.

Not the least spectacular part of the experience is the astonishingly engineered two-stage cable-car to the Aiguille du Midi from the edge of town. At the top, a tunnel cut in the ice leads to a long, steep, narrow ridge with terminal drops on either side; you have to clamber down this ridge, usually with the help of makeshift steps and a rope, before putting on skis, and for most non-mountaineers it is an uncomfortable few minutes. A guide can provide useful advice, help carry skis and even rope groups together. Courmayeur-based skiers can enjoy the Vallée Blanche without having to submit to this ordeal – see next chapter.

From the bottom of the ridge, the long run cruises off through a white wilderness of ice, snow and rock, with long stretches where speed has to be kept up, not down. The most awkward section is a junction of glaciers known as the Salle à Manger, where steeper terrain breaks up the ice with huge crevasses gaping beside the narrow path where queues of skiers build up. Even here the skiing is not technically difficult. The glacier section of the run ends with a walk uphill off the Mer de Glace on to terra firma; again queues can be a problem. From here, it is a long ski down around the mountain to Chamonix, mostly a path across the steep hillside, very messy when short of snow – progress is often impeded by an abundance of stones, mud, tree roots and the Montenvers railway track. Opening the railway in winter, as planned ('soon'), would extend the Vallée Blanche season greatly.

For those who want greater excitement than the normal Vallée Blanche run can offer, there are several severe and perilous crevasse-hopping descents from the Aiguille du Midi. Those who just want to get away from the beaten track can take ski touring equipment and branch off (under guidance) from the main trail to explore other facets of this vast area of glacier. With an early start it is possible to climb on skins up to the Col de Toula, ski down on the Italian side of the massif, return by lift and then ski the Vallée Blanche to Chamonix, a spectacular long day's skiing.

Courmayeur Italy 1230m

Good for *Mountain restaurants, beautiful scenery, après-ski, off-piste skiing, ski touring, easy road access, short airport transfers, cross-country skiing, Alpine charm, woodland runs, artificial snow*
Bad for *Skiing convenience, nursery slopes, tough runs, easy runs*

The British love Courmayeur, despite competition from more modern resorts (particularly more convenient ones)and the considerable impact on the village of the Mont Blanc tunnel road. Its ski area is attractive and varied, with lots of restaurants and beautiful changing views, and with some spectacular and exciting higher runs served (not very reliably) by the top cable-cars – plus a separate chain of cable-cars scaling Mont Blanc. Lift queues are not now the problem that they used to be, and the resort has invested in an extensive network of snow-making machinery. The village and its friendly inhabitants add considerably to the appeal for our many reporters: it is stylish without being exclusive, lively without being rowdy – one of the most attractive of Italian resorts. But it is not for everyone; the ski area is not very big and has no challenging pistes, few that are very gentle, few very long ones and normally none back to the resort, most of which which is separated from the skiing by the truck-bearing Mont Blanc tunnel road.

The tunnel makes Courmayeur the closest Italian resort to the Channel. Having a car is not particularly useful (the village is vigorously policed) except for excursions. The main lift pass encourages trips to Cervinia and Chamonix, which is much closer (and can be reached by bus without difficulty). La Thuile is also nearby, and worth a day-trip.

The skiing top 3452m bottom 1293m

Most skiers start and end the day on the vast cable-car which spans the river valley, linking the edge of the village with the edge of the **Plan Checrouit** plateau, where skis and boots can be deposited without hassle. The walk from the top of the cable-car to the lifts and runs is annoying, first and last thing. Alternatives are a short drive or bus-ride, either across the valley to Dolonne for the old gondola to Plan Checrouit, or to the Val Veny cable-car, near Entrèves. The east-facing Checrouit bowl has a large number but hardly a great variety of intermediate runs, none of which is very long, served by a variety of lifts including a six-seater gondola. The pistes are often crowded, especially near the bottom where they meet. There are surprisingly steep, narrow passages even on some of the variants graded blue.

The wooded north-west-facing **Val Veny** side of the mountain, linked in a couple of places with the Checrouit bowl, has beautiful, longer and more varied runs, with some challenging bumpy trails taking the hillside

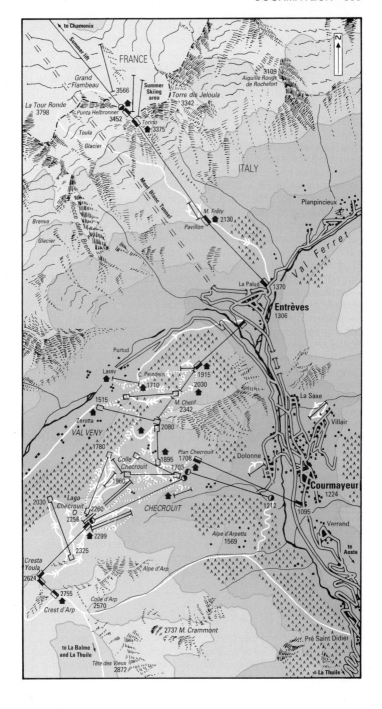

to Chamonix

Summer lift

FRANCE

Grand Flambeau

3566

Summer Skiing area

3109
Aiguille Rouge de Rochefort

Torre dis Jeloula
3342

La Tour Ronde
3798

Punta Helbronner
3452

Torino
3375

Toula Glacier

ITALY

Planpincieux

Mont Blanc Tunnel

M. Fréty
2130

Pavillon

Brenva

Rocce della Brenva

Glacier

Val Ferret

La Palud 1370

Entrèves
1306

Purtud

Lassy

C. Peindein
1710

1915

2030

La Saxe

1515

M. Chetif
2342

Villair

Zerotta

VAL VENY

2080

1780

1895

Plan Checrouit
1708

Dolonne

Colle Checrouit

1703

Courmayeur
1224

1960

2030

Lago Checrouit
2256

2260

CHECROUIT

1212

1095

Verrand

2299

Alpe d'Arpetta
1569

2325

to Aosta

Cresta Youla
2624

Alpe d'Arp

2755

Colle d'Arp
2570

Crest d'Arp

2737 M. Crammont

Pré Saint Didier

to La Balme and La Thuile

Tête des Vieux
2872

La Thuile

fairly directly and an easy, wide, winding path at the northern end of the area. The pistes served by the new Gabba chairs to the west of Lago Checrouit are reported to keep their snow well. In places, there are dangerously steep slopes beside the pistes (notably piste 19).

The very inefficient Youla cable-car above Lago Checrouit opens up a deep and sheltered bowl, usually keeping good snow, and a single uncomplicated run back down, with plenty of space for short off-piste excursions. A further short cable-car to Cresta d'Arp (where there are beautiful views) gives access to the serious off-piste skiing, principally a long and beautiful run (1500m vertical) down a secluded valley, via an awkward and not at all obvious path through steep woods to Dolonne. Other off-piste runs from this area go to Val Veny (to the north) and La Balme, near La Thuile (to the south). There are no pistes from Arp.

The three-stage **Mont Blanc** cable-car climbs over 2000m to Punta Helbronner, giving easy access to the famous Vallée Blanche run – see the Chamonix chapter preceding this one. There is an afternoon bus back from Chamonix. The off-piste run down the Italian side of the massif is very steep at the top (a rope is followed by a long exposed staircase) and often dangerous. By contrast the run down the bottom stage of the cable-car is a long, straightforward, and rarely skied piste.

Mountain restaurants are remarkably numerous, with lots of mostly very welcoming chalets and converted cow-sheds dotted around; but several reporters have complained of mediocre food, slow, surly service and only snacks available. Plan Checrouit is a proper little Hochcourmayeur, with accommodation and ski shops as well as a number of bars and restaurants. The Château Branlant serves full meals with waiter service and 'heavenly desserts', the Christiana (downstairs) and La Baita are also recommended. Other recommendations: the Petit Mont Blanc at Zerotta, where the pasta is home-made, the Altiport for 'coffee breaks and sun-worshippers' and Pré du Pascal for bargain hot wine. On the Mont Blanc side, there are bars at each lift stage, and an excellent restaurant and sun terrace at Pavillon.

The Checrouit cable-car is a long walk from the centre, but fairly free of **queues** except at weekends, when there is an influx from Turin and Milan if conditions are good, and long waits can be expected for the ride down from as well as up to the skiing. Other bottlenecks also become evident; the main black spots are Zerotta, the Youla cable-car, and the Pra Neyron chair at Plan Checrouit.

There is a large **artificial snow** installation covering several pistes down to Plan Checrouit and, over the mountain, down to Val Veny, which has proved its worth for long periods during recent seasons.

The resort

Courmayeur is a long village which now merges with its neighbouring hamlets Verrand, Villair and La Saxe, all of them quiet and prosperous second-home areas with some beautiful old rough-stone buildings. Some haphazard and unbecoming expansion has taken place along the

Verrand road near the cable-car, about half a mile from the old centre – now just an open space beside the main busy road. The heart of the old village is a delightful maze of cobbled alleys partly reserved for pedestrians, full of a very attractive variety of shops and bars, from typical Italian cafés to pubs and fast-food counters. Self-caterers are advised to shop at the supermarket on the Via Regionale directly above the cable-car station. The main resort bus service, serving cable-cars and the cross-country area, runs about every 15 minutes. There are less frequent buses to Dolonne, where the gondola for Plan Checrouit starts – a very convenient base for skiers, very inconvenient for après-skiers.

There is a great variety of **accommodation**, mostly not well situated for the main lift. Several reporters stress the undesirability of hotels located on the main road (not the main street through the village). The Pavillon is the best situated of all the hotels, and one of the most

---

Facts on Courmayeur Val d'Aosta **Italy**

Prices in lire
Ski Club represented

Tourist office
Via Circonvallazione, 100
Postcode 11013
Tel (165) 842060
Fax (165) 842072
Tlx 215871

Getting there
By road 921km from Calais. Via Macon/Geneva and Mont Blanc Tunnel; chains rarely needed.
By rail Pré-St-Didier (5km); 12 daily buses from station.
By air Geneva; transfer 2hr. (Or Turin; almost as convenient as Geneva.)

Staying there
Visitor beds 20,000; breakdown: 2,600 in hotels, 17,400 in chalets/apartments.
Package holidays Bladon Lines (hc) Chalets and Hotels "Unlimited" (h) Citalia (hs) Collineige Ski (h) Crystal (h) Enterprise (h) Falcon (h) Inghams (hs) Interski (hs) Mark Warner (j) Neilson (hs) Ski West (hcs) SnowRanger (hs) Thomson (h) .
Medical facilities In resort: Doctors, dentists, chemists. Hospital: Aosta (36km).

Non-skiing activities
Indoor Swimming/sauna in Hotel Royal and at Pré-St-Didier (5km), skating rink, Alpine museum, cinema, bridge.
Outdoor Walking paths in Val Ferret and Dolonne, paragliding, tennis.

Kindergartens
Kinderheim
Tuition: No. Hours: 9.00-4.00. Ages: 3-12. Cost: 150,000.00 per week (with lunch).

Special skiing facilities
Summer skiing Small area on the Colle del Gigante glacier (3 lifts), at around 3400m, ski school available.
Cross-country Several, 3km to 20km, in Val Ferret. 5km (difficult) and 3km (easy) at Dolonne. Instruction available.

Lift passes
Val Veny
Covers all the Val Veny and Checrouit lifts. (22 lifts in total.)
Cost 6 days 178,000.00 (£83.18). Low season: 150,000.00 saving 16%.
Credit cards accepted Yes.
Free pass for children under 1 metre in height.
Notes Passes of 6 days or more allow one day in Cervinia and one of the resorts on the Mont Blanc lift pass (Chamonix, Megève and neighbours).
Beginners Free nursery lifts at Plan Checrouit and top of Val Veny cable-car (which can be paid for by the ride).
Short-term passes Half-day; points tickets; single ascents on some main lifts.
Other passes Valle d'Aosta pass covers Courmayeur, La Thuile and Pila (6 days 184,000.00 for adults, 156,000.00 for children).
Other periods Passes for 8 non-consecutive days available.

Ski school
Monte Bianco
Classes 3hr: am only. Cost: 140,000.00 (6 half-days).
Lift priority No.
Children's classes Ages: over 6. Cost: 140,000.00 (6 half-days).
Private lessons available Hourly. Cost: 35,000.00 per hour. 1-2 people.

What was new in 91
New Plan de la Gabba chair-lift replaces old double drag-lifts.

comfortable and expensive; it has a very good pool and sauna. In the old village, the Cristallo is very attractive and comfortable; the Edelweiss is friendly, cosy, and less expensive. Two well placed hotels are the Cime Bianche ('exceedingly friendly staff') and the Hotel des Glaciers ('comfortable, substantial meals'). Cheaper B&B places which have been recommended include the Bar Roma, Pension Agip and the Croux – all simple but adequate. The Telecabine in Dolonne, run by UK operator, Mark Warner, has its own crèche, highly thought of by at least one reporter.

Après-ski resides mainly in the many bars and restaurants. The Bar Roma with its comfortable sofas and armchairs is the most popular and lively place in the early evening. Other recommended bars include Ziggi's and Steve's American Bar. There are a few discos – the Clochard in Dolonne (with restaurant) the most popular, the Etoile 'best for the early hours' – and lots of restaurants, including cheap places to fill up with pizza or pasta, nowhere cheaper or heartier than the Turistica. The Pizzeria du Tunnel is highly recommended. Of the more ambitious restaurants the most famous are the Maison de Filippo in Entrèves, a splendid place for an empty stomach and an unfussy palate. K2 at Villair and the beautiful Chalet Proment at Planpincieux in Val Ferret lay on similarly gargantuan set menus, and are much less busy. Two reporters view the Pierre Alexis as 'the best in town in terms of quality, service and value'. The ice-rink is open every evening until midnight, with disco music and lights.

The main **cross-country** trails involve a bus ride but are excellent – long, varied and beautiful, but not out of avalanche range, on last season's evidence. A large group of skiers were killed on-trail last February. For **non-skiers** there are plenty of interesting excursions (Aosta is recommended for sightseeing and cheap shopping) and good walks. In fine weather the cable-car ride to Punta Helbronner is spectacular, and many mountain restaurants are accessible to non-skiers. The Alpine museum is recommended.

Nursery slopes at Plan Checrouit are cramped by all the buildings and milling skiers. The progression to the rest of Courmayeur's skiing is also not an easy one. There are quieter nursery areas at the top of the Val Veny cable-car and at Dolonne.

We have a large number of contradictory reports on the **ski school** classes, recently more bad than good ('a "we've got your money, sod you" attitude'). Most reporters seem to agree that private instructors and guides are excellent value. Together with the local mountain guides the school runs programmes of off-piste skiing (including Vallée Blanche outings) and heli-skiing. Courmayeur is a famous mountaineering centre, and the scope for ski touring is vast.

Follow the herd

La Thuile Italy 1450m

Good for *Beautiful scenery, easy runs, skiing convenience, short airport transfers, lift queues, woodland runs*
Bad for *Tough runs, après-ski, not skiing, Alpine charm*

La Rosière France 1850m

Good for *Beautiful scenery, easy runs, lift queues, nursery slopes, family holidays, sunny slopes*
Bad for *Tough runs, après-ski, not skiing, woodland runs*

Of all the Alpine passes over which Hannibal may have driven his elephants, the Little St Bernard is the most likely candidate. Nowadays the pass is closed in winter, but lifts across the open slopes above it enable skiers to follow in Carthaginian footsteps while exploring the long and interesting ski area shared by La Thuile in the Italian Val d'Aosta and La Rosière in the French Tarentaise.

If you equate the Tarentaise with all that is biggest and best in skiing, it may come as a surprise to learn that La Rosière is the minority shareholder in this international joint venture. Italy has a larger percentage of the skiing and the best of it, with very long and beautiful intermediate runs, a few good blacks in the woods and a reputation for extreme cold. But La Rosière's skiing is far from negligible: it consists of an open, very sunny and mainly easy area on the south-facing side of the Isère valley, high above Bourg-St-Maurice, plus a couple of steeper trails through the woods below the resort. It is an excellent resort for novices and families – the village is quiet, friendly and (by local standards cheap). And for more experienced skiers there is the opportunity to make day trips to Les Arcs, La Plagne, Val d'Isère and Tignes (no more than an hour's drive away) and, of course, La Thuile (no more than an hour's ski away).

La Thuile itself is less appealing than its skiing: an odd combination of a depressingly run-down old mining village and an ambitiously large and fairly stylish new hotel and apartment complex, complete with conference halls, cavernous car parks and long echoing corridors. Someone has invested a lot of money in the belief that La Thuile is going to catch on in a big way. So far, it hasn't: even in high season the resort is quiet except at weekends, when there is an invasion from Turin.

Motorists in La Thuile are well placed for excursions to Courmayeur and Chamonix.

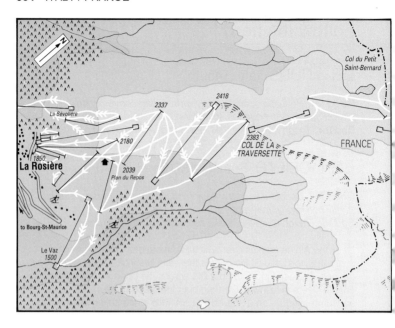

The skiing top 2642m bottom 1450m

La Thuile's ski area consists of steep wooded slopes above the resort, a wide and gentle east-facing mountainside above the trees and steeper north-facing slopes from the top lifts down towards the Little St Bernard road. On both sides of the mountain the steeper slopes are skirted by very long intermediate pistes, giving a good variety of runs of different grades back down to the resort, although the gentler ones are graded red because of their great length. La Rosière's area is a wide, mainly south-facing mountainside criss-crossed by easy intermediate runs, giving a vertical range of little over 500 metres. Of more interest to competent skiers are the runs through the woods below the village, offering greater scope and vertical range. The crests at the top of each resort's ski slopes are separated by a wide, pylon-scarred area above the pass in the shadow of Mont Blanc, where lifts have been installed to bridge the gap.

A fast stand-up gondola and a chair-lift climb steeply from the edge of La Thuile to **Les Suches** (2200m), a cluster of buildings above the woods where the mountain flattens out. Two blacks plunge back down through the woods, splendidly steep and kept in good condition by the shade; No 2 has the additional help of snow guns. Red 4 provides an easier option back to the resort. Above Les Suches an area of very easy runs opens out into a wider bowl of intermediate skiing beneath the rocky peaks of **Belvedere** and **Chaz Dura**, the high points of the ski area. Most of the runs are wide and very gentle under the long Belvedere and Cerellaz chair-lifts, slightly steeper on the slopes of Chaz

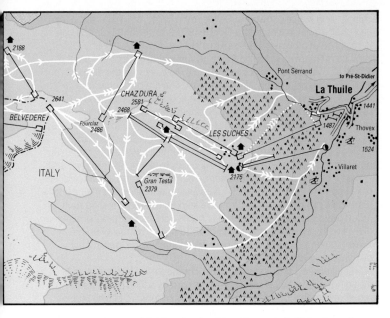

Dura. The wide mogul field under the Chaz Dura chair-lift is about the only run which is not constantly groomed. From the higher slopes there are magnificent views, including a vast wave of glacier on the Rutor (much used for heli-skiing) and the south side of Mont Blanc. On the easterly side of the ski area is a very long and satisfying home run down through the woods: it is very beautiful, with magnificent views of sunset on the Grandes Jorasses, and surprisingly little skied.

Some of La Thuile's best skiing is on the rocky north-facing slopes above the St Bernard road, served by a chair-lift and accessible from both Chaz Dura and, by a less than terrifying black, from Belvedere. There is good off-piste skiing as well as reds and blacks, and the slope offers a worthwhile drop of some 600m. The least direct route, a run of 11km for 1100m vertical, is a wide, easy and panoramic red piste, which cruises on past the chair-lift station and follows the road gently around the mountain to La Thuile, where it is joined by the steeper and more direct descents from Les Suches. A new three-seat chair-lift from the Col du Petit St Bernard to a ridge below Belvedere opened in 1990, adding a wide new area of intermediate pistes, including one not very demanding black. It has also greatly improved links between the two resorts, which are due for another boost by the construction of a chair-lift from **the** top of the existing chair-lift up the Bellecombe valley to Belevedere this year. This should provide a more direct route into La Thuile's ski area from La Rosière; the existing route can be tedious and bitterly cold. Several sections of the main run down to the Fourclaz chair require a fair amount of poling.

The Belvedere chair is the only way back to La Rosière. A 50-metre slog round the shoulder of the mountain will bring you to the top of an achingly long schuss down the Bellecombe valley, from where a steep quad chair-lift hoists you to the **Col de la Traversette** (2383m), a gap in the rocky crest crowning La Rosière's ski-fields, complete with dilapidated Napoleonic fortifications commanding the pass. From the col and all over the ski area there are fine views across the deep Isère valley to Les Arcs and the Aiguille Rouge. The run back down the col is a hairpin track, which has been recently moderated and graded red, not black. Intimidated beginners can ride down on the Chardonnet chair. Passing below the fort is a long blue run, La Choucas, which traverses the mountainside and leads directly to La Rosière village; tedium is relieved by numerous piste crossroads. Alternatively you can zigzag up and down the various lifts beneath the crest, exploring the red runs and a single moderate black beside them. This is a wide and uncomplicated area of open, very sunny intermediate skiing, with short easy runs and nursery lifts near the village. From the altiport, two more testing runs, graded red and black, skirt the pretty hamlet of Les Eucherts, ending up below it at the bottom of a chair-lift at 1500m. There must often be excellent spring-snow skiing all over the mountainside, particularly down this gully to Le Vaz at 1500m.

Directly above La Rosière is a wide, thoroughly blue slope, excellent for beginners and ski school classes, served by a long chair- and drag-lift. From the top of the chair, two straight-forward blacks plunge down the south-west face of the mountain, across the road leading up to the pass, and into the woods. They become red and weave through the trees down to **Les Ecudets** at 1150m, from where a new quad chair and a steep drag-lift bring you back to the wide blue run home.

There are several **mountain restaurants** on the Italian side; the largest (and ugliest) is a characterless self-service place at Les Suches, serving home-made pastas and soups. Le Foyer in the middle of the upper La Thuile bowl has a sunbathing terrace and a good restaurant, managed by a grumpy Italian, beneath a large bar with an open fire. Other recommendations include the Off Shore at the Belvedere chair and the Roxi bar at the Fourclaz chair – 'a delightful stopping-off point on the gentle run down to La Thuile'. There are several sunny places to eat and drink at the foot of La Rosière's pistes, but only one mountain restaurant, the Plan Repos, which is 'cosy and pleasant', serving 'huge and delicious portions'.

Queues in either resort are rare, accept at weekends when the linking lifts become bottle-neck at peak times. In La Thuile, access to Les Suches is no longer a problem, thanks to the very efficient 25-person gondola from the resort; the Fourclaz chair up to Chaz Dura, often busy with skiers returning from La Rosière, will be greatly relieved this year by the Bellecombe chair-lift up to Belvedere.

There is **artificial snow** on a fair length of north-facing piste down to La Thuile via Les Suches. La Rosière has one moveable cannon on the main slope above the village.

La Thuile

La Thuile stands in a rather austere and enclosed setting a few miles from Pré-St-Didier beside the Little St Bernard road, which climbs no further than the resort in winter. Strung out beside road and river, the old village's peeling and abandoned buildings have now been bought by the community for restoration. The disused mining buildings are to be turned into a national sports academy, and renewal has already started with the creation of a new La Thuile, above the old village at the foot of the ski slopes. This is a handsome and harmonious complex of modern buildings with a vast hotel, a huge area of underground parking, a shopping precinct with some fashionable boutiques, and apartment buildings with good indoor sports facilities. All it lacks is the breath of life.

For the purposes of British package holiday-makers, who now account for 20 per cent of La Thuile's custom, **accommodation** is mainly in the modern apartments, which are convenient for skiing, shopping, swimming and skating. Particularly recommended are the apartments in the Planibel Complex; 'spacious, chalet-style studios,

Facts on La Thuile Val d'Aosta **Italy**

Prices in lire

Tourist office
Postcode 11016
Tel (165) 884179
Fax (165) 885196

Getting there
By road 938km from Calais. Via Macon/Geneva and Mont Blanc tunnel; chains may be needed.
By rail Pré-St-Didier (10km).
By air Turin; transfer 2½hr. (Or Geneva.)

Staying there
Visitor beds 4,000; breakdown: mainly in hotels and apartments.
Package holidays Falcon (s) Ski Valkyrie (has) SnowRanger (hs) Snowbugs (hs) .
Medical facilities In resort: Fracture clinic, doctor, chemist.

Non-skiing activities
Indoor Squash, artificial skating rink, 2 swimming pools, bowling, sauna, gym, jacuzzi, massage, amusement arcade, billiards.
Outdoor Paragliding, walks.

Kindergartens
Other childcare facilities
Baby-sitters available, contact Tourist Office.

Special skiing facilities
Summer skiing Heli-skiing on the Rutor glacier till April/May.
Cross-country Loops of 1km (easy), 3km (medium), 5km (medium), 7½km (difficult) and 10km (difficult).

Lift passes
Area pass
Covers all La Thuile/La Rosière lifts. (34 lifts in total.)
Cost 6 days 160,000.00 (£74.77). Low season: 139,000.00 saving 13%.
Credit cards accepted Yes.
Beginners One baby-lift in village; day pass for nursery lifts (12,000.00); points cards.
Short-term passes Half-day (from 1.00pm); single and return tickets on main cable-car.
Other passes Valle d'Aosta pass covers La Thuile, Pila and Courmayeur (6 days 184,000.00 for adults and children).
Other periods Passes available for 8 non-consecutive days.

Ski school
Rutor
Classes 2½hr: am only. Cost: 118,000.00 (6 half-days). 2hr classes if fewer than 5 pupils. Beginners classes start on Mondays.
Lift priority Yes.
Children's classes Ages: 5 up. Cost: 118,000.00 (6 half-days).
Private lessons available Hourly. Cost: 35,000.00 per hour. 1-2 people.
Special courses Heli-skiing on the Rutor glacier from Dec to Apr. Day trip costs about 170,000.00.

What was new in 91
1. New triple chair-lift from the Col du Petit Saint-Bernard to just below the Belvedere ridge.
2. New black (Roc Noir) and red run (Dahu) down either side.

built around a courtyard very near main gondola', 'two bathrooms for a 4-6 person apartment, massive cupboard space'. The Planibel also has a vast, comfortable, expensive business-style hotel of nearly 300 rooms, often used by large conference groups. The hotel serves good buffet breakfasts and has a piano-bar, a disco and its own pool with water slide. Guests get free entry to all the Planibel's sports facilities. Among the old hotels, the simple Edelweiss is a good choice, well placed at the top of the village beside the runs down from the pass. In the old mining village, half a mile from the lifts, the Pension Rolland is 'modern, clean and friendly', the Rollands themselves 'excellent hosts'.

The good sports facilities in the Planibel Complex are open to the public but do not in themselves make La Thuile a good resort for **non-skiers**. They are useful as a substitute for **après-ski,** of which there is not much, with the notable exception of La Bricole, a beautifully converted old building between old and new parts of the resort. It has a bar, a crypt disco and a smartly rustic restaurant ('expensive but good', 'book at least 2 days in advance'). Other recommendations include Les Marmottes ('excellent food and service'), the pizzeria Lo Creton ('cheap, good quality and atmosphere') and the Relais in the Planibel Complex ('friendly service, very reasonable *menu turistica*'). The Gelateria at the bottom gondola station is a favourite tea-time spot, justly famous for its superb ice-cream and cakes.

Cross-country trails are not enormously extensive but attractively set in the wooded valley that runs down from the Rutor to La Thuile. The trails are directly accessible from the Planibel complex and link up with an open area of sunny loops on the other side of the river, location of the main cross-country centre and the resort's one instructor.

There is a small area of **nursery slopes** near the main lift station on the edge of the new part of the resort and a more extensive nursery area on the wide, easy slopes above Les Suches. We have had enthusiastic reports of the **ski school**; 'class allocation was thorough, groups were very small, instructors spoke reasonable English'. In the latter part of the season the school organises heli-skiing from the Rutor Glacier down to La Rosière.

La Rosière

La Rosière is little more than a gathering of mostly traditional-looking buildings around the hairpin bends of the road up to the Little St Bernard. It is not particularly villagey, but there are several old hamlets dotted around the sunny slopes nearby, and the style of the place is generally attractive. In winter the road ends with a snow bank at the top of the village beside a pen containing a few sunbathing St Bernard dogs (and a husky) which line up obligingly at the sight of a camera. Access to the skiing area is from the roadside at the top of the village, where the first lift was installed in 1962 behind the Relais du Petit St Bernard, last post on the French side of the border. **Accommodation** slowly grew up below the Relais but the major building boom which so affected the other Tarentaise resorts largely passed La Rosière by, and although a number of not unattractive apartment blocks have sprung up in recent years, most of the resort's regular visitors stay in private wooden chalets, hidden in the trees, in an area below the main street called Le Gollet. A regular free bus service connects Le Gollet and the outlying hamlet of Les Eucherts to the main ski area. Several reporters have remarked on the delightful friendly bus drivers. Unfortunately the buses stop soon after the lifts close, and any night-time excursions from Le Gollet require an exhausting hike up one of the 'short cuts' to the main road. There are a number of simple, convenient hotels providing accommodation nearer the ski area, including the original Relais (which also has a very popular bar) and the Plein Soleil. Several reporters recommend the family-run Belvédère ('traditional charms of mountain life'), despite its location several kilometres away on the road to Bourg. The new Terrasse apartments are convenient for the slopes and village but conditions are fairly cramped. Self-catering visitors have been

---

Facts on La Rosière   Savoie **France**

Prices in francs

Tourist office
Postcode 73700
Tel 79068051
Fax 79068320

Getting there
By road 930km from Calais. Via Macon/Annecy; chains often needed from Bourg-St-Maurice.
By rail Bourg-St-Maurice; frequent buses to resort.
By air Geneva; transfer 4½hr. (Or Lyon.)

Staying there
Visitor beds 7,500; breakdown: 3,000 in apartments, 400 in hotels, rest in private accommodation.
Package holidays Enterprise (hs) Quest Travel (schools) (h) Ski Chamois (hs) Ski Club of GB (a) Ski Club of GB (a) Ski Olympic (c) SnowRanger (s) .
Medical facilities In resort: Doctor, chemist. Dentist: Seez; Hospital: Bourg-St-Maurice.

Non-skiing activities
Indoor Fitness Club – body-building, aerobics, sauna, jacuzzi, hammam, massage; cinema, museum, library, table tennis.
Outdoor Paragliding, cleared paths, husky walks, floodlit skiing, luge run, ski jump, flights over Mont Blanc, heli-skiing.

Kindergartens
Baby Club
Tuition: No. Hours: Full- or half-day. Ages: 1-3. Cost: 300.00 (6 half-days). Lunch available.

Special skiing facilities
Summer skiing Heli-skiing till May.
Cross-country 12km of trails through the woods, graded green to black; tuition available.

Lift passes
La Rosière
Covers all lifts in La Rosière and the ski bus within the resort. (16 lifts in total.)
Cost 6 days 495.00 (£51.03). Low season: 420.00 saving 15%.
Credit cards accepted Yes.
Senior citizens 327.00 (over 60) saving 34%.
Children 327.00 (under 12) saving 34%. Free pass up to age 6.
Notes Daily extensions for La Thuile lifts (68.00 for adults, 45.00 for children); passes for a week or more allow one day in Les Arcs.
Beginners Free baby-lifts below the St Bernards' kennels; half-day or day pass for limited beginners' area.
Short-term passes Half-day and day pass.
Other passes Domaine International covers all lifts in La Rosiere and La Thuile (6 days 680.00 for adults, 449.00 for children).

Ski school
ESF
Classes 9.15-11.45 and/or 2.30-5.00. Cost: 485.00 (6 full days).
Lift priority Yes.
Children's classes Ages: 4-12. Cost: 450.00 (6 full days).
Private lessons available Hourly. Cost: 115.00 per hour. Up to 2 people.
Special courses Heli-skiing on three glaciers: the Ruitor, the Ormelune and Mt Miravidi; day trip costs from 780.00; surf courses between 12.30 and 2.30, 5 lessons cost 350.00.

What was new in 91
New 3-seater San Bernardo chairlift on La Thuile side.

What is new for 92
Bellecombe 2 chair-lift link between La Rosière and La Thuile.

impressed with the choice and prices in the local supermarket and the tri-weekly street market.

Après-ski usually begins directly after the lifts close at the Relais bar (aka Toni's), whose balcony is absolutely packed on fine evenings with people enjoying the view, the vin chaud and the excellent pizzas. There are various other popular bars including Arpin's next to the Relais and Le Dahu which has a games room, and some good restaurants. Particularly recommended are the Eterlou (for 'wide-ranging menu, excellent pizza'), the Pitchounette (for 'succulent steaks but interminable service'), and the Plein Soleil (for 'French home-cooking, very reasonable, closes early'). La Chaumière, in the nearby village of Montvalezan, is an ancient Savoyard farmhouse with bags of atmosphere, excellent food and prices to match. There are a couple of discos, reportedly fairly dead; Toni's bar has a disco night on Tuesdays which is very popular with locals, chalet staff and holiday-makers alike.

There is very little to amuse **non-skiers**, although the Tourist Office arranges weekly events such as husky walks. Other popular walks include the scenic 8km stroll to the Italian border. There is a small and expensive fitness club, recommended by a couple of reporters. Regular buses provide excursion opportunities to Bourg-St-Maurice and other towns and villages dotted around the Isère valley. There is a straight-forward 12km **cross-country** trail with various blue, red and black options, beginning at the resort centre and winding through the woods.

La Rosière is close to being and ideal resort for beginners, with excellent **nursery slopes** directly above the resort and around the altiport, served by a number of easy lifts. The pistes are kept immaculately groomed (frustratingly so for non-beginners) and there is an easy slalom course on the blue Renard run. Unlike La Thuile, La Rosière offers a local lift pass, about 30 per cent cheaper than the overall area pass and definitely worthwhile for inexperienced skiers.

Just below the St Bernards' pen is a tiny roped-off area with a short tow, used by the **kindergarten**, which is reportedly 'competent and caring'. We've had similarly good reports of the **ski school**; one complete beginner was happily skiing into Italy after a few lessons. One reporter complains of wasted time.

Le ski rules, OK?

Val d'Isère France 1850m

Good for *Big ski area, easy runs, tough runs, off-piste skiing, late holidays, resort-level snow, après-ski, lift queues, sunny slopes, summer skiing, chalet holidays, artificial snow*
Bad for *Alpine charm, mountain restaurants, short airport transfers, easy road access, not skiing, skiing convenience, woodland runs*

Tignes France 2000m

Good for *Big ski area, off-piste skiing, tough runs, late holidays, resort-level snow, lift queues, skiing convenience, summer skiing*
Bad for *Alpine charm, après-ski, not skiing, easy road access, short airport transfers, mountain restaurants, woodland runs*

These two very different resorts share an almost inexhaustible, high-altitude ski area which has established itself as one of the world's premier destinations for keen skiers. Opinions about the relative merits of the two resorts vary, but our scores of reporters are almost unanimous in their approval of the skiing and in their desire to return for further exploration of it. L'Espace Killy (as it is now styled, in honour of local hero Jean-Claude) has everything: good nursery slopes, mile upon mile of motorway piste including huge expanses at glacier level, long and steep mogul fields and, not least, enormous off-piste and ski touring potential. Queues are rarely a problem except in bad weather (when there is very little skiing to be done, especially at Tignes). If the skiing has a drawback it is that those in charge of it seem indifferent to the needs of timid skiers; piste grading is unreliable, and grooming is casual. There is precious little point in adopting the helpful French system of four grades of piste if some of the greens incorporate mogul fields.

Both Val and Tignes are skiers' ski resorts; you don't have to be an expert, but you do have be keen. Anyone who wants to do more on a winter holiday than ski, drink, eat, dance and sleep should not be tempted. Tignes is the very model of a modern French resort, built up rapidly and not at all prettily from nothing in the pit of a huge treeless horseshoe of mountains, beneath the glaciers of the Grande Motte, one of Savoie's highest and most shapely peaks. It is a large, mostly self-catering resort split into three parts around a small lake. It now has a range of sports facilities, but is fairly quiet after dark. Most of the resort is ideal for convenience skiing. On paper, there is more to find fault with in Val d'Isère; the resort is a styleless traffic-filled straggle, the lifts aren't central, and the runs down to the valley are difficult. But at least it feels like a village, and is increasingly lively in the evenings. Several reporters have disagreed with our 'bad for skiing convenience' verdict; certainly some parts of the resort (eg La Daille) are convenient, but most parts are not. The resort is beginning to invest in its appearance, preparatory to world-wide TV exposure at the Olympics this season, and seems to be moving upmarket. It still attracts young enthusiasts from all over the world, but an older and more affluent clientele (including Americans) is also evident.

The resorts are not easy to reach by car, but having one facilitates day-trips to Les Arcs, La Rosière, Sainte-Foy and La Plagne, and makes it possible for skiers based in Tignes to have a bit of fun in Val d'Isère. Buses between the two resorts are neither frequent nor cheap. Taxis can be extortionate.

The skiing top 3439m bottom 1550m

L'Espace Killy divides naturally into at least six separate sectors. On the Val d'Isère side, the sectors of Col de l'Iseran/Pisaillas, Solaise and Bellevarde are strung in a row along the curving road to Le Fornet, served by efficient ski-buses through the resort. The first two sectors are linked by lift at altitude; Solaise and Bellevarde only at valley level, just beside Val d'Isère. Bellevarde links up over the Tovière ridge with Tignes, which has skiing around all sides of a horseshoe, in three main sectors – Tovière, Grande Motte (going up to the glacier), and Palet/Aiguille Percée. Behind the Aiguille Percée there is still more skiing down to the hamlets of Les Brévières and Les Boisses.

The **Solaise** cable-car was Val d'Isère's first lift, installed in 1943. Two chair-lifts, one a new covered four-seater, run parallel to it, giving access to the Tête de Solaise. Under these lifts are some steep, awkward and often bare runs through the trees. Above the tree-line, underneath the top half of the cable-car, and served by its own chair-lift is Val d'Isère's most famous run: the Plan, or simply the Bumps – a wide mogul-field, not particularly long or steep (patches of over 30° are few, and short), but a cult. Bumps are left to grow to very impressive dimensions. Descending to the left of the cable-car, missing out most of the bumps run, Piste S is one of the most difficult in the area, very often just as bumpy as the Plan but longer, steeper and narrower – a run to sort out real skiers from Solaise swanks. Beyond the Tête de Solaise, a high, long, gentle bowl provides a lot of long, easy runs (green and blue) complicated only by piste crossroads. Around the steep rims of the bowl there is a lot of off-piste skiing, often dangerous. The long Cugnaï chair-lift gives access to runs down a beautiful off-piste back bowl – often skied into a piste-like state – leading to the chair-lift back up from Le Manchet. There are open, intermediate runs down either side of this lift, which are often allowed to grow into tricky mogul fields.

From behind Tête de Solaise there is some particularly beautiful, uncrowded skiing down to Le Laisinant (between Le Fornet and Val d'Isère) where you pick up the bus. The runs are marked red and blue, but the blue is not as easy as the blues higher up, and long. This is another area for excellent off-piste skiing of varying difficulty, the major hazard being unexpected cliff edges.

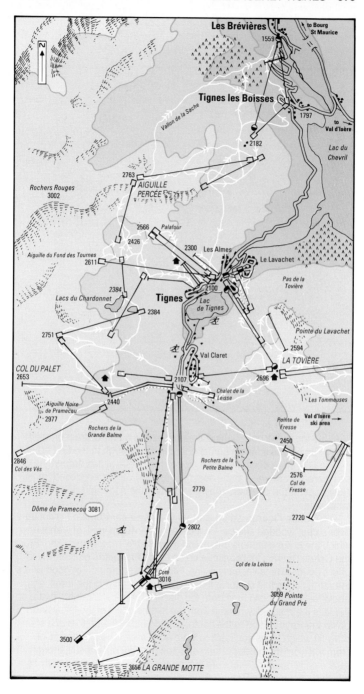

Les Brévières

to Bourg
St Maurice

1559

Tignes les Boisses

1797

to
Val d'Isère

Vallon de la Sache

Lac du
Chevril

2182

2763

*AIGUILLE
PERCÉE*

Rochers Rouges
3002

2566 *Palafour*

2426

2300 Les Almes

Le Lavachet

Aiguille du Fond des Tournes

2611

Pas de la
Tovière

2384

Lacs du Chardonnet

Tignes

2100

2384

Lac
de Tignes

Pointe du Lavachet

2751

2594

Val Claret

LA TOVIÈRE

COL DU PALET
2653

2107

*Chalet de la
Leisse*

2696

Les Tommeuses

Val d'Isère
ski area

Aiguille Noire
de Pramecou
2977

2440

Pointe de
Fresse

*Rochers de la
Grande Balme*

2450

2846
Col des Vés

*Rochers de la
Petite Balme*

2576
Col de
Fresse

2779

2720

Dôme de Pramecou 3081

2802

Col de la Leisse

Cote
3016

3059 *Pointe
du Grand Pré*

3500

3656 *LA GRANDE MOTTE*

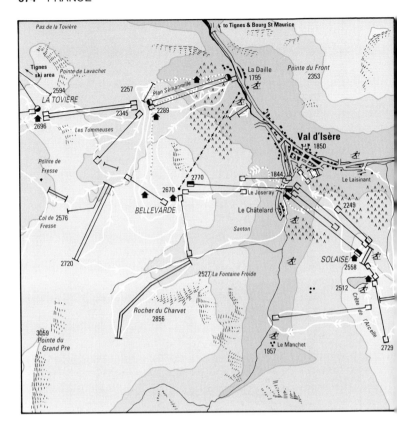

At the top of the bowl behind Solaise there is a short, steep drag-lift with a run beside it, and a tunnel near the top through to the Le Fornet ski area. The run down the other side to the gentle pistes around the Col de l'Iseran is awkward at the best of times and very often closed; most skiers opt for the dramatic chair-lift ride over the ridge and down the other side.

The **Col de l'Iseran** skiing starts with a cable-car from Le Fornet up over steep, wooded slopes – in this case only 400m vertical – above which the ground flattens out, giving a lot of easy motorway skiing. From the Col de l'Iseran, lifts continue up on to the **Pissaillas** glacier, which offers open, extensive, easy skiing, winter and summer. For good skiers the attraction of this sector is the off-piste skiing among the trees, and above all the off-piste runs from the glacier. The most straightforward of these is the much-skied route from the highest point of the lift system down the Pays Désert to the south, coming out at the bottom of a short drag-lift which takes you back to the glacier area. The so-called Col Pers run from the glacier is long and beautiful but not difficult, though guidance is needed. There are two routes down, the more easterly of which ends up at the Refuge de Prariond, a popular ski touring base.

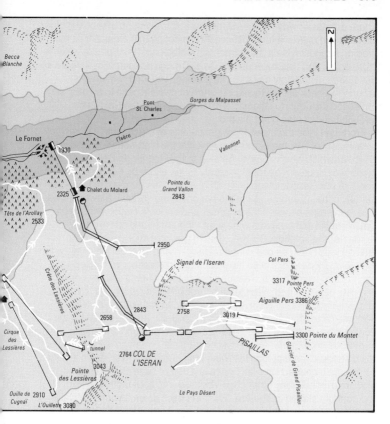

The Refuge serves drinks and simple meals on its sunny terrace. From here it is a schuss back to Le Fornet with one steeper section through a scenic gorge. The off-piste routes behind the Signal drag-lift into the Grand Vallon are much more open, and much steeper, ending in the woods above Le Fornet. From the glacier, blue motorways descend to the top of the Le Fornet cable-car, from where there is a choice of runs to the valley; the blue consists of a lot of traversing, with some awkward passages, the more direct black is narrow and testing, often bare and icy, and usually mogulled.

The Rocher de **Bellevarde** rises steeply and impressively on the western side of Val d'Isère, and a long cable-car climbs quickly from the same station as the Solaise lift on the edge of town to near the peak, over 900m above the resort. The runs directly down from Bellevarde to Val d'Isère, under the cable-car, are long, steep and demanding – about the most difficult piste skiing in the area. It is here that the new Olympic course for the men's downhill has been created. Controversially steep at the top, the 3 km run descends to the village beside the new Santel Express chair-lift. There is also some very good off-piste skiing. Bellevarde gets a lot of sun, and snow tends to deteriorate quickly.

There are easier ways to the village, but a narrow gunbarrel on the blue Santons run makes it more difficult than most people expect or its blue grading suggests. Near the Santons is a black run (the Épaule) which is more open, and has fewer people on it. Though no match for the face of Bellevarde, it certainly deserves its grading. The long twin drag-lift around the back of the Rocher du Charvet gives access to an off-piste run called the Tour du Charvet, similar in appeal to the Col Pers – beautiful and not too difficult although often dangerous.

From La Daille the other, more gentle side of the mountain is served by a variety of lifts, the quickest of which is the high-speed, underground funicular which whisks passengers up to the Rocher de Bellevarde in a mere five minutes. The more leisurely route, either by the old access gondola (the second stage of which has been dismantled) or by a parallel chair-lift, brings you to the bottom of the sunny Bellevarde area. The many runs between the funicular and gondola stations above La Daille are spread around a wide area, and are nearly all very easy except for the splendid OK run, (the old downhill race course, quite often closed because of avalanche danger) and Orange, which hugs the Bellevarde rock and is in some ways more interesting, with steeper pitches and fewer skiers. The area below the gondola station mostly consists of pistes and off-piste runs through trees, which are the main characteristic and attraction of the area, along with splendid views northwards to Mont Blanc. The runs to La Daille are the easiest ways down to the valley but often unpleasantly crowded and icy despite numerous snow guns. An interesting off-piste excursion is the so-called Piste Perdue, more or less following the course of a river, down a gully.

The main connection with Tignes is a pair of triple chair-lifts (long, slow, and – like many other chair-lifts here – without footrests) from the top gondola station to **Tovière**. The runs back down towards La Daille are tricky blues, and a short red. There is a good open off-piste area down from Tovière to La Daille, left of all the lifts and the Piste Perdue.

The Val d'Isère Downhill: Bell's view

Val holds the first big race of the World Cup downhill season, in early December. It's always been like a home race for me because there are so many British tourists around – there are louder cheers for me than for the French racers! Also I know the old OK downhill course really well: they used to hold the British championships there, and it was the first downhill I ever did when I was 14. The 1992 Olympic downhill will be held here, but on a new course on a quite different part of the mountain.

The old course is what you might call a motorway course – very fast, with long turns – not at all like the tight ones at Kitzbühel, where you just slam on the edges. At Val d'Isère you had to be very slow and smooth in your movements in the turns. Fast skis counted for a lot at the top, which is pretty flat and straight. The new course is very different, and is going to favour different kinds of racer.

The main lift out of Tignes for Tovière is now an efficient stand-up gondola, the aéro-ski (from Tignes-le-Lac). The run straight back down under the lift is a very good one – black with a steep mogul field at the bottom – and there is the possibility of an even steeper variant on the top section (the Mur de Paquerettes). The blue alternative, which follows a path for much of the way, is often dangerously crowded in the late afternoon. Other less severe runs (but facing the afternoon sun, and often icy in the mornings) lead to Val Claret, joining up with the fairly straightforward run down from the Col de Fresse and merging, to the discomfiture of beginners, with the Val Claret nursery lifts. To the south of the Col de Fresse run is a narrow, off-piste gully which provides an excellent, traffic-free alternative route.

The new funicular to the **Grande Motte** should be operational in time for the Olympics but serious engineering problems have cast a shadow of doubt on whether it will be. In time, the notorious pair of old gondola lifts, which always seem to be overcrowded or breaking down, will be dismantled, as will the long two-stage chair-lift running parallel to them. But until the funicular is in full working order, these are the two routes to the main congregation area at about 3000m.

The Grande Motte cable-car, which is rarely open early in the season, serves a run which is easy, but more interesting than most of the pistes on Val d'Isère's Pisaillas glacier. On the far side of the glacier, beside the summer ski drag-lift, is a marvellous off-piste descent to the bottom of the double Leisse chair-lifts, which should only be attempted with a guide and great care because of the vast ice-falls on the edge of the glacier. The Leisse chairs serve a broad piste down to the east of the main glacier lift stations; graded red, it is blue in character for most of its length, but ends in a fierce little mogul field.

From the main glacier lift stations, a pleasant, wide slope, often mogulled at the bottom, descends down the north-face of the mountain beside twin drags and a chair-lift back up. You can continue to Val Claret down a long and not too difficult red, often extremely crowded. Next to it is the Wall, a run for good skiers to tick off, which is just what it sounds like: a short but very steep drop over the end of the glacier. More straightforward ways down are the blue runs down the north-west side of the Motte, which connect with the Col de Fresse lifts taking you back to Val d'Isère. A particularly fine off-piste run crosses the glacier high up below the Dôme de Pramécou. A ten-minute plod brings you to a col behind the Rocher de Grande Balme, from where it is possible to join up with the skiing below Col du Palet. This area will become more accessible when the planned cable-car from below the Grand Motte mid-station to the Dôme de Pramécou is built.

The **Col du Palet/Aiguille Percée** area above Val Claret and Tignes-le-Lac is probably the least exciting skiing in Tignes, but there is a lot of it. It is very sunny and rarely crowded, with lots of runs which do not differ greatly – nearly all in the blue or easy red category, with a few steeper pitches. The twin drag-lifts up the Aiguille du Chardonnet have been replaced by a quad chair-lift, which has speeded up the flow of skiers from Val Claret to the Aiguille Percée. There is a superb, very long and beautiful piste down from Aiguille Percée to

Tignes-les-Brévières (La Sache, graded black but not difficult, until the final steep descent to the village which is often icy). Several off-piste alternatives, starting with steep drops off the ridge running west of the Aiguille Percée, follow similar routes to the valley. There is also a blue via Tignes-les-Boisses, which at the bottom may be icy and so not as easy as a blue run should be. The Col du Palet is the starting point of long and beautiful off-piste runs down to Champagny and Plan Peisey, not difficult on firm late-season snow, according to one report.

Val and Tignes still have a long way to go in the provision of inviting **mountain restaurants**, of which there are precious few. Recent reports suggest that there have been some improvements, although several reporters disagree with the tourist office view that working loos are no longer hard to find, and all are indignant at having to pay 25p for the use of them. Individual restaurants worth picking out are those at the top of Tovière and on the Grande Motte (crowded but particularly good views), the Marmottes in the gentle bowl between Bellevarde and Col de Fresse (free loos!), and the one below Col du Palet. (The latter two are not reliably marked on piste maps.) La Savouna under the Palafour chairs above Tignes-le-Lac is particularly recommended, as are the restaurants at the top and bottom of the Le Fornet cable-car; the former has good but pricey dishes, the latter hot meals, cooked to order, and draught lager. There are several recommended villagey places in Les Brevières.

The lift system is well conceived and continually improved, so that when everything is working **queues** should not be a problem. The main recent black-spots have been the return to Tignes via Tovière in the afternoon, and all the lifts out of Val Claret, particularly for the Grande Motte. There are often queues for the Grande Motte cable-car, higher up. The new Solaise Express chair-lift should relieve the peak-time queues for the cable-car. The funicular at La Daille is not always queue-free and reportedly breaks down quite frequently. The Bellevarde cable-car was shut for most of last season so inevitable queues built up at the Bellevarde chair-lifts. This should not be a problem when the cable-car is back in action and the upper of the two chairs has been replaced by a quad, like the lower. A greater problem than queues is piste congestion, especially on the Grande Motte, Solaise and runs to La Daille. The piste map is difficult to follow, attempting to cover too much in a single view.

Among off-piste skiers this is a pilgrimage resort thanks to the sheer extent of the skiable region and the number of open slopes you can reach by lift, many of them skiable (with guidance) by non-experts. The area has a reputation for avalanches, but this may have a lot to do with the numbers of people who go off-piste skiing. In our experience the authorities take the dangers seriously and work very hard, not only to make the mountains secure, but also to inform skiers about off-piste as well as piste conditions. But some visitors are confused by the resorts' policy of permanently marking all the many known off-piste runs as closed and dangerous.

There is **artificial snow** on the OK run from Bellevarde to La Daille and on the lower parts of the runs under the La Daille gondola, and on the bottom runs to Val d'Isère on both the Solaise and Bellevarde sides. Tignes has installed new snow guns in three areas; the resort run from Col du Palet, the lower part of the red from the Motte and the run beside the nursery slope chair-lift in Val Claret.

Val d'Isère

Val d'Isère is set in a remote steep-sided valley, beyond the reservoir which drowned the old village of Tignes 40 years ago. The road emerges from a series of tunnels into the valley at La Daille, little more than a cluster of modern apartment buildings at the foot of the pistes. Val d'Isère proper starts half a mile or so up the road, a gathering density of mostly ugly blocks and a few chalets. The road becomes a long, wide main street, with shops, bars, and hotels on either side and parking in the middle where once was the river. A fine old 11th-century Savoyard church and some rough old buildings huddled around it are all there is to old Val d'Isère. A new Val d'Isère has recently emerged next to it in the shape of Val d'Isère Village – a handsome rough-stone shopping and apartment precinct at the foot of the nursery slopes, built over the road out to the main lift stations. This is a very welcome development, making the village a much more attractive place to return to on skis. The resort is long and strung-out, but it is not huge, and nowhere is far from the main-road bus route; it is also flat, so walking is no great hardship. Although the road goes only to Le Fornet (the Col de l'Iseran, Europe's highest pass, is closed in winter), there are always lots of cars and buses around – far too many for comfort, according to a recent reporter: 'You are more likely to come to harm crossing the main road than you are on the ski slopes'. The shopping is good for gourmet self-caterers (expect queues at peak times), and at the end of the season for equipment bargain-hunters. There is a street market on Mondays.

There is a free and frequent ski-bus service along the valley which is invaluable, although a terrible crush at peak times (skis have to be taken inside). There is a less frequent evening service to La Daille.

There is a much wider choice of **accommodation**, and many more hotels, than in most purpose-built resorts. Central hotels and residences are within easy walking range of the main cable-car station and nursery slopes; from other places you either face longer walks or the bus. There are no really luxurious hotels but plenty of small, simple ones offering good value. At the top end of the range are the rather soulless Sofitel and the 'excellent' Latitudes. Of the other hotels, we have favourable reports of the four-star Christiania ('traditional decor, helpful, friendly staff'), the Sorbiers ('small-scale, modern but cosy, popular with Americans') and the Tsanteleina ('recently upgraded, big rooms, excellent food'), and an unfavourable report of the Bellier ('not worth its three stars'). A large number of reporters stayed in chalets or chalet hotels; most were satisfied with the standard of accommodation and facilities. We have several enthusiastic reports of Mark Warner's chalet-hotel the Cygnaski ('hard to find a better place'); it has particularly

Facts on Val d'Isère Savoie **France**

Prices in francs
Ski Club represented

Tourist office

Postcode 73150
Tel 79061083
Fax 79411206
Tlx 980077

Getting there

By road 960km from Calais. Via Macon/Lyon;
chains often needed. Horrific peak weekend
traffic jams.
By rail Bourg-St-Maurice (33km); four buses
daily from station.
By air Geneva; transfer 4½hr. (Or Lyon.)

Staying there

Visitor beds 24,500; breakdown: 2,500 in hotels,
22,000 in apartments.
Package holidays Bladon Lines (hcjs) Brittany
Ferries (s) Chalets and Hotels "Unlimited" (hcs)
Chalets and Hotels "Unlimited" (hcs) Club Med
(h) Crystal (hcs) Enterprise (hs) French
Impressions (s) Horizon (hs) Hoverspeed
Ski-Drive (hs) Inghams (hs) Made to Measure
(hs) Mark Warner (cj) Neilson (hs) Quest Travel
(schools) (h) Sally Holidays (s) Silver Ski (c) Ski
Alternatives (h) Ski Equipe (hc) Ski Europe (h) Ski
Valkyrie (hs) Ski West (hcjs) Ski Whizz Small
World (c) SkiBound (h) Skiworld (hcjas) Snobiz
(s) SnowRanger (s) Snowbugs (cs) Supertravel
(hcjs) The Ski Company Ltd (c) Thomson (hs)
Touralp (hs) Tracer Holidays (s) Vacations (hs).
Medical facilities In resort: Fracture clinic,
doctor, dentist, chemist. Hospital:
Bourg-St-Maurice (33km).

Non-skiing activities

Indoor Balneothermic centres in the hotels Le
Brussels and Sofitel Therapeos (sauna,
hammam, jacuzzi, body building, massages etc);
cinemas, bridge (courses available), dance,
aerobics, sauna, massage, solarium, gym.
Outdoor Walks in Le Manchet valley and Le
Fornet, natural skating rink (free), curling,
hang-gliding, motor-trikes, ice-driving,
snowmobile rides, paragliding.

Kindergartens

ESF (Centre and La Daille)

Tuition: Yes. Hours: 6 mornings. Ages: 3 up. Cost:
406.00 per week (without meals). 'Mini
champions' ski course for over children 4yr costs
930.00 for 6 full days.

Le Petit Poucet

Tuition: Yes for children between 4 and 8, group
lessons with ESF. Hours: 8.30-5.30. Ages: 2½-8.
Cost: 1,200.00 per week (meals included). Will
pick up children before 9.00 and return them after
5.30.

Isabelle

Tuition: Yes. Hours: 8.30-5.30. Ages: From 2.
Cost: 1,200.00 per week (meals included). Will
pick up children before 9.00 and return them after
5.30.

Special skiing facilities

Summer skiing Extensive, on Pissaillas (2700m
to 3300m, open from end of June to mid-Aug).
Cross-country 15km of easy trail around the
resort and towards La Daille. Instruction available.

Lift passes

L'Espace Killy
Covers Val d'Isère, Tignes and resort buses. (206
lifts in total.)
Cost 6 days 760.00 (£78.35).
Credit cards accepted Yes.
Senior citizens 540.00 (over 60) saving 29%.
Children 540.00 (under 13) saving 29%. Free
pass up to age 5.
Notes Pass allows one day in La Plagne and Les
Arcs; Passes of 7 days or more give free access
to swimming pool.
Beginners 7 free beginners' lifts on main nursery
slopes.
Short-term passes Half-day and day pass.

Ski school

ESF
Classes 5hr: 2½ am and/or pm. Cost: 868.00 (6
days).
Lift priority Yes.
Children's classes Ages: 4 up. Cost: 605.00 (6
days). Classes available for 14 to 18 year olds.
There are a variety of children's courses on offer
at every level; accommodation available if
desired.
Private lessons available Hourly. Cost: 151.00
per hour. Private instructor for groups of 4 costs
718.00 for morning, 401.00 for afternoon.
Special courses 'Grand Ski' – 4hr off-piste, 6
mornings (9.00-1.00) from 955.00.
Snow-Fun
Classes 3hr am. Cost: 470.00 (6 half-days).
Video sessions once a week.
Lift priority Yes.
Children's classes Ages: 6-13. Cost: 470.00 (6
half-days).
Private lessons available 1½hr (8.45-10.15).
Cost: 200.00 per session.
Special courses New 'Ski Prestige' courses, 6
per group, 21hr tuition, costs 840.00 per week.
Top Ski
Classes 9.00-1.00. Cost: 1,080.00 (6 mornings).
Initiation to off-piste skiing.
Lift priority Yes.
Children's classes Ages: 3-12. Cost: 600.00 for
6 mornings (afternoons cheaper).
Private lessons available 2 hr, full- or half-day.
Cost: 350.00 per 2 hours. 1-2 people.
Special courses Inter-resort tours, 6 full days,
1,800.00; improve your technique, 6 afternoons,
720.00; heli-skiing, day trip 995.00.

What was new in 91

Solaise Express – new 4-seater high-speed
covered chair-lift parallel to Solaise cable-car.

good family facilities including a highly recommended nanny service. Recommended apartments are Maeva, close to the nursery slopes, the Rocher Soleil residence, the central Residence de l'Isère and the new Jardins de la Balme. The Picheru apartments are very scruffy. The new funicular confirms La Daille as the most convenient place to stay from the skiing point of view; as well as direct access to Bellevarde, there is fairly quick access to Tignes. But après-skiers without cars will find La Daille dull. Most accommodation is in apartments – the Pierre et Vacances ones are reportedly 'fairly cramped'. There is a small and generally 'excellent' supermarket, though one reporter complains of it running out of stocks.

For those who prefer a quieter, more villagey atmosphere, there are chalets and hotels in Le Fornet and a comfortable new hotel, Le Becca, in Le Laisinant.

Après-ski is plentiful and varied, with more excellent restaurants than you are likely to need, even for a holiday of great indulgence. None is friendlier than the Bar Jacques, supported by recent reporters. The Grande Ourse by the nursery slopes is in some eyes the best in town. The Perdrix Blanche does 'excellent seafood'(book in advance). In La Daille, La Vieille Maison is a lovely friendly place, serving 'well presented food' and the Crech'Ouna, just above the bottom gondola station (accessible by ski in the day-time), is atmospheric and popular. One of the less expensive eating places is Chez Nana (near Dick's) – 'excellent pizza and cheese fondue, good choice of wine'. La Florence and La Luge both have a good atmosphere and sensibly priced set menus.

The variety and entertainment value of bars is as good, some totally British, others hardly at all (and more expensive). Dick's Tea-Bar is reportedly less of a forum for piste-chat and more of a slick disco; it's easy to find – underneath the searchlight. Play Bach is recommended for music and meals, and popular with the British, as is the very pub-like Morris pub which has live bands and karaoke nights. G-Jays, in Val d'Isère village, has a lively happy hour and fills up with chalet staff. A couple of reporters recommend the new, equally British, Pavilions. Slightly more French places include the Taverne Alsace ('busy and animated, good bar snacks') and Knack. Discos are unsurprisingly expensive; the small Club 21 has 'good atmosphere and music'. Tea-time favourites are the Dégustastion ('great coffee and cakes') and Bananas ('small wooden shack with a cellar bar').

Despite the various provisions for **cross-country** and **non-skiing** activity, serious practitioners of either should look elsewhere. The new ice-rink is small – 'a joke', says one reporter. We have a favourable report on the parascending school. Apparently bungy jumping is now available for a considerable fee.

Val d'Isère's main **nursery slopes** are conveniently located (between the old village and the Solaise cable-car station), and quite gentle, with plenty of bars and restaurants nearby. La Daille has a smaller area. There is enormous scope for near-beginners way up on the Iseran glacier, on the slopes above La Daille and on Solaise.

We have generally favourable reports on the several **ski schools**, and particularly on children's classes. There is enthusiastic support for Snow Fun's off-piste guiding. Perhaps this is their strength, as we have had mixed reports on their group classes, which inconveniently start at 10.30. We've had a glowing report of Pat and Jean Zimmer's Top Ski school (groups are small, teaching excellent but unorthodox, emphasis on mountain safety, lots of off-piste skiing) and another on Fred Foxon's one-week course. There is huge potential for day-trip ski tours – some into the nearby Vanoise National Park, and many skiable by non-experts. Val d'Isère is full of freelance instructors, including off-piste specialist teams. Heli-skiing on nearby Italian mountains can be arranged.

Tignes

The setting of Tignes is austere, with no woodland to relieve the bare mountain scenery. Its high and open situation makes it a good place to ski late in the season, but not a good place in bad weather. The centre is Tignes-le-Lac, beside the lake, already rather shoddy but at least with some variety of building style and the usual selection of bars, restaurants and shops (including at least one selling excellent Savoyard specialities). There are some sunny restaurant terraces. Le Lavachet is a nearby but inconvenient satellite which is linked by ski-lift shuttle. Val Claret is a cluster of tall, modern blocks at the foot of the Grande Motte lifts. From here there is easy access to all skiing areas, and reporters found they were able to satisfy all their material requirements without straying far from the building where they were staying.

There is a free shuttle bus around the resort until midnight ('very, very crowded at peak times'). There is also a bus service between Les Boisses, Les Brévières and Tignes, which is not free and is much less helpful; don't rely on finding space on the last run of the day (in either direction).

Accommodation, at least that offered by UK operators, is largely self-catering or staffed apartments. Most of the hotels are in Tignes-le-Lac and are neither attractive nor luxurious. One exception in all respects is Le Ski d'Or, an expensive, very comfortable modern chalet hotel in Val Claret. Most of the self-catering accommodation is in Val Claret and Le Lavachet. We have a comprehensively negative report on the rooms and studios in the Chalet Club Hotel (half-board or self-catering) in Val Claret. The Hameau de Borsat apartments nearby are 'convenient for the lifts, not so convenient for the shops'. On the other side of Val Claret, a cosy small hotel, 'not for the young', is the Névada. In Le Lac, the Arbina and The Alpaka are recommended, the latter for 'good, friendly service and huge breakfasts'). Les Brévières is attractive, and suits some reporters well as a base. **Après-ski** is generally quiet – you have to search for the action – but there are plenty of restaurants and a few nightclubs in all sectors. Of the restaurants, Le Ski d'Or in Val Claret is outstanding in cost and quality. Reporters recommend the Boeuf Mich, at least on weekdays, and La Pignatta. In Le Lavachet the English-run Poêle d'Or is a favourite. In Le Lac, the Clin

Facts on Tignes   Savoie **France**

Prices in francs
Ski Club represented

Tourist office
Postcode 73320
Tel 79061555
Fax 79064544
Tlx 980030

Getting there
By road 960km from Calais. Via Macon/Annecy or Lyon/Chambéry; chains often needed. Horrific peak weekend traffic jams.
By rail Bourg-St-Maurice (25km); 3 daily, 10 at weekends from station.
By air Geneva; transfer 4½hrhr. (Or Lyon.)

Staying there
Visitor beds 21,300; breakdown: 1,200 in hotels, 20,100 in apartments.
Package holidays Bladon Lines (hcs) Chalets and Hotels "Unlimited" (has) Club Med (h) Crystal (hs) Enterprise (hs) Falcon (s) French Impressions (s) Inghams (s) Kings Ski Club (jas) Made to Measure (hs) Neilson (hs) Quest Total Ski (h) Sally Holidays (s) Ski Alternatives (h) Ski Club of GB (h) Ski Europe (h) Ski Valkyrie (hcs) Ski West (hcs) Skiworld (cas) Snobiz (cs) SnowRanger (s) Supertravel (hc) Thomson (hs) Top Deck (cs) Touralp (s) Tracer Holidays (js) .
Medical facilities In resort: Doctor, fracture clinic, dentist, chemist. Hospital: Bourg-St-Maurice (25km).

Non-skiing activities
Indoor 'Vitatignes' in Le Lac (balneotherapy centre with boiling baths, sauna etc); 'Espace Forme' in Le Lac, Fitness Club in Val Claret (body-building, aerobics, squash, golf practice, sauna, hammam, Californian baths); cinema, tennis, bowling, climbing wall.
Outdoor Natural ice-rink, hang-gliding, delta-planes, paragliding, helicopters, snow scooters, husky-drawn sleigh rides, diving beneath ice on lake, heli-skiing.

Kindergartens
ESF
Tuition: Yes. Hours: 3hr (am and/or pm), 5 days. Ages: 4-12. Cost: 700.00 per week (without meals). At Le Lac.
SEI - Club Formula
Tuition: Yes. Hours: 9.00-5.00. Ages: Any. Cost: 1,100.00 per week (with meals). At Val Claret.
La Rotonde
Tuition: Yes, from age 3. Hours: 8.30-5.00, 6 days. Ages: 3 mth up. Cost: 1,250.00 per week (with meals). At Val Claret.
Les Marmottons
Tuition: Yes, from age 3. Hours: 8.45-5.00. Ages: 2½-10. Cost: 1,250.00 per week (with meals). At Le Lac.

Special skiing facilities
Summer skiing Extensive, on Grande Motte (2700m to 3656m, open all year).

Cross-country 15km of easy trails around Lac and at Les Boisses. Summer trail on the glacier. Instruction available.

Lift passes
L'Espace Killy
Covers all lifts and resort buses in Tignes and Val d'Isère. (206 lifts in total.)
Cost 6 days 760.00 (£78.35).
Credit cards accepted Yes.
Senior citizens 540.00 (over 60) saving 29%.
Children 540.00 (under 13) saving 29%. Free pass up to age 5.
Notes Pass allows one day in La Plagne and Les Arcs.
Beginners Free lifts on all main nursery slopes; special beginners' half-day pass.
Short-term passes Half-day (from 12.30) and day pass; single ascents to Palafour.
Other periods Passes for 14 non-consecutive days available.

Ski school
ESF
Classes 9.00-12.00 and/or 1.45-4.45. Cost: 800.00 (6 days).
Lift priority Yes.
Children's classes Ages: 4-12. Cost: 700.00 (6 days). Special courses for ages 15 to 20, 5 days cost 475.00.
Private lessons available Between 9.00-4.45. Cost: 145.00 per hour.
Special courses 'Discovery' courses (off-piste explorations), 5 days cost 1,000.00; 'Ski Emotion' (advanced course skiing couloirs), 5 days cost 1,200.00; surf, mono or telemark courses, 6 mornings cost 475.00; heli-skiing, day trip from 1,000.00.
Evolution 2 (Lac/Val Claret)
Classes am or pm. Cost: 450.00 (5 half-days). Beginner's Gold course (with video). Technique course for intermediates costs 450.00 (4 half-days).
Lift priority Yes.
Children's classes Ages: 5-14. Cost: 390.00 (5 half-days).
Private lessons available Per day or hour. Cost: 140.00 per hour.
Special courses Many courses on offer such as off-piste tours, 9-valley ski safari, heli-skiing, ski and rafting, speed skiing.

What was new in 91
1. 70 snow-cannons at the bottoms of all main lifts.
2. Col du Palet: Grattalu drag-lifts replaced by enclosed 4-seater chair-lift.
3. Claret drag-lift replaced by a more up-to-date tow for beginners.

What is new for 92
1. Funicular will replace the gondolas up to the Grand Motte (6 mins to Panoramic restaurant).
2. New high-speed chair-lift to replace top half of gondolas.
3. Plans to double-up the drag-lift on glacier.

Le Lavachet the English-run Poêle d'Or is a favourite. In Le Lac, the Clin d'Oeil is also popular. For livelier places reporters recommend La Corniche ('fondue parties, live singers') and the Playboy ('strippers and girlie shows') in Val Claret and Key West in Lac, a chalet-girl favourite.

Even more emphatically than Val d'Isère, this is no place for **cross-country** skiers or **non-skiers**, despite the construction of an 'excellent' new sports centre providing tennis and many other activities. The ice rink is reportedly 'appallingly maintained' and there is no swimming pool. Skidoo rides are generally popular.

Tignes' **nursery slopes** are very reliable for snow, but tend to be crowded – especially at Val Claret – and bumpy.

Recent reports are generally enthusiastic about the **ski schools** both for classes and private lessons. The schools can provide guides for the very attractive excursion to Champagny or Plan Peisey via the Col du Palet, and will arrange transport back. Ali Ross's ski clinic earns high praise. We have no recent reports of the **ski kindergartens**.

Learn to ski fast – 200km/hr

Les Arcs France 1600–2000m

Good for *Ski évolutif, tough runs, big ski area, off-piste skiing, skiing convenience, family holidays, freedom from cars, late holidays, resort-level snow, sunny slopes, rail access*
Bad for *Alpine charm, mountain restaurants, après-ski, not skiing, short airport transfers, easy road access*

Les Arcs is a modern, predominantly self-catering resort in three parts: Arc 1600 (or Arc Pierre Blanche) and Arc 1800 are close neighbours on the broad flank of the main Isère valley above Bourg-St-Maurice; Arc 2000 is in a secluded high bowl of its own, at the heart of the skiing. Although development is still going on, particularly at 2000, it is essentially a first-generation purpose-built resort, which means that it is not pretty; but it is by no means as hideous as some competitors.
 The skiing is extensive, interesting and suitable for all grades of skier, with plenty of easy runs above 1800 and 2000, and more than enough challenge on the slopes of the Aiguille Rouge for most skiers. The lift system is well thought-out and accommodation is nearly all conveniently placed for skiing. But for après-ski and non-skiing facilities the resort scores low marks – a view which only those with an interest in the matter dispute. One of Les Arcs' greatest selling points is the *ski évolutif* method of tuition which was introduced to Europe here.
 Les Arcs can be conveniently reached by funicular, which departs from behind the railway station in Bourg-St-Maurice and takes seven minutes to reach Arc 1600, with one mid-way stop at the villages of Les Granges. Bourg is a real town with a good Saturday market, real locals and reasonable prices, not least in its restaurants and hotels. Les Arcs also has piste links with the neighbouring wooded ski area of Peisey-Nancroix Vallandry – an asset in bad weather for skiers based in 1800.
 Cars have to be parked at the edge of each complex, but having one is handy for exploring the three resort centres, for making use of the pass-swapping arrangement with other resorts and perhaps for trips down to the supermarkets and specialist shops of Bourg.

The skiing top 3226m bottom 1100m

The broad north-west-facing mountain flank above Arc 1600 and Arc 1800 is well served by chairs and drag-lifts to a ridge of rocky peaks with skiing up to about 2400m. On the other side of this ridge is a wide bowl with Arc 2000 in the pit, lifts up from it to over 3000m, and ski runs below the resort to Le Pré above Villaroger, a hamlet beside the road to Val d'Isère (and lifts back up – handy for Val-based excursionists).
 The runs above **Arc 1800** are open and relatively easy, even those

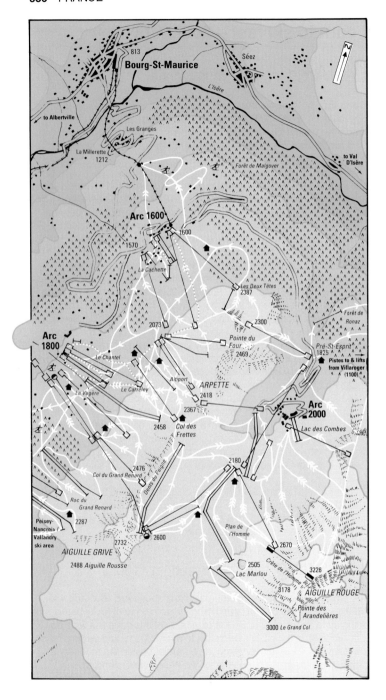

Bourg-St-Maurice

Séez

813

L'Isère

to Albertville

Les Granges

Forêt de Malgover

to Val D'Isère

La Millerette
1212

Arc 1600

1570

1600

La Cachette

Les Deux Têtes
2387

2073

2300

Pointe du Four
2469

Forêt de Ronaz

Pré-St Esprit
1825

Pistes to & lifts from Villaroger (1100)

Arc 1800

Le Chantel

Altiport

ARPETTE

La Vagère

Le Carreley

2418

2367

2458

Col des Frettes

Arc 2000

Lac des Combes

2476

Col du Grand Renard

Dents du Peigne

2180

Roc du Grand Renard

Peisey-Nancroix Vallandry ski area

2287

2732

2600

Plan de l'Homme

2670

Crête de l'Homme

AIGUILLE GRIVE

2488 *Aiguille Rousse*

2505
Lac Marlou

3226

3178

AIGUILLE ROUGE

Pointe des Arandelières

3000 *Le Grand Col*

marked red. These slopes, on which many inexperienced skiers rely, get a lot of afternoon sun, and late in the season tend to be icy in the morning and slushy in the afternoon. The skiing connects with lifts up from Vallandry, Plan Peisey and Nancroix, between Les Arcs and La Plagne. This is an excellent area for skiing in bad weather, with plenty of good runs on and off the piste in woodland. Plans are afoot to link this area with that of neighbouring Montchavin, which would give skiers from Les Arcs access to the La Plagne domain.

The skiing above **Arc 1600** is steeper and more wooded. There are some excellent broad, fairly steep trails, and there is some good off-piste skiing between them. Most runs are accessible from the high-speed quad Cachette chair-lift, which whisks skiers from the funicular station on the edge of the village to a point just south of Les Deux Têtes, also reached by chair-lift from 1600). Timid intermediate skiers can take a blue run down from the top of this sector to the bottom or over to Arc 1800, but even this run has a few awkward passages. In good conditions it is possible to ski down towards Bourg-St-Maurice, joining the funicular at Les Granges for the return to the village.

The bowl above **Arc 2000** has easy runs down into it from several points along the ridge reached from Arc 1600 and Arc 1800, and some not so easy – the piste de l'Ours (from Arpette) deserves its black grading, as does the run to Pré-St-Esprit down the Comborsière valley – a piste with many off-piste variants available, now reached by chair-lifts from both sides of the ridge. The red run down from Col des Frettes has challenging options near the top, and goes through a scenic, often crowded, narrow valley lower down.

The bowl, a splendid area for inexperienced skiers to enjoy a lot of space, good snow and beautiful scenery, now served by an efficient quad chair replacing the old drags, is dominated by the Aiguille Rouge on the far side. It is this, one of the most consistently steep lift-served mountains in the Alps, that makes Les Arcs special. Unfortunately it is often closed when conditions are not good. From the exposed open peak there are magnificent views across to the glaciers of the Mont Pourri (3782m). Off-piste slopes are in many places so steep and rocky that they are skiable only by very expert skiers. Pistes are long and challenging; the red from the top is not in itself difficult, but skirts some very steep slopes marked with dramatic warning signs – rather unnerving if visibility is not good. There is a run of exceptional length (over 2100m vertical) from the top down to Le Pré, near Villaroger; it covers an enormous variety of terrain, and for much of its course is dark red to black – and unlike some other such epic runs is often enjoyable from top to bottom. The lower half is easily accessible from Arc 2000 by means of the recently built Lanchettes chair-lift.

The face of the Aiguille Rouge above Arc 2000 is the setting of the Olympic speed-skiing run, recently shifted across the hill slightly. The combination of an extremely steep slope (about 45 degrees), long flat runout and high altitude for low air resistance is just what speed-skiers need. With their rubber suits, streamlined helmets and 240cm skis, they make a very impressive spectacle, especially from the Dou de l'homme chair-lift; 200km/hr is the going rate these days, but even greater speeds are expected at the Olympics.

There are plenty of challenging runs not served by the cable-car. The Dou de l'Homme chair-lift up to the bottom station gives access to several black pistes offering long slopes of sustained steepness and usually formidable bumps. The drags to the Grand Col on the south shoulder of the mountain serve good, high red and black pistes, and the red from there back to the middle of the bowl has the option of a big mogul-field which keeps its snow very well. Exciting off-piste runs start from the Grand Col (going behind the Aiguille Rouge to Villaroger), and from beside the Aiguille Grive (going in the other direction to Nancroix and Plan Peisey). These runs are a long way from pistes and should not be attempted without guidance.

Mountain restaurants are very few and far between and of varying quality – 'the resort's weakest point' according to one reporter. Most people return to the resort complexes for lunch, particularly in bad weather when the several open-air, sit-on-the-snow snack bars are ruled out. Above Arc 2000 such bars are the only sources of refreshment, but the runs below 2000 and down to Le Pré are the best-equipped in the whole area, with at least three attractively rustic restaurants – the Belliou la Fumée at Pré-St-Esprit (not to be confused with the much larger utilitarian place next door), the cosy little Solliet on the Villaroger run, and the Aiguille Rouge in Le Pré (recommended 'for a leisurely blow-out lunch'). In the Peisey-Nancroix Vallandry sector (where prices are lower) reporters repeatedly recommend Chez Felix ('the best in this area'), Le Blanchot and La Poudreuse ('spartan, good chef, large portions').

For a new French ski resort, Les Arcs' lift system is surprising: it is all chairs and drags except for the single cable-car on the Aiguille Rouge and the funicular up from Bourg-St-Maurice. The lift system generally works well, but a recent low-season inspector confirms the views of a number of high-season reporters, who complain of serious **queues** to get from 1600 and 1800 to 2000 in the morning, to get anywhere in the Arc 2000 bowl at lunch-time and to get back from there in the afternoon, despite the number of efficient chairs up to the dividing ridge. The new gondola from the southern end of 1800 to the Aiguille Grive, via the Col du Grand Renard, due to open during the 91/92 season, should relieve this problem. There are also queues for the Aiguille Rouge cable-car when conditions at altitude are good and serious queues for the one lift up from Peisey-Nancroix. Queues in 1800 to buy lift passes at weekends can be serious; if driving, leave your car in the huge free car park at the Bourg-St-Maurice funicular station and buy your pass at the office there. (The funicular runs from approximately 7.30am to 7.00pm).

Rather late in the day, the resort has started installing **artificial snow** on two runs directly above 1800, on the long piste to 1600 served by the Cachette chair and on one nursery slope in 1600. Each part of the resort has a floodlit piste.

The resort

Despite recent expansion at Arc 2000, most of the accommodation and most of the package holidays are concentrated in Arc 1600 and Arc 1800. Both command magnificent views north-west across to Mont Blanc, and west along the valley into the setting sun. They are both compact clusters, with curving forms hugging the mountain, designed to make sure that many of the apartments and hotels have sunny terraces and balconies. Wood has been widely used, but the original buildings were poorly finished and are now beginning to look tatty. Each centre has an adequate range of shops, but we have reports of post-skiing supermarket queues in 1600 and 1800. There are several supermarkets in Bourg and a hypermarket on the outskirts of the town.

Frequent day-time buses run between Arc 1600 and Arc 1800 until 8pm, and occasionally to Arc 2000 until 6pm.

Of the two main units, Arc 1800 is bigger and has most of the bars and shops, restaurants and apartment blocks. It is itself split into two main sectors – Le Charvet and Les Villards – each with a supermarket in easy reach of all the apartments, and a third more diffuse residential area to the south, Charmettoger. Le Charvet is the most animated part. Arrangements for getting luggage across the resort from the car parks to the more remote apartments are imperfect. Arc 1600 is smaller and quieter than 1800, and although the standard brochure term 'villagey' is misleading, the bars and restaurants are smaller and more personal. At the heart of it is a horseshoe of buildings around the Hotel La Cachette, with sunny terraces in front of the shops and restaurants. Arc 2000 is a growing assortment of large, squarish blocks (including the Club Méditerranée). It did not impress a recent visitor, who complains that the buildings were dirty, the facilities broken and the resort noisy. Despite ambitious development plans and recent spurts of hotel-building, Arc 2000 is still a long way from becoming the major Arc.

Most reporters took self-catering **accommodation** in Arc 1800 and one or two were disappointed at having to walk up from the lower blocks to the slopes. The standard of apartments varies little – most are tight on space, unluxurious, in some cases shabby, with limited cooking facilities. There is a widespread use of bunk beds and the usual sofa beds in living areas. Plenty of apartments get a lot of afternoon sun, but promises of day-long balcony sunbathing should be treated sceptically. The Archeboc apartments in Charmettoger are reportedly more spacious than most. Les Arcs' smartest existing hotel is in Le Charvet (1800) – the Golf. The Latitudes, near the new gondola station in 1800, is recommended for 'excellent food'. The Trois Arcs in 1600 is a modest hotel that has had complimentary reports. Recommended hotels in 2000, especially good for families, are the Aiguille Rouge and Eldorador. A recent reporter was not impressed by the scruffy Le Varet apartments in 2000.

People not self-catering who like France (as opposed to French ski resorts) should consider staying in Bourg-St-Maurice. There are a number of small hotels including the Concorde, the Relais des Villards

Facts on Les Arcs   Savoie **France**

Prices in francs
Ski Club represented

Tourist office
Postcode 73700
Tel 79077373 (1600). 79072600 (1800).
79073255 (2000)
Fax 79074596
Tlx 980347
This resort is represented in Britain by the
specialist tour operator Touralp, 197B Brompton
Rd, London SW3 1LA (071-589 1918)

Getting there
By road 937km from Calais. Via Macon/Annecy;
chains often needed from Bourg-St-Maurice.
Horrific peak weekend jams.
By rail Bourg-St-Maurice; frequent buses and
direct funicular to resort.
By air Geneva; transfer 4½hr. (Or Lyon,
Chambery.)

Staying there
Visitor beds 23,850; breakdown: 2850 in hotels,
21,000 in apartments.
Package holidays Brittany Ferries (s) Chalets
and Hotels "Unlimited" (hc) Club Med (h) Crystal
(hjs) Enterprise (hs) Falcon (s) Horizon (hs)
Hoverspeed Ski-Drive (hs) Made to Measure (hs)
Neilson (hs) Quality Ski Tours (h) Sally Holidays
(hs) Skiworld (cs) SnowRanger (hs) Thomson
(hs) Touralp (hs) .
Medical facilities In resort: Doctor, dentist (Arc
1800), chemist. Hospital: Bourg-St-Maurice.

Non-skiing activities
Indoor Squash (3 courts 1800), Chinese
gymnastics, saunas (1600, 1880), solaria,
aquavision, multi-gym, (1800), bridge (1800,
1600), cinemas, amusement arcades, music,
concert halls, fencing (2000).
Outdoor Natural skating rinks in all centres,
floodlit skiing, luge run, speed skiing (2000),
ski-jump, climbing wall (1800), organised
snow-shoe outings, 10km cleared paths (1800
and 1600), hang-gliding, horse-riding, sleigh
rides, helicopter rides to Italy.

Kindergartens
1600: Baby Club La Cachette (5th floor)
Tuition: No. Hours: 8.30am-6.00pm. Ages: 4mth
to 1yr. Cost: 1,171.00 per week (lunch and
lunch-time supervision 404.00). Baby-sitting
service available.
1600: Mini Club
Tuition: Yes. Hours: 9.00-5.00, 6 days. Ages: 3-7.
Cost: 2,042.00 per week (lessons and equipment
included, lunch and lunch-time supervision
341.00).
1800: Nursery Les Lauzieres
Tuition: No. Hours: 8.30-6.00. Ages: 1-3. Cost:
755.00 per week (lunch and lunch-time
supervision 300.00).
1800: La Nova
Tuition: Yes. Hours: 8.30-6.00. Ages: 3-6. Cost:

735.00 per week (lunch and lunch-time
supervision 300.00).
2000: Grand Baby-Club
Tuition: Yes. Hours: 8.30-6.00. Ages: 1-3. Cost:
1,021.00 per week (lunch and lunch-time
supervision 404.00).

Special skiing facilities
Summer skiing No.
Cross-country 15km of trails in all from the 3
centres.

Lift passes
Area pass
Covers all lifts in Les Arcs and Peisey-Nancroix,
including funicular from Bourg-St-Maurice. (74
lifts in total.)
Cost 6 days 770.00 (£79.38).
Credit cards accepted Yes.
Senior citizens 680.00 (over 65) saving 12%.
Children 680.00 (under 12) saving 12%. Free
pass up to age 7 (if parent buying a pass).
Notes Passes of 7 days or more allow one day in
La Plagne, Val d'Isère, Tignes, La Rosière and La
Thuile; 10% reduction for families with 3 or more
children.
Beginners Limited day pass for lower lifts of
each resort centre.
Short-term passes Half-day.
Other passes Forfait Ski Plus includes ski pass
and guide for 6 days, and trips to Tignes, La
Thuile etc, costs 1,380.00.

Ski school
ESF in each centre
Classes 3hr am and/or 2hr pm. Cost: 725.00 (6
full days).
Lift priority Yes.
Children's classes Ages: 4-11. Cost: 625.00 (6
full days). Teenage classes for 14 to 16 yr olds, in
1600 and 1800, costs from 720.00 per week.
Private lessons available Hourly. Cost: 150.00
per hour. 1-4 people.
Special courses 'Ski Evolutif' - 5hr per day, costs
1,298.00 per week with equipment hire and lift
pass.

What was new in 91
1. New quad chair-lift, the Plagnettes, replaces
double drag-lift from above Arc 2000 to Col de la
Chal.
2. Grand Renard piste descending towards Arc
1800 has been improved to make it more
technical and challenging.

What is new for 92
1. New 12-man 2-stage gondola set to open at
beginning of next season, taking passengers from
Arc 1800 to the Aiguille Grive via the Col du
Renard.
2. Link between Les Arcs and La Plagne set to
open.

and the Gateau de Savoie, which offer cheap rooms or half-board and are not too far from the funicular station. It is also possible to rent apartments.

Après-ski is limited, but we gather improving. The popular night-spots in 2000 are: the Red Rock ('casual bar/formal dining room, live music'); St Jacques ('small, cosy instructors' hangout'); and the Marloup ('live jazz and fondue'). In 1800 the British congregate at the Pub Russel, where 'it all happens'; there is a karaoke evening once a week. 1800 restaurants include: l'Onglet ('great steaks'), the Gargantus ('gigantic portions of pizza and pasta'), the Auberge Rouge ('expensive, suspicious of pre-opened wine') and the Green at the hotel Golf ('if you want to rub shoulders with celebrities'). There is a noisy disco beneath the Nova apartment block. In 1600 the most popular bar is the Abreuvoir ('live band, sometimes too loud for conversation'); La Cabouche is smaller and quieter. The Aquarius nightclub stays open late.

Les Arcs is not recommended either for **cross-country** skiers or **non-skiers**. Several reporters have regretted the lack of a swimming pool. Availability of skating is unreliable. An English woman in 1600 apparently organises horse-riding. Excursions to Bourg and other towns and villages in the valley are possible.

For adult beginners (but not children), **ski school** means *ski évolutif*. A reporter speaks with awe of the 'spectacular progress' made by his novice companions. Though there is a theoretical class size limit of 10 people, reporters say that this is disregarded ('regularly 14 or 15 pupils'). One family found it difficult to arrange children's classes out of French school holiday time. Reports of off-piste guiding are enthusiastic. An interesting new development is the *Carte Blanche* programme – a combination of ski school and other activities (day-time and après-ski). We have glowing reports of Club Med tuition at Arc 2000. The Mini-club **ski kindergarten** operates in all three resort centres, and has been found to 'cater well for children at modest charge'. The 1800 one is run by 'delightful, caring bilingual teachers who got our four-year-old going in no time'. There are also nurseries for pre-skiing children, and a Baby Club for babes-in-arms at 1600.

It is perhaps just as well that *ski évolutif* does not involve long days spent on **nursery slopes**, as Les Arcs is not ideally provided with these. Areas are roped off near the resort for the first stages of *ski évolutif* and for children's ski playgrounds. Arc 1800, in particular, does cater well for near-beginners, with a long, wide, easy, varied slope above the resort.

Le Pré 1200m

One reporter this year stayed at the delightful village of Le Pré, above the equally delightful Villaroger, connected to the Les Arcs lift system by the chairs up the north slope of the Aiguille Rouge. Le Pré has no shops or equipment hire places but it does have two day-time restaurants, one of which is sometimes open at night. Visitors stay in chalets or private accommodation. Chalky White runs some of his off-piste courses from here. There is a kindergarten area on the gentle slopes above the village.

Ski yourself to sleep

La Plagne France 1800–2100m

Good for *Nursery slopes, easy runs, big ski area, skiing convenience, family holidays, late holidays, off-piste skiing, resort-level snow, freedom from cars, beautiful scenery, sunny slopes*
Bad for *Après-ski, not skiing, Alpine charm, short airport transfers, easy road access, mountain restaurants*

Linked resorts: Montchavin, Les Coches, Champagny, Montalbert

La Plagne, 30 years old in 1991, represents the state of the art of resort-building. It is a large and very fragmented place, confusing at first, but very straightforward in its appeal. The skiing is enormous in extent and vertical range; few of the pistes are challenging, but the off-piste skiing is excellent. Snow conditions are reliable except at the lower extremes of the network. Nursery slopes are abundant and immediately accessible, and child-care facilities are excellent. Nearly all accommodation is in modern apartments, conveniently placed for getting to and from skiing. And there you have it – apart from some lift bottle-necks which manifest themselves in the peak holiday season, a perfect recipe for a rather limited winter holiday that suits many skiers very well indeed.

The main resort centres making up La Plagne are on gentle slopes above the tree-line, dominated by the huge monolith of Aime la Plagne, where thousands of skiers can be pigeon-holed and processed under one roof. In the most modern of these centres the designers have tried, with some success, to reproduce some village atmosphere. There are also smaller resort components much lower down, some of them modified old villages, others new developments. These lower resorts – Montchavin, Les Coches, Champagny, Montalbert – are not directly below the main parts of La Plagne, but are reached by first taking lifts up to the rim of the wide bowl around the resort centre. In bad weather, these lifts are liable to close, making the low, sheltered skiing inaccessible to centrally based skiers.

The lift pass is wide-ranging, and a car is helpful in making full use of it on excursions to Les Arcs and Val d'Isère (though for little else).

The skiing top 3250m bottom 1250m

The core of La Plagne's skiing is a central area above Plagne Centre and its close neighbours Plagne Villages, Bellecôte and Belle Plagne, all of them set between 1900m and 2050m. The western side of this basin is dominated by the single building of Aime la Plagne (at 2100m), from which it is easy to ski down to Centre. Below it is Plagne 1800, the newest of the resort units. There are three other facets to the skiing: through woods behind Aime la Plagne as far as Montalbert; south-facing slopes above Champagny, on the side of an entirely different valley; and, at the eastern end of the skiing area, a high area of glacier skiing leading down to a low area of woodland runs above Montchavin and Les Coches. From the glacier to Montchavin gives an enormous descent of 15km and 2000m vertical, but there are no prepared pistes down, and an indirect chain of six lifts up.

The central basin above the five residential units provides timid skiers with a very extensive range of not very long, not at all steep runs with a vertical range of about 500m. Above **Plagne Bellecôte** and **Belle Plagne** is a big area of almost entirely gentle runs, some of them satisfyingly long, with more challenging runs (on- and, particularly, off-piste) from Roche de Mio, reached by a sequence of slow chairs as an alternative to the busy gondola. There are easier ways back from Roche de Mio, too, offering intermediates an early taste of skiing away from the lifts. The pistes converging on **Plagne Villages** and **Plagne Centre** are a bit steeper, and include some genuine reds down from the rim of the bowl and lower points. Immediately above Centre is an unusual area of mini-canyons, with pistes and off-piste routes winding through them. On the open slopes between Centre and **Aime la Plagne** are some of the most consistently challenging red runs, with roundabout blue alternatives.

One neglected and exceptional feature of this area is the long runs directly down from Aime la Plagne, through woods past Plagne 1800 – far enough (to 1400m) to give a long and challenging run (the black Emile Allais). Behind the Biolley lifts above Aime la Plagne there are stiff runs with pitches of over 30°, initially west-facing and liable to be icy and very difficult in the mornings. After this steep open slope a gentle trail through woods links with the Emile Allais run or with the Les Adrets lift to the rounded peak of Le Fornelet (1970m) for a gentle run through the woods to **Montalbert**. There is a new chair-lift from Montalbert back up to Le Fornelet, and the link with Aime and Centre has also been improved by the new Coqs chair out of the intervening valley to a point high above Aime.

The south-facing slopes above **Champagny** can be reached from several points above the central resort units without any great difficulty; from Grande Rochette, Col de Forcle and (particularly) Roche de Mio there are splendid intermediate runs away from lifts. For good skiers the toughest skiing and usually the best snow is in the area beside the long, steep Verdons lifts (a four-seater chair has for practical purposes replaced the original long drag); from here a splendid red run goes all the way down to Champagny, with the return as far as the tree-line now achieved by an efficient gondola. The rest of Champagny's skiing is easy, sunny and not very extensive.

The **Bellecôte** glacier is the ace in La Plagne's hand. Unlike many glacier skiing areas it opens up plenty of challenging skiing, with long and wide black runs of nearly 1000m vertical and even longer off-piste runs down to Les Bauches, where there are lifts back towards Plagne Bellecôte and an easy piste on down to Montchavin. There are more adventurous things to be done under guidance, including very long runs down towards Peisey and the Champagny valley, and there is also a

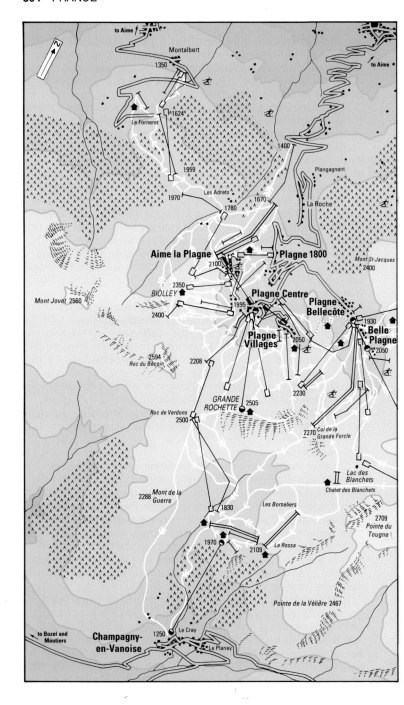

to Aime

Montalbert
1350

Le Forneret

1624

to Aime •

1400

1959

Plangagnant

Les Adrets

1970

1780

1670

La Roche

Aime la Plagne

2100

Plagne 1800

Mont St-Jacques
2400

2350

BIOLLEY

Mont Jovet 2560

Plagne Centre

2400

1995

Plagne Bellecôte

1930

Belle Plagne

2050

Plagne Villages

2050

2594
Roc du Bécoin

2208

GRANDE ROCHETTE

2505

2230

Roc de Verdons
2500

Col de la Grande Forcle
2270

Lac des Blanchets

Chalet des Blanchets

2288 Mont de la Guerre

1830

Les Borseliers

2709
Pointe du Tougne

1970

2109

La Rossa

Pointe de la Vélière 2467

to Bozel and Moutiers

1250

Le Cray

Champagny-en-Vanoise

Le Planay

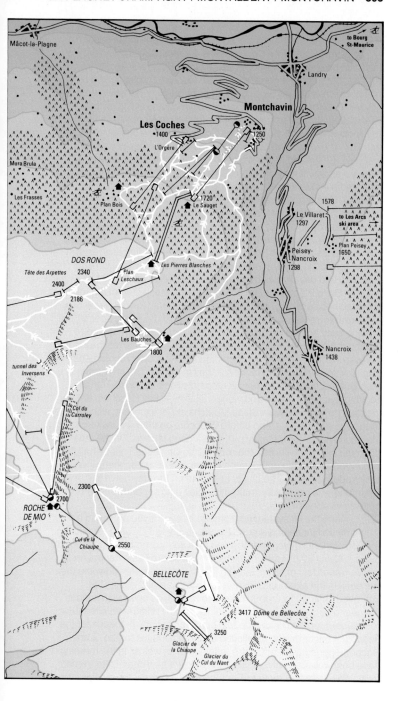

moderately easy red run from the glacier to the Col de la Chiaupe. The lifts are unfortunately often closed, particularly early in the season.

The **Montchavin/Les Coches** runs are most directly reached from the main bowl by an improved chair-lift from Plagne Bellecôte to Arpette, but also by a good, long, open red from Roche de Mio (the top half of which is served by a chair-lift) or by off-piste run down from the glacier. They provide plenty of variety of woodland skiing, with a drop of over 1000m vertical from the Arpette chair-lift to Montchavin. Getting up to Arpette from Montchavin or Les Coches is a slow business, involving four lifts. The woodland pistes below Pierres Blanches (excellent in poor visibility) are graded red and blue, but none of the blues is easy: where they are steepest they are also rather narrow, to the discomfort of timid intermediate skiers (particularly when the pistes are busy at the end of the day). One reporter recommends the off-piste skiing among the trees between the pistes in this sector. The two drags above Pierres Blanches serve broad open slopes, gentle except for tricky bits above the restaurant. The runs down from the flanks of Dos Rond into the bowl above Les Bauches are steeper than their blue grading suggests; further round the bowl, the run served by the recently built Crozats chair is easier, and usually has better snow. The Crozats chair also provides a link with Belle Plagne (not reliably open – the steep start of the run is vulnerable to sunshine) and to the Inversens chair for Roche de Mio.

Mountain restaurants are not very many and not very special, but there is easy access to restaurants in the many bits of resort dotted around the ski area, and the layout of the area encourages the idea of skiing from one village to another for lunch. A reporter recommends the English-run Bon Coin in Plagne Villages for value. The restaurant at Plan Bois, above Les Coches, is recommended for 'good French cooking, excellent prices and wonderful views'. Les Bauches, on the long run down from Bellecôte to Montchavin, is 'excellent, with a sunny terrace'. L'Alpette, last stop before Bellecôte on the way back from Montachavin, is competently run, with a good terrace. On the other (Central) side of Bellecôte, the scruffy little Chalet de Trieuse has its supporters. We have enthusiastic reports of the 'atmospheric local bar' at Grande Rochette. The chalet at 1830m on the way down to Champagny is reportedly 'authentic'. (See also separate sections on the outlying villages.)

In general the lift system runs smoothly, even if you do spend a very long time on lifts getting around the widely spread ski area. But during the February holidays, **queuing** can be a serious problem in particular places. About 80 per cent of the resort's beds are in the central area, which means lots of skiers leaving it in the morning and crowding the lifts back in the afternoon. Plagne Bellecôte is a bottleneck; the improved chair-lift to Arpette seems to have done away with serious queues to get to the Montchavin sector, and by offering an alternative roundabout route to Roche de Mio has even cut down queues for the gondola – but certainly not eliminated them. Queues for the Grande Rochette gondola out of Centre (after lunch as well as in the mornings) have been relieved only partly by the efficient new chair-lift to Verdons, giving an alternative route to Champagny. Of course, the glacier attracts crowds when snow elsewhere is poor. More than one reporter has noted that numerous large groups of very tiny children are taken up to gentle high-level pistes, which can as a result become 'clogged with skiers trying to avoid infants – a really miserable experience for all concerned'.

There is **artificial snow** on a short length of piste at Belle Plagne and the final approach to Montchavin (from a point level with Les Coches), but we have complaints about reluctance to use it (at least in Belle Plagne) when the resort is not entirely full.

The resort

All the central bits of La Plagne are linked by bus or lift from 8am until about 1am, covered by the lift pass. The cable-car which is the link between Centre and Aime la Plagne is covered by some passes but not all.

The original 1960s development is Plagne Centre, still the main centre for shopping, entertainment and après-ski. The buildings are big, square blocks, many of them linked by covered walkways. The hub is a dark and dank underground commercial precinct with lots of shops, bars and restaurants in little cubicles. The other units are all largely colonies of self-catering **accommodation**. Aime la Plagne and Bellecôte consist of large blocks. Bellecôte is recommended by several reporters – convenient for skiing, shopping second only to that of Centre, a skating rink and a swimming pool; but for a convenience resort it is irritatingly inconvenient, with the lifts starting uphill of the building. A recent inmate of Aime la Plagne was not at all enamoured of it. Belle Plagne, Plagne Villages, Plagne 1800 and brand-new Plagne Soleil all have smaller buildings less densely concentrated; they have less shopping and entertainment, but are linked to Bellecôte and Centre. The most popular unit with British skiers (and much the most popular with our reporters) is Belle Plagne, which has a more colourful and fanciful design than the others; it is convenient for skiing, especially for Roche de Mio, and has adequately comfortable and quiet apartments – those approved by reporters include Emerald, Centaur, Maeva, Croix du Sud and Nereides (at the top of the resort, with 'great' views but a stiff walk up from the centre). The Eldorador hotel is recommended this year for its food, rooms and live music. Although rather out of the way (and generally not very convenient for skiing – you have to take lifts up via Aime to get into the main ski area), Plagne 1800 has the attraction of individual chalet-style buildings, and the standard of the apartments is reported to be high. Plagne Soleil's style is relatively uncompromising, and the unit is both limited in its facilities and isolated; but the Residence Le Cervin is rated 'excellent'. A reporter says that English is more widely spoken in 1800 than in Centre and Bellecôte. We deal separately with the lower satellite villages at the end of this chapter. There is some staffed chalet accommodation in Centre (as there is in 1800), as well as a few functional hotels. The Graciosa, on the edge of the resort, is small and friendly, and its restaurant, the Etoile d'Or, highly reputed. The big

Facts on La Plagne Savoie **France**

Prices in francs
Ski Club represented

Tourist office

Postcode 73210
Tel 79097979
Fax 79097010
Tlx 980973
This resort is represented in Britain by Erna Low
Consultants Ltd, 9 Reece Mews, London, SW7
3HE. Tel 071-584 2841

Getting there

By road 934km from Calais. Via Macon/Annecy;
chains often necessary. Horrific peak weekend
jams.
By rail Aime (18km); frequent buses from station.
By air Geneva; transfer 4 1/2hr. (Or Lyon.)

Staying there

Visitor beds 45,000; breakdown: mainly in
hotels, apartments and chalets.
Package holidays Brittany Ferries (s) Chalets
and Hotels "Unlimited" (hc) Club Med (h) Crystal
(cs) Enterprise (hs) Falcon (s) Horizon (s)
Hoverspeed Ski-Drive (s) Inghams (hs) Made to
Measure (hs) Neilson (hs) Quality Ski Tours (s)
Quest Total Ski (h) Silver Ski (c) Ski Beat (c) Ski
Global (hs) Ski Red Guide (s) Ski Valkyrie (hcs)
Ski West (hs) Ski Whizz Small World (c) SkiTonic
(hcs) Skiworld (cs) SnowRanger (hs) Thomson
(hs) Touralp (hs) Tracer Holidays (cs) Vacations
(hs) .
Medical facilities In resort: Doctors, chemists.
Hospital: Bourg-St-Maurice (35km). Dentist: Aime
(18km).

Non-skiing activities

Indoor Swimming, sauna, solarium in each
centre, skating (Plagne Bellecôte), squash
(1800), fitness centre (Belle Plagne, Plagne 1800,
Plagne Centre, Plagne Bellecôte), cinemas.
Outdoor Bob-sleigh (La Roche), 30km marked
walks, paraskiing, skidoos, rafting, climbing,
skating, hang-gliding.

Kindergartens

In all centres
Tuition: available with ESF. Hours: 9.00-12.00,
2.00-5.00. Ages: depends on centre – 2-6yr in
Plagne Centre, Plagne Villages, Aime la Plagne,
Plagne Bellecôte, and Champagny; 18mths to 6yr
at Belle Plagne; 18mths to 8yr at Montchavin and
Les Coches; 3mths to 6yr at Plagne 1800; 4 to
5yr at Montalbert. Cost: 1,050.00 per week (with
meals and lunch-time supervision).

Special skiing facilities

Summer skiing Small area on the Bellecôte
glacier (3000m to 3250m) served by 6 lifts.
Cross-country Trail linking Plagne Bellecôte with
Montchavin, trails from Montchavin to Peisey
Nancroix. Cleared and maintained paths at all six
centres; 54 km at Plagne Villages, Plagne
Bellecôte and Belle Plagne. A further 35 km of
trails at Champagny-le-Haut.

Lift passes

La Plagne pass
Covers all lifts in La Plagne and the ski bus. (105
lifts in total.)
Cost 6 days 770.00 (£79.38). Low season:
620.00 saving 19%.
Credit cards accepted No.
Senior citizens 575.00 (over 60) saving 25%.
Children 575.00 (under 13) saving 25%. Free
pass up to age 6.
Notes Passes of 7 days or more allow one day in
Les Arcs, Val d'Isère or Tignes.
Beginners Free baby-lift in each centre.
Short-term passes Half-day. A few lifts can be
paid for by the ride.
Other passes Limited passes available in the
four main areas (Central La Plagne, Champagny,
Montchavin and Montalbert). 'Discovery' passes
in each area. Also combined pass/ski school
deals in low season.

Ski school

ESF
Schools in all centres: Plagne Centre, Plagne
villages, Plagne 1800, Plagne Bellecôte, Aime la
Plagne and Belle Plagne.
Classes 4 1/2hr to 5 1/2hr (depending on season
and location). Cost: 630.00 (6 days). Lunch-time
classes possible during peak periods.
Lift priority Yes.
Children's classes Ages: Up to 14. Cost: 660.00
(6 days).
Private lessons available 1 or 2 hr. Cost: 155.00
per hour.
Special courses Off-piste course, 6 days
1,260.00; race training, 6 days 960.00; ski
touring, 6 days 1,220.00.
Le Ski Puissance
Classes 2 1/2 or 5 hr. Cost: 775.00 (6 full days).
Lift priority Yes.
Children's classes Ages: Up to 14. Cost: 685.00
(6 full days).
Private lessons available Per hour or 1 1/2
hours. Cost: 155.00 per hour.

What was new in 91

1. Mélèzes chair-lift from below Centre giving
quick connection to Bellecôte.
2. Bouclets chair-lift replacing a short drag below
Aime.
3. Long Coqs chair-lift serving black runs behind
Aime
4. Fornelet chair-lift replacing drag above
Montalbert.

France has been recommended – 'spacious rooms, excellent dinners, outrageously expensive wine.'

Après-ski activity is very limited. There are bars and restaurants in all the residential units, piano bars in Centre and Bellecôte, and a few discos, the greatest selection being in Centre; but not many places with any character or animated atmosphere. The Grande Rochette gondola is sometimes open in the evening, with fondues and *braserades* served at the mountain restaurant at the top. Plagne 1800's one bar, the English-run Tom's, is pivotal for young Brits – music, dancing, videos of the bar's own weekly slalom race; open until the early hours (but disco prices after 10pm). The same people run Froggies, a cheap-and-cheerful restaurant. Also in 1800, the Loup Blanc is reported to do a good *braserade*. In Belle Plagne, the Mouflin and Matafan bars are lively in the early evening. The several restaurants here are generally regarded as good but pricey: La Cloche ('informal, reasonably priced, excellent *pierrade*'), the Matafan ('excellent and often fully booked'), the Vieux Tyrol ('good Alpine fare') and the Pasta ('welcoming pizzeria'). The Cor Caroli nightclub has a karaoke night for the British community. Karaoke is also to be had in the one bar of Plagne Soleil, the English-run Lincoln.

In general, the high units of La Plagne are suitable only for downhill skiers. Montalbert and Champagny are better for **cross-country** skiing. **Non-skiing** facilities have been improved, but they do not add up to a great deal, and La Plagne remains a skiers' resort.

Nursery slopes are generally very good. Plagne Centre, Plagne Villages, Belle Plagne and Bellecôte are the most suitable of all, with gentle surrounding slopes, very reliable for snow.

Recent reports on La Plagne's various **ski schools** (the great majority relating to Belle Plagne) are generally favourable, typically complimenting organisation, tuition and spoken English, but with the very occasional reservation about 'follow-me' tuition and limited spoken English. Facilities for children are generally excellent, with nurseries and **ski kindergartens** in all the main resort units. Reports on these and on children's classes are generally though not entirely favourable.

Minor resorts

Montchavin   1250m

Montchavin is a little old village which had most of its rustic wrinkles ironed out when it was transformed into a miniature ski resort in the early 1970s; but it is still undeniably attractive, with the pistes down from Arpette ending in an orchard in front of jolly restaurant terraces. And it has some village atmosphere in its bars and restaurants in the evening. Practically all the accommodation is in apartments and chalets (much of it up the steep slope to the east of the home pistes), but the Bellecôte is a small, simple hotel close to the centre – 'pleasant room, friendly staff, good food'. There are adequate shops, and a kindergarten. This all sounds appealing for families, and perhaps for novice skiers who would be happier in a backwater than in the mainstream of La Plagne. But there are snags, not only with the skiing (see above) but also with the lifts: access to the gentle upper slopes is normally via an unnerving dog-leg drag, difficult for children. When snow is short at village level, beginners go up to Plan Bois, above Les Coches.

Tourist office ✆ 79078282.
Package holidays Made to Measure (hs) Simply Ski (hcs) Ski Esprit (cj).

Les Coches 1450m

One of the newest components of La Plagne, Les Coches was purpose-built in the early 1980s, in a sympathetic style and on a human scale – not unlike Belle Plagne. Small though it is, the village is broken into three 'hamlets'; the main one is Hameau du Carreau, at the foot of the main lift, with a sunny restaurant terrace facing up the wooded slopes. All the accommodation is in apartments and chalets. There is a ski kindergarten. A 'train' runs a shuttle service by road between Les Coches and Montchavin for the benefit of non-skiers (eg to get to the bank and better shops). The Pierre et Vacances apartments are generally approved of. La Taverne du Monchu is repeatedly recommended for good food at modest prices, and friendly service. When snow is short on the village nursery slopes, classes move up to a large area of gentle skiing at Plan Bois, at the top of the chair-lift out of the village.

Tourist office ✆ 79078282.
Package holidays Hoverspeed Ski-Drive (s) Made to Measure (s) Simply Ski (cs) Ski Esprit (cj) Ski Olympic (c).

Champagny 1250m

A peaceful collection of hamlets, some of them old, in a secluded valley. The main community (Champagny-le-Bas) is linked to the La Plagne ski area by a chain of lifts starting a stiff walk above the village centre. Of Champagny's four hotels, the simple Les Glières is convenient for the chair-lift. Several reporters have mentioned the boisterous warmth of the lunchtime atmosphere and excellent value for money at Chez Thérèse in the Hotel Bouquetin. Beyond the village the mountains form a narrow gateway into a beautiful lonely upper valley (Champagny-le-Haut, 1450m) – an excellent place for cross-country skiing. Champagny has a disco, ten ski instructors (some English-speaking), ski and non-ski kindergartens

Tourist office ✆ 79220953.
Package holidays Sally Holidays (hs) Ski Jeannie (cs).

Montalbert 1350m

Montalbert is a tiny (1,650-bed) purpose-built satellite below Aime la Plagne, on the western extremity of the ski area. Its position is a key factor: the skiing immediately above the resort is limited (and exposed to the afternoon sun), and connections with the more extensive areas beyond Plagne Centre are time-consuming (though recently improved). All the accommodation is in apartments. A long cross-country trail climbs through woods along the mountainside past Les Coches to Peisey-Nancroix. There is a ski kindergarten (Le Gros Calin).

Tourist office ✆ 79097733.
Package holidays Ski-Tal (hc)

Les Trois Vallées: big is beautiful

Courchevel France 1300–1850m

Good for *Nursery slopes, easy runs, big ski area, skiing convenience, après-ski, resort-level snow, chalet holidays, family holidays, lift queues, tough runs, woodland runs, artificial snow*
Bad for *Alpine charm, short airport transfers, easy road access, not skiing*

Méribel France 1450–1700m

Good for *Big ski area, lift queues, sunny slopes, chalet holidays, resort-level snow, mountain restaurants, artificial snow*
Bad for *Short airport transfers, nursery slopes, easy road access, not skiing*

Val Thorens France 2300m

Good for *Big ski area, tough runs, off-piste skiing, late holidays, nursery slopes, skiing convenience, summer skiing, resort-level snow, lift queues*
Bad for *Not skiing, Alpine charm, après-ski, short airport transfers, easy road access, woodland runs*

Les Menuires France 1850m

Good for *Big ski area, tough runs, off-piste skiing, skiing convenience, resort-level snow, artificial snow*
Bad for *Not skiing, Alpine charm, après-ski, short airport transfers, easy road access, woodland runs*

Linked resort: La Tania

'Le plus grand domaine skiable du monde' is the rather nebulous catchphrase of one of the skiing industry's biggest conglomerates. Four important resorts share an enormous linked ski area (at the latest count, some 200 lifts and over 600km of piste) which in one holiday many skiers can barely come to terms with, never mind exhaust. The *domaine skiable* may or may not be the biggest in the world, or even in the Alps, but it is certainly one of the most impressive and dynamic.

Parisians who can afford it fly with their poodles to **Courchevel**, stay in comfortable hotels, and dine and dance without counting the *centimes*. For them, Courchevel is one of the best equipped of all French resorts; and for skiing gourmets it is without doubt the best resort in the world (which is not saying much). Its slopes offer enormous scope for beginners and timid skiers, and enough variety of difficulty and terrain to satisfy experts. The major drawback of staying here is remoteness from the high-altitude skiing of Val Thorens – though access has been much improved by new lifts along the way. Courchevel is split into several parts, usually referred to by numbers approximating to altitude; the resort centre is at 1850, the highest part. None of the parts is pretty, despite recent and current cosmetic improvements.

Méribel, in the central valley, is a British favourite – many reporters find the British presence unpleasantly dominant at times. The French, at least, don't seem to mind: several reporters note that by French standards the local people are friendly. The resort consists of two separate villages, both purpose-built. Méribel-les-Allues (now generally called Méribel) celebrated its 50th birthday in 1989. Despite its youth, it is inoffensive to the eye and resembles a real village, its chalets and chalet-style blocks sprawling widely across a steep hillside; parts of it are very convenient for skiers, but most parts are not. Méribel-Mottaret (Mottaret), further up the valley, was initially designed very much for skiing convenience, but with more care over appearance than that usually implies; recent development has diluted the convenience somewhat, but Mottaret remains the best location from which to explore the whole of the enormous ski area. Recent reports suggest that the après-ski in both villages is less limited than it used to be, despite the large numbers of chalet- or apartment-based guests.

On the road between Méribel and Courchevel is the new resort of **La Tania**, a small modern development of not unattractive apartment blocks and hotels, supposedly for press use during the Olympics. A new stand-up gondola connects La Tania with the Courchevel ski area, on the north-facing slopes below the Col de la Loze.

The appeal of **Val Thorens** is simple: snow. It is the highest resort in Europe, and its moderately steep slopes face mainly away from the sun. They generally offer good skiing conditions down to resort level at times when the sunnier, lower slopes of Les Menuires and Méribel, in particular, are alternating between slush and ice. Visitors to lower resorts have in the past found Val Thorens a very valuable snow guarantee. The resort's setting is remote and bleak, and the buildings are little more than functional, but Val Thorens is less of an eyesore than many such resorts, and aims to sell not just on price but on quality of facilities. As a result it attracts a significant German and Scandinavian trade. It has declared itself traffic-free; it is not, and recent reports suggest that the steps taken to keep cars out of the resort are often ignored.

Les Menuires is one of the ugliest blots on the Alpine landscape – a cheerless, functional scattering of shopping blocks, lift pylons and apartment blocks, providing many ordinary French (and a few British) families with economical and convenient apartment accommodation.

St-Martin-de-Belleville, some way down the valley but linked to both Les Menuires and Méribel by a series of chair-lifts, is a sharp contrast – a quiet, small, friendly village where skiing does not dominate.

The skiing   top 3200m   bottom 1270m

The Méribel and Courchevel valleys are well linked by lifts and pistes up and down the ridge separating the two, mainly via La Saulire but now via the back-door Col de la Loze as well. Les Menuires and Val Thorens are not quite so well connected to Méribel, because they are set much further up their valley.

The **Courchevel** skiing is spread widely across the mountainside with a great variety of terrain and orientation. The shape of the mountains is concave, with the steeper runs around the rocky rim dividing Courchevel from Méribel, and a huge area of gentle slopes just above the resort which gives rise to the idea that the skiing consists entirely of nursery slopes. This is far from the truth.

Saulire From the big central station in Courchevel 1850 the left-hand gondola goes up to Verdons, where a 150-person cable-car climbs quickly to the top of the skiing at Saulire. This is the only lift from Courchevel which gives access to the three notorious couloirs dropping from the mountain crest, scoffed at by connoisseurs as being neither long nor steep nor narrow, but as graded pistes indisputably severe – the Téléphérique, next to the cable-car, is the steepest piste we have had the doubtful pleasure of measuring, at 38°. The couloirs are reached from the cable-car by a narrow, lumpy and dangerous piste along the ridge to the right, which is the most awkward part for many skiers making for the furthest of the three, the Grand Couloir – relatively wide, and 'only' 36 at its worst. Good snow, shaded from the sun, helps a lot.

All the other runs served by the cable-car can also be reached from the alternative gondola from Verdons to Vizelle, from where you have the choice of continuing over to Méribel, taking one of the steepish red or genuinely black alternative ways back to Verdons, skiing the black north-east face of the mountain under the high-speed Suisses chair or entering the beautiful wide Vallée des Creux and from there skiing either down to 1550 (a tediously flat trail) or, via linking lifts, back to 1850 or over to 1650. These are long runs with plenty of opportunity for exploration (by no means always safe) near the pistes on the top half.

Les Creux Each of the three chair-lifts from Lac des Creux serves interesting, challenging skiing. The Creux Noirs chair-lift also opens up an off-piste run to Mottaret. The Chanrossa lift serves an impressive, wide slope of about 500m vertical; the black piste is only moderately steep but the heavily skied off-piste area is steeper. Chanrossa gets a lot of afternoon sun and the snow deteriorates. Behind Chanrossa, harmless red runs lead into the extensive Courchevel 1650 skiing.

Courchevel 1650 Most of the runs down to 1650 are wide, open and easy, but there are some more challenging pitches particularly down the Roc Mugnier coomb. A gondola, now accessible by two-way escalator from street level, climbs from the village to Mont Bel Air. Below this knoll, where lifts from the lower slopes converge, the short Petite Bosse drag provides a link with Praméruel for the trip back to 1850, and long parallel drags give access to the Roc Mugnier coomb and connect with other

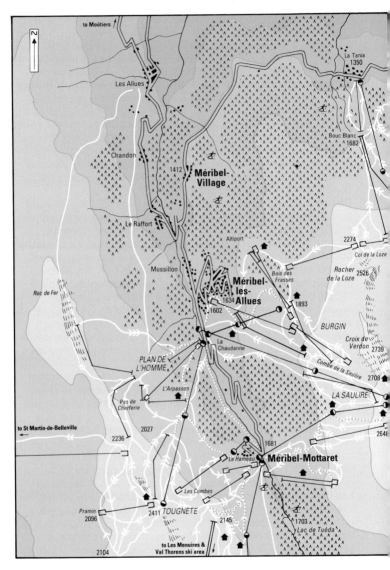

drag-lifts, serving the confidence-building runs below the Col de Chanrossa and more interesting runs down the north-face of the Signal. **Col de la Loze** The right-hand gondola from 1850, and several drag-lifts nearby, serve the skiing below the Col de la Loze. Long black trails of nearly 900m vertical go down through thick woods to Le Praz (1300) – consistently challenging runs, with the occasionally severe pitch of up to 35. These pistes and their red variants are a great asset in bad weather, and the slopes also offer plenty of off-piste scope.

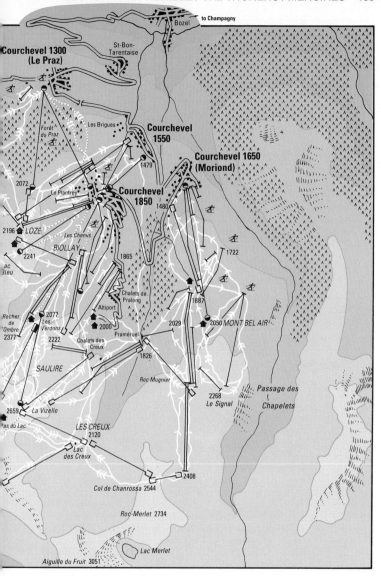

Gondolas from Le Praz and the new stand-up gondola from La Tania, which links with the Bouc Blanc drags, serve the forest pistes and give access to Courchevel 1850.

There is some less demanding skiing in this sector – enjoyable runs in the morning sun down to 1550 and easy blue pistes and green paths back to 1850. From the Col de la Loze itself, an attractive piste – not difficult but often with poor snow – leads to Méribel Altiport, whence a four-seater chair-lift takes you back to the Col and so to Courchevel.

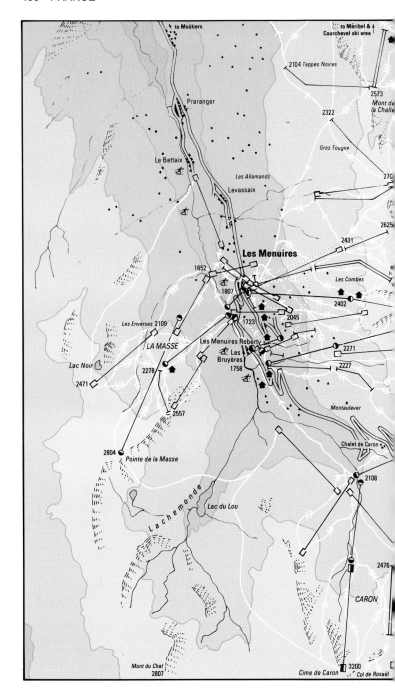

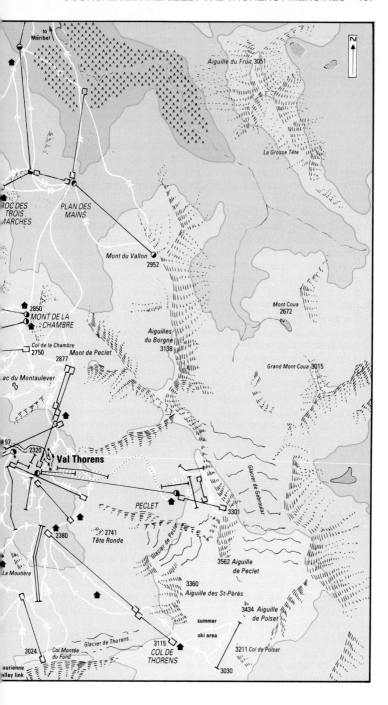

to Méribel

Aiguille du Fruit 3051

La Grosse Tête

ROC DES TROIS MARCHES

PLAN DES MAINS

Mont du Vallon 2952

Mont Coua 2672

MONT DE LA CHAMBRE 2850

Aiguilles du Borgne 3138

Col de la Chambre 2750

Mont de Peclet 2877

Grand Mont-Coua 3015

Lac du Montaulever

497

2320

Val Thorens

Glacier de Gebroulaz

PECLET

3301

2380

2741 Tête Ronde

Glacier de Peclet

3562 Aiguille de Peclet

La Moutière

3360 Aiguille des St-Pères

3434 Aiguille de Polset

summer

ski area

3024 Col Montée du Fond

Glacier de Thorens

3115 COL DE THORENS

3211 Col de Polset

aurienne alley link

3030

For many years the skiing of the **Méribel** valley was largely confined to the two flanks, facing roughly east and west, between Méribel and Mottaret – ideal for sunny skiing morning and afternoon. In this area there is no difficulty in getting across from one side to the other or making the links along the mountainsides above the two resorts. The slopes are open, and wooded only above Méribel. Most of the runs are intermediate, with blue runs that are often unpleasantly difficult, and black runs which are mostly not. Mottaret and Méribel are linked directly by a very easy, wide green run, the Truite.

Only in the last few years have lifts been installed to open up the head of the valley, beyond Mottaret – first the Plattières gondola to Roc des Trois Marches above Les Menuires, and more recently a stand-up gondola on the opposite side of the valley, going up to over 2900m on the virgin Mont-Vallon.

Saulire Above Mottaret there are many variants of the open runs directly down from Saulire, mostly stiff red but with some winding routes which are just about blue. The slopes face south-west, and snow conditions are often treacherous, despite the large numbers of snow cannon which line many of the runs. In good conditions, the little-used Grande Rosière run is a splendid sustained black. The excellent black race-course down to Méribel is rarely open to holiday skiers.

Burgin The runs in the Burgin sector immediately above Méribel are mostly shorter and easier, and have more reliable snow. Above the Altiport is a particularly fine long green run for near-beginners. The new Rhodos two-stage gondola from Chaudanne to the Altiport makes this area easily accessible to beginners, and also provides a quick alternative to the traditional Saulire route to Courchevel via the Rocher de la Loze chair-lift. From Rond-Point, at the top of the village, a not-easy piste runs down through the trees beside the resort.

Tougnète The east-facing slopes are more varied and fragmented, with little bowls and ridges out of the way of the piste network. Above Méribel the long two-stage gondola to Tougnète serves a long black run back down to the base station – a short steep mogul-field at the top, an easy middle section with connections to Mottaret, and a steeper run down through the woods under the bottom section of the lift, often short of snow. The easy black and enjoyable red runs served by the Mont de la Challe drags (seen most clearly on the Les Menuires map) often provide good snow when it's in short supply. There is a large, uncrowded area of easy and intermediate runs in the Plan de l'Homme sector, and now a black run from the Roc de Fer drag (La Face) which is reportedly a 'fast, steep motorway'; it will be in use this season as the women's Olympic downhill course. The Pas de Cherferie drag is now linked to a couple of lifts and runs over the ridge, above St-Martin-de-Belleville, including a sweeping red, Jerusalem, which is often blissfully free of traffic and ends near a delightful restaurant. A blue run continues on down to the village.

Plattières and Mont-Vallon At the head of the valley, beyond Mottaret, the three-stage Plattières gondola ascends to the Roc des Trois Marches on the ridge dividing Méribel and Les Menuires; it has a gloriously wide, easy blue trail beside the first two sections; facing north and usually immaculately groomed, this is an ideal run for timid novices, and largely compensates for the absence of gentle nursery slopes in Mottaret. Under the top section of the gondola, by contrast, is a short, unprepared black pitch which needs good snow to cover its rocks and is then heavily mogulled; the alternative Mouflon piste, joining the blue part-way down, is an interesting red which often has good snow. From the Roc de Tougnes and Roc des Trois Marches there is plenty of scope for finding off-piste ways down between the runs; some of these slopes can be dangerous. The base of the Mont-Vallon gondola can be reached from the top or the second station of the Plattières gondola, or from the top lifts of Val Thorens and Les Menuires. Most of these splendid runs (which mostly have steep starts) are still classified as *itinéraires* – that is, off-piste – despite their justifiable popularity and much improved access. From the top of Mont-Vallon, red runs descend either side of the gondola. That on the south side is unremarkable, and starts with an unpleasant shelf around the mountain before descending to Plan des Mains, for the chair up to the Plattières gondola (and its piste home to Mottaret) or further rides on the Vallon gondola. The other is a long, mogully piste, properly graded red and very enjoyable in good snow conditions; it rejoins the old *itinéraire* about half-way to Mottaret; if you carry on down from there, you have a lot of skating and poling ahead; but there is now the more attractive alternative of a high-speed chair back up the valley to Plan des Mains.

The skiing of **Les Menuires**, like that of Méribel, is spread over two sides of a valley, but here connections from one side to the other are awkward, especially when snow is poor. Above the resort are various long runs, facing south-west, of about 1000m vertical from Roc des Trois Marches and Mont de la Chambre (the main links with Méribel). The many variants are stiff intermediate runs, often made more difficult and unpleasant by poor snow and crowds of skiers in transit. The link with Val Thorens has been greatly improved by the installation last year of a stand-up gondola starting well to the south of the queue-prone original, but arriving at the same point on the Mont de la Chambre. On the slopes directly above the village is the new Olympic slalom course, served by a drag-lift.

La Masse Opposite Les Menuires, La Masse is a much more tempting mountain for good skiers. The old two-stage gondola has recently been replaced by a longer stand-up version which conveniently starts just below the Enverses chair-lift. The slopes of La Masse face north-east and usually have much better snow than elsewhere in the valley; the runs are long (again about 1000m vertical) and tough, including some genuine blacks – the Dame Blanche is about the steepest in this valley – and are not busy with transit crowds. The main off-piste run to La Châtelard and St-Martin-de-Belleville runs high along the crest of the mountains. Another run drops down into the valley between La Masse and the Cime de Caron (in which lifts will surely appear before long).

Val Thorens is set at the head of the Belleville valley and is tightly enclosed by a horseshoe of mountains with slopes facing south, west and north. Most of the lift departures are below the resort, and the lower slopes are gentle; streams (and associated ice) are a hazard. The skiing divides into four main sectors, of which the most compelling is the Caron area, to the south of the resort.

Caron The main focus of the Val Thorens ski area is the 160-person Cime de Caron cable-car, which climbs swiftly to the highest point of the Trois Vallées' winter skiing, and opens up some magnificent runs of almost 900m vertical. An easy track runs around the back of the peak with a long off-piste run down into the valley between Caron and La Masse. The black north-facing piste is a long, wide, open, steep slope reached by an awkward shelf, and the main red run on the shoulder of the mountain is full of challenge; the variant to the left on the top half is unsigned, often closed, narrow and pointless. The drags to the east of Caron serve north-facing slopes which are enjoyable for their reliably good snow, and the higher Montée du Fond chair-lift serves a pair of mogulled reds. But the main alternative interest for good skiers is the several pistes which have been opened up recently by lifts starting well below the resort – first, a chair east of the Caron access gondola, going up to La Moutière, and then the Boismint and Plan de l'Eau chairs opening up the virgin mountainside to the west. All serve testing red runs which have added considerably to the area's attractions.

Maurienne The Montée du Fond chairlift at the eastern extremity of the Caron area gives access, via a long slog around the shoulder of the mountain, to south-facing skiing down the other side of the mountain into the Maurienne valley, previously an off-piste preserve but now equipped with a speedy four-seater chair-lift and a straightforward red run of 660m vertical to a sunny restaurant (which is also a refuge, with 40 beds). This area is to be extended by further chair-lifts to a 1,000-space car park in the valley bottom, giving access to the Trois Vallées for skiers based in the many small resorts of the Maurienne region and for the lucky residents of Turin, no more than 1hr away by road through the Fréjus tunnel. When these lifts open, weekend crowds are certain.

Col de Thorens By comparison with Caron, the rest of Val Thorens' skiing seems ordinary. Runs on the glacier from the Col de Thorens are wide and easy, though there is a well marked off-piste diversion on to a moderate mogul field on the edge of the glacier.

Péclet There are generally more challenging runs on Péclet, a wide bowl served by a chair-lift and offering a range of red pistes with good snow despite the afternoon sun. The old access gondola has been replaced by a very capacious stand-up affair. Like some other recent high-capacity gondolas, it runs on two cables instead of the usual one – but in this case they are widely separated, with the aim of keeping the cabins steady in high winds. The return run to the resort can be tricky when conditions are not good. The chairs on the north side of the village serve sunny, moderately steep pistes, as well as giving access to the Méribel valley.

   Mountain restaurants are more numerous in the Trois Vallées than in many modern resorts, and recent additions have improved matters further. Few are particularly attractive in terms of interior style, but several are well sited – notably La Sittelle, just above the first mid-station of the Plattières gondola, which has a splendid view of the

Aiguille du Fruit. There are good views also from Saulire, Roc des Trois Marches and Mount Bel-Air. Reporters' recommendations in Courchevel include: Altitude 21 above Courchevel Altiport ('superb sundeck, great griddle cooking, delicious hors d'oeuvres'), Chalet des Pierres half-way down the Verdons run ('the sweet table was out of this world') and Le Casserole on the 1650 slopes; in Méribel: La Chardonneray at the Pas de Lac gondola mid-station ('waitress service, sun trap'), the cabin near the top of the Tougnète gondola ('best hot chocolate in Trois Vallées'),and the Rhododendrons above the Méribel Altiport ('lovely atmosphere, delicious fresh food, reasonable prices'); in Les Menuires: the mid-station of the Masses and the Chardon Bleu above St-Martin-de-Belleville ('delightful stone cabin with balcony, large portions of home-made food'); and in Val Thorens: La Moutière between the Montée du Fond chair-lifts ('log fire, fresh flowers, excellent vin chaud') and the restaurant at the bottom of the La Moraine chair-lift.

The Trois Vallées lift system copes with the enormous numbers of skiers remarkably well. The main **queue** black spots are the major lifts out of Courchevel (the Verdons gondola) and Les Menuires at peak periods – though the latter has been greatly relieved by the alternative Bruyères gondola. Mottaret's Pas-du-Lac gondola also gets crowded by skiers making for or returning to Courchevel – the improved alternative route via Méribel (Col de la Loze) is often quicker. One of the delights of the system is the exemplary use of cable-cars to Cime de Caron and La Saulire: not only are they huge, but also their journeys are short and steep, and they serve testing pistes, not quickly skied. The new Peclet gondola in Val Thorens had a few teething troubles at the beginning of last season and reporters complained of queues building up even when the old gondola was still in use.

There are substantial **artificial snow** installations in all three valleys – in Courchevel on a long piste down from Verdons and two shorter pistes from Loze to 1850, and then on down to 1300; in Méribel on the final sections of all the main pistes down to the lift station at La Chaudanne, including the run under the new Rhodos gondola; at Mottaret, virtually all the way down from La Saulire on one side and from Tougnète on the other, and on the lowest section of the Plattières gondola run; in Les Menuires on several west-facing runs immediately above the village and down to the valley bottom; and in Val Thorens from the Peclet glacier down to the village. A tour of the Tarentaise resorts last season impressed on us how much better the piste grooming is, at least in Méribel and Courchevel, than in other major resorts of this region.

Courchevel

Courchevel consists of a string of communities along the road which winds up one flank of the wide Bozel valley. 1300, 1550 and 1850 are stacked up the same hillside, with lift and piste connections between each other; 1650 is out of the way on the other side of a river gorge. A bus shuttle service (not covered by the general lift pass) links the different parts of the resort. There is an hourly service until about 10pm.

Facts on Courchevel Savoie **France**

Prices in francs

Tourist office

Postcode 73122
Tel (33)79080029
Fax (33)79083354
Tlx 980083

Getting there

By road 925km from Calais. Via Macon/Annecy; chains may be needed. Horrific peak weekend jams.
By rail Moûtiers (25km); frequent buses.
By air Geneva & Lyon; transfer 3½hr. (Or Lyon. Direct flights from Paris twice daily, and from Lyon and Geneva on Saturdays.)

Staying there

Visitor beds 32,432; breakdown: 5,400 in hotels, 26,400 in apartments/chalets.
Package holidays Activity Travel (hcs) Bladon Lines (hc) Brittany Ferries (s) Chalets and Hotels "Unlimited" (cs) Crystal (hcs) Enterprise (hcs) French Impressions (s) Inghams (h) Le Ski (hcs) Made to Measure (hs) Silver Ski (c) Ski Alternatives (h) Ski Chamois (cj) Ski Esprit (c) Ski Red Guide (cs) Ski Unique (h) Ski West (hcjs) Ski Whizz Small World (hc) SnowRanger (hs) Supertravel (hcjs) .
Medical facilities In resort: Doctors, chemists, dentist. Hospital: Moûtiers (25km).

Non-skiing activities

Indoor Artificial skating rink, bridge, chess, squash, swimming and saunas (hotels), gymnasium, exhibitions (galleries in 1850 and 1650), cinema, games rooms, billiards, language courses.
Outdoor Hang-gliding, joy rides, flying lessons, ski-jumping, parachuting, scooter rides, nights in an igloo, floodlit skiing, toboggan runs, snow-shoe excursions, snowmobile rides, dog-sleigh rides, 35km cleared paths, 2½km toboggan run.

Kindergartens

Village des enfants (Forum 1850)
Tuition: Yes. Hours: 8.00-8.00. Ages: 2-12. Cost: 840.00 per week (meals cost 55.00 per day).
Vacances des Petits (1650)
Tuition: Yes. Hours: 9.00-5.00. Ages: 2-7. Cost: 960.00 per week (with meals).
Jardin d'enfants-in all centres
Tuition: Yes. Hours: 9.30-5.00. Ages: from 3 (1850 from 4). Cost: 850.00 per week (meals available).

Special skiing facilities

Summer skiing No.
Cross-country 10 trails, totalling 50km; mostly easy, in woods above Le Praz and at each resort centre. Instruction available.

Lift passes

Three Valleys pass
Covers all lifts of Courchevel, Méribel, Les Menuires and Val Thorens. Does not include buses. (220 lifts in total.)
Cost 6 days 880.00 (£90.72). Low season: 792.00 saving 10%.
Credit cards accepted Yes.
Senior citizens 693.00 (over 60) saving 21%.
Children 693.00 (under 16) saving 21%. Free pass up to age 5.
Notes One-day extension for Three Valleys (88.00).
Beginners Limited area passes.
Short-term passes Half-day (from 12.30) available for Vallée de Courchevel pass, Courchevel 1850, 1550 and 1300 lifts only, and Courchevel 1650 lifts only.
Other passes Vallée de Courchevel (6 days 750.00 for adults, 544.00 for children); Courchevel 1850, 1550 and 1300 (6 days 675.00 for adults, 472.00 for children); Courchevel 1650 (575.00 for adults, 415.00 for children).

Ski school

ESF in 1850
Classes 9.30-12.00 and/or 2.45-4.45. Cost: 780.00 (6 full days).
Lift priority Yes.
Children's classes Ages: from 4. Cost: 600.00 (6 full days).
Private lessons available Hourly. Cost: 160.00 per hour.
ESF in 1650
Classes 9.30-12.00, and/or 2.45-4.45. Cost: 735.00 (6 days).
Lift priority Yes.
Children's classes Ages: from 3. Cost: 560.00 (6 days).
Private lessons available Hourly. Cost: 155.00 per hour.
Special courses Mono and Surf courses, 150.00 per day.
ESF in 1550
Classes 3hr am or pm. Cost: 530.00 (6 mornings). 450.00 (6 afternoons).
Lift priority Yes.
Children's classes Ages: From 3. Cost: 450.00 (6 mornings).
Private lessons available 3hr. Cost: 630.00 for 3hr am, 520.00 for 3hr pm.

What was new in 91

1. New resort, La Tania, on road beween Meribel and Courchevel 1300. New 12-man gondola from resort to Bouc Blanc, just below Col de la Loze.
2. Improvements to the Suisses and Marmottes slopes above 1800.
3. 1850: The Forum, a vast sports and recreational complex with an Olympic-sized skating rink and new kindergarten facilities, Village des Enfants.
4. 1300: New ski-jumping stadium at 1300 for the Olympics.
5. Renovations to many existing hotels. Two new hotels, the Grandes Alpes (1850) and the Golf (1650).
6. 2-way escalator to lift terminal in 1650.

If you go up to 1850 from the lower stations you can always toboggan, slide or ski back down if the moon is out. For après-ski excursions a car is of value.

1300 (Le Praz) is an attractive hamlet with a few hotels and a couple of restaurants at the bottom of the skiing, handy for the cross-country trails. A large new stadium has been built in the village for the Olympic ski jumping competitions. 1550 is more of a resort, but a characterless one – a dormitory suburb, by-passed by the road, by most skiers and by all serious après-skiers. It has some inexpensive hotels and restaurants. 1650 (Moriond) is a straggle of roadside apartment blocks and hotels; recently some cosmetic effort has been made to create a more Alpine look.

The main focus is 1850; it was built without much style in the early days of French purpose-building (the late 1940s) and has been much added to since. Only very recently has there been any advance in aesthetic achievement – and a recent campaign of 'embellishment' has had some effect in softening buildings and taming traffic. It is now a large resort spread between 1700m and 1900m, above and below the original site on a wide shelf about on the tree-line. The hub is a huge lift-station complex known as La Croisette. Either side of it there are lively and very smart shopping streets. The centre is reasonably compact, but chalets and hotels are spread far and wide across the hillsides, mostly on or near an easy piste. Car parking is said to be a 'nightmare'.

Accommodation is in staffed chalets, apartments in chalets, and lots of hotels. Most chalets used by UK operators are on the east side, if not in the centre. In general, standards of accommodation are high, and hotel prices are high too. No less than four of the better hotels have restaurants with Michelin rosettes. Recent recommendations include the Airelles in the Jardin Alpin area for 'excellent cuisine', Crystal 2000 despite its inconvenient position on the edge of town, and the chalet-hotel Saint Louis. At the cheaper end of the market are the Courcheneige – 'superior to its two-star rating' – and the Potinière. In 1550, the Chanrossa is 'very friendly, with excellent dinners' and well-placed for lifts and the L'Adret is a friendly French place with 'little spoken English'. One reporting family were disillusioned with the Floride in 1650 and recommend the nearby Golf. There are good food shops, at least in 1850.

When the French are on holiday there is a lot of expensive, chic, late **après-ski**. One reporter summed up the discos as 'the best I've ever encountered – expensive, stylish and yobbo-free'. There are places with a more Alpine atmosphere, relaxing piano bars,and many good restaurants; Le Bercail is recommended for 'excellent seafood' and the Chabichou for 'an expensive and delicious blow-out – nine courses!'). Livelier bars include Jack's (very British) and l'Arbe ('good simple bar with snacks'). Popular spots in 1650 are the Albatross ('noisiest, and by far the most popular with the British'), the Yeti and the Green Club disco ('little atmosphere'). The Ambassador serves a good and reasonably priced Plat du Jour. Outings down to Le Praz are popular – the Bistrot du Praz is an 'expensive but very good' restaurant, the Kinou a popular crêperie, the Mammoth a bar-restaurant frequented by chalet girls. The resort is quieter when the après-ski depends more on the British; several reporters have commented on 1550 being 'dead' at night. The cinema in 1850 shows a different film each night, often in English. An exceptional facility is the 400-seat auditorium in the Jardin Alpin area, where classical concerts are given on high-season Wednesdays.

Courchevel is not a very attractive resort for **non-skiers** although the construction of the massive new 'Forum' sports and recreational complex in 1850 will no doubt improve matters. Interesting excursion possibilities are few, but there are said to be lovely walks in the woods and organised snow-excursions. There are quite extensive **cross-country** trails there too.

There are very good **nursery slopes** – both 1850 and 1650 have huge areas of very green skiing immediately above the resort.

Reports on what is supposedly Europe's biggest **ski school** indicate that its various branches are engaged in healthy competition, and that the 1550 school has considerable attractions for British skiers – exclusively English-language lessons in the afternoons (whereas English may be difficult to find in the other schools). We've also had a number of favourable reports on the independent school, Ski Cocktail. The **ski kindergarten** is 'virtually a mini-resort in its own right, with its own runs and lifts, right in the middle of the village'.

Méribel

Méribel spreads steeply from about 1400m, beside the river, up the west-facing side of the valley to about 1700m, with large chalet-style buildings all along the road which winds up the hillside and continues past the top of the resort (Rond-Point, where the ski school meets) on through the woods to the Altiport. Life revolves around the hectic little square at the bottom of the village, now fully surrounded by timber cladding as a result of new building on the downhill side. A recent effort to smarten up the streets leading to and from the square (by using less salt and grit on the roads and installing decorative new street lights) has made a significant difference to the town centre. Having a car is a considerable advantage, especially for those who want to go out in the evening to eat, drink or dance. There is an expensive daytime bus service between Mottaret and Altiport via Méribel, not covered by the lift pass.

Accommodation is mostly in apartments and staffed chalets, of which there is an enormous choice. There can be long walks to and from skiing unless you are based close to the village piste. Of the hotels, the Orée du Bois is conveniently placed at Rond-Point, and is straightforwardly comfortable. The Adray is isolated but very on-piste. The Altiport is comfortable, expensive and very isolated, whereas the Grande Coeur is comfortable, expensive and central, with excellent food and service. The Allodis and the smart Le Chalet with its half-indoor, half-outdoor pool are both new chalet-style hotels in an area above the nursery slopes that has been developed for the Olympics.

The Saulire is recommended for 'unbeatable value, friendly staff, relaxed atmosphere'.

Après-ski has greatly improved and there are now several discos,

Facts on Méribel   Savoie **France**

Prices in francs

Tourist office
Postcode 73550
Tel 79086001
Fax 79005961
Tlx 980001

Getting there
By road 920km from Calais. Via Macon/Annecy; chains may be needed. Horrific peak weekend jams.
By rail Moûtiers (18km); 6 buses a day from station (10 a day at weekends).
By air Geneva; transfer 3½hr. (Or Lyons.)

Staying there
Visitor beds 27,000; breakdown: 2,000 in hotels, 24,200 in apartments and chalets.
Package holidays Abercrombie and Kent Travel (c) Activity Travel (hcs) Bladon Lines (hcs) Brittany Ferries (s) Chalets and Hotels "Unlimited" (hcs) Collineige Ski (s) Crystal (hs) Enterprise (hcs) French Impressions (s) Horizon (hs) Inghams (hs) Made to Measure (hs) Mark Warner (cj) Meriski (c) Neilson (hs) Sally Holidays (s) Silver Ski (cj) Ski Alternatives (ha) Ski Chamois (s) Ski Peak (s) Ski West (hcjs) Ski Whizz Small World (cj) SkiBelAir (hc) Skiworld (hcas) SnowRanger (hs) Snowtime (hcjs) Supertravel (hcjs) The Ski Company Ltd (c) Thomson (hs) White Roc Ski (hc) .
Medical facilities In resort: Doctors, chemist, dentist. Hospital: Moûtiers (18km).

Non-skiing activities
Indoor Parc des Sports Méribel (skating rink, swimming pool), Club Forme Mottaret (spa, sauna, solarium, gym), library, billiards, video club, bridge, fitness centres, sauna, jacuzzi, planetarium, 2 cinemas, concert hall.
Outdoor Flying lessons and joy rides, scooters, snow-shoe excursions, paragliding, hang-gliding, 10km cleared paths, motor trikes, sleigh rides.

Kindergartens
Club Saturnin (Meribel)
Tuition: Yes, from age 4. Hours: 9.00-5.00. Ages: 2-8. Cost: 1,014.00 per week (with meals).
Les Pingouins (Mottaret)
Tuition: Yes. Hours: 9.00-5.00. Ages: 3-8. Cost: 1,030.00 per week (with meals).
ESF-Mini Club
Tuition: Yes. Hours: 9.00-5.00. Ages: 4-12. Cost: 470.00 per week (with lunch).

Special skiing facilities
Summer skiing No.
Cross-country 6km blue track and 2km green track at Mottaret; 10km red, 5km blue, 1½km green track near Altiport, above Méribel and

intinerary from Altiport to Courchevel 8km long. Instruction available.

Lift passes
Three Valleys pass
Covers all lifts in Courchevel, Méribel, Les Menuires, Val Thorens. (220 lifts in total.)
Cost 6 days 880.00 (£90.72). Low season: 792.00 saving 10%.
Credit cards accepted Yes.
Senior citizens 693.00 (over 60) saving 21%.
Children 693.00 (under 16) saving 21%. Free pass up to age 5.
Notes One-day extension for Three Valleys (88.00).
Beginners Coupons valid for a limited area. One free lift in Mottaret and one in Méribel.
Short-term passes Half-day (from 12.30pm) available for Vallée de Méribel pass, Mottaret lifts only and Méribel lifts only.
Other passes Vallée de Méribel (6 days 750.00 for adults, 544.00 for children); Mottaret only (day pass 125.00 for adults, 87.00 for children); Méribel only (day pass 120.00 for adults, 82.00 for children).

Ski school
ESF in Méribel and Mottaret
Classes 9.45-12.15 and 2.45-5.00 in Méribel, 9.30-12.00 and 2.45-5.00 in Mottaret. Cost: 700.00 (5 days, Mon-Fri). Beginners' course costs 1,050.00 including lift pass.
Lift priority Yes.
Children's classes Ages: up to 12. Cost: 580.00 (5 days, Mon-Fri).
Private lessons available Hourly. Cost: 145.00 per hour. Private instruction for groups of up to 6.
Special courses Slalom and powder courses, 5 days 1,050.00.
Ski Cocktail
Classes 2hr am or 3hr pm. Cost: 670.00 (6 mornings, Sun-Fri). 5 mornings or 4 afternoons cost 580.00.
Lift priority Yes.
Children's classes Ages: up to 12. Cost: 760.00 (5 mornings, Mon-Fri).
Private lessons available 2hr, 3hr, 4hr or full day. Cost: 165.00 per 2 hours.
Special courses On request.

What was new in 91
1. 3 new runs in the Meribel-Mottaret sector: a blue allowing easy access to the Mont Vallon sector, a blue giving direct access to the Mont Vallon gondola and a red transit run from the top of the Roc des Trois Marches lift.
2. New snow guns installed on runs down to Meribel and Mottaret, bringing total to 325.

various British-dominated piano and video bars and a range of restaurants. Reporters recommend the Aussie-run Pub for 'costly giant cocktails, big-screen videos, live rock music and karaoke', the French Connection bar which is 'very lively at Happy Hour and has live rock music three times a week' and the Marquis' video bar. Of the restaurants, we have good reports of Pinocchio's, Le Refuge, Chez Kiki in Morel ('top quality food, fun atmosphere'), and the central Santa Marina for 'delicious French cuisine'. The tiny Galette (must book) is said to have 'good atmosphere, excellent food and reasonably priced wine'.

The **cross-country** trails in the woods around the Altiport are in beautiful surroundings and suit not very ambitious practitioners well. Méribel does not have a lot to offer **non-skiers** apart from swimming and skating, facilities for which (already good) are being improved for the Olympics. A new rink and stadium has been built at Chaudanne for the ice-hockey competition; it will eventually be connected with the Olympic village, Brides-les-Bains, by gondola.

The main **nursery slopes** at Rond-Point are too steep and busy for comfort – though the excellent long green run at Altiport is some compensation. Reports on the two main **ski schools** are generally not very complimentary – 'enormous classes of up to 18', 'the instructor arrived late and finished early', 'a nearly three-hour break over lunch totally disrupted the day'. Ski Cocktail is more expensive but much more flexible; instructors visit the chalets each week to recruit new arrivals. New Zealander Pat Graham, affilliated to the ESF, runs five-day ski clinics for all levels. One reporter's four-year old progressed fast at the **ESF's ski kindergarten**, despite seemingly shambolic organisation.

Mottaret is better placed for skiing links with Courchevel and (especially) Les Menuires. The main accommodation area, Le Laitelet, climbs high up the side of the valley – in this case the east-facing side, up to 1850m – and again there is a piste down the southern side of the centre (access to which is easy); further hotel and apartment building (Le Chatelet) is going on 200m south, up the valley, this time on the west-facing side, and this section also has easy ski links with the centre. Other new development is going on a little way down the valley, which is less convenient. Accommodation is mostly in apartments although there are several hotels; Les Arolles is particularly recommended – 'worth more than three stars, delicious five-course dinners' – as is the Tarentaise, under the same ownership. Most reporters stayed at the top of the resort in the Hameau complex. Many of the well-fitted apartments have balconies with splendid views of the piste; there is an underground car-park. There is not much après-ski here – just a few restaurants (Le Ty Sable is 'intimate, with Savoyard specialities', the Crocodile bar has 'an excellent braserade') and a big, anonymous congregation area with an open fire, two pool tables and an expensive bar. There are more stylish restaurants and bars in the centre of Mottaret but it is a steep 20-minute hike up a series of metal staircases for anyone staying at Le Hameau (the village lift, the Chalets, which shuttles back and forth between Le Hameau and Mottaret centre, stops running at 7.30pm). A good compromise is to eat at the hotel Les Arolles, half-way down. The centre, which consists of a shopping arcade, bank, post office and well-stocked supermarket, has several worth-while restaurants; reporters recommend the Plein Soleil and the Petite Rosière (further down the road to Méribel). The new development on the Courchevel side of the resort includes several new shops as well as the smart hotel Mont Vallon, and is convenient for the main lifts. Night-life revolves around the basement Down Town bar and the Rastro, a rustic place a few minutes' walk from the centre, usually packed with chalet-staff and Brits.

Mottaret's nursery slopes are even less comfortable than those of Méribel, but classes appear to be taken up the Plattières gondola at an early stage. Two of our reporters had impatient instructors and gave up ski school after a couple of days. We have very favourable reports of the Pingouins ski kindergarten at Le Hameau – 'very friendly staff, almost all English-speaking'.

Val Thorens 2300m

Val Thorens is all-new, and built with at least some concern for appearance. It is not very large – two loosely-grouped clusters of tall, white-and-wood blocks built along a winding spine of road, with pistes on all sides (and through the middle), most of them broad and easy; skiing to and from most residences is possible, and for skiing purposes location is unimportant. In the lower part of the resort is the very smart sports complex, and lower still, in a rather isolated position, is another smart new development, the imaginative Temples du Soleil residential complex. Cars are exiled to parks outside the resort after unloading (unless you have a garage space at your accommodation), at a cost of £15 a week in the open, £30 to £35 under cover. Car-parks on the edge of the resort fill up very quickly in high season. A recent reporter was banished to car-park 3, nearly a kilometre below the resort and connected by a free shuttle bus that stopped running at 7.30pm. Hardly surprisingly, the no-cars-in-the-village rule is not strictly obeyed and many are left outside apartments.

All the **accommodation** is convenient for skiing and shopping. We have had mixed reports about the quality of apartments and the service provided by the rental agencies; the Altineige and Cheval Blanc apartments seem to get the thumbs' up , the Temples du Soleil block the thumbs' down ('cramped, noisy, lifts vandalized'). Few reporters stayed in hotels, but those that did recommend the upmarket Val Thorens ('lovely staff, great food, comfortable rooms'), the Val Chavière, the modern Bel Horizon and particularly the Sherpa ('very friendly, lovely atmosphere'). There are a few enticing food shops (one reporter warmly recommends the cheese shop just up from the cinema, another the Belle en Cuisse smoked meat shop; both offer free samples), and new supermarkets have improved the outlook for self-caterers. The one in the Peclet centre is apparently a better bet than the two in the Caron centre. A regular reporter was over-charged on two consecutive days in the Sherpa supermarket. It is possible to borrow raclette sets from the

Facts on Val Thorens Savoie **France**

Prices in francs
Ski Club represented

Tourist office
Postcode 73440
Tel 79000808
Fax 79000004
Tlx 980572

Getting there
By road 940km from Calais. Via Macon/Annecy; chains may be needed. Horrific peak weekend jams. Covered parking available.
By rail Moûtiers (35km).
By air Geneva; transfer 4hr. (Or Lyon.)

Staying there
Visitor beds 17,000; breakdown: 600 in hotels, several thousand in apartments.
Package holidays Brittany Ferries (s) Crystal (hjs) Enterprise (hs) Falcon (s) Horizon (hs) Hoverspeed Ski-Drive (s) Inghams (hs) Made to Measure (hs) Neilson (hs) Quest Travel (schools) (a) Sally Holidays (s) Ski Alternatives (h) Ski Club of GB (h) Ski Club of GB (h) Ski Global (hs) Ski Unique (hs) Ski Valkyrie (hs) Skiworld (s) Snobiz (hs) SnowRanger (hs) Thomson (hs) Touralp (s) Tracer Holidays (s) Vacations (hs) .
Medical facilities In resort: Doctors, dentist, chemist. Hospital: Moûtiers (35km).

Non-skiing activities
Indoor Club Pierre Barthes (tennis school, squash, golf practice and simulator, swimming pool, saunas, jacuzzi, gym), games rooms, music recitals, cinema.
Outdoor Walks, snow scooters, hang-gliding, flying school.

Kindergartens
ESF-Mini-Club
Tuition: Yes. Hours: Sun-Fri. Ages: 3 up. Cost: 1,070.00 per week (with meals).
ESF-Baby-sitting
Tuition: No. Hours: 5 days. Ages: 3mths up. Cost: 920.00 per week (with meals).
Other childcare facilities
Marielle Goitschel's Children's Village: self-contained holiday centre for children, 6 days with meals 1,300.00. Accommodation available.

Special skiing facilities
Summer skiing Extensive, on 2 flanks of Aiguille de Péclet; several chairs and drags 2800–3300m.

Cross-country Several km, down the valley. Instruction available.

Lift passes
Three Valleys pass
Covers all lifts of Courchevel, Méribel, Les Menuires and Val Thorens. (220 lifts in total.)
Cost 6 days 880.00 (£90.72). Low season: 792.00 saving 10%.
Credit cards accepted Yes.
Senior citizens 693.00 (over 60) saving 21%.
Children 693.00 (under 16) saving 21%. Free pass up to age 5.
Notes Family reductions.
Beginners 2 free lifts in Val Thorens.
Short-term passes Half-day pass available for Val Thorens lifts only and Vallée de Belleville pass.
Other passes Val Thorens lifts only (6 days 620.00 for adults, 435.00 for children); Vallée de Belleville (6 days 785.00 for adults, 640.00 for children).

Ski school
ESF
Classes 2 or 3 hr, am or pm. Cost: 500.00 (5 days, Mon-Fri).
Lift priority Yes.
Children's classes Ages: up to 12. Cost: 410.00 (5 days, Mon-Fri).
Private lessons available Hourly. Cost: 150.00 per hour. 1-2 people. Private instruction available for groups of up to 5.
Special courses Race training courses.
Ecole de Ski Internationale (Ski Cool)
Classes 3hr, am or pm. Cost: 530.00 (5 days). Special 6-day course with video sessions (600.00 for adults, 580.00 for children).
Lift priority Yes.
Children's classes Ages: up to 12. Cost: 510.00 (5 days).
Private lessons available Hourly. Cost: 165.00 per hour. 1-3 people.
Special courses Mono and surf courses available, 5 days 600.00.

What was new in 91
Nothing.

What is new for 92
Ice-driving circuit.

butchers if you buy meat and cheese from them. There is a small market twice a week.

Après-ski is limited, though there are more bars and restaurants (several with music) than in many resorts of this kind, and a couple of discos. Among the 'trendiest' of the bars are the 'excellent' Lincoln Inn (serves Whitbread, should you require it), Champagne Charlie's and the Malaysia bar ('an odd mixture of chic and theme; occasional live jazz'). A smaller, cheaper bar is the Chantenca. Restaurant recommendations include the Scapin ('very friendly, excellent food and service'), Tino's trattoria ('very filling pizza and spaghetti') and La Pause, at the top of town ('quiet, good value'). The most popular nightspot appears to be the Agora. Despite the impressive sports facilities, the resort cannot be recommended for **non-skiers** and there is no ice-rink, though one is planned. Skidoo rides (at nearly £30 an hour) and snow-shoe walks are available. There is **cross-country** skiing down the valley to Les Menuires and beyond.

The **nursery slopes** are spacious and gentle, and have reliably good snow; but they are much used by non-nursery skiers. Reports on the ESF **ski school** are not altogether favourable; there have been complaints of large classes, irresponsible staff, much waiting around and 'boring' childrens' classes. In contrast, we've had largely enthusiastic reports of Ski Cool; 'we learnt more in one descent than in a week with the ESF'. The extensive **ski kindergarten**, which is under the direction of the famous racer Marielle Goitschel is 'expensive but worthwhile'.

Les Menuires 1850m

Les Menuires has five major components (though more can be distinguished), all of them ranged along the east side of the valley. The centre is La Croisette, a crescent of linked blocks with cars and road outside and an open, snowy plaza of lifts, pistes and café sun-terraces inside. Most of the entertainment and shopping facilities are here, although Reberty, a satellite village about 1km south, (most often offered by British operators), has a fair amount of services including branches of the two ski schools, an ice-rink, swimming-pool and two cinemas. Reberty gives easier and less crowded access to Val Thorens, but is rather isolated. (The free shuttle bus around the resort stops about 7.30.) The lower satellite of Preyerand is connected to La Croisette by a gondola which runs until midnight.

We have reports of cramped self-catering **accommodation** in Reberty, but two recent commendations of the Les Lauzes apartments ('good sized, with superb views up to Caron'). Another reporter recommends staying on the La Masse side of the valley, which is relatively uncrowded. There are a few hotels in three of the five centres; the recently built L'Ours Blanc in Reberty is apparently 'excellent in every respect, superb cuisine, friendly and helpful staff'. We lack reports on any of the others.

There are plenty of bars and restaurants for **après-skiers** but they tend to lack life. Particularly recommended is the Deux Frères crêperie – 'cheerful and not too expensive'. There are two discos, three cinemas (often showing very up-to-date films), and various post-skiing activities such as torchlit descents. Despite reasonable sports facilities, Les Menuires has little to offer the **non-skier**. There are 28km of **cross-country** trails along either side of the valley, catering for all skiing levels.

The **nursery slopes** are broad, gentle and sunny, and right in the heart of the resort, but they are often hideously crowded and in the past

Facts on Les Menuires   Savoie **France**

Prices in francs

Tourist office
Postcode 73440
Tel 79007300
Fax 79007506

Getting there
By road 928km from Calais. Via Macon/Annecy; chains may be needed; horrific peak weekend jams.
By rail Moûtiers, regular buses from station.
By air Geneva; transfer 4: Direct buses to resorthr. (Or Lyon, Champery.)

Staying there
Visitor beds 22,000; breakdown: mainly in hotels and apartments.
Package holidays Brittany Ferries (s) Club Med (h) Crystal (hs) Enterprise (hs) Hoverspeed Ski-Drive (hs) Inghams (hs) Made to Measure (hs) Quest Total Ski (h) Quest Travel (schools) (h) Ski Club of GB (h) SnowRanger (hs) Supertravel (h) Touralp (hs) .
Medical facilities In resort: Doctor and chemist in resort. Hospital, Moûtiers, 27km.

Non-skiing activities
Indoor Sports Club, gym, body-building, table tennis, library, games room, theatre, 3 cinemas.
Outdoor 2 outdoor swimming pools, plane and microlight rides, hang-gliding, guided walks, scooters, skating rink, snow-shoe excursions.

Kindergartens
Le Village des Schtroumpfs
Tuition: Yes. Hours: 9.00-5.00. Ages: Nursery 3mth-2½, Garderie 2½-10, Jardin d'Enfants 4-6. Cost: 580.00 per week (lunch extra 70.00). Children can be collected from their accommodation.

Special skiing facilities
Summer skiing At Val Thorens.

Cross-country 3.2km green, 3.5km blue, 20km red in valley.

Lift passes
Three Valleys
Covers all lifts in Courchevel, Méribel, Val Thorens and Les Menuires. (220 lifts in total.)
Cost 6 days 880.00 (£90.72). Low season: 792.00 saving 10%.
Credit cards accepted Yes.
Senior citizens 693.00 (over 60) saving 21%.
Children 693.00 (under 16) saving 21%. Free pass up to age 5.
Notes One-day extension for Val Thorens (65.00), for Three Valleys (88.00). New family reductions for families of 5 or more.
Beginners Points cards, single gondola tickets.
Short-term passes Half-day pass available for Les Menuires and St Martin de Belleville and Vallée de Belleville pass.
Other passes Les Menuires and Saint-Martin de Belleville (6 days 685.00 for adults, 515.00 for children); Vallée de Belleville (6 days 785.00 for adults, 640.00 for children).

Ski school
ESF
Classes 3hr am and/or 2½hr pm. Cost: 740.00 (6 days). 6 half-days 590.00.
Lift priority Yes.
Children's classes Ages: up to 15. Cost: 615.00 (6 full days). 508.00 (6 half-days).
Private lessons available Hourly. Cost: 135.00 per hour.
Special courses Race training, 6 days 1,100.00; surf and mono courses, from 1,600.00 per week including lift pass.

What was new in 91
1. New 12-person gondola to replace old gondola up La Masse.
2. New snowboard centre run by the ESF.

have been prone to ice, despite large snow-making installations. The few reports we have of the **ski school** (including one from a contented school-party leader) are favourable. At La Croisette there is an all-day **kindergarten**, which greatly impressed one reporting family.

Not just a pretty place

Valmorel France 1400m

Good for *Lift queues, sunny slopes, skiing convenience, family holidays, freedom from cars, resort-level snow, nursery slopes, Alpine charm*
Bad for *Mountain restaurants, not skiing, après-ski*

Linked resort St-François-Longchamp

If any purpose-built resort can claim to be villagey, it is Valmorel, a small new development not far from Les Menuires and Val Thorens – resorts from which it could hardly be more different in spirit. Ever-so-tasteful residential 'hamlets' of wood-and-slate chalet-style apartments are grouped around the home piste, leading down to a colourful, traffic-free, toytown shopping street – the whole laid out so ingeniously that there is no loss of convenience for skiers. In other respects Valmorel is typical of small modern French resorts: it mainly appeals to car-borne self-catering French families and to British package tourists on a budget (who are present in considerable numbers), and there is not much to do but ski. The resort is noticeably cheaper to live in than its more prestigious neighbours (Méribel and so on).

Valmorel is linked to St-François-Longchamp, a bitty little resort to the south of the Col de la Madeleine. The resulting ski area – Le Grand Domaine – is uncrowded and varied, and fairly *grand* except by the exalted standards of the Tarentaise. St-François-Longchamp's slopes are sunny and gentle, and include excellent nursery slopes. Valmorel's side is more reliable for snow, more extensive and more challenging – many runs are more difficult than their gradings suggest. But quite a number of recent reporters were disappointed by the limited extent and difficulty of the skiing, particularly when the snow was sparse in the village and rapidly 'skied out' at altitude.

The skiing top 2550m bottom 1250m

Valmorel sits at the foot of a horseshoe of ski-fields with slopes facing north, west and east. Although there are links, the skiing above the village splits naturally into two main sectors, which we've labelled Mottet and Beaudin.

The **Mottet** sector offers the highest lift in the Valmorel horseshoe by a wide margin, and (facing mainly north) also has the best snow. Lifts from the top of Valmorel (Hameau du Mottet) give access to the Col du Gollet, the eastern extremity of the system. This is a fine open slope with off-piste or black and red runs which get the afternoon sun, and is also the start of the Nine Valleys route, with an off-piste descent towards Les Menuires.

The main lift from the top of the village, the Pierrafort gondola, serves

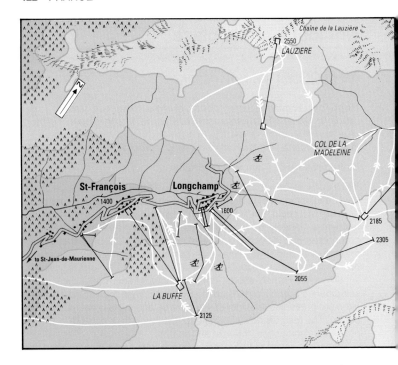

a broad slope with long blue runs which are not of trivial difficulty, and leads to a chair-lift which climbs over the most challenging pistes (and often the best snow) of the ski area to the local high-point, the Col du Mottet (2400m). The wide mogul field under the top part of the chair is genuinely black but not intimidating (about 33°, more in places) except at the awkward start; there is a roundabout alternative red, which also gives access via a short drag to an excellent, long, less daunting black into the Celliers valley. The lower part of the run down the Mottet chair consists of a consistently challenging, mogulled red.

A long chair-lift from the centre of the village goes up to the rounded **Beaudin**, where three long drag-lifts serve long, easy runs on top. The blue runs down into the Celliers valley are again not trivial, particularly in the mornings, when they may have hard moguls. Another long drag brings you back up to the Combe de Beaudin and from here it is an easy run to the Montagne de Tête. The morning-sun side of the Tête provides good scope for off-piste skiing and some tough intermediate runs below the chair-lift. The other side has a very long green trail though the woods to Combelouvière.

From the Celliers valley an ingenious two-speed three-seater chair-lift reaches the broad ridge above the road pass of the **Col de la Madeleine** (closed in winter). The two red runs beside it could well be black, with several pitches of nearly 30°, but there are blue alternatives. On the sunny side of the ridge the runs down to Longchamp are open and very gentle. A combination of schuss and plod takes you from the

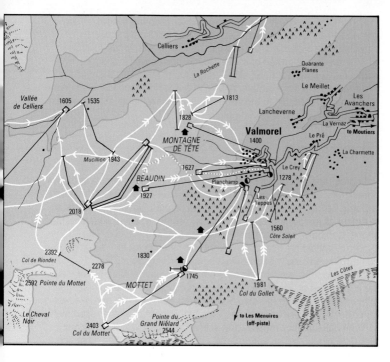

top of the chair to the col, and beyond it to the four-seater **Lauzière** chair, which goes up to 2550m on the Longchamp side of the road pass but is covered by the Valmorel Domaine ski-pass. The black run down from this chair is not particularly steep but faces south and is often slushy by late afternoon; the red back to the Col deserves its grading. There are several ways back to Valmorel; one of them, via the Côte 2305 drag-lift to the top of the Madeleine chair, involves a particularly nasty piece of blue run which two reporters would grade dark red – 'narrow, mogulled and terrifying'. A new chair-lift from Longchamp up to the Col, improving access to Valmorel, is supposedly planned.

The west-facing slopes above the road linking St-François and Longchamp are little skied and include some wide, entertaining intermediate runs through light woods above the road and down to the village. It is an area that suits timid novices very well – even the blacks are not very steep.

The area's **mountain restaurants** have improved in both quantity and quality in recent years but they are still not over-abundant (particularly in the St-François-Longchamp sector). The Pierrafort gondola is best-served, with pleasant enough chalets at the top (L'Altipiano) and part-way down (Le Prariond). A regular reporter thoroughly recommends Les 2 Mazots at the Col de la Madeleine – 'great ambience and decor, *croûte du fromage* is superb'. The Banquise Rose in Longchamp and the Chough in Combelouvière are also recommended. The piste map lists mountain loos.

The area is generally free of **queues** except during school holidays, when St-François-Longchamp and the lifts back from there get crowded. The Beaudin chair-lift from the village is very queue-prone when there is a shortage of snow. The ski area is well managed, particularly on the Valmorel side – at the top of major lifts there are information huts, for example. **Artificial snow** has been installed on the blue run from Beaudin to the village; it proved invaluable at the end last season.

The resort

Valmorel has runs and lifts reaching down into the very centre and down both flanks, and tentacles of road reaching up. At the base of the resort is Bourg-Morel, its commercial centre – a colourful arcaded pedestrian street full of restaurants, shops (including some excellent specialist food shops) and bars, with café terraces at the foot of the pistes. The supermarket did not impress a recent self-catering mum – 'meat good quality but particularly expensive, vegetables very poor'. The spit-roasted take-away chickens are highly recommended. Nearby is the impressive children's ski-village, Saperlipopette – the spiritual heart of the resort, catering for up to 300 children from an early age. Recent reporters have been impressed by the friendliness of all the resort staff.

Nearly all the **accommodation** is in apartments, well liked by our reporters when sold as apartments – not so well liked when advertised as chalets. Most of the 'hamlets' are served by a free shuttle lift (Télébourg) from Bourg-Morel, where there are small specialist food shops. The Planchamp and Fontaine apartments are surprisingly spacious and well equipped, the Ruisseau ones are 'rather compact'. There are three hotels, rather expensive and functional. The Planchamp, a little way above Bourg-Morel, is the best in town, but not as good as it thinks it is. Normally, only the Hôtel du Bourg, in the heart of the village, offers rooms by the night. It has received mixed reports from recent visitors; some were seriously unimpressed, others were extremely enthusiastic. Skiers with cars can stay much more cheaply in the delightful hamlet of Les Avanchers, at the little (and fairly simple) Cheval Noir.

Although **après-ski** is limited, it suited most recent reporters well – 'relaxed and informal, no wild discos, not for poseurs or lager louts'. Apparently noise restrictions are enforced after 8pm for the benefit of families. There are plenty of satisfactory restaurants, a disco (Jean's Club) and some quite lively bars (some with occasional live music). Le Grenier is an instructors' haunt and has a friendly atmosphere, and the bar of the La Vadrouille restaurant (by the Scotty dog sign) is an old favourite with most reporters. Recommended restaurants include Chez Albert for 'fabulous' pizzas, La Vadrouille for 'unpretentious French food, good pub atmosphere, often crowded' (the patron sings), La Flambée and the Petit Prince for crêpes, and Le Creuset for 'a real treat'. The Perce Neige has not impressed. Street musicians play in the main square. There is floodlit skiing once a week.

Recent improvements have made Valmorel a more appealing place for cross-country skiers and non-skiers. There are now 20km of cross-country trails in three areas, connected by a shuttle bus, and several kilometres of cleared, sign-posted walks at the top of Beaudin and Lanchettes. There are two popular toboggan runs and full-day snow-shoe excursions, as well as joy-rides (or skiing trips) to other resorts from the recently opened air-strip. The resort does not have a swimming pool, but there is a keep-fit centre and sauna. The cinema shows up-to-date films with English sub-titles.

The dense network of pistes just above the village gives inexperienced skiers no easy options. But there are good, specially contoured **nursery slopes** with three lifts, away from the main pistes.

Our several recent reports on the **ski school** are all complimentary. Although classes tended to be big (10-15 pupils), instructors generally spoke excellent English and were great fun and safety-conscious. Para-skiing is available, and guides lead tours of the Tarentaise valleys

Facts on Valmorel Savoie **France**

Prices in francs

Tourist office

Postcode 73260
Tel 79098555
Fax 79098529
Tlx 980321

Getting there

By road 910km from Calais. Via Macon and Lyon.
By rail Moutiers, 4 buses from station on weekdays, more at weekends.
By air Geneva; transfer 4hr. (Or Lyon.)

Staying there

Visitor beds 8,500; breakdown: 8,200 in apartments, 300 in hotels.
Package holidays Brittany Ferries (s) Crystal (hcs) Enterprise (hs) French Impressions (s) Hoverspeed Ski-Drive (s) Inghams (s) Made to Measure (hs) Neilson (hs) Quality Ski Tours (as) Quest Travel (schools) (a) Sally Holidays (s) Simply Ski (hcs) Ski Party Snow World (hs) Ski Red Guide (as) SnowRanger (s) Thomson (hs) Touralp (hs) .
Medical facilities In resort: Doctor, physiotherapist, chemist. Hospital: Moûtiers.

Non-skiing activities

Indoor Keep-fit club, sauna, gym, cinema.
Outdoor Snow-shoe outings, walks, tobogganing, floodlit skiing.

Kindergartens

Saperlipopettes
Tuition: Yes (but not obligatory). Hours: 8.30-5.00.
Ages: 6mth-1½yr nursery, 1½-3 and 3-8.
Playrooms and snow garden. Cost: 620.00 per week (meals 55.00 per day).

Special skiing facilities

Summer skiing No.
Cross-country 20km of tracks in 3 areas, Aigle Blanc, Les Avanchers and Le Rocher, connected by shuttle bus. Instruction available.

Lift passes

Grand Domaine
Covers all lifts in Valmorel and St-François-Longchamp. (47 lifts in total.)
Cost 6 days 698.00 (£71.96).
Credit cards accepted Yes.
Senior citizens 595.00 (over 60) saving 15%.
Children 595.00 (under 13) saving 15%. Free pass up to age 4.
Beginners One free drag.
Short-term passes Half-day (from 12.00 noon); single and return tickets on some lifts.
Other passes Valmorel Domaine covers 24 lifts in Valmorel (6 days 658.00 for adults, 557.00 for children).

Ski school

ESF
Classes 2½hr am (advanced) or pm (others). Cost: 450.00 (6 full days). Beginners' course costs 846.00 including lift pass.
Lift priority Yes.
Children's classes Ages: 4-13. Cost: 409.00 (6 days).
Private lessons available Per 90 mins. Cost: 142.00 session.
Special courses 7-day ski safari; powder courses 6 days 450.00; snowboard 6 days 450.00.

What was new in 91

New snow guns on 3km run from Beaudin to the village.

and other areas. The Saperlipopette **ski kindergarten** is greatly liked, to the extent that one reporter who had left her child at home regretted the decision. It has 'spacious accommodation, a huge selection of activities and endlessly energetic English-speaking instructors'. Mid-march reporters last year found its snow garden totally devoid of snow. Book in advance, especially at weekends. Once children reach ski-school age, they progress to their own nursery slope, separate from the adult one.

St-François-Longchamp   1450–1650m

Valmorel's partner is a succession of hamlets along the Col de la Madeleine road, linked by a free ski-bus which runs reliably to a spacious timetable. They attract few non-French visitors and the atmosphere is far from festive. The top hamlet, Longchamp, is an ugly group of modern buildings below the pass, surrounded by sunny slopes. It has a kindergarten, a natural ice rink, a piano bar and a couple of discos. There are two or three small supermarkets, and some good specialist food shops. St-François is a cluster of simple old hotels and *colonies de vacances*.

Tourist Office ✆ 75591056. Tx 309951.

All things in moderation

Valloire France 1400m

Linked resort: Valmeinier
Separate resort: Les Karellis

Valloire is an old village tucked away in a secluded bowl high up above the Maurienne valley, beside the road up to the very high Col du Galibier (closed in winter), where the *département* of Savoie meets Hautes-Alpes. It has developed gradually as a resort over the 60 or 70 years since skiing became popular with the local military. Although not a strikingly picturesque village, it has retained the spirit and looks of a real French community, and combines village atmosphere with a fair amount of mostly intermediate skiing and moderate prices. It is generally quiet, but liable to be invaded by crowds of boisterous Italians at holiday times.

Valloire's **skiing** is spread over five sides of two neighbouring mountains and gives plenty of variations of terrain, with long runs of nearly 1000m vertical. There is no very difficult skiing (the black runs are not steep). The two main areas – Setaz and Crey du Quart – are served by lifts starting only a few minutes' walk from the centre and going up to almost 2500m, but most of the skiing is below 2000m. Each area has a small nursery area beside a restaurant part-way up – useful when the very convenient village-level slopes are washed out. Lift queues are not normally a problem in the village except during French school holidays, but can arise higher up when the drag-lifts fail to cope with peak loads. On the far side of Crey du Quart, pistes descend towards Valmeinier 1500, though the village itself, at the foot of its own little ski area on **Gros Crey**, is reached by a lift from the foot of the pistes across a narrow valley. The lift passes of Valloire and Valmeinier both cover the Crey du Quart sector, with the exception of the lower lifts out of the other resort – though supplements can be paid by the day for the use of all the other resort's lifts, and Valmeinier is among several resorts where you can ski for a day on the strength of a six-day Valloire pass.

The **Setaz** sector is reached from the village by a six-person gondola over a narrow north-facing slope – more of a mountain-end than a mountainside. Various descents go through the woods to the resort (one, La Marmotte, equipped with snow-guns) or down the steeper sides of the mountain – easy ones from the restaurant, tougher ones starting higher up. The downhill race-course starts near the top – a 3.8km run for 920m vertical. The west-facing slope goes down to Les Verneys, beside the Galibier road (1560m); beyond it, on the Crey Rond massif, is a small nursery area and a chair-lift up to 1912m which opens up a very worthwhile expanse of off-piste skiing. The east-facing slope of Setaz is linked at Pragontier (1750m) to the **Crey du Quart** sector – a broad, open, sunny hillside, lightly scrub-covered lower down. This sector is also reachable directly from the village by a chair-lift to Pré-Rond (1750m). There is some excellent easy skiing on the gentle, spacious top half of the mountain, but much of it gets strong afternoon sun and conditions deteriorate during the day; the run to Pragontier making the link back to Setaz can be particularly tricky as a result (there is the alternative of a chair-ride down the lower half). There may also be some more demanding slopes on the bottom half, but on our visits they have been unskiable. Conditions are more reliable on the north-facing runs from here towards Valmeinier – again, satisfying length and varying difficulty, from easy blue to a genuine black mogul field down to the valley. Valmeinier's skiing on Gros Crey is served by three chair-lifts going up to 2575m, more than 1000m above the village. But the slopes get a lot of sun, and suffer accordingly.

The Setaz area is adequately served by its two mountain restaurants, the most popular of which is the Thimel. The Crey du Quart area has one at Pré-Rond and a small new place on the ridge below Crey du Quart (not yet marked on the resort piste map).

Long and varied cross-country trails climb south from Valloire to Les Verneys and on to Plan Lachat (1961m), past several restaurants. The easiest loops are at Les Verneys, reached by bus from Valloire.

There are several modest, inexpensive hotels and unobtrusive apartment buildings in the resort. Attractive hotels include the Christiania – simple but adequately comfortable, and conveniently placed on the main shopping street – and the Grand ('very convenient for the nursery slopes and Crey du Quart lifts, excellent rooms, good authentic food served in front of an open fire'). The Plein Sud is a 'good budget hotel'. We have an unfavourable report of the 'very cramped and tatty' Cassettes studios.

The evening ambience is subdued, but there is no shortage of welcoming bars with music or videos. Recommendations include the Touring Bar, the American Dodgers, which has live music on Thursdays and Fridays, and the bar of the Plein Sud. The two discos, Charley's and Le Mammouth (in the basement of the Rapin hotel) are apparently lively. There are a few good restaurants including a very popular pizza place in the new shopping precinct and an 'excellent' take-away for self-caterers. The range of shops is reported to be good – one reporter recommends the cheese shops in the precinct which give free cheese samples with glasses of wine – and there is a weekly market. The precinct incorporates a launderette. There is an Olympic artificial ice-rink, little used but reportedly 'very good'. The village styles itself a *station d'art*, and among its winter attractions is an international snow sculpture competition, held in late January. Each contestant (and there are many, from at least fifteen nations and from as far afield as Mexico) is provided with a four-metre solid cube of snow in which to sculpt. Their spectacular creations are then judged and prizes awarded; even the public have a vote. According to January reporters, the sculptures are 'extremely impressive and really add to the resort atmosphere'. The basement of the central Rochevert building houses an excellent photographic exhibition in very civilised surroundings.

There are two ski schools; both are said to be well organised and have English-speakers (some Antipodean). One group of beginners with the Ski Ecole de Valloire felt that they could have done with more tuition and less guiding. There are ski and non-ski kindergartens, apparently good fun.

Tourist office ✆ 79560396. **Package holidays** Enterprise (hcs) SkiBound (hjs) Thomson (hcs)

Valmeinier   1500m

Valmeinier is a small and traditional-looking village with a direct lift up into its local skiing but also a higher mountainside satellite village at the foot of most of the pistes (1800m). Extensive building (40 wooden chalets) is going on in the upper village. The plans to link Valmeinier 1800 with the Valfréjus are, for the moment, on hold. It is unlikely that they will be realized for another couple of years.

Tourist office ✆ 79568048. **Package holidays** Quest Total Ski (h) SnowRanger (s)

Les Karellis   1650m

The Valloire lift pass gives limited access to Les Karellis, a small modern resort less than an hour's drive north-west of Valloire. Les Karellis consists of a handful of apartment blocks perched in tiers on a ledge above the Maurienne valley. Its narrow ski area, on the relatively snow-sure north-facing slopes of three adjacent mountains, is varied and interesting, with a range of wide open red and blue runs of 900m vertical, some shorter stretches of genuine black and a couple of scenic cross-country trails.

Main access to the intermediate slopes of the Tête d'Albiez (2472m) and the Casse-Massion is by new quad chair-lift to Plan du Four, where there is a restaurant, Le Vinouva. From just below Plan du Four, the Chaudannes chair ascends to the resort's high-point (2520m) and serves easy blue slopes down the shoulder of the mountain and through the woods back to the resort. The resort itself has about 2,650 beds, mostly in apartments. There are adequate facilities, a handful of bars and restaurants and one disco. Baby-lifts serve nursery slopes in the village and just above it; there is a Club Enfant for children between three and twelve years old, and a nursery for toddlers. Reporters who have made the day-trip to Les Karellis from Valloire have generally thought it well worthwhile.

Tourist office ✆ 79595036. Fax 79595042.

A star is marketed

Valfréjus France 1550m

The brain-child of an Alpine entrepreneur who has had a lot to do with the development of Tignes, Valfréjus was launched a few years ago with all the hype usually reserved for new blockbusters of romantic fiction, and soon found its way into a number of UK package holiday brochures. Needless to say, the product does not live up to all the claims made and implied by its promoters. It is not yet a vast ski area to rival the biggest and best in the Alps; it is not the favourite rendezvous of the ultra-chic and those smart enough to jump on bandwagons before they start rolling; and it is not super-reliable for the deepest and freshest of snow. So what is it? A very small, smartly and attractively styled modern resort with a small but tall, varied and uncrowded ski area. When compared with other small resorts of the southern French Alps, it emerges as a very worthwhile and interesting new development, gaining in substance and efficiency each year. And in two or three year's time it should be able to offer a much enlarged ski area. Although some of the resort literature shows the long-projected lifts intended to link with an even greater number of non-existent lifts above Bardonecchia to the south, there are more concrete plans for links westward towards Valloire and Valmeinier.

The resort stands in a narrow but not oppressively enclosed wooded setting at the top of a steep hairpin road from Modane, at the French end of the Fréjus road and rail tunnels. At the foot of the main lifts and pistes is a precinct of sensitively styled buildings incorporating lots of new wood, balconies and colourful decoration. There are smart shops as well as apartments in the main building (Le Thabor) framing the foot of the pistes and lift station; skiers pose quite a threat to pedestrians. Two nearby hotels have opened recently; the Relais de Valfréjus is attractive, comfortable (although rooms are not large) and fairly expensive. The Chavière block (which houses the Vita hotel) is about to be extended to incorporate new Vita Parc apartments. Opposite it, a new ice-rink with underground parking is planned. There is more accommodation dotted around the road which loops through the resort, including another hotel up the hillside and the so-called Chalet Club, a sizeable and very clubby institution with small apartments modestly equipped and thus encouraging use of the two in-house restaurants. There are squash courts, a free swimming pool and jacuzzi, disco-aerobics sessions and evening entertainment. As well as those in the Chalet Club, there are several other reasonable restaurants in the resort; the Bardonecchia has à la carte and self-service restaurants and plays live music; the Etagne serves good crêpes and has a 'disco-style' bar downstairs; the Piccolina and Bois Brûlé are both recommended pizzerias. The Sun-Rise pub is about the most popular bar for the younger generation. There are piano bars at both the Relais de Fréjus and the Chalet Club. There is a lively disco, the Sphinx. Operators organise day-trips to Valloire and evening excursions to Bardonecchia. There are nursery and ski-kindergarten facilities (in roped-off areas) for children of three months upwards. There are two ski schools; English is adequate but not widely spoken. For a small resort the shopping is reportedly quite good, though the supermarket is said to be pricey.

It is quite a walk up from here up the road to the main centre and lift station but a couple of lifts make it possible to ski across and have also created short easy runs above the Club.

The ski area is served by a long two-stage six-seater gondola, climbing over north-west-facing slopes. Below the mid-station at Arrondaz (2200m) the slopes are steep and wooded, with a difficult red run including a serious pitch of about 28° which we found in a dangerously icy and stony condition and causing widespread misery. There were no warning signs. There is a black variant on the top part. A long track provides a gentle route down.

Around Arrondaz is a flat open area with a popular waiter-service restaurant, some nursery lifts and steeper short drags. The gondola continues up a splendid steep coomb to Punta Bagna (2737m), a panoramic peak with a restaurant on top, and offers the choice of the direct black run down the front, which is less awesome than it looks from below, or easier runs (blue and red) of about 400m vertical in the wide, beautiful and sunny bowl behind Punta Bagna, the Combe du Fréjus. The most roundabout run goes down via the Col du Fréjus (2540m), from where it is possible to ski down to Bardonecchia off-piste, returning by train and bus. There is a chair-lift back up to Punta Bagna from the bottom of this back bowl (Pas du Roc, 2350m), which is also linked to the Arrondaz mid-station by a chair-lift up and over the Col d'Arrondaz (2500m), with a disembarkation point at the col and short intermediate runs on both sides. The alternative way home is a long, beautiful and not difficult blue run back to the resort, ending up with a long track through the woods. The top half of the run has some good off-piste variations.

Tourist office ✆ 79053400. Tx 980150.

Package holidays Made to Measure (h) Quest Total Ski (h) Ski Global (hs) Ski Party Snow World (hs) Ski Red Guide (cs) SnowRanger (s).

Reformed character

Sauze d'Oulx Italy 1500m

Good for *Big ski area, woodland runs, mountain restaurants, sunny slopes, short airport transfers*
Bad for *Not skiing, skiing convenience, resort-level snow, late holidays, tough runs, freedom from cars*

Linked resorts: Sansicario, Sestriere, Jouvenceaux

For many years Sowzy Doo was one of the most popular of Alpine resorts among young British skiers. Its simple recipe was cheap hotel accommodation and cheap and extremely cheerful nightlife, combined with an entertaining area of intermediate skiing ideal for sunbathing and bombing through the woods. But recent reporters have been pleasantly surprised to find the resort as a whole far from rowdy, and on a recent high-season visit we too found the resort more Italian and more dignified than of old. The influence of the British clientele is nevertheless clear; many people speak English, and ski equipment is priced (and paid for) in sterling in some shops. Sauze's fall from favour with the British mass market may be connected with the very thin snowfalls it suffered in the mid-1980s; now that everywhere else has had thin snowfalls – and now that all the lifts of Sauze and Sestriere are run by one apparently business-like company – it may be due for a revival of interest.

The resort does have drawbacks, however: steep and icy walks around town, and a local lift system that seems to be unchanged since the 1960s – slow, rusty chair-lifts, some of them singles, where you might hope for a gondola. There is a slightly picturesque old village backwater with a fine old church; but apart from this Sauze is an undistinguished mess of modern buildings, particularly in the centre – there are smarter areas of apartment blocks (little used, as far as we can see) spreading across the wooded mountainside.

Sestriere was the first purpose-built ski resort, a joint venture between Mussolini and Agnelli – hand-built by fascist robots. After a period of neglect, it has recently been bringing itself up to date by demolishing ancient cable-cars and investing heavily in artificial snow equipment; when coupled with its altitude (around 2000m), this must make Sestriere one of the most snow-sure resorts in the Alps. It is not the most appealing of resorts in other ways – all-modern, and spread across a very high, wide and windy pass. Traditionally fashionable with Italian skiers, it still attracts smart weekenders and second-home owners from Turin, which is only a couple of hours away by car, but is pretty lifeless most of the time and especially so in low season.

Some of the smart crowd have forsaken Sestriere for neighbouring Sansicario, a stylish, small, modern development with a good skiing area of its own, linked to Sestriere and Sauze on the one side, and Cesana Torinese on the other.

Sauze is one extremity of the Milky Way ski area; Montgenèvre in

France is the other. A car is helpful in exploring the whole of the system, and facilitates trips beyond Montgenèvre to Briançon and Serre-Chevalier, only a few miles further away to the west.

The skiing top 2820m bottom 1390m

The Sauze d'Oulx ski area occupies a quarter-circle of mountainsides facing west and north, the lower two-thirds or so wooded. Lift departures are awkwardly sited, and the ski area is broken up by gullies – though no longer by fragmented ownership of the lifts.

The sunny woodland clearing of **Sportinia** is at the heart of the skiing. It has a couple of hotels, a small and crowded nursery area, and a circle of restaurants. Above it there is a wide expanse of good, open intermediate skiing on gently undulating terrain around the top of Triplex, and beyond it another extensive open bowl offering spacious intermediate skiing. This is served by several drag lifts, one giving access to Col Basset and the run down to Sestriere, and another going up an entertaining shaded mogul slope to the shoulder of Monte Fraiteve, a windy peak (with panoramic views of French mountains) where the ski areas of Sauze d'Oulx, Sestriere and Sansicario meet. Fraiteve is the start of the famous Rio Nero off-piste run, which follows a river gully down to the Oulx–Cesana road, 1600m below.

Below Sportinia there are excellent wide runs back through the woods – marked red and black, quite steep in places but never really difficult. Runs down to Jouvenceaux are graded blue and black, but are reported to be less different than that suggests.

The **Genevris** lift system (no longer independently owned) starts with a chair-lift a long way from most hotels and is usually approached via Clotes instead. From the Belvedere mid-station there are drag-lifts serving gentle runs below Monte Genevris; below Moncron are Sauze's most challenging pistes, where the difficulty is often accentuated by the effect of the sun.

The run down to **Sestriere** from Col Basset goes down a valley which is splendid for off-piste exploration when conditions are good, but offers only a tedious but well-graded winding road to the mid-station of the return six-seat gondola when they are not.

The bulk of the Sestriere skiing is on mainly north-and west-facing slopes on two mountains (Sises and Banchetta) separated by a deep valley. Above Sestriere itself, Sises is a good slalom hill, with short steep runs below Alpette. The top drag-lift may offer some good off-piste skiing on the shady side of the peak, but the gorge between the two ski areas does not look hospitable. There are intermediate runs down to Grangesises and the Hotel Principi. Banchetta is a better holiday skier's mountain, with longer and more varied runs down to the roadside mini-resort of Borgata. The steep Motta drag-lift and parallel chair serve the highest and toughest of Sestriere's skiing, with slopes of about 30°, often mogulled, beside the drag. You don't have to tackle these to reach the wide and beautiful west-facing red run (dotted on the piste map, so presumably an itinerary rather than a piste) down into the dividing valley

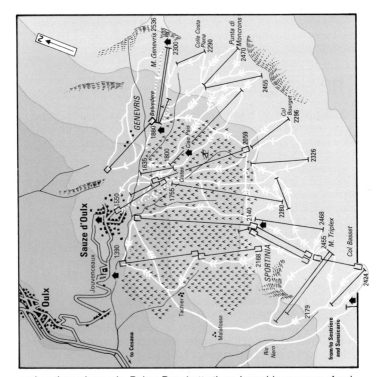

and on through woods. Below Banchetta there is a wide expanse of red and blue pistes and some entertaining off-piste hollows and ridges above the sunny Anfiteatro area. The wooded north-facing slopes above Borgata are steep, but beside the road there are drag-lifts up to Sestriere and very easy runs down – ideal for near-beginners.

The easiest way back to Sauze is via the Col Basset gondola from Borgata, but you can also start from Sestriere itself, where chair-lifts go up to Fraiteve with easy south-facing slopes on the Sestriere side, and runs from the top down to Sansicario and Sauze.

The open slopes above **Sansicario** are fairly steep at the top, and the run all the way down to Sansicario, starting off black or red, is a challenging and satisfying descent. Most of the rest of the west-facing skiing is wide, intermediate to easy woodland trails. There are some good long off-piste runs (including the Rio Nero) to points along the Cesana–Oulx road and an infrequent bus service back to the lifts at Cesana. Runs to La Combe, beside Cesana, get progressively steeper as they go down; the section below the bottom chair-lift is never easy and is often too bare to be skied.

Distribution of **mountain restaurants** in the area as a whole is rather is very patchy, with none at high altitude, and a general shortage (apart from two good restaurants above Borgata) at Sestriere. But Sauze has some memorable restaurants, some of them hotels: the old Capanna Kind and the Monte Triplex at Sportinia; the expensive Ciao Pais tucked

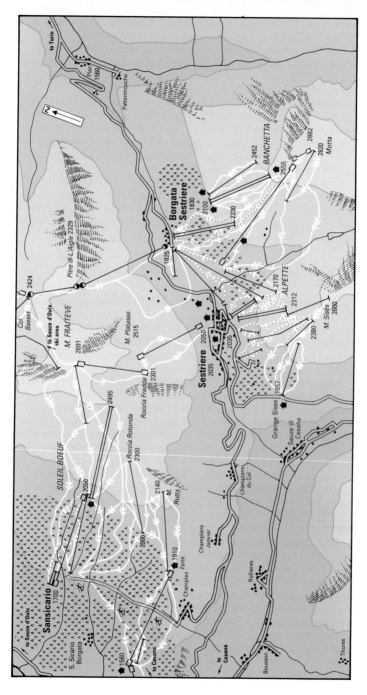

away below Moncrons; and the smart and expensive Capricorno at Clotes. The Soleil Boeuf above Sansicario is recommended.

The main **queue** problems are on the Sauze side of the mountain, with Sportinia being the main bottleneck, but all our recent reports relate to times when conditions were poor or skiers few. A reporter based in Sansicario found that taxis were the best way to get to the Clavière/Montgenèvre skiing. Several reporters have commented on the low standard of piste marking at Sauze d'Oulx. The woodland runs are quite similar and it is surprisingly easy to get lost – particularly when (as on our most recent visit) the lift pass office is unable to provide a piste map. The map is not very helpful, failing to identify pistes and to explain the meaning of the many dotted runs.

Sestriere has a big **artificial snow** installation, covering many of its north-west-facing pistes, from 2500m down to Borgata at about 1800m. Sauze has guns on the runs from Clotes to the village and on the runs beside the double drag up Monte Genevris. Sansicario has guns on two pistes from the mid-station of Soleil Boeuf to the village.

The resort

Sauze stands on the sunny west-facing flank of a wide valley junction. It is built on a steep slope; it is also quite large, and almost everywhere seems to be a long, steep walk from everywhere else – including the three widely separated lift stations. An oversubscribed and unpredictable ski-bus covered by the lift pass does a circuit around the village and its lift stations until early evening.

Accommodation is mostly in cheap hotels, which reporters generally find adequate. By far the best location is around Piazzale Miramonti, between the Clotes and Sportinia lifts. The only attractive hotel in this area is the small Hermitage, in a sunny open situation overlooking the village slopes. The San Giorgio is far from luxurious and badly placed, but friendly and inexpensive. The Palace is the biggest, the most comfortable and the most expensive hotel, but not particularly stylish. There is a variety of high-altitude accommodation. The Capricorno at Clotes is expensive and attractive, and being open only to guests and diners is entirely lout-free. You can be first on to the nursery slopes by staying at Sportinia – the Monte Triplex or even the old Capanna Kind. The Ciao Pais above Clotes also offers cheap, simple accommodation.

There seems little doubt that **après-ski** in Sauze is not what it was. It can still be called cheap and cheerful, but not offensively rowdy. There is plenty of organised après-ski – meals out, torchlit descents, tobogganing and Miss Sauze competitions – but there is plenty of life in the bars and discos in any event. Favourite British haunts are the Derby hotel bar and neighbouring Moncrons cocktail bar; other recommendations: the New Life disco, Max bar, Cotton Club ('yuppyish'!), Frigo cocktail bar, La Grigla for pizzas and Gossips for spare ribs. The Andy Capp at the foot of the home piste may still be 'lager-lout territory', but we saw little evidence of that on our recent early-evening visit.

Facts on Sauze d'Oulx Torino **Italy**

Prices in lire

Tourist office

Piazza Assietta
Postcode 10050
Tel (122) 85497
Fax (122) 85497

Getting there

By road 999km from Calais. Via Chambéry/Fréjus tunnel; chains occasionally needed.
By rail Oulx (5km); frequent buses.
By air Turin; transfer 2hr.

Staying there

Visitor beds 10,000; breakdown: 1,800 in hotels, 8,200 in apartments.
Package holidays Enterprise (hs) Neilson (hs) Ski Global (h) Thomson (h) .
Medical facilities In resort: Doctor, chemist. Hospital: Sulsa (29km). Dentist: Oulx (5km).

Non-skiing activities

Indoor Tennis, bowling, cinema, artificial ice rink, swimming pools, tennis, volleyball and squash courts, gym, sauna, massage.
Outdoor Natural skating rink, floodlit tobogganing, torchlit descents, hang-gliding, parapenting, heli-skiing.

Kindergartens

Proloco
Tuition: Yes. Hours: 9.00-3.00. Ages: 6mths-6yrs. Cost: 200,000.00 per week (Meals are not provided and must be supplied).

Special skiing facilities

Summer skiing No.
Cross-country Green run to Pian della Rocca (4km).

Lift passes

La Via Lattea
Covers Sauze, Sansicario, Clavière, Cesana and Sestriere lifts. (27 lifts in total.)

Cost 6 days 180,000.00 (£84.11). Low season: 165,000.00 saving 8%.
Credit cards accepted No.
Children 180,000.00 saving nothing. Free pass up to age 7.
Notes Includes one free day in Alpe d'Huez, Les Deux Alpes, Serre-Chevalier, La Grave and Puy-St-Vincent.
Beginners One free lift at Sauze and Sestriere; points cards.
Short-term passes Half-day pass.
Other passes Montgenèvre extension costs 12,000.00. Walking pass valid on some lifts 12,000.00.

Ski school

Sauze Project
Classes 10.00-1.00. Cost: 140,000.00 (6 half-days). 2 hr lessons also available, 95,000.00 for 6 days.
Lift priority Yes.
Children's classes Ages: Any. Cost: 140,000.00 (6 half-days).
Private lessons available Hourly. Cost: 30,000.00 per hour. 1-2 people; 39,000.00 for up to 4 people; peak times are more expensive.
Special courses Surf, mono and freestyle courses.
Sauze Sportinia
Classes 10.00-1.00. Cost: 135,000.00 (6 half-days).
Lift priority Yes.
Children's classes Ages: Any. Cost: 135,000.00 (6 half-days).
Private lessons available Hourly. Cost: 30,000.00 per hour.
Special courses Racing courses, guided tours around Milky Way.
Sauze d'Oulx
Classes 10.00-1.00. Cost: 135,000.00 (6 half-days).
Lift priority Yes.
Children's classes Ages: Any. Cost: 135,000.00 (6 half-days).
Private lessons available Hourly. Cost: 30,000.00 per hour.

Walking around Sauze is no great pleasure, and there are few **non-skiing** facilities. The ice rink is operated 'conditions permitting'. Nor can the resort be recommended for **cross-country** skiers. **Nursery slopes** are adequate – the main slope is at Sportinia, open and very sunny but very crowded. There are also nursery areas at Belvedere on the Genevris side, and in the village (if there's snow). We have mainly enthusiastic reports on the standard of instruction in the Sportinia **ski school**; there is no shortage of English-speaking instructors. The school quickly brings beginners off the nursery slopes on to real pistes, so they need a lift pass. Ski school races are a popular weekly event.

Jouvenceaux 1380m

This small and charming hamlet is just below Sauze d'Oulx, and is growing up the road from Oulx to meet it. At the bottom of the lift up to Sportinia is a delightfully unspoilt maze of crumbling alleys with old fountains and medieval paintings on the wall of the church. Most of the Jouvenceaux accommodation is quite a walk or a bus ride from its lift, and does not share the charm of the old village.

Sestriere 2035m

Sestriere is a bleak and often windswept place, spread around the wide col with a scattering of thin larches around the bottom of the mountain flanks. The great landmarks are the tall, round towers of the Torre and the Duchi d'Aosta hotels (now occupied by Club Med), and the Gothic turrets of the recently restored Principi di Piemonte hotel, some way from the resort centre but with its own lift access to the Sises ski area. Buses run to and from Borgata, Grangsises and the end of the Rio Nero run (on the Oulx–Cesana road). Accommodation is in the form of hotels, apartments in large new complexes, and Club Med. Apart from the Principi, the most luxurious hotel is the modern low-rise Sestriere. The Savoy Edelweiss is simple and central. The Miramonti is not very well situated, but friendly, attractive and good value. Après-ski is moderately lively and stylish when the Italians are in residence at weekends and in holiday periods. An ice driving course can be included in the hotel-plus-lift-pass formula. The resort is not appealing for cross-country skiers or non-skiers. The wide Col de Sestriere provides excellent nursery slopes, and very easy runs between the resort and Borgata.
Tourist office ✆ (122) 755444. Fax (122) 755171.
Package holidays Club Med (h) Quest Total Ski (h) SnowRanger (hs).

Sansicario 1700m

Sansicario has a sunny position half-way up a west-facing mountainside, well placed for exploring the Milky Way. It consists mainly of apartment buildings below a neat commercial precinct to which they are linked by a shuttle lift. Facilities are generally good for beginners, especially children (a good skiing and non-skiing kindergarten providing all-day care plus lunch if required). Cross-country skiers are reasonably well catered for, with a 10km loop across the hillside from the resort. Non-skiing and après-ski facilities are good, but there is little variety – a disco, three restaurants, three bars (including a piano bar which serves draught Guinness, but 'would be improved by the presence of a pianist'), tennis, swimming, sauna, massage, gym, riding and even ski-jöring. Accommodation is of a high standard, mostly in apartments, but with a few comfortable, expensive hotels, of which the most attractive is the Rio Envers Gallia, a bit of a walk from the centre.

Montgenèvre France 1850m

Good for *Big ski area, resort-level snow, easy runs, skiing convenience, woodland runs*
Bad for *Not skiing, après-ski, late holidays, mountain restaurants, tough runs, freedom from cars*

Linked resorts: Clavière, Cesana Torinese

A border village beside a main road at a high pass is an unpromising specification for a resort, and Montgenèvre, just inside France on its border with Italy, looks messy and unappetising as you drive through it. A long line of busy bars and restaurants with sunny terraces has developed along the roadside in recent years. But around the church, just off the road, is an attractively unspoilt old village. And the skiing here (mainly north-facing, with a high base altitude) often has the best snow conditions in the region; as a result, at times of general snow shortage the resort fills to bursting with skiers from large Italian resorts nearby (Sauze d'Oulx and Bardonecchia). Not surprisingly, Montgenèvre is also popular with local weekenders from both sides of the border (Briançon and Turin). There is cheap self-catering accommodation as well as good-value hotels, the skiing and nursery slopes are conveniently arranged, and Montgenèvre would attract the 'family resort' label but for the main road running between village and slopes – less main since the opening of the Fréjus road tunnel a few miles to the north, but still busy.

Montgenèvre's local skiing is rather limited in extent and mostly easy but there are links with other resorts, providing a large and reasonably varied area: it is the minority French sector of the Milky Way (Voie Lactée/Via Lattea), a long chain of linked skiing which makes it possible, snow and the customs permitting, to ski to Sauze d'Oulx or Sestriere, via Clavière, Cesana and Sansicario (all in Italy). It is quite an expedition to the more remote Italian resorts, and a car is a great help in exploring them – and French resort reached via Briançon.

The frontier is actually a mile and 100m vertical down the road at Clavière, which would be in France if the border did not loop around the village to put it in Italy. It is a quiet place except at weekends, which our few reporters have found a pleasing base.

The skiing top 2600m bottom 1350m

Montgenèvre has ski slopes on both flanks of the pass. The south-facing side, Chalvet, is marginally higher (up to 2600m) and usually less crowded than the north-facing slopes (which form the main link with the Italian Milky Way resorts), but is expanding into what may soon be the more interesting of the two halves. It also provides an easy

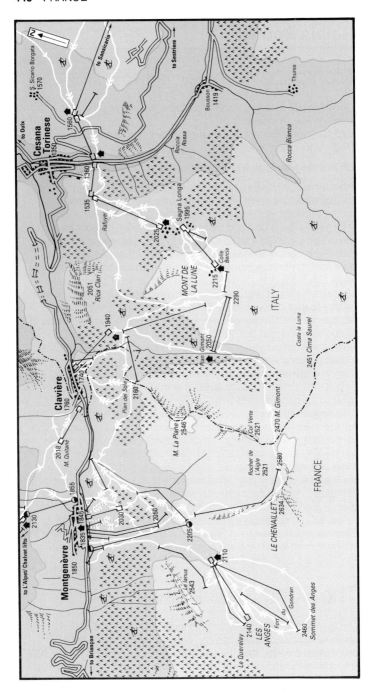

low-altitude route to Clavière.

A few minutes' walk east of the centre is the gondola for **Chalvet**, where two chairs and three drag-lifts now serve treeless, mostly easy runs with one or two more difficult runs and also some off-piste skiing down to Montgenèvre from the Bélier drag (2365m). There is a fairly easy red and a long green run back to the bottom. The blue run beside the drag-lift to the Col de l'Alpet (2430m) is very gentle, but the lift gives access to Montgenèvre's interesting new ski area. Already the north-east-facing slope behind the col has a chair-lift with black and red runs beside it and a long easy run round to Clavière. Future lifts up to 3000m will open up much more skiing, apparently challenging. This side of Clavière can also be reached by a long traverse from the top of the Chalvet gondola. Its lift, the Montquitaine chair, has an awkward short black beside it, but is mainly used for access to Montgenèvre, another very gentle traverse.

On the other side of the pass, a gondola from the Briançon end of the village and drag-lifts from the centre serve easy runs through woods opening out into wide nursery slopes above the road. From the top of the gondola there is a choice of three skiing areas. The wide, sheltered bowl of **Le Querelay/Les Anges** has eerie ruined fortress buildings around the crests and some red and black runs beneath them; but there is really no difficult skiing. The Brousset drag-lift serves some challenging skiing in the woods. The long dog-leg drag-lift through impressive rocky scenery to Rocher de l'Aigle has a red run beside it, awkwardly narrow in places, but is mainly used for access to Clavière. The Milky Way link starts with a poorly signed traverse around the mountain, easily missed in bad visibility. In other respects it is not at all difficult, and leads to a long Italian run (initially red, later green) past the Gimont drag-lifts and down to Clavière. The more obvious run down from Rocher de l'Aigle is a splendid off-piste bowl which leads, via some scrub, to the Brousset drag.

The north-facing slopes of **Mont de la Lune** above Clavière and Cesana offer some of the best skiing in the Milky Way: fast sweeping trails through the woods (none of them easy) and some good off-piste skiing. The bottom section below Rafuyel is often bare, calling for a lift ride down to La Combe, just outside Cesana. The steep slopes opposite, where a long succession of lifts spans the Sestriere road on the way up to Sansicario and Fraiteve (the link with Sauze and Sestriere ski areas), are even less often in good condition and are little skied. Clavière's few lifts provide the necessary links to ski back to Montgenèvre, up and down along the steep wooded slopes beside the road and cross-country tracks. In good snow the runs are not particularly difficult, but there is no genuinely easy way back except via Montquitaine, involving a long walk.

Montgenèvre is seriously short of **mountain restaurants**. The excellent and inexpensive bars and restaurants above Clavière (particularly La Coche) offer some consolation.

Queues in Montgenèvre are bad only at weekends and when snow in nearby resorts is poor. There is now **artificial snow** on several of the lower slopes.

The resort

Montgenèvre is spread along the north side of the busy main road across the high col, now also the main street, with a customs hut at the Italian end of it. On the south side of the pass are open fields, with a row of lifts and a wide area of **nursery slopes**, admirable except for the amount of non-nursery skiing traffic and wind they receive. (Montgenèvre is itself more windswept than its main ski areas, which are relatively sheltered.) There are three supermarkets but shopping facilities are limited; there is a weekly market, 'fun' but 'not cheap'. There is apparently no bureau de change.

   Accommodation is mostly in apartments widely spread along the road, in the old village and on the lower south-facing slopes; there are also a few catered chalets. Access to skiing is easy from most places,

---

Facts on Montgenèvre   Hautes-Alpes **France**

Prices in francs

Tourist office
Postcode 05100
Tel 92219022
Fax 92219245
Tlx 440440

Getting there
By road 979km from Calais. Access via Fréjus tunnel or Grenoble/Briançon. Chains may be needed.
By rail Briançon (10km) or Oulx (17km); 3 or 4 buses per day from station.
By air Turin; transfer 2½hr. (Or Grenoble; transfer 3hr. Lyon; transfer 4hr.)

Staying there
Visitor beds 7,500; breakdown: 400 in hotels, 7,100 in flats.
Package holidays Enterprise (cs) Made to Measure (hs) Quest Total Ski (h) Quest Travel (schools) (h) SkiBound (a) SkiTonic (h) Thomson (cs).
Medical facilities In resort: Doctors, chemist. Hospital and dentist: Briançon (10km).

Non-skiing activities
Indoor Library, cinema.
Outdoor Natural skating rink (open until 11pm), curling, hang-gliding, paragliding, snow scooters.

Kindergartens
Jardin d'enfants
Tuition: Yes. Hours: 9.00-noon, 2.00-5.00. Ages: 3-5. Cost: 620.00 per week (without meals). Closed Sun am and Sat pm.
Halte-garderie
Tuition: No. Hours: 9.00-5.30. Ages: 1-4. Cost: 400.00 per week (without meals). Open all week.

Special skiing facilities
Summer skiing No.

Cross-country Total 50km on either side of the pass, and at Les Alberts (7km away). 20km down the alpine runs at Montgenèvre.

Lift passes
Local pass
Covers Montgenèvre lifts only. (23 lifts in total.)
Cost 6 days 500.00 (£51.55). Low season: 400.00 saving 20%.
Credit cards accepted Yes.
Senior citizens 375.00 (over 60) saving 25%.
Children 375.00 (under 12) saving 25%. Free pass up to age 4.
Notes Local pass allows one free day in Serre-Chevalier and Puy-St-Vincent. Extensions available for rest of Voie Lactée Sud (60.00 per day) or just Mt de la Lune and Sansicario (55.00 per day). Family reductions available.
Beginners One free drag-lift. Day passes for limited area.
Short-term passes Half-day (from 1.00pm); single ascents.
Other passes Grande Galaxie pass (one day in Serre-Chevalier, Voie Lactée Sud, Puy-St-Vincent, 2 days in Les Deux Alpes and Alpe d'Huez).

Ski school
ESF
Classes 2½hr am or pm. Cost: 460.00 (6 half-days). Lunchtime lessons available in high season.
Lift priority Yes.
Children's classes Ages: 5-11. Cost: 430.00 (6 half-days).
Private lessons available Per hour. Cost: 140.00 per hour. 1-2 people.
Special courses Off-piste courses (with snow scooters) from 180.00 per trip.

What was new in 91
New chair-lift replaced two old drag-lifts from village to Le Prarial.

but the Italian end of the village is the more convenient, the French end more remote from the church bells. A large new resort development is planned here, along with a new access lift for the south-facing side of the ski area. The pick of Montgenèvre's few and unluxurious hotels are the Napoléon, convenient and fairly comfortable, and the more attractively rustic Valérie, near the church. Prospective guests in chalet Le Boom ('well placed in village centre') should note the comments below.

There is not a wide range of **après-ski** activity, but there is a good choice of inexpensive bar-restaurants in which to make merry and three of them have disco-nightclubs attached. That the Le Boom chalet is 'cheap' but 'grotty'; Stevie Nick's is British-run. The Ca del Sol is a popular bar in the centre; La Graal revolves around satellite TV.

Montgenèvre is better than other resorts in the Milky Way for **cross-country** skiing, with a fair extent of easy trails beside the road to Clavière (more attractive than that sounds) and some more advanced runs in the woods on the Briançon side of the resort. There is very little for **non-skiers** to do, though the skating rink is a good one.

Most recent reports speak well of the **ski school** – 'friendly, helpful, good English' – for all grades of skier and for private lessons.

Clavière Italy 1750m

Clavière is very much a border village, with the customs post in the middle, and a row of shops on the Italian side specialising in food and cheap Italian alcohol, with prices in francs and lire. There are a few quiet and not unattractive hotels along the road. The village is tightly enclosed by wooded slopes, and the nursery slope is small and steep. Lifts give access to the skiing above Montgenèvre and Cesana, with easy runs back from both. There is a cross-country trail up to Montgenèvre and back. Clavière's après-ski is very limited – half a dozen bars, one disco – and it is no place for non-skiers. The ski school has some English-speaking instructors and, outside high season, mainly English-speaking pupils. Weekend queues and traffic are serious problems.

Tourist office ✆ (122) 8856. **Package holidays** Quest Travel (schools) (h).

Cesana Torinese Italy 1350m

Cesana is an attractively dilapidated old village on a busy road junction at the foot of the Italian approach to the Montgenèvre pass. It is rather confined and sunless, and accommodation is limited. More holiday-makers go to the hotels and chalets dotted around the ski slopes (mainly at Sagna Longa, 2000m). The chair-lifts up to the skiing above Clavière and Sansicario are a long walk from the centre, and the place can be safely recommended only to those with a car for access to other resorts.

Tourist office ✆ (122) 76698. **Package holidays** Ski Europe (h).

Serre-Chevalier France 1350m – 1500m

Good for *Big ski area, off-piste skiing, nursery slopes, cross-country skiing, lift queues, woodland runs*
Bad for *Skiing convenience, Alpine charm, resort-level snow, freedom from cars*

Linked resort: Briançon

Serre-Chevalier is not a village but a mountain, which stands above Briançon, the highest town in Europe, privileged in the amount of good skiing on its doorstep (and now with lifts of its own up to the eastern extremity of Serre-Chevalier). The slopes have been a playground for local skiers for over half a century, and both the ski area and the resort villages at its feet have developed in a messy, unplanned way; the diffuse, car-oriented nature of the place is superficially reminiscent of America. Despite a growing international clientele, it still has the atmosphere of a place for locals, and this is one of the key attractions for our rapidly growing band of enthusiastic reporters.

The skiing certainly deserves to be more widely known. As well as a large area of mostly intermediate pistes, there is a huge amount of unpisted, skiable north-facing mountain within striking range of the lifts. Serre-Chevalier cultivates a reputation as a resort for the connoisseur of off-piste skiing. In this sense, too, it is a place for locals (or skiers with local guides) – the best runs are not always obviously visible.

The slopes of Serre-Chevalier and its neighbours drop down to the Guisane valley, where no less than 13 villages and hamlets make up the modern ski resort. There are three main ones, styled for skiers as Serre-Chevalier 1350, 1400 and 1500 but normally known by their proper names: Chantemerle, Villeneuve-la-Salle, and Monêtier-les-Bains. The lower two share most of the accommodation, resort facilities and the larger half of the ski area. But Monêtier is the only one of the three with any village atmosphere, and it also has the most difficult skiing. Unfortunately it is the least convenient. All the main villages suffer from traffic on the main Grenoble to Briançon road. Briançon makes an interesting departure from ski-resort norms, its fortifications enclosing a maze of ancient narrow streets.

There are complicated lift-pass-sharing arrangements with several other major ski areas in the region, which operate under the Grande Galaxie umbrella. Briançon and Serre-Chevalier are well placed for exploration by car, with Montgenèvre and the Italian border not far to the east, Puy-St-Vincent to the south, Les Deux Alpes and Alpe d'Huez to the west. Another excellent excursion is to the off-piste mountain at La Grâve (on the way to Les Deux Alpes, and described in the same chapter), which participates less fully in the galactic lift-pass-sharing arrangements. Having a car is handy locally too, allowing you to pick accommodation without worrying too much about location in the resort.

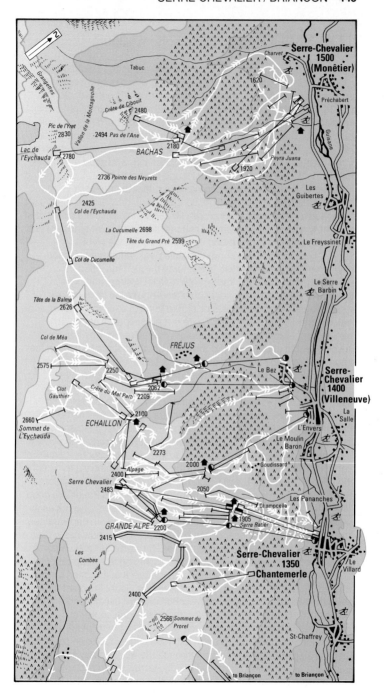

The skiing top 2780m bottom 1350m

Most of the lifts and pistes are concentrated above the neighbouring villages of Chantemerle and Villeneuve, in a linked network covering a series of valleys of open, mostly intermediate skiing between 2000m and 2500m, with longer runs of varying difficulty down through thinly wooded lower slopes dotted with chalets and farm buildings and with rough roads that make easy alternatives to the direct descents to the valley floor. Monêtier's distinct but now linked sector, at the western end of the area, is in many ways the most appealing, with good red runs in the woods, a couple of testing blacks and the best of the off-piste skiing.

Above **Grand Alpe** is an open basin of rather featureless intermediate runs with a good but congested nursery area at the top of the gondola. The double Prorel drag-lift serves intermediate pistes, and below it is an isolated four-seater chair-lift serving two 'magnificent and often deserted' red pistes dropping 500m through the woods. Serre-Chevalier itself is an unremarkable peak, but there are good views from the top and a fast race-course through the woods.

Prorel is also the top of the recently built lift system starting in **Briançon**. A 12-person gondola from the edge of the town centre serves an east-facing red piste of 1150m vertical back to the town, snow (natural or artificial) permitting. There is a nursery area at the mid-station (1625m) and a black slalom course (served by a drag) finishing at that same point. On the open south-east facing flank of the mountain are long runs – red at the top, green and blue lower down.

The **Fréjus/Echaillon** sector above Villeneuve provides more interesting runs for good skiers, with short, fairly steep unprepared pistes beneath the crest of the mountain chain. There are splendid views southwards and a beautiful black run (L'Isolée, well named) along the narrow ridge from Eychauda towards Echaillon. In good snow conditions, inexperienced skiers can enjoy very long runs to the valley.

Monêtier's network of lifts is linked to the Fréjus sector by a series of high chair-lifts, one of which goes to the high-point of the system on the shoulder of the Pic de L'Yret (2830m), giving runs of 1300m vertical to the valley. The black and red pistes from here towards Fréjus are good runs when conditions are right, but both get a lot of sun. The link as a whole is high and exposed – unpleasant or impossible in bad weather. The wide and beautiful east-facing bowl above Fréjus now has a piste – the excellent red Vallon de la Cucumelle. The Yret chair makes some favoured off-piste runs easily accessible, including the steep (about 35°) face under the lift – much skied (despite the fact that it is often fenced off) and often a formidable mogul-field, 'without doubt the most difficult run in the resort'. Fortunately snow conditions are usually good. From Bachas at 2180m down to the valley there is a wide choice of intermediate pistes through the larch woods, with plenty of off-piste scope. None of these runs is easy, although a blue has been contrived. Tabuc is a splendid long black run through the woods away from the main ski area, with one or two awkwardly narrow steep sections.

Mountain restaurants are to be found at most of the main lift stations; but Monêtier has only two, one new last season. Reports suggest that standards have generally improved and that many restaurants have been extensively refurbished. Recommendations include the old chalet-hotel Serre-Ratier, Le Pi-mia at the foot of the Vallon de la Cucumelle run, the newly rebuilt Aravet restaurant (allows picnics) and Jack's bar ('good atmosphere, busy, live music').

Lift **queues** are not generally a problem, provided runs down to the valley are skiable – Villeneuve and Chantemerle now have three access lifts each, and the resort as a whole can now shift over 10,000 skiers an hour from the valley floor. As a result, main pistes around Grand Alpe and Fréjus can be very congested and the drags above Fréjus can develop queues. The slopes of Monêtier and Briançon are generally the least crowded. Streams and hillocks make it difficult or impossible to traverse across the natural balcony at around 2000m. There is an enormous range of lift passes, including ones covering the Briançon Prorel area; limited-area passes can be extended by the day. A recent reporter complains about lifts shutting early (about 4.15pm in March) – a nuisance if you want to visit the other villages.

There is **artificial snow** on two runs from the Grande Alpe mid-station to Chantemerle, on the lower slopes at Monêtier and from about 2000m down to Briançon. Villeneuve now has a 95m half-pipe for the amusement of surfers. There is floodlit skiing on the nursery piste.

The resort

Chantemerle (1350) is only 5km out of Briançon and serves mainly as a service area for skiing commuters; space between main road and river is limited and parking facilities are inadequate. **Villeneuve** (1400) is more spread out, with a narrow high street on one side of the river and more spacious resort development (commercial centre and apartment buildings) beside what was the main road at the foot of the slopes on the other side (a bypass now skirts the area). If there is any centre of Serre-Chevalier, this is it. Near the Fréjus lifts, the old hamlet of **Le Bez** has been converted to serve as a resort community without losing all its charm. **Monêtier** (1500) is a quiet rural spa village with some delightful huddles of old buildings between road and river. The lift starts on the other side of the river, quite a walk away.

Ski-buses tour the villages and lift stations – free if you have the right lift pass – and have been found adequate by most reporters, with some complaints about long intervals. The service to and from Monêtier is limited. Ordinary buses also run along the valley and into Briançon.

Accommodation consists of apartments and about 30 hotels, mostly small and simple, evenly distributed between the three resort centres, and in many cases run and staffed by British operators. Most self-catering accommodation in Chantemerle is reported to be out of the centre, on a steepish hill. Hotel Le Clos is in a superb position and serves good food, but has some drawbacks (shabby rooms, limited hot water). A better bet is the spotless but characterless Plein Sud. Villeneuve is arguably the best location for skiing convenience. A little tractor-drawn train provides free transport around the village. The Lièvre Blanc hotel has been repeatedly recommended – 'bags of character, brilliant bar'. The Christiana is a simple, friendly and reasonably priced hotel between the two main lifts. On the other, quieter side of the village, La Vieille Ferme is a long walk from skiing, but rewards the effort with interesting décor, a warm welcome and good food. The Aigle du Bez is a clean and functional new woody hotel at Le Bez, very convenient for the Fréjus lifts, mainly used by school parties. In Monêtier the simple

Facts on Serre-Chevalier Hautes-Alpes **France**

Prices in francs
Ski Club represented

Tourist office
Postcode 05240
Tel Chantemerle 92240034; Villeneuve 92247188; Le Monêtier 92244198
Fax 92247618
Tlx 400152

Getting there
By road 1,004km from Calais. Via Grenoble/Col du Lautaret or Chambéry/Fréjus tunnel/Briançon; chains may be needed.
By rail Briançon (5km); 7 daily buses from station.
By air Lyon; transfer 3½hr. (Or Grenoble; transfer 2½hr. Also Turin.)

Staying there
Visitor beds 30,000; breakdown: mainly apartments.
Package holidays Bladon Lines (c) Chalets and Hotels "Unlimited" (hcs) Enterprise (hs) Kings Ski Club (jas) Made to Measure (hs) Quality Ski Tours (h) Quest Total Ski (h) Quest Travel (schools) (h) Sally Holidays (s) Sarac Ski (cs) Ski Global (hs) SkiTonic (h) SnowRanger (s) .
Medical facilities In resort: Doctor, chemist, dentist. Hospital: Briançon (5km).

Non-skiing activities
Indoor Swimming pool and sauna, fitness centres, cinemas, bridge.
Outdoor At Chantemerle: skating rink, ice-circuit, paragliding, cleared paths, snow-shoe walks. At Villeneuve: horse-riding, cleared paths, parapenting, snow-shoe walks. At Monêtier: skating rink, cleared paths. Also hang-gliding, delta-planes rides, husky dog sleigh rides.

Kindergartens
Les Poussins (Chantemerle)
Tuition: Yes. Hours: 9.00-5.00. Ages: From 8mths. Cost: 960.00 per week (with meals).
Les Schtroumpfs (Villeneuve)
Tuition: Yes. Hours: 9.00-5.00. Ages: From 6mths. Cost: 840.00 per week (without meals).
Pré-Chabert
Tuition: Yes. Hours: 9.00-6.00, per day. Ages: From 2. Cost: 690.00 per week (without meals).

Special skiing facilities
Summer skiing La Grave.
Cross-country About 45km of trails (mixed abilities) along valley floor from Briançon to beyond Le Casset (west of Le Monêtier).

Lift passes
Grand Serre-Che pass
Covers all Serre-Che lifts, Villeneuve pool, one session in fitness centre and ski buses. (65 lifts in total.)
Cost 6 days 680.00 (£70.10).
Credit cards accepted Yes.
Senior citizens 505.00 (over 60) saving 26%.
Children 505.00 (under 16) saving 26%. Free pass up to age 4.
Notes Daily extensions available for whole area, and for Voie Lactée or Montgenèvre. Passes of 6 days or more give one day in each of Les Deux Alpes, Alpe d'Huez, Puy-St-Vincent, Voie Lactée Sud (Montgenèvre/Sansicario) and Bardonecchia.
Beginners Free lift at Chantemerle; beginners' day passes for valley lifts at Villeneuve and Monêtier.
Short-term passes Half-day (for morning or afternoon).
Other passes Various different passes covering the Serre-Che and Briançon lifts – the Grand Serre-Che/Briançon pass covers them all, 6 days cost 750.00 for adults, 560.00 for children; the Serre-Che pass just covers 1350 and 1400, 6 days cost 580.00 for adults, 435.00 for children; the Monêtier pass just covers the 1500 lifts, 6 days cost 525.00 for adults, 380.00 for children. Passes available for non-skiers.
Other periods Passes available for 8 non-consecutive days.

Ski school
ESF (in all centres)
Classes 3hr am or 2hr pm. Cost: 430.00 (6 days, afternoons cheaper).
Lift priority Yes.
Children's classes Ages: 4-16. Cost: 375.00 (6 days, afternoons cheaper).
Private lessons available Hourly. Cost: 135.00 per hour.
Special courses Premier ski – a special course for beginners, costs 1040.00 for 6 full days; mono, surf and telemark courses on request.

What was new in 91
1. New artificial ice-rink at Chantemerle.
2. New restaurant at Fréjus.

Alliey is very charming and central; the Auberge du Choucas is a welcoming, recently restored old farmhouse.

Après-ski is quiet except at weekends, and the resort only just escapes a 'bad for après-ski' verdict. There are plenty of restaurants (the Serre and the Marotte in Villeneuve, and the Bidule in Le Bez are recommended) and a few discos, of which the Baita (Villeneuve) and Serre-Che (Chantemerle) attract most of the local young. Recommended bars include the Pub ('good noisy cellar bar, log fire, half-price drinks until 10pm') and the bar of the Clos hotel ('disco for residents three times a week') in Chantemerle; and the Iceberg ('popular with British, live music, videos') and the Lièvre Blanc ('excellent bar with open fire, very reasonable prices') in Villeneuve.

The **cross-country** skiing is good (provided that there is snow in the valley), especially west of Monêtier (the best base for this purpose) where the valley is less built up; long off-piste excursions towards the Col du Lautaret are possible.

There is a fair range of activities to amuse **non-skiers**, and (unlike the resort villages), the old hamlets dotted along the valley floor have some charm. Excursions to Briançon are 'a must'.

Nursery slopes are good, with open areas at the foot of Villeneuve and Monêtier slopes, and higher up at the top of the Fréjus and Grand Alpe gondolas. There are very long green runs down to the valley floor, especially the one from Col Méa to Villeneuve.

There are several **ski schools;** we have reasonable reports of the ESF ('good use of time, English and organization poor') and mixed reports of the small but flexible Ecole du Ski Buissonnière, which meets at Aravet, a much less attractive nursery area than Fréjus because of its steep drag-lifts. The schools organise day excursions.

Briançon   1325m

Briançon sells its distinctive brand of skiing under the slogan 'Le Ski et La Ville'. It certainly makes an unusual ski resort; the streets are lined not with ski shops but with the ordinary food shops that make French towns so compelling for the British visitor, while up the hill is a fortified old town for après-ski sightseeing. The ramparts give a good view, past the towers of the church and across the roofs of the town, of Le Prorel, Briançon's ski hill, and the rest of the Serre-Chevalier ridge stretching away to the west. The town's twelve-person gondola rises from a new complex (with covered and open car-parks) only a short walk from the centre of the town. The Auberge le Mont-Prorel is a simple tin-roofed chalet hotel (a Logis de France) right next to the lift station; the Parc is a smarter modern hotel with brasserie attached, a short walk away near the central crossroads; the Vauban, a little further away and a little less modern, is about the most comfortable. There are reasonable sports facilities – a pool, an Olympic skating rink (with a big-league hockey team), a climbing wall – and a modest range of cultural activities. The kindergarten at the Prorel complex takes children from six months.
Tourist office ✆ 92210850.
Package holidays   Sally Holidays (h) Ski Europe (h) SnowRanger (s).

Alpe d'Huez France 1850m

Good for *Nursery slopes, beautiful scenery, big ski area, tough runs, off-piste skiing, resort-level snow, family holidays, sunny slopes, artificial snow*
Bad for *Alpine charm, freedom from cars, woodland runs*

Linked resorts: Auris-en-Oisans, Villard-Reculas, Vaujany, Oz Station

Alpe d'Huez is a big modern resort spread widely across a treeless hillside in an outstandingly open and sunny yet sheltered setting, high up on the northern wall of the Romanche valley, east of Grenoble. The most immediately striking feature of the skiing is the vast areas of green runs at just above resort level, but there is also a lot of interesting intermediate skiing, and for experts there are some steep mogul slopes, the longest black runs in the Alps and some very long, exciting off-piste runs. But there is a snag: how much of this skiing is in practice available, and how much of it is enjoyable, depends on what effect the strong southern sun, of which the resort is so proud, has had on the mainly south- and west-facing slopes.

Like Les Deux Alpes (a close neighbour as the helicopter flies), Alpe d'Huez is mainly an early post-War development, which means it has grown up piecemeal, and has hotels as well as apartments, and animated après-ski – at least at holiday times, when it has quite a chic French clientele. It also means that it is not particularly convenient for skiing: for many residents, there are walks to and from skiing, or lifts for which there may be queues. Although mainly modern, the resort is architecturally not at all new or stylish (apart from its beautiful church), and more than one reporter has likened the village to a building site. But, in compensation, others have noted a friendly welcome for British skiers. The resort projects a very dynamic image and appears to be reaping the benefits. In our first edition, six years ago, we said the place attracted few non-French visitors, and listed only two small-scale British tour operators going there. This year, operators number over 20, and we have a healthy number of readers' reports.

Already impressive and well equipped with modern lifts, Alpe d'Huez's ski area has recently been augmented considerably by a further wave of investment in new lifts, mechanising a big area of north-west-facing slopes above Vaujany and Oz-en-Oisans. The village of Vaujany is an appealing base for those who don't mind finishing as well as starting their day with a lift ride. Oz Station is a ski-in lift-out skiers' dormitory a long way up the mountain from the village of Oz.

Again like Les Deux Alpes, Alpe d'Huez has limited lift-pass-sharing arrangements with several other resorts in the area – Les Deux Alpes is nearest, but Serre-Chevalier and Montgenèvre, close to Briançon, are within reach by bus or car. In the resort itself, a car is no great asset for most visitors.

The skiing top 3330m bottom 1100m

The skiing around Alpe d'Huez itself can be divided into three areas, two of them (Pic Blanc/Clocher de Mâcle and Signal) accessible from the top point of the roughly triangular resort and via subsidiary lifts from points down the two flanks. The third area, Signal de l'Homme, is separated from the resort by the Sarenne gorge, but can be reached by riding a fast high-capacity chair-lift (from the eastern Bergers part of the resort) down into the gorge and then up again, or in a very roundabout way on skis. The new lifts above Vaujany have effectively added a fourth area to the north, connected at two points to the Pic Blanc sector.

Most of the skiing takes place immediately north-east of the resort, on the sunny lower and middle slopes of **Pic Blanc**, served by the impressively efficient two-stage 25-person Grandes Rousses gondola. The first section of the gondola climbs only 240m over the enormous area of green runs and walks next to the resort. Above it, the rocky massif steepens, and the second stage serves red and blue runs of 600m vertical – interestingly varied, but often too busy for comfort. It also gives access to the cable-car to Pic Blanc itself.

Behind the Pic Blanc cable-car station is the south-facing, crevasse-free Sarenne glacier, which starts with a fairly steep (around 28°), often stony and usually crowded mogul-field immediately below the lift station. The view is enormous and so are the runs – only blacks, of which two are notorious. (In summer, the glacier provides easier short runs.) One run is the mogul-slope under the cable-car, reached via a tunnel through the mountain and an awkward path at the end of it. Although this is steep, it is much less fearsome than it looks from below; but it gets the afternoon sun, and in sunny weather may be closed until the moguls have softened (around lunch-time).

The alternative way down from Pic Blanc is to take one of the runs all the way down the glacier and into the Sarenne gorge, at about 16km the longest black runs and possibly the longest pistes in the Alps, mainly thanks to the very long, gentle run-out beside the river and down into the gorge. They are superb trails, wild and beautiful, of over 1800m vertical, but snow conditions below glacier level are often difficult and the runs are not reliably open. The main run is the Sarenne, on which the only properly black passage is a short but steep (34°) mogul slope a little way below the initial one; this levels off into a long fast-cruising stretch, after which the run becomes an interesting alternation of more and less steep sections, some of the former rather narrow but none of more than red difficulty. When short of snow these narrow bits are dreadful bottle-necks. The Chateau Noir is a less popular piste variant to the left of the Sarenne; the Combe du Loup, to the left again, is now off-piste, and a much more serious proposition than the main runs.

Pic Blanc is also the point of departure of some long and spectacular off-piste runs, both on the Alpe d'Huez flank of the Grandes Rousses where many of the runs lead down towards Vaujany, and on the other side towards Clavans and other points of no return. Some involve precipitous walks and very steep slopes, and guides are essential.

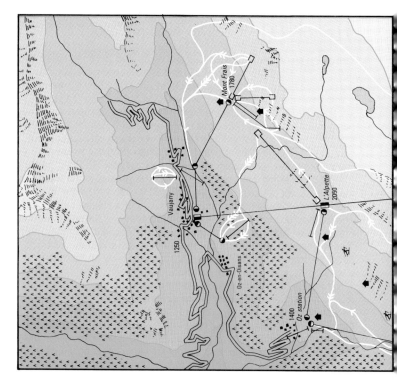

From the mid-station of the main gondola, the Lièvre Blanc chair-lift gives access to a lot of good, challenging skiing. It serves its own red piste, but also gives access to another more notable red, the satisfyingly secluded Balme, down to Alpe d'Huez. Above it, a further chair-lift goes on up to **Clocher de Mâcle**, where a trio of interesting black runs begin. These include a beautiful long run (the Combe Charbonnière) past Europe's highest disused coal-mine and from there either round to the resort or down into the Sarenne gorge. A more direct descent is the downhill race-course. The short run down from Clocher de Mâcle to Lac Blanc is steep (33˚), but snow is usually good. There are reportedly some challenging off-piste variants.

The mid-station of the main gondola (at 2100m) is also accessible from the east end of Alpe d'Huez via the Flèche Sarenne gondola, which at present terminates at Plat des Marmottes (2300m). This lift also serves worthwhile pistes of its own, including the self-explanatory red Canyon, and the planned second stage will lead directly to the Sarenne glacier, currently accessible only by the Pic Blanc cable-car.

Vaujany's home slopes are on a mainly gentle mountain shelf, with much steeper and rockier terrain above and below, reached by a six-seat gondola to Montfrais (the nursery and main congregation area) or by the first stage of the 160-person cable-car to the higher point of L'Alpette.

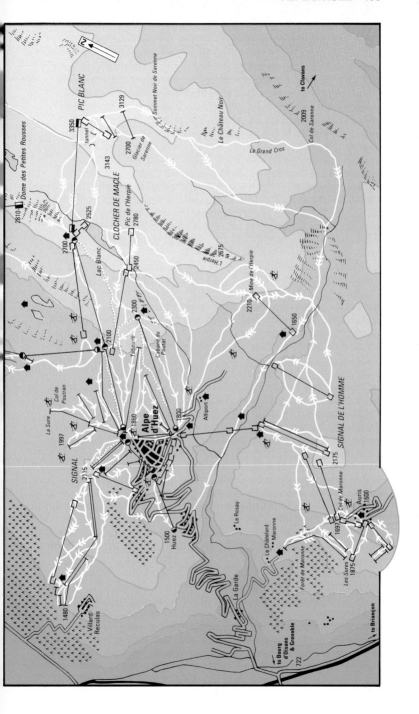

Four short lifts fan out from Montfrais, serving wide, easy nursery slopes and one or two intermediate variants, with plenty of friendly lightly treed areas in which to get some off-piste experience. The Vallonnet chair at the northern extremity of the area gives access to red and black runs to the valley; the black Roche Melon is a local favourite. These runs merge with the blue from Montfrais to terminate at the gondola mid-station, near La Villette. A chair-lift connects Montfrais with the cable-car mid-station at L'Alpette, with an easy, attractive, away-from-the-lifts blue going back down. L'Alpette has another short beginners' lift, and an easy cross-country trail leading across the undulating shelf towards the mid-station of the Grandes Rousses gondola. There is no piste to Vaujany itself, but in good conditions a black is intended to go down from L'Alpette to the lower point of L'Enversin (the low-point of the whole area), whence a short multi-cabin cable-car will (from this winter) go across the valley bottom and up to the village. A red run, open at the top but confined to a narrowish shelf lower down, descends to Oz-Station, with a 12-person gondola going back up to L'Alpette.

Another fast gondola (the Poutran) from Oz goes up in two stages to the mid-station of the Grandes Rousses gondola; the red run back down a shady valley to Oz is one of the most rewarding in the area. When snow in the area as a whole is suffering from the sun, the shady top section often has better-than-average conditions; but when the problem is lack of snowfall, the rocky terrain can be a problem. You have to take a short drag beside the Perce-Neige restaurant to get to the mid-station of the Oz gondola, also giving access to a little-skied blue variant on the bottom section, which joins the run from L'Alpette to Oz.

The other way into the Alpe d'Huez skiing for skiers based in Vaujany or Oz is the second stage of the Vaujany cable-car to the Dôme des Petites Rousses – at 2800m, slightly higher than the top of the Grandes Rousses gondola and linked to it by an open red run which is easy apart from a short steepish pitch near the start. The return to L'Alpette is via a good, testing red run which often has the best snow in the area. Petites Rousses is the start of several classic off-piste descents, including a long itinerary route down the Couloir de la Fare, which brings skiers back to the mid-station of the Montfrais gondola at La Villette.

The **Signal** drag-lifts climb to a rounded peak not very far above the top of Alpe d'Huez with open, easy and intermediate runs back to the resort beside the numerous lifts. Behind Signal, longer runs drop down the open west-facing slopes above the hamlet of Villard-Reculas. There are gentle runs at the top served by the Petit Prince drag, but no easy way down to the bottom – even the green alongside the lowest drag (Cloudit) may be 'a giant mogul field'.

On the other side of the resort and of the Sarenne gorge, the **Signal de l'Homme/Auris** sector is not very large, but its wide open north-facing slopes are a valuable resource in this sunny ski area. The whole hill is of intermediate steepness, and much of it becomes covered in moguls, on- and off-piste. An easy path links up with the run down the Sarenne gorge, leading to the Chalvet chair-lift and thus to pistes down to the Bergers end of Alpe d'Huez (or a long off-piste traverse to the top end of the resort). In the opposite direction, a splendid long red goes down from Signal de l'Homme to Le Châtelard; the return drag-lift and black run beside it are both steep, albeit briefly. Most of the short intermediate runs served by chair-lifts above the new resort of Auris do not enjoy very reliable snow cover; but the Crocus run gets less sun than the others and now has artificial snow (as well as evening illumination).

Mountain restaurants away from the resort itself have recently increased in number; even now they cannot be called numerous, but a high proportion are small and attractive. Practically all have terraces sited to make the most of the resort's sunny orientation, and some are appealing in poor weather too. The Bergerie just above Villard-Reculas is one of the most attractive, and has a ski-in outdoor bar where you can sit down with skis on; the Forêt de Maronne hotel at Le Châtelard is another. For serious lunching, it is difficult to beat the very welcoming Chalet du Lac Besson, in an out-of-the-way position among the cross-country trails between Alpe d'Huez and Vaujany; with a bit of effort, downhillers can get to Lac Besson from the Chamois piste (look for signs), but snowmobile lifts can be arranged; table reservations are often necessary (© 76806537). Other recommendations: the cosy Combe Haute in the Sarenne gorge at the foot of the Chalvet chair-lift; the Perce-Neige, just below the mid-station of the Oz Poutran gondola, on the red run to Oz-Station; the Alpette (Chez Passoud), just below the mid-station of the Vaujany cable-car, on the way down towards Oz; Les Airelles, at the top of the Montfrais nursery drag above Vaujany. The otherwise inhospitable Marmottes, at the top of the Flèche Sarenne gondola, has a large terrace with what is claimed (with some justice) to be the best view in the area.

Alpe d'Huez is not plagued by **queues**, nor is it free of them. The main apparent black spots are the gondolas out of the resort and the Pic Blanc cable-car. But the queue for the capacious Grandes Rousses gondola moves very quickly (particularly on the right); and both sections of the gondola are avoidable, the lower one by a triple drag and the upper by the little-used Plates chair. The Lièvre Blanc chair from the Grandes Rousses mid-station generates queues, partly because it serves a lot of good skiing and partly because joining the gondola at the mid-station is difficult. The lifts above Villard-Reculas are prone to queues; a powerful new chair is promised for next season. Several of the drag-lifts on the lower slopes are now doubles or triples. It is not unusual to find queues to get through the tunnel leading from the glacier to the slopes above the resort, especially when (in the late afternoon) the glacier runs close before the cable-car; there is no sign of the promised duplicate tunnel. In holiday periods there are queues for the bucket lift which runs between the bottom and the top of the resort, particularly at its mid-station; some families have found it awkward – it slows down, but it doesn't stop. This lift is crucial for easy access to the slopes from many lower parts of the resort; but the Flèche Sarenne gondola at the east end of the resort has improved access to the main ski area from there (and is itself not immune from queues as a result). In several places piste gradings understate difficulty.

There is an impressive **artificial snow** installation on easy pistes down to the resort from the top of the main gondola, on a blue piste to the resort served by the Flêche Sarenne gondola, on a linking piste across from the Flêche Sarenne to the main gondola, and down to the resort from Signal. Auris has guns on one easy run just above the resort. There is a floodlit half-pipe for surfers to play on at the foot of Signal.

The resort

Alpe d'Huez has spread over a large area of steepish hillside in a triangular shape with the main lift departure at the top. At the eastern end, Les Bergers is a recent extension which forms a second centre of shops and other facilities, including the most widely recommended supermarket. And down the hill a little is a further satellite, L'Eclose, linked by lifts to Les Bergers and the bottom of the main resort; this has its own shopping centre, judged adequate for self-catering by our reporters. There is a complicated one-way system, often choked with traffic in icy conditions. There is a shuttle bus service, not much used, and a bucket lift running up through the western fringes of the resort, with several stations.

Accommodation is in apartments and plenty of small and medium-sized hotels; mainly modest, though there are two four-star places and a new five-star hotel opens this season. The growing band of UK tour operators offer a range of both, and one or two have managed to find chalets. The resort is large, and the best location for skiing purposes is right at the top of it, near the lift station – though Les Bergers has its supporters. The Christina is friendly and charming and one of the few attractive, chalet-style buildings at the top end of the resort. The nearby Chamois d'Or is a bright, comfortable modern hotel with a highly regarded restaurant. Après-skiers may prefer to be nearer the bottom of the resort. The comfortable Vallée Blanche is well placed and has its own disco. Reporters recommend Le Petit Prince ('good hotel, friendly people'), the Belle Aurore ('best we've stayed in – excellent food, very friendly staff, bright and warm lounges; bedrooms a bit small'), the Refuge ('simple, convenient, friendly and cheap'), the Beau Soleil and the Christiania in Les Bergers ('right on the piste'). Apartments in the resort vary considerably in age and comfort, and in shopping convenience. Recent reports from self-caterers are mixed; Le Hameau is approved of. The Rocher Soleil Aparthotel in Les Bergers 'cannot be recommended highly enough – superbly convenient location, spacious, well equipped.'

Après-ski is lively, particularly during the New Year, February and Easter holidays when there are plenty of French as well as British visitors in town. The resort has a range of good restaurants, the most highly regarded being the Lyonnais and that in the Chamois d'Or; the Edelweiss is recommended for 'amazingly good value', the British-run Lincoln (with a favourite bar) for 'steaks above a lively disco' (and for karaoke), the Pinocchio for 'wonderful' pizza, the Pomme de Pin for 'a last night splurge'. There are piano bars, and several hotels have live bands or discos. Bar recommendations include the Cactus ('full of chic, popular with instructors'), the Avalanche ('popular disco-bar, good singer') and the Igloo cocktail bar and disco ('jungle-like decor, run by a crazy American'). There are also a few fast-food counters and one or two simple, inexpensive bars.

Facts on Alpe d'Huez   Isere **France**

Prices in francs
Ski Club represented

Tourist office

Postcode 38750
Tel 76803541
Fax 76806954
Tlx 320892

Getting there

By road 916km from Calais. Via Lyon/Grenoble; chains may be needed.
By rail Grenoble (65km); daily buses from station.
By air Lyon; transfer 2½hr. (Or Geneva; transfer 2½hr. Grenoble; transfer 1½hr.)

Staying there

Visitor beds 31,500; breakdown: 36 hotels, 25,000 beds in apartments.
Package holidays Activity Travel (hcs) Brittany Ferries (s) Club Med (h) Crystal (hjs) Enterprise (hs) Horizon (hs) Hoverspeed Ski-Drive (s) Inghams (hs) Kings Ski Club (jas) Made to Measure (hs) Neilson (hs) Quest Total Ski (h) Quest Travel (schools) (h) Sally Holidays (s) Ski Europe (hy) Ski Peak (s) SkiBound (has) Skiworld (hs) SnowRanger (s) Thomson (hs) Vacations (hs) Winter Adventure Holidays (hs) .
Medical facilities In resort: Doctors, dentists, chemists. Hospital: Grenoble (65km).

Non-skiing activities

Indoor Artificial ice rink (skating and curling), sports centre (tennis, gym, squash, aerobics, body-building, climbing wall, sauna, jacuzzi).
Outdoor 30km cleared paths, swimming pool, shooting range, hang-gliding, paragliding, ice-driving.

Kindergartens

Baby Club des Mickeys/SEI
Tuition: Yes. Hours: as adult classes. Ages: 3-4. Cost: 740.00 per week (no meals). Lunch-time care available.
Club des Marmottes/SEI
Tuition: Yes. Hours: as adult classes. Ages: 4-12. Cost: 740.00 per week (no meals). Lunch-time care available.
Les Eterlous
Tuition: Possible. Hours: 8.30-6.00. Ages: 3mth up. Cost: 1,200.00 per week (with meals).

Special skiing facilities

Summer skiing Sarenne Glacier, 2700m–3300m, 3 lifts.
Cross-country Short beginners' loop, 6.3km and 8.2km blue loops, 16.4km red loop above resort.

Lift passes

Grandes Rousses
Covers all Alpe d'Huez lifts, swimming pool and skating rink. (85 lifts in total.)
Cost 6 days 750.00 (£77.32). Low season: 563.00 saving 25%.
Credit cards accepted Yes.
Senior citizens 600.00 (over 60) saving 20%.
Children 600.00 (under 13) saving 20%. Free pass up to age 5.
Notes Passes for 6 days or more give one day in Les Deux Alpes, Serre-Chevallier, Puy-St-Vincent, Montgenèvre/Sansicario, Bardonecchia. Passes of over 11 days valid for 2 days in each centre.
Beginners 3 free lifts; day pass for beginners covers 15 lifts.
Short-term passes Half-day pass for Grandes Rousses area.
Other passes Auris pass (6 days 416.00 for adults, 366.00 for children), Oz-Vaujany pass (6 days 550.00 for adults, 468.00 for children).

Ski school

ESF
Classes 9.45-11.45 and 2.30-5.00. Cost: 670.00 (6 days).
Lift priority Yes.
Children's classes Ages: 3-12. Cost: 550.00 (6 days). Extra hourly lessons in the middle of the day during school holidays and week-ends.
Private lessons available Per hour at lunch-time. Cost: 140.00 per hour. 1-2 people.
Special courses Racing courses, 6 days 890.00; daily off-piste tours.
SEI
Classes 2½hr am and 2hr pm. Cost: 1,895.00 (6 days). Price includes tuition, lift pass and ski hire.
Lift priority Yes.
Children's classes Ages: 3-12. Cost: 1,556.00 (6 days). Price includes tuition, lift pass and ski hire.
Private lessons available Hourly. Cost: 150.00 per hour. 1-2 people.
Special courses Ski Evolutif courses.
Fun Altitude
Snowboard school.
Classes 4½hr/day. Cost: 900.00 (5 days, Mon-Fri). Packages of tuition and equipment hire.
Lift priority Yes.
Children's classes Ages: Any. Cost: 900.00 (5 days, Mon-Fri).
Private lessons available Hourly. Cost: 140.00 per hour.
Special courses Surf, mono.

Alpe d'Huez is very much a resort for skiers, and cannot safely be recommended for a **cross-country** skiing or for a **non-skiing** holiday. But it is a question of atmosphere rather than shortage of facilities: there are long cross-country trails and splendid walks high up in the main ski area, and the sports facilities are good, and being improved; the pool and rink are covered by the lift pass.

Nursery slopes are exemplary: very spacious, very extensive, very gentle and adjacent to the resort. The two **ski schools** meet at the top and bottom of the resort. Reports are favourable, and parents have been impressed by the school's handling of children, and the 'wonderful' mountain guides. The **kindergarten** arrangements are said by some reporters to be less impressive than they seem; in particular, it can be difficult to arrange care for children not old enough to fend for themselves. But Les Eterlous in Les Bergers is said to be family-run and good, and used to English-speakers.

Vaujany   1240m
Vaujany is a sleepy little mountainside village – a handful of simple hotels, one grocery shop, one ski shop – which (thanks to the community's rake-off from the local hydro-electric scheme) is extravagantly over-equipped with major lifts; on a recent high-season visit, we never encountered a full cabin on the cable-car, let alone a queue. Small-scale apartment-block developments are going on, but nothing that seems likely to have much impact on the present privileged state of affairs. It is not a pretty or notably charming place (many of the roofs are of rusty corrugated iron) nor a convenient one (the village spreads up a steep hillside) but its simplicity and seclusion make it a much more desirable base for many people than Alpe d'Huez. There are three simple hotels in the village centre. The Etendard, closest to the lift station, is the après-ski hub, both at tea-time and later on, when the other hotel bars have closed; but last season (at least) its rooms were filled by Belgian package holiday-makers. The Rissiou considers itself best in town, but the friendly little Cimes across the road gets our vote. There is a disco in the basement of the less central Grandes Rousses hotel, of varying liveliness. Shopping is limited to a single grocery and a single ski shop (inconveniently positioned in the new development right at the top of the village). Last season, at least, the ski school included an enthusiastic American instructor. The school runs a ski-kindergarten on the nursery slopes at Montfrais; these are reached by gondola, but are otherwise good – spacious, gentle, north-facing but not excessively shady, with refreshments on hand; it is a pity that they are so exposed to speeding skiers.
Tourist office ✆ 76807878.
Package holidays   Made to Measure (h) Ski Peak (hcs).

Oz-Station   1350m
The mountainside satellite of Oz-en-Oisans consists of a cluster of modern, timber-clad apartment buildings with steeply pitched roofs, secluded in the woods at the foot of two impressively efficient gondolas, making it an excellent base for keen skiers. There is one 'very expensive' grocery and one ski shop, and several quiet bar-restaurants,

but no ski school.
Tourist office ✆ 76807801 Fax 76807283.

Villard-Reculas 1450m

Villard-Reculas is a rustic old village with one hotel and a new but sympathetically styled apartment development at the foot of the slopes and lifts. There is one small supermarket and one ski shop in this development, and a couple of small bar-restaurants.

Auris-en-Oisans 1600m

Although it does not attract much custom from Britain, Auris is the biggest of the mini-resorts on the fringes of Alpe d'Huez, with almost 4,000 visitor beds and a bit more evening animation than the others. It is not nearly so well placed for the bulk of the Alpe d'Huez skiing as Vaujany or Oz, but better placed for outings by car to Les Deux Alpes, Serre-Chevalier and so on. Auris-Station, at the foot of the lifts and piste, is a modern development of apartments with pitched roofs, incorporating several ski shops, a couple of food shops and a hotel – the Beau Site. Down the hillside in the original village of Auris (away from the lifts) are a couple of more traditional hotels – the Auberge de la Fôret and Les Emaranches – and chalets and gîtes to rent. Over the hill behind the resort and served by pistes and a lift, the welcoming Forêt de Maronne hotel at Le Châtelard is another attractive option. There are several cafés and restaurants in the resort, a cinema and a disco. There is a branch of the Alpe d'Huez ski school (ESF), and a kindergarten, Les Marmottes, which is reported to be very good and runs a jardin des neiges for the older children.
Tourist office ✆ 76801352.

Les Deux Alpes France 1650m

Good for *Easy runs, off-piste skiing, beautiful scenery, sunny slopes, après-ski, late holidays, summer skiing*
Bad for *Alpine charm, mountain restaurants, not skiing, freedom from cars, woodland runs*

Linked resort: La Grave

We reported favourably on this big modern resort in previous editions, and return visits (admittedly in good conditions) have not dimmed our enthusiasm. It is now well and truly discovered by the British. (In only a few years it has gone from being almost unknown here to a position of such prominence that the list of British tour operators offering it is among the longest in these pages.) But it does not appeal to everyone; and, perhaps more importantly, it does not satisfy everyone to whom it does appeal.

The village is strikingly lively, with many more bars, restaurants and colourful shops lining its long main street than is normal in a modern French resort; it has a lot of hotels, and some are inexpensive. To the south, it has the mightily impressive scenery of the Ecrins national park. On the other hand, it is ugly and full of hazardous and smelly traffic, and very strung out – although it is not too inconvenient for skiing.

The skiing goes very high, with a magnificent easy glacier area, a row of challenging runs immediately above the resort and some skiing below it – though without the shelter of dense forest. The lift system gives access to good off-piste runs, long and short. But it is the skiing, above all else, that leads to disappointment. Some skiers go expecting a ski area comparable in size to Val d'Isère/Tignes or the Trois Vallées, which it is not. Others find that their enjoyment of the high easy runs is spoilt by difficult conditions on the lower slopes at the end of the day. A lack of snow low down also leads to disappointment for good skiers looking for tough pistes. The reservation that we endorse most wholeheartedly is that the narrowness of the ski area makes it difficult to escape people and pylons, and limits the variety of the skiing. Les Deux Alpes offers a foretaste of what skiing may be like in the 1990s in many other big resorts: efficient lifts relieving queues but causing overcrowded pistes.

One sure way to escape the problem is to ski to La Grave, a famous mountaineering resort to the north-east of the glacier with a very long lift serving an uncompromisingly wild, unpisted ski area and leading to tamer skiing on the Glacier de la Girose, recently linked to Les Deux Alpes' Glacier du Mont de Lans. The La Grave lift company is anxious to resist the obvious pressures to make its main ski area safe for piste skiers escaping the overcrowded runs of Les Deux Alpes – and, for that matter, piste skiers tempted to descend on skis from La Grave's own glacier runs. Keen off-piste skiers and local mountain guides will hope that they succeed.

Alpe d'Huez is less than an hour away by road (and only minutes by helicopter), and Serre-Chevalier is not much further away to the east; taking a car is worthwhile for such excursions, which are encouraged by lift-pass-sharing arrangements.

The skiing top 3568m bottom 1270m

As far as skiing goes, Une Alpe et Demie would be a more appropriate name. The western side of the skiing climbs only a few hundred metres above the resort to the shoulder of **Pied Moutet** (2100m) and is not heavily used, despite the attraction of a long north-facing unprepared run down to the small village of Bons (1300m). The blue run down to the Venosc end of Les Deux Alpes is steep.

The skiing that matters is on the eastern side of the resort. The lower slopes are broad – running the whole length of the long resort – and above nursery-slope level are seriously steep; the remote upper ones, on the glacier, are broad and gentle; between the two, from 2200m to 3200m, is a large area of narrower middle slopes where the ground is too broken up to provide a network of runs, although some good north-facing slopes have been opened recently, and another such development is planned. This area has bottle-necks, with congested pistes, particularly in the afternoon.

The first section of skiing immediately above the resort, with main access gondolas going up from the middle of the resort and from the southerly Alpe-de-Venosc, and a chair from Le Village in the north, is a broad, steep, open, west-facing mountainside, terraced for safety, with a spacious open ridge at the top where very easy runs and a number of lifts link the two gondola stations. There is little variety in the runs to the village, and all are steep except for a narrow track (graded green) which zigzags down at the northern end of the ridge, and from which it is possible to traverse to most parts of the resort. When crowded at the end of the day, this run is no fun at all, and a traverse across the open mountainside is preferable. The nearby unbashed run down to the bottom of the skiing at Mont-de-Lans presents an amusing route-finding challenge away from the crowds when conditions are right.

Behind the ridge above the village is the Combe de Thuit, a deep, steep bowl with the peaks of Rachas, Tête Moute and **Diable** at its head. The four-seat Diable gondola from the south end of the village and chair above it lead directly to Tête Moute, from where the black Diable run gives an equally direct 1200m descent to the village, only the top half of which is marked black on the resort piste map. The top pitch of this run is seriously steep – about 35˚ – and it exceeds 30˚ for much of its length down to the top of the Diable gondola. Below that the gradient eases off, but the run is often covered in big moguls which are inclined to be icy at beginning and end of the day; it can be an extremely taxing way home.

The Thuit chair-lift (from the pit of the bowl up to the top of the Diable gondola) has opened up some steep off-piste skiing here, and serves a long blue run with a steepish mogulled start. (Skiing down to take this lift

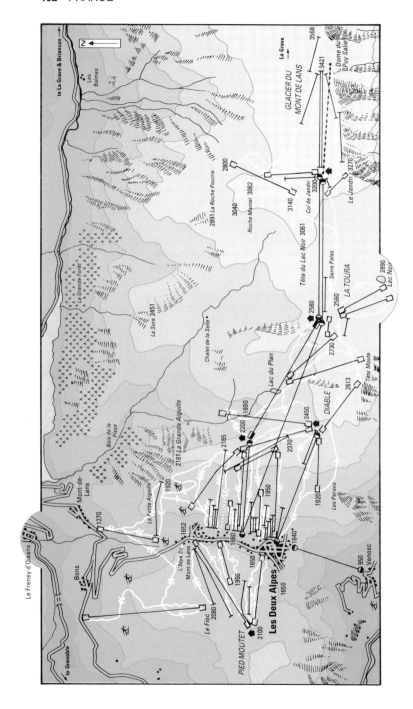

also provides an alternative to the narrow, crowded track around the bowl which is the main way home from higher areas). From Tête Moute there are excellent steep (up to 35°) north-facing runs off-piste between the rocks, as well as a more roundabout blue piste, down to Lac du Plan. From here, chairs go back up to the shoulder of Tête Moute and to the major mid-mountain lift station at 2580m, for access to the gondolas up to the Col de Jandri and the glacier. The alternative is to carry on down to the Thuit chair, or to take the broad terrace run around to the eastern side of the coomb. Beyond this gondola station at 2580m a diverging pair of chair-lifts serve open north-facing runs on **La Toura**, steeper than their blue grading suggests, with interesting off-piste variants. There are splendid views from the top of both these lifts, across and steeply down into the Vénéon valley. Long runs of over 1000m vertical are possible from here down into the coomb.

The top section of the gondolas up to **Col de Jandri** span a larger open area of intermediate skiing centred on an excellent, long but crowded blue with a short awkward section at the end (which can be avoided by branching left). To the north of the Col are gentle north-facing runs on the fringe of the glacier, served by chairs. Above it, to the south, a chair serves a short but challenging mogul field. All these chairs can be very cold to ride.

The **Glacier du Mont-de-Lans**, to the east of the col, is now served by the new Dôme Express underground funicular up to the Dôme de la Lauze, only about 200m above Col de Jandri but almost 2km distant. On the next-door Glacier de la Girose, **La Grave** has constructed a drag up to the Dôme from Col des Ruillans (3200m), the top of its cable-car. The two lift systems are separated by a 10-minute plod, but disregarding that the two resorts now share one of the best summer skiing areas in Europe: a wide expanse of long, easy runs between 2780m and 3568m, with magnificent views and highly reliable snow conditions. Naturally, the glacier area is inhospitable in bad weather; but it is open in winter when conditions permit. From the top, you have the opportunity to notch up the biggest on-piste descent in the Alps – 2300m vertical down to Mont-de-Lans, all of it manageable by even a timid intermediate skier when snow conditions are favourable. The runs back to the Col constitute a vast nursery slope. There is a less gentle run across the glacier to the Roche-Mantel chair-lift, and excellent, steep off-piste skiing down to the lower Signal chair.

The Col des Ruillans (3200m) is the start of various long and very beautiful off-piste runs down to La Grave (1500m). The safe ways down are not obvious; do not attempt the trip without a guide. The ski school takes groups regularly when conditions are good. Les Deux Alpes' very long and narrow lift system gives some other opportunities to go off-piste, but many come into the category of ski mountaineering.

This is not a resort for lunchtime *gourmands* – **mountain restaurants** are few, uninviting, expensive and crowded, the main exception being La Pastorale at the bottom of the Diable run ('good atmosphere, the least expensive', but 'slow service' and 'a lot of noise from clanking lifts'). Many restaurants do have large terraces, and good views; the mid-mountain one at 2600m is 'friendly, with prompt waiter service'. The higher restaurants charge for the use of loos. Lunch on the way down to La Grave is an attractive proposition, at the Etienne Chancel refuge ('superb location, very friendly')

Thanks to the Jandri Express 20-person gondola, going up is now easier than finding space in the restaurants or on the pistes back down to the resort in the afternoon; the lift system generates **queues** mainly when skiers are being bussed in from elsewhere. But it is not perfect. There were acute problems last season on the crowded beginners' area atop the ridge above the village, with 'appalling crushes' on the Séa chair and long queues for the cable-car to 2600m. There are queues for the Signal and Roche Mantel chair-lifts in fine weather and for the Thuit, La Noir, La Toura and Jandri 4 chairs in late afternoon. The glacier funicular seems to have relieved the pressure on the existing drag-lifts to a lesser extent than might have been hoped. The piste map has been redrawn from a new perspective to show the La Grave skiing, and is improved in other ways, but still 'requires the use of some imagination'. There is no **artificial snow**.

The resort

The setting of Les Deux Alpes is a remarkably symmetrical one, with steep drops to the north and south of the flat col on which it sits, and steep walls climbing evenly to the east and west. Originally two communities – the Alpes were the summer pastures of Mont-de-Lans to the north and Venosc to the south – it is now one long village, with concentrations of development around the central gondola station and in Alpe-de-Venosc – the most compact, stylish and lively part, splendidly set on the southerly ledge above the very steep Vénéon valley. At the northern end, in Clos-des-Fonds, a traffic-free development called Le Village is growing up the eastern hillside (and now has its own access lift to the ridge above). There is now a free resort bus service of which some reporters have made good use; a few complain that it is unreliable. Shopping is limited in Le Village, good in the main resort.

Accommodation is mostly in apartments, but there are also lots of small hotels, mostly simple and friendly – and UK tour operators' holidays employ a range of both, plus an increasing number of catered chalets – though a common complaint is of apartments masquerading as chalets. For skiing the best location is right in the centre near the main Jandri lift station. The central Brunerie is recommended by several reporters for 'friendly service and excellent facilities', though the dining room is 'rather austere'. The Edelweiss is 'extremely homely, food excellent'. Attractive hotels at the Venosc end include the Chalet Mounier – 'excellent, with very good nouvelle cuisine', 'good cocktails, live music' – Pied Moutet and Belle Etoile. The Marmottes is out of the way but runs a courtesy bus and can be reached on skis, and offers 'excellent food, facilities, accommodation and service'. The Champame apartments are rather a hike from the Jandri gondola, but otherwise recommended – 'spacious and well equipped, with good views'. Apartments in Le Village seem to satisfy their occupants, but the

Facts on Les Deux Alpes   Isere **France**

Prices in francs

Tourist office

Postcode 38860
Tel 76792200
Fax 76790138
Tlx 320883

Getting there

By road 928km from Calais. Via Lyon/Grenoble; chains may be needed.
By rail Grenoble (75km); 4 daily buses from station.
By air Lyon; transfer 3hr. (Or Geneva; transfer 3hr. Grenoble; transfer 1½hr.)

Staying there

Visitor beds 30,000; breakdown: 6,000 in hotels, most in apartments.
Package holidays Bladon Lines (hcs) Brittany Ferries (s) Chalets and Hotels "Unlimited" (hcs) Crystal (hcjas) Enterprise (hcs) Horizon (hs) Hoverspeed Ski-Drive (s) Inghams (hs) Made to Measure (hs) Neilson (hs) Panorama's Ski Experience (hs) Quest Total Ski (h) Quest Travel (schools) (h) Sally Holidays (s) Ski Alternatives (h) Ski Club of GB (h) Ski Global (hs) Ski Party Snow World (hcs) Ski Valkyrie (hcs) SkiBound (hs) SkiTonic (h) Skiworld (cas) SnowRanger (hs) Thomson (hs) Tracer Holidays (cs) Vacations (hs) .
Medical facilities In resort: 5 doctors, 1 dentist, 2 chemists. Hospital: Grenoble (75km).

Non-skiing activities

Indoor 2 Alpes Tonic centre (gym, dance, body-building, Californian baths, sauna, hammam, solarium); Club Forme Le Village (squash courts, swimming pool, jacuzzi, solarium, sauna, hammam); Swimming Pool Complex (swimming pool, artificial skating rink, jacuzzi, sauna – free entry with lift pass); Tanking centre, bowling, cinemas.
Outdoor Hang-gliding, paraskiing, heli-skiing, 4-wheel bikes, curling.

Kindergartens

ESF-Jardin de neige
Tuition: Yes. Hours: 9.15-12.15 and 2.30-5.00.
Ages: 4-6. Cost: 750.00 per week (meals and lunchtime supervision can be arranged).
SEI-Jardin de neige
Tuition: Yes. Hours: 9.30-12.00 and 2.30-5.00.
Ages: 3-6. Cost: 770.00 per week (without lunch). Sun am or pm 75.00 extra.
Bonhomme de Neige
Tuition: No, but delivery to lessons possible.
Hours: 9.00-5.30. Ages: 2-5. Cost: 900.00 per week (with meals). Must bring innoculation book.
La Crèche du Village
Tuition: No. Hours: 8.30-12.30 and 1.30-5.30.
Ages: 6mths-2yr. Cost: 1,020.00 per week (with meals). Must bring innoculation book. Reductions for second child.

Special skiing facilities

Summer skiing Extensive area with 12 lifts, 2780m to 3568m.
Cross-country 1km, 2km, 3km and 8km loops, northern end of resort (Petit Alpe and La Molière). 4km and 8km trails at Venosc (reached by gondola) with links to Bourg d'Oisans.

Lift passes

Red 'Super Ski'
Covers all lifts, ski-bus, entry to swimming pool and skating rink, and discounts at the fitness centre. (63 lifts in total.)
Cost 6 days 740.00 (£76.29). Low season: 630.00 saving 15%.
Credit cards accepted Yes.
Senior citizens 560.00 (over 60) saving 24%.
Children 560.00 (under 13) saving 24%. Free pass up to age 4.
Notes Main pass of 6 days or more includes one day's skiing in each of the following resorts; Alpe d'Huez, Serre-Chevalier, Montgenèvre, Clavière, Cesana, Sestrière, Sansicario and Sauze d'Oulx. Passes of 11 days or more include 2 days in each resort.
Beginners 2 free lifts, and blue 'Ski première trace' pass.
Short-term passes Half-day.
Other passes 3 limited area passes: blue 'ski première trace' covers 19 lifts (68.00 per day), pink 'ski sympa' covers 27 lifts (88.00 per day), yellow 'grand ski' covers 39 lifts (110.00 per day). Ski Tonic pass (6 days, 895.00) gives morning access to fitness centre and afternoon access to lifts.

Ski school

ESF
Classes 9.15-12.15 and/or 2.30-5.00. Cost: 590.00 (6 mornings). 490.00 afternoons.
Lift priority Yes (small groups only).
Children's classes Ages: 6-13. Cost: 460.00 (6 mornings). 380.00 6 afternoons. 750.00 6 full days.
Private lessons available 1½hr over lunchtime or all day Sunday. Cost: 140.00 per hour. 1-2 people.
Ski Ecole Internationale de St-Christophe
Classes 9.30-12.00 and/or 2.30-5.00. Cost: 530.00 (6 half-days). 6 full days cost 1,020.00. Package of tuition and lift pass 1,640.00 per week.
Lift priority Yes (small groups only).
Children's classes Ages: 6-13. Cost: 405.00 (6 half-days). 6 full days 770.00.
Private lessons available Hourly. Cost: 165.00 per hour. 1-4 people.

What was new in 91

New snow machines at bottom of runs to village.

location is reportedly far from ideal when snow conditions are poor.

Après-ski is plentiful and lively, with a number of interesting and good restaurants, entertaining bars (many with happy hours, some with live music, others video) and discos – the high entry charges of which may be halved by means of tour operators' discount tickets. Recommended bars are the noisy Mike's, near the Jandri station ('very British, ESF prize-giving venue') and the Windsor (aka the Pub); and the Rodeo at the Venosc end – 'loud, rowdy and messy', 'cheapest beer and slammers in town', 'good table service' and 'an amazing mechanical bull'. Of the restaurants, Le Bambon offers 'attentive service and good raclette', the Crêpes a Gogo is an old log cabin doing 'excellent food at reasonable prices', Smokey Joe's Café is recommended for 'English food with tomato sauce' and Le Petit Marmite for a friendly French atmosphere and food. The Belle Auberge is a 'super formal' restaurant. Le Pregentiz near the Jandri station is highly recommended for 'fantastic cakes and ice-creams'.

Les Deux Alpes is not ideal for **cross-country** skiers but Venosc has a long network of peaceful cross-country trails in the Vénéon valley (below Les Deux Alpes at the low altitude of around 950m, reached by gondola). It is not a resort in which **non-skiers** are likely to feel at home, though they too can enjoy outings to the valley and there are good sports facilities (including some in Le Village); there is even a pass available combining morning access to the 2 Alpes Tonic sports complex and afternoon access to the ski-lifts.

Nursery slopes are at the foot of the steep slopes on the west-facing side of the village beside Alpe de Venosc. Although not a very extensive area, these serve the purpose well enough. But the huge area of easy skiing on the glacier and the long runs below it makes this very much a resort where beginners should be encouraged to get up the mountain at an early stage.

We have generally encouraging reports on both **ski schools**. A local ex-champion freestylist runs courses of adventure skiing, including freestyle, monoski and off-piste.

La Grave 1450m

A pleasant alternative to staying in Les Deux Alpes is La Grave, a little village straddling the road up to the Col du Lauteret which has a number of small, simple hotels – one reporter recommends the Edelweiss. There are a couple of cafés and bars – including a popular crêperie – and several shops (both food and sports). The ski school uses the nursery slopes at Le Chazelet (opposite the main Meije gondola), but La Grave is far from ideal for beginners. The local mountain guides are highly regarded but apparently expensive.

Tourist office ✆ 76799005. **Package holidays** Chalets and Hotels Unlimited (h) Fresh Tracks (h) Quest Travel (schools) (h) Ski Challenge (hs).

Short-circuit skiing

Risoul, Vars France 1850m

Risoul and Vars are two very different resorts sharing the biggest linked ski area in the southern Alps (south of Briançon). Among the drawbacks, reporters note the long airport transfers (four hours plus from Grenoble, slightly less from Turin).

Vars, which attracts a chic French clientele, is the longer-established and larger of the two and has more skiing. It has more to it than ski-fields and apartments – varied shopping, lively après-ski, some attractive hotels, good walks and cross-country trails, and several mountain restaurants. But it is ugly, and set in a rather enclosed position.

Risoul is a new resort in a beautiful open situation with splendid views over a once-strategic junction of valleys (complete with fortifications) towards the highest peaks of the southern Alps. It resembles a real village, with large wood-clad buildings grouped loosely around a main street, and an annoying amount of traffic. At the top of the village and the foot of the pistes is a broad, sunny plateau with an arc of apartment buildings and café terraces. Risoul is small, but less claustrophobic and better equipped with bars and restaurants than many similar places. There is skating, and long cross-country trails around the mountain. Reporters staying in the Club Leo Legrange seemed content with its food and facilities (including crêche and free disco). The conveniently situated Melezes apartments are apparently 'spacious and beautifully equipped'; but avoid the restaurant underneath them. Reporters recommend La Bergerie for good food and service, and the Oasis for 'delicious specialities'. There is a disco in the hotel Dahu.

The ski area consists mainly of broad bowls above the two resorts, facing east and north respectively. They are nearly back-to-back, but the neighbouring peaks at the top of the two areas are separated by a saddle, now equipped with lifts. Neither area is very large, and few of the runs are challenging or long – the lifts above the two resorts approach 2600m, with a chain of drags on the extremity of the Vars area reaching 2750m; but, provided the links are open, there is plenty of scope for energetic intermediate skiers. Most of the Risoul side is gentle and particularly suitable for inexperienced skiers, with an excellent, sunny, secluded beginners' area. Vars also has some attractive woodland runs on the opposite side of its valley. One recent reporter found the drags linking Risoul with Vars were too steep for children and beginners, which rather limited the area they could ski in.

There are kindergartens in both resorts, and SEI as well as ESF ski schools. We have favourable reports of both adult and children's classes – 'they transformed our sons' ideas of ski school'.

Tourist offices Risoul ✆ 92460260; Vars-les-Claux ✆ 92465131.

Package holidays Risoul: Quest Travel (schools) (h) SkiBound (jas) SnowRanger (s) Thomson (hcs); Vars: Chalets and Hotels Unlimited (hcs) Sarac Ski (cs) Ski Bound (hj) SkiTonic (h) SnowRanger (s).

Pra-Loup France 1600m

Linked resort: La Foux d'Allos

Pra-Loup is one of the major resorts of the southern French Alps, second only to Serre-Chevalier and Vars in its number of lifts and visitor beds, and is linked by lift and lift pass to La Foux d'Allos. The main centre, Pra-Loup 1600, is a compact village on a mountain shelf above the Ubaye valley, purpose-built (mainly in the 1960s) with no regard for appearance. Pra-Loup 1500 is a smaller, less concentrated development on the road up. The ski area is best suited to intermediates; wide, varying terrain both above and below the tree-line. The slopes immediately above 1600, lightly wooded and facing north-east, are reached by gondolas from either end of the village, supplemented by chairs and drags at resort level and higher up, with a top height of around 2100m. The runs are easy and intermediate, the only black not difficult. Further chairs and drags link around the flanks of the mountain to the higher points of Le Péguieou and Le Lac (both around 2500m); from the former there are wide and sunny green and blue runs towards 1500, and from the latter red pistes go off southwards to connect with La Foux d'Allos via Les Agneliers. The area has a few friendly mountain restaurants; particularly recommended are the Costebelle and the Dalle en Pente, at the top of the two gondolas. Queueing is not usually a problem but some of the lifts are old and slow and need to be upgraded. Reports of the ski school are mixed; most are complimentary, some are critical of large classes and disorganisation.

There is not much to do but ski; 1600 has a natural ice rink, 1500 an indoor tennis hall. Nightlife revolves around hotel bars, restaurants and discos. Notable exceptions are Gray's bar and the Shamrock disco in 1600 centre and a good pizzeria, Le Pinguouin, overlooking the ice-rink. Accommodation is in hotels and apartments. The Marmotel hotel is convenient but fairly basic and used by school groups, as are Les Bergers and Les Airelles. There is a fair-sized shopping arcade and a reasonably stocked supermarket. Buses run infrequently down to the nearby town of Barcelonnette.

Although only a few miles to the south of Pra-Loup, La Foux d'Allos is not linked to it by road in winter but is approached from the south; flights go into Nice, and the three-hour transfer is 'not for the nervous or travel-sick'. It is a purpose-built resort, but neither as convenient nor as hideous as many others. The most recent developments, in particular, have plenty of pitched roofs and wood cladding. Reporters have commented on the friendly attitude of the locals towards the considerable influx of British visitors. Accommodation (hotels and apartments) is all convenient for the ski lifts; the Sestrière hotel is the most upmarket. There is not much to interest non-skiers (an ice rink and snow scooters) and only a couple of discos for après-skiers; but our reporters enthuse about the range and value of restaurants and the modest prices in the bars. Particularly recommended are the Thai restaurant and the British-run Verdon and Aiglon. We have no recent reports of the ski school or ski-kindergarten.

The skiing has much in common with that of Pra-Loup a mixture of lightly wooded and open slopes, with green, blue and red runs served by drags and chairs. A gondola goes up to the high point of the system at 2600m, giving a black north-east-facing descent of 800m to the village. Other slopes face all points of the compass, but most of the skiing, to the north of the resort on the way to Les Agneliers and so Pra-Loup, is sunny to some degree. A new drag-lift and a replacement four-seater chair-lift have improved the links to Pra-Loup.

Tourist offices La Fous d'Allos ℭ 92838070. Fax 92838627. Pra-loup ℭ 92841004. Fax 92840293.

Package holidays La Foux d'Allos Vacations (hs). Pra-loup Quest Total Ski (h), Ski Party Snow World (h), SkiBound (hj).

Island of dreams?

Isola 2000 France 2000m

Good for *Nursery slopes, skiing convenience, resort-level snow, sunny slopes, family holidays, freedom from cars*
Bad for *Alpine charm, not skiing, tough runs, après-ski, easy road access*

Isola 2000 is one of the southernmost of Alpine resorts, only an hour and a half from Nice up the tortuous gorges of the Tinée as the local taxis fly, but inaccessible from the north, which rules out the airports usually used by British tour operators. Despite this, British skiers account for a big chunk of the winter business, especially in low season.

The resort was created by a British property company in the 1960s. The present (Lebanese) owners value our custom, and to encourage it are happy to play along with tour operators' demands to run their own ski schools; they claim to be in a strong enough position to fend off the widely publicised attention of the French ski instructors' union which has been so disruptive elsewhere in the Alps.

Like other small resorts of its generation, Isola was conceived, with skiing families in mind, as a super-convenient all-in-one complex of shops, bars, economically designed apartments and hotels immediately beside the lift station and a sunny nursery area. This building (Front de Neige) survives as the heart of the resort, as convenient but also as dismally cheerless as ever, despite periodic refurbishings. In an attempt to raise the tone, the resort has added less convenient but prettier new colonies (Le Bristol, Le Hameau and Les Adrets) on the slopes behind Front de Neige, with bigger and better flats; and, most recently, an unashamedly luxurious chalet hotel, discreetly set up the hillside. Isola is a more interesting and less claustrophobic resort as a result, with an exceptionally wide range of accommodation. The ski area is rather less wide-ranging, but nicely varied, and well suited to beginners, leisurely intermediate skiers and families with small children.

Unlike other southern resorts, Isola is high enough for its owner to scorn artificial snow and yet offer a worthwhile snow guarantee: a free lift pass on another occasion if you can't ski down to Front de Neige or if less than half the lifts are working. Most of the lifts are clustered in the densely mechanised central sector above Front de Neige, so it is possible for two out of the ski area's three sectors (and most runs of interest to good skiers) to be closed without triggering the guarantee. Last winter Isola reported excellent conditions well into spring, but claims that its microclimate brings ultra-reliable snow conditions should be treated with scepticism – like all such claims. The resort's unique sun guarantee is offered only to self-caterers: a free week's accommodation another time, if the resort's heliograph registers no sun for more than three consecutive days in a week.

Despite its name, Isola is not entirely isolated. Skiers with a car may

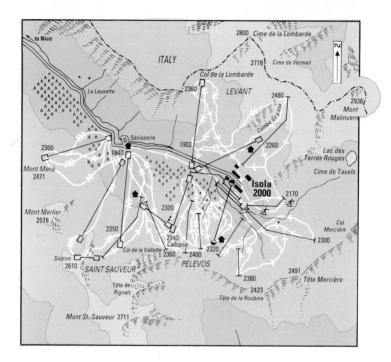

be tempted by a day in Auron (with skiing which is reportedly less convenient than Isola's, and certainly less reliable for snow, but more challenging).

The skiing top 2610m bottom 1800m

The resort's piste map employs a sensible division of the skiing into three areas, though all are linked – the south-west-facing slopes of Domaine du Levant, and the north-east-facing slopes split by the Tête de la Cabane into the Domaine du Pélevos, immediately above the resort, and the Domaine du Saint Sauveur, further west.

The **Pélevos** area is densely equipped with pistes and lifts, the major one being a gondola which departs directly from the resort building. From the top (2320m) there are satisfyingly varied easy and intermediate runs back down through the patchy trees, and links in both directions to drags which go slightly higher. If you go east, you can get to a long green run, well away from the lifts, which is splendid for near beginners in the right conditions, but hard work if there is new snow. If you go west, a drag gives access to further varied runs to the resort and makes the link with the Saint Sauveur area. Skiing down to the big car park at 1900m (the main way into the skiing for day visitors, below the resort) brings you to a chair which forms another link with the Saint Sauveur area as well as serving its own worthwhile red and black runs.

Saint Sauveur is the serious sector, with satisfying skiing for intermediates and experts. The skiing in this area has been modified in recent years, with existing lifts lengthened and shortened, new lifts added and pistes rearranged. A drag and short chair take you to the high point of Isola's skiing, the Cime de Sistron (2610m), on the flank of Mont Saint Sauveur. There are red and blue variants of the run back down, and off the back of the mountain is a short black leading to a long red down and a return drag on a partly wooded slope which until recently accommodated three black runs and no lifts. Further across the mountainside is the chair-lift towards Mont Mené, which has now been abbreviated to cut out the problematic area at the summit, which was very exposed to wind. There are black and red variants of the run to the bottom of the chair, not greatly different in difficulty. The return from this whole sector to the slopes above the resort depends on the Génisserie chair, once a famous bottle-neck but now tripled in capacity.

Once back up the Génisserie chair, a choice of lifts takes you back over la Cabane to the Pélevos slopes, and runs either to the resort or down to 1900m, where the main chairs go up to the Levant area – the Col de la Lombarde and Combe Grosse. These serve south- and south-west-facing slopes which are distinctly gentler than those opposite, mainly on open mountainsides above the trees. Easy traverses from this area link with drag-lifts at the head of the valley serving long, flat green runs which are an uphill extension of the nursery slopes.

The lift system works well enough, and as far as we know **queues** are only a problem at weekends. Two evenings a week the Belvedere slope immediately above the resort is floodlit. There is no **artificial snow**, but there is an unusual snow guarantee (see introduction).

Mountain restaurants are few, but adequate for a small ski area with good lifts out of the resort, permitting trouble-free lunching at base. The Génisserie (at the bottom of Saint Sauveur) is stylishly rustic.

The resort

The 'resort' consists mainly of a zigzag series of modern blocks linked by a meandering spinal corridor which will convey you to wherever you want to go within the main complex, including no fewer than 30 shops which are sufficiently flashy to betray Isola's second role as a venue for weekend sprees from the Côte d'Azur. Residents of Le Hameau have their own supermarket, ski shop and restaurant, but for other requirements are dependent on the mother ship. To get to and from it they are now provided with a free funicular.

Accommodation is mainly in apartments, though there are hotels. The three original hotels are spaced along the Front de Neige building, arranged in price order from up-piste, down-market Le Druos ('warm, nice atmosphere, plenty of hot water') via the Pas du Loup to down-piste, up-market Le Chastillon. Out on a sunny limb (although only a short traverse from an easy piste) stands a handsome new chalet hotel, the Diva, neither grand nor conventionally luxurious but very expensive (£70 to £130 a night for half-board), and excellent in all respects – beautiful bedrooms, impeccable service and outstanding food from an alumnus of Le Gavroche. The resort brochure contains detailed plans of apartments; those in Les Adrets have impressed reporters although one complains of traffic noise at anti-social hours, those in Le Hameau have not. A handful of individual chalets have been built, and more are on the way. The Bristol apartments are new and claim to be luxurious.

Apart from the hotel Diva, where there is a a piano bar, **après-ski** is confined to Front de Neige. The bars do good business in the early evening (the Rendezvous is 'very friendly'), as (we are assured) do the two discos later on at weekends and peak holiday times. At other times, Isola winds down from quiet to silent at an early hour. 'Après-ski hardly exists', reports a regular New Year visitor. Of the restaurants in and

---

Facts on Isola 2000   Alpes-Maritimes **France**

Prices in francs
Ski Club represented

Tourist office
Postcode 06420
Tel 93231515
Fax 93231425
Tlx 461644

Getting there
By road 1,325km from Calais. Via the Côte d'Azur (roads from the north-west which look more direct on the map are in practice very slow); chains often needed.
By rail Nice; 2 or 3 buses daily from station.
By air Nice; transfer 1½hr.

Staying there
Visitor beds 8,220; breakdown: 220 in hotels, 8,000 in apartments.
Package holidays Made to Measure (has) Neilson (hs) Ski Party Snow World (s) Thomson (h) Vacations (hs) .
Medical facilities In resort: Medical centre with doctor and chemist. Ambulance helicopter. Hospital: Nice (85km).

Non-skiing activities
Indoor Swimming-pool, fitness centre (sauna, weight-training, boxing, yoga, aerobic and stretching classes), cinema, concerts.
Outdoor Natural ice-rink (skating, curling, football), hang-gliding, ice driving, motor trikes, snow-scooters, paragliding, cleared walks, floodlit skiing.

Kindergartens
Caribou
Tuition: Yes. Hours: 9.00-5.15. Ages: 3-10. Cost: 850.00 per week (with meals).
Les P'tites Canailles
Tuition: Possible. Hours: 8.30-5.30. Ages: 2 up. Cost: 700.00 per week (lunch available on request).
Other childcare facilities
Baby-sitting service available from Tourist Office.

Special skiing facilities
Summer skiing No.
Cross-country 4km long, above the village.

Lift passes
Isola 2000
Covers all Isola lifts. (22 lifts in total.)
Cost 6 days 577.00 (£59.48). Low season: 520.00 saving 10%.
Credit cards accepted Yes.
Senior citizens 455.00 (over 60) saving 21%.
Children 455.00 (under 12) saving 21%.
Notes Students (12-24) 520.00 all season.
Beginners Limited area Mini-Pass (97.00 per day).
Short-term passes Half-day (from 12.30) and weekend passes available.

Ski school
ESF
Classes 2hr am and/or pm. Cost: 430.00 (6 days). Group Ski – groups of 4 or 5, 2½ hr per day for 6 days, costs 540.00.
Lift priority Yes.
Children's classes Ages: Up to 12. Cost: 430.00 (6 days).
Private lessons available Per day. Cost: 145.00 per hour. Up to 3 people.

What was new in 91
1. New 550-place car park.
2. New drag-lift providing better access to the Chastillon beginners' slope.
3. New 4-seater chair-lift Pignalls to replace old lift in St Sauveur sector.

What is new for 92
Replacement 4-seater chair-lift, and a new drag-lift planned.

around Front de Neige, the Cow Club in the middle of the nursery slope usually has the best atmosphere; the pizzas are good, too. There are weekly torchlit descents and fireworks. Baby-sitting can be arranged by the tourist office.

It is not a good resort for **cross-country** skiers or **non-skiers** – though the facilities for non-skiing activities are being improved. The small swimming-pool has already been replaced by a larger one (though it remains outdoor) and there is a new ice rink; like the old one it is positioned, logically but depressingly, in the shade of the main building.

The **nursery slopes** are superb, running the length of the resort, and the progression to real pistes is so gradual as to be imperceptible.

For most recent British visitors to Isola, ski instruction has been provided by the tour operator, usually with a mixture of British and local instructor seconded from the ESF and able to provide specialist instruction – in monoski and surf for example. Whether this harmonious co-operation will survive the current campaign to preserve French instructors' jobs for French instructors remains to be seen. Reporters have certainly found the tuition satisfactory in both Vacations and Neilsons' **ski schools**. The ESF uses Ski Evolutif (short skis) for beginners. The **ski kindergarten** takes the form of a 'children's village', with indoor as well as outdoor activities, and for younger children there is a new nursery (with beds) which the tourist office says is 'very well equipped'. Reports are favourable.

Pyrenean preamble

Reflections on the view that small is friendly

Early editions of the *Guide* provoked tourist offices, tour operators and readers alike to tell us that we had not done justice to the delights of Pyrenean skiing, more particularly French Pyrenean skiing. We had reports of enviably happy holidays in resorts plentifully supplied with snow and, to their mind, not short of charm either. They told us that any idea that Pyrenean snow is unreliable is quite unfounded, that the people are welcoming, and that the price is right. We duly returned for a Pyrenean tour of duty in early February 1987, and found snow conditions that gave us every incentive to reflect on these important matters while sitting in bars. Since then, the interest of UK tour operators and (to judge by the reports we receive) of *Guide* readers in minor Pyrenean resorts has dwindled. But here, as a preface to our reports on the few resorts on which readers do report, are some wide-ranging observations on Pyrenean skiing in general.

First, the contentious subject of snowfall. There is no evidence of less precipitation in the Pyrenees than in the Alps. If anything there is more, especially in winter. But there is plenty of evidence that the Pyrenean winter is significantly milder than the Alpine one, not because the region is further south, but because it is further west and nearer the warm Atlantic. As well as snow it sees plenty of rain and rapid thaw, and even in the depths of winter it is often mild.

The Pyrenees also have a more pronounced influence on the climate than the Alps. Simply stated, the ski resorts on the northern side of the chain (the French resorts, plus Spanish Baqueira-Beret) are much more reliable for snow than those on the southern side. Then, the Mediterranean side of the Pyrenees is much drier than the Atlantic side. The main French resorts are concentrated in a relatively small area at the centre of the chain. The Spanish resorts are more spread out and there may be a greater divergence between their snowfall, something which is hard to assess when there is little snow at any of them (except Baqueira). On the Spanish side the ski area closest to the Med is that of La Molina and Masella, a notoriously risky place for snow. Although nearly all of Andorra is on the southern side of the Pyrenees, and closer to the Mediterranean than the Atlantic, its main ski areas are high and straddle the mountain barrier. Good snow conditions are by no means exceptional.

Brochures have traditionally made a big thing of how welcoming local people are in the Pyrenees. Sceptics may read between the lines and conclude that there are few good things to be said about more tangible aspects of Pyrenean resorts. But there is no denying the importance of the atmosphere in a resort in determining the success or failure of most people's ski holidays. It is what the enduring popularity of many small Austrian resorts is based on, and it is what counts more than anything else in the Pyrenees. People seem to be genuinely pleased to receive visitors and anxious to make sure that they enjoy themselves. This helps to compensate for the lack of the frills that adorn the well-wrapped Austrian tourist package, with its sleigh rides, ice-rinks, saunas, whirlpools, tea dances and Tyrolean evenings.

For many people the most important part of the Pyrenean welcome is ski school. Following the example of Andorra, where the British-run school has made a great success of ensuring that people enjoy learning to ski, schools in several of the French resorts are listening to what the British operators tell them. The instructors are being made to learn English and organise separate classes for British skiers, and are not too proud to mix with the tourists in the evenings. This is all old hat in the Tyrol, of course; perhaps for that very reason there seems to be an enthusiasm in these Pyrenean resorts that may be lacking in resorts where they have been going through the routine for decades.

Equally important is straightforward friendliness. In too many upmarket Alpine resorts, the skier with money to spend is clearly regarded as someone to be milked as speedily as possible, while the skier without money to spend is regarded as a waste of expensively furnished space. And there is no doubt in our minds that this is not true of the Pyrenees. People go to Spain in summer because they do not get this kind of reception; the atmosphere is usually relaxed and friendly. For skiing purposes this is almost as true on the French side of the Pyrenees as in Spain. Cheap-and-cheerfulness is an even greater part of the appeal of duty-free Andorra. Perhaps too many of us succumb to the temptation of cheap-skate holidays (self-catering) in expensive resorts where we are out of place and grumpy. In a cheaper resort we could relax, enjoy ourselves and perhaps find to our surprise that the limitations of the skiing weren't so intolerable after all.

Part of the reason that the Pyreneans are pleased to see the British is that we represent the only foreign business they can hope to attract. It may or may not be a plus point that in the resorts served by British operators almost all non-natives are British, apart from some Spaniards in France, a few French in Spain, and both in Andorra. Outside Andorra the British presence is small in absolute numbers; but it can still be quite dominant, especially out of season.

If your picture of a mountain village has the timbered prettiness of Switzerland and Austria, the Pyrenees may come as a bit of a shock. The usual building material is stone, and even the most handsome old villages are not colourful. In France you face an unappealing choice between grey spas (Barèges and Cauterets) and purpose-built resorts which are no more attractive than their Alpine counterparts (La Mongie, Piau-Engaly, Pla d'Adet). Only St-Lary has any charm as a village. In Spain the purpose-built resorts (Formigal and Baqueira) are more stylish, and the old village resorts (notably Cerler) are much more appealingly rustic. There are some beautiful old buildings in Andorra, but generally the Principality seems an architectural rubbish heap.

Barèges France 1250m

Good for *Big ski area, short airport transfers, sunny slopes, nursery slopes, Pyrenean charm*
Bad for *Tough runs, resort-level snow, late holidays, not skiing, mountain restaurants*

Linked resort: La Mongie

Many a skier disillusioned by anonymous French ski resorts must have wondered where to go in search of somewhere combining the charm of a real unspoilt French country village with the sport of a large, varied ski area. Our shortlist of possible answers (and it would be short) would include a few Alpine resorts and Barèges, which is among the friendliest Pyrenean resorts and has a half share in the largest Pyrenean ski area. A dull-looking grey spa, it is not at all institutional and has a cheerful, intimate atmosphere, partly due to its very small size. All our recent reporters have enjoyed being in a 'real French village' and have commented on the friendliness of the 'real French people' in it. Prices are low by French standards. But there is not much to do apart from ski and soak up the sulphur in the spa-water pool.

Barèges was one of the first ski resorts in the Pyrenees, with some famous long runs through the woods to the village. These now form only a small part of a long lift system following the course of a road which in summer leads over the Col du Tourmalet to the modern resort of La Mongie. Although hardly the Trois Vallées, the area offers plenty of variety of slope, scenery and, usually, snow conditions.

La Mongie is larger and higher than Barèges but has no more facilities to offer. It has the less varied half of the ski area, and lacks the charm of Barèges. We have reports that La Mongie is much less unfriendly than it looks; it could hardly be more so. It makes a better choice for novices, with easy slopes around the resort that keep their snow relatively well. The lifts linking the two resorts can be closed in bad weather, and the taxi-ride home is reported to cost £60.

The skiing top 2350m bottom 1250m

An approximately M-shaped arrangement of two hills immediately above Barèges offers the only woodland skiing, reached by either of the two access lifts from the resort. The **Ayré** funicular climbs steeply in two stages through the woods and serves fine red and black runs down to the Lienz clearing – about the most satisfying skiing in the area, especially when conditions are good all the way down to the resort. The trees help to conserve the snow, at least on the upper parts. Although these sweeping runs are not terrifyingly steep there is no easy way down from Ayré; but inexperienced skiers can make their way easily

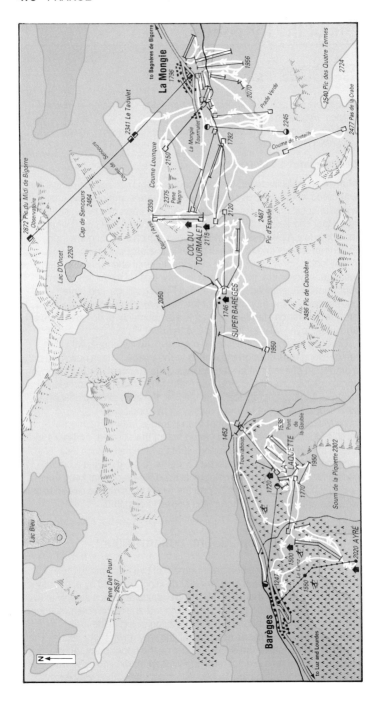

across from the mid-station, mainly used by cross-country skiers, to Lienz. Of the two runs from there down to Barèges, the green is a road starting with an uphill section and is rarely used, the red is fairly straightforward but often has unreliable snow near the bottom.

The **Laquette** gondola is the busiest of the access lifts, being the most direct route towards La Mongie as well as the way up to the ski school meeting place, a congregation area on a knoll with restaurant and nursery area. A variety of short intermediate pistes, from green to red, covers the flanks of the hill, west-facing down to Lienz and east-facing down to Tournaboup, but there are no runs through the woods below the lift directly down to Barèges.

Tournaboup is where the Col du Tourmalet road ends in winter, and is also the end of the woods. There is a small nursery area beside a large car-park, and a long chair-lift over a wide, moderately steep west-facing mountainside, unpisted but tempting and much skied in good conditions. From the top of the lift an uncomplicated link run leads on to **Superbarèges**, a grand name for what is no more than an undistinguished restaurant in the pit of a wide theatre of snow-fields. There are fairly steep west-facing slopes below the Col du Tourmalet, including some short, stiff mogul-fields (well worth avoiding in the morning) and some easier blue and green runs. A new development to the north of Superbarèges, below the Lac d'Oncet, will add a new dimension to this area. Below Superbarèges, the run back to Tournaboup and Barèges is a very long path beside road and river (and across both), a pretty enough way home into the sunset, but not very interesting skiing and often crowded. Being so flat, at least it holds the snow fairly well; but in sticky snow it is hard work.

As the toiling Tour de France cyclists probably have little chance to appreciate, there are fine long views east and west from the ridge beside the **Col du Tourmalet**, although the mountains themselves are not particularly beautiful. The eastern slopes are gentler and all the runs directly down to **La Mongie** are wide and generally easy. The rocky slopes flanking the resort and road, facing north and south, are steeper and both have lifts, although the terrain does not allow a very wide network of skiing. The main lift on the north-facing side is a gondola serving a blue run down, a long gully which sees almost no sun. The 4 Termes chair-lift has added to this run and also gives access to a very long (and by all accounts beautiful) off-piste itinerary down the Aygues Cluses valley, ending up at Tournaboup. The most challenging piste skiing in this area is beneath the Prade Berde chair-lift, on steep runs that are often closed.

On the south-facing side of La Mongie the Pic du Midi cable-car is a ski-lift only as far as the first station (2340m). There are plans to allow skiers up to and down from the observatory on top (2877m), which would add an exciting new dimension. The slopes beneath the nearby Sud chair-lift are not gentle, and the single blue run down includes an awkward and unavoidable narrow section. On this sunny side of the mountains, the most interesting runs are reached from the top of the Coume Louque drag and chair, a splendid viewpoint. One run follows a valley back down to La Mongie, the other leads down a wide south-west facing coomb to Superbarèges; the start is exposed and followed by a sequence of pitches steep enough to be graded black. Here, too, morning ice is to be expected. A variant is another favourite off-piste itinerary, round to the Lac d'Oncet, a good place for spring snow (often in midwinter). The proposed development up this valley has begun with the construction of the Toue drag-lift.

Mountain restaurants are adequate in number, at least above Barèges, and inexpensive (by Alpine standards), but not particularly appealing, with the notable exceptions of the delightful Chez Louisette at Lienz and the recently reopened restaurant at the Col du Tourmalet. Of several sunny places in La Mongie, Le Yeti is recommended.

As usual in the Pyrenees, **queues** can be a serious weekend problem and a very serious Sunday one. Barèges itself cannot cope with many cars, and the lifts from the top of the village and from Tournaboup are oversubscribed. The Col du Tourmalet can be a bottle-neck in either direction. The queues are reportedly 'refreshingly orderly'. Two regular visitors say that money is not being invested in the present lift system and that the lifts are 'outdated and slow'. There is no **artificial snow**.

The resort

Barèges is a tiny village, little more than a single street climbing steeply beside a river, narrowly enclosed at the feet of wooded mountainsides. This is no place for a village, and none would have grown up had it not been for the hot springs, which became famous in the 17th century. But it was not until the 19th century that avalanche barriers allowed the construction of permanent buildings, which stand today grey and undistinguished (except for the spa itself, a mixture of smart renovation and grand old church-like buildings at the top of the village).

Having a car is of no great value in Barèges, and parking space is limited. The ski-bus, covered by the lift pass, cannot cope when runs to the village are closed and many skiers end up at Tournaboup.

Accommodation is in simple, ordinary, old-fashioned, inexpensive hotels, none with more than two official stars. At least one has been given over to British use on a chalet basis. We have mostly enthusiastic reports on the Europe and the Richelieu, neighbours not too inconveniently placed just below the funicular station and about five minutes' walk (uphill) from the main lift station. The Central is pleasant but old-fashioned, the Poste rather neglected. We have consistently good reports on the English-run Les Sorbiers, a cross between a chalet and a small hotel – 'high standard of accommodation, good food and atmosphere'. Self-caterers will find Barèges limited, both for shopping ('very basic') and eating out. We have a favourable report of the 'excellent' bakery in the village.

Après-ski consists of nothing more than a few bars (including one run by the mayor, so behave), a couple of restaurants and two discos. About the liveliest place is the Oncet. Restaurant recommendations include Le Ranch ('delicious kebabs', 'very good five-course menu') and

La Rozelle ('for fondues and crêpes'). The main organised event is an evening, usually very jolly, up at Chez Louisette organised by the ski school (Pyrenean meal – 'so much food it was obscene!' – and torchlit descent). The Barèges locals party late; the discos don't open till 11.00pm and don't fill up till 1.00am. Hotels facing on to the main street are frequently disturbed when they empty in the early hours. There is a cinema.

There are reasonable **cross-country** possibilities, on and off piste, in woods around Lienz. Although there are lots of easy, beautiful walks, Barèges is not recommended for **non-skiers**. Skiers can show off bruises in the warm, smelly, 'immaculately kept but expensive' spa pool, open every evening. There is also a small swimming pool, and a second one, complete with jacuzzi, is being built.

Facts on Barèges Hautes-Pyrenees **France**

Prices in francs

Tourist office
Postcode 65120
Tel 62926819
Fax 62926660
Tlx 521995

Getting there
By road 1,135km from Calais. Via Toulouse, Tarbes. The road up from Luz (6km) is narrow, but chains are rarely needed.
By rail Lourdes (37km); SNCF bus to resort, 4 daily.
By air Lourdes; transfer 1hr. (Or Tarbes; transfer about 1hr.)

Staying there
Visitor beds 2,000; breakdown: 1,500 in apartments, 500 in hotels.
Package holidays SnowRanger (hs) Thomson (hs) Winter Adventure Holidays (hs) .
Medical facilities In resort: Fracture clinic, doctors, chemist.

Non-skiing activities
Indoor Sauna, massage, spa bath, cinema, casino.
Outdoor Hang-gliding, parascending, tennis.

Kindergartens
Hospitalet
Tuition: No. Hours: 9.00-5.00. Ages: 2-8. Cost: 720.00 per week (meals available).
Le Club Marmotte
Tuition: Yes. Hours: 9.30-4.30. Ages: 3-7. Cost: 540.00 per week (with meals).

Special skiing facilities
Summer skiing No.
Cross-country 15km near Lienz, reached by funicular.

Lift passes
Barèges-La Mongie
Covers all lifts in Barèges, Tourmalet and La Mongie and the ski bus. (56 lifts in total.)
Cost 6 days 540.00 (£55.67). Low season: 517.00 saving 4%.
Credit cards accepted Yes.
Free pass up to age 6.
Notes Reductions for children and OAPs on day pass.
Beginners Beginners' card (57.00) covers Laquette or Lienz and their drag lifts.
Short-term passes Half-day for Barèges only; single ascents on the Lienz funicular.
Other passes Barèges-Tourmalet, covers 27 lifts, costs 445.00 per week; can be extended to cover La Mongie.

Ski school
ESF
Classes 2hr: 10.00-12.00 or 2.00-4.00 (school holidays only). Cost: 270.00 (6 half-days). Substantial price difference during French school holidays (6 days 320.00).
Lift priority Yes.
Children's classes Ages: up to 12. Cost: 260.00 (6 half-days). Lunch 50.00.
Private lessons available Hourly. Cost: 130.00 per hour. 1-2 people. 170.00 for 3-5 people.
Special courses Parapenting school, 350.00 per day.
Ecoloski
Classes 3hr: 9.00-12.00 and/or 2.00-5.00. Cost: 350.00 (5 days).
Lift priority Yes.
Children's classes Ages: up to 12. Cost: 350.00 (5 days).
Private lessons available Hourly. Cost: 130.00 per hour. 1-3 people.
Special courses 2-day ski touring course, night in refuge hut, 500.00; 'Touche à Tout', 3-day course with parapenting, 1,000.00.

What was new in 91
New teleski de Toue to 2,050m south of Super Bareges.

Barèges has **nursery slopes** in all the main areas, except on the edge of the village itself. The main one is at the top of the Laquette gondola. There is no shortage of long green runs.

We continue to receive glowing reports of the commitment, enthusiasm and entertainment value of the small band of instructors at the Ecoloski **ski school** – 'they efficiently and quietly separated the groups, gave fantastic tuition and an excellent video review; I shall be back'. Equally enthusiastic reports of advanced classes – 'lots of off-piste, moguls, couloirs, and lots of fun' – contrast with our one recent lack-lustre report of the ESF.

La Mongie 1800m

La Mongie is an all-modern but far from new roadside resort in a high, bleak, treeless setting. Two resort units are linked by a bucket lift (day-time only) and an expanse of almost flat nursery slopes, which suffer only from being a thoroughfare. The main centre is the lower one, its focus a south-facing semi-circle of restaurants, shops and hotel buildings with a car park in the middle, lift stations nearby and a large number of dogs on the scrounge. As a whole La Mongie is a styleless and messy place, but it has a greater variety of bars, shops and restaurants than most small purpose-built resorts. There is almost nothing for non-skiers to do. The upper resort, known as Tourmalet or La Mandia, is a long angular modern complex with a three-star hotel, a restaurant and apartments, mostly with south-facing balconies. There are ski school and lift pass offices at both resort centres, and a kindergarten at the lower one. The road up from Bagnères-de-Bigorre is extremely busy on Sundays, and may be closed when the resort is deemed full.

Tourist office ✆ 62919415.

Andorra's box – duty-free-for-all

Soldeu, El Tarter, Pas de la Casa, Grau Roig, Arinsal, Pal, Arcalis

Note There are some general observations about skiing in the Pyrenees starting on page 475.

Andorra differs from the rest of the Pyrenees in being even cheaper (lifts, lessons and equipment are cheap, as well as meals and drinks), and in being very popular with British skiers and après-skiers, who have the benefit of a ski school run extremely well by the British, for the British. Throughout the principality the Anglo-influence runs deep, with lots of British and colonial expatriates living in retirement or running hotels, bars, restaurants, development companies and ski schools. Everyone seems to know everyone else and there is a very easy-going, friendly atmosphere which sets Andorra apart.

None of Andorra's ski areas is very large or challenging, but that doesn't seem to matter. You don't go there for tough skiing – or for comfortable accommodation, haute cuisine, charming surroundings, ice rinks, snowy paths, smooth-running bus services or comfortable sheltered gondola lifts. You go for sun, fun, a cheap holiday and lively après-ski. The recipe suits lots of young skiers (and lots of not so young ones) well. Après-ski revolves around bars, restaurants and discos. As well as ski-school celebrations, tour operators organise fancy dress parties, fondue outings, and bar crawls. Bar prices are very low, and skiers used to Alpine resorts, especially big French and Swiss ones, are amazed at how friendly and relaxed the atmosphere is, with free drinks flowing at the slightest excuse and lots of entertaining characters on both sides of the bar.

Andorra is a small duty-free principality with French and Spanish co-rulers. Spanish language (Catalan) and currency prevail, except in the north-east around Pas de la Casa, where the skiing and the supermarkets serve French weekenders. The single main road (42km long) carries heavy traffic from the Spanish border (850m) through the capital, Andorra La Vella, over the Port d'Envalira (2408m) to the French border at Pas de la Casa (2095m). La Vella is towny, characterless and a permanent traffic jam, and the road is lined by a succession of very ugly, shoddy modern villages – 'all the same, like abandoned building sites,' wrote one reporter. One of them is Soldeu (1800m), a small roadside development at the foot of the main ski area. Most British operators send their clients to hotels there or in Encamp (which has no skiing), about 20 minutes down the road. The side valleys north of La Vella have been more recently developed, with less ugly results. The main skiing here is near Arinsal. There is some accommodation in the village, and apartments within walking range of the lifts, but most packages to Arinsal use accommodation in La Massana a few miles towards La Vella. There is also skiing at Pas de la Casa and at two new developments, in their own side-valleys – Pal, close to La Massana, and Arcalis, further away to the north.

Andorra does not have much appeal for non-skiers, but there are reportedly good sports facilities La Massana and La Vella. Shopping is Andorra's main industry and tourist attraction. La Vella is a supermarket city where well-known brands of gin and whisky can be found for about £5 a litre and less well-known ones for a lot less. Bargains in ski equipment depend on special offers and haggling.

Access for air travellers is most convenient from Barcelona. Twice-daily 'service taxis' are affordable when shared. Transfer time is about 3 hours. Transfers from Toulouse (about 4 hours, 'very scenic') and coach trips from Britain are vulnerable to closure of the road; our

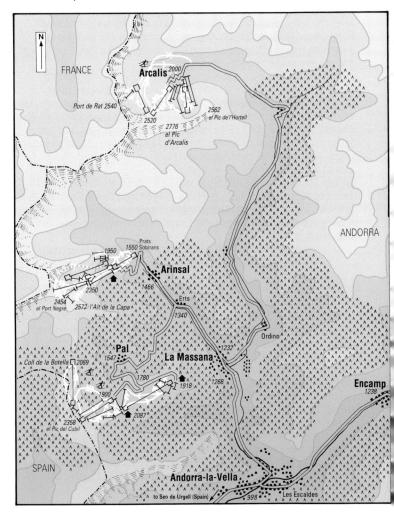

inspector endured a 17-hour journey to Toulouse via a rail-only tunnel. There are overnight trains from Paris to L'Hospitalet, with connecting buses.

For all skiers not staying in Soldeu, private transport is vital. Those with a car can reach all the skiing from a single base, but most skiers rely on tour operators' shuttle services, which do not allow much flexibility. There are public buses, but they are unreliable and infrequent and of most use to skiers based in La Vella. No lift pass covers all of Andorra, and skiers keen to explore have to use day passes.

The biggest and best of Andorra's ski areas is shared by Soldeu and its lower neighbour, El Tarter (1700m), a car park and lift station beside the road between Soldeu and Encamp, with a few hotels nearby. For those based in Soldeu, skiing starts with a precarious walk across a bridge from the village to the lifts, where skis and boots can be deposited. From here a two-stage chair-lift ascends to Pla dels Espiolets, a wide, sunny and varied nursery area with a restaurant, where prices are reported to be unreasonably high and the staff unpleasantly surly; most people take their own picnics which can be left at the ski school meeting place until lunch-time. Lifts in all directions serve a broad area of mostly easy open skiing between 2100m and 2560m, with some good, though short, off-piste runs in the basin beneath the rounded Tossa del Llosada. There are some longer and tougher runs, and some off-piste skiing, through the woods down to Soldeu and El Tarter. Several of the pistes to the village have artificial snow. The slopes are mostly north-facing and in good conditions,

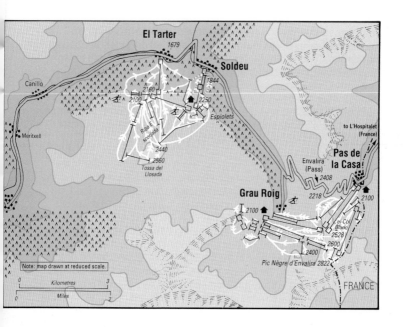

Soldeu provides excellent skiing for beginners and leisurely intermediates, including a 6km green run from top to bottom.

Visitors staying at Encamp are usually bussed to the other point of entry to the ski area, the chair-lift up from El Tarter. This connects with another long chair-lift up a flattish wooded slope (mainly used for cross-country skiing) to Pla dels Espiolets. Alternatively, a series of drags take you from the plateau above El Tarter to the area of open skiing below Tossa del Llosada. The only other mountain restaurant in the ski area is at the top of the El Tarter chair-lift; it is newer and much more pleasant than the one at Pla dels Espiolets, but no less expensive. From here, you have a choice of green or black runs back down to El Tarter. Queues are not normally a problem, except at weekends (when there are invasions from France) and half-term (when there is an invasion from Britain). Many of the lifts are old and slow and in need of modernisation. Recent reporters have complained of queues for the long drag-lift which connects Soldeu's nursery slopes with the main intermediate skiing above them. Reporters have been generally unimpressed by piste maintenance: 'Grooming was slow after two days of snowfall; the authorities seemed to be somewhat overwhelmed with the task'.

Soldeu itself is an unattractive ribbon development along a busy main road. There is one 'rather limited' supermarket and no bank in the village. **Accommodation** used by British operators is mostly very basic, and some of it primitive. About the best hotel in Soldeu is the new Sport, widely recommended, especially by families, for 'comfortable rooms and a good restaurant'. The Naudi is also a good choice.

Like Soldeu, Encamp has little to recommend it. Amongst the unattractive hotel blocks are a lot more half-built ones. Apparently the work-forces have recently been transferred to the Olympic sites in Barcelona, leaving many buildings unfinished. Of the hotels in Encamp, neither the Comtes de Foix nor the Hotel Encamp are recommended – the latter has 'grotty rooms, slow service, pathetic breakfasts'.

El Tarter has little accommodation at the moment, but this may soon change when the newly constructed 'mini resort' around the lift station is completed. We have a very enthusiastic report of two hotels in El Tarter: the Sant Pere and its neighbour El Chalet, another small family hotel, 'extremely comfortable and well run' by a British couple.

Après-ski starts at teatime in the Sol y Nieve (near the bottom main chair-lift up from Soldeu) or in popular bar of the hotel Bruxelles in the village itself. Restaurant recommendations include L'Squirrol (in Soldeu), Mephisto's and the Cava Pierrott (both in Encamp). The El Pi in Encamp offers a good four-course menu. Later on, the Edelweiss Lounge (opposite the Sport hotel) has Irish folk music or karaoke on offer. Bars in Encamp include Tito's and the Whiskey. Discos rarely get going much before midnight; entrance is often free, and the price of drinks not much higher than in the bars. El Duc is apparently the one 'real disco' in Soldeu, the Pussycat is also recommended. The Comtes de Foix in Encamp is lively but 'cramped and stuffy'. Several reporters complain of 'excessive rowdiness' when the bars and discos close in the early hours.

One of the big attractions of Soldeu is the excellent ski school staffed by English-speaking instructors of many nationalities, predominantly Australasian and British. A reporter's claim that it is 'the best ski school I have ever come across' is reflected by most other visitors. There is also an excellent children's ski school and a good kindergarten.

The most convenient access point for the **Pas de la Casa** skiing is Grau Roig (2040m), a collection of buildings near the main road. Ski-lifts climb up to the high ridge from both sides, providing a simple arrangement of open runs (about 500m vertical) facing west above Grau Roig, and north-east above Pas de la Casa (2095m). Development of the slopes to the west of Grau Roig has also begun and there are ambitious plans to eventually link it up with the Soldeu ski area. The scenery is bare and severe, and the terrain is not very varied, but snow is reliable and there is plenty of space. There are nursery slopes in Pas de la Casa and Grau Roig, and a cross-country trail in the latter. The ski school and kindergarten are well thought of.

Arinsal's skiing is at present much more confined, a narrow east-facing coomb with descents from about 2500m to a congregation area with ski deposit at 1950m, at the top of the chair-lift from the valley (1550m). To the right of this area are easy nursery slopes, served by four drags. To get back to the valley, there is a black run under the main chair, and an indirect blue route down. Plans to develop the neighbouring coombs are underway. One long blue run from the top has artificial snow. Arinsal is another blot on the Andorran landscape – 'we weren't expecting any Alpine charm, but it still came as a bit of a shock'. The Solona hotel is recommended ('excellent value, good food, service with a smile') as are the Prats Sobirans apartments, close to the lifts. Although Arinsal village now has about 4,000 beds, many people stay in nearby La Massana, which has a better choice of hotels, shops, bars and restaurants. Hotels include La Massana and the Rossell; the latter has 'three-foot baths and cardboard walls'.

New **Pal** is a smartly equipped skiing area with a greater variety of skiing in prettier scenery than most of the Andorran resorts, between 1810m to 2350m. There are attractive nursery runs on woodland clearings and a few gentle longer runs, most of them wooded. The area extends across a north-facing hillside, and involves a lot of traversing from lift to lift. There is some artificial snow.

In the far north, **Arcalis**, difficult to reach even at the best of times (the bus goes hourly) is in an even more embryonic state. It already provides some interesting skiing between 1940m and 2550m around a rugged north-facing bowl. English-speaking instruction here is uncommon.

Tourist offices Encamp ℰ 31405; La Massana ℰ 35693; Soldeu ℰ 51151.
Package holidays Arinsal: Andorra Holidays (has) Crystal (hs) Enterprise (hs) Neilson (hs) Thomson (hs); Encamp: Falcon (h) Top Deck (h); Pas de la Casa: Crystal (hs) Enterprise (hs) Horizon (hs) Neilson (hs); Soldeu: Crystal (hs) Enterprise (hs) Falcon (h) Freedom Holidays (hjas) Panorama's Ski Experience (hs) Ski Global (h) Skiworld (hs) Thomson (hs) Top Deck (hs).

Baqueira Beret Spain 1500m

Baqueira is a genuinely exclusive resort in the Spanish Pyrenees – a small modern development without any cheap hotels, and with more than its fair share of Ferraris, furs and leather. It lies at the head of the beautiful Val d'Aran, near Viella on the northern side of the Pyrenees, which means easy access from France and more reliable snow than in other Spanish resorts. Its skiing is interesting – a reasonably large and attractively varied area with a mixture of wooded and open ground and both gentle and steep runs. At the foot of the lifts is the original resort development – modern, uncompromising apartment blocks and hotels. Many regular visitors prefer to stay in the more traditional hotels further down the valley. There are 'particularly fine' Paradores in Viella and Arties. Because it is not cheap, Baqueira attracts few British tour operators. But its small British following is a fiercely loyal one; many swear by it, and almost all say they will return.

The ski area is divided into two halves by a narrow valley. The main hill, Cap de Baqueira (2500m), is directly above the resort and consists of a compact network of chairs and drags serving mainly intermediate runs on the west face of the mountain. The recent construction of three triple chair-lifts below the Cap de Argulls has added a significant new area on the right-hand side – mainly blue runs, with a couple of steeper pitches, graded red and black. There are some longer, challenging pistes on the north side of the Cap de Baqueira and a couple of itineraries down the wooded valley that separates it from the the wider and gentler slopes above Beret – a car park and restaurant complex at 1850m. From Orri (in the valley) a series of chair-lifts and easy pistes between 1800–2500m take you across the open mountainside to the furthest point of the lift system, Tuc det Dossau, which has two steep descents and an indirect blue one. Except on public holidays, queues are not a problem. The lift system (apparently modelled on that of Vail) is impressively efficient and has more than its fair share of fast quad chairs (including a new one from Baqueira to the nursery slopes at Torre de Control). We have enthusiastic reports of the ski school (although there is little spoken English) and ski kindergarten.

The resort itself lies beside the road up to the very high Bonaigua pass, often but not always closed in winter. Recent sympathetic development has increased its appeal as a base (there are some excellent shops, hotels, restaurants and leisure centre) and it apparently 'exudes a relaxed and friendly atmosphere'. Après-ski is genuinely Spanish; the numerous *tapas* bars fill up as soon as the lifts close. Despite its exclusive reputation, our reporters were pleasantly surprised to find resort prices lower than they expected.

Tourist office℗ (73) 645025
Package holidays: Ski Miquel (hcs).

Sun and snow (and wind)

Sierra Nevada Spain 2100m

Sierra Nevada is a high mountain range in the very south of Spain, near the ancient Moorish city of Granada; its skiing used to be marketed under the name of Sol y Nieve (Sun and Snow), and to add further to the confusion the purpose-built resort in which most skiers are accommodated (at 2100m) is known as Pradollano. The ski area is more than usually vulnerable to bad weather, and the mountain range as a whole is very exposed to Atlantic gales. When the weather here is bad, everything stops. But when conditions are good (and they often are), the skiing can be excellent and the views stunning. Because of the proximity of Granada (only 32km away) and the Costa del Sol, the resort suffers from extreme crowding at weekends and holiday times.

The main skiing area is reached by a new stand-up gondola or chair-lift from the edge of the village. To the right of the top gondola station (and 'cheap and cheerful' Borreguiles restaurant) is a small nursery area, consisting of short green runs served by baby drag-lifts and a chair. Most of the skiing is on the wide easy and intermediate slopes of Veleta (3470m), above Borreguiles. Of more interest to experts is the skiing around Loma de Dílar, a ridge served by chairs and drags with short, steep black runs down the face. These blacks provide some challenge, but the resort is more suited to beginners and intermediates.

Most of the Pradollano's buildings date from the 1960s and 1970s, but some is more recent . It is not an attractive place – 'just like Torremolinos with snow and litter' – but it is a bit livelier than many small purpose-built resorts, with a reasonable choice of nightlife . Bars fill up as soon as the lifts close. Crescendo Lodge is one of the liveliest. There is an impressive range of restaurants – local, French, Turkish, Italian. The Borreguiles is one of the most popular; arrive early – it is often full. Of the discos, the Sierra Nevada 53 is recommended. Accommodation is mainly in hotels; the Melia Sol y Nieve and the Melia Sierra Nevada, both near the main square, are convenient and pleasant. The Telecabina is not recommended. The chalet-style Parador, set on its own above Pradollano (accessible by chair-lift and piste), is fairly functional but has exceptional views. A recent reporter was unimpressed by their so-called luxury apartment – 'sparsely furnished and lacking basic equipment'. There are competing ski schools, and no shortage of spoken English. Recent reports suggest that standards vary from instructor to instructor. There is a kindergarten in the resort, and a ski kindergarten up at Borreguiles.

Apart from the obvious excursion to Granada (and the Alhambra), there is nothing for non-skiers to do. Shopping is limited, and reportedly expensive. The tortuous road up from Granada is beautiful but not for the nervous.

Tourist office ✆ (958) 480500. **Package holidays** Ski Global (h), Thomson (h).

Scotland: an overview

Last season was a good one for Scottish skiing, with plentiful snow in the New Year coinciding with anxiety about foreign travel to bring record numbers of skiers to the five areas. In order of skier volume, these are: Cairngorm, near Aviemore; Glenshee, near Braemar; Aonach Mor, six miles east of Fort William; The Lecht, between Grantown and Braemar; and Glencoe, south of Fort William. As in continental Europe, the later part of the season was too mild for the good of the snow.

The winter brought relief to an industry down on its luck after a run of bad seasons, and investment plans to improve and extend the ski areas may be brought down from the shelf. But these will not include the once-controversial Lurcher's Gully plan at Cairngorm; the Lurcher's file is now closed. The winter also brought an unprecedented number of reports from readers, mostly on the new area, Aonach Mor, which impressed most visitors with the style if not the extent of its skiing.

As usual, complaints centred on the shortcomings of Scottish piste marking, mapping, maintenance and hazard warnings, about 'staff unfriendly at best, generally unhelpful and occasionally abusive' (a report from Glencoe), and about queues on the slopes and in mountain restaurants. Overall, few reporters regretted their visit: most of them are regulars and know what to expect. 'I like the "natural" (ie bloody awful) conditions which prevail,' wrote one.

Welcome new developments have not changed the basics of Scottish skiing. Snow beats plastic hands down: having real ski slopes close to home is great good fortune for keen skiers who do live nearby, especially if they have the flexibility to be able to ski in mid-week and thereby avoid the crowds; and skiing adds greatly to the holiday appeal of the Highlands, which have many other attractions. But it would be risky to book a Highlands holiday expecting six days a week of intensive skiing, which most keen skiers undoubtedly want. For them, Scotland is no substitute for a ski holiday in Europe or America.

The drawbacks are the weather and the physical limitations of the ski areas themselves. As the map in the next chapter shows, Scotland's main ski destination, Aviemore/Cairngorm, is small. Glenshee now has a greater number of lifts, but is not appreciably bigger. These areas cannot rival the main Alpine resorts that attract keen British piste bashers, and they get very crowded at weekends. The ski areas are comparable in size to those of the smallest Alpine resorts – Alpbach or Niederau, for example. But these places rely for their appeal on the traditional charm of an Alpine village, which few Highland villages, least of all Aviemore, can match. None of the Scottish ski areas has a resort (or even US-style accommodation) at the foot of the slopes.

'Weather as always unpredictable,' reports a regular visitor, 'varying from glimpses of sun to severe blizzard' – often several times a day. As Cairngorm's Customer Services Manager, Tim Whittome, told us: 'We are at the same latitude as Labrador, and above 2000 feet (which is where skiing takes place) the climate is pretty similar.' The vagaries of Scottish weather make booking a holiday in advance even more of a lottery than it has currently seems to be in the Alps. Our maritime climate gives a low proportion of the stable, dry, bright weather that contributes so much to the beauty of the Alpine winter, and a high proportion of wind and cloud. Skiing often takes place in extremely unfriendly conditions, with no shelter provided by trees, higher mountains or enclosed lifts (the gondola at Aonach Mor is for access to the skiing, not a part of it). Weather conditions change very rapidly. It is vital to dress appropriately: forget the fashion fabrics and wear lots of layers beneath 100% waterproof outer shell garments (including hood). Cairngorm operates an admirably compassionate unwritten policy of offering partial refunds when the weather deteriorates significantly during the day.

As a supplement to skiing abroad, Scottish skiing has some advantages – mainly the advantages of not being abroad. A ski school staffed by native English-speakers has more than a head start over the foreign variety. Lift queues are as orderly as only British queues can be. Shop prices are much the same as at home, and so is the cost of evening entertainment. There is a great sense of camaraderie, and the après-ski ambience is friendly, sometimes becoming rowdy. For those living in Scotland and northern England, travelling to and from skiing is cheap and usually straightforward.

The Scottish ski season rarely starts before New Year and often lasts well into April and even May, at Cairngorm, Aonach Mor and Glencoe, anyway – Glenshee and the Lecht almost always close earlier. Although it was not the case last Easter, conditions are often at their best in the late season. With the aid of snow fences beside runs and lift tracks, snow accumulates in gullies and persists long after most of the slopes are bare. Daylight hours are longer in spring, and conditions on the mountain are less likely to be unbearable than in the depth of winter. And from Easter onwards, the range of other tourist attractions in the Highlands widens significantly.

For southerners tempted to sample the Scottish ski experience, there are very convenient overnight trains from London to Aviemore and Fort William. Bus services to local ski areas, however, are not the height of efficiency, and the great majority of skiers arrive by car or private coach.

The addition of Aonach Mor to the list of Scottish ski areas has added to the appeal of combining all the areas in a touring holiday: clockwise, it is 40 minutes from Glencoe to Aonach Mor, 1 1/2 hours on to Cairngorm, an hour on to The Lecht, another hour on to Glenshee. In practice, conditions are often much better in either east or west: plans to visit all the centres may be discarded in favour of staying where the snow is best. Useful, frequently updated Scottish snow reports on Ski Hotline 0898 654 654. General holiday information from Ski Holiday Scotland 0349 65000.

The next chapter looks at Aviemore/Cairngorm in detail, as in earlier editions. After that comes a round-up of the other Scottish ski centres.

White heather club

Aviemore Scotland

Note There is a general review of Scottish skiing in the preceding chapter, and a summary of the alternative venues in the following one.

Aviemore is still the major Scottish ski centre, accounting for over half the total market, despite the recent challenge from Aonach Mor, and the fact that Glenshee now has a greater number of lifts. It is not a ski resort in the usual Alpine sense; it is a valley village which became established as a summer resort in the middle of the last century and found itself well placed to adapt to winter tourism in the middle of this one by virtue of proximity to the Cairngorm mountains. It sits in the broad Spey valley between Perth and Inverness, about three hours by coach from Edinburgh or Glasgow (the main road along the valley is a very good one, though occasionally blocked), and is not surprisingly highly popular with the residents of those cities, and others within weekend driving range, when conditions are attractive.

General proximity to the Cairngorms does not mean particular proximity to the Cairngorm Chairlift Company's installation, which is nearly 10 miles away, to the east, beneath the summit of Cairngorm itself. By Alpine (or even Pyrenean) standards it is a modest area; but compared with the dry slopes with which most English skiers have to be content for 50 weeks of the year, it is mightily impressive, with top-to-bottom runs approaching 3km in length (when snow conditions permit) and a lift-served vertical drop of 550m.

The skiing top 1100m bottom 550m

The Cairngorm ski area consists of four chair-lifts and thirteen drag-lifts on two flanks of Cairngorm, the Coire Cas and Coire Na Ciste. There is a car park and ticket office at the bottom of each sector, and the two meet at the top on gentle ground around the igloo-shaped Ptarmigan, Britain's highest restaurant. There is now also a two-way link between the two bowls lower down, often lacking snow on the Day Lodge side.

The higher car park, beside the offices, shops and various shelter and refreshment facilities of the Day Lodge (655m), is the main starting point. The lower lifts serve easy slopes below Shieling and the Fiacaill ridge. From Shieling, the White Lady tow and, wind permitting, chair continue up to the high nursery area at Ptarmigan and themselves serve stiffer intermediate runs, often mogulled. The M1 run is an approved race-course and often used for training or racing, with special hardener added to the snow for extra speed. From Ptarmigan, keen skiers can hike up to Cairngorm summit (1245m) and tackle the steep slopes of the headwall, which lead down into Coire Cas and its western neighbour Coire-t-Sneachda. Avalanches are a risk in this sector.

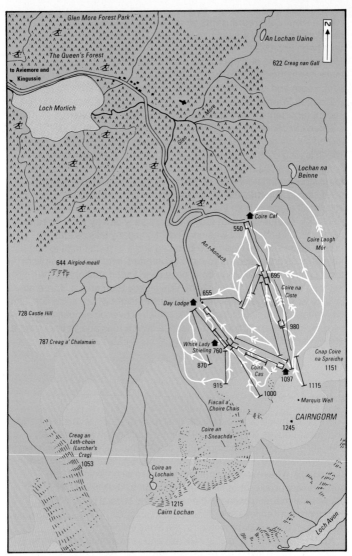

From the lower car park, apparently called Coire Caf (550m), a similar arrangement of lifts – a two-stage chair, with assorted tows – reaches Ptarmigan via the narrower and longer Coire Na Ciste, which has Cairngorm's toughest run, the West Wall: black-graded, and potentially dangerous when hard (there are several gentler alternatives). The gullies beneath the ridge on the extreme northern side of the ski area (marked as a blue run on the plan) often provide good skiing, but it may be necessary to walk to and from them. It is often not possible to ski back to the lower car park.

If the **mountain restaurants** were inviting, they would add greatly to the appeal of the ski area in bad weather. They aren't, though there have been improvements. Full meals are now available in the Day Lodge restaurant, and the bar beneath it has a log fire. There is a small snack bar at the Coire Caf car park. Higher up, there is only the Shieling picnic room and snack bar (with beer on sale if you buy food), and the unlicensed Ptarmigan snack bar, renovated to provide extra seating. Recent reporters are unimpressed by facilities and food alike.

When the car parks are full the ticket offices close. When skiers are spread evenly across the whole area, **queues** rarely exceed 15 minutes (which is long considering the length of the runs) even on a busy day. Congestion can be much more serious when the ski area is only partly open: strong winds often close the chair-lifts or confine skiers to the lower slopes. Alternatively, poor snow cover closes the lower runs and limits uplift capacity from the car park ('It's often quicker to walk up to Shieling'). Queueing is conducted in a uniquely orderly way – in ranks, so that piste-space is not wasted. The lift company tells us that dangerous skiers are vigorously pursued and that piste marking and maintenance have also improved, but reporters continue to complain about Cairngorm's failure to bash pistes and flatten sections of the daunting mogul-fields for which the White Lady is notorious. There are limits to what can be done: in general, the runs are where snow lies, and the prevailing strong winds mean that patchy cover on exposed ridges is the rule, not the exception. Snow fences beside runs and lift tracks are a further hazard, although an invaluable aid to durable snow.

There is no **artificial snow**.

The resort

There is not much of an old village, just rows of shops, with a few hotels and guest-houses lining the road near the station; the resort largely consists of a modern development – the Aviemore Centre – which has extensive facilities, including a dry ski slope, a go-kart circuit and a huge skating rink. These really come into their own when skiing is not possible, especially for families with children to keep occupied. There are several morning buses to the slopes, and several back in the afternoon, but services are reported to be sporadic. There are also daily buses from more distant villages in the Spey valley.

Accommodation is mainly in hotels and self-catering apartments in Aviemore Centre itself. There are several simple B&B houses in the village. The Coylumbridge is a large, comfortable and self-contained hotel with a holiday-camp atmosphere, outside Aviemore on the way to the ski area; it has a log-cabin bar and dancing in the evening, and its own pool and tennis courts. Outside Aviemore, the Osprey in Kingussie and the Ard-Na-Coille in Newtonmore are excellent small family hotels. There are several other villages and towns in the Spey Valley, less obviously affected by tourism but offering good accommodation, ski school and hire shops.

Aviemore **après-ski** can be very jolly, with live entertainment and

Facts on Aviemore Highlands **Scotland**

Prices in £

Tourist office
Postcode PH22 1PP
Tel 0479 810363
Fax 0479 811063

Getting there
By road A9.
By rail Aviemore.
By air Inverness; transfer 1hr. (Or Edinburgh.)

Staying there
Visitor beds 12,000; breakdown: 5,000 in self-catering, 4,000 in hotels, 1,600 in B&B, 550 in youth hostels, 850 in tents.
Medical facilities In resort: Health Centres in main villages. Hospital in Inverness, 40 miles.

Non-skiing activities
Indoor Skating and curling (Aviemore Centre rink), badminton, sauna, whirlpools, multigym, squash, cinema.
Outdoor Dry-skiing, fishing, clay-pigeon shooting, karting, mountain biking, pony trekking, 4-wheel-drive courses, adventure playground, tennis, Visitor's Centres at Carrbridge and Rothiemurchus Estate, Strathspey Railway, whisky distilleries, golfing, folk museum.

Kindergartens
Penguin Ski School
Tuition: Yes. Hours: 10.30-12.30 and 1.30-3.30. Ages: 5-7. Cost: 68.00 per week (without meals). Part of Aviemore Ski School. Extra helper in each class.
Cyril the Squirrel's Nut House (Coylumbridge Hotel)
Tuition: No. Hours: 10.00-8.00 (school holidays), 12.00-7.00 (low season). Ages: 5-12. Cost: 60.00 per week (without meals). Staffed (but not supervised) play area with lots of facilities. Special sessions for mums and toddlers.

Other childcare facilities
Crèche facilities at the Aviemore centre.

Special skiing facilities
Summer skiing No.
Cross-country 45 km of trials in the Glenmore forest, and at Glenmulliach (about an hour away) and Huntly (about 2 hours away). Instruction and hire widely available.

Lift passes
Cairngorm
Covers all lifts. (17 lifts in total.)
Cost 6 days 65.00. Low season: 52.00 saving 20%.
Credit cards accepted Yes.
Senior citizens 43.50 (over 60/65) saving 33%.
Children 43.50 (under 18) saving 33%.
Beginners Limited area pass.
Short-term passes Half-day (from 1.00pm); single and return tickets on 4 chairlifts.
Other passes Limited area covers 10 lifts (Day Lodge to Sheiling and Coire Na Ciste), costs 8.70 for adults and 5.80 for children per day.

Ski school
Aviemore Ski School
One of many ski schools (including a snowboard school and one specialising in telemark), all offering similar packages.
Classes 10.30-12.30 and 1.30-3.30. Cost: 50.00 (6 days). Half-day classes possible from 10.15-1.15 on Sat and Sun. Packages of instruction, ski hire and lift pass cost 130.00 per week.
Lift priority No.
Children's classes Ages: 8-17. Cost: 50.00 (6 days).
Private lessons available Full- or half-day. Cost: 80.00 per hour. Full day, up to 4 people.

---

reasonably priced drinks in hotel bars. There is a disco and skating disco in the Centre, a cinema, and several restaurants, from fish and chips to medium-haute cuisine. The Tavern is recommended for 'excellent authentic Italian food', the Cairngorm hotel for bar meals and comfort. Evening (and early morning) rowdiness has provoked complaints from reporters in the past; as part of a police campaign to eliminate it, the Chippy has had to curtail its opening hours. Après-ski shopping is limited; good sports shops, but not much else.

When there is a lot of snow, the forest land around Glenmore provides plenty of scope for **cross-country** skiing, as the mountains do for Nordic ski-touring and winter climbing. Dangers resulting from the unpredictability of the weather should not be underestimated. Access to the cross-country trails is at Inverdruie, just outside Aviemore.

There is some compensation for Aviemore's lack of charm in the extent of its facilities for **non-skiers** (or for skiers on non-skiing days). Apart from all the activities at Aviemore centre, there are beautiful walks and excursions in the neighbourhood, including Loch-an-Eilean (with its picturesque ruin) and Loch Garten, where ospreys come to nest in spring. We have good reports of riding, clay-pigeon shooting, go-karting and whisky-tasting.

The **nursery slopes** are good, though often crowded, and bleak weather does not provide very favourable conditions to learn in. There are several **ski schools** in Aviemore and many others based in nearby villages. Reports are generally favourable – 'we progressed well and confidently and thoroughly enjoyed ourselves'. All the ski schools offer packages of equipment hire, tuition and lift pass, costing about £100 for five days (excluding weekends).

Scotland's other resorts

The main rival to Aviemore/Cairngorm is **Glenshee**, whose 24 lifts and 40 km of runs create an extensive up-and-down system, a small-scale three-valleys arrangement, with the A93 and Aberdeenshire/Perthshire border running through the middle (and reaching 640m at the pass – access is sometimes difficult). All Glenshee's lifts are drags, less vulnerable than chair-lifts to closure by wind. The lifts are reported to 'open before it's properly light, and carry on until dusk'. Lacking both snow-holding gullies and exceptional altitude, Glenshee has a short season, rarely extending into April.

The runs are short, but there is plenty of scope for an entertaining day's skiing in fine weather, and a broad range of difficulty and slope orientation. The short Tiger run can be a fearsome proposition in icy conditions, but the most satisfying runs for good skiers are on the slopes of Glas Maol (1068m) at the far end of the larger (Aberdeenshire) sector. These slopes hold snow well without snow-fences, and there is usually a choice of possible ways down, including a steep speed-skiing track. There are good nursery slopes near the car park. The new restaurant near the Cairn Aosda lift is reported to be 'excellent, not smelling of cheap cooking like the car park cafe'. But, considering the extent of the ski area, there is still a shortage of cafés; and there is no shelter at all in the Glas Maol area. Ski hire and ski school are on-site. The main accommodation base is the village of Braemar, 9 miles away. The Fife Arms is Braemar's closest approximation to après-ski, popular for cheap, filling bar meals, and with an occasional disco. The Invercauld Arms has a more expensive restaurant, reportedly good. There are various isolated hotels and pubs closer to the ski area, including the Dalrulzion, recently recommended for 'good food, regular live entertainment and a drying room.' A few miles south of Glenshee, Glenisla has cross-country skiing.

Aonach Mor has now completed two winters of operation. It is an impressive set up, as it should be at a cost of over £8m: in 12 minutes, Scottish skiing's only gondola hoists skiers and summer visitors from a valley-floor car park (at 90m, the world's lowest base ski lift station) to the slopes of Snowgoose bowl, served by a chair and various drag-lifts. Reporters were generally surprised to encounter few lift queues (except to descend to the car park, from about 3.30) and unanimously impressed by the quality of piste preparation, setting a new standard for Scotland: 'beautifully combed runs, Alpine-style; other resorts, take note'.

It is rarely possible to ski down from Snowgoose to the car park. The vertical range of the ski area is 1191m (30m below the summit of Aonach Mor) to 686m, a long run by Scottish standards. Restaurants (and bar) at top and bottom of the gondola are inviting. It all looks new, smart, something to be proud of. What's more, the views from the slopes are magnificent – Ben Nevis, the Great Glen, various lochs and the mountains of Skye in the distance. Cairngorm has nothing like this.

The main drawbacks are that the gondola and thus the entire ski area are vulnerable to closure in high wind – the lift company reports seven full days lost last season; and that in its present state the ski area is small – 'basically one intermediate run', reports an unimpressed visitor, a regular skier in Scotland. This is a bit unfair, but it is true that Snowgoose is just one broad open face, with more and less gentle facets providing good beginner slopes near the restaurant (snow permitting) and a greater challenge near the top of the bowl, especially if you ski along Lemming Ridge and down Nid Wall, which is steep enough for speed skiing. Snowgoose is unusually wide and open for Scotland, where skiing is typically confined to narrow snow-filled gullies. The top tow is also reported to be prone to closure, in which case the range of runs is very limited and the Goose run is overcrowded. Queueing arrangements are reported to be less well organised than elsewhere, with congestion common between the Snowgoose T-bar and Summit poma.

There are firm plans to extend the lift system into the vast bowl immediately behind Aonach Mor's summit ridge. At the moment this is a challenging and potentially dangerous off-piste area reached from the summit ridge in a number of places, varying from moderately steep to extreme. Returning to the restaurant involves a long traverse and some walking. Ask a patrolman's advice before setting off over the back.

One of the best things about Aonach Mor is Fort William, an old lochside town at the foot of Ben Nevis well used to tourism, although not in winter. It combines a degree of holiday resort liveliness (including karaoke, of course) with the unaffected atmosphere of an ordinary small country town – solid hotels and a range of everyday shops and pubs. Reporters recommend the Crannog Seafood restaurant on the pier and the Indian Garden restaurant. The Snowgoose restaurant is often open in the evening, with weekend discos and ceilidhs, and no charge for the gondola ride. The Lochaber Leisure Centre has a good pool, squash courts, sauna and a climbing wall. The bus to the ski area leaves from outside Presto, near the Nevisport centre, a complex of bar, café, bookshop and sports shop at the heart of town. The overnight sleeper from Euston pulls in to the centre of Fort William at nine in the morning and the return leg reaches London at eight. Motorists are warned to 'watch out for policemen with speed guns in and around Fort William'.

The smaller partner in Ski Lochaber, the White Corries ski area at **Glencoe**, is now open five days a week (not Tuesdays and Wednesdays). An access chair-lift (335 to 671m) from an isolated roadside car park leads to a shelf ironically known as The Plateau to generations of Scottish skiers who had to trudge uphill across it. Beyond this lies the main ski area, between 716m and the 1109m summit of Meall A' Bhuiridh, served by a chair and two short stages of tow. Previously primitive, Glencoe has progressed to basic, with a renovated mid-mountain cafe ('less squalid than the old one, but not much') supplying snacks, a hot drinks machine, seating for about 80, and loos; but no smoking and no alcohol. More important, the old access chair has been replaced and extended, and a new drag-lift has been installed on the Plateau, which is no longer a walk but a good nursery slope (snow permitting). The other lifts remain unconvincing, awkward to ride, and jerky.

Although the ski area is small, it can boast genuinely easy runs on the Plateau, a short sharp challenge in the Flypaper run from the summit, and intermediate runs in the corries above the café. Nor is it exceptional to be able to ski all or most of the way down to the car park, making a long top-to-bottom run of nearly 800m vertical. The slope under the access chair should be considered off-piste, the main hazard being streams. The slopes have few snow fences, minimal hazard warnings and according to a recent visitor 'a tremendous amount of hardware left to rot on the mountain – a real eyesore and often an danger to skiers'. There is a ski hire and ski school office at the car park, and some isolated accommodation nearby: the King's House Hotel, which claims to be Scotland's oldest inn, is about a mile from the lift. There is simple accommodation at Glencoe village, and a wider choice at Fort William, a beautiful half-hour's drive away along Glencoe.

The **Lecht** (near Tomintoul, between Grantown and Braemar) is a small area most suitable for complete and near-beginners: a series of ten parallel tows on one side of the valley, and one on the other side. There is a café and ski school, creche and ski hire facilities on site.

Latitude, not altitude

Norway

Norway, they say, is due for a revival of interest. In the 1960s, it attracted 15,000 skiers a year from Britain; by the late 1980s, despite growth of the UK skiing market, that number had fallen as low as 1,500. In 1988, a campaign was launched to reverse the decline, by persuading more tour operators that they could market Norway successfully and by putting its resorts back in the public eye.

The effort certainly seems well timed. The depressing lack of reliable snow in the Alps and Pyrenees has not been shared to anything like the same degree by Norway, and snow is clearly quite an asset when selling skiing holidays. And the country is preparing to host the 1994 Winter Olympics.

For cross-country skiers (particularly hardy types able to countenance cross-country tours carrying packs) it has enormous appeal: eminently suitable terrain, long prepared trails, a developed system of huts for refreshment purposes, reliable snow and, not least, a culture in which cross-country skiing is the norm and downhill skiing is the curiosity.

Even some downhillers may find this last refreshing. But there are other aspects to skiing in Norway that many downhill-skiing holiday-makers accustomed to Alpine resorts would be likely to find disappointing. The scenery has none of the drama of the Alps (or the Pyrenees). The skiing itself, by the same token, tends to be a bit tame, and in many resorts limited in extent. The resorts rarely present either the picture-postcard charm of Austria or the effortless transition from ski-room to snow that is characteristic of France. The range of non-skiing activities they offer does not compare well with the facilities of the all-round winter resorts of the Alpine countries. The weather (which can of course be wonderful at times) does not so often reflect the stable high-pressure conditions that skiers have traditionally hoped to find in the Alps in the latter part of the season (and now, it must be admitted, dread finding in the early part of the season). Last, but by no means least in many eyes, prices are high in restaurants and bars; in particular, the peculiar Scandinavian approach to the taxation of alcohol means that even a modest level of consumption becomes spectacularly expensive, while anything approaching indulgence is ruinous.

But people do go to Norway for downhill skiing, and like what they find. They are people for whom the above-mentioned factors matter less than being received by courteous (although not always demonstratively friendly) natives, many of whom speak excellent English, and spending time in ski areas which (away from holiday weekends) are free of crowds and queues, both on the lifts and on the pistes.

Geilo (800m) has cleverly achieved prominence in the British marketplace by arranging to have a Ski Club rep stationed in the resort, thus ensuring multiple mentions in the British press. For downhill skiers it is a rather limited place, with descents no longer than 1.5km in length and 265m vertical – by Alpine standards, very small beer indeed. Most of the skiing is easy; there are some black pitches which just deserve their grading, but they are short. Queues are normally negligible. The village is high up on the Oslo-Bergen railway line, some way east of the line's 1300m high-point; it sits to one side of a broad, shallow valley, with ski slopes in two areas – one immediately adjacent to the village, the other (Vestlia) a bus-ride away across the valley. The resort has no real centre, though the railway station is the obvious focus; it is not a village of any great charm, though pleasant enough on a snowy sunlit day. Hotels and other lodgings are widely spread around, including some at or close to the foot of each main ski area. Dr Holm's Hotel is in a league of its own: a splendidly smart, stylish and spacious place, immaculately white-painted without, warmly welcoming within. The Geilo hotel, handy for one of the main lifts, is traditional in style, comfortable and helpfully run, and very welcoming to children. Après-ski is quiet; a reporter recommends the Vestlia hotel's Scottish comedian; the Highlander bar; and the Bardolla's disco.

Voss is also on the Bergen-Oslo line, but west of the mountains, not far from Bergen. The lakeside town itself is practically at sea level, but the skiing takes place on the elevated, uncrowded slopes of Hangur, reached from the town by a cable-car (which produces slight queues) or by chair-lift from the satellite community of Bavallen. The lift system is modest and the top height is only 945m, but there is skiing down through woods to 300m when snow permits. It is a real town, where skiing does not dominate.

Hemsedal (650m), not far north of Geilo, has impressed reporters with the variety of slopes served by its dozen lifts; it provides runs of up to 4km in length and a healthy 750m vertical. The resort is rather spread-out, making buses (which do not run very frequently) essential.

Lillehammer, more-or-less directly north of Oslo, will be the host town of the 1994 Winter Olympics. Many new facilities are being constructed in preparation, with the Alpine courses concentrated about 15km away at Hafjell. Our reporters recommend the area (and particularly Nordseter) for 'family holidays late in the winter, doing cross-country with occasional days of downhill, and staying in a rented chalet/hut'; and for 'ski touring over a very large area'. One reporter based in a Lillehammer hotel is very critical of the poor bus services.

Trysil (600m), over on the Swedish border, may now be Norway's biggest downhill resort, with runs up to 4km in length and 650m vertical on the part-wooded, part-open slopes of Trysilfjellet (1132m), the lifts starting several kilometres from Trysil itself. Recent additions to the lift network have brought the piste total to over 60km. Our reporters have all been happy with its varied runs and lack of crowds.

Package holidays   Geilo: Made to Measure (hs) Norwegian State Railways (hs) Norwegian Travel Service (has) Ski Sutherland (hy) Winter Adventure Holidays (hs). Voss: Color Line (hsy) Dawson and Sanderson (hasy) Made to Measure (h) Neilson (h) Norwegian State Railways (h) Norwegian Travel Service (has) Ski Sutherland (hy). Hemsedal: Headwater (h) Made to Measure (hs) Norwegian State Railways (hs) Norwegian Travel Service (hs). Lillehammer: Made to Measure (h) Norwegian State Railways (h) Norwegian Travel Service (h); Trysil: Norwegian Travel Service (hs) Ski Global (hs) Ski Sutherland (h).

Orientation tour

Eastern Europe

Yugoslavia, Bulgaria, Romania, Czechoslovakia, Poland

Downhill skiing on a serious scale – with established resorts served by extensive lift systems – can be found in many European countries other than the Big Four of Austria, France, Italy and Switzerland, and on many mountain ranges other than the Alps. Such skiing is often of no more than local interest, but it is not always so. Elsewhere in the *Guide* we describe the Pyrenean resorts of tiny Andorra, which tend to attract inexperienced skiers in search of a jolly holiday at keen prices. The other direction in which skiers on a budget tend to look is eastwards, to Bulgaria and Romania, and to their close neighbour Yugoslavia, which at its north-western extremity borders Italy and Austria. Czechoslovakia, which briefly appeared on the British package market, and Poland are also attracting handfuls of adventurous skiers.

As you might expect, the Eastern European countries have quite a lot in common with one another, and are in some ways quite different from the major Alpine countries – or, for that matter, from Pyrenean ones. The skiing of some resorts can compete with that of minor resorts in Austria, for example, and the accommodation is built to match the expectations of foreign visitors, but in other respects Eastern Europe – and particularly Bulgaria and Romania – can be disappointing. The heart of the matter is that, for a variety of reasons, these countries do not offer the opportunities for self indulgence that many skiers have become used to in resorts elsewhere. Although this matters a lot to some skiers, it matters much less to others – leaders of school parties, for example, may consider a shortage of tempting bars rather a blessing.

The vast numbers of reports we've received this year indicate that the upheavals in Eastern Europe in 1989/90 have affected the popularity of these countries as skiing destinations. Not only do they offer a cheap holiday and a 'unique cultural experience', but there is also the potential for combining a sight-seeing trip with a few days' skiing. The local people are trying hard to adjust to the rapid changes, and particularly to a market economy. Things do not always run as smoothly as tourists come to expect – there are still shortages, delays, slow service, and sometimes only basic facilities. The conflict between low local standards and visitors' high expectations and evident affluence sometimes leads to resentment on both sides, occasionally aggravated, as one reporter put it, by 'ostentatious disregard for the plight of the locals'. We have had reports this year of visitors being ripped off by locals, and worse still, a thirteen year old boy being threatened on the ski slopes by Bulgarian teenagers who demanded his bum-bag. But the majority of reporters have been exceptionally impressed by the friendliness and generosity of the Eastern Europeans.

Yugoslavia

Yugoslavia's best-known resort, offered by mainstream tour operators as well as the Eastern Europe specialists, is **Kranjska Gora** (810m), on the south-east extremity of the Alps, close to both the Italian and Austrian borders (the excursion agenda includes Villach and Venice). The village is inoffensive – its chalets slightly more severe than their Tyrolean equivalents, and its setting, in a flat-bottomed valley between craggy, wooded mountains, a pretty one. But it is a difficult resort to recommend to any category of skier except dedicated ski school pupils who are content to perfect their turns on a limited range of pistes. There are wide and gentle nursery slopes right on the edge of the village, but the transition to real pistes is rather abrupt – the mountains rise quite steeply from the valley floor. There are lots of drag-lifts serving intermediate pistes on the Vitranc, but they go no more than half-way up what is in any case a small mountain – which means not only limited skiing but also a pronounced danger of poor snow. A two-stage chair-lift goes further, to 1570m, giving a fairly challenging descent of over 750m vertical to the valley; but that is all there is for the competent skier to enjoy. A couple of new pistes are said to be opening this year. There are swimming pools and saunas in several of the slightly institutional hotels, and discos and bars in which a festive atmosphere can be made to prevail. The bar of the Slavec hotel is said to have a good local atmosphere. The hotel Larix has been recommended by reporters for its location, rooms and facilities – 'good family rooms, lovely bar overlooking nursery slopes'. The Garni is equally conveniently situated for the nursery slopes and is clean and spacious. One reporter commends the Lek for its 'outstandingly helpful and pleasant service'. The Prisank has good food but not much variety. Other restaurant recommendations include Pino's pizzeria ('about £2 for a delicious family-size pizza') and the Spaghetti House, just outside the village. We have had a favourable report of the ski school – 'tuition sound, English adequate, allocation tactful, private lessons available'.

Of the other resorts in the Yugoslavian Alps accessible to the British package-holiday skier, **Bovec** (520m), just south of Kranjska Gora, is the most interesting from a skiing point of view. It does not have many lifts, but they include a three-stage gondola rising 1750m and serving some moderately challenging slopes. If and when there is snow down to the village, the run from top to bottom must be memorable. Bovec itself was rebuilt after World War II and is a town, rather than a resort. Après-ski revolves around hotels and lively local bars.

Also in northern Yugoslavia is the picturesque town of **Bled** (880m), set against the backdrop of the Julian Alps. The town looks on to a 17thC church on an island in the middle of a lake. There are plenty of excursion possibilities available (to local sights and further afield). One regular reporter recommends staying in the Golf, a quiet hotel set slightly away from the main centre. Bled's skiing is at **Zatrnik**, a short bus ride away – 'good, regular and comfortable buses'. Zatrnik has only five lifts serving easy wooded slopes, ideal for beginners in good snow conditions but providing little challenge to intermediates. The skiing areas of Mt Vogel and Mt Kobla are also within easy reach and have more scope and better snow records. There is accommodation available to British package holidaymakers right at the base of Mt Vogel, in the Zlatorog hotel near the Vogel cable-car station, recommended for 'good family rooms and a great swimming pool'. This hotel is undeniably convenient for the slopes, but is rather isolated in the evenings as it is not really part of a village. Other reporters have preferred the more lively Kompas and Jezero hotels, in a village about 5km away on the other side of Bohinj lake. According to the proposals on the 1991 piste map, another cable-car will soon connect these hotels with the small, north-facing ski area on Mt Vogel (1800m), but for the time being, a regular bus shuttles skiers to the access cable-car near the Zlatorog hotel. From the top station, seven lifts conveniently connect a handful of easy and intermediate runs and a small nursery area. More runs and lifts are planned. There are two mountain restaurants which serve 'good basic fare'. Reports of the ski schools are generally favourable – English is widely spoken and video analysis is said to be helpful. The other skiing area of interest to people staying around Bohinj lake is that of Mt Kobla and the adjacent mountain Savnik; it consists of a mixture of easy and intermediate runs, entirely below the tree-line between 550–1500m. The 1991 piste map shows more projected than actual lifts. Kobla is quick to fill up at weekends. The only tour operator who presently offers holidays at Mt Vogel and Mt Kobla sells them under the collective title of **Bohinj**. There are said to be lovely walks and cross-country skiing along the valley floor.

The Yugoslavia's newest and most extensive resort is to the south: **Kopaonik** (1620m), a purpose-built skiing centre in the heart of Serbia (about level with Florence). One of its drawbacks is the long airport transfer (about 3 hours from Nis, 5 from Belgrade) but it does have about the best range of downhill and cross-country skiing in the country and is described by our several reporters as 'an excellent resort for families, beginners and intermediates'. A small network of lifts (a short walk from the hotels) serve the main mountain above the resort (Suvo Rudiste, 1975m). Mainly blue and red pistes descend on three sides of the mountain, with a maximum vertical drop of 520m. Further lifts stretch out across a wooded ridge, giving access to more challenging runs (graded black, but not difficult) to the valley at Brzece. There are several mountain huts but only one, the Rtanj, near the bottom of lift 8, is recommended – 'a rustic gem, home-made food'.

The resort has been thoughtfully (though not attractively) developed on a wooded plateau. The hotel Atlas is 'a cut above the rest – excellent food, quiet location, restrained live music'. The nearby Konaci apartments are owned and run by by the same team, but a recent group of self-caterers found the range of food available very limited – 'a preponderance of pickled vegetables'. The recently refurbished and extended Grand hotel is reportedly 'ideal for families' and has ample, under-used sports facilities (sauna, jacuzzi, squash courts, indoor tennis courts, swimming pool) and spacious public rooms but not much atmosphere. Nightlife revolves around bars, restaurants and the Yugotours Holiday Club (lively disco, draught beer). One reporter recommends the restaurant and nightclub of the Baciste. The Grill Bar

Zurk and Omorika Serbian restaurant are also worth a visit; the latter has a folk trio playing Slavonic songs at each table. The Red Bull at the back of the Konaci apartments serves good sweet and savoury pancakes. A recent reporter returning to Kopaonik after an absence of two years found that the food and drink prices had quadrupled; they are still cheap by Austrian and Italian standards, but not by Eastern European ones. Snowmobile trips are popular, as are excursions to the 12thC monastery at Studenica. The ski school is highly praised – 'conscientious instructors with a good command of English', 'good use of video cameras'. Children's facilities are reportedly excellent.

Despite the eminence it achieved in hosting the Winter Olympics in 1984, **Sarajevo** (on about the same latitude as Kopaonik, but much nearer the Adriatic) is not really a ski resort. Like Innsbruck, it is a valley town with skiable mountains nearby, and the accommodation for skiers is concentrated at the foot of the pistes in Jahorina (1530m) and Bjelasnica (1270m), a long way out of town (and widely separated). The lifts of the former go up to just over 1900m, those of the latter to almost 2100m, with runs of up to 800m vertical. Most of the skiing is of intermediate difficulty, on open slopes. Life revolves around the hotels, purpose-built for skiers. According to one reporter, they have 'good food, typical Slavonic hospitality and entertainment with an oriental flavour'. There are some simple non-skiing sports facilities at Jahorina, and very extensive cross-country skiing trails near Bjelasnica.

Package holidays Kranjska Gora: Enterprise (hs) Neilson (hs) Thomson (h) Yugotours (hs). **Bled**: Balkan Holidays (h) Neilson (h) Thomson (h) Yugotours (hs). **Bohinj**: Yugotours (h). **Bovec**: Yugotours (h). **Kopaonik**: Neilson (hs) Thomson (hs) Yugotours (hs)

Bulgaria

Anyone planning a holiday in Bulgaria should first find out what they're letting themselves in for. Most of our reporters this year were seriously shocked by the level of poverty in the country. It is worth listing a number of primary concerns. First, currency: due to continual devaluation, reporters found the Bulgarian lev had little value and that hard currency was much sought after. The official rate of exchange in February 1991 was about 30 lev to the pound, but pounds were in such demand that you could easily get 50 lev on the so-called black market (which reportedly involves any and every Bulgarian you meet). Some hotel bars and restaurants would only accept hard currency. Secondly, medical facilities: a couple of reporters who had the misfortune to end up in Bulgarian hospitals found them very basic, unclean and lacking facilities that we in the West take for granted. One reporter had to have medicines flown out from England for his one-year-old daughter who was detained in the hospital at Samakov. On the other hand, all those who saw mountain rescues taking place were impressed by the efficiency of the rescue teams, and minor injuries were treated speedily and effectively. Thirdly, food: no one goes to Eastern Europe expecting gourmet dinners, but we have had a higher-than-usual number of complaints about the food. Reporters did not go hungry but were very unhappy about the quality and variety of what they were eating – 'a hunk of unrecognisable meat and boiled potatoes every night'. Even the better (and more expensive) restaurants serve the same because that is all they can get hold of. Bear in mind that to most locals this would be a feast. If you know what to expect, you won't be disappointed. Fourthly, fuel: there was a major shortage in Bulgaria last season due to the Gulf war. Tourist buses were unaffected but local transport was occasionally disrupted and understandably expensive. Occasionally hotel central heating systems were affected. If you are concerned by the considerations above, you should perhaps consider a skiing holiday elsewhere. To most of our reporters they mattered very little and were superseded by the beauty of the country, the friendliness of the people, the variety of the skiing and the excellence of the ski schools. One word of advice from a reporter who visited Vitosha is 'take a travel kettle, a supply of tea, coffee and soup, and any pharmaceuticals and toiletries that you might need – if you don't use them, you can give them away'.

Judging by the number of reports we've received in the last couple of years, **Borovets** (1323m) is the most popular British destination in Eastern Europe. None of our reporters regretted their choice. Spectacularly situated among pine forests high in the Rila mountains, the resort is more a scattered collection of hotels than a village. But with a highest ski point of 2430m, reached by the formidable three-mile Yastrebets six-seater gondola, Borovets' skiing compares favourably with that of many of the smaller Alpine resorts. It is divided into three areas: a variety of wooded runs on the mountain directly above the resort; wooded intermediate runs reached by gondola to the right of the resort; and open skiing between 2150m and 2540m, above the top gondola station, served by a series of parallel drag-lifts. There is a limited nursery area at the foot of the main mountain and some long meandering blue trails, including one 6km one from the top of the 'antique' single chair, but the skiing is generally more suited to intermediates, who have the choice of some fairly testing red and black runs; there is little in the way of real challenge or off-piste scope for the expert. Mountain restaurants are not over-abundant and are basic but incredibly cheap ('15p a dish'). There is a lovely old house/café on the 6km blue run which is well worth a visit. There are rarely lift queues. The ski school is unanimously praised by reporters, and kindergarten arrangements are apparently satisfactory.

Most of the hotels are within five minutes' walking distance of the slopes and lifts. Horse- or donkey-drawn carts do a circuit of the main hotels. The Rila is situated right at the foot of the mountain opposite the main chair-lift and convenient for the gondola and nursery slopes but is huge and rather impersonal ('the reception area looks like an airport lounge'). The recently built Samakov (with swimming pool) is reportedly attractive and comfortable, with good food by local standards, but is again rather large and impersonal. The smaller twin hotels of Ela (the ski school HQ) and Mura also offer comfortable accommodation close to the lift network. Après-ski relies almost entirely upon the hotel bars, discos and floor-shows, with the Rila and Samakov acting as the principal entertainment centres. The Ela has an English bar with English prices to match. One reporter recommends the small but cosy bar of the

Breza. The ski instructors put on a ski-jumping show once a week. Apart from a few excursions (the Rila monastery is popular), there is little for non-skiers to do. There are very few shops but some market stalls selling local crafts (particularly wood-carving and lace). Three short cross-country trails commence 2km from the resort, accessible by bus.

South-west of Borovets is **Pamporovo** (1620m), a fairly large resort better suited to first-time skiers. The nearest airport, Plovdiv (about 1¾ hours away) is very basic with limited facilities (so say several reporters who were delayed there for 6 hours). The resort consists of a handful of rather unattractive modern hotels, lacking atmosphere but offering a surprisingly high standard of accommodation, some five minutes' (free) bus-ride from the slopes. Most reporters stayed at the adequate Perelik. Some ate at the Rohzen – food better, rooms more basic.

The lift system consists entirely of chairs and drags serving mainly easy pistes on Snezhanka mountain (1925m). There are several good nursery areas and a number of delightful confidence-building blue pistes down through the trees, including one from the top height of 1925m to the low point of the system at 1450m. There are two black runs, including the 'Wall', which is not as steep as it sounds but is used as a slalom race-course; advanced skiers would probably find little to maintain their interest after the first two or three days. Snack bars on the mountain are apparently numerous but of poor quality. One reporter recommends the pizza caravan near Stoudenets. Rental equipment is first-class, and we have very favourable reports of the ski school – the instructors take an obvious pride in their command of English, and instruction is reportedly clear, technically sound and patient. Pamporovo is the southernmost mountain resort in Eastern Europe, and snow conditions can be unreliable in the latter part of the season.

Cross-country trails of 4km, 16km and 18km start in the resort, with instruction in cross-country techniques available. Après-ski, in Alpine terms, is limited to a few 'folksy' restaurants and hotel discos, although there are night clubs at the hotel Perelik and at the Smolyan (45 minutes' bus ride away). One reporter recommends the bar at Molina. Also thoroughly recommended are the traditional local evenings laid on for tourists; folk barbeques at the Cheverme restaurant, 'game' evenings sampling local fare, and meals in the homes of Bulgarian families – 'traditional food, unlimited home-brewed spirits, music and dancing'. The ski instructors apparently put on a cabaret evening which is 'highly entertaining'. Non-skiing activities include indoor bowling and swimming at the Perelik; there are also excursions to various local points of interest, including the capital, Sofia, and Plovdiv.

Bulgaria's highest resort is on Mt **Vitosha**, overlooking Sofia. The resort, at 1800m, consists of a couple of comfortable hotels (the Proster is the larger and has more facilities, eg swimming pool and sauna), a hire shop and lift station on a wooded ledge. Most of the skiing is intermediate level, on north-facing slopes above the tree-line; it is served by a small network of lifts which was greatly improved for the World Student Games in 1984. The lifts are apparently closed one day a week for maintenance work. Vitosha's proximity to Sofia means that it is inundated with people at weekends and lift queues become a serious

problem. The ski school is 'excellent – tuition in six languages'.
Package holidays Borovets: Balkan Holidays (hca) Enterprise (h) Falcon (h)
Inghams (h) Ski Global (ha). **Pamporovo**: Balkan Holidays (hca) Enterprise (h)
Falcon (hs) Quest Total Ski (h) Quest Travel (schools) (h) Ski Global (ha)

Romania

Romania's most serious ski resort is **Poiana Brasov** (1020m), about
two hours north of Bucharest in the centre of the country. It is an
unusual resort – purpose-built, with its hotels and other facilities dotted
around a wooded plateau at the foot of the skiing, rather like an
enormous holiday camp, and not at all like a village. This is no doubt an
excellent arrangement in summer, when walks in wooded surroundings
are what people go for. In winter it means that life for many skiers
revolves around buses, which are said to be 'intermittent'. Of the hotels,
the Alpin is particularly recommended ('large rooms with balconies,
pleasantly furnished, constant hot water'); the Teleferic is 'adequate, but
basic'. Non-skiing and après-ski facilities are fairly limited; there is a big
public pool, other sports facilities including skating and bowling, and a
range of nightlife from discos to 'very racy cabarets'. Excursions are
organised to 'Dracula's castle', which is undergoing renovations.

The main ski area is reached by gondola or cable-car (don't expect
them both to be running at the same time though) up to 1775m and
consists of three main elements: satisfying intermediate runs
approximately following the line of the lifts from top to bottom; a good,
open nursery area at altitude; and a longish roundabout run away from
the lifts – graded black only because it is not prepared, has one
moderately steep pitch towards the end, and is used as a downhill race
course. There is also a separate gentle nursery area down in the resort.
Mountain restaurants are reportedly grim; the Outlaws hut is about the
best of the bunch and apparently serves bear meat. There is no
shortage of ski school instructors who speak excellent English.

Sinaia (800m) is a small town stretching along the main road through
the mountains from Bucharest to Brasov, its role as a ski resort relatively
minor. A two-stage cable-car from the town (its top section duplicated by
a chair-lift) serves long intermediate runs down the front of the mountain
which are quite challenging (particularly in poor visibility, as they are
poorly marked), but for most skiers the main area is the exposed,
treeless slopes behind the mountain and on subsidiary peaks beyond –
short intermediate runs with some variety, and plenty of scope for skiing
off-piste. The town is quiet, and although there are a few bars and
restaurants, in practice après-ski revolves around tour operators' hotels.

Prices in Romania are even lower than Bulgaria. All our reporters
found it very difficult to spend £20 in a week's holiday. Some prices
quoted by them are: 15p for chicken and chips, £1.20 for a bottle of
champagne, £1 for a sledge, £20 for new ski boots.
Package holidays Poiana Brasov: Balkan Holidays (h) Enterprise (h) Inghams (h).
Sinaia: Ski Party Snow World (h).

Czechoslovakia

At the moment no tour operators offer holidays in Czechoslovakia.
Thomsons pioneered two resorts in the Tatra mountains in 1988/89 but

have now pulled out and Inghams cancelled their programme last year due to poor sales. Of the two areas, the **South Tatras** are the more serious proposition. There is no village to speak of – just hotels dotted along the valleys to the north and south of the pine-clad main mountain, Mt Chopok (2045m). On the north side there is a fairly extensive and varied ski area, vulnerable to wind. The only way down is by black run or chair-lift.

Poland

As far as we know, no tour operators have yet ventured into Poland's leading resort, **Zakopane**, on the Polish side of the Tatra mountains. But, if the verdicts of our two enthusiastic reporters are anything to go by, they soon should. Zakopane is about two hours' drive south of Krakow, right on the Czechoslovakian border. It is surrounded by breathtaking scenery, an abundance of flora and fauna and delightful outlying villages, with traditionally carved and decorated wooden churches. The village organises complimentary coach tours around the area. Other excursions are possible (eg to Auschwitz) .

Our reporters were informed that the village had changed dramatically over the past year. 'The main street, Krupowki, was full of small shops, all bursting with goods. Food was plentiful, easy to buy and incredibly cheap'. A 'marvellous meal' with French wine in the government-run Orbis hotels cost about £8 a head. At the other end of the scale, a drink or meal in the delightful local cafés cost just a few pence; opinions on the quality of the food differ. The Poles rise and retire early, so you won't find much going on after 9pm. From the hotels at the centre of the village the slopes are best reached by taxi (skis and poles are shoved in the boot).

The skiing comprises four small separate areas. The main area, Kasprowy Wierch (1985m), is reached by a cable-car which ends on the Czech border. From here, you can ski intermediate runs on either side of the mountain, served by antiquated chair-lifts. Deciphering where the runs are is another matter – 'one could designate the whole area off-piste; piste-bashers do not appear to have reached Poland yet'. The second area, Gubalowka, is reached by funicular from the bottom of the high street. A pleasant run down a straightforward slope brings you to the end of the lift queue. The steep Nosal runs are Zakopane's main racing slopes and are reserved in the morning for slalom practice. In bad conditions, which are not uncommon at this low altitude, the resort relies on two snow-guns. One reporter found the ski school instructors helpful. Day lift passes are uneconomical; it is better to pay by the ride.

Our reporters agree that Zakopane has the potential to become an impressive resort. But 'for the present, its appeal must lie with the recreational skier who wishes to combine his holiday with an insight into a rapidly developing country'.

Skiing in America

In our 1990 edition, with concern mounting about the unreliable nature of European snow, we gently introduced American skiing to the Guide with a round-up of the most popular resorts in the States. This year we have detailed reports on four major American resorts: Vail, Breckenridge, Park City and Jackson Hole. Those reports follow this chapter, in which we aim to explain how American skiing differs from European, and to convey something of the range of experiences it offers. After the four detailed resort chapters comes a revised round-up of other resorts.

Erratic snowfalls in Europe have spoilt many ski holidays in recent years. As a result, more and more British skiers have looked to the United States, where snow cover is perceived as more reliable. In the West, the great wall of the Rockies draws huge quantities of snow out of clouds formed over the Pacific. The eastern mountains, where moisture cannot be relied on from the sky, have a different ace to play: consistently low temperatures, which mean that snow-guns are effective in guaranteeing skiable snow.

Until 1988, most of the British who skied in the States did so as a side trip to a business or social visit. Then the improving exchange rate and a big drive by the American resorts to attract foreign skiers (their own market had levelled off and they needed more customers to finance expansion) encouraged tour operators such as Thomson to provide packages. The most successful were Ski the American Dream, who tailor-make packages, combining the advantages of block bookings of accommodation and flights with a fair amount of flexibility.

The whole development of skiing in the States came about quite differently from that in Europe. A very few resorts – such as Stowe in Vermont – began, as resorts did in Europe, with people skiing experimentally on long boards. The majority developed because people who had learned to ski in Europe found mountains suitable for skiing which were conveniently close to deserted mining towns. Aspen, Breckenridge, Copper Mountain and Park City were all brought back to life in this way. Now there are also purpose-built resorts – Snowbird started as a sort of American Flaine, with concrete lift station and multi-purpose plaza; until quite recently, Squaw Valley in California was simply a cable-car serving Olympic slopes above.

Quite often, skiers have to base themselves some way from the slopes: as the mountains are on National Forest land, building there is restricted. Most skiers take their cars, and they are well catered for, with promptly cleared roads and big car-parks. Where shuttle services are needed to go from the accommodation (or even just from the car-parks) to the slopes, this is swift and reliable, employing a wide variety of 'people-movers'. Car-hire and petrol are cheap, so anyone not travelling on an all-in package can afford to hire a 'skierized' vehicle (equipped with chains, ski rack and strong anti-freeze) and enjoy the freedom it provides. Since the resorts are rarely linked by trails (they don't use the word piste) or lifts, but are often only a short distance apart by road, a car has obvious attractions.

But it's wrong to think of US ski areas as coming from a single mould. They vary as much as the European ones do – the Alps, Pyrenees and Dolomites are no more different than the Colorado Rockies, the Adirondacks in the East, the Wasatch Mountains of Utah or the Sierra Nevada of California. There are smart and less smart villages. Northstar at Tahoe, for example, is a quiet family resort, where all the runs end in the village and children cannot get lost. At the other extreme, perhaps, is Aspen, with its four separate mountains each catering for a different skier, shopping malls to satisfy the millionaires and small corner restaurants to please gourmets.

In the East – close to the big centres of population – the cold is intense. This means that snow-making is reliable, so the resorts regularly open in November and do not close until June. Throughout that time, snow cover is good – kept that way by a barrage of snow-guns, and a fleet of tillers (as they call piste-bashers). Since American skiers are quick to sue the resorts if they so much as trip on a rock or root, trail grooming is meticulous.

Another result of this passion for litigation is that each resort is surrounded by a fence, and if you are found outside it you lose your lift pass. So high-mountain touring in the European sense is practically impossible, though in some areas you can hire a guide to take you outside the defined ski area. The Utah Interconnect is exceptional in offering the opportunity to ski from resort to resort (see the Park City chapter).

This does not mean that virgin powder is impossible to find. The fabled snow of the Rockies does have an uncanny way of falling at night, leaving clear sunny days between. Every resort leaves untracked powder between pistes or in high bowls, but there is great competition to reach it on the early-morning lifts, and it is quickly skied out. Colorado and (particularly) Utah are best for this light powder; California snow is despised as 'sierra cement' by connoisseurs.

Après-ski entertainment has a flavour all its own in the States. The converted mining towns offer bars reminiscent of miners' saloons, with bluegrass music beating out through the wooden half-shutter doors. The Tram at Snowbird swings at night in spite of (or perhaps because of) Utah's archaic (but changing) drink laws. The Million Dollar Cowboy Bar in Jackson – with its long bar studded by silver dollars and its resident population of seven-foot cowboys stomping on the dance floor or sitting hunched around the blackjack tables – has all the atmosphere of a hundred years ago, coupled with a lot more liveliness. In Nevada, casinos and cabarets take the place of the usual ski-resort discos.

American accommodation is amazingly spacious compared with that in Europe, and not expensive. At least three French apartments would fit into the standard 'condominium', and fittings such as microwave ovens, washing-up machines, clothes washers and driers are commonplace. It is not unusual to find spa baths and saunas in the condominium buildings, and within the last couple of years health centres have been appearing in the smarter resorts.

Because the condominiums are so cheap and well equipped, they are understandably popular. But there are also hotels offering MAP (Modified American Plan) – dinner, bed and breakfast. Food is good – though breakfasts seem to take forever as you are quizzed as to which of fifteen ways you want to eat your egg each day. Practically everyone eats on the mountain, where the 'lodges', though few in number, are big, clean and efficient. You will not find cosy little wood-beamed restaurants as in Zermatt or Cortina, but you will find hamburgers or pastrami or chilli con carne served hot and fast in spotless surroundings. The plumbing, needless to say, is beyond comparison with the Alpine equivalent.

The American ski areas are usually much smaller than their counterparts in Europe. There are no huge linked expanses such as the Three Valleys, for example. Runs, too, are generally quite short: three or four miles is considered a long run, compared with two or three times that length in Europe. But the efficiency of the lift system does mean that skiers can cover just as many miles in a day.

An efficient network of fast lifts is a high priority. Some resorts use gondolas as the main way up the mountain, but chair-lifts are much the most common type of lift. (Cable-cars – contrarily called trams, just as the San Francisco trams are called cable-cars – are on the other hand quite rare.) The advent of the detachable quad (a four-person chair-lift which travels at gondolas speeds but slows to let you on and off) has helped to melt away the queues.

Even those queues which remain move fast, and a few pieces of rope and strategically sited poles organise the queues ('lines' in local parlance) in a wonderfully civilised fashion. In the States, no one would dream of queue-barging, let alone scrambling over another's skis. There are separate queues for single skiers (as opposed to those who insist on riding with their companions); those skiing alone move into the singles line, to catch an early chair with spaces. This system works well, and ought to be adopted in Europe – practically all chairs go up the mountain with a full complement.

Riding American chairs can be a cold business, but some of the newer ones, such as the Vistabahn at Vail, have plastic covers which come down to seat level. Many chairs have no safety bar and no footrest and, as they swing high up on the pylons, can give rise to vertigo. The lift operators insist that they are safer than chairs with bars because you cannot get tangled up in them. There is no doubt that their lack of complication and weight also makes them cheaper to build and operate. But this doesn't result in cheap lift passes – a pass for 6 days in big resorts cost around £110 in 1990-91.

The main resorts of Colorado, Utah and California lie south of the 40° latitude line – about level with Naples. The tree-line is twice the height of that in the Alps, so most of the runs are cut through forest. This is helpful in bad weather, improving shelter and visibility, and latterly the planners have left islands of trees in the middle of trails, to break the monotony. Some resorts, such as Vail, Breckenridge and Park City, have opened up high bowls where there are no trees, and these are usually kept for good skiers to enjoy especially after a snowfall.

The American resorts are actively marketed, and the marketing men quickly realised that to attract parents they must provide day-long care for children. They realised, too, the long-term value of treating children well. If children enjoy a resort they will probably come back again when the choice is theirs; in due course, they'll come back with *their* kids. So special areas are set aside for children, special instructors look after them, either on the slopes or in special compounds, and even the grown-up restaurants offer special child-size menus. Sometimes the camps resemble gold mines, Indian camps or cowboy corrals. Disneyland also plays its part.

Ski schools operate just as in the Alps, with regular classes and also special or private lessons if you can afford them. If you do not want lessons but do want some help in getting your bearings, you can take advantage of the free 'meet-the-mountain' tours which most resorts offer once or twice a day, designed to familiarise new arrivals with the lift network and the best areas to ski at different times of the day.

America is truly the country of communications. Lift maps (as well as tissues, and tools for fixing bindings) are stacked by every lift queue. Signposting on the trails is excellent. Often, 'the easiest way down' is marked as well as black diamonds, blue squares or green circles. (There are no red runs in the States – easy blacks or blues take their place.) Places which cater for a lot of first-time skiers, such as Killington in the East, also employ pictograms – so you follow a trail of bears, suns or snowflakes down to the bottom of a run. On the trails there are frequent warnings to slow down and look out for trails crossing ahead. There are often telephones alongside the trails as well as at lift stations. Boards at lift stations carry chalked messages to friends to arrange meeting places during the day.

Patrols are efficient, and rescue sledges take injured skiers off the mountain without charge. Sometimes skiers are invited (as at Arapahoe Basin) to inspect the patrol huts where, as well as shovels and avalanche equipment, modern communication systems and sophisticated medical supplies are to be found, including defibrillators.

Perhaps the greatest difference between American and European resorts is simply the way holiday skiers are treated. 'Have a good day' may sound trite when you hear it each time you climb on a chair-lift, but the sentiment is echoed all over the mountains and in the resorts by people who really seem to care that you should enjoy yourself. Maybe it comes as an order from the marketing directors, but it works.

Vail Colorado 2500m

Good for *Resort-level snow, Alpine charm (sic), off-piste skiing, easy runs, big ski area, woodland runs*
Bad for *Tough runs, mountain restaurants*

Separate resort: Beaver Creek

If you're going all that way and paying all that money to get there, you may as well splash out and go for the best. This is an understandable approach to skiing in North America, similar to that adopted by many Americans crossing the Atlantic in the opposite direction. And if that's your approach, Vail has a fair claim on your attention. Opinions about the best in American skiing vary as much as they do about European resorts. But for all-round excellence many votes would be cast for Vail which, thanks to new lifts extending its famous back bowls, has recently usurped Mammoth Mountain's position as the biggest ski mountain in North America. Even this is not enormous by the standards of the big linked lift systems in Europe; nor will Vail's vertical drop of a little under 1000m impress connoisseurs of big-drop Alpine resorts.

In the States, sophistication tends to be borrowed from Europe, and this is the hallmark of the resort, which has been built from nothing over the last thirty years in a style apparently aiming to persuade its visitors they are in a transatlantic Tyrol. With its Gasthofs, sleigh rides, wedel courses, Wein Stube Continental restaurants, piano bars and wine snobs, Vail may seem a little pretentious and disappointingly lacking in denim and stetson clad bourbon-swilling cowpokes. But it is no more contrived than many modern resorts in Austria and Switzerland.

To European eyes the scenery gives no indication of great altitude: rolling, round-topped hills, tree-covered from top to bottom. From summit clearings there are enormous views over the folds and undulations of a gentle mountain landscape. Like the resort, it will remind many skiers of Austria, as will the background row of genuinely mountainous rocky peaks of the Gore range.

Vail has generated numerous reports and a remarkable unanimity of enthusiasm. No reporters regretted their choice, and few expressed reservations, except about the mountain restaurants and general lack of any Wild West atmosphere. Even the lift queues added to the holiday satisfaction of one reporter: 'a civilised delight'. More than one reporter was pleasantly surprised at the variety of skiing, and at the extent of off-piste skiing available in Vail.

Vail is jointly owned (and shares a lift pass) with Beaver Creek, a younger and smaller resort 10 miles to the west which cultivates an even more exclusive image. Beaver Creek has runs as long as any at Vail, can boast the tougher pistes (its so-called Birds of Prey runs) and is less crowded at busy times. But the ski area is smaller and for the moment has nothing to compare with the Vail bowls.

The skiing   top 3490m bottom 2500m

The quality of Vail's skiing lies in a well-balanced mixture of easy and intermediate runs on the front of the mountain, which is mostly woodland; comfortable, modern and efficient lifts, almost all chairs, which must be a mixed blessing in cold weather; and a vast area of more open ground at the back, almost entirely reserved for off-piste skiing. These are the 'back bowls', said to occupy two-thirds of Vail's 3,700 skiable acres. They give the lie to any suggestion that American resorts place too many constraints on skiers' freedom, and for good skiers they amply compensate for Vail's relative lack of challenging pistes. All the back bowl routes are marked black on the map, which looks unnecessarily daunting as a result. (So, perhaps, does our own map: bear in mind that skier consensus finds the US blacks dark red in European terms, and the blues usually easy.)

The back bowls are not terrifyingly steep, and popular routes are skied into a piste-like state soon after a snowfall. There are also a few genuinely easy groomed runs punctuating the wide slopes.

Lift access is from both ends of the long resort to various points along a broad ridge punctuated by four top lift stations: Eagles Nest in the west, at the top of the Lionshead gondola; Wildwood and Summit (or PHQ, for Patrol Headquarters), both reached from Vail Village and Mid-Vail, a teeming concourse at the heart of the ski area; and a slightly lower point, known as the Far East.

The upper half of the front side of the mountain has short runs in two main bowls: in the North East bowl between Summit and Far East the Highline chairlift serves the most difficult of Vail's pistes, short sharp double-black mogul-fields of about 300m vertical. The runs down to Mid-Vail from Wildwood and PHQ are mostly wide and easy, apart from a couple of steep pitches ('Look Ma') for exhibitionists in sight of Mid-Vail. Swingsville and Racetrack runs are used as timed race-courses, the first a simple coin-operated self-timing system, the second a more competitive (and more expensive) race against a time set by a top racer, with daily prizes (the Nastar system).

Near-flat panorama runs (and walks) follow the ridge: the Minturn Mile from Summit along to Wildwood followed by the almost as gentle but consistently downhill Eagle's Nest ridge run or Lost Boy (a slow-skiing run) which makes a tour of the western perimeter of the ski area, down to the bottom of Game Creek bowl, a side rather than a back bowl. Blue runs branch off from Lost Boy and on the other side of Game Creek bowl steeper runs drop down from Eagle's Nest ridge.

For longer runs the most satisfying options are those that drop from Eagle's Nest ridge (or the lift station itself) all the way to the resort. The most direct of these, from the top of the new Avanti express lift, is used as a Women's World Cup downhill. There are various snaking catwalk alternatives to the two steepish runs down to the Vail Village lift stations, and it is not difficult to ski back to any part of the resort, including the zone west of Lionshead, which has its own access chairlift and a gentle path home through the woods. On the eastern side of Mid-Vail most

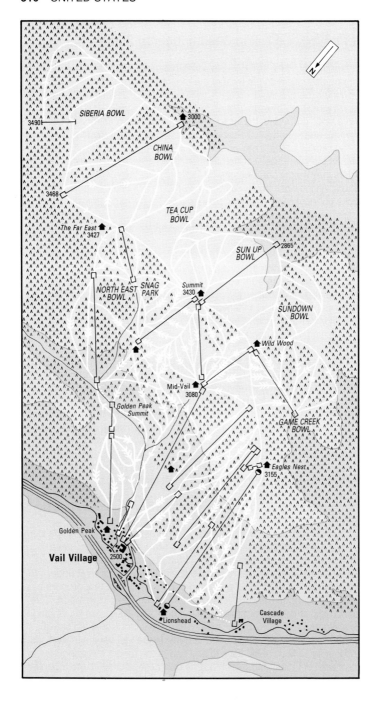

N

SIBERIA BOWL

3490⊢⊣ 3000

CHINA BOWL

3468

TEA CUP BOWL

The Far East 3427

SUN UP BOWL 2865

NORTH EAST BOWL SNAG PARK Summit 3430

SUNDOWN BOWL

Wild Wood

Mid-Vail 3080

Golden Peak Summit

GAME CREEK BOWL

Eagles Nest 3155

Golden Peak

Vail Village 2500

Lionshead

Cascade Village

routes home converge with Riva Ridge, which changes from ridge to funnel on its way down and, like many of Vail's runs, has the disconcerting habit of changing colour (from blue to black and back). Flapjack followed by Riva Ridge, from the top of the Highline chair to the resort, is said to be Vail's longest run, 7km. Prima/Pronto/Log Chute is about the toughest option on the mountain.

The back bowls are the entire ski area on the south-facing side of the main summit ridge, reached from Wildwood, PHQ, the Far East and numerous drop-off points along the crest. Unsurprisingly, light untracked powder does not last long. In the beginning there was just one lift, the High Noon chair, which returns skiers about 600m vertical to PHQ up the broad dividing ridge between Sun Down and Sun Up bowls, which have about 10 named runs each. In the nature of bowl-shaped ski areas, there is a wide range of orientation and, usually, snow conditions, though the bowls are in general sunny. The last places to be tracked out involve a lot of traversing for only short sections of interesting skiing before joining the Sun Up and Sun Down catwalks back to the chair-lift. Snow conditions being equal, the steepest and best runs are close to the lift on the eastern side of Sun Down bowl.

To the east of Sun Up, a huge new area has been opened up by the installation of a new high-speed chair-lift, the Orient Express, far away to the east of The Far East. The whole new area is usually known as China Bowl (apparently the rocky crest at the furthest eastern boundary of the ski area reminded someone of the Great Wall), but the undulations of the mountain divide the new zone into five identifiable sectors: the main bowl (China) with the chair-lift up its eastern flank; Siberia, Inner Mongolia and Outer Mongolia to the east, the most distant corners of Vail's ski area, served by a short linking drag-lift which has taken Vail's top altitude up to 3490m; and, tucked away between China and Sun Up, dainty little Tea Cup, where all the runs have sponsored brand names. Silk Road isa very gentle run making a huge tour to the east of the new area, as is Poppy Fields, a groomed piste from top to bottom of the Orient Express lift down the heart of China Bowl. The western side is not quite go-as-you-please territory, for there are rocks and cliffs in the vicinity of Dragon's Teeth. The biggest and steepest slopes are Jade Glade and the mighty Genghis Khan, which is less precipitous than it looks from the Orient Express lift, but plenty steep enough to keep the avalanche patrol busy after a snowfall.

Vail is tremendously proud of its high-speed four-seater chair-lifts. Our many reports suggest that **queues** are rarely a serious problem but are not unknown; twenty-minute waits at some bottle-necks have been encountered at peak times (weekends and college breaks). The busiest lifts are up to Summit and in the bowls when conditions are good.

There are mountaintop **restaurants** at the Far East, Wildwood and Eagles Nest but the main lunchtime congregation point is Mid-Vail. The choice is between the self service Look Ma Grill, which does good business at breakfast time as well as at lunchtime, and the elegant Cook Shack restaurant downstairs, where tables should be reserved. Reporters agree that on-slope catering is Vail's weakest point. The new Far East restaurant next season will be welcome.

The resort

Vail is a post-War creation, strung out for well over a mile between Interstate 70 and the foot of wooded mountainsides, exactly 100 miles from Denver; it is to the west of the Continental Divide, which is valuable for snowfall but sometimes complicates access: the road is good, but can be treacherous on the descent from Vail Pass.

Vail has none of the dreary functionality many skiers will associate with modern ski resorts: instead of big grey blocks of flats, sprawling lodges and luxury chalets are widely spread out, their polished timber and white stonework spruce and well kept. Wooded slopes climb from the edge of the village, covered footbridges span the Gore Creek which winds through the resort, traffic-free shopping streets are lined with

Facts on Vail   Colorado USA

Prices in dollars

Tourist office
Postcode 81657
Tel (303) 949 5750
Fax (303) 949 4699

Getting there
By road 100km from Denver. Interstate 70 west to Vail village.
By rail Denver, Union Station.
By air Denver; transfer 1.5hr.

Staying there
Visitor beds 25,000; breakdown: mainly in hotels, lodges and apartments.
Package holidays Activity Travel (hs) Bladon Lines (hs) Crystal (h) Falcon (hs) Hickie Borman (h) Inghams (h) Key to America (h) Made to Measure (hs) Neilson (h) Powder Byrne (h) Ski Club of GB (h) Ski Vail (hrcas) Ski Whizz Small World (c) Ski the American Dream (hs) SkiBound (hs) SnowRanger (h) Supertravel (h) Thomson (h) .
Medical facilities In resort: Vail Valley Medical Centre. Hospital; Denver.

Non-skiing activities
Indoor Athletic clubs, spas, massage parlours, museum, cinema, tennis courts, artificial skating rink, library.
Outdoor Hot-air balloons, skating, ice hockey, heli-skiing, sleigh rides, fishing, mountaineering, snowmobiles, snow-shoe excursions, snow-cat rides.

Kindergartens
Small World Play School
(at Golden Peak and Beaver Creek)
Tuition: No. Hours: 8.00-4.30. Ages: 2mths up.
Cost: 270.00 per week (with lunch).
Children's Centres
(at Golden Peak, Lionshead and Beaver Creek)
Tuition: Yes. Hours: 10.30-3.00. Ages: 3-12,.
Cost: 288.00 per week (with lunch).

Other childcare facilities
Lists of baby-sitters available from most lodges.

Special skiing facilities
Summer skiing No.
Cross-country 30km of trails at McCoy Park , Beaver Creek.

Lift passes
Area pass
Covers all Vail and Beaver Creek lifts. (20 lifts in total.)
Cost 6 days 210.00 (£109.38).
Credit cards accepted Yes.
Senior citizens 168.00 (over 65) saving 20%. Over 70s free.
Children 150.00 (under 13) saving 29%.
Notes Lift pass is fully interchangeable with that of Beaver Creek.
Beginners Lift pass is included in price of ski school.
Short-term passes Half-day (from 12.00pm).

Ski school
Vail and Beaver Creek
Four locations for ski school – Vail Village, Lionshead, Golden Peak and Beaver Creek.
Classes 10.00-3.45. Cost: 205.00 (3 days). Price includes lift pass. 'Learn to ski' course costs 170.00 for 3 days.
Lift priority Yes.
Children's classes Ages: 12. Cost: 155.00 (3 days). Price includes lift pass.
Private lessons available Between 8.30-3.45. Cost: 85.00 per hour. 1-5 people.
Special courses Style, bumps/powder and video race workshops, half-day costs 40.00; snowboarding (from 10 years old), 57.00 per day; Wedel weeks; weeks for the over 50s.

What is new for 92
1. New ski area on Grouse Mountain, adjacent to Beaver Creek, giving six new advanced and intermediate trails served by a quad chair-lift.
2. New self-service restaurant in Far East bowl.

elegant window displays and punctuated by small squares full of sculptures, and a photogenic central clock-tower stands outlined against the jagged peaks of the Gore mountains. This is Vail Village, at the eastern end of the resort. If not convincingly villagey, it is certainly easy on the eye. The other focus of resort life is the main lift station, Lionshead, which is similar in style and has the resort's main 'parking structure' near the Interstate exit. Free buses run every few minutes between Vail Village and Lionshead lift stations, via the parking structures and information centres. Traffic is banned from the central precinct from 8.30 to 10.30 in the morning and 2 to 5 in the afternoon. There is an efficient bus service to Beaver Creek.

Shopping in Vail is expensive but full of variety and curiosity value: as well as art galleries and expensive clothes shops there is an Alaskan craft shop, a splendid hattery and a DIY T-shirt emporium. Even the ski shops are full of all sorts of gadgets that seldom reach Europe.

The main thing to worry about when choosing **accommodation** is location. The luxury option is the Lodge, ideally placed next to the Vail Village lift station and with a large steaming outdoor pool, or the Westin, out on its own to the west of Lionshead, with its own link lift into the system. Both are wonderfully pampering and extremely expensive. At a less elevated price level, the Tyrolean Inn and Gasthof Gramshammer are well placed in Vail Village and welcoming in imported Alpine style. Infra-dig development on the wrong (north) side of the road provides relatively cheap accommodation; the Roost Lodge (recommended by several reporters) has a minibus service to the lifts. Skiers with cars (or happy to rely on bus services, which are not free) can stay, shop and eat cheaply down the valley in Eagle or Avon.

Vail is a complete resort and does not lack facilities for **cross-country** skiing (riverside trails on and around the golf course at the eastern end of the resort) or for **non-skiers**: three sports centres, with tennis courts (and special depressurised balls for use at high altitude), squash courts and all sorts of high-tech fitness/aerobics rooms.

Après-ski begins early, with 'buzzing' bar-life between 4 and 6pm. Lionshead has a 'Teen Cafe and Hangout' for 6- to 19-year-olds, with pool, video games and music, sodas and snacks. The smartest restaurants are in the two grand hotels: the Lodge's excellent Wildflower Inn and Alfredo's at the Westin. There are several fast food outlets. For a bit more atmosphere and a lot more food, there is no beating the uproarious Saloon Mexican restaurant at Minturn where they serve gargantuan plates of gooey enchiladas and margeritas by the litre. Alternative ethnic dining possibilities include the Nozawa (Japanese) in the Inn at Vail and the Mataam Fez Moroccan restaurant where you sit on the floor, eat with your fingers and watch belly-dancing. Mickey's piano bar in the Lodge is a fashionable place for the well heeled and sedentary to be seen over an after-dinner drink. Cyrano's is recommended for good food and the best dance music. Minimum-age rules (usually 21) are strictly enforced in discos and clubs.

There are **ski school** meeting places at Lionshead and Vail Village. The verdicts of the many reporters who took lessons ranged from the merely 'good' to the emphatically 'brilliant'. The school is huge, and large classes were never reported. Kindergarten arrangements are splendidly entertaining, with costumed characters and adventure trails. Free Meet the Mountain Tours start at 1pm on Sundays Mondays and Tuesdays, at Wildwood. **Nursery slopes** at valley floor level are between the Vista Bahn and Golden Peak lift stations at Vail Village and are mainly used as a children's playground. There is another nursery area at the top of the Lionshead gondola, and plenty of very easy longer runs in all sectors of the front side of the mountain.

Beaver Creek 2470m

Beaver Creek is a new resort, nearing the end of its first decade, 10 miles to the west of Vail and about a mile from the Interstate-side dormitory of Avon, a useful if unexciting holiday base. The resort itself is a straightforward collection of handsome new buildings and stylish shopping precincts at the foot of the slopes, now centred on the 300-room, $65m Hyatt Regency hotel, which offers inmates a ski concierge (to clean your skis and warm your boots overnight), 14 shops, 7 jacuzzis, 3 restaurants and a huge ballroom opening on to the slopes.

Beaver Creek already has a very worthwhile ski area, to be augmented this winter by a new hill (Grouse Mountain) with a high-speed quad, six runs (mostly advanced) and a 550m vertical drop. The main ski hill is served by two chair-lifts from the village to the summit (3490m) via a mid-station/restaurant area, Spruce Saddle, nearer the top than the bottom (3110m). The most direct complete descent is the 1989 World Championship mens' downhill course, Centennial, which sweeps down below the access chair-lift. As at Vail there are more roundabout and gentler alternative ways down.

Between the summit and Spruce Saddle the terrain is gentle and the upper runs make an ideal confidence-building area for near-beginners: provided, that is, they don't strike off to the left down the flank of the mountain on the double-black Birds Of Prey runs – Goshawk, Peregrine and Golden Eagle – long, steep trails (over 600m vertical) through the woods, often fiercely mogulled. There is a blue run down into this valley from Spruce Saddle, and a chair-lift (Westfall) back up to the summit. This is also the base of the new Grouse Mountain lift, to 3260m.

The valley divides Beaver Creek's main ski mountain from a broader and gentler ski area, served by two lifts: one from the resort, the other linking up with the Westfall and Grouse Mountain lifts. As well as intermediate trails beneath the lifts and a catwalk linking the two, there is an area of cross-country trails (30km in total) on the broad plateau behind the two top lift stations, McCoy park, at an average altitude of about 3000m. This zone is also the idyllically tranquil setting of a luxurious private chalet, Trapper's Cabin, bookable by the night, far from any pistes but accessible on skis. Near the bottom of the other lift (Larkspur) is another Beaver Creek institution: Beano's Cabin, favoured lunch spot among local big wheels who stump up the annual sub of some $10,000 to join the Beaver Creek Club. Beano's is less exclusive by night, when dinner excursions by snowmobile are organised.

Package holidays: Bladon Lines (hs) Falcon (h) Hickie Borman (h) Inghams (h) Key to America (h) Neilson (h) Ski Equipe (has) Ski the American Dream (hs) SnowRanger (s) USAirtours (h).

Breckenridge Colorado 2925m

Good for *Easy runs, tough runs, resort-level snow, lift queues, family holidays, woodland runs, artificial snow*
Bad for *Mountain restaurants*

Breckenridge is not one of the super-smart resorts that force themselves to international attention. It is not a resort that expert skiers normally have at the top of their North American agenda (although, as our verdicts suggest, there are runs to suit them). It is not a notably big ski area, even by American standards (its ski terrain is quoted as being less than half the size of Vail's, which itself only just qualifies for our 'big ski area' award). But we have many reports from enthusiastic visitors, most of whom were even more impressed than other visitors to America by the friendliness and helpfulness of the people, and particularly the lift staff.

The resort combines the attributes (spelled out elsewhere) common to most American resorts with some others which are less universally shared. The first is that the mountains here look vaguely mountainous to European eyes; there are no particularly distinctive peaks, but above the trails through evergreen forest there are open slopes, and views of rocky outcrops, and not just more rounded wooded hilltops. Secondly, the slopes and the town are not widely separated. Depending on where you choose to stay and where you choose to start or finish skiing, it can be a quite inconvenient resort; but it can also be just as convenient as the most carefully designed European resort – there is a lot of accommodation on or close to the slopes. Thirdly, the town is in the main visually inoffensive (even picturesque, if you don't react against its somewhat extravagant pastiches of 19th-century styles), distinctively American (rather than pseudo-Tyrolean), and lively without being intimidatingly ritzy or unreasonably expensive.

By the standards of European skiing, the piste network is very dense; the strips of forest left standing are sometimes narrower than the pistes they separate, and one piste usually seems much like its neighbours. But all these pistes add up to a lot of ground, which keeps the density of skiers happily low. None of the runs is long; on smoothly groomed blue and green runs, a moderately competent skier can go from the top to the bottom of any of the three 'peaks' in a few minutes. On the other hand, there are plenty of genuinely challenging and time-consuming mogul slopes. What the skiing perhaps lacks is a supply of intermediate slopes of the kind that make up the staple skiing diet of so many resorts in Europe, where they are graded red. Here, none of the blues are that difficult, and few of the blacks are that easy.

Breckenridge operates under the Ski the Summit umbrella, along with Keystone/Arapahoe Basin and Copper Mountain, about an hour away by reliable free shuttle buses. They do not share a lift pass but operate a tiresome system of interchangeable vouchers. Trips further afield (to Vail, for example) are possible, and car or minibus hire is easily arranged.

The skiing top 3720m bottom 2925m

Breckenridge's skiing is spread across the faces and flanks of three adjacent mountains, facing mainly north-east: Peak 8, Peak 9 and (you guessed) Peak 10, ranged from right to left as you look up the lifts. Peak 9 is directly accessible from the fringes of the town, and offers mainly easy skiing (except in one small area) from the top height of just under 3500m down to the resort. Peak 10, to the left, is a one-lift hill reached by descending the flank of Peak 9; it goes up to a similar altitude but has a broader range of difficult skiing. Peak 8 can also be reached from Peak 9 on skis, but also has direct access from a resort outpost, the Bergenhof. This is the experts' mountain, though it also has plenty of easy runs, even from the top altitude of 3720m.

Most skiers get on to **Peak 9** by means of the Quicksilver four-seat

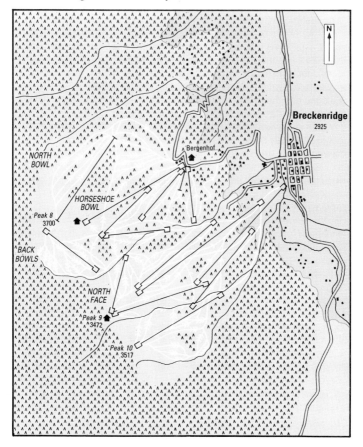

high-speed chair, starting a short walk up the nursery slopes from the edge of the resort. There is quite a lot of accommodation on the uphill side of the chair, notably the big Beaver Run apartment-hotel complex, from which you can either ski down to the Quicksilver or take another fast chair (Mercury) from higher up the hill. Each of these chairs serves a network of broad, very easy green trails through the forest, and gives access to higher chairs going up to the top (or nearly the top) of the mountain. The half-dozen higher runs on the front of the mountain are blues, but still smooth and easy. On the north side of the hill is a fierce little area of double-diamond 'expert only' trails, no more than 300m vertical, with entertainingly threatening names, served by their own chair-lift.

Runs of every grade drop down into the valley on the south side of Peak 9 for access to the one lift up **Peak 10** – another 'detachable quad'. Here again there are easy blues down the front of the mountain, but a choice of short but serious blacks on either flank – most with pitches in excess of 30°. On the north flank is The Burn, an entertaining area of off-piste skiing where most but not all of the trees were lost in a fire. At various points on this flank there are ways back across to Peak 9, the higher ones leading to the high Lift B rather than back to the resort and the Quicksilver lift and giving access to a long green traverse run, Union, which cuts right across Peak 9 to link with Lift 4 on Peak 8, which takes you to the tree-line.

Peak 8 has its greens and blues, served by another high-speed quad, on the front face, and it has serious double-diamond runs down the forested flank into the valley between it and Peak 9. But it also has distinctive features: easy blacks through the woods on the front face (reds, in European terms); an area of lightly wooded real blacks (gradients between 30° and 35°) high up on the south side of the peak, called the Back Bowls (not to be confused with Vail's); and twin bowls on the front of the mountain, above the trees (Contest and Horseshoe) offering 400m vertical of double-diamond – wide slopes, often with the best snow around, but uncompromisingly steep and often with big moguls. These and the Back Bowls are reached by the only lift in the resort which is not a chair – a T-bar drag.

As usual in America, **mountain restaurants** are few in number (two – Peak 10 has only a 'warming hut') and functional in nature; but there is no denying that they feed large numbers of people efficiently and well – particularly the Vistahaus (Peak 8), which is recommended for its pizza and soup.

The lift system normally works well and is mainly free of **queues** except at weekends (Denver is close) and during college breaks in late March. The Peak 8 T-bar and lift C on Peak 9 are occasional troublespots. A new lift is planned to extend the high bowl skiing on Peak 8, serving an area reachable at present by climbing. Lifts close early by European standards, even late in the season. There are free 'meet the mountain' tours, and timed race courses (including Nastar ones) on Peaks 8 and 9. Heli-skiing is available in the area and is highly recommended for skiers who don't need to count the pennies, even if they have little off-piste experience. There is extensive machinery for making **artificial snow**, particularly on Peak 9, but it is not always used as skiers would wish.

The resort

Breckenridge is an old gold-mining town, and the resort makes the most of it. As well as some genuinely old wooden buildings, around the long main street there are lots of not-so-old dinky retailing developments in vaguely 19th century styles, some quite tasteful, others conspicuously vulgar. There are various efficient free bus services run by the resort and by individual hotel/apartment complexes such as Beaver Run. Getting around is not a problem unless staying on the outskirts.

The slopes start a bit of a walk from the main street, and much of the

Facts on Breckenridge   Colorado **USA**

Prices in dollars

Tourist office

Postcode CO 80424
Tel (303) 453 6018
Fax (303) 453 7238

Getting there

By road 85km from Denver. Interstate 70 to exit 203, then Colorado Highway 9.
By rail Denver, Union Station.
By air Denver; transfer 1.5hr.

Staying there

Visitor beds 23,000; breakdown: mainly in hotels.
Package holidays Activity Travel (hs) Chalets and Hotels "Unlimited" (s) Crystal (hs) Falcon (hs) Hickie Borman (hs) Inghams (hs) Key to America (h) Made to Measure (hs) Powder Byrne (h) Quest Total Ski (h) Quest Travel (schools) (h) Ski Club of GB (h) Ski Whizz Small World (c) Ski the American Dream (hs) Ski-Tal (h) Skiworld (hcs) SnowRanger (hs) Snowbugs (hcs) Thomson (h) USAirtours (hs) Winter Adventure Holidays (hs) .
Medical facilities In resort: Medical and physio centres, chemists.

Non-skiing activities

Indoor Sports clubs, swimming, sauna, massage, jacuzzi, cinema, theatre, art gallery, library, indoor miniature golf course.
Outdoor Heli-skiing, horse and dog sleigh rides, rafting, fishing, ice skating (peak 9), snowmobiles, snow coach rides, toboggans, scooters.

Kindergartens

Snow Play (at Peak 8 and 9)
Tuition: No. Hours: 8.30-4.30. Ages: 2-5. Cost: 204.00 per week (with lunch and snacks).
Junior Ski School (at Peaks 8 and 9)
Tuition: Yes. Hours: 8.30-4.30. Ages: 4 and 5. Cost: 252.00 per week (with lunch). Special classes for 3yr olds as introduction to skiing, costs 37.00 per day, includes 1 1/2hrs tuition and meals.

Special skiing facilities

Summer skiing No.
Cross-country 35km of trails from Frisco centre, along the shores of Lake Dillon. Instruction available.

Lift passes

Area pass
Covers all lifts. (15 lifts in total.)
Cost 6 days 168.00 (£87.50).
Credit cards accepted Yes.
Senior citizens 78.00 (over 60) saving 54%. Over 70s free.
Children 78.00 (under 13) saving 54%. Free pass up to age 5.
Beginners 2 beginners' lifts. Beginners in ski school (levels 1-4) do not need a lift pass when with an instructor.
Short-term passes Half-day (from 12.00pm).
Other passes Ski the Summit – booklets of coupons which are interchangeable at Breckenridge, Copper Mountain, Keystone and Arapahoe Basin (6 out of 7 consecutive days 162.00 for adults, 84.00 for children).

Ski school

Breckenridge Ski School
Classes Full- or half-day, from 10.15 or 1.45.
Cost: 168.00 (6 days). Special women's classes, taught by female instructors.
Lift priority Yes.
Children's classes Ages: 6-12, teenagers 13-17. Cost: 168.00 (6 days). Lunches cost 5.00. Special 5-day package with meals 180.00.
Private lessons available Hourly. Cost: 65.00 per hour. Each additional person costs 20.00.
Special courses Daily ski clinics on one of the following: racing, style, powder, bumps, the Diamond challenge (tough runs). Telemark and snowboarding courses also available.

What was new in 91

New high-speed quad chair-lift, replacing old 2-seater chair on Peak 9.

accommodation is between the two. Practically all our reporters were enthusiastic about their accommodation. Beaver Run Resort is a massive hotel/apartment complex with easy access to the slopes, splendid rooms, 'wonderful' outdoor hot tubs and an efficient bus service. Just down the hill, the Hilton is widely recommended – 'superb rooms, superb breakfasts'. The Village is ideally placed between the town and slopes; the Lift condos and Liftside Inn are recommended. Breckenridge Mountain Lodge offers 'good, cheap accommodation a short walk from the centre'; rooms are small by local standards. Powderhorn apartments are 'brilliant', Pine Ridge condos 'massive and excellent'.

There is quite a range of **après-ski** activity, including snowmobile tours, forest sleigh rides involving steak dinners, 'super' ice-skating on the village pond and shopping until 9pm or 10pm. The resort organises quite a few special events, sporting and otherwise, including a well established January carnival, the Ullrfest, with parades, ice sculptures, fireworks and so on. There are plenty of bars with happy hours and happy customers from mid-afternoon onwards; recommendations include Jake T Pounders ('owned by a dog, live music, free popcorn') and Joshua's. There is a wide range of restaurants ('everything except a curry house'), which tend to fill up early when the resort is busy; many are reluctant to take reservations, so you eat early (from tea-time) or late, or wait for a table. Mi Casa is a popular bar with a long and lively happy hour (margeritas by the litre), and a good-value Mexican restaurant. The Cajun Cafe is repeatedly recommended for 'genuine southern food'. Other recommendation include: the Whale's Tail ('loads of atmosphere, good food, half-price kids' portions'); May Palace ('great Chinese, huge portions'); the lively Italian/American Hearthstone; the Red Orchid (Chinese); Horseshoe II (popular with families); Pierre's (French); the Prospector. The Brewery, which is a brewery, does 'the best beer in town' and 'reasonably priced snack meals'. Some reporters had difficulty tracking down discos, but they do exist.

Non-skiers should be able to keep themselves amused in Breckenridge, and can always resort to excursions to Vail or Aspen for celebrity-spotting or window-shopping, or to Boulder for actual shopping. **Cross-country** skiing is quite well provided for locally, and there are other centres nearby.

There are gentle (partly flat) **nursery slopes** at the foot of both Peak 8 and Peak 9. With one or two exceptions, our many reporters are uniformly enthusiastic about **ski school** classes and private tuition, and especially about the school's flexibility in meeting every conceivable tuition need. There are good kindergarten arrangements at Peak 8 and Peak 9 for children from the age of 2 months; advance booking is necessary.

Rich vein

Park City Utah, USA 2100m

Good for *Easy runs, resort-level snow, family holidays, tough runs, off-piste skiing, nursery slopes, short airport transfers, woodland runs, artificial snow*
Bad for *Mountain restaurants, skiing convenience, freedom from cars*

Separate resorts: Deer Valley, Park West

Like Utah skiing in general, Park City lags some way behind many other American resorts – in particular, those of neighbouring Colorado – in European promotion. Or perhaps we should say it has lagged some way behind: by the time this edition is published, Park City's hitherto low profile may have become much heightened. By now, the International Olympic Committee should have picked a venue for the 1998 Winter Games; one of the strongest contenders was Salt Lake City, Utah, which (like Albertville, France) is a hook on which to hang the sporting facilities of several nearby ski resorts; chief among them is Park City.

'Nearby' is, in this case, no exaggeration: Salt Lake City (a metropolitan area of some three-quarters of a million people) is privileged to have half a dozen serious ski resorts within three-quarters of an hour's drive.

The town grew up as a base for silver mining, and strives to preserve its 19thC heritage. One of its attractions as a resort is the lively, colourful Main Street, much of which looks as if it dates from the mining days, even if it doesn't. Silver mining is never far out of mind while you're skiing, either, with runs bearing names like Claimjumper, Shaft and Dynamite, and old mines (mostly disused, one ready for re-use when the price of silver gets high enough) dotted around the valleys. Sadly, the days are gone when you got up the hill by riding a mining train a couple of miles into the mountain and then taking an elevator up to the foot of the Thaynes chair-lift.

The Park City ski area comes from the classic Rocky Mountain mould. It is not large (compare the map with those of some major European resorts), and the terrain is neither dramatic nor notably varied; but its ridges, flanks and valleys provide the requisite range of gradients and they are laced with runs, so there is a lot of skiing to be done at all levels of competence (and navigation can be tricky). Most of the skiing is in the trees, but at the top of the system where the trees thin out are several steep faces and bowls with great appeal to good skiers.

Although only a mile from Park City, linked by the ski-bus and dependent on Main Street for nightlife, Deer Valley is in other ways a distinctly separate resort. Like many American resorts, it essentially has one owner; there is no easily skied link to Park City, and no shared lift pass. Nor is there a shared market niche; in 1991, Deer Valley celebrated its 10th year of selling itself on 'service, luxury and convenience'. Not surprisingly, it is relatively expensive. The accommodation is mainly in upmarket houses and apartments, with a couple of smart hotels half-way up the mountain, and the skiing consists mainly of beautifully groomed blues (which in America means intermediate runs, remember) – though there is also a range of genuine blacks.

Just down the road from Park City (off the area covered by our piste map), Park West occupies a contrasting market slot, selling itself mainly to Utahans on price – '$25 a day: Utah's best ski value'. (Deer Valley's daily lift pass, for comparison, cost $39 last season). Its ski area is small but adequately varied, with some challenging black pistes and off-piste runs; the resort is accessible on the ski-bus, so anyone who is thinking of splitting their time between Park City and Deer Valley can easily take in a day here as well.

Several other resorts are within easy reach by road: Brighton, Solitude, Alta and Snowbird – the latter two of particular interest to powder freaks (and covered in our USA round-up chapter a few pages after this one). There are effective bus services, but exploration-minded reporters have found car hire cheap. You can also ski to these resorts by signing up for the Utah Interconnect guided day-tour.

The skiing top 3050 bottom 2100m

The central physical feature of the ski area is a rounded mountain spur which starts out as Pioneer Ridge at the top, runs north-east through the major meeting point of Summit House and goes on down as Crescent Ridge. Park City is on the east side of this ridge, and most of its skiing is spread along its two flanks. The afternoon-sun side flanking Thaynes Canyon is fairly straightforward; the morning-sun side is complicated mainly by Treasure Hill, between the main ridge and the town. At the top of Thaynes Canyon is a lift serving the extensive, entirely off-piste skiing of Jupiter Peak and Jupiter Bowl.

For practically all skiers except the few with downtown accommodation, the base of the skiing is Resort Center, on the north-west fringe of the resort. The obvious way up the mountain from here is the four-seat gondola, which terminates 730m higher and 23 minutes later at the inaccurately named Summit House (2830m), having changed direction at the mid-mountain Angle Station. But there are various alternative routes using chairs.

The Town chair up to Angle Station gives direct queue-free access to the skiing from downtown Park City, and is usually quiet because there is no large-scale car parking nearby; both pistes back to the town are blue, but you can ride the chair down if you prefer.

The Pay Day triple chair goes to the top of Treasure Hill and serves a range of runs on the north-west-facing flank; the main run back down to Resort Center is the smooth, sweeping blue of the same name, chiefly remarkable as the longest night-skiing run in the West (about 2km, 390m vertical); it is illuminated from 4pm to 10pm, every night from Christmas to the end of March.

The Ski Team chair, starting a little walk above Resort Center (and therefore relatively queue-free) serves a sector of the main ridge facing north-east which is consistently quite steep, and the location of the resort's race-courses. (Erika's Gold is named after Erika Hess, who won both the Slalom and GS in the resort's first World Cup event, in November 1985.) Some of the other runs (such as Shaft) go directly down the hill and are only a couple of moguls wide.

The north-west-facing slopes of Thaynes Canyon are served by four chairs. At the north end of the valley, close to its mouth, the King Consolidated lift serves a range of similar broad intermediate pistes which get gradually steeper towards the northern end – those at the limit of the ski area just shading into a black grading. The efficient detachable quad Prospector chair is a great lift for intermediates, serving several harmless blue alternatives and the long, looping Claimjumper green, which for much of its length is out of sight of any lift. Motherlode serves a mix of steep blues and not particularly steep blacks – Glory Hole, for example, does not exceed 30°, although it is often heavily mogulled. The Thaynes chair serves the steepest pistes in the area, not because the mountainside as a whole is particularly steep but because The Hoist run, in particular, takes the form of a giant staircase and offers short pitches of up to 38° – a more typical gradient on the steeper stretches would be 35°.

At the top of Thaynes Canyon is the Jupiter chair, giving access to the experts-only off-piste skiing from Jupiter. The least steep section up here is the West Face of Jupiter Peak, a lightly wooded slope of around 38–40° which is reached by skiing down the ridge to the east past several alternative steeper 'shots' (to use the local term). A stiff half-hour walk up from the low point of the ridge – about 700m, climbing about 60m (at an altitude of 3000m) – brings you to Park City's steepest skiing, on the treeless East Face – a row of daunting couloirs, ranging from over 40° to (we are told) in excess of 51°. (Detailed topographical maps confirm these figures: most of this face has a gradient in excess of 1-in-1, or 45°.) The East Face leads down the less precipitous Puma Bowl, and off to the east of that is yet another mainly treeless area, McConkey's Bowl; all of this north-east-facing skiing ends up at the Pioneer chair. If you go north-west from the top of Jupiter lift instead of east, you have the options of the relatively tame Shadow Ridge or the steeper Portuguese Gap and Scotts Bowl.

As well as providing the return link for the bravo skiing on and below Jupiter's East Face, the Pioneer chair serves a range of intermediate runs on the south-east flank of Pioneer Ridge and, on the other side, the seriously steep Blueslip Bowl (named after the slips terminating the employment of resort staff caught skiing it when it was out of bounds, before a satisfactory exit had been created).

By American standards, the quantity of **mountain restaurants** is impressive: three (unless, like the resort literature, you count the one in the bottom gondola station). All have sunny terraces, but little else to recommend them; all are self-service, with an uninspiring range of fast food. Snow Hut, at the foot of the Prospector chair, has the redeeming feature of being built of logs. The uncompromisingly modern Summit

House has a good location – high, with big views, and at a convenient crossroads; in good weather, there is a barbecue on the sun terrace. An even bigger new restaurant is planned for this point when the new gondola is built (see below). The locals are tremendously proud of Mid-Mountain restaurant, an old mining lodge which a few years ago was moved three-quarters of a mile up the mountain to a position near the bottom of Pioneer lift; it seems a lot of effort for an unremarkable result.

Most reporters have found no worrying queues except for lift passes. Most of the major lifts are triple chairs without footrests or guard rails and an hourly capacity of 1,800 skiers; the recently built Prospector is a

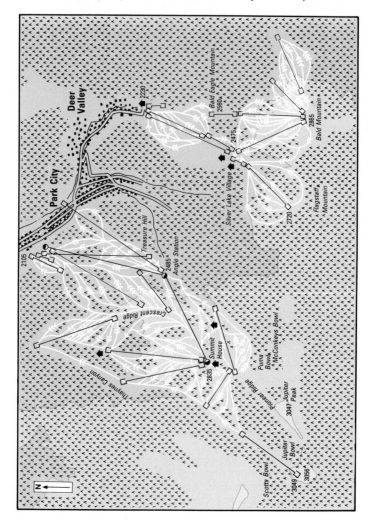

detachable quad carrying 2,800 an hour. A big new gondola is planned for the near future, running up and over Crescent Ridge from Resort Center.

There is an impressive **artificial snow** installation on a range of runs from top to bottom of the piste network.

The resort

Although Park City has a compact centre, consisting mainly of its pleasantly 'historic' Main Street, the resort as a whole spreads widely across the flat ground at the foot of the hills. There is good shopping in Main Street for clothes and gifts, and out-of-town supermarkets for food and everyday goods. Although there is a lift from the foot of Main Street, the main lifts start half a mile from the centre at Resort Center – a skiers' restaurant/shopping complex, smartly brick-built in post-modern style, with large car parks. Frequent free buses link the ski lifts, the centre and the suburbs from before 8am until after midnight, and a free reproduction trolley-car shuttles up and down Main Street.

There is some **accommodation** within walking distance of the lifts, but not much; the Silver King hotel and Silver Cliff condos, about 150 yards from the lifts, are recommended. The Prospector Square is a bus-ride away, but also recommended; it has the town's 'most complete fitness facility'. There are some small hotels and guest-houses occupying historic buildings around the old part of town, notably the Washington School Inn. Cross-country skiers and downhillers unconcerned about driving to the slopes should consider staying 20 minutes away in the Heber Valley at the secluded Homestead, a cluster of charmingly furnished old buildings forming a polished and relaxing hotel.

Most visitors seem to retire early to their condos, but for those who want it there is **après-ski** activity of various kinds along Main Street. To the relief of Utah's tourist trade, the Mormon state's booze laws are gradually being relaxed; but the sale of drink stronger than beer is still limited to 'private' clubs (temporary membership is easily obtained); the minimum age for drinking is 21, and anyone who looks under 30 may be asked for identification. Connoisseurs of real ale should make an early acquaintance with the products of the Wasatch Brew Pub – a bar, restaurant and mini-brewery producing (in sharp contrast to Messrs Budweiser, Coors and so on) tasty lagers and ales. Connoisseurs of ski resort dives should not miss a game of pool at the Alamo. There is a wide range of competent restaurants; reporters recommend the Barking Frog for 'modest prices and star-spotting', Alex's, Riverhouse Café and Claimjumper. Gamblers can take half-day or all-night excursions across the state line into Nevada.

There is some good **cross-country** skiing terrain, though the best of it is away from the downhill skiing and from the resort; the city golf course provides loops closer to hand. It is not a particularly good resort for **non-skiers** despite the availability of interesting excursions (to Salt

Facts on Park City Utah **USA**

Prices in dollars

Tourist office
Postcode UT 84060
Tel (801) 649 8111
Fax (801) 649 5964

Getting there
By road 30 miles east of Salt Lake City on
Interstate I-80.
By air Salt Lake City; transfer 45 mins.

Staying there
Visitor beds 10,000; breakdown: mainly in hotels
and apartments.
Package holidays Activity Travel (hs) Hickie
Borman (h) Made to Measure (hs) Ski the
American Dream (hs) SnowRanger (hs) Tailor
Made (hs) Thomson (h).
Medical facilities In resort: Doctor, dentist, optician
and physiotherapist. Hospital in Salt Lake City.

Non-skiing activities
Indoor Park City Racquet Club – 4 tennis courts, 2
racquetball courts, basketball, gymnasium,
aerobics; Prospector Athletic Club – racquetball
courts, weights room, swimming pool, whirlpool,
sauna; art galleries.
Outdoor Snowmobiles, hot-air balloons, sleigh
rides, fly and ice fishing, steam train rides.

Kindergartens
Kinderschule
Tuition: Yes. Hours: 8.30-4.30. Ages: 3-6. Cost:
250.00 per week (with snacks, lunch and lessons).
Other childcare facilities
Several companies offer day-care and baby-sitting
services, including K.I.D.S. Resort at the
Prospector Square Hotel and Miss Billie's Kid's
Kampus.

Special skiing facilities
Summer skiing No.
Cross-country 2 cross-country areas; Jeremy

Ranch (8 miles from Park City) has 65km of trails
for all standards; White Pine touring centre has
10km of trails on Park City golf course. Tuition and
hire available.

Lift passes
Park City
Covers all lifts in Park City ski area. (13 lifts in total.)
Cost 6 days 212.00 (£110.42).
Credit cards accepted Yes.
Senior citizens 96.00 (over 65) saving 55%. Over
70s free.
Children 104.00 (under 13) saving 51%.
Notes Main pass is for 6 out of 7 days.
Beginners Lift pass is included in ski school
package.
Short-term passes Half-day passes from 1.00pm.
Other passes Multi-area books contain vouchers
that can be swapped for day-passes in Deer Valley,
Park West or Park City (6 out of 7 days costs
216.00 for adults and 108.00 for children). Night
pass for floodlit trails costs 8.00 for adults and 5.00
for children.
Other periods Passes of 3 days or more allow you
one non-skiing day.

Ski school
Park City Ski School
Classes 10.00-12.00 and 2.00-4.00. Cost: 150.00
(5 days). Beginners' classes cost 295.00 for adults
and 221.00 for children.Price includes lifts, lessons
and ski hire.
Lift priority No.
Children's classes Ages: 7-12. Cost: 238.00 (5
days). 331.00 with supervised lunches.
Private lessons available Per hour. Cost: 55.00
per hour.

What is new for 92
Increased snow-making capacity.

Lake City, for example). Snowmobiling in deep snow in the back-country woods is an advance on the usual Alpine offering.

There are gentle **nursery slopes** at the foot of the mountain, and the opposite end of the car park from Resort Center are two chairs serving an excellent network of easy pistes (on the gentle Three Kings ridge) reserved for novices – mainly greens, with a couple of blues for confidence-building purposes.

We lack first-hand reports on the ski school, but classes are reportedly small even in high season.

Deer Valley 2200m
Deer Valley is a diffuse resort – smart condos and chalet-equivalents spread over and around a broad meadow – at the foot of a compact ski area run by the Norwegian Olympic champion Stein Eriksen. It is famed for the perfect grooming of its pistes, but not all the runs are groomed every day, so there can be excellent skiing in fresh deep snow after a

fall. From Snow Park Lodge, a chalet-style restaurants-and-shops complex where valets look after your skis while you park your car, chair-lifts old and new go up to Bald Eagle Mountain serving intermediate pistes with one or two more difficult variants. Beyond the rounded summit is Silver Lake Village, a mid-mountain resort (reachable by road) which is the obvious place for lunch (Snow Park Lodge being the only alternative). Beyond Bald Eagle Mountain, chairs go up from two points to the high point of the system, Bald Mountain (2870m); it is on the various flanks of this hill that good skiers will spend most of their time. The more direct runs served by the three most easterly lifts are all deservedly black-graded, and Mayflower bowl at the south-eastern extremity of the area is a double-diamond off-piste area. The two lifts up from Silver Lake Village – one to Bald Mountain, the other opening up the new area of Flagstaff – serve gentler slopes.

The return to the valley (for skiers not staying in Silver Lake Village) involves taking one of two short chairs up to the top of Bald Eagle, and then choosing from a range of blue pistes, a single green (Success) or a single black – Know You Don't, with a modest maximum gradient of 30˚.

There is some very impressive accommodation to be rented here, at some very impressive prices. The preferred location except for those wanting quick access to Park City's Main Street is Silver Lake Village. The places to stay are both imported and both very comfortable and attractive – the convincingly Norwegian Stein Eriksen Lodge and the only slightly less authentically Austrian Goldener Hirsch, complete with working Alpine horn.

Park West 2075m

Park West is a mini-resort four miles away from Park City, and linked to it by regular shuttle buses. There is some accommodation dotted around the broad valley at the foot of slopes, but most visitors are based in Park City or Salt Lake.

Above the base station at 2075m there are three short chair-lifts serving the easy, open lower slopes, and then four linked longer chairs going up to a top height of 2745m on Ironhorse Peak. A potentially confusing development here for European skiers is that there are runs graded red, which are expert-only, ungroomed runs, like the double-diamond blacks elsewhere in the USA. But, as a reporter points out, any uncertainty about the nature of the runs disappears as you ride the long Ironhorse chair-lift across them. The main ski area encompasses three ridged hills, each with blue runs down the ridge and steeper runs through woods down the flanks.

Snowboarding, not permitted at the other local resorts, is encouraged here – there is an area specially designed for practice and tuition, including two half-pipes.

Jackson Hole Wyoming 1920m

Separate resort: Grand Targhee

With two mountains rising straight from the rolling cowboy-country sage-brush of the valley, Jackson Hole is big, bold and impressive. It has one of the biggest vertical drops in the United States (1620m) and, according to several enthusiasts, 'unparalleled expert skiing'. The ski areas are divided logically, with an 'aerial tram' (cable-car) serving the extensive black areas on Rendezvous mountain to the left and the intermediate area (Casper bowl) in the centre, and two chair-lifts giving access to the beginners' area on Apres Vous mountain to the right. The village has a 'unique, down-to-earth charm' – no expensive or classy nightspots, but an impressive choice of restaurants and two 'Wild West' saloons with tremendous atmosphere.

Rendezvous mountain seems to have a mixture of everything: moguls, couloirs, tree-skiing and open powder slopes. From the top of the Tram (where there is a warming hut, serving soup and hot drinks), there are a series of steep and testing bowls, served by two lifts (of which the Rendezvous drag only operates between 11am-2pm and in good conditions). Rendezvous bowl, a wide, open mogul field, drops into the narrower tree-lined Cheyenne bowl, through the narrow Cheyenne Gully. To the left of Cheyenne bowl, the Bivouac black run provides some of the most challenging tree-skiing in the area. On the other side of Cheyenne, underneath the Sublette quad chair, is Laramie bowl, not as steep, but with longer runs and two 'suicidal' chutes off the dividing ridge. It is possible to ski over to the central ski area from here, or continue to more moderate black runs lower down, the north and south Hobacks and half a dozen runs down the face of the mountain. After a fresh snowfall, these runs provide some of the best powder skiing on the mountain, but they are also the first to suffer in less-than-ideal conditions.

Underneath the Thunder chair, which links Casper bowl with Rendezvous, is the notorious Thunder bumps run. Also accessible from the Thunder chair are two narrow couloirs – 'a warm up', says one reporter, 'for Corbet's Couloir which involves a sharp drop over a twenty foot cornice into a narrow chute'. **Casper bowl**, reached either from the tram or from two chairs from the village, has a variety of good intermediate pistes and long trails through the woods. **Apres Vous** mountain is also less severe than Rendezvous, though you can come across the occasional steep pitch or short mogul field, and there is plenty of scope for off-piste skiing between the trees. The majority of the skiing is easy and pleasant, with enticing sheltered bowls and extensive nursery runs to the village.

There is no big city nearby, so weekend crowds are not usually a problem, but there are usually 15-30 minute queues for the tram in the morning and after lunch (most skiers eat in the village, rather than in the one, no-more-than-adequate mountain restaurant at the base of Casper bowl). A dispute over the ownership of the resort has prevented any recent development, and many of the chair-lifts are old and slow. The Thunder chair is particularly queue-prone. Reporters have been very impressed with piste information and safety. Noticeboards at the village indicate which runs have been groomed in the last eight or sixteen hours. Any rocks are marked with red dye. The outer boundaries of the ski-area are clearly marked and anyone found skiing outside them can be fined $400. There is artificial snow in two areas above the village.

'Ski hosts' offer free guided tours around the resort every day. Reports of the ski school are enthusiastic – classes are small by European standards. The Ski Wee kindergarten is also recommended; kids are transported around the slopes in eight-seater buggies which keep them free of the lifts and provides the necessary impetus of fun. All-day nursery care is also available.

Teton Village, the resort at the foot of the slopes, is tiny. There are a few houses built among the aspen trees on the slopes but the village consists mostly of a tiny horseshoe of hotels. Of these, the Mangy Moose is the most popular. It serves enormous breakfasts and has a great lunch-time bar. The elegant Alpenhof has apparently deteriorated and one regular visitor was recently disappointed by the slow service at its restaurant, Dietrich's. The Sojourner is a good alternative, with popular fondue nights.

For shops and nightlife, you need to take the bus into the town of **Jackson** itself, twelve miles away. The Start bus service shuttles back and forth between the two resorts 'matching Swiss efficiency for time-keeping and cleanliness'; any journey costs $1, a book of ten tickets costs $7. You may have to wait a few minutes at peak times as the buses are not allowed to carry standing passengers. Jackson is a town of saloons with swinging doors where you can gamble or sip your beer seated in a leather saddle at the bar. There are lots of traditional 'Wild West' shops selling leather goods and Indian pottery and jewellery at uninflated prices. One reporter was delighted to find Timberland boots at about half the UK price. Another suggests searching out the highly original Jackson Hole Hat Company.

Most places in the town are within easy walking distance of each other, and never far from the bus route to Teton. The Wort hotel is apparently the most glamorous, but according to our reporters, you won't do better than the Parkway – 'excellent, friendly, very comfortable, lots of facilities (sauna, hot spa, gym etc)'. A simpler alternative is the Inn. Neither serves food, but this is no problem; there are about 40 restaurants in the town, most of which offer good value and real atmosphere. Our reporters are unanimously impressed. Particular recommendations are: for breakfast, Bubbas and the Bunnery ('healthier options'); for snacks, the Sizzler fast-food bars; for dinner, the 'quaint' Sweetwater, just off the main square, JJ's Silverdollar at the Wort hotel ('pleasant and quiet, food has a local emphasis, eg buffalo and elk'), the Blue Lion ('posh, but worth it'), the Cadillac Grille ('1940s atmosphere, excellent variety of meals') and Anthony's Italian restaurant ('extremely popular with locals, book well in advance'). Jackson has two exceptional bars, the Million Dollar Cowboy Bar and the Rancher, which seem to be the focus of the town. Both have pool tables, live music and bags of cowboy atmosphere. Between 7pm and 9pm on Thursdays, you can learn how to dance 'Western swing-style' in the Million Dollar bar.

There is plenty to tempt the non-skier. Apart from the many sports and bathing facilities, there are 'unmissable' day-trips to Yellowstone Park by snowmobile or husky-drawn sledge, tours around the Elk refuge on the edge of town and snow-shoe excursions in the stunning Grand Teton National Park. Cross-country enthusiasts have a choice of 25km of groomed trails at Teton or 10km of 'rolling terrain' at Grand Targhee. Several reporters have commented on the abundance of visible wildlife in the area – coyotes foraging near the village and moose and deer on the slopes. A car is not necessary to enjoy the local sights, but one reporter was very glad to have hired one and gained the freedom to explore this beautiful area.

All our reporters have commented on the cheapness of the resort. With the exception of the lift pass (which is expensive for what it is, even by US standards), resort prices were considerably lower than expected. The tram costs $2 per ride on top of the lift pass.

On the edge of Jackson is the Snow King ski area, a small mountain with a vertical rise of about 500m, served by two chair-lifts and a short drag. It is a very suitable area for beginners, with plenty of easy wooded trails, but there are also enough steep pitches at the top to keep a seasoned skier occupied for half a day. Twice a week, Wednesdays and Saturdays, there is night skiing on the lower slopes.

Tourist office ℗ (307) 7332292

Package holidays Activity Travel (hs) Chalets and Hotels Unlimited (h) Collineige Ski (s) Fresh Tracks (h) Hickie Borman (hs) Made to Measure (hs) Neilson (h) Ski Club of GB (h) Ski Scott Dunn (hs) Ski the American Dream (hs) SnowRanger (hs) Supertravel (h) Tailor Made (hs)

Grand Targhee 2420m

The Grand Targhee ski area, 42 miles away from Jackson and reachable by daily bus, has an excellent powder reputation and is 'definitely worth a visit' according to several enthusiastic reporters. The resort consists of little more than a large car-park fronted by a handful of buildings, which include a lodge and three restaurants. A steep climb from the car-park brings you to the Bannock chair-lift, which climbs to an elevation of just over 3000m (it is possible to get off, but not on, half-way up). It serves a vast array of predominantly black runs on sparsely wooded and 'completely uncrowded' slopes and a long, scenic green trail which skirts the main ski area and descends down a valley to the base-station. To avoid queues at Bannock, you can take a short chair above the beginners' area and traverse across to the Blackfoot lift, which provides access to the runs at the northern end of Targhee. Exposure to wind can sometimes be a problem. The neighbouring mountain is reserved for snowcat powder skiing which needs to be booked at least a day in advance and costs about $160 per day (including a champagne lunch).

United States: other resorts

Vail, Breckenridge, Park City and Jackson Hole (the subject of the four chapters before this one) are not in a league of their own; there are plenty of other resorts worth considering, most of them now available through UK tour operators. This chapter, based on an introduction to American skiing contributed to the *Guide* a couple of years ago by Elisabeth Hussey, outlines the main contenders. We have added some short summaries of reporters' views; in doing so we have not repeated endlessly remarks (about friendliness, scenery, piste-grooming and so on) that are valid for America in general – see page 510.

California

Squaw Valley
For a long time after the excitement of hosting the 1960 Olympics, Squaw did not develop very fast as a resort. It did not need to – skiers were drawn by its difficult slopes (KT22 is named after the 22 kick-turns made by a panic-stricken intermediate trying to get down), vertical drop of 870m (reached by a 150-person cable-car), and extensive area for hotshots, mostly high above the tree-line.

Now, however, a huge and impressive lodge has been built at Gold Coast, a convenient mountain meeting-place with beginner and intermediate area nearby. A great deal of artificial snow-making has also been added, following a snow drought in 1988. Hotels have now been built at the bottom of the cable-car; the Olympic Village Inn, the Olympic Plaza Bar and restaurant, and the Squaw Valley Lodge are all ski-in, ski-out. A triple chair, five minutes down the road from the cable-car, now links the big complex of Squaw Creek to the ski area. With 405 bedrooms and luxurious facilities, it provides plenty of accommodation. Many skiers, however, still prefer to stay on Lake Tahoe, with the chance to visit 21 nearby resorts. In Reno accommodation is remarkably cheap – they expect to take the money off you at the gambling tables.

Experts will still go to Squaw and even walk a little from the top lift to reach the 300m-long cliff of Palisades, but their less expert friends and relations will also enjoy easier trails.

Heavenly Valley
Heavenly has one face of its mountain in California and the other in Nevada. It also has the most amazing scenery, with Lake Tahoe, glittering blue-green, below it on the California side, while the Nevada desert stretches away to the east. The resort has the largest ski area in North America, with a vertical drop of over 1000m. It is mostly well groomed and equipped with snow-making, but there are unpisted areas such as Mott Canyon. Recently built lifts, such as the Comet detachable quad, are thinning the crowds which pour up from the cities of California and Nevada. Like Squaw Valley, Heavenly looks after its beginners at

the top of the mountain where the snow is lighter. But it's wise to ride the chair down – some of the moguls down towards the lake are huge.

As at Squaw, nearby towns such as Tahoe City tempt you to stay by offering cheap rates, hoping their one-arm bandits and blackjack tables will make up the difference. Cabarets introduce the top names in international show business. Not the best place for families, Heavenly is for those who want to ski hard and have a good time.

What particularly impressed our reporters was the scenery – 'fabulous, even better than expected'. What didn't was the lack of snow last year.

Mammoth Mountain

In California's Sierra Nevada range, Mammoth Mountain's slopes lie alongside a rising valley road, which at weekends is packed with cars from San Francisco and Los Angeles. But chair-lifts at intervals along the road spread out the crowds, so there is no central bottleneck, and the city crowds disappear during the week.

Thirty lifts, including five speedy quads, cover 150 trails. The vertical drop of nearly 1000m includes steep chutes and powder bowls at the top, then the trails reach the trees and funnel into mogul slopes, intermediate runs and easy motorways, so that all skiers can take their choice. Thanks to a breathtaking top altitude of 3370m and extensive artificial snow on the lower slopes, the season lasts normally from November to June.

Dave McCoy, who founded the resort and runs it with his family, is a stickler for appearances. Instructors and resort staff have to look clean and tidy (no moustaches allowed). The family influence is pervasive; Mammoth is recognised as one of the top US resorts for families.

The Mammoth Mountain Inn is right across the car park from several lifts and has a good restaurant, bar and accommodation, though not much nightlife. For that, Mammoth Lakes, (four miles down the road) offers excellent restaurants and bars. Those without cars who want to return to Mammoth Mountain Inn should ask the time of the last shuttle-bus to avoid a lonely walk home.

The McCoy family also own June Mountain, 20 minutes' drive away, and the lift passes are interchangeable. About a sixth the size of Mammoth Mountain, it offers a good day's skiing and has shops, ski-hire and child-care. Despite its name, June Mountain closes usually in early May.

Package holidays Ski the American Dream (h).

Colorado

Aspen

Richest (and probably most expensive) of the United States ski resorts, Aspen started life as a tough mining town. It was deserted when the silver market slumped in 1893, and started its new life in the 1930s when the first trails were laid out by André Roch of Switzerland.

The town was lovingly restored by Walter Paepcke, a Chicago

millionaire who saw its potential as a summertime music camp and started by distributing pots of paint to the owners of dilapidated mining shacks. Now the town is laid out in a colourful patchwork of low-rise clapboard houses. The flights into its little airport from Denver, Chicago and Los Angeles are usually crowded with the rich and famous. In the evening the glittering malls are thronged with well dressed skiers.

Most skiers have to walk (or take the bus) for some distance to reach the slopes. Aspen has no less than four skiing mountains. Aspen Mountain rises from the town itself with big bold runs including the World Cup men's downhill course. Aspen Highlands, only recently included on the lift pass, is less developed, with a variety of ungroomed powder chutes and bowls. Snowmass, a bus-ride away, is the perfect intermediate mountain – neat, manicured, with lower slopes lined with ski-out, ski-in condominiums. Buttermilk, on the outskirts of the town, is for beginners and children, keeping them safely away from the bombers. Experts should stay in Aspen itself – the old four-square Hotel Jerome if they can afford it or the Christiania Lodge or Alpine Club Lodge if their budgets are tighter. Restaurants tend to fill up early in the evening so it is advisable to book in advance.

Reporters approved of the lack of queues, but regretted the lack of good mountain restaurants; one was disappointed by the dreary appearance of the village – 'neither pretty nor expensive-looking'.

Package holidays Bladon Lines (hs) Crystal (hs) Inghams (hs) Made to measure (hs) Neilson (h) Ski Club of GB (h) Ski the American Dream (hs) SnowRanger (hs) Supertravel (h) Thomson (h).

Copper Mountain

In the same Ten Mile Mountain Range as Breckenridge, Copper Mountain forms part of the Ski the Summit area, which includes Keystone and Arapahoe Basin on its lift pass, and makes a comfortable base from which to visit all the Ski the Summit resorts, with eight mountains, 56 lifts and 268 trails. There is a free Summit Stage shuttle bus. Keystone is worth visiting for the night skiing as well as by day and A-Basin (to use the local abbreviation) rises above the trees to 3890m, staying open until June. But there is enough local skiing to satisfy the fastest piste-basher for a week or more. The skiing has been laid out to a careful plan. It has three base areas – one for beginners, one for intermediates and one (with 840m vertical drop) for experts. Reporters came across several lift queues but not many mountain restaurants.

The village started as little more than a Club Méditerranée hotel but now a new Hyatt and condominiums form a compact living area with the Resort Racquet and Athletic Club providing pools, hot tubs, saunas, gyms, indoor tennis, a nursery and a restaurant. The village still does not amount to much – there are few shops, even fewer restaurants.

Package holidays Club Med (h) Inghams (hs) Ski the American Dream (hs) SnowRanger (hs) USAirtours (hs).

Steamboat

Billy Kidd, winner of a silver medal in the 1964 Olympics and a gold in the World Championships at Val Gardena in 1970, is the front man for Steamboat and everyone's ideal 'nice guy'. He waits at 1pm each day to ski down with anyone who cares to share his mountain, and his stetson has become the town's trademark. (The resort's 'cowboy' feel is actively encouraged – they run a stampede there each spring, and a joke ski race for cowboys each January.) Billy likes powder, so a certain amount of the terrain is kept unbeaten and the Powder Cats will, at a price, take skiers up to the Buffalo Pass to ski the powder all day long.

The town of Steamboat Springs, a couple of miles from the slopes, got its name from the gurgling noise made by the local springs, which sounded like steamboats. The thermal water now refreshes skiers after they have spent a strenuous day on the mountain. Steamboat developed first around a ski jumping area called Howelsen Hill, which is now lit for night skiing. Most of accommodation for skiers has been built at the bottom of the ski area, some of it ski-in-ski-out. The Ski-Inn Condos are recommended. There are some lively bars and restaurants, and a modest amount of shopping.

The slopes have plenty of blue and green trails, and a reasonable amount of more challenging skiing, including entertaining wooded glades. Billy Kidd's feel for the family makes it a good place to take children. They have a stay-and-ski-free arrangement of their own.

Steamboat is quite a long drive from Denver, but you can take connecting flights, or fly direct from many other airports in the States.

We have a fat file of reports, all from very satisfied customers, but very few identifying pros and cons particular to Steamboat.

Package holidays Bladon Lines (hs) Crystal (hs) Falcon (hs) Inghams (hs) Ski Whizz Small World (c) Ski the American Dream (hs) SnowRanger (s) Supertravel (h).

Idaho

Sun Valley

Created by Averall Harriman during the depression of the 1930s, to encourage passengers on to the Union Pacific Railroad, Sun Valley had a stylish start to life. Harriman hired a good publicity man, who saw the advantages in advertising sun rather than snow – hence the name. He also arranged for a couple of films to be made here, and then many movie stars were invited to the resort. Their photographs still give an old-time glamour to the Sun Valley Lodge, matching its wide corridors, big-tapped baths and curious concrete construction. To avoid the ugliness of concrete the mixture was poured into wooden moulds and painted to look like immense logs. Surprisingly, it works.

As befits the resort which in 1936 installed the first chair-lift in the world, Sun Valley has a well connected system of chairs, including three quads. It covers a well balanced ski area with a vertical drop of over 1000m, catering for all standards.

The best way of getting to Sun Valley is to fly in a Dash 7 from Boise, Seattle or Salt Lake City. Within the resort, buses shuttle to the ski mountains and around the various lodges. Our one recent reporter was disappointed by very poor snow in December, and by the reluctance of the resort's new management to use their snow-making facilities.

Package holidays SnowRanger (h).

New Mexico

Taos Ski Valley

The slopes of Taos (at the same latitude as Tunis) are breathtaking in height and challenge, descending from over 3600m. Ernie Blake, its founder, deliberately left areas unreachable except on foot, so that some powder is kept for those energetic enough to work for it.

He also refused to build too large a resort village, so unless you book early you will find yourself staying down in the valley and driving up to ski each day. This is not too much of a hardship, since Taos itself is no featureless valley settlement but a Hispano-Indian adobe town full of history, where many painters and writers (including DH Lawrence) have made their homes at one time or another. There are 80 fine art galleries and the shops are full of Indian rugs and jewellery.

Huge moguls greet you as you reach the resort's car-park (you can sneak off to the side to avoid them) and, up above, the powder among the wooded glades is unaffected by the blazing sun (the tree-line here is twice as high as in the Alps). Ernie Blake's sense of humour pervades the slopes. At the top of the more difficult glades, glass jugs of martini are hidden – find them and you can imbibe a bit of courage to help you down. The runs are called after pioneers and revolutionaries – one steep traverse is named Sir Arnold Lunn. It's a resort for good skiers, though Kachina Peak has a whole network of interesting and fairly easy trails. Practically everyone who goes there goes to ski school and Jean Mayer, head of it, employs instructors who can teach at any level (and are just as likely to discuss world affairs as the quality of snow).

Taos is reached by flying to Albuquerque and then on to the resort's airfield. The resort is unique, and worth the trip. Our most recent reporter says that the skiing 'takes some beating' for the better skier, but that the intermediate areas are rather limited (and crowded).

Package holidays Ski Club of GB (h) Ski the American Dream (hs) SnowRanger (h).

New York

Lake Placid

Lake Placid still dreams of the two Winter Olympics it hosted, in 1932 and 1980. For the winter sports enthusiast this Olympic past has advantages. Not only are there the big bold slopes of Whiteface Mountain to ski, but all the other Olympic facilities to try out as well.

The ski jumps are out of bounds to beginners but there is a lift enclosed in glass to take sightseers to the top for a peer down the vertiginous slide. On the luge run you can steer the final five turns yourself. The half-mile bobsled descent is perhaps the most exciting event of all. There are miles and miles of prepared cross-country trails through the Adirondack National Park (the biggest of such parks in the States). Three big skating rinks are open to the public when not in use for exhibitions, competitions and ice hockey matches.

Lake Placid is a pretty town, set by Mirror Lake, with white-painted houses and a bustling air. Whiteface Mountain, a bus-ride away, has a much more vigorous climate – the same contrast as is found between Aviemore and Cairngorm. Whiteface rates high for the quality and extent of its difficult terrain, so it attracts good skiers. In 1988 it opened a new intermediate run from the top to the base – over three and a half miles, with a vertical drop of 980m. Over 90% of the skiable area is covered with snow-making, which had its first big test (passed with flying colours) at the 1980 Olympics. One recent reporter found the ski area fairly limited.

The town is quite extensive, with good shops, plenty of restaurants, three cinemas and several nightclubs. It is quite innovative, too, in providing amusement for its visitors. Husky dogs draw sleighs full of people on the lake and lessons are given in driving them.
Package holidays Hickie Borman (h) SnowRanger (h).

Utah

Alta and Snowbird are close together amid the startlingly beautiful scenery of Little Cottonwood Canyon, just 40 minutes drive from Salt Lake City. Their small ski areas contain a lot of skiing, and a lot of it appeals to experts – partly because of their reputation for exceptional amounts of exceptionally light powder snow. A glance at our piste map tells you that these are highly unusual places. The two resorts are not linked (except by frequent shuttle-bus), although it is possible to ski between the two with guidance.

Alta
This resort dates back to 1938 and has not changed much in 20 years. There are no trams or high-speed quads, but the skiing is for the

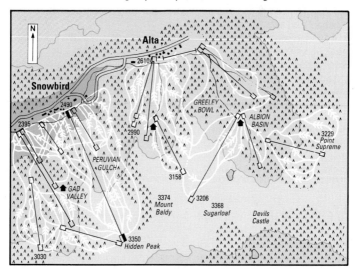

connoisseur. The first thing you notice is that there is no village – just a few buildings dotted around the valley; many skiers drive up from Salt Lake. The second is Alf's High Rustler – over 350m of moguls straight to your feet.

There are two ski areas, divided by a high ridge ending in the aforementioned Rustler run. The main area, in a valley beneath Mt Baldy, has blue runs down the middle and steep black pistes and off-piste areas on either side. Greeley Bowl, on the other side of the dividing ridge, is off-piste and genuinely black, but beyond it Albion basin is gentler, with excellent green motorways leading back to the canyon. The total vertical drop of around 600m is modest, but within it there is a lot of skiing to be done. The ski school is famous, organised by Norwegian Alf Engen and specialising in powder technique. Master it here and you will have no trouble anywhere else.

A few hotels and condominiums are spread along the base of the mountain, linked by a rope tow in both directions from which small tows go up to the lodges. The Alta Lodge looks the best. The lift pass is very cheap by Utah standards.

Snowbird

A modern resort built on stark concrete lines, reminiscent of Flaine, Snowbird taps a different market: it has much more accommodation, and is a place for good skiers who like luxury. Dick Bass, the Texan oil millionaire who directs the resort, has grandiose ideas and Cliff Lodge, the main hotel, is a vast 500-bed place complete with conference centre, two floors dedicated to health and fitness, restaurants and a 12-storey glass window (the atrium) looking straight out at the white slopes, quilted with gentle moguls. The mixture of concrete walls inside and Chinese treasures brought back from Dick Bass's travels is curious but effective. There are three cheaper condominium lodges – Iron Blosam, The Lodge and The Inn – which are comfortable but not reachable on skis.

A 125-person cable-car rises from the resort's central plaza to Hidden Peak at 3350m, from which there is a choice of going down blue or black pistes into Peruvian Gulch, or black piste into Gad Valley, or along the ridge that separates the two before plunging down off-piste on one side or the other. This is all above the tree-line. Gad Valley has several chairs serving a lot of black and blue piste skiing, and lower down a dense network of greens across the mountainside. Trees are scarce because avalanches have taken them away; there are just sufficient on the lower slopes to give definition to the runs. The total vertical here is a little more – about 950m.

Package holidays Activity Travel (hs) Fresh Tracks (hc) Hickie Borman (hs) Made to Measure (hs) Ski Club of GB (h) Ski the American Dream (hs).

Vermont

Killington

Close to the big cities of the east, Killington can draw thousands of desk-bound workers longing for holidays with exercise and adventure – provided that snow can be guaranteed and that learning to ski there is fun. Temperatures regularly plummet below zero from October to May, so Killington soon became expert in the use of computerized snow-guns and the tillers necessary to keep the snow in good order. They also thought up a system which took the fear out of learning. Videos explain what is going to happen; people-movers take beginners with unwieldy equipment to their first slope; there is a high proportion of teachers to learners. As a result, the resort can guarantee to get novices skiing down from the top of the mountain within three days.

But Killington is not just for beginners. With 77 miles of trails stretching over six peaks, the resort prepares a full range of slopes and its teaching system extends to small areas all over the place where instructors specialise in more advanced technique. The whole area is beautifully signposted so that you can follow pictures of bears or suns down the appropriate trails, including 'the easiest way down'. Chair-lift riding in extremely low temperatures is a chilly business – warm clothes, face-masks and hand-warmers are essentials.

Killington is also easy to reach for a few days skiing to add to a business trip. It is 85 miles from Burlington airport and 39 from Rutland, from both of which you can hire a car. The Vermont inns are cosy and picturesque, and in Killington village itself there are quite attractively built condominiums. The Pickle Barrel, the Wobbly Barn and the Nightspot all provide live music.

Recent reporters were critical of the 'drab' buildings, appalling mountain restaurants and weekend lift queues.

Package holidays   Hickie Borman (hs) Ski the American Dream (hs) SnowRanger (h) Thomson (hs).

Stowe

The old village of Stowe is a pleasure to visit, with clapboard houses, country inns and old-fashioned corner shops clustered around the white-spired church which is its emblem. Stowe has been famous for skiing since the 1920s and has the oldest ski school in the States.

The two ski areas lie a bus-ride away from the village, though there are a couple of hotels on the slopes looking after golfers in summer, skiers in winter. The two areas are not yet connected (there are plans for a ski link) but their lower slopes are close. Some fearsome trails (including The Front Four) cascade down from the top of Mount Mansfield. The snow-making guns and intense cold can turn the surface into boilerplate at times. A detachable quad has cut the queues, though some remain. On Spruce Peak the skiing is easier.

Cross-country is excellent – you can stay at the Trapp Family Lodge (of Sound of Music fame) which is surrounded by trails. A free shuttle bus operates from many of the inns, which, with deep leather chairs and roaring fires, steak-and-kidney pie or Highland Haggis, provide country comfort. Burlington airport is less than an hour away by car.

Our one recent reporter was extremely impressed by the ski school, but disappointed by the lack of facilities for non-skiers.

Package holidays   Ski the American Dream (hs) SnowRanger (h) Thomson (hs).

Heaven on earth

Whistler British Columbia, Canada 652m

Separate resort: Blackcomb

Whistler is the name of the mountain (2178m) that towers above two resort villages – Whistler Creek and Whistler Village – about 75 miles north of Vancouver on the Sea to Sky highway. The first ski lifts were built here 27 years ago and Whistler soon became Canada's number one resort, but it is only in the last few years that it has gained an international reputation and attracted increasing numbers of British skiers. Its ski area is not particularly big or particularly high, and it is prone to bad weather due to its proximity to the Pacific coast. The main resort, Whistler Village, is purpose-built, charmless and, because of its low altitude, often snowless. In recent years it has been inundated by Japanese tourists and the latest saying in the resort is 'the Canadians ski here, the Australians work here and the Japanese buy here'. So where do the British fit in? Many of them, tempted by the resort's reputation for deep snow, wide range of skiing, and proximity to Vancouver, ventured across the Atlantic for the first time last season. None was disappointed. The words of one sum up their collective opinion: 'Having skied in Austria, France, Switzerland and Colorado, I found that Whistler combined the best of European scenery, variety and memorable runs with the best of American efficiency, politeness, friendliness, space, snow and ski school'. Although there are several excursion possibilities, there is not much here to tempt non-skiers.

Whistler Village shares a lift pass with the small neighbouring resort of Blackcomb, which has a similar, compact ski area, linked to Whistler by a single chair. The lift pass is the only thing the resorts share; Blackcomb has its own management, lift company, ski school, even piste map. The fierce rivalry between the two (which are only a short walk apart) may seem strange to people used to cooperative, multi-linked European resorts. But it does add a healthy element of competition, the results of which are abundantly evident in both resorts, in the form of new lifts, each one better and faster than the last.

Whistler's main access lift is the 5km-long 10-person gondola from the edge of the Village to Roundhouse Station (1810m). There is a mid-station for access to the nursery slopes and baby-lifts around Olympic Station. To the left of Roundhouse Station, three chairs serve short intermediate runs with some steeper, moguly pitches through the trees. To the right, longer runs descend to Whistler Creek under the old gondola (due for renovation next year) and parallel chair. In bad weather and poor visibility, reporters have been very glad of these extensive, sheltered woodland runs. In good weather, most head for the upper bowls above Roundhouse, resulting in long queues for the Peak chair. The views from the top are spectacular and the runs down equally breathtaking, especially after fresh snow.

Blackcomb's skiing is reached by a series of quad chairs. Like Whistler, it is divided between open and wooded slopes, with many green paths and some truly black descents, including the (officially) steepest piste in North America – the Saudan couloir. Blackcomb has now installed snow guns to protect its lower slopes, but when conditions are mild and humid (which they often are) these are not much use. Neither mountain has an adequate supply of restaurants. Whistler has two adjoining ones at Roundhouse which are said to serve fast food on plastic plates. Pika's has open-air barbecues. Cristal Ridge is about the best on Blackcomb; it is 'a small, jolly cabin serving buffalo burgers, soups and sandwiches'. The resorts' main ski schools are both highly praised. There is a third school, Ski Esprit, run jointly and operating over both ski areas, which is reportedly 'first class, tremendous fun, the best I've ever experienced'. There is a high proportion of Aussie instructors. Kindergarten facilities are superb and cater for children of 18 months up. On sunny weekends queues can be a problem, particularly for the main gondola and the two highest lifts in each resort (the Peak and 7th Heaven chairs) but in general the lift system is efficient and the lifts (many of which are quad chairs) are very speedy. Our reporters have been unanimously impressed with the maintenance of both lifts and runs. It is possible to organise heli-skiing trips from either resort – one reporter had a memorable trip with Tyax Helicopter Skiing. Blackcomb has summer skiing on the glaciers.

Most visitors stay in Whistler Village. Whistler Creek, a couple of miles away, is rather isolated and limited, and is bisected by the Sea to Sky highway. The highway skirts Whistler Village whose central areas are traffic-free and lined with smart shops. Accommodation is of a high standard. We've had glowing reports of the Nancy Greene Lodge, named after and run by the former Canadian gold medallist, and recommendations of the Delta Mountain Lodge. There are a variety of condominiums ranging from 'standard' to 'very luxurious', and a number of European-style catered chalets. One reporter raves about the chalet Saulire, run by Colin Cannon, who also provides a ski guiding service.

The cosmopolitan nature of the village is reflected by the wide range of bars and restaurants. There are two recommended Japanese sushi restaurants, one of which (the Teppan Village) prepares the meal at your table. Umberto's is a popular Italian restaurant, and Araxis serves 'excellent but expensive' Mediterranean cuisine. Two reporters commend the Keg steak house. A lively tea-time bar is the Longhorn at the bottom of Whistler's home run. Later in the evening the Savage Beagle, Buffalo Bill's and Garfunkle's come into their own.

The most popular place to stay in Blackcomb is the luxuriously modern Chateau Whistler. Its Wildflower restaurant has 'an interesting menu and excellent wine list'.

Tourist reservations office Whistler℗ (604) 932 4222. Blackcomb℗ (604) 932 3141.
Package holidays Canada Air Holidays (hs), Chalets and Hotels "Unlimited" (c), Hickie Borman (h), Neilson (hs), Piste Artistes (c), Ski Highlife (hs), Ski-Tal (cas), SnowRanger (h), Top Run (hcas).

REFERENCE SECTION

Up to this point, the *Guide* has been devoted more-or-less to one end: helping you decide where to go skiing. But there are other considerations involved in arranging a skiing holiday, and we deal with them in this final section of the *Guide*.

Skiing safety

It may take a scare in bad weather, or a real tragedy witnessed at close quarters to bring home the fact that the mountains in winter are a hostile place. Here are some pointers to help you deal with the dangers.

Weather and exposure

Exposure to bad weather can be more than just unpleasant – if protracted it can result in frostbite (which in extreme cases can lead to tissue loss) or hypothermia (which can be fatal).
Frostbite is the excessive cooling of small areas of the body – usually of the fingers, toes, nose, cheeks or ears. The affected tissue first goes white and numb; this first-degree frostbite can be dealt with simply by immediate gentle re-warming – by putting your hands under your armpits, for example.
Hypothermia is the condition resulting from a drop in the temperature of the body as a whole. It is difficult to diagnose; some of the more obvious symptoms are out-of-character behaviour, physical or mental lethargy, slurring of speech, sudden spurts of energy, and abnormality of vision.

Accident procedure

When an accident occurs, it's important to act quickly.
■ Mark the accident site by placing crossed skis about ten metres uphill of the casualty.
■ If the casualty is not breathing, administer artificial respiration – the kiss of life, for example; make sure that no foreign bodies are lodged in the mouth or throat.
■ If the casualty is breathing but unconscious turn him on to his side to minimise the risk of choking; first protect any fractured limb against movement.
■ Stop any bleeding by applying direct pressure to the site of the wound, using some sort of cloth pad if possible.
■ If there is an injury is to the lower leg *do not* remove the ski boot – it has the effect of a splint.
■ Keep the casualty warm, comfortable and cheerful, and set about contacting the ski patrol.

■ If the casualty shows signs of shock – going pale, cold and faint – he should be encouraged to lie with his head lower than his feet; don't give him any food or drink.

Safety on the piste

A set of rules for skiers has been drawn up by the Fédération International du Ski (FIS), with the aim of keeping skiing accidents to the minimum. Not only do these rules offer worthwhile guidance, but they are increasingly forming the basis of legal judgements in both civil and criminal actions in Continental courts. If you cause an accident while in breach of these rules, you could be in trouble. The FIS Rules are reproduced on the facing page.

Safety off-piste

Serious off-piste skiing, well away from the beaten track, can have many dangers – avalanches, crevasses on glaciers, the possibility of losing your way, for example. If you lack experience, don't go far off-piste without a guide. In any event:
■ ski in a group
■ always ski in control
■ use safety straps or, preferably, visibility tapes to make skis easier to find after a fall
■ carry a map and compass *and* know how to use them
■ be wary of slopes where the run-out is not obvious from the start
■ always assess the risk of avalanche
■ if possible, carry an avalanche cord and an avalanche transmitter-receiver to steer rescuers towards you if you are buried.
Avalanche transmitter-receivers are now commonplace, and it is difficult to justify skiing off-piste without one. The Ski Club hires out Autophon transmitter-receivers, which are the devices most widely used in Europe.

FIS Rules for the conduct of skiers

The rules are reproduced below exactly as published in English by the FIS; the *Notes* are our own observations, drawing on the FIS Commentaries.

Rule 0

Skiing is a sport and as all other sports, it has a risk element and certain civil and penal responsibilities.

Notes Skiers are expected to know the FIS Rules and to follow them. If you do not, you lay yourself open to legal action in the event of an accident.

Rule 1 – Respect for others

A skier must behave in such a way that he does not endanger or prejudice others.

Notes The FIS Rules apply to all skiers, including ski school pupils and racers. Instructors must respect the rules, teach them, and enforce them.

Rule 2 – Control of speed and skiing

A skier must adapt his speed and way of skiing to his personal ability and to prevailing conditions of terrain and weather.

Notes Speed should take account not only of the need to stay in control, but also of the prevailing speed of skiers on a run. It is normal to go fast on a run generally used by accomplished skiers – a black or a red run – and slow skiers must not obstruct such runs. It is normal to go slowly on an easy run generally used by beginners – a blue or a green run – and fast skiers must allow for inexpert skiers. All skiers must go slowly in narrow passages and at the bottom of runs and near lift departures. You must be able to stop or make a turn within your range of vision.

Rule 3 – Control of direction

A skier coming from above, whose dominant position allows him a choice of path, must take a direction which assures the safety of the skier below.

Notes Skiers are expected to allow for those ahead of them to stop suddenly, but are not expected to allow for sudden turns to right or left. There are no 'rules of the road' (such as keeping to the right or left); skiers must decide responsibly for themselves how to handle situations as they arise. You must take account of skiers alongside you on a run as well as those in front.

Rule 4 – Overtaking

It is permitted to overtake another skier going down or up – to the right or to the left, but always leaving a wide enough margin for the overtaken skier to make his turns.

Notes An overtaking skier must not cause any difficulties for the skier being overtaken, whether stopped or moving.

Rule 5 – Duties of a skier crossing the course

A skier wishing to enter a course or passing a training ground must look up and down to make sure that he can do so without danger to himself or others. The same applies when starting again after a stop on the course.

Notes Any manoeuvre on a ski run other than normal skiing down it can be dangerous, and implies the need for special care.

Rule 6 – Stopping on the course

If not absolutely necessary, a skier must avoid a stop on the course, especially in narrow passages or where visibility is restricted. In the case of a fall, a skier must leave the course free as soon as possible.

Notes If you stop, do so at the side of the run. Adding to the danger of skiing difficult slopes (for example, narrow passages with bad visibility from above) by obstructing the run could be considered an offence.

Rule 7 – Climbing

A climbing skier must keep to the side of the course and in bad visibility keep off the course entirely. The same goes for a skier who descends on foot.

Rule 8 – Respect for signals

A skier must respect the signals.

Notes Signs indicating that runs are closed or marking dangerous points must be respected.

Rule 9 – Conduct at accidents

At accidents, everybody is duty-bound to assist.

Notes The FIS hopes that irresponsibly leaving the scene of a skiing accident will be considered equivalent to leaving the scene of a road accident.

Rule 10 – Identification

All witnesses, whether responsible parties or not, at an accident must establish their identity.

Notes The reports of witnesses to an accident can be of great importance if there is any dispute about liability.

Package holidays

The resort chapters of the *Guide* contain lists of companies offering package holidays to each resort. After the name of each operator in the list (in brackets) we say what kinds of accommodation the operator offers in that resort; we use the following abbreviations:

h: hotels and hotel-like guest-houses
c: catered chalets
j: 'jumbo' or 'club' chalets
s: self-catering apartments
r: rooms in private homes
a: catered apartments.
y: youth accommodation

Here we give profiles of the operators, listed in alphabetical order. If you can't find a particular operator under its main name (eg Global), try looking under 'Ski'. After the address and phone numbers, there are six headings under which we give information for all operators – sales, bonding, surcharges, insurance, travel and accommodation. Then there are four headings which appear only when there is something to say – children, ski guiding, tuition and snow guarantee. All of these headings are explained here. The resort lists and the operator profiles given here are based on the latest information available to us in April 1991; some operators were able to tell us about their 1991-92 programmes, but in most cases the information relates to the 1990-91 season.

Sales

Many operators sell their holidays both through agents and directly to the customer. We say what each operator's main or only sales channel is, and in brackets the secondary channel if there is one.

Bonding

We list only those operators whose holidays are bonded, or who accept payment by credit card. In both cases the money you pay for the holiday before you go is protected in the event of the financial failure of the company. If buying a holiday from one of the many small-scale operators who are not bonded, make your payment by credit

card *direct to the operator*. Then, if the operator goes under, you can claim your money back from the credit card company. Note that American Express and Diners Club are not credit cards, and do not offer this protection.

The letters ABTA signify that the operator is a member of the Association of British Travel Agents. ABTA members' holidays are fully protected, whatever mode of travel is used.

The letters ATOL signify that the operator has a licence from the Civil Aviation Authority to run air-travel package holidays using charter flights; such holidays are protected, but bear in mind that an ATOL gives no protection for holidays based on coach travel, self-drive or scheduled airline flights – and that an operator may offer unprotected and protected holidays in the same brochure.

The letters PSA signify membership of the Passenger Shipping Association's bonding scheme.

The letters AITO signify membership of the Association of Independent Tour Operators. Members are required to have bonding up to ABTA standards, and the Association offers a bonding scheme of its own.

Surcharges

'None' means that the price you see in the brochure (or, at worst, the price you are invited to pay when you come to make a booking) will be the price you pay for your holiday. Anything else means that you may be asked to pay more; we say in what circumstances, and up to what amount. 'Within ABTA guide-lines' means that the company's surcharge policy is that promoted by the trade association ABTA. Which is:

The price of your holiday is subject to surcharges on the following items: Government action; currency; aircraft fuel; overflying charges; airport charges and increases in scheduled airfares. Even in this case, we will absorb an amount equivalent to 2% of the holiday price which excludes insurance premiums and any amendment charges.

Only amounts in excess of this 2% will be surcharged; if this means paying more than 10% on the holiday price, you will be entitled to cancel your holiday with a full refund of all money paid, except for any premium paid to us for holiday insurance and amendment charges. Should you decide to cancel because of this, you must exercise your right to do so within 14 days from the issue date printed on the invoice.

Note that in addition to the surcharge itself there may be an 'administration' charge – anything from a merely irritating 50p to a not negligible £10.

Insurance

All the operators we list provide travel insurance; we say here whether it is optional, normally compulsory (meaning that you must take it unless you provide evidence of comparable insurance) or absolutely compulsory (meaning that you must take it whether or not you already have comparable insurance).

Travel

We say first what style of travel the operator's holidays are mainly based on; where appropriate, we then give UK departure points (airports or coach pickup points). If there are alternative styles of travel, they are listed in brackets. Many operators sell charter flight seats without the other components of a package holiday. Such deals formally count as packages, which means that they can be sold at low prices, undercutting fares on scheduled airlines. We tell you if flight-only seats are available; we also say if supplements are payable for regional departures and if a charge is made for ski-carriage.

Accommodation

We say first what kind of accommodation the operator mainly offers. If there are alternative kinds, they are listed in brackets.

Children

If the operator offers any special arrangements for families – such as nurseries or baby-sitting in its chalets – we note it here.

Ski guiding

If the company provides people to guide you around the slopes, we describe the nature of the service. If guiding is important to you, check with the company to establish precisely what is provided; guiding is often limited by resort authorities, and the limits can change from season to season.

Tuition

If the operator provides ski tuition routinely or organises special packages involving tuition, we note it here.

Snow guarantee

If the operator provides some sort of insurance against a lack of snow, we summarise it here. Note that the small print of these guarantees can be important: if you care about such things, check the terms of the guarantee in the operator's brochure before you book.

Other points to note

There are many agencies which have self-catering accommodation to let independently rather than as part of a package holiday. Much the biggest is Interhome, whose brochures are worth getting before you look elsewhere: ring 081-891 1294 or write to 383 Richmond Road, Twickenham TW1 2EF.

Abercrombie and Kent Travel

Holidays in Morocco, France, Canada
Sloane Square House, Holbein Place, London, SW1W 8NF
Reservations 071-973 0492.
Fax 071-730 0376, Tx 3813352.
Sales Direct. (Agents.)
Bonding ABTA.
Surcharges Due to currency changes.
Insurance Compulsory.

Travel Air, departing Heathrow, Gatwick. Supplements payable for regional departures.
Accommodation Refuge, self-catering, hotel.
Ski guiding Fully qualified ski and mountain guides lead groups throughout the area with avalanche receivers.
Tuition Mountain craft, and ski mountaineering techniques.

Activity Travel

Holidays in big-name resorts
19 Castle Street, Edinburgh, EH2 3AH
Reservations 031-225 9457. Also
London: 081-541 5115; Manchester:
061-236 7498.
Fax 031-220 4185, Tx 728290.
Sales Direct. (Agents.)
Bonding ABTA, ATOL.
Surcharges Within ABTA guide-lines.
Insurance Compulsory.
Travel Air, departing Prestwick, Gatwick,
Edinburgh, Glasgow, Newcastle,
Manchester. Supplements payable for
regional departures. Flight-only seats
available. (Self-drive.)
Accommodation Catered chalets.
(Hotels, self-catering.)
Ski guiding Representatives provide
introduction to the ski area.

Adventure Unlimited

Chalet holidays in Chamonix
c/o Spicer Travel, 3 Madoc Street,
Llandudno, Gwynedd, LL30 2TL
Reservations (0492) 77968.
Fax (0492) 77968.
Sales Direct.
Bonding Credit cards accepted.
Surcharges No more than 5%, and
none after final payment
Insurance Compulsory.
Travel Air, departing Heathrow, Gatwick;
others on request. Supplements payable
for regional departures. (Self-drive.)
Accommodation Catered chalet.
Children Baby-sitting can be arranged.
Ski guiding 5 days a week guides will
lead groups to best skiing; private
guiding can be booked.
Tuition Off-piste and touring.

Allez France

Hotel holidays in Chamonix
27 West Street, Storrington, West
Sussex, RH20 4DZ
Reservations (0903) 745793.
Fax (0903) 745044.
Sales Direct.
Bonding ABTA, ATOL, AITO.
Surcharges Will pass on excess (or
refund) costs if currency rate changes by
8%, but will absorb the first part
equivalent to 2% of basic holiday costs.
Insurance Normally compulsory.
Travel Air, departing Gatwick, Heathrow,
Manchester. Supplements payable for
regional departures. (Self-drive.)
Accommodation Hotel.
Ski guiding Guides provide transport
and lead guests on the slopes.

Alpine Life

Holidays in Argentière
27 Ribble Close, Chandlers Ford,
Hampshire, SO5 2NQ
Reservations (0703) 269658.
Fax (0703) 270789.
Sales Direct.
Bonding Credit cards accepted.
Surcharges Will pass on increases over
5% due to currency changes.
Insurance Normally compulsory.
Travel Air, departing Heathrow, Gatwick,
Manchester, Edinburgh, Glasgow.
Supplements payable for regional
departures. Supplement payable for ski
carriage. (Coach, self-drive.)
Accommodation Catered chalets.
(Self-catering.)
Tuition Powder initiation, problem clinics.

Alpine Tours

Holidays in Austrian Tirol
54 Northgate, Canterbury, Kent, CT1
1BE
Reservations (0227) 454777.
Fax (0227) 451177.
Sales Agents and direct.
Bonding ABTA, ATOL, AITO.
Surcharges None.
Insurance Optional.
Travel Air, departing Gatwick,
Manchester, Stansted, Leeds-Bradford.
Supplements payable for regional
departures. Supplement payable for ski
carriage. (Coach, self-drive.)
Accommodation Hotels. (Snow homes,
self-catering, catered apartments.)
Children Nursery and babysitting.
Tuition Kneissl racing camp, powder
clinic, mogul clinic, snowboard camp.
Snow guarantee If all lifts are closed for
any reason for a whole day, transport will
be provided to alternative resort and new
lift passes paid for; if no alternative, will
pay £15 compensation per day.

Andorra Holidays

Holidays in Andorra
PO Box 2, Dalbeattie, DG5 4NT
Reservations (038 778) 684.
Fax (038 778) 283.
Sales Direct.
Bonding ATOL.
Surcharges Due to factors beyond
control e.g. currency movements, airline
charges, up to max 15%. No further
increases after final invoice.
Insurance Normally compulsory.
Travel Air, departing Gatwick,
Manchester, Glasgow. Supplements
payable for regional departures.

Flight-only seats available. (Self-drive.)
Accommodation Catered apartments.
(Self-catering, hotels.)
Ski guiding For an additional fee, and
using company's minibus, guides lead
intermediate and advanced groups
throughout the ski area and indicate the
best mountain restaurants.
Tuition Learn-to-ski weeks, race training
for advanced skiers.

Austrian Holidays

Hotel holidays in Austria
50-51 Conduit Street, London, W1R 0NP
Reservations 071-439 7108.
Fax 071-437 0343, Tx 21757.
Sales Agents and direct.
Bonding ABTA, ATOL.
Surcharges Up to 10% due to fuel
prices, currency changes, government
action and other costs. No surcharge on
holidays booked and paid for before Dec.
Insurance Optional.
Travel Air, departing Heathrow.
Supplements payable for regional
departures. Flight-only seats available.
Accommodation Hotels.

Austro Tours

Wide range of Austrian holidays
5 St Peter's Street, St Albans, Herts,
AL1 3DH
Reservations (0727) 838191.
Fax (0727) 838196, Tx 298822.
Sales Agents. (Direct.)
Bonding ABTA, ATOL, AITO.
Surcharges Within ABTA guide-lines.
Insurance Normally compulsory.
Travel Air, departing Gatwick, Heathrow,
Birmingham, Manchester. Flight-only
seats available. (Self-drive.)
Accommodation Hotels.
Snow guarantee If all lifts closed in
resort, transport will be provided to
alternative resort; if no alternative, will
pay £20 compensation per day

Autotours

Coach operator with one skiing
destination
20 Craven Terrace, London, W2 3QH
Reservations 071-258 0272.
Fax 071-706 0988, Tx 22359.
Sales Direct.
Bonding Credit cards accepted.
Surcharges Due to currency changes
and fuel costs.
Insurance Optional.
Travel Coach, departing London
Paddington. (Self-drive.)
Accommodation Hotels.

Balkan Holidays

Holidays in Bulgaria, Yugoslavia and
Romania
Sofia House, 19 Conduit Street, London,
W1R 9TD
Reservations 071-493 8612.
Tx 262923.
Sales Direct and agents.
Bonding ABTA, ATOL.
Surcharges None.
Insurance Normally compulsory.
Travel Air, departing Gatwick,
Manchester. Supplements payable for
regional departures.
Accommodation Hotels. (Club chalet
and catered apartments.)
Children Will book nursery and
kindergarten facilities.
Tuition Learn-to-ski weeks.
Snow guarantee With insurance policy:
if no snow, transport will be provided to
another resort; if no alternative will pay
£15 compensation per day.

Beach Villas

Small but wide-ranging programme
8 Market Passage, Cambridge, CB2 3QR
Reservations (0223) 311113.
Fax (0223) 313557, Tx 817428.
Sales Direct. (Agents.)
Bonding ABTA, ATOL, AITO.
Surcharges Over 2% and not more than
7%, due to currency, VAT, aviation
costs, overflying charges or airport tax
changes.
Insurance Normally compulsory.
Travel Air, departing Gatwick, Luton;
Manchester, Birmingham on request.
Supplements payable for regional
departures. (Self-drive.)
Accommodation Catered chalets.
(Self-catering, hotels.)
Children Limited baby-sitting by own
staff.
Ski guiding In Méribel, Morzine and
Arabba, ski companions guide groups to
the best snow, and organise ski races
and picnics.
Snow guarantee If schools and lifts are
closed for a whole day, transport will be
provided to alternative resort; if no
alternative, will pay £15 compensation
per day. Optional snow insurance
(premium £25): if, 3 days prior to
departure, less than 10% runs are open,
can cancel with refund, less £25 excess.

Bladon Lines

Major operator, emphasis on chalets
56/58 Putney High Street, London,
SW15 1SF

Reservations 081-785 3131.
Fax 081-788 3543, Tx 295221.
Sales Agents and direct.
Bonding ABTA, ATOL, AITO.
Surcharges Within ABTA guide-lines.
Insurance Optional.
Travel Air, departing Bristol, Gatwick,
Luton, Manchester, Glasgow.
Supplements payable for regional
departures. Flight-only seats available.
(Self-drive, rail.)
Accommodation Catered chalets, club
chalets. (Hotels, self-catering.)
Children Free nursery booking service.
Ski guiding In many resorts, full-time
guides are provided; in some resorts,
part-time guides are provided; in all
resorts, guides organise après-ski
activities.
Snow guarantee For chalets and chalet
hotels: if, 3 days prior to departure, less
than 10% lifts and runs are operating,
alternative accommodation will be
arranged; if no alternative, can cancel
with full refund, less insurance premium
and £25 excess.

Brittany Ferries

Self-drive holidays in France
The Brittany Centre, Wharf Rd,
Portsmouth, PO2 8RU
Reservations (0705) 751833.
Fax (0705) 811053, Tx 86878.
Sales Agents and direct.
Bonding PSA, credit cards.
Surcharges Due to factors beyond
control e.g. government action; may
cancel with full refund.
Insurance Normally compulsory.
Travel Self-drive/ferry, departing
Portsmouth.
Accommodation Self-catering.

Canada Air Holidays

Holidays in Canada
50 Sauchiehall Street, Glasgow, G2 3AG
Reservations 041-332 1511. Also
(0345) 090905.
Fax 041-333 0503, Tx 817428.
Sales Agents and direct.
Bonding ABTA, ATOL.
Surcharges None.
Insurance Optional.
Travel Air, departing Heathrow,
Manchester, Glasgow. Flight-only seats
available.
Accommodation Hotels. (Self-catering.)

Chalet Morzine

Small chalet operator, mainly in Morzine
134 Lots Rd, London, SW10 0RJ
Reservations 071-351 2993.

Fax 071-351 5044, Tx 893851.
Sales Direct.
Bonding Credit cards accepted.
Surcharges Any increases over 5% will
be passed on.
Insurance Optional.
Travel Air, departing Gatwick; others on
request. Supplements payable for
regional departures. (Self-drive.)
Accommodation Catered chalets.
(Self-catering, hotels.)
Children Free kindergarten service.
Ski guiding Representatives are willing
to ski with guests and arrange
excursions, picnics and slalom races,
take videos and photographs for guests.

Chalets and Hotels 'Unlimited'

Wide-ranging programme
50A Friern Barnet Lane, London, N11
3NA
Reservations 081-368 4001.
Sales Direct. (Specialist agents.)
Bonding Credit cards accepted.
Surcharges Due to currency changes,
government action or flight costs; once
full cost paid, no further surcharges on
accommodation.
Insurance Normally compulsory.
Travel Air, departing Gatwick,
Manchester, Glasgow, Heathrow.
Supplements payable for regional
departures. Flight-only seats available.
(Self-drive, coach.)
Accommodation Catered chalets,
self-catered chalets. (Hotels, catered
apartments, self-catering.)
Children Kindergartens, nannies and
baby-sitting can be arranged.
Ski guiding In some resorts; services
vary.
Tuition Learn-to-ski courses, safari
weeks with mountain guides.
Snow guarantee For extra payment on
insurance: where more than 80% of lifts
in the booked resort are not operating
within 48 hours of departure, can cancel
with full refund less insurance premiums;
in resort, travel to alternative resort will
be provided; if no alternative, will pay
£10 compensation per day.

Citalia

Holidays in Italy
Marco Polo House, 3/5 Lansdowne
Road, Croydon, Surrey, CR9 1LL
Reservations 081-686 5533.
Fax 081-686 0328, Tx 8812133.
Sales Agents and direct.
Bonding ABTA, ATOL, AITO.
Surcharges Within ABTA guide-lines.

Insurance Optional.
Travel Air, departing Gatwick,
Manchester. Supplements payable for
regional departures. Flight-only seats
available. Supplement payable for ski
carriage. (Self-drive.)
Accommodation Hotels. (Self-catering.)
Snow guarantee If insufficient snow,
transport will be provided to alternative; if
no alternative, will pay £30
compensation per day.

Club Med

All-inclusive holidays in 'ski villages'
106 Brompton Road, London, SW3 1JJ
Reservations 071-581 1161.
Fax 071-581 4769, Tx 299221.
Sales Agents and direct.
Bonding ABTA, ATOL.
Surcharges None.
Insurance Compulsory.
Travel Air, departing Heathrow, Gatwick,
Manchester. Supplements payable for
regional departures. (Rail, self-drive.)
Accommodation Hotels.
Children Nursery and nanny service in
some resorts.
Ski guiding Guides lead groups of
every level.
Tuition Beginners, intermediate,
advanced, monoski, surfing instruction.

Collineige Ski

Small but wide-ranging programme
32 High Street, Frimley, Surrey, GU16
5JD
Reservations (0276) 24262.
Fax (0276) 27282.
Sales Direct.
Bonding Credit cards accepted.
Surcharges Any costs received which
affect the price of the holiday will be
passed on.
Insurance Optional.
Travel Air, departing Heathrow,
Manchester. Supplements payable for
regional departures. (Self-drive, rail.)
Accommodation Catered chalets.
(Hotels, self-catering.)
Children Qualified nanny service,
baby-sitting.
Ski guiding In Chamonix, for an
additional fee, a guide with minibus
leads and instructs groups of 6-8 people
throughout the ski area.
Tuition Tailor-made instruction
programmes.

Color Line

Holidays in Voss, Norway
Tyne Commission Quay, North Shields,
Tyne and Wear, NE29 6EA

Reservations 091-296 1313.
Fax 091-296 1540, Tx 537275.
Sales Direct and agents.
Bonding PSA.
Surcharges Due to factors beyond
control up to 1 month before departure;
no surcharges once final invoice paid.
Insurance Optional.
Travel Self-drive/ferry, departing
Newcastle.
Accommodation Hotels. (Self-catering,
youth hostels.)

Contiki

Coach-travel holidays for 18-35s in
Hopfgarten
Wells House, 15 Elmfield Road,
Bromley, Kent, BR1 1LS
Reservations 081-290 6422.
Fax 081-290 0282, Tx 21127.
Sales Agents and direct.
Bonding ABTA, ATOL.
Surcharges Due to fuel costs only.
Insurance Normally compulsory.
Travel Coach, departing London. (Air.)
Accommodation Club chalets. (Hotels.)
Tuition Learn-to-ski holidays.

Crystal

Major mainstream operator
The Courtyard, Arlington Rd, Surbiton,
Surrey, KT6 6BW
Reservations 081-399 5144.
Fax 081-390 6378, Tx 265284.
Sales Agents.
Bonding ABTA, ATOL.
Surcharges None.
Insurance Normally compulsory.
Travel Air, departing Gatwick, Exeter,
Leed/Bradford, Manchester, Luton,
Bristol, Glasgow, Birmingham,
Newcastle, Southampton, Southend.
Supplements payable for regional
departures. Flight-only seats available.
Supplement payable for ski carriage.
(Coach, self-drive, rail.)
Accommodation Hotels. (Catered
chalets, self-catering, catered
apartments, club chalets, snow homes.)
Ski guiding In some resorts, guides
lead groups to the best skiing.
Tuition Learn-to-ski holidays.
Snow guarantee If take insurance
policy, and if insufficient snow, transport
and pass will be provided for alternative
resort; if no alternative, will provide £20
compensation per day.

Dawson and Sanderson

Holidays in Voss, Norway
60 Middle Street, Consett, County
Durham, DH8 5QE

Reservations (0207) 591261.
Fax (0207) 591262.
Sales Agents and direct.
Bonding ABTA, ATOL.
Surcharges Within ABTA guide-lines.
Insurance Normally compulsory.
Travel Air, departing Heathrow,
Newcastle, Manchester. Supplements
payable for regional departures.
Flight-only seats available.
Accommodation Hotels. (Self-catering,
catered apartments, youth hostels.)
Tuition Learn-to-ski weeks.

Enterprise

Major mainstream operator
Groundstar House, London Road,
Crawley, RH10 2TB
Reservations 071-221 0081. Also
Manchester: 061-831 7000; Glasgow:
041-204 2552; Birmingham: 021-666
7000.
Fax (0293) 543414.
Sales Agents. (Direct.)
Bonding ABTA, ATOL.
Surcharges None.
Insurance Optional.
Travel Air, departing Gatwick, Heathrow,
Manchester, Bristol, Glasgow,
Birmingham, Stansted, Newcastle.
Supplements payable for regional
departures. Flight-only seats available.
Supplement payable for ski carriage.
(Self-drive, rail.)
Accommodation Hotels. (Self-catering,
catered chalets.)
Children Own kindergartens in selected
hotels.
Ski guiding At many resorts, and
usually for 4 days a week, free guides
lead intermediate and advanced groups
and organise ski races.
Tuition Learn-to-ski holidays,
intermediate and advanced courses.
Snow guarantee Transport will be
provided to alternative resort; if no
alternative, will pay £10 compensation
per day up to cost of holiday.

Falcon

Minor mainstream operator,
wide-ranging programme
33 Notting Hill Gate, London, W11 3JQ
Reservations 071-757 5400. Also
Manchester: 061-831 7000; Birmingham:
021-666 7000; Glasgow: 041-204 0242.
Sales Agents. (Direct.)
Bonding ABTA, ATOL.
Surcharges None.
Insurance Optional.
Travel Air, departing Gatwick,
Manchester, Glasgow, Bristol,

Birmingham. Supplements payable for
regional departures. Supplement
payable for ski carriage. (Rail.)
Accommodation Hotels. (Self-catering.)
Tuition Learn-to-ski holidays. Fine Skills
workshop in Tignes run by Evolution 2.
Snow guarantee Transport will be
provided to alternative resort and cost of
lift pass and school covered if
pre-booked in UK; if no alternative and if
lose 3 or more days skiing, will pay
compensation of 3 times daily cost of
holiday including ski pack costs but
excluding insurance; if unable to ski for
whole holiday, will make complete
refund of holiday cost excluding
insurance.

Freedom Holidays

Holidays in Andorra and Châtel
224 King Street, London, W6 0RA
Reservations 081-741 4686. Also
Manchester: 061-236 0019.
Tx 892928.
Sales Direct. (Agents.)
Bonding ABTA, ATOL, AITO.
Surcharges Within ABTA guide-lines.
Insurance Normally compulsory.
Travel Air, departing Gatwick,
Manchester, Heathrow. Supplements
payable for regional departures.
Flight-only seats available. Supplement
payable for ski carriage. (Self-drive.)
Accommodation Self-catering. (Hotels.)
Children Nursery for 3-6 year olds.
Ski guiding Guides provide introduction
to area and mountain restaurants plus
circuit of Portes du Soleil.
Tuition Learn-to-ski weeks.
Snow guarantee If take insurance
policy, and if all lifts closed due to
insufficient snow, and no alternative
resort available, will pay £15
compensation per day.

French Impressions

Holidays in France
31 Topsfield Parade, London, N8 8PT
Reservations 081-342 8870.
Fax 081-342 8860.
Sales Direct.
Bonding Credit cards accepted.
Surcharges Due to currency changes;
no surcharges less than 8 weeks prior to
departure.
Insurance Optional.
Travel Self-drive. (Air, rail.)
Accommodation Self-catering. (Hotels.)
Children Baby-sitting in some properties.
Snow guarantee If resort is totally
closed, will provide £5 a day for transport
to alternative resort; if no alternative will

pay £20 compensation per day.

Fresh Tracks
Holidays with off-piste guidance
McMillan House, Cheam Common Rd,
Worcester Park, Surrey, KT4 8RH
Reservations 081-335 3003.
Fax 081-330 6819, Tx 928618.
Sales Direct. (Agents.)
Bonding ABTA.
Surcharges Within ABTA guide-lines
Insurance Optional.
Travel Air, departing Gatwick, Heathrow,
Manchester. Supplements payable for
regional departures.
Accommodation Hotels. (Self-catering.)
Ski guiding Internationally qualified
mountain guides lead intermediate and
advanced groups on- and off-piste.
Tuition Learn-to-powder ski courses; ski
touring courses.

Headwater
Cross-country skiing holidays
146 London Rd, Northwich, Cheshire,
CW9 5HH
Reservations (0606) 48699.
Fax (0606) 48761.
Sales Direct.
Bonding ABTA, ATOL, AITO.
Surcharges None.
Insurance Normally compulsory.
Travel Air, departing London,
Manchester, Newcastle, Glasgow,
Belfast. Supplements payable for
regional departures. (Rail, self-drive.)
Accommodation Hotels. (Self-catering.)
Children Baby-sitting in French resorts.
Ski guiding Guides accompany groups
on outings and organise après-ski
activities.

Hickie Borman
Holidays in America and Canada
56 High Street, Ewell, Surrey, KT17 1RW
Reservations 081-393 0127.
Fax 081-394 1373, Tx 919535.
Sales Agents and direct.
Bonding ABTA.
Surcharges Within ABTA guide-lines.
Insurance Optional.
Travel Air, departing Heathrow, Gatwick,
Manchester, Glasgow. Supplements
payable for regional departures.
Flight-only seats available.
Accommodation Hotels. (Catered
chalets.)
Snow guarantee From Dec to Mar, if
conditions unskiable due to insufficient
snow, will refund accommodation costs
for each day lost.

Horizon
Major mainstream operator
Broadway, Edgbaston Five Ways,
Birmingham, B15 1BB
Reservations 021-632 6282. Also
081-200 8733; 061-236 3828.
Sales Agents.
Bonding ABTA, ATOL.
Surcharges None.
Insurance Optional.
Travel Air, departing Gatwick,
Birmingham, Manchester, East
Midlands, Bristol, Luton, Stansted,
Cardiff, Leeds Bradford, Newcastle,
Glasgow. Supplements payable for
regional departures. Flight-only seats
available. (Self-drive.)
Accommodation Hotels. (Self-catering.)
Children Pre-bookable crèche.
Ski guiding In 12 resorts free guides
lead groups of similar ability.
Tuition Ski clinic, learn-to-ski holidays in
10 resorts, via local ski school.
Snow guarantee If insufficient snow,
transport will be provided to alternative
resort; if no alternative, will pay £30
compensation per person per day.

Hoverspeed Ski-Drive
Self-drive holidays, mainly in France
Maybrook House, Queens Gardens,
Dover, CT17 9UQ
Reservations (0304) 240241. Also
London: 081-554 7061; Birmingham
021-236 2190; Manchester 061-228
1321.
Fax (0304) 240099, Tx 965915.
Sales Agents and direct.
Bonding PSA.
Surcharges Due to currency changes; if
more than 10%, can cancel and claim
refund. No surcharges within 10 weeks
of departure.
Insurance Optional.
Travel Self-drive/hovercraft/Seacat/ferry,
departing Dover, Folkestone, Newhaven,
Portsmouth.
Accommodation Self-catering. (Hotels.)

HuSki
Holidays in Chamonix
63a Kensington Church Street, London,
W8
Reservations 071-937 5171.
Fax 071-938 2312.
Sales Direct.
Bonding Credit cards accepted.
Surcharges Any flight cost increases
will be passed on.
Insurance Optional.
Travel Self-drive, departing Dover,

Folkestone, Newhaven. (Air.)
Accommodation Catered chalets.
(Self-catering.)
Ski guiding Guides introduce groups to
the pistes and organise video recording
Tuition Off-piste and mountain-guiding
trips with Yak and Yeti.

InStyle

Holidays in Italy
6A Blackboy Road, Exeter, EX4 6SG
Reservations (0392) 70131.
Fax (0392) 70136, Tx 42560.
Sales Agents. (Direct.)
Bonding ABTA, ATOL.
Surcharges Within ABTA guide-lines.
Insurance Optional.
Travel Air, departing Exeter. Flight-only
seats available.
Accommodation Hotels.
Tuition Learn to ski weeks.
Snow guarantee To be announced

Inghams

Major mainstream operator
10-18 Putney Hill, London, SW15 6AX
Reservations 081-785 7777.
Fax 081-785 2045, Tx 25342.
Sales Agents. (Direct.)
Bonding ABTA, ATOL.
Surcharges None.
Insurance Optional.
Travel Air, departing Gatwick, Heathrow,
Luton, Stansted, Bristol, Birmingham,
Manchester, Newcastle, Glasgow,
Dublin. Supplements payable for
regional departures. Flight-only seats
available. Supplement payable for ski
carriage. (Rail, self-drive.)
Accommodation Hotels. (Self-catering,
catered apartments, snow homes.)
Tuition Learn-to-ski holidays.
Snow guarantee If take insurance
policy, and if there is a total closure of
the area/resort lift system due to
insufficient snow, transport will be
provided to alternative resort; if no
alternative, will pay £30 compensation
per day.

Interski

Holidays in Courmayeur
95 Outram Street, Sutton-in-Ashfield,
Notts, NG17 4BG
Reservations (0623) 551024.
Fax (0623) 440742, Tx 378424.
Sales Direct.
Bonding ABTA, ATOL.
Surcharges None.
Insurance Normally compulsory.
Travel Coach, departing throughout
Britain. Flight-only seats available. (Air,

self-drive.)
Accommodation Hotels. (Self-catering.)
Children Kindergartens and baby-sitting
can be arranged.
Tuition Own instructors, learn-to-ski
holidays, snowstart weeks.
Snow guarantee If, 48 hours prior to
departure, resort has insufficient snow,
will either: pay £10 compensation per
day when skiing not possible; or rebook
holiday for alternative date; or allow
client to cancel with full refund less costs
e.g. admin charges, travel cancellation
charges.

Key to America

Holidays in America
15 Feltham Rd, Ashford, Middlesex,
TW15 1DQ
Reservations (0784) 248777. Also
081-202 2196.
Fax (0784) 256658.
Sales Agents. (Direct.)
Bonding ABTA, IATA.
Surcharges But price guaranteed if pay
in full at time of booking.
Insurance Optional.
Travel Air, departing Heathrow, Gatwick.
Accommodation Hotels and
self-catering.

Kings Ski Club

Holidays in Austria and France
24 Culloden Rd, Enfield, Middlesex, EN2
8QD
Reservations 081-342 0303.
Sales Direct.
Bonding Credit cards accepted.
Surcharges None on coach holidays;
surcharge only on flight holidays
Insurance Normally compulsory.
Travel Coach, departing London;
regional departures for large groups on
request. (Air, self-drive.)
Accommodation Club chalets. (Catered
chalets, self-catering, hotels.)
Ski guiding Guides lead groups for all
levels of skier above beginner,
throughout the ski area.
Tuition Race training camps.
Snow guarantee If take insurance
policy, transport will be provided to
alternative resort and additional lift pass
paid for; if no alternative resort,
alternative wintersports will be arranged;
if neither of thes options are possible,
will pay £15 compensation per day.

Kuoni

Holidays in Switzerland
Kuoni House, Dorking, Surrey, RH5 4AZ
Reservations (0306) 881002.

Fax (0306) 740328, Tx 859445.
Sales Agents.
Bonding ABTA, ATOL.
Surcharges Within ABTA guide-lines.
Insurance Optional.
Travel Air, departing Heathrow, Gatwick,
Manchester, Birmingham. Supplements
payable for regional departures.
(Self-drive.)
Accommodation Hotels. (Catered
apartments.)
Children Free kindergartens at some
hotels.
Tuition Ski safari weeks.

Le Ski

Holidays in Courchevel
65 Ashbrow Road, Huddersfield, HD2
1DX
Reservations (0484) 548996.
Fax 0484 548996.
Sales Direct.
Bonding ATOL.
Surcharges Due to government action
only; no currency surcharges.
Insurance Normally compulsory.
Travel Air, departing Gatwick,
Manchester, Edinburgh, Glasgow,
Bristol, Newcastle. Supplements payable
for regional departures. Supplement
payable for ski carriage. (Self-drive,
motorail, coach, rail.)
Accommodation Catered chalets.
(Self-catering, hotels.)
Ski guiding Free guides lead groups of
similar ability to the best skiing.

Made to Measure

Wide variety of tailor-made holidays
43 East Street, Chichester, West
Sussex, PO19 1HX
Reservations (0243) 533333.
Fax (0243) 778431, Tx 869205.
Sales Direct and agents.
Bonding ABTA, ATOL.
Surcharges Within ABTA guide-lines,
but no surcharges if pay full price within
7 days of receiving the invoice.
Insurance Optional.
Travel Air, departing Heathrow,
Manchester, Gatwick, Birmingham.
Supplements payable for regional
departures. Flight-only seats available.
(Self-drive, rail.)
Accommodation Hotels. (Self-catering.)
Children Some hotels have
kindergartens, nanny service and
baby-sitting; special brochure 'Made for
Pleasure Family Skiing'.
Tuition Fun ski courses, Altenmarkt,
Austria; ski improvement courses,
powder snow courses, ladies ski weeks.

Mark Warner

Chalet holiday specialist
20 Kensington Church Street, London,
W8 4EP
Reservations 071-938 1851.
Fax 071-938 3861.
Sales Agents and direct.
Bonding ABTA, ATOL.
Surcharges Within ABTA guide-lines.
Insurance Optional.
Travel Air, departing Gatwick, Heathrow,
Manchester, Glasgow. Supplements
payable for regional departures.
Flight-only seats available. (Self-drive.)
Accommodation Catered chalets and
club chalets.
Children Own nanny service, crèches,
baby-sitting in Verbier, Val d'Isère and
Courmayeur.
Ski guiding 5 days a week in France
and Italy, 2 days a week in Switzerland,
guides lead groups of similar ability
throughout the ski area.
Snow guarantee If, 3 days prior to
departure, less than 15% of all runs and
lifts in resort are open, an alternative
resort will be found; if not possible, can
cancel with full refund less insurance
premium, and less 10% of final invoice
with a min. of £30.

Meriski

Chalet holidays in Méribel
72, Brocklebank Rd, Earlsfield, London
SW18 3AX
Reservations 081-874 0015.
Sales Direct.
Bonding Credit cards accepted.
Surcharges No currency surcharges,
but will pass on price increases over 2%
due to government action, aircraft fuel,
overflying charges and airport charges; if
more than 10% can cancel with refund
less insurance and amendment fees.
Insurance Optional.
Travel Air, departing Heathrow, Gatwick.
Accommodation Catered chalets.
Children Nanny service in chalet.
Ski guiding Free guides lead groups
throughout Les Trois Vallées, starting
from Méribel.
Tuition Ski Venture specialist tuition.

Mogul Ski Holidays

Mainly Austrian hotel holidays
Royal Chambers, Station Parade,
Harrogate, Yorks
Reservations (0423) 569512.
Sales Direct and agents.
Bonding ABTA.
Surcharges Within ABTA guide-lines.

Insurance Normally compulsory.
Travel Coach, departing throughout UK.
Supplement payable for ski carriage.
(Air.)
Accommodation Hotels, snow homes.
(Self-catering.)
Ski guiding Free guides show groups
round the main ski areas, on-piste.
Tuition Ski clinics, race training.
Snow guarantee Transport will be
provided to alternative resort, up to max
cost of £15; if no alternative, will pay £15
compensation per day up to max £75.

Neilson

Major mainstream operator
Arndale House, Otley Rd, Headingley,
Leeds, LS6 2UU
Reservations (0532) 744422.
Fax (0532) 752609.
Sales Agents.
Bonding ABTA, ATOL.
Surcharges None.
Insurance Optional.
Travel Air, departing Gatwick, Heathrow,
Luton, Stansted, Bristol, Birmingham,
Manchester, Newcastle, Glasgow,
Leeds-Bradford. Supplements payable
for regional departures. Flight-only seats
available. Supplement payable for ski
carriage. (Coach, rail, self-drive.)
Accommodation Hotels. (Self-catering,
snow homes.)
Children Free kindergartens in some
resorts.
Ski guiding Ski leaders lead groups of
similar abilities throughout the ski area.
Tuition Own ski school in some resorts.
Snow guarantee If take insurance
policy, transport will be provided to
alternative resort; if no alternative, will
pay £25 compensation per day.

Norwegian State Railways Travel Bureau

Holidays in Norway
21-24 Cockspur Street, London, SW1Y
5DA
Reservations 071-930 6666.
Fax 071-321 0624.
Sales Agents. (Direct.)
Bonding ABTA, ATOL.
Surcharges Within ABTA guide-lines.
Insurance Optional.
Travel Air/rail, departing Heathrow.
Flight-only seats available. (Ferry/rail.)
Accommodation Hotels. (Self-catering.)

Norwegian Travel Service

Holidays in Norway
Church Gate, Church Street, Woking,
Surrey, GU21 1DJ

Reservations (0483) 756871.
Fax (0483) 755120, Tx 859397.
Sales Agents and direct.
Bonding ABTA, AITO.
Surcharges Within ABTA guide-lines.
Insurance Normally compulsory.
Travel Air, departing Heathrow, Gatwick,
Newcastle, Manchester, Birmingham,
Aberdeen, Glasgow. Supplements
payable for regional departures. (Ferry.)
Accommodation Hotels. (Self-catering,
catered apartments.)
Children Ski kindergarten in Geilo,
Trysil and Hemsedal.

Over the Hill

Holidays for older skiers
The Barns, Collops Lane, Stebbing,
Dunmow, Essex CM6 3SZ
Reservations (0371) 856214.
Fax (0371) 856562.
Sales Direct.
Bonding ATOL, credit cards.
Surcharges Due to increases in
scheduled airfares (if more than 5%);
once paid in full, no further surcharges
Insurance Normally compulsory.
Travel Air, departing Gatwick,
Manchester. Supplements payable for
regional departures. Flight-only seats
available.
Accommodation Hotels.
Ski guiding Fully qualified French ski
instructors teach/guide 6 hours per day
with 6 people per group, both on- and
off-piste.
Tuition Fully qualified ski instructors
teach/guide 6 hours per day with 6
people per group, both on and off-piste.

PR Christian Holidays

Christian holidays in Switzerland
95 Mount Pleasant Road, Camborne,
Cornwall, TR14 7RJ
Reservations (0209) 715359.
Sales Direct.
Bonding Credit cards accepted.
Surcharges None.
Insurance Normally compulsory.
Travel Coach, departing Cornwall,
Bristol, London, Ramsgate/Dover.
Accommodation Hotels.

Panorama's Ski Experience

Budget-oriented holidays
29 Queens Road, Brighton, BN1 3YN
Reservations (0273) 206531.
Fax (0273) 205338, Tx 877593.
Sales Agents. (Direct.)
Bonding ABTA, ATOL, AITO.
Surcharges Within ABTA guide-lines.

Insurance Optional.
Travel Air, departing Gatwick, Manchester. Supplements payable for regional departures. Supplement payable for ski carriage. (Self-drive.)
Accommodation Hotels and self-catering.
Snow guarantee If take insurance policy, transport will be provided to alternative resort within 2.5 hours drive; if no alternative, will pay £20 compensation per day.

Piste Artistes

Holidays in Champéry and Whistler
3rd floor, Shirehorn Centre, 34 Prospect Street, Hull HU2 8PX
Reservations (0482) 20601.
Fax (0482) 20509.
Sales Direct.
Bonding Accept credit cards.
Surcharges Due to flight cost increases only
Insurance Optional.
Travel Air, departing from any airport. Flight-only seats available. Supplement payable for ski carriage. (Self-drive.)
Accommodation Catered chalets and hotels.
Children Nursery and nanny services.
Ski guiding Guides lead groups on the slopes to different destinations each day, and makes videos for each party.
Tuition Skiing instruction for all levels.

Poles Apart

Chalet holidays in Argentière
119 Hampstead Way, London, NW11 7JN
Reservations 081-455 2214.
Fax 081-455 2214.
Sales Direct.
Bonding Credit cards accepted.
Surcharges Airline surcharges only
Insurance Normally compulsory.
Travel Air, departing Heathrow, Manchester, Birmingham. Supplements payable for regional departures. (Self-drive, rail.)
Accommodation Catered chalets. (Self-catering.)
Children Crèche, nannies and babysitters can be provided.
Ski guiding 5 mornings a week, free guides provide transport and lead groups throughout the ski area. French qualified guide takes groups off-piste.
Tuition Off-piste weeks.

Powder Byrne

Mainly holidays in Switzerland
50 Lombard Rd, London, SW11 3SU

Reservations 071-223 0601.
Fax 071-228 1491.
Sales Direct.
Bonding Credit cards accepted.
Surcharges Due to currency changes.
Insurance Optional.
Travel Air, departing Heathrow. Supplements payable for regional departures. (Self-drive.)
Accommodation Hotels. (Catered chalets, self-catering.)
Children Nanny service can be arranged; Junior Club in school holiday periods.
Ski guiding Ski instructors guide and instruct intermediate and advanced groups daily throughout the ski area, and participate in après-ski activities; qualified mountain guides lead off-piste skiing.
Tuition Off-piste tuition and advanced programmes; own ski instructors; intensive piste instruction; weekend tuition.

President

Holidays in Turkey
542, Kingsland Rd, Dalston, London E8 4AH
Reservations 071-249 4002.
Fax 071-923 1856, Tx 883613.
Sales Direct.
Bonding ABTA, ATOL.
Surcharges None.
Insurance Optional.
Travel Air, departing Gatwick.
Accommodation Hotels.

Quality Ski Tours

Small but wide-ranging programme
Unit 7, Innovation Centre, Pottery Lane, Whittington Moor, Chesterfield, S41 9BN
Reservations (0246) 550066.
Fax (0246) 550064, Tx 547530.
Sales Direct. (Agents.)
Bonding ABTA, ATOL.
Surcharges None.
Insurance Optional.
Travel Air and coach, departing Gatwick, Manchester and Birmingham. Flight-only seats available.
Accommodation Hotels. (Self-catering, catered apartments.)
Snow guarantee Transport will be provided to alternative resort

Quest Total Ski

Group-holidays offshoot of dominant schools operator
Olivier House, 18 Marine Parade, Brighton, East Sussex, BN2 1TL
Reservations (0273) 677777.

Fax (0273) 600999, Tx 87374.
Sales Direct. (Agents.)
Bonding ABTA, ATOL, AITO.
Surcharges None if payment deadlines met.
Insurance Normally compulsory.
Travel Air, departing Gatwick, Luton, Manchester, Stansted, Belfast, Bristol, Glasgow, Newcastle, Teeside. (Coach.)
Accommodation Hotels. (Self-catering.)
Tuition Own ski instructors in many French resorts.
Snow guarantee If ski school and all lifts closed, transport will be provided up to £20 per day; if no alternative, will arrange alternative facilities up to £20 per day or will pay £20 compensation per day.

Quest Travel

Dominant schools operator
Olivier House, 18 Marine Parade, Brighton, East Sussex, BN2 1TL
Reservations (0273) 677777.
Fax (0273) 600999, Tx 87374.
Sales Direct.
Bonding ABTA, ATOL, AITO.
Surcharges None if payment deadlines met.
Insurance Compulsory.
Travel Air, departing Gatwick, Luton, Manchester, Stansted, Belfast, Bristol, Glasgow. Supplements payable for regional departures. (Coach.)
Accommodation Hotels. (Catered apartments.)
Snow guarantee If ski school and all lifts closed, transport will be provided up to £15 per day; if no alternative, will arrange alternative facilities up to £15 per day or will pay £15 compensation per day.

Ramblers

Cross-country holidays
Box 43, Welwyn Garden City, Herts, AL8 6PQ
Reservations (0707) 331133.
Fax (0707) 333276, Tx 24642.
Sales Direct. (Agents.)
Bonding ABTA, ATOL.
Surcharges None.
Insurance Optional.
Travel Air, departing Gatwick, Heathrow.
Accommodation Hotels.
Ski guiding Guides lead groups cross-country.

Sally Holidays

Self-drive holidays, mainly in France
81 Piccadilly, London, W1V 9HF
Reservations 071-355 2266.

Fax 071-355 3008, Tx 291860.
Sales Agents. (Direct.)
Bonding ABTA.
Surcharges None.
Insurance Optional.
Travel Self-drive/ferry, departing Ramsgate.
Accommodation Self-catering. (Hotels.)
Ski guiding Provide session and day trips according to grade of skiers.

Sarac Ski

Holidays in Serre-Chevalier and Vars
18 Fawsey Leys, Rugby, Warwickshire
Reservations (0788) 812633.
Sales Direct.
Bonding Credit cards accepted.
Surcharges Only due to government action.
Insurance Compulsory.
Travel Air, departing Gatwick, Manchester. Supplements payable for regional departures. Flight-only seats available. (Self-drive.)
Accommodation Catered chalets. (Self-catering.)
Ski guiding Free guides lead groups throughout the area.
Snow guarantee Compulsory insurance policy includes piste closure compensation for up to £25 per day.

Scandinavian Seaways

Holidays by sea to Sweden
Scandinavia House, Parkeston Quay, Harwich, Essex, CO12 4QG
Reservations (0255) 241234. Also Newcastle: (091) 2960101; London: 071-493 6696.
Fax (0225) 240268, Tx 987542.
Sales Agents and direct.
Bonding PSA.
Surcharges Due to currency changes and fuel oil price increases. No surcharges within 30 days of departure.
Insurance Normally compulsory.
Travel Self-drive/ferry, departing Harwich.
Accommodation Self-catering.

Silver Ski

Chalet holidays, mainly in France
Conifers House, Grove Green Lane, Maidstone, ME14 5JW
Reservations (0622) 35544.
Fax (0622) 38550.
Sales Direct. (Agents.)
Bonding ABTA, ATOL, AITO.
Surcharges Due to fuel costs only if increase more than 10%
Insurance Compulsory.
Travel Air, departing Gatwick,

Manchester, Glasgow. Supplements payable for regional departures. (Self-drive, rail.)
Accommodation Catered chalets.
Ski guiding Guides lead groups to the best snow avoiding queues, and indicate the best mountain restaurants.
Snow guarantee If less than 10% lifts are open, transport will be provided to alternative resort

Simply Ski

Holidays in France
8 Chiswick Terrace, Acton Lane, London, W4 5LY
Reservations 081-742 2541.
Fax 081-995 5346, Tx 8955503.
Sales Direct. (Some agents.)
Bonding ABTA, ATOL, AITO.
Surcharges Surcharges passed on directly with no profit.
Insurance Optional.
Travel Air, departing Gatwick, Heathrow, Manchester. Supplements payable for regional departures. Flight-only seats available. (Self-drive, rail, coach.)
Accommodation Catered chalets. (Self-catering, hotels.)
Children Nursery, crèche, kindergarten, baby-sitting.
Ski guiding Guides lead groups throughout the ski area, and off-piste only if clients accept full responsibility.
Snow guarantee If all lifts are closed, transport will be provided to alternative resort; if no skiing at all, will pay £20 compensation per day.

Ski Alternatives

Up-market hotel holidays
17 Montpelier Street, London SW7 1HG
Reservations 081-785 7771.
Fax 081-788 3543, Tx 295221.
Sales Agents and direct.
Bonding ABTA, ATOL, AITO.
Surcharges Due to government action only
Insurance Normally compulsory.
Travel Air, departing from any airport. Supplements payable for regional departures.
Accommodation Hotels. (Catered chalets, self-catered chalets.)
Children Professional nanny service.
Snow guarantee If, 3 days before departure, less than 10% lifts and 10% runs are in operation, can cancel with full refund less insurance premium and £25 excess.

Ski Beat

Chalet holidays in La Plagne

57 York Road, Montpelier, Bristol, BS6 5QD
Reservations (0272) 557361.
Fax (0272) 557361.
Sales Direct.
Bonding Credit cards accepted.
Surcharges Over 2% due to currency changes up to max £10.
Insurance Optional.
Travel Air, departing Gatwick. Supplements payable for regional departures. (Self-drive, rail.)
Accommodation Catered chalets.
Children Cots and babysitters.
Ski guiding Guides lead groups 3 days a week.
Tuition Surf, mono, off-piste and parapente on request.

Ski Challenge

Holidays in La Grave and Serre-Chevalier
Milber Cottage, Manor Road, Seer Green, Beaconsfield, Bucks, HP9 2QU
Reservations (0494) 670270.
Fax (0494) 676669.
Sales Direct.
Bonding Credit cards accepted.
Surcharges None.
Insurance Normally compulsory.
Travel Air, departing Heathrow. (Self-drive.)
Accommodation Hotels and self-catering.
Ski guiding In La Grave, guides lead groups of all abilities throughout ski area, and off-piste for groups of sufficient ability.
Tuition Minimum 6 half-days of tuition included in holiday price.
Snow guarantee If insufficient snow, accommodation cost will be refunded plus £25 compensation per day.

Ski Chamois

Coach-based and other holidays in France
18 Lawn Road, Doncaster, DN1 2JF
Reservations (0302) 369006.
Fax (0302) 326640.
Sales Direct.
Bonding Credit cards accepted.
Surcharges Due to currency changes, government action or any other increase.
Insurance Compulsory.
Travel Coach, departing Newcastle, Scotch Corner, Leeds, Doncaster, London, Dover, Ramsgate. Supplement payable for ski carriage. (Air.)
Accommodation Catered chalets. (Catered apartments, club chalets, hotels, self-catering.)

Ski guiding For at least 4 days a week, guides lead intermediate and advanced groups.
Snow guarantee If insufficient snow, transport or accommodation will be provided for alternative resort.

Ski Club of GB

Holidays geared to skiers of particular standards
118 Eaton Square, London, SW1W 9AF
Reservations 071-245 1033.
Fax 071-245 1258, Tx 291608.
Sales Direct.
Bonding ATOL 1489 - through Hamilton Travel.
Surcharges Due to factors beyond control e.g. air transport increases, fares, but not currency.
Insurance Optional.
Travel Air, departing Gatwick, Heathrow, others on request. Supplements payable for regional departures.
Accommodation Hotels. (Catered chalets, catered apartments.)
Ski guiding Guides lead groups to the best snow, off-piste with groups of sufficient ability; provide instruction on technique. Ski safaris.
Tuition Special clinics with BASI trainer and instructors. Beginners and off-piste weeks.

Ski Equipe

Holidays in a few big-name resorts
1 Higher Road, Urmston, Manchester, M31 1AB
Reservations 061-748 2947.
Fax 061-755 3362.
Sales Direct. (A few agents.)
Bonding Credit cards accepted.
Surcharges Due to currency fluctuations, min £5
Insurance Normally compulsory.
Travel Air, departing Gatwick, Manchester; others on request. Supplements payable for regional departures. Flight-only seats available. Supplement payable for ski carriage. (Self-drive, rail, coach.)
Accommodation Chalets and self-catering. (Hotels.)
Ski guiding Provide introduction to the slopes on first 2 days of holiday.
Tuition Special course weeks offered by Verbier ski school. Special powder weeks.

Ski Esprit

Chalet holidays, especially for families
Austen House, Upper Street, Fleet, Hampshire, GU13 9PE

Reservations (0252) 616789.
Fax (0252) 811243.
Sales Direct. (Agents.)
Bonding ABTA, ATOL, AITO.
Surcharges None.
Insurance Optional.
Travel Air, departing Gatwick. Flight-only seats available. (Self-drive.)
Accommodation Catered chalets.
Children Qualified British nannies in all resorts; in-chalet crèches, snow club for 5-8 year olds, free baby-sitting.
Snow guarantee If snow conditions make skiing impossible, will move clients to chalets in resorts with better snow; if not possible will arrange transport to open snowfields – at clients' expense; if take insurance policy, and if 90% ski lifts closed in resort, will pay £20 compensation per day.

Ski Europe

School group holidays
Northumberland House, 2 King Street, Twickenham, Middlesex, TW1 3RZ
Reservations 081-891 4400.
Fax 081-892 3454.
Sales Direct. (Area reps.)
Bonding ABTA.
Surcharges Only if booking conditions not complied with or if booking by air: within ABTA guide-lines
Insurance Optional.
Travel Coach, departing throughout UK. (Air, rail.)
Accommodation Hotels. (Youth hostels.)
Tuition Own ski school in most resorts. Ski Master Programme of pre-course tuition and high-level tuition in resort.
Snow guarantee For coach holidays only: transport will be provided to alternative resort, but not additional lift pass/school.

Ski Global

Major mainstream operator
26 Elmfield Rd, Bromley, Kent, BR1 1LR
Reservations (0274) 736403. Also Birmingham: 021-454 6677; Bradford: (0274) 736403; Newcastle: 091-281 8131; Cardiff: (0222) 345121; Glasgow: 041-332 4466; Belfast: (0232) 320340; Bristol: (0274) 214503.
Fax 081-464 3441, Tx 8953010.
Sales Agents. (Direct.)
Bonding ABTA, ATOL.
Surcharges None.
Insurance Normally compulsory.
Travel Air, departing Gatwick, Manchester, Birmingham, Luton, Cardiff, East Midlands, Glasgow, Belfast,

Newcastle, Leeds-Bradford, Bristol. Supplements payable for regional departures. Flight-only seats available. Supplement payable for ski carriage. (Coach, rail, self-drive.)
Accommodation Hotels. (Self-catering, catered apartments, snow homes.)
Ski guiding In many resorts, free ski escorts lead groups of similar standard for half or whole days.
Tuition Learn-to-ski holidays.
Snow guarantee If all lifts close, transport will be provided to alternative resort; if no alternative, will pay £30 compensation per day.

Ski Highlife
Holidays in Whistler
Churchill House, 7 George St, Dewsbury WF13 2LX
Reservations (0924) 430500.
Fax (0924) 460039.
Sales Direct.
Bonding ABTA.
Surcharges Due to flight cost increases only
Insurance Compulsory.
Travel Air, departing from any airport on request. Flight-only seats available.
Accommodation Hotels. (Self-catering apartments and chalets.)
Tuition Heli-skiing days.

Ski Hillwood
Specialists in family holidays
2 Field End Road, Pinner, Middlesex, HA5 2QL
Reservations 081-866 9993.
Fax 081-868 0258.
Sales Direct.
Bonding ATOL.
Surcharges Over 5%, due to factors beyond control e.g. currency changes, government action, fuel costs.
Insurance Compulsory.
Travel Air, departing Luton, Birmingham, Gatwick. Supplements payable for regional departures. Flight-only seats available. (Self-drive.)
Accommodation Hotels. (Self-catering, snow homes.)
Children Crèche, 9am to 5pm, Sunday to Friday, for children from 6 weeks old; baby patrol most evenings.
Ski guiding Free guides lead intermediate and advanced groups.
Tuition Summer race training on Stubai glacier.

Ski Jeannie
Holidays in France and Switzerland
21 London Rd, Great Shelford,

Cambridge, CB2 5DB
Reservations (0223) 840680.
Fax (0223) 845835, Tx 81277.
Sales Direct. (Exhibitions.)
Bonding ATOL.
Surcharges None.
Insurance Normally compulsory.
Travel Air, departing Gatwick (Manchester and Glasgow on request). Supplements payable for regional departures. Flight-only seats available. (Self-drive.)
Accommodation Catered chalets. (Hotels, self-catering, catered apartments.)
Children Baby-sitting.
Ski guiding Guides lead groups from intermediate upwards, organise torchlight descents, slalom races.

Ski La Vie
Holidays in Switzerland
28 Linver Road, London, SW6 3RB
Reservations 071-736 5611.
Fax 071-381 6955.
Sales Direct.
Bonding ATOL, credit cards accepted.
Surcharges None.
Insurance Optional.
Travel Air, departing Gatwick, Heathrow; others on request. Supplements payable for regional departures. (Self-drive.)
Accommodation Catered chalets. (Self-catering, hotels.)
Children Norland nannies available day or night for any period of time.
Ski guiding Free guides lead groups of similar ability throughout ski area, and off-piste at own risk and in no official capacity.
Snow guarantee If less than 15% of the lifts in the Champery/Les Crosets skiing area are not open due to lack of snow, will provide transport to glacier skiing at Les Diablerets; may also transfer to accommodation in Les Diablerets if possible, and refund any difference in price.

Ski M & M
Holidays in the Portes du Soleil
12A North Junction Street, Edinburgh, EH6 6HN
Reservations 031-555 1717. Also 081-977 8757; 0272 290124.
Tx 934999.
Sales Direct.
Bonding ATOL and credit cards.
Surcharges Will only pass on flight cost increases.
Insurance Compulsory.
Travel Air, departing Gatwick,

Manchester, Glasgow, Bristol. Supplements payable for regional departures. Flight-only seats available. Supplement payable for ski carriage. (Self-drive.)
Accommodation Catered chalets. (Hotels, self-catering, catered apartments, snow homes.)
Children Nanny service for ages 3 months to 4 years in both resorts.
Ski guiding Free ski leaders lead groups for all abilities, except complete beginners.
Tuition Ski instruction weeks, specialist mogul clinics, advanced ski clinics, intermediate ski clinics, potential instructor clinics, perfect your parallels clinics, snowboard clinics.
Snow guarantee Transport will be provided to alternative resort.

Ski Miquel

Holidays in the Spanish Pyrenees as well as the Alps
460 Corn Exchange, Manchester, M4 3BY
Reservations 061-832 2737.
Fax 061-835 1517, Tx 665114.
Sales Direct.
Bonding ATOL.
Surcharges None.
Insurance Compulsory.
Travel Air, departing Gatwick, Manchester. Supplements payable for regional departures. Flight-only seats available. Supplement payable for ski carriage. (Self-drive.)
Accommodation Hotels. (Catered chalets, self-catering.)
Ski guiding Representatives offer to introduce groups to the ski area.
Snow guarantee If resort closed, transport will be provided to alternative resort; if no alternative, will pay £20 compensation per day plus unused lift passes, lessons and ski hire costs refunded.

Ski Morgins

Holidays in Morgins
Raughton Head, Carlisle, Cumbria, CA5 7DD
Reservations (06996) 258.
Sales Direct.
Bonding Access accepted.
Surcharges If currency falls by more than 10%; no surcharges once full payment received.
Insurance Optional.
Travel Air, departing All major UK airports. (Self-drive, rail, coach.)
Accommodation Chalets.

(Self-catering, hotels.)
Ski guiding Provide guide to slopes 4 days a week and evening entertainments programme.
Tuition Off-piste, race training and mogul clinics.
Snow guarantee Transport to nearest snow is provided to clients without own means of transport.

Ski Olympic

Holidays in France
Rhossili, Barnsley Rd, Doncaster, S Yorks, DN5 8RB
Reservations (0302) 390120.
Fax (0302) 390120.
Sales Direct. (Agents.)
Bonding ABTA, ATOL, AITO.
Surcharges Within ABTA guide-lines.
Insurance Normally compulsory.
Travel Coach, departing M1, M25, Dover. Flight-only seats available. (Air (Manchester, Gatwick), self-drive.)
Accommodation Catered chalets. (Self-catering.)
Children In-chalet nanny service on special weeks.
Ski guiding Guides lead groups throughout the ski area and organise après-ski activities.
Tuition Learn-to-ski holidays and intermediate weeks in La Rosière.

Ski Oui

Holidays in the Chamonix valley
56 Bower Street, Maidstone, ME16 8SD
Reservations (0622) 763745.
Sales Direct.
Bonding Credit cards accepted.
Surcharges Will pass on any increased costs
Insurance Normally compulsory.
Travel Air, departing Gatwick; others on request. (Self-drive, rail.)
Accommodation Catered chalets. (Self-catering.)
Children Own nannies for ages 6 months to 2 years.
Ski guiding Ski companions lead groups of different abilities to the best skiing and arrange races and picnics.
Snow guarantee If take insurance policy, will pay piste closure compensation of up to £20 per day.

Ski Partners

Holidays in Austria
Friary House, Colston Street, Bristol, BS1 5AP
Reservations (0272) 253545.
Fax (0272) 293697, Tx 445960.
Sales Direct. (Agents.)

Bonding ABTA, ATOL, AITO.
Surcharges Within ABTA guide-lines.
Insurance Compulsory.
Travel Air, departing Luton, Gatwick, Bristol, Manchester, Belfast. Supplements payable for regional departures. Flight-only seats available. (Coach.)
Accommodation Hotels.
Tuition 6 x 2 hour lessons included in holiday price; beginners weeks, snowboarding weeks, cross country weeks.
Snow guarantee If all lifts closed, transport, passes and school will be provided for alternative resort, up to £15 per day.

Ski Party Snow World
Holidays for groups
34-36 South Street, Lancing, West Sussex, BN15 8AG
Reservations (0903) 765581.
Fax (0903) 750325, Tx 877437.
Sales Direct.
Bonding ABTA.
Surcharges Within ABTA guide-lines.
Insurance Compulsory.
Travel Air, departing Gatwick, Manchester, Glasgow, Belfast. Supplements payable for regional departures. Flight-only seats available. (Coach, self-drive.)
Accommodation Hotels. (Self-catering, catered apartments and chalets.)
Children Can arrange crèche.
Ski guiding In selected resorts guides offer introduction to ski area and give specialist ski tips.
Tuition Learn-to-ski holidays; own instructors in some resorts.
Snow guarantee Transport will be provided to alternative resort; if no alternative, will pay £10 compensation per day or provide alternative recreational programe.

Ski Peak
Holidays in France
Hangerfield, Witley, Surrey, GU8 5PR
Reservations (0428) 682272.
Fax (0428) 685369.
Sales Direct.
Bonding Credit cards accepted.
Surcharges Due to factors beyond control; no surcharges once full payment received.
Insurance Normally compulsory.
Travel Air, departing Gatwick, Manchester. Supplements payable for regional departures. Flight-only seats available. (Self-drive.)

Accommodation Catered chalets. (Self-catering, hotels.)
Children Nanny service in Jan and Apr.
Ski guiding Ski representatives arrange ski lessons and passes, and introduce groups to the best skiing.
Tuition Free 2 hour private ski lesson included. Ski mountaineering tuition weeks.
Snow guarantee For £3.50 insurance premium, will pay £15 per day if piste closed.

Ski Red Guide
Mainly holidays in France
Permanent House, 18/20 Clifton Street, Blackpool, Lancs, FY1 1JP
Reservations (0253) 23939.
Fax (0253) 752401, Tx 67453.
Sales Direct.
Bonding Credit cards accepted.
Surcharges Up to 10%, due to currency changes and other factors beyond control.
Insurance Normally compulsory.
Travel Coach, air, departing London, Birmingham, Manchester, Preston, Blackpool, Penrith, Carlisle, Glasgow, Dover, Knutsford, Edinburgh, Crooklands. Supplements payable for regional departures. (Self-drive, motorail.)
Accommodation Catered chalets. (Hotels, self-catering.)
Children Baby-sitting.
Ski guiding Free guides lead groups of all standards throughout the ski area.
Tuition Learn-to-ski weeks.
Snow guarantee If lack of snow is known before departure, alternative accommodation will be arranged; once in resort, transport will be provided to alternative resort; if neither possible, will pay up to £30 compensation per day to those with insurance policy.

Ski Scott Dunn
Holidays in Switzerland and America
Fovant Mews, 12A Noyna Rd, London, SW17 7PH
Reservations 081-767 0202.
Fax 081-767 2026.
Sales Direct.
Bonding ATOL.
Surcharges Due to currency, flight and government action; no surcharges once final payment made.
Insurance Normally compulsory.
Travel Air, departing Gatwick, Glasgow; others on request. Supplements payable for regional departures. Flight-only seats available. (Self-drive.)
Accommodation Catered chalets.

(Hotels, self-catering.)
Children Nanny service, Snoopy miniclub.
Ski guiding Guides lead groups throughout the ski area.
Tuition Alternative ski school in Champery. Heliskiing in Zermatt and Jackson Hole.
Snow guarantee If 80% or more of ski lifts and runs are closed at mid-day, 3 days before departure in European resorts, will either refund the total holiday cost less 10% excess and insurance premium or relocate chalet guests to another resort where the above conditions are not met at no additional cost to guest.

Ski Sutherland

School group holidays
Church Gate, Church Street West, Woking, Surrey, GU21 1DJ
Reservations (0483) 770383.
Fax (0483) 755120, Tx 859397.
Sales Agents and direct.
Bonding ABTA.
Surcharges None.
Insurance Compulsory.
Travel Air, departing Heathrow, Gatwick, Manchester, Birmingham, Newcastle, Glasgow. (Coach, rail.)
Accommodation Hotels.

Ski Tips

Holidays in Morzine
Oasis Hotel, Marine Parade, Great Yarmouth, NR30 2EW
Reservations (0493) 855281.
Fax (0493) 330697.
Sales Direct.
Bonding ATOL.
Surcharges Due to fuel and aviation cost increases up to £10, and government action, but not currency changes.
Insurance Normally compulsory.
Travel Air, departing Gatwick, Manchester, Glasgow. Supplements payable for regional departures. (Self-drive, coach.)
Accommodation Catered chalets. (Club chalet, hotels.)
Ski guiding Guides introduce groups to the ski area and arrange après-ski activities.

Ski Total

Minor mainstream operator
10 Hill Street, Richmond, Surrey, TW9 1TN
Reservations 081-948 6922.
Fax 081-332 1268, Tx 94013570.

Sales Direct. (Agents.)
Bonding ATOL, AITO.
Surcharges Due to government action only.
Insurance Compulsory.
Travel Air, departing Gatwick, Manchester, Edinburgh, Glasgow. Flight-only seats available. (Self-drive.)
Accommodation Catered chalets. (Club chalets, self-catering, hotels.)
Children Baby-sitting.
Ski guiding 4 days a week free guides introduce groups to the ski area, both on and off-piste.

Ski Unique

Minor operator, wide-ranging programme
Church Gate, Church Street West, Woking, Surrey, GU21 1DJ
Reservations (0483) 755766.
Fax (0483) 755120, Tx 859397.
Sales Agents and direct.
Bonding ABTA.
Surcharges Within ABTA guide-lines.
Insurance Compulsory.
Travel Air, departing Heathrow, Birmingham, Manchester.
Accommodation Hotels. (Self-catering.)
Snow guarantee For an extra insurance premium.

Ski Vail

Holidays in Vail
Brunswick Court, 12-14 Brunswick Place, Hove, East Sussex BN3 1NA
Reservations (0273) 746971.
Fax (0273) 554445.
Sales Direct.
Bonding Credit cards accepted.
Surcharges For cost increases of more than 2%; if more than 10% can cancel with full refund.
Insurance Normally compulsory.
Travel Air, departing Gatwick.
Accommodation Catered chalets. (Self-catering.)
Children Nannies and baby-sitters can be arranged.

Ski Valkyrie

Mainly holidays in France
56 Bower Street, Maidstone, Kent, ME16 8SD
Reservations (0622) 763745.
Fax (0622) 690964.
Sales Direct.
Bonding Credit cards accepted.
Surcharges Will pass on any increased costs
Insurance Normally compulsory.
Travel Self-drive. Flight-only seats available. (Air, rail.)

Accommodation Catered chalets. (Hotels, self-catering.)
Snow guarantee If take insurance policy, will pay up to £20 compensation per day for piste closure.

Ski Weekend

Specialists in weekend and ten-day holidays
3 Maple Cottages, Canada Lane, Faringdon, SN7 8AP
Reservations (0367) 241636.
Fax (0367) 242820.
Sales Direct.
Bonding Credit cards accepted.
Surcharges Due to currency changes only.
Insurance Compulsory.
Travel Air, departing Manchester, Heathrow, Gatwick. Supplements payable for regional departures. (Self-drive.)
Accommodation Hotels. (Catered chalets.)
Children Crèche facilities available.
Ski guiding Representatives provide an initial orientation morning.
Tuition Mountain awareness instruction.

Ski West

Mainly chalet holidays
1 Belmont, Lansdown Rd, Bath, BA1 5DZ
Reservations (0225) 444516.
Fax (0225) 444520, Tx 44680.
Sales Direct. (Agents.)
Bonding ABTA, ATOL, AITO.
Surcharges For government action only
Insurance Normally compulsory.
Travel Air, departing Gatwick, Luton, Manchester, Bristol, Glasgow, Newcastle. Supplements payable for regional departures. Flight-only seats available. (Coach, self-drive.)
Accommodation Catered chalets. (Hotels, club chalets, self-catering, snow homes.)
Snow guarantee If, 3 days prior to departure, less than 10% of runs are open, alternative accommodation will be offered, or can cancel with full refund, less insurance premium.

Ski Whizz Small World

Chalet holiday specialist
13 Hillgate House, Hillgate Street, London, W8 7SP
Reservations 071-221 1121.
Fax 071-792 3145.
Sales Direct. (Agents.)
Bonding ABTA, ATOL, AITO.
Surcharges None.
Insurance Optional.

Travel Air, departing Gatwick. Supplements payable for regional departures. (Self-drive, rail.)
Accommodation Catered chalets. (Club chalets.)
Children Nanny service in all resorts; child-minding chalets in 3 resorts.
Ski guiding Snowmen lead groups to the best skiing for their ability.
Tuition Special off-piste ski guiding in Chamonix.

Ski the American Dream

Holidays in America
Station Chambers, High Street North, London, E6 1JE
Reservations 081-552 1201.
Fax 081-552 7726, Tx 8952436.
Sales Agents and direct.
Bonding ABTA, AITO.
Surcharges Within ABTA guide-lines.
Insurance Normally compulsory.
Travel Air, departing Gatwick, Heathrow, Manchester, Glasgow. Supplements payable for regional departures.
Accommodation Hotels. (Self-catering.)
Tuition Ski improvement courses, back country skiing.

Ski-Tal

Minor mainstream operator
2 Criterion Buildings, Wintersbridge, Portsmouth Road, Thames Ditton, Surrey, KT7 0SS
Reservations 081-398 9861.
Fax 081-398 7153, Tx 94014959.
Sales Direct.
Bonding ATOL.
Surcharges Due to currency changes (if more than 5%).
Insurance Normally compulsory.
Travel Air, departing Gatwick. Supplements payable for regional departures. Flight-only seats available. (Self-drive.)
Accommodation Catered chalets. (Hotels, self-catering, catered apartments.)
Children Informal child-minding by chalet staff.
Ski guiding Guides organise passes, schools and equipment hire, introduce groups to the best runs according to ability and organise tours for intermediates and advanced groups.

SkiBelAir

Holidays in Méribel
43 Elvaston Place, London, SW7 5NP
Reservations 071-251 2077.
Fax 071-792 3142.
Sales Direct.

Bonding Credit cards accepted.
Surcharges Due to fuel price increases only
Insurance Optional.
Travel Air, departing Gatwick; others on request. Supplements payable for regional departures. Supplement payable for ski carriage. (Self-drive.)
Accommodation Catered chalets. (Self-catering by arrangement, hotels.)
Children Nanny service can be arranged for children of all ages.
Ski guiding Guides lead groups of all levels except beginners.
Snow guarantee If, between 3 and 14 days prior to departure, less than 10% of lifts are operating in the Méribel valley, can cancel with refund of up to £500 per person; applicable between 1 Jan and 30 Apr

SkiBound

Group and schools holidays
Blenheim House, 120 Church Street, Brighton, Sussex, BN1 1WH
Reservations (0273) 676123.
Fax (0273) 676410, Tx 877658.
Sales Agents and direct.
Bonding ABTA, ATOL, AITO.
Surcharges Over 2% and up to max £10 per person, due to currency, aircraft fuel, airport charges and government action.
Insurance Compulsory.
Travel Air, departing Gatwick, Manchester, Belfast, Glasgow. Supplements payable for regional departures. Flight-only seats available. Supplement payable for ski carriage. (Coach, self-drive.)
Accommodation Hotels. (Club chalets, self-catering, catered apartments.)
Tuition Learn-to-ski weeks; own ski schools in some resorts.
Snow guarantee Dec and Jan departures only: if all lifts and/or the ski school are closed due to insufficient snow, transport and pass will be provided for alternative resort; if no alternative, alternative accommodation may be arranged, or will pay £15 compensation per day. Other times: transport will be arranged but client pays.

SkiGower

Schools holidays in Switzerland
2 High Street, Studley, Warwickshire, B80 7HJ
Reservations (052 785) 4822.
Fax (052 785) 7236, Tx 94070135.
Sales Direct.
Bonding ABTA.

Surcharges Within ABTA guide-lines.
Insurance Compulsory.
Travel Coach, departing throughout UK.
Accommodation Youth centres. (Hotels.)
Tuition Own British ski instructors.

SkiTonic

Mainly group holidays
2 Church Street, Chesham, Buckinghamshire, HP5 1HT
Reservations (0494) 773388.
Tx 848210.
Sales Agents. (Direct.)
Bonding ABTA, ATOL.
Surcharges None.
Insurance Normally compulsory.
Travel Air, departing Gatwick, Manchester, Glasgow. Supplements payable for regional departures. (Self-drive.)
Accommodation Hotels. (Catered chalets.)
Ski guiding Guides lead groups throughout ski area.
Tuition Learn-to-ski weeks.
Snow guarantee If take insurance policy and if insufficient snow, £5 will be provided for transport to alternative resort; if no alternative, will pay £15 compensation per day.

Skiworld

Minor mainstream operator
Skiworld House, 41 North End Road, London, W14 8SZ
Reservations 071-602 4826.
Fax 071-371 1463.
Sales Direct. (Agents.)
Bonding ABTA, ATOL, AITO.
Surcharges Within ABTA guide-lines. Anyone taking the Skiworld insurance will not be surcharged.
Insurance Optional.
Travel Air, departing Gatwick. Supplements payable for regional departures. Flight-only seats available. (Rail, self-drive, coach.)
Accommodation Self-catering. (Hotels, catered chalets, catered apartments.)
Ski guiding Guides introduce groups to the ski area and offer informal guiding during the rest of the week.
Tuition Advanced technique holidays in Tignes.
Snow guarantee If take insurance policy, and if resort closed all day due to insufficient snow, transport will be arranged to alternative resort, or will provide vouchers worth £10 per day towards a future holiday.

Snobiz

Holidays in Austria and France
11 Liston Court, High Street, Marlow,
Bucks SL7 1ER
Reservations (0628) 890797.
Fax (0628) 898366, Tx 848717.
Sales Agents and direct.
Bonding ABTA, AITO.
Surcharges None.
Insurance Normally compulsory.
Travel Air, rail, departing Gatwick,
Heathrow, Birmingham, Manchester,
Glasgow. Supplements payable for
regional departures. Flight-only seats
available. (Self-drive.)
Accommodation Hotels. (Catered
chalets.)
Children Nursery.
Tuition Learn to ski holidays.
Snow guarantee If take additional
insurance: if there is insufficient snow in
resort causing all lifts to close, transport
will be arranged to alternative resort; if
no alternative, will pay £20
compensation per day

SnowRanger

Very wide range of holidays
Suite 228/9, Linen Hall, 162 Regent
Street, London, W1R 5TB
Reservations 071-439 1255.
Fax 071-434 4078, Tx 919170.
Sales Direct.
Bonding Credit cards accepted.
Surcharges Due to currency changes (if
more than 5%), or government action.
Insurance Optional.
Travel Air, rail, departing Heathrow, Gatwick,
Bristol, Luton, Birmingham, Manchester,
Edinburgh, Glasgow. (Self-drive, rail,
coach.)
Accommodation Hotels. (Self-catering.)
Tuition Powder snow , ski touring,
off-piste holidays, heliskiing.

Snowbugs

Holidays in France, Italy and America
3 The Bigg Market, Newcastle upon
Tyne, NE1 1UN
Reservations 091-222 1535.
Fax 091-222 1284.
Sales Direct. (Agents.)
Bonding ABTA, ATOL.
Surcharges None.
Insurance Normally compulsory.
Travel Air, departing Gatwick,
Newcastle, Glasgow, Manchester.
Supplements payable for regional
departures. Flight-only seats available.
(Self-drive, rail.)
Accommodation Catered chalets.

(Hotels, self-catering apartments.)
Ski guiding Lead groups of all abilities
from intermediate to advanced.
Tuition Learn-to-ski weeks.
Snow guarantee If less than 5% of lifts
are working due to lack of snow, free
transport will be provided to alternative
resort.

Snowcoach Club Cantabrica

Minor mainstream operator
Holiday House, 146-148 London Rd, St
Albans, Herts AL1 1PQ
Reservations (0727) 866177.
Fax (0727) 43766, Tx 8814162.
Sales Agents and direct.
Bonding ABTA, ATOL.
Surcharges Within ABTA guidelines
Insurance Normally compulsory.
Travel Coach, departing throughout
England and Wales.
Accommodation Hotels. (Snow homes,
catered chalets.)
Children Own child-minders in some
resorts in Andorra and Italy, normally for
children aged 1.5 years to 8 years, 4
days and 2 half-days a week; 2 evenings
child patrol.
Ski guiding Guides sort equipment and
passes for beginners, lead groups of
intermediates, and find the best snow for
advanced groups.
Snow guarantee If take insurance
policy, transport will be provided to
alternative resort.

Snowline

Holidays in Portes du Soleil
460 Corn Exchange, Manchester, M4
3BY
Reservations (0625) 616489.
Sales Direct.
Bonding Credit cards accepted.
Surcharges Over 2% and up to 10%,
due to currency changes.
Insurance Normally compulsory.
Travel Air, departing Manchester,
Birmingham, Gatwick, Glasgow.
Supplements payable for regional
departures. Supplement payable for ski
carriage. (Self-drive.)
Accommodation Catered chalets.
(Hotels, self-catering.)
Children Mini-club for ages 4 to 12.
Ski guiding Guides lead intermediate
and advanced groups for half and full
days, on- and off-piste.
Snow guarantee Transport will be
provided to alternative resort, or will pay
up to £20 compensation per day.

Snowtime

Holidays in Méribel
96 Belsize Lane, London, NW3 5BE
Reservations 071-433 3336.
Fax 071-433 1883, Tx 267707.
Sales Direct.
Bonding ATOL.
Surcharges Due to fuel increases
passed on by airline
Insurance Optional.
Travel Air, departing Gatwick,
Manchester, Glasgow. Supplements
payable for regional departures.
Flight-only seats available. (Self-drive,
rail.)
Accommodation Catered chalets. (Club
chalets, self-catering, hotels.)
Children Norland nanny available; own
crèche in hotel.
Ski guiding 5 days a week, free guides
lead groups to the best skiing, both on
and off-piste.
Snow guarantee If, due to lack of snow,
less than 15% of the lifts are operating in
the valley of Meribel for more than 3
days on a one week holiday or more
than seven days on a two week holiday,
and provided all bookings are received
10 weeks prior to departure and fully
paid for 8 weeeks before departure: will
provide similar holiday for the equivalent
date during the following season, or will
provide a full credit towards a holiday
later in the same season.

Sportsworld Travel

Holidays in Canada
New Abbey Court, Stert Street,
Abingdon, Oxon OX14 3JZ
Reservations (0235) 554844.
Fax (0235) 554841, Tx 838813.
Sales Direct. (Agents.)
Bonding ABTA, ATOL.
Surcharges Within ABTA guide-lines.
Insurance Normally compulsory.
Travel Air, departing Gatwick, Heathrow;
others by request. Supplements payable
for regional departures. Flight-only seats
available.
Accommodation Hotels. (Self-catering.)
Tuition Heliskiing packages.

Summit

Holidays in Morgins
PO Box 729, Hove, East Sussex, BN3
4FY
Reservations (0273) 733143.
Sales Direct.
Bonding Credit cards accepted.
Surcharges Over 2%, due to currency
changes.

Insurance Normally compulsory.
Travel Air, departing Heathrow, Gatwick,
Manchester, Glasgow. Supplements
payable for regional departures.
Supplement payable for ski carriage.
(Self-drive.)
Accommodation Catered chalets.
(Hotels.)
Children Nursery, baby-sitting, mini-club.
Ski guiding Ski leaders lead groups of
5-10 throughout the Portes du Soleil;
also lead groups off-piste.
Tuition Mogul weeks, powder weeks
and beginner (learn to ski) weeks.
Snow guarantee If all lifts are closed,
transport will be provided to alternative
resort.

Supersports Ski Chalets

Chalet holidays in Les Gets
331 Lymington Road, Highcliffe, Dorset
Reservations (0425) 273435.
Sales Direct.
Bonding ATOL and credit cards.
Surcharges None.
Insurance Normally compulsory.
Travel Air, departing Gatwick.
Supplements payable for regional
departures. Flight-only seats available.
(Self-drive, coach.)
Accommodation Catered chalets.
(Self-catering.)
Children Baby-sitting.
Ski guiding Guides lead groups of
similar ability 4 days a week.
Snow guarantee Transport will be
provided to alternative resort if available
within 1½ hour journey.

Supertravel

Major operator, specialising in chalets
22 Hans Place, London, SW1X 0EP
Reservations 071-584 5060.
Fax 071-581 3831, Tx 263725.
Sales Direct. (Agents.)
Bonding ABTA, ATOL.
Surcharges Within ABTA guide-lines.
Insurance Normally compulsory.
Travel Air, departing Gatwick,
Manchester, Glasgow, Heathrow.
Supplements payable for regional
departures. Flight-only seats available.
(Self-drive, rail.)
Accommodation Catered chalets,
hotels. (Self-catering.)
Children Baby-sitting, nanny service.
Ski guiding Guides lead intermediate
and advanced groups.
Tuition Ali Ross skiing clinics, heliskiing
in Europe and Canada, off-piste courses
in Val d'Isère.

Swiss-Ski

Holidays in Switzerland, mainly in hotels
Bridge House, Ware, Herts, SG12 9DE
Reservations (0920) 463971.
Fax (0920) 487943, Tx 81633.
Sales Direct.
Bonding ABTA, ATOL.
Surcharges None.
Insurance Optional.
Travel Air, departing Heathrow, Gatwick,
Birmingham, Manchester. (Self-drive.)
Accommodation Hotels. (Self-catering
apartments.)
Snow guarantee If take insurance
policy, and if all lifts are closed for a day
or more, will pay £15 compensation per
day, up to £105.

Tailor Made

Specialists in Davos and other Swiss
resorts
Erlysmead House, 20 Farleigh Wick,
Bradford-on-Avon, Wiltshire, BA15 2PZ
Reservations (0225) 859598; (0491)
25063.
Fax (0225) 858796; from Dec-May:
(0491) 33836.
Sales Direct.
Bonding Credit cards accepted.
Surcharges Due to factors beyond
control.
Insurance Normally compulsory.
Travel Air, departing Gatwick, Heathrow,
Birmingham, Manchester. (Self-drive.)
Accommodation Hotels. (Self-catering.)
Ski guiding Guides can be arranged,
on- or off-piste.
Tuition Advanced, off-piste, powder
initiation courses; problem clinics,
heliskiing.

The Ski Company Ltd

Very upmarket holidays in France
41 Hyde Vale, Greenwich, London,
SE10 8QQ
Reservations 081-692 3955.
Fax 081-692 3815.
Sales Direct. (Agents.)
Bonding ATOL.
Surcharges Up to £10, due to flight
charges only.
Insurance Optional.
Travel Air, departing Heathrow.
Supplements payable for regional
departures.
Accommodation Catered chalets.
Children Nannies provided or own
nanny can be brought at low cost.
Ski guiding 6 days a week, professional
guides from local ski school.
Tuition Off-piste, powder instruction

weeks, ski touring.
Snow guarantee If, 8 days prior to
departure, 50% of lifts are closed due to
insufficient snow, can cancel with refund
less £30 excess (provided bookings
made 8 weeks prior to departure).

Thomson

The market leader
Greater London House, Hampstead Rd,
London, NW1 7SD
Reservations 021-632 6282.
Fax 071-387 8451.
Sales Agents.
Bonding ABTA, ATOL.
Surcharges None.
Insurance Normally compulsory.
Travel Air, departing Gatwick, Heathrow,
Stansted, Luton, Cardiff, Bristol,
Birmingham, East Midlands,
Manchester, Leeds-Bradford, Newcastle,
Glasgow. Supplements payable for
regional departures. Flight-only seats
available. Supplement payable for ski
carriage. (Self-drive.)
Accommodation Hotels. (Self-catering,
catered chalets, snow homes.)
Children Children's clubs for non-skiing
children in selected resorts.
Ski guiding In 49 resorts free guides
lead experienced groups.
Tuition Learn-to-ski weeks.
Snow guarantee If insufficient snow,
transport or accommodation will be
provided for alternative resort ; if no
alternative will pay £30 compensation
per day.

Top Deck

Holidays in Andorra and elsewhere
133, Earls Court Rd, London, SW5
Reservations 071-370 4555.
Fax 071-373 6201, Tx 8955339.
Sales Agents. (College ski clubs.)
Bonding ABTA, ATOL, AITO.
Surcharges None.
Insurance Optional.
Travel Air, departing Gatwick,
Manchester. Supplements payable for
regional departures. Supplement
payable for ski carriage. (Coach,
self-drive, rail.)
Accommodation Hotels. (Club chalet,
self-catering.)
Tuition Snowboarding tuition and
snowboarding weeks.
Snow guarantee If lifts are closed due
to insufficient snow, transport will be
provided to alternative resort; if no
alternative, will provide a voucher worth
£10 per day (max £30) for use towards a
future Top Deck holiday.

Top Run

Holidays in Whistler
21 Garrick Street, London WC2E 9AX
Reservations 071-836 8121.
Fax 071-240 5795, Tx 299798.
Sales Direct.
Bonding ABTA.
Surcharges None.
Insurance Normally compulsory.
Travel Air, departing Gatwick,
Manchester.
Accommodation Hotels, self-catering
apartments. (Catered chalets.)
Children Nannies, baby-sitters.
Tuition Heliskiing, powder, moguls
workshops.

Touralp

Holidays in major French resorts
197B Brompton Road, London, SW3 1LA
Reservations 071-589 1918.
Fax 071-823 8938, Tx 269710.
Sales Direct. (Agents.)
Bonding ABTA, ATOL.
Surcharges None.
Insurance Normally compulsory.
Travel Air, departing Gatwick, Heathrow,
Manchester. Supplements payable for
regional departures. Flight-only seats
available. (Coach, self-catering, train.)
Accommodation Self-catering. (Hotels.)
Snow guarantee If all pistes closed due
to too much or too little snow, will pay
£25 compensation per day; if less than
25% lifts operating between 14 days and
24 hours prior to departure, can cancel
with refund less insurance premium and
£30 excess.

Tracer Holidays

Holidays in France
131A Heston Road, Hounslow,
Middlesex, TW5 0RD
Reservations 081-577 1200.
Fax 081-572 9788, Tx 892512.
Sales Direct. (Agents.)
Bonding ATOL.
Surcharges Within ABTA guidelines
Insurance Normally compulsory.
Travel Air, departing Gatwick. Flight-only
seats available. (Self-drive, rail, coach.)
Accommodation Catered chalets. (Club
chalets, self-catering, hotels.)
Ski guiding One day a week free guides
give introductory tour of pistes.
Snow guarantee If no snow, will move
clients to alternative resort

USAirtours

Holidays in America
295 Eastern Avenue, Gants Hill, Ilford,
Essex, IG2 6NT
Reservations 081-550 8866. Also
Birmingham: 021-550 7775; Cardiff:
(0222) 377091; Manchester: 061-456
2515.
Fax 081-551 2000, Tx 94016230.
Sales Direct.
Bonding ABTA.
Surcharges Within ABTA guide-lines.
Insurance Normally compulsory.
Travel Air, departing Gatwick;
Manchester on request.
Accommodation Self-catering. (Hotels.)

Vacances Elite

Upmarket holidays in Verbier and
Kashmir
Meadbank, 12 Parkgate Rd, London,
SW1 4NN
Reservations 071-223 8655.
Fax 071-738 9171, Tx 262964.
Sales Direct.
Bonding Credit cards accepted.
Surcharges Due to currency changes,
government action, aviation costs, civil
unrest or any other factor beyond control.
Insurance Optional.
Travel Air, departing Heathrow.
Supplements payable for regional
departures. (Self-drive.)
Accommodation Catered chalets.
(Hotels.)
Ski guiding Guides lead groups to the
best skiing and organise extra-curricular
activities.

Vacations

Mainstream operator
30-32 Cross Street, London, N1 2BG
Reservations 071-359 3511.
Fax 071-359 3465.
Sales Agents. (Direct.)
Bonding ABTA, ATOL.
Surcharges Due to aviation fuel and
government action.
Insurance Compulsory.
Travel Air, departing Gatwick, Heathrow,
Stansted, Birmingham, Manchester,
Glasgow. Supplements payable for
regional departures. Flight-only seats
available. Supplement payable for ski
carriage. (Self-drive.)
Accommodation Self-catering. (Hotels,
club hotels.)
Ski guiding Free guides introduce ski
areas and lift system.
Tuition Own ski school in 5 resorts ski
progress, advanced workshop, surf and
mono courses.
Snow guarantee If, within 2 weeks of
departure, due to lack of snow, there is
less than 10% lifts open, will transfer to

better resort; if during stay, lift sytem is closed due to lack of snow, free transport will be provided to alternative resort.

Waymark

Cross-country skiing holidays
44 Windsor Rd, Slough, SL1 2EJ
Reservations (0753) 516477.
Fax (0753) 517016.
Sales Direct.
Bonding ATOL.
Surcharges Due to airfare increases only.
Insurance Optional.
Travel Air, departing Heathrow, Gatwick, Birmingham, Manchester, Newcastle, Glasgow. Supplements payable for regional departures.
Accommodation Hotels. (Mountain huts.)
Ski guiding Guides lead groups cross-country and give tuition.
Tuition Learn-to-instruct course.

White Roc Ski

Holidays in France
69 Westbourne Grove, London, W2 4UJ
Reservations 071-792 1188.
Sales Direct.
Bonding Credit cards accepted.
Surcharges Due to currency changes (if more than 5%).
Insurance Normally compulsory.
Travel Air, departing Heathrow, Birmingham, Manchester. Supplements payable for regional departures. (Self-drive.)
Accommodation Catered chalets. (Hotels, self-catering.)
Children Free nursery booking service.
Tuition Off-piste powder skiing instruction with guide in Chamonix valley.
Snow guarantee If, 2 days prior to departure, more than 75% lifts are not operating, can cancel with full refund less insurance premium and £25 excess. In resort, transport will be provided up to £10 per day to alternative resort; if no alternative, will pay £25 compensation per day.

Winter Adventure Holidays

Mainly holidays in France
1-5 Lower High Street, Burford, Oxon, OX8 4RN
Reservations (0993) 822019.
Fax (0993) 823352.
Sales Direct.
Bonding Credit cards accepted.
Surcharges None if pay on time
Insurance Normally compulsory.

Travel Coach, departing London, Watford, Dover. Supplements payable for regional departures. (Air; self-drive.)
Accommodation Hotels. (Self-catering.)
Ski guiding Group leaders ski with groups all day and organise free après-ski activities.
Snow guarantee Compulsory insurance policy includes cash compensation for each day's skiing lost.

Winterworld

Chalet and self-catering holidays in Villars
8 Deanwood House, Stockcross, Newbury, Berks, RG16 8JP
Reservations (0635) 44684.
Fax (0635) 35434, Tx 846811.
Sales Agents.
Bonding ABTA, ATOL, AITO.
Surcharges Within ABTA guidelines.
Insurance Normally compulsory.
Travel Air, departing Gatwick, Heathrow, Manchester. Supplements payable for regional departures. Supplement payable for ski carriage. (Self-drive.)
Accommodation Catered chalets. (Self-catering, hotels.)
Children Free baby-sitting in catered accommodation.
Ski guiding Free guides help clients to explore the ski area.
Snow guarantee Provides private mini-bus to take clients to glacier 20 mins away.

Yugotours

Holidays in Yugoslavia
Chesham House, 150 Regent Street, London, W1R 6BB
Reservations 071-439 7233. Also Glasgow: 041-226 5535; Manchester: 061-228 6891; Birmingham: 021-233 3001.
Fax 071-439 7321, Tx 263543.
Sales Agents.
Bonding ABTA, ATOL.
Surcharges None.
Insurance Normally compulsory.
Travel Air, departing Gatwick, Heathrow, Manchester, Glasgow, Birmingham. Supplements payable for regional departures.
Accommodation Hotels. (Self-catering, catered apartments.)
Children Kindergarten and special ski school can be arranged.
Snow guarantee If insufficient snow, transport will be provided to alternative resort; if no alternative, will pay £20 compensation per day and arrange other activities.

Insurance

Skiing can be a hazardous sport: some of the people who do it get hurt, and some seriously. The risks are often exaggerated – only a small percentage of those who go skiing suffer any injury at all – but they should not be ignored. The UK's National Health Service will provide free treatment for skiers injured on the Scottish slopes, regardless of the fact that the injuries may be self-inflicted. Abroad, you can often call on reciprocal medical care deals in which the UK is a partner. But the bureaucracy surrounding that system is a big hurdle to have to get over – and most ski-resort clinics are in any case privately run, which means that reciprocal care deals are worthless. Also, medical attention isn't the only cost which can arise on a skiing trip. Some of the risks you run may be covered by a policy you have already taken out – loss of luggage, for example – but others are most unlikely to be covered. Your travel plans may have to be changed; you may break or lose your skis; or you may have to pay for a rescue. As a result you need winter sports insurance.

Most tour operators have their own policies arranged direct with an insurance company. Some make their cover compulsory – though its cost is rarely included in the package holiday price; others insist that you take it unless you provide evidence that you have bought equally good cover elsewhere. These days the obvious differences between one policy and another may not seem huge. But the less obvious differences are not trivial – they may matter enough to steer you away from the tour operator you first thought of, or to make you decide to buy your insurance independently. Surprisingly three seasons of high insurance claims – snow guarantees, head and knee injuries, rock-damaged equipment – do not seem to have resulted in inflated premiums. On the contrary, they appear to have stimulated increased competition in the insurance market. Shopping around rather than blindly accepting the tour operator back-of-the-brochure policy might save you money and get you exactly what you want or need.

In this section we outline the variations, so that you can weigh up the policies which are thrust at you. We take in turn each of the kinds of cover you can expect to find. We divide policies into those offered by tour operators and those sold separately – 'independent'

policies. Where we say 'all policies', strictly speaking we mean all those we've looked at, which is not all those that exist but a great many. It's vital to check that the policy you're about to buy will suit **you**.

First, a bit of key terminology. Under many sections of a policy, the amount that's paid out in settlement of a claim will be less than the amount you've lost. The difference, called an **excess**, varies between policies and between sections, but is often £25 per claim. Every separate incident is considered as a separate claim. For example, if your ski bag is damaged on the journey out and you lose your ski poles at a later stage of the holiday, you will be making two claims, and you will have to bear two excesses.

As well as setting out the reasons for which you'll be able to claim, a policy will have **exclusion clauses** – these tell you about circumstances in which the insurance company won't pay up. You should carefully check these exclusions before buying a policy. You'll often find that you won't be covered if you take part in very risky sports – for example, ski-jumping, racing in major events, ice hockey or bob-sleigh riding. More alarmingly, some policies now exclude off-piste skiing. Since the line between piste and off-piste skiing is very unclear

(and many insurance companies are unable to define it satisfactorily), any mildly adventurous skier who might be tempted off-piste should steer clear of such policies. There are plenty of companies that offer fully comprehensive skiing cover and some that actually make a feature of off-piste skiing, ski-touring and helicopter rescue. **Watch out** Some policies exclude off-piste skiing.

Although everyone should read policies carefully, there are two groups who should be particularly wary. Those who are over 65 should bear in mind that some policies have an age limit, usually 70 or 75 years; others have an age exclusion in respect of medical and cancellation expenses only. Those for whom pregnancy is a possibility should be on the lookout for exclusions relating to that eventuality: policies vary a lot in this respect.

Watch out Some policies have exclusion clauses relating to illnesses you've suffered in the past.

You should tell the insurance company about any health problem you have when you take out the policy. If you don't, a subsequent claim could be turned down.

Claims involving expenditure should always be supported by receipts. And claims must always be submitted within a reasonable time of your return.

In most countries, UK citizens are entitled to treatment by the local national heath service, either free or at reduced cost. DHSS leaflet SA30 has details. Do *not* take this to mean that you can manage without insurance.

There are particular groups of skiers who would definitely benefit from taking out independent policies. One is the family. An independent family policy could work out considerably cheaper than taking out individual cover for the children – but remember that claims (and their cash limits) will be calculated per family as opposed to per individual. Another is the keen skier who plans more than one trip a year. There are several policies available that give cover for the whole season (or for thirty days during it) and which work out much cheaper than buying a series of separate policies.

Several companies now produce insurance cards, which can not only be waved at whoever is rescuing or treating you as evidence of your cover, but in some cases can also be used like a credit card; the insurance company is billed directly from the resort, saving you from having to fork out the cash at the time and claim it back later. The best-known of the card schemes is Carte Neige in France, which will guarantee you treatment without bills or hassle in any French resort. Benefits also include low premiums, discounts on facilities in many French resorts, and public liability cover, but not cover for cancellation or baggage loss. Various UK companies operate insurance card schemes, but only one of these, Fogg Travel, actually provides the credit-card-type service. **Carte Neige** is most easily bought in the resort. **Fogg Travel** are on (0623) 631331.

Cancellation

What it's for To repay money you've paid in advance for a holiday you're unable to go on.

Do you need it? Yes, unless you're making no advance bookings.

Who offers it? All policies.

When it applies Most policies pay up if you are prevented from travelling by your own illness (including pregnancy), or the illness or death of a close relative of yourself or of another member of your holiday party. Most pay if any member of the party is called for jury service or is required to appear in court as a witness. Many policies will pay out if you decide to cancel your holiday after a delay in departure of at least 12 hours (usually 24 hours). Some pay if you have to cancel because a close business associate or someone you plan to stay with while on holiday is ill, if you're made redundant or if your home is made uninhabitable by fire, flood or burglary.

What you can claim Whatever amounts you have paid out that you can't get back. An excess will usually be deducted – it may be lower than usual if you claim only the deposit. (You don't get your insurance premium back, of course.)

How much cover? Tour operators' policies generally cover the cost of the holiday; others set a limit – usually between £1,000 and £3,000. Obviously you need to make sure that the limit is high enough to meet the full cost of your holiday. Some policies incorporate cancellation with medical expenses, thus setting a much higher upper limit.

Watch out Some policies won't pay out if you cancel your holiday because of an injury while taking part in a 'hazardous activity' – eg mountaineering.

Curtailment

What it's for To repay a proportion of money you've paid for a holiday you have to cut short, and extra costs arising from an early return home.

Do you need it? Yes, unless you're making no advance bookings.

Who offers it? All policies.

When it applies If you have to come home early for the kinds of reason set out under Cancellation.

What you can claim A proportion of the pre-paid cost of the holiday, according to the length of time on holiday you've lost, and reasonable additional expenses for travel and accommodation to get you home. Most policies have an excess.

How much cover? Generally, the same limits apply here as under Cancellation. Some tour operator policies cover you for only a proportion of the amount you have spent on your holiday, while others set a limit equal to the cost of the holiday – either may be too low if you have to fly back soon after you arrive. Narrow cash limits may be similarly inadequate – look for a limit of at least twice the holiday cost. Quite a few policies now include curtailment with medical expenses.

Medical expenses

What it's for To meet costs arising from illness or injury.

Do you need it? Yes, even in countries where there are good reciprocal health care agreements.

Who offers it? All policies.

When it applies If you fall ill or injure yourself during the holiday, either on or off the slopes, or require emergency dental treatment.

What you can claim All treatment expenses – doctors' fees, hospital bills, prescription charges etc – plus any additional accommodation and travel costs resulting from your illness or injury, including the costs of a person to accompany you (on medical advice) and of mountain rescue in normal circumstances. Many policies will pay to bring you back home (by air ambulance if necessary) for medical treatment if it would be better for you (or cheaper for the insurance company). Most policies will not pay the additional cost of private-room accommodation in hospital unless your doctor thinks it is necessary. Some policies will not cover surgery or treatment which can reasonably be delayed until you return to the UK, where you can be treated under the NHS or your own medical bills insurance. Other policies provide for any expenses incurred up to 12 months after the time when you are injured or fall ill.

In the event of death all policies will meet 'reasonable' costs for burial or cremation locally or for transport of the body or ashes to the place of residence in the UK.

How much cover? Anything from £50,000 to £1 million, sometimes even an unlimited amount. If you're going to North America you should aim for £1 million. If you have insufficient cover, you will become personally liable for any costs incurred.

The limit on for funeral expenses abroad is usually £1,000.

Watch out A claim may be refused if you were under the influence of drink or drugs at the time of the accident.

Injury/illness benefit

What it's for To cheer you up.

Do you need it? Not really.

Who offers it? Several policies.

When it applies Generally, if you have to spend at least 24 hours in hospital as a result of an injury or illness outside the UK. One or two policies (which call this cover 'Inability to ski') pay out if you can produce a medical certificate to say that you cannot ski.

What you can claim A specified amount (usually £10, sometimes more) for every 24-hour period in hospital.

How much cover? Most policies set a total claim limit – often £200, but sometimes as low as £120 or as high as £600.

Personal accident

What it's for To compensate you for disablement, or to compensate your heirs for your death.

Do you need it? Not as part of a skiing policy. If you think you need insurance against disability or death, you should have a year-round policy (probably at a much higher level of cover).

Who offers it? Nearly all policies.

When it applies If you are killed or suffer a specific injury, eg loss of a limb or an eye, or permanent total disablement. Most policies will pay compensation for disablement occurring up to twelve months after the date of the accident. Some also offer a weekly benefit for temporary total disablement.

What you can claim A fixed lump sum, according to the injury you suffer.

How much cover? The size of the

lump sum varies considerably; it's usually at least £5,000, can be as much as £25,000, but is more commonly £15,000. Death benefit for children (and in some policies, for elderly people) is much lower, often only £1,000 or even £500.

Personal liability

What it's for To meet claims made against you by others for damage to themselves or their property for which you are legally liable.

Do you need it? Yes and no: this sort of insurance is valuable at any time, so you really should have a permanent policy. Household contents insurance normally provides it.

Who offers it? All policies.

When it applies If an individual successfully makes a claim against you for damages. Many policies won't cover claims made by members of your own family or by someone you employ. And watch out if you hire a car – you will need separate cover.

What you can claim Any damages awarded against you (and legal costs of disputing the claim), but not the costs of defending yourself in criminal proceedings.

How much cover? Usually £500,000, sometimes £1 million. Insist on the higher figure for North America.

Watch out A few policies exclude claims made in overseas courts – these are not recommended.

Personal money

What it's for To replace lost or stolen money, and other things which can be used in exchange for goods or services.

Do you need it? Yes, unless you have an existing policy which covers you all the time for such risks.

Who offers it? All policies – though some include it within the Baggage and personal effects section.

When it applies If your cash, travellers' cheques, credit cards are stolen, lost or destroyed. Such things as air and other travel tickets, insurance Green Card, petrol coupons and vouchers will also be covered. Some specialist policies specifically cover the loss of your lift pass, but this would otherwise be dealt with as a travel ticket. A few include the cost of recovering a lost or stolen passport.

What you can claim The value of whatever you have lost.

How much cover? The limit of cover varies from £200 to £500, but is usually in the £200 to £250 range. There are usually separate limits for loss of cash, and for ski passes – this varies widely, from £75 to £200.

Watch out Claims will normally be met only if the incident has been reported to an appropriate authority (usually the police) within 24 hours.

Baggage and personal effects

What it's for To replace lost or damaged belongings.

Do you need it? Probably, though many of your possessions may be already covered if you have a house contents and/or an all risks policy. Some independent policies offer a substantially reduced premium (up to a third off) in this case.

Who offers it? All policies.

When it applies If any of your possessions are lost, stolen or damaged – with certain exceptions. Contact lenses and documents are excluded by virtually all policies, as are fragile things (eg binoculars, souvenirs) which get broken.

What you can claim Usually just the actual value of what you lose (ie its second-hand value). Some policies, however, allow for replacement with something new (although cash limits will still apply).

How much cover? Often £1,000, though it could be as low as £750 or as high as £1,500, occasionally higher. It's important to work out how much it would cost to replace your belongings should the whole lot be lost – it may be more than you think, particularly if you're relying on the holiday policy to cover such things as your jewellery and cameras as well as clothes and suitcases. And many policies also cover ski equipment in this section. Most policies have a limit on what will be paid for any one item, often somewhere in the £200 region. A pair of skis, bindings and ski sticks is usually counted as one item, as is a camera together with its lenses, flash unit and so on. Some policies also have a limit to what they will pay out in total for valuables such as jewellery, cameras etc – £200 or £300 say.

Watch out All policies expect you to take 'reasonable care' of your possessions. Some specifically say they won't pay if unattended belongings go missing.

Delayed baggage

What it's for To tide you over until your delayed bags turn up.

Do you need it? It can certainly help.

Who offers it? Most policies.

When it applies If your baggage is delayed for 12 hours or more.

What you can claim The cost of essential items. If you have a tour operator policy, the rep should give you the necessary cash; if your baggage never turns up, the money you've been given will be deducted from your claim for the loss. If you have an independent policy, you will have to use your own money and claim it back on your return to the UK. If your skiing equipment is delayed you will be entitled under some policies to the cost of hiring replacements until it shows up.

How much cover? The limit on what you can claim ranges from £50 to £300.

Ski equipment

What it's for To replace lost or damaged ski equipment.

Do you need it? Yes, if ski equipment is excluded from cover under Baggage and personal effects; hired equipment is likely to be excluded from that section, even if your own equipment is not.

Who offers it? Some tour operators and specialist skiing policies; others include it as a subsection of Baggage and personal effects.

When it applies If your skis, ski sticks, bindings or ski boots are lost, stolen or damaged. Some policies which cover loss or theft of hired equipment will not cover *breakage* of hired skis.

What you can claim Some companies pay the cost of replacement, or repair if that is practicable, others pay only the market value, allowing for wear and tear. Although some companies say they will pay only for the one broken ski, in practice this is often not the case – you will be covered for the pair. If it's your own equipment that's lost or broken, some policies will cover the cost of hiring replacements for the remainder of your holiday (as well as paying for the eventual purchase of a replacement set).

How much cover? Cover for your own skis is usually limited to between £200 and £400. This is more than enough for a cheap set of equipment, but not for a flashy set. Cover for hired skis is much less: usually £100 or £150. Some policies offer no cover for skis hired in the USA.

Watch out Some companies insist you bring broken skis home with you, so that they can satisfy themselves that they are beyond repair.

Ski pack / Inability to ski

Note: the cover offered under these two headings is essentially the same, except that 'Ski pack' covers only those skiing facilities booked in advance through the operator in the form of a Ski pack. Some policies use the 'Inability to ski' heading for cover that we describe as 'Injury/illness benefit'.

What it's for To repay a proportion of what you have paid for equipment hire, lessons and lift pass if you become unable to make use of those facilities.

Do you need it? Worth having.

Who offers it? Some tour operators.

When it applies If you fall ill or are injured during the holiday.

What you can claim A proportion of what you have paid out, depending on how long you spend out of action.

How much cover? Usually £100 to £200.

Travel delay

What it's for To compensate you for big delays in your journey.

Do you need it? It's less fuss than seeking compensation in other ways.

Who offers it? Most policies, although with some it's an optional extra.

When it applies If you're delayed for more than twelve hours – often only if the delay is for a specified reason – usually including strikes, mechanical breakdown and bad weather.

What you can claim A specified daily amount during the delay or, if you wish to cancel your holiday, the total cost of it.

How much cover? Usually £20 (occasionally more) for the first 12 hours, £10 for each subsequent 12 hours, up to a maximum of £60 or £100. If you cancel your holiday, the limit of cover in the Cancellation section will usually apply – although some policies set a different limit.

Missed departure

What it's for To meet the costs which arise if you miss the outward flight.

Do you need it? Seems worthwhile.

Who offers it? Mostly tour operator policies, and a few independent ones.

When it applies If public transport fails to deliver you to the airport or other departure point in time to join the booked trip – provided you allowed a reasonable

time to get there. Some policies also cover you if you miss the flight because of a car accident or breakdown.

What you can claim The cost of extra transport to get to your resort, and accommodation if necessary.

How much cover? Varies a lot; from £200 to £350 for trips within Europe, £500 to £800 for trips to the USA.

Interruption of transport

What it's for To compensate you if you're marooned in your resort.

Do you need it? Doubtful; it's the tour operator's responsibility to get you home once they've got you out to a resort.

Who offers it? Several policies have variations on the same theme.

When it applies There are policies which will cover you for hi-jacks, avalanches, landslides, riots, strikes or civil commotions provided that they occur within the period of insurance. Some tour operators have a *weather extension* which covers you only if the difficulties are attributable to the weather. Several tour operators include something under other policy sections.

What you can claim What you have to spend while marooned, up to a limit.

How much cover? The cover limit varies from £150 to £300. Some policies also place a separate limit on the cost of a new flight home.

Snow guarantee

What it's for To meet the cost of getting to snow or lifts if your resort lacks either, or to compensate you for their absence.

Do you need it? Not essential, but valuable if you think there is a risk of extremely bad skiing conditions.

Who offers it? Only a few policies, but many tour operators now offer snow guarantee separate from their insurance policy – see 'Package holidays' chapter.

When it applies If all or a defined (high) proportion of the lifts in the resort are shut (though in some policies this is not necessarily justification for cover) and it's impossible to ski – either because of the weather or because of a shortage of snow.

What you can claim The cost of getting to and skiing in a nearby resort – in practice your operator will probably arrange everything, and no money will change hands. If that's not possible, some will pay compensation – often £15 or £20 a day, though you may get no money for the first two days and may not get any until after you've returned home.

How much cover? Some place a limit of £100, but others go as high as £500, and some offer the option of a higher limit on payment of a higher premium.

Legal expenses

Note: one or two policies bracket this cover with 'Legal advice', which means you have access to free advice on any legal problem which arises while you are on holiday.

What it's for To meet the cost of claiming damages or compensation from third parties following injury or death.

Do you need it? Sounds a good idea: the high cost of legal action can otherwise prevent your pursuing a strong legal claim against someone who has caused an accident.

Who offers it? Several policies.

When it applies If you are injured or killed on holiday and you or your heirs wish to pursue a civil claim against whoever was responsible.

What you can claim Legal costs and expenses.

How much cover? A wide range, from £5,000 to £25,000.

Getting there

Whether you are buying a package or aiming to travel independently, this chapter and the following one are designed to speed you on your way. This chapter covers travel by air, rail or coach; the next chapter offers advice on going by car.

Going by air

Air travel is the normal way of getting from Britain to the skiing mountains, and practically all the tour operators listed in the Package holidays chapter offer holidays based on it. Many of them also sell charter flight seats without accommodation, at prices well below those charged for normal scheduled flights.

UK airports

When departure day arrives, it may be worth giving your departure airport a call to check that your flight is not delayed. We give the phone number for any general enquiries.

Belfast Aldergrove
✆ (0849) 422888
Buses every half hour Mon-Sat from Glengall St bus staion.
Long-term car-park: £2.50 per day (up to 7 days), £5.00 plus 80p per day over 7 days.

Birmingham
✆ 021-767 7145/6
Passenger transit system links airport with Birmingham International railway station (free). Regular buses from city centre.
Long-term car-park: £2.50 per day (open air), £3.50 (multistorey).

Bristol Lulsgate
✆ (0275) 474444
Local buses from Bristol bus station every 2 hours.
Long-term car-park: £1.80 per day

Cardiff Wales
✆ (0446) 711111
X51 bus from the bus station (opposite railway station) approximately every hour.

Long-term car-park: £2.00 per day

East Midlands (Derby)
✆ (0332) 810621
Buses every 15 minutes from Derby bus station.
Long-term car-park: £2.30 per day (up to 7 days), £2.10 per day (over 7 days)

Edinburgh
✆ 031-333 1000
Buses every 15 minutes from Waverly bridge.
Long-term car-park: £3.75 per day

Glasgow
✆ 041-887 1111
Buses every half hour Mon-Sat from Buchanan St and Anderson bus station.
Long-term car-park: £4.50 per day (under 7 days), £2.80 per day (7 days and over)

Leeds/Bradford
✆ (0532) 509696
Buses every hour from Leeds and Bradford bus stations.
Long-term car-park: £1.80 per day

London: Gatwick
✆ (0293) 531299
Non-stop Gatwick Express every 15 minutes from Victoria (journey time about 30 minutes). Carriage of skis will cost you about £3.20. Direct trains also from London Bridge. Flightline 777 coaches (operated by Greenline) from Victoria. Coaches and trains from many points in south. Coach station is in the South Terminal, which is linked to the North Terminal by an automatic rapid transit every 3 minutes.
Long-term car-park: Car-parks at both terminals. Regular courtesy buses will take you to your terminal. £3.30 per day.

Childcare facilities: South Terminal –
small, unmanned soft play area. North
Terminal – Play Bus (run by a local play
group) during holiday periods has a
multitude of activities for one to
eight-year-olds.
London: Heathrow
℗ 081-759 4321
Heathrow has two separate stations on
the underground Piccadilly Line, with
one serving Terminals 1-3 and another
serving Terminal 4. Trains run about
every 5 minutes at peak times and every
9 minutes at other times, (Allow at least
an hour to get out from Central London.)
There are regular Airbuses from various
points in central London to all Terminals,
and Railair Links from British Rail
stations at Reading and Woking.
Regional coaches arrive at Heathrow's
Central Bus Station (at Terminal 1-3).
Regular buses connect Terminals 1-3
and 4.
Long-term car-park: Separate car-parks
for Terminals 1-3 and 4. Regular
courtesy coaches will take you to your
Terminal. £6.40 per day (up to 7 days),
£4.25 per day (over 7 days). One reader
suggests parking near Hounslow West
tube station (2 stops from Heathrow). It
may be slightly inconvenient but could
save you a lot of money.
Childcare facilities: Terminal 4 –
Play-Care Centre, staffed by trained
nursery nannies, has a variety of
facilities including a Wendy house, slide,
toys and computer games.
Luton
℗ (0582) 405100
Frequent trains from Kings Cross and St
Pancras, shuttle service to airport on
Luton Flyer. Buses every hour from
Victoria
Long-term car-park: £2.90 per day
Manchester
℗ 061-489 3000
757 shuttle service from the train and
bus stations.
Long-term car-park: £2.80 per day
Newcastle
℗ 091-286 0966
Express bus link and metrolink from
Newcastle train station. Hourly buses
from bus station.
Long-term car-park: £2.25 per day (up to
7 days), £1.90 (over 7 days)
Stansted
℗ (0279) 662520
Buses from Victoria and Cambridge
every 2 hours.
Long-term car-park: £2.15 per day

Foreign airports
We list below the airports most
commonly used by skiers.

Austrian resorts
Munich Convenient for resorts around
and west of Innsbruck. ℗ (01049)
899211. Airport bus to station; buses to
Kitzbühel, Innsbruck and Dolomites.
Innsbruck Convenient for resorts in the
Tirol. ℗ (01043) 51282376. Buses to
Mayrhofen
Salzburg Convenient for eastern
Austrian resorts including the Zillertal
and Grossraum. ℗ (01043) 6628055.
Airport buses to station. Buses to
Innsbruck.

French resorts
Chambéry Convenient for the
Tarentaise resorts. ℗ (01033) 79544605.
Geneva Convenient for the northern
French resorts. ℗ (01041) 227993111.
Buses to Chamonix, Courmayeur, the
Tarentaise resorts, resorts in the Portes
du Soleil, La Clusaz, Megève and Flaine.
Grenoble Convenient for resorts in the
southern Alps. ℗ (01033) 76654848.
Buses to Alpe d'Huez and Les Deux
Alpes.
Lyon Convenient for the Tarentaise
resorts. ℗ (01033) 72227221. New
charter terminal opened in 1990 in
preparation for the Olympics. Shuttle bus
to all main resorts. Direct trains from
Lyon to Moûtiers and Bourg-St-Maurice.
Nice Convenient for Isola 2000 and
southern French resorts. ℗ (01033)
93213030. Buses direct to Isola.
Toulouse Convenient for Pyrenean
resorts and Andorra. ℗ (01033)
61424464.

Italian resorts
Milan Convenient for resorts on the
Italian/Swiss border. ℗ (01039) 24851.
Bus from airport to town centre; resort
buses form bus station.
Turin Convenient for resorts on the
Italian/French border. ℗ (01039)
115778431. Buses to town centre; resort
buses from bus station.
Venice Convenient for resorts in the
Dolomites. ℗ (01039) 5216333. Buses to
town centre; resort buses from bus
station.

Swiss resorts
Geneva Convenient for western Swiss
resorts. ℗ (01041) 227993111. Airport
buses to train stations; bus links to many

French, some Italian and some Swiss resorts.
Zurich Convenient for resorts on Swiss/Austrian border and Jungfrau. ℂ (01041) 18127111. Train to railway station; buses to western Austrian resorts.

USA
Denver Convenient for most Colorado resorts. ℂ (0101) 303 2701300. Buses to all main resorts.
Salt Lake City Convenient for all the main Utah resorts. ℂ (0101) 801 5752400. Buses to all main resorts.

Going by coach

International Express, the Continental arm of National Express, offer scheduled through routes all over Europe, using a number of European coach operators. Services start from London Victoria with UK services timetabled to connect with European departures. Their Eurolines service 131 runs three times a week to Chamonix with stops at Grenoble, Chambéry, Annecy, Annemasse and Geneva. Total journey time is 22 hours. Tickets are available from reservation centres in major cities or from a travel agent. ℂ 071-730 0202.

A growing number of tour operators offer coaches either as their main mode of transport or as a cheaper alternative to flying. Coach travel has in the past been associated with budget holidays and school or student parties; it should not necessarily be. Many companies now offer a highly sophisticated, highly efficient service which has several advantages over air travel, not the least being an extra day in the resort (coaches usually arrive early Saturday morning

and leave the following Saturday evening). Operators offer reductions of between £20-£40 per person for coach travel and often have several pick-up points in the UK. The coaches are usually equipped with videos, toilets, reclining seats or bunk beds, and hostesses serving microwaved meals and hot drinks.

Operators that use coach travel:
Alpine Life, Alpine Tours, Autotours, Chalets and Hotels Unlimited, Contiki, Crystal, Ski Europe, SkiGower, Interski, Kings Ski Club, Le Ski, Mogul Ski Holidays, Neilson, PR Christian Holidays, Quality Ski Tours, Quest, Simply Ski, Ski Bound, Ski Chamois, Ski Equipe, Ski Global, Ski Party Snow World, Ski Partners, Ski Olympic, Ski Red Guide, Ski Sutherland, Ski Tips, Snowcoach Club Cantabrica, SnowRanger, Supersports Ski Chalets, Top Deck, Touralp, Tracer Holidays, Ski West, Skiworld, Winter Adventure Holidays.

Going by rail

Going by train has been warmly recommended by several reporters, particularly those travelling with young families, who have found it easier and more efficient than going by air (provided that you don't have many changes):

■ you save money
■ you don't have to worry about the number or weight of your bags
■ a family can take over a whole couchette compartment (6 beds)
■ there is usually a bar with snacks on board
■ resort transfers from stations are relatively short (usually no longer than an hour)
■ you get at least an extra day's skiing

Under the heading 'By Rail', each resort factbox lists the nearest railway station and the number of buses from that station to the resort each day. Here we list major resorts with railway stations in them, and give approximate journey times from London and the number of changes of train involved, excluding that for the Channel crossing.

Switzerland
Andermatt 20hr, two changes
Arosa 21hr, one change
Davos, 19hr, one change
Grindelwald, 19hr, two changes
Gstaad, 18hr, two changes
Klosters, 19hr, two changes
Murren, 19hr, three changes
St Moritz, 20½hr, one change
Villars, 18hr, two changes
Wengen, 19hr, two changes
Zermatt, 19hr, one change
Austria
Badgastein, 24hr, direct
Kitzbuhel, 23hr, one change
Mayrhofen, 24½hr, two changes
St Anton, 20½hr, direct
Zell am See, 24hr, one change
Zell am Ziller, 24 hr, two changes
France
Chamonix, 21hr, one change
Scotland
Aviemore, 10hr, direct

Snow Train

Over the past few years, the tour operator 'snow train' option has become a popular alternative to flying to the Alps. There are now Friday night direct trains from Calais to the Tarentaise resorts in France and to a number of resorts in Austria. Some tour operators will book train-only tickets for you.

The French service leaves Calais at about 9.15pm every Friday during the skiing season and arrives in the Tarentaise by 9.00am the following morning, stopping at Moûtiers (for transfers to the Trois Vallées or Valmorel), at Aime (for transfers to La Plagne) and at Bourg-St-Maurice (for transfers to Val d'Isère, Tignes, Les Arcs and La Rosière). Independent travellers can have their cars conveyed (see Motorail section in the next chapter).

The Austrian service leaves Calais at 7.00 every Friday evening and arrives at St Anton by 8.00am on Saturday, Ötztal by 9.00am (for transfers to Sölden and Obergurgl), Innsbruck by 9.30am (for transfers to Igls, Seefeld and the Zillertal) and Wörgl by 10.15am (for transfers to Kitzbühel and the Grossraum resorts). This is not a Motorail service.

The following tour operators offer the snow train option:
Bladon Lines, Collineige Ski, Crystal, Enterprise, Falcon, French Impressions, Headwater, Inghams, Le Ski, Neilson, Poles Apart, Silver Ski, Simply Ski, Ski Beat, Ski Europe, Ski Global, Ski Oui, Ski Red Guide, Ski Sutherland, Ski Valkyrie, Ski Whizz Small World, SnowRanger, Snobiz, Snowbugs, Snowtime, Supertravel, Top Deck, Tracer Holidays, Skiworld.

Rail enquiries

British Rail International, International Rail Centre, Victoria Station, London SW1V 1JY ✆ 071-834 2345.
French Railways, 179 Piccadilly, London W1V OBA. ✆ 071-409 3518.
German Railways, 18 Conduit Street, London W1R 9TD ✆ 071-499 0578 .

Going by car

Most British skiers travel to their chosen ski mountains by air, on package deals. But taking a car has clear advantages, particularly to skiers who like to get around in search of new challenges or the best snow. This chapter is designed to help.

Getting prepared

Breakdown insurance

The two main motoring organisations – the AA and RAC – offer various services to members (eg advice on route-planning and road conditions). Several reporters have recommended their personalised route planning service, whereby you specify your destination and for a sum of between £10 and £15, they come up with a computer print-out of your exact route. The AA, RAC and several other organisations also offer insurance against some of the cost and inconvenience of breakdowns and accidents abroad. Contact details and premiums are given below. Breakdown insurance is an expensive way of buying peace of mind, but you may feel it's worthwhile – particularly in winter, when roads are at their most dangerous and cars perhaps at their least reliable. Some of the deals on offer can (or must) include personal insurance for medical expenses and so on.

Most of the following types of cover are included in all the policies we looked at, though the amounts you can claim vary from company to company:

■ assistance if you break down either in the UK or abroad including towing to, and storage in, a garage
■ emergency labour charges
■ the cost of despatching any spare parts, including communication costs but not the cost of the parts themselves
■ additional hotel and travel expenses
■ hire of replacement vehicle

■ all necessary costs to bring your vehicle home but not including cost of repairs or sea passage
■ chauffeur to drive vehicle home if only driver is medically unfit
■ legal cover, including bail bond.

In addition, both the AA and RAC offer emergency credit vouchers. If you plan to drive abroad twice or more in one year, it may well be worth your while to take out annual insurance cover, which most companies also offer. There are also big savings to be made on family policies.

Automobile Association (AA)
✆ (0256) 20123; Fanum House, Basing View, Basingstoke, Hampshire RG21 2EA. Their 5-Star service costs £34.50 for 6–12 days. There's an extra charge of £3 for non-members. Personal cover costs £11.95 per adult, double that if you include winter sports cover.

Royal Automobile Club (RAC)
✆ 081-686 2525; RAC House, Brighton Road, South Croydon, Surrey CR2 6XW. Their Eurocover Motoring Assistance costs £33.45 for standard cover (6–10 days). There's an extra charge of £3 for non-members.

Europ Assistance ✆ 081-680 1234; Europ Assistance House, 252 High Street, Croydon, Surrey CR0 1NF. Their Motoring Emergency Service costs £31.50 for 6–12 days. Additional medical and personal travel cover costs an extra £17.80 per person. Note that their medical cover excludes injuries sustained whilst skiing.

National Breakdown Recovery Club
✆(0532) 393666; PO Box 300, Leeds LS99 2LZ. They offer members vehicle

protection as part of a package – you have to take out their medical insurance as well. For 5–9 days, two adults in a car pay £29 for vehicle protection and £25.50 for medical cover. A further £20 each will cover winter sports.

Mondial Assistance ✆ 081-681 2525; Leon House, 201-241, High Street, Croydon, Surrey CR0 1QR. Their Motorists Emergency Service costs £32.50 for 11–17 days, with an additional cost of £29.80 per person for personal and medical cover.

Autohome Limited ✆ (0604) 232334; 202/204 Kettering Road, Northampton, Northants NN1 4HE. 6–10 days Motoring Assistance cover from their Autohome Continental policy costs £25.30 for a car and £11.50 per adult for medical and travel insurance. There is a 5% discount for members.

The mechanics

When going to the mountains in winter, the likely weather and road conditions make special preparations necessary:

- if your car engine is water-cooled, make sure the anti-freeze is strong enough; this is particularly important if the car is going to be left outside at night, when the temperature may drop as low as −30˚C
- don't forget you'll need a strong solution of winter screenwash, too
- if you have any doubts at all about the condition of your battery, have it tested before you set off; and consider buying 'jump leads' so that you can start your engine from another car's battery
- check the car handbook to see whether thinner oil is recommended for very cold conditions, and whether you need to adjust the engine air intake
- if you can arrange it, get some experience on a skid pan before you go – on snow-bound roads in the Alps, skidding to some degree is inevitable
- if your car's headlights throw a lot of light upwards (rather than having a very sharply defined beam) consider fitting special fog lamps – night driving in falling snow is a nightmare without good lights
- take a small shovel for getting out of roadside drifts; if you have a tow rope, take that, too.

Snow-chains

If you expect to find snow on the pistes in your resort, it's reasonable to expect snow on the roads as well. And if there is snow on the roads you'll need chains for the car's driving wheels – not only to keep going on hills but also to satisfy the local laws. (In Austria, the police have a habit of obliging chainless motorists to buy chains from them, at punitive prices.) Chains tend to be expensive (up to £50.00) and difficult to get hold of in Britain; in and around the Alps they're easy to find at much lower prices (about £12.00-20.00 in most large supermarkets or service stations). You might find that the common car sizes are out of stock. It is possible to hire chains in the UK, eg from the AA for around £20.00 per week (they can also supply ski racks and ski boxes).

You should put your chains on before they become absolutely necessary; if you wait until the car slithers to a standstill you may find yourself putting them on in an acutely inconvenient and dangerous place, perhaps blocking the road. It helps if you practise putting them on as soon as you buy them – not only to make sure that you know how, but also to make sure that you've got all the bits.

You can keep chains on while driving on ordinary roads, but only for short periods and at very low speeds – the limit should be specified in the instructions. People who live in or near the Alps avoid the tedious and messy business of repeatedly applying and removing chains in one of two ways. The first is by fitting special winter tyres with chunky treads and often with metal studs; these are meant to be used at higher speeds on normal roads, but aren't a practical (or economic) proposition for a trip across the Continent. The second is by owning a four-wheel-drive car (normally also fitted with chunky tyres); four-wheel-drive is a huge advantage, making chains unnecessary in all but the most extreme circumstances and giving much more control when going downhill, where chains don't help all that much – particularly on a rear-wheel-drive car. If you have a choice of front- and rear-wheel-drive, take the front-wheel-drive.

Continental ferries

When planning winter crossings to the Continent, bear in mind the possibility of bad weather. If there are heavy seas hovercraft services are more liable to interruption than conventional ferries; while long ferry crossings can seem (or even be) interminable.

In our experience, most drivers plan to get an early start on the Continent, hoping to get as far as they can in the day's driving. Our table of ferry information below deals only with crossings that fit this approach: we list early or overnight arrival times on the Continent (in local time). We also give phone numbers, routes, duration of the crossings and the approximate return prices for car and passenger. (These are the basic prices for 1990/91 – there is a surcharge for cabins on overnight crossings, and no doubt increases for 1991/92).

Channel ferry services

Company	Crossing	Dur-ation	Return fares		Outward arrivals on Cont-inent	Return departures from Cont-inent
			car	adult		
		hr.m	£	£	a.m.	p.m.
Brittany Ferries (0705) 827701	Portsmouth –Caen	6.00	65*	33	6.30	16.30
Hoverspeed (0304) 240241	Dover–Calais (Hovercraft)	0.30	70	30	9.30 11.00	16.30 18.00
	Dover–Boulogne	0.35	70	30	11.35	17.05
North Sea Ferries (0482) 77177	Hull–Zeebrugge	13.30	98	86	8.30	18.00
	Hull–Rotterdam	13.00	98	86	8.00	18.00
Olau Line (0795) 666666	Sheerness–Vlissingen	8.30	84	50	7.00	22.30
P&O European Ferries (0304) 203388	Portsmouth–Le Havre	5.45	65	32	7.00	23.30
	Dover–Calais	1.15	62	24	8.15 11.15	19.45 21.15
	Dover–Boulogne	1.40	62	24	10.55	18.30 20.45
	Dover–Zeebrugge	4.30	62	24	10.00	18.30
	Felixstowe–Zeebrugge	5.45	62	30	8.00	23.59
Sally Line (0843) 595522	Ramsgate–Dunkerque	2.30	50	24	12.30 23.59	20.30
Sealink Stena Line (0233) 647047	Dover–Calais	1.30	76	16	8.30 10.30 12.00	18.45 20.45 22.45
	Folkestone–Boulogne	1.50	76	16	10.35	20.45 23.15
	Harwich–Hook	8.00	114	60	7.00	22.30

* £10 extra for car with roofrack

Ferry packages

Several of the ferry companies put together packages for independent travellers during the skiing season . They include return ferry crossings and breakdown insurance, and may include snow chains, Green Card, winter sports insurance and accommodation. The packages offered in 1991 were:

Ski Fare (P&O European Ferries) Return ferry, AA 5-star vehicle cover and winter sports insurance – £156 for car and 2 adults, £47 for additional adults, £37 for additional children.

SkiLink (Sealink Stena Line) Return ferry, breakdown insurance, Green Card and winter sports cover – £149 for car and 2 adults, £44.50 for additional adults, £34.50 for additional children.

Ski Drive (Sally Ferries) Return ferry, RAC Eurocover Motoring Assistance and snow chains – £132 for 2 adults and up to 3 children.

Brittany Ferries and **Hoverspeed** do not offer special fare/insurance deals, but do sell package holidays – see appropriate section.

Take it easy

There are several ways in which to cut down the time and stress involved in getting to your resort.

Motorail services

One alternative to driving all the way is to put your car on a car-carrying train, although getting to the starting point of the service may involve quite a bit of driving.

French railways run several services from the Channel ports (Calais, Boulogne and Dieppe) – destinations include St-Gervais (between Megève and Chamonix), Moûtiers (for Tarentaise resorts – Valmorel, Méribel, Courchevel, La Plagne, Les Arcs, Tignes, Val d'Isère), Grenoble (for Les Deux Alpes, Serre-Chevalier and neighbours), Nice (for Isola and neighbours) and Narbonne (for the Pyrenees). There are also services from Paris to Gap (Southern Alps), Lyons (Alps) and Tarbes (Pyrenees) and also to Milan and Munich.

By far the most popular of the French motorail services is the one that leaves Calais at 9.15am every Friday during the skiing season and arrives at Moûtiers by 9.00am (or Bourg-St-Maurice by 10.00am) on Saturday. The train is heavily used by tour operators and has a bar and disco on board. A car and driver costs approximately £250, additional adults are £62 each and children £31 each. Couchettes (6 bunkbeds per cabin) cost a further £12 (1st class) and £9 (2nd class). Note that these prices do not include ferry crossings; you can secure special Motorail fares with Sealink. For further information ring 071-409 3518.

German railways run a day service from Cologne to Munich and night services from Dusseldorf or Paris to Munich. Some of these trains continue on to Innsbruck (for the western Austrian resorts) and Bolzano in northern Italy (for those in the Dolomites). There are also services from Brussels or Cologne to Salzburg (for the eastern Austrian resorts) and from Cologne to Basel (for the Swiss ones). For further information ring 071-499 0578. Approximate fares for a car and 2 adults, including return ferry and couchettes, are:
Dusseldorf–Munich £240;
Dusseldorf–Innsbruck £312;
Brussels–Salzburg £340.
Some services run daily or several times a week, others only once a week. It's advisable to book as early as possible – up to six months in advance – to be sure of getting in.

Motorway tolls

You have to pay tolls on most motorways in France, Italy and Spain, and on sections in Austria and Yugoslavia. These can add up to quite an amount over a long journey so it's worth doing your sums. Calais to Chamonix adds up to FF255; Calais to Albertville 228FF (the new piece of motorway between Chambéry and Albertville will be toll-free); Calais to

Grenoble 222FF. If you're coming from the Normandy and Brittany ports, the prices will be marginally lower (Caen-Chamonix 226FF). Toll booths in France generally accept Visa and Access cards – no signature necessary. The Brenner Pass motorway, south of Innsbruck and over the Italian border to Bolzano and the Dolomite resorts, costs AS130. The Tauern motorway between Salzburg and Villach costs AS120. In Switzerland, foreign motorists using motorways must buy and display a windscreen sticker (valid 12 months) which costs SF30 at the border (or £12.50 from the Swiss Tourist Office, AA or RAC in the UK).

Tunnels

There are several tunnels which help you avoid making a detour or travelling over a mountain pass. Some, but not all, charge a toll which varies according to size of car; we give one-way tolls based on a family car. The rail tunnels listed have car-carrying shuttle trains.

Fréjus Road tunnel between Modane (France) and Bardonecchia (Italy), 13km long, cost FF140.

Mont Blanc Road tunnel between Chamonix (France) and Entrèves (near Courmayeur, Italy), 11.5km long, chains are occasionally required for the approaches in winter, customs are on the Italian side of the tunnel, cost FF140.

Grand St Bernard Road tunnel between Bourg St Pierre (south of Martigny, Switzerland) and Aosta (Italy), 6km long, cost SF32.

St Gotthard Road tunnel south of Andermatt (Switzerland) on motorway to Milan, 16 km long, open all year, chains may be required on approaches but are not permitted in tunnel, free, but requires motorway tax sticker – see tolls.

San Bernardino Road tunnel south of the resorts around Chur (East Switzerland), 6.5 km long, free, but requires motorway tax sticker.

Arlberg Road tunnel parallel to the Arlberg Pass between St Anton and Bludenz (Austria), 14 km long, cost AS150.

Felber Tauern Road tunnel on pass between Kitzbühel and Lienz (Austria), return ticket AS100 (AS180 in summer). In addition there are the following rail tunnels where cars are transported through the tunnel on a train.

Lötschberg Rail tunnel between Kandersteg in the Jungfrau and Goppenstein, giving access to the southern resorts (Zermatt and Saas Fee).

Simplon Rail tunnel between Brig, north of Saas Fee (Switzerland) and Iselle (Italy).

Furka Rail tunnel between Andermatt and Brig (Switzerland).

Check that any **mountain passes** on your route are open before you attempt them. The following mountain passes are usually closed between November and April; the Arlberg (use tunnel), the Furka (use rail tunnel), the Great St Bernard (use tunnel), the Grossglockner (between Zell am See and Lienz), Mt Cenis (between Chambéry and Turin), Petit St Bernard (between Bourg-St-Maurice and Aosta), San Bernardino (use tunnel), Simplon (use rail tunnel), Splügen (between Splügen and Madesimo), St Gotthard (use tunnel), Stelvio (between Bormio and Trafoi).

Hiring a car

If you don't want the effort of driving to the Alps but would like the luxury of having a car while you are there, the obvious solution is to hire one. Being able to transport yourselves to areas of snow in the unreliable conditions of the past few years can make the difference between a mediocre holiday and a superb one. And, if you go about it the right way, hiring need not add a huge amount to the cost of a holiday, particularly if it is split between a group. But it is important to shop around, as the amounts you can pay tend to differ widely. The rates commonly charged for the provision of ski racks and snow chains are outrageous – often the charge per week is more than enough to cover the cost of buying the equipment. Look out for special deals of one sort or another. Of the four big international rental companies (Avis, Budget, Europcar and Hertz), Budget have a Holiday Drive Ski package (car hire, unlimited mileage, Collision Damage Waiver, snow tyres or chains and a ski rack) and Hertz have some special ski rates – and will include free chains and racks if you reserve them in advance. Snow tyres or chains are standard equipment on all hire cars in Switzerland. From our experience, four-wheel-drive vehicles are charged at rip-off rates and need to be booked well in advance. We list here the four major companies.

Budget Rent-a-Car 41 Marlowes, Hemel Hempstead, Herts HP1 1LD ✆ (0800) 181181
Hertz Radnor House, 1,272 London Rd, Norbury, London SW16 ✆ 081-679 1777

Europcar 2nd Floor, Bank House, Park Place, Leeds LS1 ✆ (0532) 422233
Avis Reservations Office, Ground Floor, Hayes Gate House, 27 Uxbridge Rd, Hayes, Middlesex UB4 0JA ✆ 081-848 8733

Routes to the Alps

Having received a large number of reports this year from people who have driven to their skiing destinations, we have decided to cover the most popular driving routes in this section of the *Guide*. We would welcome further reports, particularly on routes to the Austrian and Swiss Alps and the Pyrenees.

French Alps

From Calais

Drivers crossing to Calais or Boulogne have the choice of two main routes:

- one entirely by autoroute via Paris
- the other mainly by autoroute via Reims

The latter is marginally slower as the non-autoroute section between Châlons-sur-Marne and Chaumont can be very tedious, but it does cost less (in terms of tolls) and you do see more (in terms of countryside). Both routes follow the A26 as far as Arras, just over an hour from Calais; those following the Reims route continue on the A26, those bound for Paris take the A1. The two routes meet up again at Beaune.

Via Paris

If you want a coffee break just north of Paris, a brief diversion off the A1 will take you into the medieval town of Senlis with its early Gothic cathedral. There are several inexpensive restaurants and cafés in the main street.

It is no longer necessary to risk life and limb on the Paris Périphérique (multi-lane ring road) on your way south. From the A1, you can circumnavigate the capital without ever having to leave the motorway by following the A3 and the newly opened A86. The A3 leaves the A1 three km after Charles de Gaulle airport, and is signed to Lyon. If you keep following the signs to Lyon you can't go wrong (or so we are told); after 10 km on the A3, take the A86 due south

for 6½ miles until you come to the A4. Head west towards Paris for about 2 miles before joining the A86 for another 7 miles to the N186. A further 2 miles west on the N186 will bring you to the A6 and the long slog south.

Once you've safely negotiated the capital, you can think about lunch. One recommended lunch-stop is the quaint village of Barbizon, about 7 km south west of the A6 on the N37. The Clé d'Or serves ample lunches at reasonable prices but if you really want to splash out, try the Bas-Breau, a beamed inn with an international reputation and prices to match. A quick stroll in the Fontainebleau Forest, and then back to the A6. Alternatively, about an hour south of Fontainebleau brings you to Auxerre (pronounced 'Orsaire'), along the tree-lined left bank of the river Yonne. The cathedral alone is well worth the 6 km detour off the autoroute and there are plenty of restaurants in the town. You can cut a corner and get back to the motorway on the N65. A further hour's drive will bring you to Beaune.

Via Reims

Two worthwhile early stops on the A26 are at Laon and Reims. Laon's lovely 12thC cathedral, perched majestically above the modern town, is just visible from the autoroute. Reims is in the heart of Champagne country and has plenty of cellars which are open to the public, and plenty of places to lunch at, including two Michelin-starred restaurants. If you don't want to stop, follow signs for the A4 and Châlons-sur-Marne. After about 20 minutes, you leave the autoroute on the N44, and it is a bendy, two-hour drive before you rejoin it again just south of Chaumont. One recent reporter stayed at a delightful hotel, Aux Armes de Champagne, 8km east of Châlons on the N8 in the little village of L'Épine – 'lovely setting and excellent food and drink'. Once back on the autoroute, you

follow signs for Dijon, first on the A26, then the A31. The motorway skirts Dijon and continues on to Beaune, where you join the A6.

From Normandy

If you're coming from the Normandy ports (Le Havre, Caen or Cherbourg), you can also miss the Paris Périphérique by doing a detour around Versailles. Turn off the A13 at the signs for Versailles and continue until you reach the N13, where you head east. After about 20km, you meet the A6 for the journey south. Versailles has a vast selection of cafés and restaurants to suit all pockets.

Nearing the Alps

Beaune is an important wine town and a beautiful city but with a dearth of reasonably-priced places to eat and stay. But at Levernois (the autoroute junction 5 km south of Beaune) the Hostellerie de Levernois is recommended as a good place for a meal, and a bed and breakfast farmhouse, Le Parc, as excellent value for a stop-over in a pleasant rural setting. Another half-hour's driving on the A6 South gets you close to Mâcon where you choose your route according to the resort you are aiming for:

■ head eastbound on the A40 Geneva autoroute for the northern French resorts, such as Chamonix and Morzine

■ continue southbound on the A6, turning on to the A43 Grenoble road at Lyon for the southern French resorts, such as Alpe d'Huez and Les Deux Alpes.

■ for the Tarentaise resorts (Val d'Isère, La Plagne, Trois Vallées etc.), the choice is not so obvious. Either of the above routes is possible. If you take the Geneva route, you need to turn off the motorway at junction 10 and follow the N508 through Annecy to Albertville. If you take the southern route, you need to follow the A43 from Lyon to Chambéry. South-east of Chambéry, you join the new (free) section of motorway to Albertville, due to be completed in time for the Olympics. There are arguments in favour of each of these two routes: the southern route is marginally shorter in terms of mileage but is not necessarily quicker, despite the new Chambéry to Albertville section of motorway, which should relieve the notorious weekend

traffic-jams around here. But the autoroute passes right through the middle of Lyon and you can be caught up in terrible city-centre traffic jams. The longer eastern route is less queue-prone, more scenic and has less heavy commercial traffic.

Southern route via Lyon

Lyon, the third biggest city in the country, is often referred to as the Manchester of France. If you want to stop, head for the old quarter on the right bank of the Saône where narrow streets are lined with beautiful Renaissance houses; there are galleries, art nouveau cafés and bistros crammed with old-world atmosphere. The original town was set on top of this hill and you can still see the remains of two Roman theatres and a museum devoted to Gallo-Roman Lyon.

Leaving the A6 at Lyon you head east on the A43 motorway, continuing all the way to Chambéry for the Tarentaise. Chambéry is a pleasant, elegant town; close to the centre we can recommend the recently renovated Princes hotel, with its excellent Michelin-starred restaurant. The N6 north-east of Chambéry crosses the new autoroute about 10km before Albertville and heads into the Maurienne for resorts such as Valloire and Valmorel. Albertville itself is a bit of a dump but blessed with one outstanding hotel-restaurant, that of Philippe Million (30 rooms). One reader stopped at Le Sapin, just off the main road, which offers a wide range of good-value meals (but service can be slow). The final stages of the journey to the Tarentaise resorts have been improved by the contruction of a fast dual carriageway to Moûtiers. Unfortunately this has not solved the weekend queue problem and several reporters have sat in stationary queues for several hours at peak holiday times. Moûtiers is an obvious target for a Friday night but is short of accommodation (especially on a Friday night); the Ibis is convenient and acceptable (60 rooms). For those heading for Val d'Isère and Tignes, there are several inexpensive places to stay in the villages up the valley. On the main road a few kilometres east of Bourg-St-Maurice (which itself has a handful of simple hotels) is Il Cappricio, a simple B&B run by a charming Italian couple, in the village of Viclaire.

If you are heading for Alpe d'Huez or Les Deux Alpes, you need to fork off the A43

and follow the A48 to Grenoble.
Grenoble is a large, lively cosmopolitan centre, the capital of the French Alps; if you want to avoid staying in the centre of town, there are some attractive places in the area, for example, the super-smart Chavant, a beautifully restored old auberge in the village of Bresson, about 5km south of the city. From the city, follow the N91, signed to Briançon, for about an hour, until you see the turnings for the resorts.

Eastern route via Annecy

If you want to spend your first – or last – night close to the Alps to give you an extra day's skiing, there are towns just off the A40 motorway east from Mâcon which offer overnight accommodation without asking ski-resort prices.

One reporter recommends the Hotel de France, right in the centre of Bourg-en-Bresse, as 'delightfully archaic, clean and comfortable'.

Bellegarde-sur-Valserine is a rather dreary town west of Geneva and Annecy but it offers some unassuming hotels with better-than-average restaurants: in the town the Michelin-starred Belle Epoch (ten rooms) and three miles west, the Auberge de la Fontaine (seven rooms).

The lovely town of Annecy, on the northern shores of a natural lake of the same name, makes a convenient overnight base and has a good range of accommodation and restaurants; for atmosphere, stay at L'Abbaye in Annecy-le-Vieux (8 rooms). The old town at the foot of the castle is best for cheap places to eat; *haute cuisine* is available at Auberge de l'Eridan.

Austrian and Swiss Alps

Although the French Alps are still more favoured by drivers, it is worth considering taking a car to Austria or Switzerland, especially as continued European road-building and tunnel-building now offer a better choice of routes.

Switzerland

The Swiss resorts can be easily reached by:

- following the French autoroutes to Geneva and then taking the motorway north of Lake Geneva into Switzerland for the Valais resorts
- following the Belgian/German motorways to Basle and then south to Berne, then taking the N6 to Interlaken, for Adelboden and the Jungfrau
- following the Belgian/German motorways to Basel, then taking the N3 via Zurich to the eastern resorts (Lenzerheide, Arosa etc.)

If you want to get from the Bernese Oberland to the Valais, don't overlook the Lotschberg car-carrying rail tunnel (see tunnels above).

Austria

The link between Switzerland and western Austria has been much improved in recent years, with motorways running across northern Switzerland and a combination of motorway and good ordinary roads on the Austrian side. The quickest route to the western Austrian resorts (St Anton, Obergurgl etc) is via Basle and Zurich, then crossing the Swiss border just north of Liechtenstein.

Most reporters bound for eastern Austria have taken the German motorway all the way from Aachen to Munich. Most have had smooth journeys, but some have been caught up in horrific queues near Munich. One reporter recommends staying in Novotels en route which can be booked ahead by the ferry company. Those in Aachen and Frankfurt are recommended by a recent reporter.

Be prepared

Here we list dry ski slopes in England, Scotland, Wales and Northern Ireland which are open to the public, and give the details for the main organisations you might want to contact when planning a ski holiday or investigating some other aspect of skiing.

Dry ski slopes

For each slope we list adult prices for peak-time skiing (usually weekends and evenings) as well as a guide to the cost of lessons (as part of a group) and private tuition (on a one-to-one basis). Prices include equipment hire unless we state otherwise. These are last season's (1990/91) prices so you can expect to pay a bit more than we say.

England

Avon

Avon Ski Centre
Lyncombe Lodge, Churchill, Bristol
BS19 5PG
✆ (0934) 852335
Practice: approx £5/hr. Lessons: £35 for 3 x 1½hr sessions. Private tuition: £18/hr. Equipment hire: 50p/hr

Berkshire

Bracknell Ski Centre
John Nike Leisuresport Complex, John Nike Way, Bracknell
✆ (0344) 860033
Practice: approx £5/hr. Lessons: £7.50/hr
Ski Carter
99-113 Caversham Rd, Reading
✆ (0734) 575589
Practice: £6/hr. Lessons: £21 for 4 x 1hr sessions

Cheshire

Ski Runcorn
Town Park, Palacefields, Runcorn
✆ (0928) 701965
Practice: £3.90/hr. Lessons: £6.50 for 1½hr. Private tuition: £15.90/hr

Co Durham

Spectrum Leisure Complex
Hunwick Lane, Willington, Crook, DL15 0JA
✆ (0388) 747000
Practice: £3.50/hr. Lessons: £5.50/hr. Private tuition: £13/hr

Cumbria

High Plains Lodge Ski Slope
High Plains Lodge, Alston
✆ (0434) 381886
Practice: about £5/hr
Kendal Ski Club
24, Michelson Rd, Collinfield, Kendal
✆ (0539) 733031
(Ski slope is at Kirkbie Kendal Lower School)
Practice: £2/hr (members £1). Lessons: £5/hr (members £3). Equipment hire: £2/hr (members £1)

Derbyshire

Swadlincote Ski Centre
Hill Street, Swadlincote, Burton-on-Trent
✆ (0283)217200
Practice: £4.40/hr (members £3). Lessons: £8.50/hr. Equipment hire: £1/hr

Devon

Exeter and District Ski Club
Clifton Hill Sports Centre, Belmont Rd, Exeter EX1 2DJ
✆ (0392) 211422
Practice: £5.50 for 2hr (members £2). Lessons: additional £1 for 1-hour's tuition within 2-hour practice session

John Nike Leisuresport Complex
Alpine Park, Marsh Mills, Plymouth, PL6
8LQ
✆ (0752) 600220
Practice: approx £5/hr. Lessons: £7.50/hr
Wessex Ski Club
Barton Hall, Kingskerswell Rd, Torquay
✆ Torquay 313350
Practice: £5/hr (full members £3.50).
Lessons: £7/hr (full members £5)

Dorset
Christchurch Ski Centre
Mantchams Lane, Hurn, Christchurch
✆ (0202) 499155
Practice: £5/hr. Lessons: £28 for 4 x 1hr
sessions. Private tuition: £16/hr
Warmwell Leisure Resort
Warmwell, Dorchester, DT2 8JE
✆ 083 632 2632
Practice: £4.80/hr. Lessons: £7/hr.
Private tuition: £18/hr

East Sussex
Borowski Ski Centre
New Road, Newhaven, BN9 0TH
✆ (0273) 515402
Practice: £5/hr. Lessons: £40 for 3 x 2hr
sessions
Stanley Deason Leisure Centre
Wilson Avenue, Brighton
✆ (0273) 694281
Practice: £4/hr. Lessons: £30 for 2 x 3hr
sessions

Essex
Brentwood Park Ski Centre
Warley Gap, Brentwood, M13 3LG
✆ (0277) 211994
Practice: £6/hr. Lessons: £45 for 3 x 2hr
sessions. Private tuition: £35/hr
Harlow Ski School
Hammarskjold Rd, Harlow, CM20 2JF
✆ (0279) 444100
Practice: £6.50/hr (members £5.50).
Lessons: £49 for 4 x 1hr sessions.
Private tuition: £26/hr

Gloucestershire
Gloucester Ski Centre
Robinswood Hill, Gloucester
✆ (0452) 414300
Practice: £5/hr. Lessons: £29 for 6 x 1hr
sessions

Hampshire
Calshot Activities Centre
Calshot Spit, Fawley, Southampton,
SO4 1BR.
✆ (0703) 892077
Practice: £4/hr. Lessons: £35 for 5 x 1hr
sessions

Southampton Ski Centre
Sports Centre
Bassett, Southampton
✆ (0703) 790970
Practice: £4.50/hr. Lessons: £30 for 4hr
of tuition (over 4 or 2 weeks)
Stainforth Ski Centre
Hurst Rd, Aldershot, GU11 2DJ
✆ (0252) 25889
Practice: £4.96/hr. Lessons: £13.28 for
2-hour session. Private tuition: £19.78/hr

Hertfordshire
Bassingbourn Ski Club
9 Claymore Drive, Hitchin, SG5 3UB
✆ (0462) 34107. (The slope itself is at
the barracks in Royston)
Practice: £6 for 2hr. Lessons: £35 for 4 x
2hr sessions (members £17.50)
Gosling Ski Centre
Stanborough Road, Welwyn Garden
City, AL8 6XE
✆ (0707) 331056/330780
Practice: £4.50/hr (members £3.80).
Lessons: £30 for 3 x 1hr sessions
(members £28)
Hemel Ski Centre
St Albans Hill, Hemel Hempstead, HP3
9NH
✆ (0422) 241321
Practice: £4.50/hr. Lessons: £8/hr.
Private tuition: £15/hr

Kent
Alpine Ski Centre
Capstone Farm Country Park, Capstone
Rd Chatham, ME7 3JH.
✆ (0634) 827979
Practice: approx £5.50/hr. Lessons: £8/hr
Bowles Ski Centre
Eridge Green, Tunbridge Wells, TN3
9LW. ✆ (0892) 665665
Practice: £4.60/hr. Lessons: £28 for 2 x
2hr sessions. Private tuition: £21/hr
Folkestone Sports Centre
Radnor Park Avenue, Folkestone
✆ (0303) 850333
Practice: £5/hr. Lessons: £8.25/hr

Lancashire
Oldham Ski Centre
Counthill School, Moorside, Oldham
✆ 061-678 4054
Practice: £5.70/hr. Lessons: £34 for 4 x
2hr sessions
Pendle Ski Club
The Clubhouse, Nick O'Pendle, Sabden,
Nr Blackburn, BB6 9HN
✆ (0200) 25222
Practice: £5 for 2hr (members £2.50).
Lessons: £5.50 (members £3).
Equipment hire: 50p extra

Ski Rossendale
Haslingden Old Road, Rawtenstall,
Rossendale, BB4 8RR
✆ (0706) 228844/226457
Practice: £4.60/hr. Private tuition: £13.20
for 50 mins. Equipment hire: £1.50/hr

Lincolnshire

Tallington Ski Centre
Tallington Lakes Leisure Park, Stamford
✆ (0778) 344990
Practice: £5/hr. Lessons: £7.50/hr

London

Alexandra Palace Ski Centre
Alexandra Park, London, N22
✆ 081-888 2284
Prices not known
Beckton Ski Centre
Mountain Top Ltd, Beckton Alps, Alpine
Way, London, E6 4LA
✆ 071-511 0351
Practice: £7/hr. Lessons: £49 for 3 x 2hr
sessions
Blue Ski Hillingdon Ski Centre
Park Road, Uxbridge
✆ (0895) 55183
Practice: £4/hr. Private tuition: approx
£18/hr
Crystal Palace National Sports Centre
London SE19 2BB
✆ 081-778 0131
Practice: £4.80/hr. Private tuition: £20/hr
Woolwich Ski Slope
Repository Rd, Woolwich, London, SE18
✆ 081-317 1726
Practice: £7/hr (members £4). Lessons:
£35 for 3 x 2hr sessions. Private tuition:
£16/hr

Merseyside

Oval Sports Centre
Old Chester Rd, Bebington, L63 7LF
✆ 051-645 0551
Practice: £2/hr. Lessons: £20 for 4 x 1hr
sessions. Equipment hire: £2/hr.

Norfolk

Norfolk Ski Club
Whitlingham Lane, Trowse, Norwich
✆ (0603) 662781
Practice: £2.50/hr (plus membership
fee). Lessons: £35 for 4 x 1½hr
sessions. Private tuition: £21/hr

Northamptonshire

Skew Bridge Ski School
Northampton Road, Rushden
✆ Rushden 59939
Practice: £6/hr. Lessons: £33 for 3x 1hr
sessions

North Yorkshire

Catterick Indoor Ski Slope
Loos Rd, Catterick Garrison, DL9 4LE
✆ (0748) 833788
Practice: £4.64/hr. Lessons: £10 for
1½hr instruction and 1hr practice
Harrogate Ski Centre
Yorkshire Showground, Hookstone
Wood, Road, Harrogate, HG2 8PW
✆ (0423) 505457/8
Practice: £7/hr (members £5). Lessons:
£50 for 4 x 2hr sessions

Nottinghamshire

Carlton Forum Leisure Centre
Foxhill Rd, Carlton, Nottingham NG4 1RL
✆ (0602) 612949
Practice: £2.40/hr. Lessons: Junior
course £15 for 4 x 1hr sessions

Shropshire

Telford Ski Slope
Court Street, Madeley, Telford TF7 5DZ
✆ (0952) 680291
Practice: £4.50/hr. Lessons: £5.60/hr

Somerset

Wellington Sports Centre
Corams Lane, Wellington, TA21 8LL
✆ (0823) 663010
Practice: £2.90/hr
Yeovil Ski Centre
Addlewell Lane, Nine Springs, Yeovil
✆ (0935) 21702
Prices not known.

South Yorkshire

Sheffield Ski Village
Parkwood Springs, Vale Road, Sheffield
S3 9SJ
✆ (0742) 769459
Practice: £6.50/hr. Lessons: £39 for 3 x
2hr sessions. Private tuition: £24/hr

Staffordshire

Festival Park Ski Slope
Festival Park, Stoke-on-Trent, ST1 5SN
✆ (0782) 204159
Practice: £5.80/hr. Lessons: £8.50/hr.
Private tuition: £25/hr

Suffolk

Suffolk Ski Club
Bourne Terrace, Wherstead, Ipswich IP2
8NG
✆ (0473) 602347
Practice: £5/hr. Lessons: £36 for 3 x 2hr
sessions. Private tuition: £12/hr

Surrey

Bishop Reindorp Ski School
Larch Avenue, Guildford
✆ (0483) 37373
Prices not known.
Sandown Ski School
Sandown Park, More Lane, Esher
✆ (0372) 465588
Practice: £5.50/hr. Lessons: £45 for 4 x
1hr sessions. Private tuition: £20/hr

Tyne and Wear

Sunderland Ski Centre
Silksworth Sports Complex, Silksworth,
Sunderland SR2 3AN
✆ 091-522 9119
Practice: £4.10/hr. Lessons: £5/hr.
Private tuition: £12/hr
Whickham Thorns Ski Club
Market Lane, Dunston, NE11 9NX
✆ 091-460 1193
Practice: £3.50/hr. Lessons: approx £8/hr

West Midlands

Ackers Trust Ski Centre
Golden Hillock Rd, Small Heath,
Birmingham, B11 2PY
✆ 021-771 4448
Practice: £5/hr. Lessons: £9/hr. Private
tuition: £25/hr

Scotland

Borders

Jedburgh Sports Complex
Jedburgh Grammar School, Jedburgh
✆ (0835) 62566
Practice: £2.95 for 1½hr

Central

Firpark Ski Centre
Hillpark Education Centre, Benview,
Bannockburn.
✆ (0786) 816205
Practice: £2/hr (+ annual membership
fee of £5.60). Lessons: £18.20 for 8 x
1hr sessions
Polmonthill Ski Centre
Polmont Farm, Polmont
✆ (0324) 711660
Practice: £3.80/hr. Lessons: £6.40 for 2hr

Fife

Fife Institute of Physical Education
Viewfield Road, Glenrothes
✆ (0592) 771700
Beginners' courses for all ages.

Grampian

Alford Ski Slope
Greystone Rd, Alford, Aberdeen, AB3
8JE. ✆ (09755) 62380/63024
Practice: £3 for 2hr. Lessons: approx
£36 for 6 x 1hr sessions. Private tuition:
£14/hr
**Craigendarroch Hotel and Country
Club**
Braemar Rd, Ballater, Royal Deeside,
AB35 5XA. ✆ (03397) 55858
Practice: £7/hr. Lessons: £40 for 10 x
1hr sessions
Kaimhill Ski Slope
Garthdee Rd, Aberdeen, AB1 7BA
✆ (0224) 311781
Practice: £2 for 1½hr. Lessons: approx
£33 for 6 x 1hr sessions. Equipment
hire: £1.30 for 1½hr

Highland

Cairdsport
The Aviemore Centre, Aviemore,
Inverness-shire PH22 1PL
✆ (0479) 810296
Practice: £5.50/hr. Lessons: £9 for 1hr
session
**Glenmore Lodge National Outdoor
Training Centre**, Aviemore,
Inverness-shire, PH22 1QU
✆ (047986) 256. Prices not known
Lochanhully Woodland Club
Carrbridge, Inverness-shire, PH23 3NA
✆ (0479) 84234
Practice: £3.50 for 1½hr. Lessons: £9
for 1½hr. Equipment hire: £3.50 for 1½hr

Lothian

Hillend Ski Centre
Biggar Road, Edinburgh
✆ 031-445 4433
Practice: £3.85/hr. Lessons: £5.85/hr.
Private tuition: £33.70/hr

Strathclyde

Bearsden Ski Club
The Mound, Stockiemuir Rd, Courthill,
Bearsden, Glasgow G61 3RS
✆ 041-943 1500
Practice: £7.50/hr (members free).
Lessons: £40 for 6 x 1hr sessions.
Private tuition: £17.50/hr (members free)
Glasgow Ski Centre
Bellahouston Park, 16 Dumbreck Road,
Glasgow, G41 5BW
✆ 041-427 4991/4993
Practice: £3 for 2hr (members free).
Lessons: £38 for 6 x 1hr sessions
(members £25). Private tuition: £17/hr
(members £13). Equipment hire: £3/hr
(members £2.50).

Tayside

Ancrum Outdoor Education Centre
10 Ancrum Road, Dundee
✆ (0382) 60719. Lessons: £21 for 2 x
2hr sessions on dry slope followed by 2
days on snow.

**Loch Rannoch Outdoor Activity
Centre**
Kinloch Rannoch, Perthshire, PH16 5PS
✆ (08822) 201
Practice: £3.50 for 1½hr. Lessons: £8
for 1½hr

Wales

Clwyd

Deeside Ski Slope
NEWI, Kelsterton Road, Connah's Quay,
Deeside, CH5 4BR. ✆ (0244) 822215
Practice: £4/hr

Dyfed

Pembrey Ski Slope
Pembrey Country Park, Llanelli
✆ (05546) 4443
Practice: £4/hr. Lessons: £5.50/hr

Gwent

Pontypool Ski Slope
Pontypool Park, Pontypool
✆ (04955) 756955
Practice: £4.80 for up to 1hr. Lessons:
about £30 for 4 x 1hr sessions

Gwynedd

Plas y Brenin
Capel Curig, LL24 0ET. ✆ (0694) 280
Practice: £6 for 2hr. Lessons: £36 for 5 x
2hr sessions

Rhiwgoch Ski Centre
Bronaber, Trawsfyndd. ✆ (076687) 578
Practice: £6/hr. Lessons: £6.50/hr

Ski Llandudno
Great Orme, Llandudno
✆ (0492) 874707
Practice: £7/hr. Private tuition: £19/hr

Powys

Dan-yr-Ogof Ski Slopes
Abercrave, Glyntawe
✆ (0639) 730284. Lessons: £7 for 1½hr

South Glamorgan

Cardiff Ski Centre
Fairwater Park, Fairwater, Cardiff
✆ (0222) 561793
Practice: £4/hr. Lessons: £40 for 4 x 1hr
sessions. Private tuition: £16/hr

Northern Ireland

Craigavon Golf and Ski Centre
Turmoyra Lane, Silverwood, Lurgan,
BT66 6NG
✆ Lurgan 326606
Practice: £3.10/hr. Lessons: £32 for 6hr
course

Ski Knockbracken
Ballymaconaghy Road, Knockbracken,
Belfast BT8 4SB
✆ (0232) 892108/795666
Practice: £4.50/hr. Lessons: £40 for 6 x
1hr sessions. Private tuition: £21/hr

Ulster Ski Club
36 Belfast Road, Lisburn, Co Antrim,
BT27 4AG
✆ (0846) 661033. Lessons: £20 for 4 x
1½hr sessions

Ski travel agents

There is a growing number of ski travel
agencies who, unlike your average High
Street agency, sell skiing holidays only.
Catering for all types of skier and
supposedly staffed by experts, they
claim to be able to match potential
clients with suitable holidays. Some also
offer discounts on the holidays if they are
booked through them. All are ABTA
members.

Ski Choice, Travellers Choice Ltd, 27
High Street, Benson, Wallingford, Oxon
OX10 6RP ✆ (0491) 37607. Fax (0491)
333836.

Ski Travel Centre, 311 Byres Road,
Glasgow G12 8UQ ✆ 041-357 3945. Fax
041-357 4283.

Ski Solutions, 206 Heythorp Street,
London SW18 5PA ✆ 081-944 1155.
Fax 081-879 1762.

Skiers Travel Bureau, Marco Polo
Travel, 79 Street Lane, Roundhay,
Leeds LS8 1AP ✆ (0532) 666876. Fax
(0532) 693305.

Snow Line, PO Box 9, Market
Harborough, Leicestershire LE16 7QS
✆ (0533) 434393. Fax (0533) 434393

Skiing organisations

British Association of Ski Instructors

Maintains standards of ski instruction; tour operators and others who provide ski tuition other than in resort ski schools often have BASI-qualified instructors.
Grampian Road, Aviemore, Inverness-shire PH22 1RL
✆ (0479) 810407

British Ski Federation

Governs the sport of competitive skiing in Britain.
258 Main Street, East Calder, West Lothian, Scotland EH53 0EE.
✆ (0506) 884343. Fax (0506) 882952.

Ski Councils

These bodies govern the sport as a whole, taking responsibility for promoting and developing skiing and skiers' interests with the aid of grants from the Sports Council. Taking the English Ski Council as an example:
■ full membership is open to clubs, colleges and youth organisations

■ associate membership is open to companies with related activities and individuals registered with the National Coaching Scheme
■ most activities – coaching, award schemes, races and so on – are based around local slopes, on snow or dry surfaces, and are organised by volunteers
■ there is a small staff who handle admin and coordination.

English Ski Council
Area Library Building, Queensway Mall, The Cornbow, Halesowen, West Midlands B63 4AJ ✆ 021-501 2314. Fax 021-585 6448.
Scottish National Ski Council
Caledonia House, South Gyle, Edinburgh EH12 9DQ ✆ 031-317 7280. Fax 031-339 8602.
Ski Council of Wales
240 Whitchurch Road, Cardiff CF4 3ND ✆ (0222) 619637. Fax same as phone number.
Ulster Ski Council
8 Abercorn Park, Hillsborough, County Down, NI ✆ (0846) 683243 (evenings only).

Ski Club of Great Britain

118 Eaton Square, London SW1W 9AF ✆ 071-245 1033. Fax 071-245 1258.
Now the dominant club for British skiers, the SCGB was formed in 1903 by a group of eleven pioneers of downhill skiing 'to encourage the sport of skiing, assist novices, give information to members and bring together persons interested in the sport'. In the Club's early days, the organisation of ski racing formed a significant part of its activities (the first World Championships in Alpine downhill and slalom racing were organised by the Club, at Mürren in 1931). Although the original aims remain, it concentrates these days on recreational skiing, and offers its members an impressive range of services and benefits to help them get the most out of their skiing holidays.

The aspect of the Club best known to non-members is its gathering of information about skiing conditions: its snow reports are widely published during the skiing season. These reports come from the Club's representatives, who are present in about 30 major resorts (listed below) throughout the season to help visiting members. The reps organise weekly programmes, as part of which they lead groups of different standards around the slopes, on and off-piste. There is more about reps' activities in 'Reading a resort entry', at the beginning of the resorts section of the book. Members who like the idea of skiing for the whole of their holiday in a compatible group led by a qualified person – perhaps with the intention of improving a particular aspect of their skiing – are catered for by the Club's programme of organised skiing parties. The Club administers the British Ski Tests, designed to provide skiers with a measure of their skiing competence. The Club runs an Information Department at its London headquarters, staffed by experienced skiers with access to extensive files of detailed information on resorts and on other aspects of skiing – equipment stockists, for example. In the associated Equipment Advisory Centre, members can examine the latest skis, boots and bindings and get advice on what would suit them.

The clubhouse is also a social centre, with a popular bar and cheap, informal restaurant. There is a year-round programme of events (social and ski-related) here and around the country – the Club has a network of regional and local representatives, and links with many dry ski slopes.

As well as an annual Members' Handbook, members receive five issues a year of *Ski Survey* – the biggest-circulation skiing magazine in Britain,

one of the brightest and for keen skiers probably the best.

Among other benefits for members are discounts – commonly five or ten per cent – on the cost of ski holidays and equipment from a wide range of suppliers, in the Alps as well as in Britain.

Resorts likely to have SCGB reps in 1992
Andorra
Soldeu
Austria
Igls, Kitzbühel, Mayrhofen, Obergurgl, St Anton, Schladming
France
Alpe d'Huez, Chamonix/Argentière, Flaine, Isola 2000, Les Arcs, La Plagne, Megève, Serre Chevalier, Tignes, Val d'Isère, Val Thorens
Italy
Cervinia, Courmayeur
Norway
Geilo
Switzerland
Arosa, Crans-Montana, Davos, Grindelwald, Gstaad, Klosters, Mürren, Saas Fee, St Moritz, Verbier, Villars, Wengen, Zermatt

National tourist offices

Andorran Delegation in Great Britain
63 Westover Road, London SW18 2RS;
✆ 081-874 4806. •
Austrian National Tourist Office
30 St George Street, London W1R OAL;
✆ 071-629 0461. Fax 071-499 6038.
Bulgarian National Tourist Office
18 Princes Street, London W1R 7RE;
✆ 071-499 6988. Fax 071-321 0025.
Canadian High Commission
Canada House, Trafalgar Square,
London SW1Y 5BJ; ✆ 071-930 8540.
French Government Tourist Office
178 Piccadilly, London W1V OAL;
✆ 071-491 7622. Fax 071-493 6594.
German National Tourist Office
65 Curzon Street, London W1Y 7PE;
✆ 071-495 3990. Fax 071-495 6129
Italian State Tourist Office
1 Princes Street, London W1R 8AY;
✆ 071-408 1254. Fax 071-493 6695
Norwegian Tourist Board
5-11, Lower Regent St, London
SW1Y 4NX; ✆ 071-839 2650. Fax
071-839 6014.

Romanian National Tourist Office
17, Nottingham St, London W1M 3RD;
✆ 071-224 3692.
Scottish Tourist Board
23 Ravelston Terrace, Edinburgh
EH4 3EU; ✆ 031-332 2433.
Fax 031-343 1513.
19 Cockspur Street, London SW1Y 5BL;
✆ 071-930 8661. Fax 071-930 1817.
Spanish Tourist Office
57 St James's St, London SW1A 1LD;
✆ 071-499 0901. Fax 071-629 4257.
Swedish Tourist Board
29-31 Oxford St, London W1R 1RE;
✆ 071-437 5816. Fax 071-287 0164.
Swiss National Tourist Office
Swiss Centre, New Coventry Street,
London W1V 8EE; ✆ 071-734 1921. Fax
071-437 4577.
United States Travel and Tourism
22 Sackville Street, London W1X 2EA;
✆ 071-439 7433.
Yugoslav National Tourist Office
143 Regent Street, London W1R 8AE;
✆ 071-734 5243. Fax 071-437 0599.

Reporting on resorts

Reporters to the *Guide* stand a good chance of winning a free copy of the next edition. Resort reports should use the structure set out below and be sent to Dept CD, Consumers' Association, FREEPOST, 2 Marylebone Road, London NW1 4DX. No stamp is needed. Please write as clearly as you can, or type your reports if possible. Use separate sheets for different resorts, however short your reports.

Resort report checklist
Basics
Your name and address.
Your GSG reporter number if known.
Your skiing background (experience, competence).
Resort name/country.
Date of visit.
Tour operator you used.
Hotel/chalet/block you stayed in.
Verdicts
Your reactions to our 'good for' and 'bad for' verdicts on the resort.
Operation of lifts
Remarks on lift closures, lift queues, lift passes and other payment systems, new developments this season or next.
Operation of runs
Remarks on piste-grooming, piste closure, artificial snow,
Information for skiers
Remarks on lift/piste summary boards, piste direction signing, piste edge marking, avalanche warnings, piste maps, piste grading.
Mountain restaurants
General comments; specific recommendations.
Ski school
Remarks on organisation, tuition, language, use of time, allocation of pupils to classes, group size etc. Cover private lessons, guiding, special courses if you tried them. Specify which school.
Children's facilities
Remarks on skiing and/or non-skiing kindergartens: facilities, staff competence and attitude, language, approach to ski tuition, meals, hours, cost etc.
Local transport
Need for transport within the resort; where you can get to, and where you can't; frequency, reliability, convenience, cost, crowding; value of having a car.

Accident/medical facilities
Your experience of mountain rescue, doctors, clinics, dentists, pharmacies efficiency, convenience, cost.
Equipment hire
Where you hired what (specify shop); choice of alternative sources; efficiency of shop you used, quality of equipment, maintenance, adjustment, cost.
Shopping
Range of everyday (food/supermarket) shops; quality, service, prices. Range of other (clothing/jewellery/gift) shopping.
Non-skiing facilities
Range, quality, convenience, price of sporting and other non-skiing facilities in the resort; excursion possibilities.
Après-ski
Range and style of bars, restaurants, discos, clubs; what happens in the resort after skiing, from tea time until the small hours; specific recommendations.
Getting there
Remarks on airport arrival/departure, coach transfer, car access/parking, rail connections.
Accommodation
Remarks on particular hotel(s), chalet(s) or apartments(s) – name them; advice on choice of location within the resort.
Prices
General observations on the cost of meals and drinks (village and mountain), food in shops, entry to and drinks in discos and clubs. Please give examples whenever possible (eg small beers 11F).
Summary
What did you particularly like and dislike about the resort?
What aspects of the resort came as a surprise (pleasant or otherwise)?
Who does the resort suit?
And who does it not suit?
On the whole, do you regret choosing this resort? If so, why?

Resort index

Resort descriptions are grouped into chapters, usually because they share a skiing area, and are arranged in a geographical sequence. First, north-east Italy is taken from east to west; then the sequence goes through the Alps in an anti-clockwise sweep from eastern Austria to southern France; then come other skiing areas. The page references given here take you to the start of the chapter in which the resort is described or mentioned.

The contents of the resorts section of the *Guide* are listed in chapter order on page 31; that's where you should look if you know roughly where you want to go. A comparative summary of major resorts starts on page 47; that's where you should look if you know your holiday needs but don't know which resorts will meet them.

Resort names starting with Le, La or Les are indexed not under L, but under the initial letter of the main part of their name.

Which? and Holiday Which?

Published once a month, *Which?* gives you comparative reports on the merits and value for money of many products and services that you buy for yourself, your family and your home.

Because Consumers' Association is an independent organisation our product testing is completely unbiased, so you can be sure you are getting the facts.

As a *Which?* subscriber, you can also get *Holiday Which?*, published 4 times a year in January, March, May and September. It reports on a wide range of holiday destinations in the UK and abroad, with details on food, excursions and sight-seeing as well as background information on climate, scenery and culture.

To claim your free trial subscription to *Which?* and *Holiday Which?* just complete and return the form opposite. No action is necessary if you wish to continue after your free trial: your subscription will bring you *Which?* and *Holiday Which?* for £16.75 a quarter until you cancel by writing to us (and to your bank to cancel your Direct Debiting Mandate), or until we advise you of a change in price. Your subscription becomes due on the first of the month, three months after the date on the mandate. If you do not wish to continue beyond the trial period, simply write and let us know before your first payment is due.

Gardening from Which?

Published 10 times a year with bumper issues in spring and autumn, this magazine aims to help you in your gardening by sharing the results of our thorough research and the experience of our gardening experts.

Every issue of *Gardening* contains something for everyone; from beginner to expert. The magazine's 80 or so comparative reports a year look at a wide variety of subjects from shrubs, flowers and cacti, fruit and vegetables to tools, techniques and equipment. So whether you've got a few window boxes, a lawn, well-established ornamental borders or a greenhouse, *Gardening* will help you to find ways of improving what you have and save you time and money.

To claim your free trial subscription to *Gardening from Which?* just complete and return the form opposite. No action is necessary if you wish to continue after your free trial: your subscription will bring you *Gardening from Which?* for £11.75 a quarter until you cancel by writing to us (and to your bank to cancel your Direct Debiting Mandate), or until we advise you of a change in price. Your subscription becomes due on the first of the month, three months after the date on the mandate. If you do not wish to continue beyond the trial period, simply write and let us know before your first payment is due.

Which? way to Health

This lively and authoritative magazine will help you and your family stay healthy. You'll find articles on staying fit, eating the right foods, early detection of any health problems, health products and how to get the best from the NHS.

This magazine is published every two months and, like *Which?*, is completely independent – bringing you unbiased facts about health in Britain today. The magazine takes a close look behind the scenes exposing bad practice and harmful products to help prevent you, the consumer, being deceived. We also report on any medical breakthroughs which could bring relief or cure for victims.

To claim your free trial subscription to *Which? way to Health* just complete and return the form opposite. No action is necessary if you wish to continue after your free trial: your subscription will bring you *Which? way to Health* for £5.75 a quarter until you cancel by writing to us (and to your bank to cancel your Direct Debiting Mandate), or until we advise you of a change in price. Your subscription becomes due on the first of the month, three months after the date on the mandate. If you do not wish to continue beyond the trial period, simply write and let us know before your first payment is due.

Consumers' Association, Castlemead, Gascoyne Way, Hertford X, SG14 1LH.

FREE TRIAL ACCEPTANCE

Please send me free the next 3 issues of *Which?* and a free issue of *Holiday Which?* as they appear. I understand that I am under no obligation. If I do not wish to continue with *Which?* and *Holiday Which?* after the free trial, I can cancel this order at any time before payment is due on the 1st of the month three months after the date shown. But if i decide to continue I need do nothing – my subscription will bring me *Which?* and *Holiday Which?* for the current price of £16.75 a quarter.

☐ Tick here if you prefer not to receive offers from third parties.

KA _ _

DIRECT DEBITING MANDATE

I/We authorise you until further notice in writing to charge to my/our account with you unspecified amounts which may be debited thereto at the instance of Consumers' Association by Direct Debit. Orignator's Ref. No. 992338

Signed	Today's date
Bank account in the name of	
Bank account number	
Name and address of your bank	
	Postcode

Banks may decline to accept instructions to charge direct debits to certain types of account other than current accounts.

YOUR NAME AND ADDRESS

Name
Address
Postcode

FREE TRIAL ACCEPTANCE

Please send me free the next 3 issues of *Gardening* as they appear. I understand that I am under no obligation. If I do not wish to continue with *Gardening* after the free trial, I can cancel this order at any time before payment is due on the 1st of the month three months after the date shown. But if I decide to continue I need do nothing – my subscription will bring me *Gardening* for the current price of £11.75 a quarter.

☐ Tick here if you prefer not to receive offers from third parties.

L_D

DIRECT DEBITING MANDATE

I/We authorise you until further notice in writing to charge to my/our account with you unspecified amounts which may be debited thereto at the instance of Consumers' Association by Direct Debit. Orignator's Ref. No. 992338

Signed	Today's date
Bank account in the name of	
Bank account number	
Name and address of your bank	
	Postcode

Banks may decline to accept instructions to charge direct debits to certain types of account other than current accounts.

YOUR NAME AND ADDRESS

Name
Address
Postcode

FREE TRIAL ACCEPTANCE

Please send me free the next 2 issues of *Which? way to Health* as they appear. I understand that I am under no obligation. If I do not wish to continue with *Which? way to Health* after the free trial, I can cancel this order at any time before payment is due on the 1st of the month three months after the date shown. But if I decide to continue I need do nothing – my subscription will bring me *Which? way to Health* for the current price of £5.75 a quarter.

☐ Tick here if you prefer not to receive offers from third parties.

E_XL

DIRECT DEBITING MANDATE

I/We authorise you until further notice in writing to charge to my/our account with you unspecified amounts which may be debited thereto at the instance of Consumers' Association by Direct Debit. Orignator's Ref. No. 992338

Signed	Today's date
Bank account in the name of	
Bank account number	
Name and address of your bank	
	Postcode

Banks may decline to accept instructions to charge direct debits to certain types of account other than current accounts.

YOUR NAME AND ADDRESS

Name
Address
Postcode

*Which? and
Holiday Which? –
details overleaf*

Consumers' Association, Castlemead,
Gascoyne Way, Hertford X, SG14 1LH.

---

*Gardening from
Which? –
details overleaf*

Consumers' Association, Castlemead,
Gascoyne Way, Hertford X, SG14 1LH.

---

*Which? way to
Health –
details overleaf*

Consumers' Association, Castlemead,
Gascoyne Way, Hertford X, SG14 1LH.